Fodor's

OREGON

5th Edition

Fodor's Travel Publications New York, Toronto, London, Sydney, Auckland
www.fodors.com

Be a Fodor's Correspondent

Share your trip with Fodor's.

Our latest guidebook to Oregon—now in full color—owes its success to travelers like you.

We are especially proud of this color edition. No other guide to Oregon is as up to date or has as much practical planning information, along with hundreds of color photographs and illustrated maps. We've also included "Word of Mouth" quotes from travelers who shared their experiences with others on our forums. If you're inspired and can plan a better trip because of this guide, we've done our job.

We invite you to join the travel conversation: Your opinion matters to us and to your fellow travelers. Come to Fodors.com to plan your trip, share an experience, ask a question, submit a photograph, post a review, or write a trip report. Tell our editors about your trip. They want to know what went well and how we can make this guide even better. Share your opinions at our feedback center at fodors.com/feedback, or email us at editors@fodors.com with the subject line "Oregon Editor." You might find your comments published in a future Fodor's guide. We look forward to hearing from you.

Happy traveling!

Tim Jarrell, Publisher

FODOR'S OREGON
Editor: Molly Moker

Editorial Contributors: Erica Duecy, Carolyn Galgano
Writers: Andrew Collins, Sarah Cypher, John Doerper, Mike Francis, Matt Graham, Brian Kevin, Janna Mock-Lopez, Kerry Newberry, Deston S. Nokes, Dave Sandage, Jenie Skoy, Allecia Vermillion, Christine Vovakes, Crystal Wood

Production Editor: Evangelos Vasilakis
Maps & Illustrations: David Lindroth, *cartographer;* Bob Blake, Rebecca Baer, *map editors;* William Wu, *information graphics*
Design: Fabrizio La Rocca, *creative director;* Guido Caroti, Siobhan O'Hare, *art directors;* Tina Malaney, Nora Rosansky, Chie Ushio, Jessica Walsh, Ann McBride, *designers;* Melanie Marin, *senior picture editor*
Cover Photo: (Heceta Head Lighthouse): Bertsch Udo/SIME/Photononstop
Production Manager: Amanda Bullock

5th Edition

ISBN 978-1-4000-0511-6

ISSN 1523-8776

SPECIAL SALES
This book is available at special discounts for bulk purchases for sales promotions or premiums. Special editions, including personalized covers, excerpts of existing books, and corporate imprints, can be created in large quantities for special needs. For more information, write to Special Markets/Premium Sales, 1745 Broadway, MD 6-2, New York, New York 10019, or e-mail specialmarkets@randomhouse.com.

AN IMPORTANT TIP & AN INVITATION
Although all prices, opening times, and other details in this book are based on information supplied to us at press time, changes occur all the time in the travel world, and Fodor's cannot accept responsibility for facts that become outdated or for inadvertent errors or omissions. So **always confirm information when it matters,** especially if you're making a detour to visit a specific place. Your experiences—positive and negative— matter to us. If we have missed or misstated something, **please write to us.** We follow up on all suggestions. Contact the Oregon editor at editors@fodors.com or c/o Fodor's at 1745 Broadway, New York, NY 10019.

PRINTED IN COLOMBIA

10 9 8 7 6 5 4 3 2 1

CONTENTS

Fodor's Features

ABOUT
THIS BOOK

Our Ratings

Sometimes you find terrific travel experiences and sometimes they just find you. But usually the burden is on you to select the right combination of experiences. That's where our ratings come in.

As travelers we've all discovered a place so wonderful that its worthiness is obvious. And sometimes that place is so experiential that superlatives don't do it justice: you just have to be there to know. These sights, properties, and experiences get our highest rating, **Fodor's Choice,** indicated by orange stars throughout this book.

Black stars highlight sights and properties we deem **Highly Recommended,** places that our writers, editors, and readers praise again and again for consistency and excellence.

By default, there's another category: any place we include in this book is by definition worth your time, unless we say otherwise. And we will.

Disagree with any of our choices? Care to nominate a place or suggest that we rate one more highly? Visit our feedback center at www.fodors.com/feedback.

Budget Well

Hotel and restaurant price categories from ¢ to $$$$ are defined in the opening pages of each chapter. For attractions, we always give standard adult admission fees; reductions are usually available for children, students, and senior citizens. Want to pay with plastic? **AE, D, DC, MC, V** following restaurant and hotel listings indicate whether American Express, Discover, Diners Club, MasterCard, and Visa are accepted.

Restaurants

Unless we state otherwise, restaurants are open for lunch and dinner daily. We mention dress only when there's a specific requirement and reservations only when they're essential or not accepted—it's always best to book ahead.

Hotels

Hotels have private bath, phone, TV, and air-conditioning and operate on the European Plan (EP, meaning without meals), unless we specify that they use the Continental Plan (CP, with a Continental breakfast), Breakfast Plan (BP, with a full breakfast), or Modified American Plan (MAP, with breakfast and dinner), or are all-inclusive (AI, including all meals

and most activities). We always list facilities but not whether you'll be charged an extra fee to use them, so when pricing accommodations, find out what's included.

Listings
★ Fodor's Choice
★ Highly recommended
⊠ Physical address
✛ Directions or Map coordinates
⌖ Mailing address
☎ Telephone
🖷 Fax
⊕ On the Web
✉ E-mail
✍ Admission fee
☉ Open/closed times
Ⓜ Metro stations
▭ Credit cards
Hotels & Restaurants
🏠 Hotel
➡ Number of rooms
⚲ Facilities
🍴 Meal plans
✕ Restaurant
⚲ Reservations
🏛 Dress code
⌇ Smoking
🆎 BYOB
Outdoors
⚐ Golf
⛺ Camping
Other
☾ Family-friendly
⇨ See also
⊠ Branch address
☞ Take note

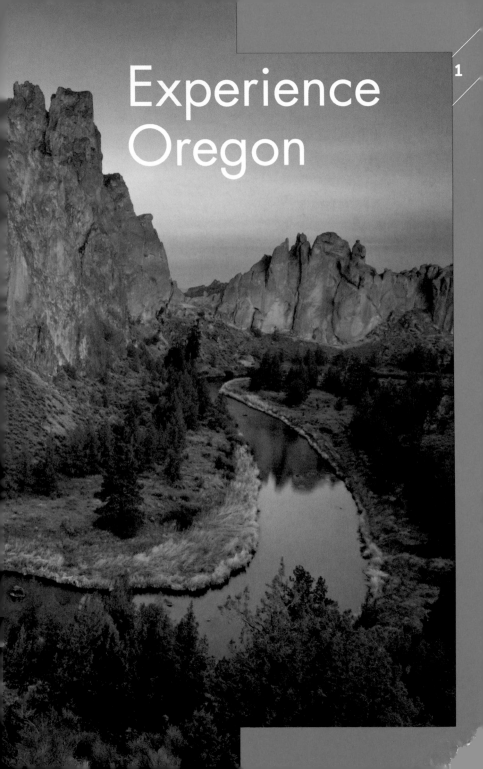

Experience
Oregon

WHAT'S WHERE

Numbers refer to chapters.

2 Portland. The state's largest city is a magnet for fans of artisanal food, beer, and wine, and its leafy parks and miles of bike lanes make it a mecca for outdoors enthusiasts.

3 The Willamette Valley and Wine Country. Just beyond the Portland city limits and extending south for 120 mi to the engaging college town of Eugene, the Willamette Valley has become synonymous with exceptional winemaking. The region is also home to Salem, the state capital.

4 The Oregon Coast. You could make a case that Oregon's roughly 300 mi of rugged coast, abundant with craggy mountains, gentle coves, historic lighthouses, and quaint fishing villages, is every bit as scenic as the more crowded and famous California coast.

5 The Columbia River Gorge and Mt Hood. Anchored by the sophisticated, historic community of Hood River, the Columbia Gorge extends for about 160 mi along the Oregon and Washington border. Wind sports and white-water rafting abound. Thirty-five miles south is Oregon's highest peak, iconic Mt. Hood, a favorite destination for hiking and skiing.

6 Central Oregon. The semiarid and generally sunny swatch of Oregon that lies immediately east of the Cascade Range takes in a varied landscape, with the outdoorsy city of Bend acting as the region's hub—it's loaded with hip restaurants and microbreweries.

7 Southern Oregon. The verdant Umpqua and Rogue valleys, popular gateways to Crater Lake, offer plenty to see and do in their own right. The Klamath Falls region provides some of Oregon's best, undervisited scenery, while artsy Ashland and Old West–looking Jacksonville abound with sophisticated restaurants, shops, and wineries.

8 Crater Lake National Park. Crater Lake is a geologic marvel and a hiker's paradise, with about 90 mi of trails. The 21-square-mi sapphire-blue expanse is the nation's deepest lake.

9 Eastern Oregon. The vast and sparsely populated eastern reaches of the state promise plenty of memorable sights and recreational opportunities for those who make the effort. The Wild West town of Pendleton—famed for its annual rodeo—and historic Baker City are just off Interstate 84.

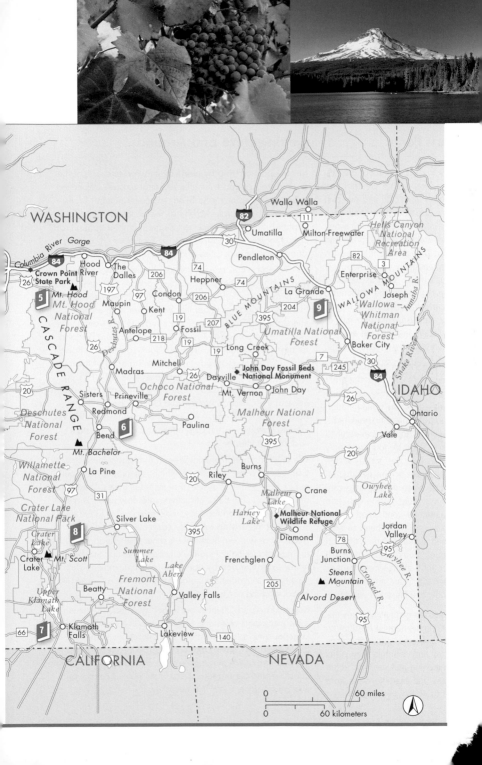

WASHINGTON

Columbia River Gorge

Walla Walla

82

11

Hells Canyon National Recreation Area

Umatilla

Milton-Freewater

84

30

Pendleton

82

3

Enterprise

Joseph

Hood River

The Dalles

206

Crown Point State Park

84

26

5 Mt. Hood
Mt. Hood National Forest

197

74

Heppner

74

La Grande

204

WALLOWA MOUNTAINS

Wallowa–Whitman National Forest

Imnaha R.

Condon

97

Maupin

206

Kent

395

9

19

BLUE MOUNTAINS

Umatilla National Forest

Baker City

CASCADE RANGE

Antelope

218

Fossil

207

19

Baker City

Deschutes R.

26

19

Long Creek

19

Snake River

Mitchell

Madras

26

Dayville

John Day Fossil Beds National Monument

245

7

84

IDAHO

Ochoco National Forest

Mt. Vernon

John Day

30

Sisters

Prineville

26

Ontario

Redmond

Malheur National Forest

Paulina

6 Bend

Deschutes National Forest

20

Mt. Bachelor

395

Vale

20

Willamette National Forest

La Pine

Burns

97

20

Riley

Crane

Owyhee Lake

31

Crater Lake National Park

Silver Lake

Malheur Lake

8

Crater Lake

Summer Lake

Harney Lake

Malheur National Wildlife Refuge

Jordan Valley

Crater Lake

Mt. Scott

Lake Abert

395

Diamond

78

95

Frenchglen

Burns Junction

Owyhee R.

Fremont National Forest

Beatty

Upper Klamath Lake

Steens Mountain

Crooked R.

205

7 Klamath Falls

66

Valley Falls

Alvord Desert

95

Lakeview

140

CALIFORNIA

NEVADA

0   60 miles

0   60 kilometers

OREGON PLANNER

Fast Facts

Packing It's all about the layers here, as the weather can morph from cold and overcast to warm and sunny and back again in the course of a few hours, especially in spring and fall. The climate also varies tremendously within relatively small areas, such as between the coast and the Willamette Valley, or between the mostly dry and sunny eastern half of the state and the cold and frequently snowy Cascade Range.

Safety The most dangerous element of Oregon is the great outdoors. Don't hike alone, and make sure you bring enough water plus basic first-aid items. If you're not an experienced hiker, stick to tourist-friendly spots like the more accessible parts of the designated parks. When driving, take care to use only designated and maintained roads and check road conditions ahead of time when planning to pass through mountainous terrain from fall through spring—many roads over the Coast and Cascades ranges are closed in winter.

Taxes Oregon has no sales tax, making it a popular destination for shoppers, although many cities and counties levy a tax on lodging and services. Room taxes, for example, vary from 6% to 9½%.

Getting Here and Around

Most visitors arriving by plane fly into Portland, site of the state's largest airport. Smaller regional airports are based in Eugene, Medford, and Bend. A smaller number of visitors arrive by Amtrak, which has major service connecting Portland, Salem, Eugene, and Klamath Falls with San Francisco, Seattle, and Spokane, or by Greyhound bus, with stops in most major cities and towns.

If traveling by car, major interstate highways connect Oregon with Washington, Idaho, and northern California, making it easy to include the state as part of a regional Pacific Northwest road trip to Seattle, Vancouver, and environs. Interstate 5 is Oregon's major north–south freeway, and Interstate 84 cuts east–west across the state from Portland through the Columbia Gorge and southeast toward Boise, Idaho. Other major roads through the state, all of them offering plenty of beautiful scenery, include U.S. 101 up and down the coast, U.S. 97 north–south along the eastern edge of the Cascade Range, and U.S. 20 and U.S. 26, both of which run east–west from the coast through the Willamette Valley, over the Cascades, and across the state's vast eastern interior.

The only destination within Oregon that's genuinely easy to visit without a car is Portland, which is served by a superb public transportation system that includes buses, streetcars, and light rail. The city's attractive, safe downtown is also easy to navigate on foot. If you do bring a car to Portland, you'll find the driving relatively easy—parking can be pricey at downtown hotels but is otherwise cheap and easy to find outside the immediate city center. A car can be useful for exploring nearby points of interest or making day trips to the Willamette wine country, Columbia Gorge, Mt. Hood, and the coast.

Beyond Portland, it's possible to get by without a car in relatively compact cities and larger towns like Ashland, Bend, Eugene, and Salem, but many key attractions in these areas lie farther afield, and a car is ideal for exploring. To reach and explore most of the state, including the beautiful coastline and the rugged, sparsely populated central and eastern portions, a car is a necessity.

1

Top Festivals

Portland is the state's festivals hub, with many events taking place downtown on the city's scenic Willamette riverfront, but you'll find plenty of engaging festivals elsewhere. Also keep in mind that Oregon is wild about farmers' markets—most towns in the state have one from spring through fall, and Portland has dozens. There's often live entertainment, arts and crafts, and prepared food at these bustling outdoor markets.

Spring Portland's **Cinco de Mayo** festival celebrates its sister-city relationship with Guadalajara, Mexico, and runs a full weekend in early May.

Summer Among the many big waterfront gatherings in Portland each summer, check out **Portland Gay Pride** in mid-June, the **Waterfront Blues Festival** over Fourth of July weekend, the **Oregon Brewers Festival** in late July, and the **Bite of Oregon** food festival in early August. Arguably the most famous event in the state, the **Portland Rose Festival** consists of numerous events and parties throughout June, culminating in a huge parade. Look high in the sky for evidence of the colorful **Tigard Festival of Balloons** in June—hot-air balloons soar above this Portland suburb throughout the weekend. Jacksonville's **Britt Festivals** bring fans of high-caliber outdoor musical and theater performances to this historic Victorian town all summer long. Wine lovers flock to McMinnville, in the Willamette Valley, to sample fine regional vintages in late July and early August during the **International Pinot Noir Celebration**. Autumn is just around the corner with the arrival of the **Oregon State Fair** in Salem in late August and early September.

Fall The **Pendleton Round-Up** is one of the most prestigious and downright fun rodeos in the country, drawing more than 50,000 participants and spectators in September. In coastal Bandon each October, the **Cranberry Festival** comprises a fair and parade. The **Sisters Folk Festival** brings top-name artists to this scenic mountain town near Bend, which hosts its bustling **Bend Fall Festival** in mid-September.

Winter Although it sounds like a short-term seasonal event, Ashland's famed **Oregon Shakespeare Festival** actually runs from mid-February through early November. In mid-February, **Bend WinterFest** celebrates the region's winter sports with a mix of outdoors activities and indoor concerts. Late February's **Newport Seafood and Wine Festival** is a tasty time to visit the coast. Also at this time is the acclaimed **Portland Jazz Festival**.

When to Go

There's no more scenic and enjoyable time to visit just about any part of Oregon than summer, which promises the driest, sunniest weather and mild temperatures, as well as lush, verdant terrain and the majority of the state's key festivals and gatherings—it's also the only time the road encircling Crater Lake is open. You should plan for occasionally intense (but dry) heat waves in the valleys, from Ashland clear north to Portland. Even in summer, fog and rain can sometimes overpower the coast for a few days at a time.

Spring and fall, however, can be just as beautiful, with blooming flowers and fall foliage, and with fewer crowds in such popular spots at the coast, Columbia Gorge, and Willamette wine country.

During the winter months, from the coast to the Cascades (including Portland and the Willamette Valley), rain and gray skies are the norm and quite common in spring and fall. On the balance, temperatures in the Willamette Valley rarely dip below freezing. Although inclement weather dominates the western third of the state, eastern Oregon is typically dry and pleasant, and there's great skiing in the Cascades. Winter is also the best time for whale- and storm-watching along the coast and bird-watching in southeastern Oregon.

WHAT'S NEW

In Portland

The city of Portland, which developed its first-rate **MAX light rail service** in the late 1970s, opened its fourth line, the Green Line, in 2009—it connects Clackamas Town Center in the city's southeastern suburbs to the downtown campus of Portland State University. The city's Tri-Met system has further plans to develop light rail lines through the city's hip Inner Southeast neighborhood to Milwaukee (to open in 2015), and expand its popular downtown streetcar line to form a loop crossing the Willamette River via a new transit bridge, providing service to Inner Southeast (to open in 2012).

Consistently named America's best airport by readers of *Condé Nast Traveler*, **Portland International Airport** added several new restaurants and shops to its terminals in the past year, as well as a massive expansion to the on-site parking garage. Several new nonstop routes have been added to Portland in recent months, including Air Canada service to Calgary and Toronto, and Alaska Airlines service to Chicago, Honolulu, Kona (HI), and Maui.

Portland has had its share of notable hotel developments. The **McMenamins Group**, known for converting historic and often quite unusual old buildings into atmospheric hotels, plans to open the new **Crystal Hotel** in early 2011. This 51-room boutique property, which occupies a century-old building with a checkered past (it's housed everything from shady flophouses to gay strip clubs), is just a couple of blocks from McMenamins famed Crystal Ballroom, and it will feature a full-service restaurant, saltwater soaking pool, and cellar bar.

The swanky 331-room **the Nines** hotel, part of Starwood's Luxury Collection brand, is Portland's fanciest new hotel. It's been created ingeniously inside the top nine floors of downtown's venerable Meier & Frank department store building—the rooftop Departure restaurant/lounge and lobby-level Urban Farmer restaurant have helped turn the Nines into one of the city's see-and-be-seen hot spots. Sleek and contemporary 174-room **Hotel Modera**, with its first-rate Nel Centro restaurant and handy location near Portland State University and the Portland Art Museum, is another notable lodging newcomer, as is the Gold LEED-certified **Courtyard by Marriott—Portland City Center.** This 256-room property is right on the new Max Green Line light rail and is home to a hip diner-inspired restaurant called The Original.

Portland's more residential and less touristy **East Side** continues to develop increased cachet among visitors seeking funky shopping, offbeat yet stellar dining, and hip lounge hopping and live music. The Hawthorne and nearby Belmont areas have long been popular for their countercultural vibes, but just to the south the adjoining **Clinton** and **Division** areas have seen an influx of cool places to eat and shop. The fringy, decidedly non-conformist **Alberta Arts District** and rapidly expanding **Mississippi Arts District** are two northern neighborhoods on the east side with plenty of distinctive new options for sipping, noshing, and browsing.

Fans of greater Portland's outstanding wineries and microbreweries are celebrating the recent development of a third component to the city's artisan-beverage reputation: **Distillery Row**, which comprises several rising stars in the craft-distillery scene on the city's inner east side (around SE 9th Avenue between SE Harrison and

SE Washington streets). Here you can sample the likes of New Deal vodka and 12 Bridges gin—most of these small-batch producers are open for tours and tastings.

Elsewhere in Oregon

One slight complaint about the wine regions in Oregon has long been the lack of upscale accommodations to match the bounty of stellar vineyards and tasting rooms. Finally, things are changing. In late 2009 the **Allison Inn & Spa** gave Oregon's Willamette Valley a resort to crow about—the 80-room property has a first-rate, full-service spa and a highly regarded restaurant. Another wonderfully received newcomer to the area, the 20-room **Inn at Red Hills** is delighting gourmands with its exquisite rooms and sterling Farm to Fork restaurant and market.

Out on the coast, in summer 2010 Astoria's exceptionally good **Columbia River Maritime Museum** launched a terrific new interactive exhibit, "Crossing the Bar, Perilous Passage," which provides an enthralling look at the dangerous Columbia River Bar—the turbulent mouth of the Columbia, which ships must navigate upon entering the river from the Pacific. The exhibit includes actual footage of rescues and dangerous crossings as well as a map locating the hundreds of wrecks that have occurred here over the centuries.

Also in Astoria in summer 2010, the town's old county jail, which was featured prominently in the quintessential '80s coming-of-age adventure movie *The Goonies*, became home to the new **Oregon Film Museum**. Memorabilia and exhibits related to several movies shot in Oregon—including *Free Willy*, *One Flew Over the Cuckoo's Nest*, *Animal House*, and *Kindergarten Cop*—fill this quirky museum.

Other developments along the coast include the addition of a new Swampland exhibit at the **Oregon Coast Aquarium** in Newport, complete with exhibits on everything from mangrove to cypress swamps, and a crew of creatures who frequent these regions, including an alligator, anaconda, red tail boas, snapping turtles, and piranhas.

Down the coast a bit, the state's most revered golfing destination, **Bandon Dunes**, opened its fourth golf course, dubbed **Old Macdonald**, in summer 2010—the rolling, windswept course overlooks the ocean and has a design inspired by one of the nation's pioneers of golf-course design, Charles Blair Macdonald. Critics have already begun hailing this challenging layout as one of the West Coast's most impressive courses.

Visitors to Lane County, which includes the city of Eugene and parts of the central coast, can plan their trips and ask for guidance at Springfield's new **Eugene, Cascades, and Coast Adventure Center**. The facility opened in summer 2010, and sells day passes to parks, beaches, and recreation areas throughout the region. It is staffed by specialists who can help visitors seeking advice on rafting, hiking, kayaking, and the dozens of other recreational opportunities that abound in this area.

On the leafy campus of the **University of Oregon** in Eugene, the **Museum of Natural and Cultural History** is in the midst of an ambitious three-part expansion. The museum's new collections center opened in 2009, a state-of-the-art exhibit hall will open in 2011, and a research wing is being added in 2012. This follows work done on U of O's similarly impressive **Jordan Schnitzer Museum of Art**, which completed a major redevelopment in 2005.

OREGON TOP EXPERIENCES

(A) Wine Tasting. Few wine-producing regions in America are more strongly identified with a single varietal than the Willamette Valley is with Pinot Noir. More than 200 vineyards here produce this rarefied wine, not to mention excellent Chardonnay and Pinot Gris. If you're short on time, drive to tiny Carlton, which has more than 20 tasting rooms.

(B) White-water Rafting. Oregon offers some of the best white-water rafting in the country; the mighty Rogue River is a thrilling ride. Several outfitters offer trips along this frothy, 215-mi river in the southwestern part of the state. Other excellent spots for rafting include the Deschutes River in Bend, and the Clackamas and White Salmon rivers near Portland.

(C) Mount Hood. Just 60 mi east of Portland, the state's highest mountain is the only place in the "lower 48" where you can ski year-round. There are five differ-

ent facilities, Timberline Lodge Ski Area being the most scenic.

(D) Crater Lake National Park. The deepest lake in the United States is also the clearest, a fact readily grasped as soon as you behold this searing-blue body of water formed from rain and snowmelt that's filled an ancient volcanic caldera. In summer this 21-square-mi lake is southern Oregon's foremost attraction, and its encircled by a well-maintained 33-mi road.

(E) The Columbia Gorge. The 75-mi section of the breathtaking Columbia River that extends just east of Portland to The Dalles provides some of the most stunning scenery in the Pacific Northwest. Towering cliffs on both the Washington and Oregon sides of the river form a dramatic backdrop, and meandering highways line both banks (on the Washington side, Hwy. 14 is slower but offers better views). Water and wind sports abound.

(F) Portland Neighborhoods. Oregon's largest city is famed for its eccentric neighborhoods, which merit at least a day of exploring. Be sure to hit Hawthorne, Mississippi Avenue, and Alberta on the east side, where vintage clothiers and organic coffeehouses abound. Just north of downtown, the more upscale Pearl District has stylish boutiques and trendy eateries—it's also home to legendary Powell's Bookstore. On weekends, don't miss nearby Portland Saturday Market, the largest arts-and-crafts fair in the country.

(G) The Oregon Shakespeare Festival. Sunny, hilly, and attractive, Ashland is a charming, small city in its own right, but attending this world-class festival, which presents plays (from Shakespeare to classic to contemporary) on three different stages from mid-February to early November, is all the more reason to go.

(H) Brewpubs. The nation's second largest producer of craft beer, Oregon has no shortage of microbreweries—many of them serving their product, along with great food. You're sure to have an authentic experience at any of the prolific and decidedly quirky McMenamins pubs and breweries throughout the state.

(I) Beachcombing. Dramatic, pristine beaches line Oregon's windswept coast, offering countless opportunities for hikes along the sand, plus surfing and swimming for the intrepid (Oregon waters are frigid, even in summer). The 41 mi of rolling bluffs that make up Oregon Dunes National Recreation Area near Reedsport are a favorite draw. Also check out the beautiful beaches near Manzanita, Yachats, and Brookings.

IF YOU LIKE

Hidden Food and Wine Finds

As the state—and especially greater Portland—continues to develop cachet for its super restaurants, farmers' markets, wineries, and microbreweries, it's worth making the effort to venture a bit off the beaten path to find some genuine only-in-Oregon culinary treats.

Burgerville, Portland. With nearly 40 locations around metro Portland, Burgerville has taken classic fast food to new heights by sourcing local, seasonal ingredients, from Washington sweet onions for its onion rings to the fresh blackberries and hazelnuts in the luscious milkshakes.

Clear Creek Distillery, Portland. Clear Creek paved the distillery way with its unique spirits—the pear brandy or cherry Kirschwasser make a perfect nightcap, and a sip of Douglas fir eau de vie will deliver you right to the heart of an Oregon forest.

Josephson's Smokehouse, Astoria. Once the heart of Oregon's salmon-canning industry, the endearingly raffish town of Astoria is still a prime destination for seafood lovers. Drop by Josephson's for hot- and cold-smoked salmon, prawns, halibut, and albacore.

Rogue River Creamery, Central Point. This small dairy in an otherwise nondescript town near Medford produces phenomenal blue cheeses in several varieties (from Smokey Blue to Oregonzola), plus a delectable lavender-infused cheddar.

Sleepy Monk, Cannon Beach. Portland's Stumptown Coffee is Oregon's most famous coffee roaster among die-hard java connoisseurs, but true aficionados rave about this tiny, organic coffeehouse in Cannon Beach—the dark, bold Bogsman Brew blend is heaven in a cup.

Offbeat Museums

Although you'll discover a plethora of art and history museums, Oregon fascinates visitors with its diverse selection of lesser-known, quirky museums.

Columbia River Maritime Museum, Astoria. The observation tower of a World War II submarine and the personal belongings of the passengers of area shipwrecks are among the exhibits inside, while outdoors on the riverside dock you can tour the lightship Columbia, which formerly plied the region's waters as a floating lighthouse.

Evergreen Aviation Museum, McMinnville. Engrossing facts about aviation complement an awesome assortment of flying machines at this expansive repository best known as the home of Howard Hughes's "flying boat," the *Spruce Goose,* which has a wingspan longer than a football field and its end zones.

Favell Museum of Western Art and Native American Artifacts, Klamath Falls. Inside this relatively small building you'll discover an astounding collection of some 100,000 Native American artifacts, plus the world's largest collection of miniature guns and a trove of Western artwork.

High Desert Museum, Bend. Evocative and intricate walk-through dioramas and an indoor-outdoor zoo with creatures great and tiny convey the high desert's past and present in a delightfully airy and family-friendly space.

National Historic Oregon Trail Interpretive Center, Baker City. With a simulated span of the legendary Oregon Trail, this well-designed museum offers a thorough and vivid look at life for the some 300,000 pioneers who entered Oregon from the Midwest during the 19th century.

Distinctive Lodging

In Oregon you can stay in hip, urban neighborhoods, along the beach, in the woods, or atop snow-covered mountains. Accommodations include elegant, full-service boutique hotels, luxury alpine retreats, historic bed-and-breakfasts, cozy ski chalets, rustic national park cabins, and funky local motels.

The Allison Inn & Spa, Newberg. Elegant yet refreshingly contemporary, this 80-room boutique resort and spa has finally given Oregon's scenic Willamette Valley accommodations worthy of the region's ethereal Pinot Noirs.

Heceta House, Heceta Head. Occupying the same dramatic promontory as a working lighthouse, this Queen Anne–style bed-and-breakfast has views of the Pacific that inspire many a marriage proposal.

McMenamins Kennedy School, Portland. The quirky McMenimans company has readapted dozens of buildings around Oregon as pubs, restaurants, and hotels—from a former asylum to this cleverly designed property in a funky northeast Portland neighborhood, a 1915 elementary school.

Sunriver Resort, Sunriver. A former military base near Bend has transformed into an almost self-contained resort village. Golf, great food, luxury rooms, and, above all, the high desert's sweeping sense of splendid isolation are the main draws here.

Timberline Lodge, Mt. Hood. This iconic 60-room lodge on the upper slopes of Oregon's highest peak is buried beneath many feet of snow for much of the year. Admire the 96-foot stone chimney in the lobby.

Majestic Mountaintops

Oregon is studded with mostly conical mountain peaks, which are strung along its Cascade Range from the Columbia River right down to the California border. The lofty summits, most of them topped with a full cover of snow all year-round, make for memorable photography subjects. Those who venture closer, however, will discover some of the state's best opportunities for recreation.

Mt. Ashland. The first soaring peak you encounter upon crossing into southern Oregon on Interstate 5, this 7,533-foot peak has great skiing much of the year, and also rewards visitors with fantastic views of the Rogue Valley.

Mt. Bachelor. This 9,065-foot peak offers some of the best downhill skiing and snowboarding in the West—consider the impressive 3,265-foot vertical drop. In summer, you can ride a chairlift to the Pine Marten Lodge for panoramic vistas across the shimmering Cascade Lakes.

Mt. Hood. One of Oregon's most recognizable land features, the snowy, conical Mt. Hood rises to some 11,245 feet (the tallest in the state).

Neahkahnie Mountain. Although it tops out at just 1,661 feet, this craggy peak is one of the most dramatic along the state's winding coastline. Trails leading to the top draw plenty of hikers from nearby Manzanita and Cannon Beach.

Steens Mountain. A striking sight in eastern Oregon's otherwise rather level high desert, this 9,700-foot peak was created from a massive block of fractured lava and is largely devoid of vegetation. Hikers here have been known to spot golden eagles and bighorn sheep.

FLAVORS OF OREGON

Short of tropical fruit, there aren't too many types of food that don't grow somewhere in Oregon. Myriad fish and shellfish species dwell off the coast, while tree fruits line the windswept Columbia Gorge, and berries grow wild and on farms in the fertile Willamette Valley. A host of other fruits, vegetables, greens, and produce thrive in the temperate climate. Ranch lands, dairy farms, and acres of wheat and other crops round out an abundance that changes with the seasons. Oregonians celebrate the state's range of ingredients in memorable dishes and drinks.

Natural Bounty

Few states can match Oregon's agricultural diversity, which is good news for both chefs and food-crazy locals.

Nuts: There's a reason why hazelnuts—also known as filberts—are the official state nut. Oregon produces 99 percent of the country's hazelnuts, which add a toasty-sweet flavor to meat, salads, desserts, coffee drinks, and more.

Berries: Blueberries, blackberries, and strawberries thrive in the lush Willamette Valley. But the state is home to lesser-known berries highlighted in local preserves, baked goods, and sweet sauces. Subtly tart loganberries are a cross between blackberries and red raspberries. Marionberries have a slightly earthy flavor, and are sometimes dubbed "the cabernet of blackberries."

Produce: Farmers' markets and restaurant menus are filled with locally grown staples like mushrooms, rhubarb, lettuce, onions, beans, potatoes, apples, and pears.

Cheese: Open an Oregonian's refrigerator and you're likely to find a fat yellow brick (or a diminutive "baby loaf") of Tillamook cheddar from the century-old collective of coastal creameries. The state's broad swaths of grazing lands generate milk that fuels artisanal cheese producers. Some of the country's best blue cheese comes from the Rogue Creamery in southern Oregon.

Microbrews: German immigrants arriving in the mid-19th century launched an Oregon tradition of transforming the state's clear, clean water supply and grain crops into distinctive brews. Today the state is home to several larger breweries, like Widmer Brothers and Bridgeport Brewing Company, and scores of smaller producers.

Seafood

With 362 mi of coastline, bays, tide flats, and estuaries, Oregon has a stunning variety of fish and shellfish off its shores. Restaurants and locals are attuned to the seasons, from the start of Dungeness season to the best months for oysters.

Salmon: Oregonians know king salmon as chinook salmon, but make no mistake—the largest Pacific salmon reigns as the prize catch of the state's native cuisine. Silvery coho salmon also swim in the state's coastal rivers. Oregon salmon is phenomenal simply grilled or roasted. Perhaps the most indigenous way to cook salmon is to smoke it, a practice that dates back to Native American dwellers.

Crab: Dungeness crab may be named for a town in Washington, but Oregon harvests more of these prized crustaceans than any other state. They are a delicacy simply boiled and served whole, but picked meat often appears in crab cakes or as a focal point in modern regional dishes.

Shellfish: Low tide on Oregon's beaches can yield thin razor clams or a variety of bay clams. Mussels also grow in clusters along rocky costal stretches. Both are

delicious steamed (perhaps in an Oregon wine or beer) or in a creamy chowder.

Ocean fish: Pacific halibut, sole, sturgeon, hake, lingcod, and the prized albacore tuna are all fished off the Oregon coast. The Columbia River also offers up freshwater favorites like steelhead trout and Columbia River sturgeon.

New American Cuisine

By now chefs across the country are in the throes of the farm-to-table movement, but in Oregon the close connection between chef and producer has long bypassed trend status. It's simply how things are done. Restaurants like **Wildwood, Higgins,** and **Paley's Place** were producing organic, locally sourced dishes long before these approaches became national ideals.

Cuisine here tends to be modern and unfussy—a simple, slightly edgy celebration of what grows nearby. Dishes can have Asian, French, or other global influences, but the ingredients ground them solidly in the Northwest. However there is perhaps no more authentically Oregon preparation of meat or fish than cooking it with a crust of hazelnuts.

Portland is assuredly the epicenter of the state's restaurant scene, but wine-country tourism has helped spread noteworthy cuisine to the Willamette Valley and the coastal wine region.

Since it was first inhabited, Oregon has looked to the ocean to feed its population. However eastern Oregon cattle ranches provide a ready supply of sustainably raised beef that chefs love to showcase. The recent nose-to-tail dining trend has generated interest in other meats, including rabbit, pork, goat, and lamb, sourced from Oregon farms.

Wine

Pinot noir grapes have been the central force of Oregon winemaking since the industry took root in the 1960s. Frustrated by Pinot's poor performance in California, a few intrepid winemakers headed north to test out Oregon's cooler climate. Since then, the state has built an international reputation as a paradise of Pinot Noir.

The Willamette Valley's climate is similar to that of France's Burgundy region, where Pinot Noir grapes have reigned for centuries. The rich farmland on the valley floor isn't optimal for grape growing; most vineyards spread across the hillsides that ring the valley, taking advantage of higher elevation, thinner soil, and cool ocean breezes.

Oregon played a central role in America's rediscovery of this famously finicky grape. Today the state is the country's top producer of Pinot Noir. Oregon has 16 official wine-growing regions, though the vast majority of wineries are clustered in the Willamette Valley. Grapes also flourish in parts of southern Oregon and the Columbia Valley along the Washington border.

After Pinot Noir, Pinot Gris is the second most prevalent wine varietal in the state. The delicate, fruity white wine is somewhat of an unsung hero, since its darker Pinot cousin earns so much acclaim. Chardonnay and Riesling round out the state's top wines. Oregon wines are generally highly affordable, and deliver a great value for the money.

Unencumbered by the winemaking traditions of France, or even California, Oregon vintners have taken the lead in growing organic grapes and producing wines using sustainable methods.

PORTLAND WITH KIDS

Adventure-driven Oregon has plenty to delight families throughout the year, and many of the state's best kids-oriented attractions and activities are in greater Portland. Just getting around the Rose City—via streetcars and light rail trains on city streets and kayaks, excursion cruises, and jet boats on the Willamette River—is fun. For listings of family-oriented concerts, performances by the Oregon Children's Theatre, and the like, check the free *Willamette Weekly* newspaper.

Museums and Attractions

On the east bank of the Willamette River, the **Oregon Museum of Science and Industry** (OMSI) is a leading interactive museum in the Northwest, with touch-friendly exhibits, an Omnimax theater, the state's biggest planetarium, and a 240-foot submarine moored just outside in the river. Along Portland's leafy Park Blocks, both the **Oregon Historical Society** and the **Portland Art Museum** have exhibits and programming geared toward kids.

In Old Town, kids enjoy walking amid the ornate pagodas and dramatic foliage of the **Lan Su Chinese Garden**. This is a good spot for a weekend morning, followed by a visit to the **Portland Saturday Market**, where food stalls and musicians keep younger kids entertained, and the cool jewelry, toys, and gifts handcrafted by local artisans appeal to teens. Steps from the market is the **Oregon Maritime Museum**, set within a vintage stern-wheeler docked on the river. And just up Burnside Street from the market, **Powell's City of Books** contains enormous sections of kids' and young adults' literature.

Parks

Portland is dotted with densely wooded parks—many of the larger ones have ball fields, playgrounds, and picnic areas. The most famous urban oasis in the city, **Forest Park** (along with adjoining **Washington Park**) offers a wealth of engaging activities. You can ride the MAX light rail right to the park's main hub of culture, a complex comprising the **Oregon Zoo, Portland Children's Museum**, and **World Forestry Discovery Center Museum**. Ride the narrow-gauge railroad from the zoo for 2 mi to reach the **International Rose Test Garden** and **Japanese Garden**. From here it's an easy downhill stroll to **Northwest 23rd and 21st avenues'** pizza parlors, ice-cream shops, and bakeries.

Outdoor Adventures

Tour boats ply the **Willamette River**, and a couple of marinas near OMSI rent **kayaks** and conduct **drag-boat races** out on the water. There are also several shops in town that rent **bikes** for use on the city's many miles of dedicated bike lanes and trails (⇨ *See our Pedaling Portland feature in Chapter 2*). There's outstanding **white-water rafting** just southeast of Portland, along the Clackamas River. On your way toward the Clackamas, check out **North Clackamas Aquatic Park** and **Oaks Amusement Park**, which have rides and wave pools galore.

Nearby **Mt. Hood** has camping, hiking, and biking all summer, and family-friendly ski resorts—**Timberline** is especially popular for younger and less experienced boarders and skiers.

From summer through fall, the pick-your-own berry farms and pumpkin patches on **Sauvie Island** make for an engaging afternoon getaway—for an all-day outing, continue up U.S. 30 all the way to **Astoria**, at the mouth of the Columbia River, to visit the **Columbia River Maritime Museum** and **Fort Stevens State Park**, where kids love to scamper about the remains of an early-20th-century shipwreck.

ECOTOURISM IN OREGON

The word *ecotourism* is believed to have been coined by Mexican environmentalist Héctor Ceballos-Lascuráin in 1983. According to Ceballos-Lascuráin, ecotourism "involves traveling to relatively undisturbed natural areas with the specific object of studying, admiring, and enjoying the scenery and its wild plants and animals." His original definition seemed a bit too general, so in 1993 he amended it with a line that stressed that "ecotourism is environmentally responsible travel."

Natural beauty abounds in Oregon, which has been a pioneer in sustainability and conservation. Famously "green" Portland is a model of eco-friendly urban planning, with its superb public transit, network of urban-growth boundaries, multitude of bike lanes, and abundance of LEED-certified buildings. Outside the city, six of the state's ski areas (Mt. Ashland, Mt. Bachelor, Mt. Hood Meadows, Timberline, and Anthony Lakes) are members of the **Bonneville Environmental Foundation's Ski Green Program** (⊕ *www.ski-green.org*).

Travel-related businesses that embrace the principles of environmental sustainability are common throughout Oregon. The state's tremendous stock of forests, parks, and preserves is a big reason there's been such a push here to balance growth with preservation.

Travel Portland, which is one of the only tourism organizations in the country with its own public relations manager dedicated solely to promoting environmentally responsible travel, lists green resources on its Web site (⊕ *www.travelportland. com/portland_resources/green-resources. html*). This compendium of eco-conscious businesses includes everything from wineries and microbreweries to hotels, restaurants, and shops.

Accommodations

Oregon has dozens of accommodations committed to sustainable design and operating practices. Many smaller properties are members of **OBBG Green** (⊕ *www. obbg.org/oregon-green-travel.php*), which is made up of more than 15 bed-and-breakfasts that qualify as eco-friendly.

Food and Beverages

Oregon has been a leader in the movement toward producing food, beer, and wine using sustainable practices and emphasis on local and organic ingredients. One excellent resource for learning about organic and sustainable pick-your-own farms and farmers' markets around the state is **Oregon Tilth** (⊕ *www.tilth.org*).

Two statewide organizations dedicated to sustainability in winemaking are **Low Input Viticulture & Enology** (⊕ *www.liveinc. org*) and **Oregon Certified Sustainable Wine** (⊕ *www.ocsw.org*). Dozens of wineries around the state have been recognized for their environmentally friendly practices. Additionally, local breweries with eco-friendly reputations include **Widmer Brothers, Deschutes, Hopworks**, and **Full Sail**.

Tours

EcoShuttle (⊕ *www.ecoshuttle.net*) is an environmentally oriented charter tour company that arranges winery, brewery, and ecotours. The popular Willamette River boat-tour company **Portland Spirit River Cruises** (⊕ *www.portlandspirit. com*) is a recognized member of Travel Portland's green resources program, as is **Portland Walking Tours** (⊕ *www. portlandwalkingtours.com*). To gain a better sense of the progress Oregon's logging industry has made toward sustainable practices, be sure to visit the **World Forestry Center Discovery Museum** in Portland's Washington Park.

GREAT ITINERARIES

BEST OF OREGON TOUR

Days 1 and 2: Portland
Start by spending a couple of days in the state's largest city, where you can tour the museums and attractions that make up **Washington Park**, as well as the **Lan Su Chinese Garden** in Old Town, and the excellent museums and cultural institutions along downtown's leafy **Park Blocks**. This city of vibrant, distinctive neighborhoods offers plenty of great urban exploring, with Nob Hill, Hawthorne, and the Mississippi Avenue Arts District among the best areas for shopping, café hopping, and people-watching. If you have a little extra time, consider spending a couple of hours just south of the city in the Willamette Valley wine country—it's an easy jaunt from Portland.

Days 3 and 4: The Coast
Leave Portland early on Day 3 for the drive west about 100 mi on U.S. 30 to the small city of **Astoria**, which has several excellent spots for lunch and the **Columbia River Maritime Museum**. Pick the main scenic highway down the Oregon coast, U.S. 101, and continue south stopping at **Fort Stevens State Park** and the **Fort Clatsop National Memorial**. In bustling **Seaside**, stroll through the touristy but lively downtown before ending the day in charming **Cannon Beach** (26 mi south of Astoria), which has a wealth of oceanfront hotels and inns, many with views of one of the region's seminal features, 235-foot-tall **Haystack Rock**.

The following morning, continue south down U.S. 101. In **Tillamook** (famous for its cheese), take a detour onto the **Three Capes Loop**, a stunning 35-mi byway. Stop in small and scenic **Pacific City** (at the south end of the loop) for lunch. Once you're back on U.S. 101, continue south

THE PLAN

DISTANCE: 1,060 mi

TIME: 10 days

BREAKS: Overnight in Portland, Cannon Beach, Florence, Eugene, Ashland, Crater Lake, Bend, Hood River

to Newport, spending some time at the excellent **Oregon Coast Aquarium** as well as Oregon State University's fascinating **Hatfield Marine Science Center**. Your final stop is the charming village of **Florence**, 160 mi (four to six hours) from Cannon Beach.

Day 5: Eugene
Spend the morning driving 20 mi south of Florence along U.S. 101 to scamper about the sandy bluffs at **Oregon Dunes National Recreation Area** near Reedsport. Then backtrack to Florence for lunch in Old Town before taking Highway 126 east for 60 mi to the attractive college city of **Eugene**, staying at one of the charming inns or bed-and-breakfasts near the leafy campus of the University of Oregon. Take a walk to the summit of **Skinner Butte**, which affords fine views of the city, and plan to have dinner at one of the excellent restaurants at the **5th Street Public Market**. Budget some additional time in Eugene the following morning to visit two excellent University of Oregon museums, the **Jordan Schnitzer Museum of Art** and the **Oregon Museum of Natural History**.

Days 6 and 7: Ashland and Crater Lake
From Eugene, take Interstate 5 south for 60 mi to historic **Oakland**, where a delicious lunch awaits at **Tolly's Restaurant and Soda Fountain**. If you're visiting in summer, continue 15 mi down Interstate 5 to Roseburg, and then head east along Highway

138 (the Umpqua River Scenic Byway), which twists and turns over the Cascade Range for 85 mi to the northern entrance of **Crater Lake National Park**. Once inside the park, you can continue along Rim Drive for another half hour for excellent views of the lake. Overnight in the park or in nearby **Prospect**.

The following morning, take the lake boat tour to **Wizard Island** and hike through the surrounding forest. In the afternoon, head southwest on Highway 62 to Interstate 5, and then on to **Ashland**, 95 mi (about two hours) from Crater Lake. Plan to stay the night in one of Ashland's many superb bed-and-breakfasts. Have dinner and attend one of the **Oregon Shakespeare Festival** productions (mid-February through early November). If it's winter and Crater Lake's roads are impassable, from Oakland (*above*) continue straight down Interstate 5, stopping to check out the towns of **Grants Pass** and **Medford**, and end Day 6 in Ashland (125 mi south of Oakland), where you can spend two evenings.

Days 8 and 9: Bend

Get an early start out of Ashland, driving east along scenic Highway 66 for 60 mi to **Klamath Falls**, where you can stop for lunch and to tour the excellent **Favell Museum of Western Art and Native American Artifacts**, and the extensive **Klamath County Museum**. Then drive north on U.S. 97, stopping if you have time at **Collier Memorial State Park**, to reach the outdoorsy resort town of **Bend**, where you can spend two nights checking out the parks, mountain hikes, microbreweries, and hip restaurants of the state's largest city east of the Cascades. Be sure to visit the outstanding **High Desert Museum**, the **Old Mill District**, and **Mt. Bach-**

elor Ski Area (which has outdoor activities year-round).

Day 10: Hood River

From Bend, continue north up U.S. 97, and then northwest up U.S. 26 to **Mt. Hood**, 105 mi total. Have lunch at the historic **Timberline Lodge**, admiring the stunning views south down the Cascade Range. Pick up Highway 35 and drive around the east side of Mt. Hood and then north 40 mi up to the dapper town of **Hood River**, in the heart of the picturesque Columbia Gorge. Spend the night at one of the attractive inns, and try one of this town's stellar restaurants for dinner. From here it's just a 60-mi drive west along a scenic stretch of Interstate 84 to reach Portland, or you could drive east through the gorge through The Dalles and on to the Wild West town of **Pendleton**, 150 mi east. The town's regional airport connects to Portland and Seattle.

Alternatives

For a fuller sense of the Oregon Coast, continue down to **Bandon** and eventually all the way to **Brookings** on Day 4, where you can spend the night. Then on Day 5, continue south to Crescent City, California, and pick up U.S. 199 northeast to **Grants Pass**, where you can continue on to Ashland and Crater Lake. From U.S. 199, note that **Oregon Caves National Monument** makes for an interesting detour. Allow an extra day or two if you go this route.

From **Bend** you could easily add two additional days to your trip by making a loop drive through eastern Oregon. Follow U.S. 26 east to **Ochoco National Forest**, **John Day**, and—via Highway 7—historic **Baker City**, 230 mi total. From here it's a 240-mi drive west on Interstate 84 to **Hood River** via **Pendleton** and the scenic **Columbia Gorge**.

FIVE SCENIC OREGON DRIVES

Cascades Lakes Scenic Byway

2 to 4 Hours This mountainous 66-mi tour, which is closed in winter due to snow, passes shimmering mountain lakes and prime geological examples of how glaciers and volcanoes have contributed to Oregon's rugged landscape. The route begins just west of **Bend** on Forest Road 46, which climbs up into the Cascades and through the towering evergreens of **Deschutes National Forest** before turning south by **Devil's Lake**. The road ends at Highway 58, about 80 mi southeast of **Eugene**.

The High Desert: Bend to Baker City

5 to 8 Hours This 230-mi drive from **Bend** across the state's consistently sunny high desert is popular year-round for its stunning big-sky panoramas. Follow U.S. 97 north to **Redmond** (from which you could easily detour to **Cline Falls State Park** for a picnic, or up to the rugged hiking of **Smith Rock State Park**). Next turn east on U.S. 26 and follow the road through verdant ranch lands around **Prineville** and into the pine-forested ridges of **Ochoco National Forest**. Continue into eastern Oregon through the **Painted Hills** unit of **John Day Fossil Beds National Monument**, with its fascinating geological formations, and on through such historic gold-mining centers as **John Day**, and—via scenic U.S. 26 and Highway 7—**Baker City**.

Historic Columbia River Highway

1 to 3 Hours Several spans still exist of this 75-mi road through the magnificent Columbia Gorge. The **Historic Columbia River Highway** (U.S. 30) opened in 1922 and is considered a masterful feat of highway engineering, as it climbs over verdant riverside bluffs and passes beside several massive waterfalls. The longest continuous stretch of road extends from **Troutdale**, just east of Portland, and climbs and dips for 22 mi parallel to the Columbia River, ending just west of **Bonneville Dam**. Be sure to stop at **Crown Point State Scenic Corridor**, with its 30-mi views up and down the gorge.

The Southern Coast: U.S. 101 from Brookings to Florence

4 to 6 Hours You'll spy some of the most majestic maritime scenery in the West on the stretch of U.S. 101 that extends north from the Oregon/California border for 160 mi to Florence. You'll first arrive in the pretty fishing village of **Brookings**, through panoramic views from **Samuel H. Boardman State Park**, quaint **Port Orford**, and **Oregon Dunes National Recreation Area** in **Reedsport**. Finish just north in picturesque Florence, which lies on the Siuslaw River and has a charming Old Town with several fine restaurants.

Washington County's Vineyard and Valley Scenic Tour

3 to 6 Hours This meandering series of country roads passes through the heart of Washington County, the nearest patch of the Willamette wine country to Portland, which makes it perfect for an afternoon drive—interspersed with some first-rate wine tasting. The 50-mi route (⊕ *www.visitwashingtoncountyoregon.com/Scenic-Tour-Route*) begins just off U.S. 26, Exit 61, in Swiss-settled **Helvetia**, turns south through **Forest Grove's** pastoral wine country, and then finishes with a turn through the fertile **Tualatin Valley**, passing by vintage general stores and historic taverns.

Portland

WORD OF MOUTH

"There are no chain restaurants, Starbucks, etc. up on Alberta but independent cafes and galleries, spread out in pockets along with 'industrial' type businesses and a big Catholic church. They have a popular monthly event there in the Alberta Arts district called 'Last Thursday' in which the street opens up like a carnival and the galleries stay open—an art walk."

—Andrew

WELCOME TO PORTLAND

TOP REASONS TO GO

★ **Unleash your inner foodie.** Don't miss an amazingly textured range of global delights, created with fresh, locally harvested ingredients.

★ **Beer "hop."** (Pun intended.) Thirty-five local microbrews and offbeat varieties with such names as Hallucinator, Doggie Claws, and Sock Knocker await.

★ **Experience McMenamins.** Visit one of the local chain's beautifully restored properties, such as a renovated 1915 elementary school turned hotel.

★ **Take a stroll through Washington Park.** The International Rose Test Garden, Japanese Garden, Oregon Zoo, World Forestry Center, and Children's Museum are all here.

★ **Peruse pages at Powell's City of Books.** The aisles of this city block–sized shop are filled with more than a million new and used books. Top off hours of literary wanderlust with a mocha or ginseng tea downstairs at World Cup Coffee and Tea House.

1 Downtown. At the center of it all, Portland's downtown has museums, clubs, restaurants, parks, and unique shops. To get around downtown quickly, take the TriMet MAX light rail for free.

2 Pearl District and Old Town/Chinatown. The Pearl District, Portland's trendy and posh neighborhood, is teaming with upscale restaurants, bars, and shopping, along with pricey condos and artists' lofts. A visit here is

3 **Nob Hill and Vicinity.** From funky to fabulous, this neighborhood is also referred to as "Northwest 23rd" or "Northwest District." The exciting shopping, restaurants, and bars draw a younger but still sophisticated crowd.

4 **Washington Park.** Keep busy at the Oregon Zoo, Children's Museum, World Forestry Center, Hoyt Arboretum, Japanese Garden, International Rose Test Garden, Vietnam Veterans Memorial, and Oregon Holocaust Memorial. Nearby Forest Park is the largest forested area within city limits in the nation.

5 **East of Willamette River.** Ten bridges span the Willamette over to Portland's east side. It offers much of what downtown does but with fewer tourists. If you visit, you'll be rewarded with under-the-radar neighborhoods such as Belmont, Eastmoreland, Hawthorne, Laurelhurst, and Sellwood in the southeast and Alameda, Alberta Arts, Irvington, and the Lloyd District in the northeast.

6 **West of Downtown.** The lush hills at the west end of downtown hold stately homes and excellent parks, and mark the starting point for much of the greater Portland metro area.

rewarded with tantalizing bakeries and chocolatiers. Old Town/Chinatown offers variety, from cutting-edge to old-fashioned. This is the area for Asian-inspired public art, the LanSu Chinese Garden, and tours of the city's Shanghai Tunnels.

GETTING ORIENTED

Geographically speaking, Portland is relatively easy to navigate. The city's 200-foot-long blocks are highly walkable, and mapped out into quadrants. The Willamette River divides east and west and Burnside Street separates north from south. "Northwest" refers to the area north of Burnside and west of the river; "Southwest" refers to the area south of Burnside and west of the river; "Northeast" refers to the area north of Burnside and east of the river; "Southeast" refers to the area south of Burnside and east of the river. As you travel around the Portland metropolitan area, keep in mind that named east and west streets intersect numbered avenues, run north to south, and begin at each side of the river. For instance, Southwest 12th Avenue is 12 blocks west of the Willamette. Most of downtown's streets are one-way.

PORTLAND EATS

Despite most restaurant menus' lack of foams or flash, Portland has quietly become a formidable food presence. The city fields a respectable number of chefs and restaurants that garner national attention and win major industry awards.

(above) Delectable eats from Portland favorite, Le Pigeon. (opposite page, top) A pie from Ken's Artisan Pizza. (opposite page, bottom) The signature dish from Nong's Khao Man Gai food cart.

While temples of fine dining are few and far between, Portland offers a lively mix of memorable food in casual digs, like popular Thai spot **Pok Pok,** and the famed street carts clustered around town. Portland also has plenty of restaurants, like the venerable **Jake's Famous Crawfish,** that celebrate its proximity to the sea by offering oysters, tuna, and other fare that was swimming off the Pacific coast the previous day.

Popular destinations like **Bluehour, Fenouil,** and **Andina,** have cemented the reputation of Northwest Portland's Pearl District as a restaurant hot spot. Otherwise, new restaurants tend to open on the east side of the Willamette River, where rents are cheaper.

– *by Allecia Vermillion*

NOSE-TO-TAIL DINING

For a famously vegan-friendly city, Portland chefs love their meat—all parts of it. Locals love dropping in to **Le Pigeon** (✉ *738 E. Burnside* ☎ *503/546–8796* ⊕ *www.lepigeon.com*) for the towering burger, or nose-to-tail plates, including pig's foot served with watermelon and feta cheese, beef cheek, lamb tongue, and sweetbreads with potatoes and capers, which also appear on the menu.

2

CURBSIDE CUISINE

The national craze for street food is reflected in a proliferation of carts dishing out increasingly exotic or high-end fare. Check out our favorites below, or go to local blog, Food Carts Portland (⊕ www.foodcartsportland.com), and Twitter thread @pdxfoodcarts, for more information on the food carts around town.

bloop oatmeal cart (✉ SW 3rd Ave. & Washington St. ⊕ www.bloopoatmeal.blogspot.com): The oatmeal dished up here weekday mornings bears no resemblance to those just-add-water microwaveable packets. Chunky oats come sweetened with almond milk and topped with combinations like peanut butter, banana, and cinnamon.

Nong's Khao Man Gai (✉ SW 10th Ave. and Alder St. ⊕ www.khaomangai.com): There's really just one menu item at Nong's, but it usually sells out by the end of lunchtime. Reminiscent of the street foods of Thailand, the steamed rice with chicken gets its horsepower from a sauce of garlic, ginger, fermented soybeans, and Thai chilies.

Potato Champion (✉ S.E 12th Ave. and Hawthorne Blvd. ⊕ www.potatochampion.com): This colorful trailer sells heaping paper cones of Belgian-style frites, with an array of dipping sauces, including pesto mayonnaise and rosemary-truffle ketchup, into the wee hours of the morning.

Tabor (✉ SW 5th Ave. and Stark St. ⊕ www.schnitzelwich.com): This Czech spot sells goulash, potato pancakes, sausages, and spaetzle-like halusky worthy of a sit-down restaurant. However people come in droves for the schnitzelwich, a horseradish-smeared ciabatta roll holding a perfectly breaded and fried pork loin or chicken breast.

The Grilled Cheese Grill (✉ 1027 NE Alberta Ave. ⊕ www.grilledcheesegrill.com): Located in a converted school bus, the grill offers playful variations of the classic sandwich. Get "the BABS," bursting with bacon, apples, and both blue cheese and Swiss.

PORTLAND PIZZA PICKS

Two east-side spots have earned a cult following among people who swear the pies are worth the consistent one- to two-hour wait for a table. Hungry diners often line up outside **Apizza Scholls** (✉ 4741 SE Hawthorne Blvd. ☎ 503/233–1286) 45 minutes before the doors open. Try a truffle-scented Tartufo Bianco, with mozzarella, pecorino Romano, and sea salt, or devise your own toppings, but exercise restraint—Apizza Scholls limits you to no more than three toppings to let the quality of the ingredients shine through. The popular Monday-night pizza at **Ken's Artisan Bakery** (✉ 338 NW 21st Ave. ☎ 503/248–2202 ⊕ www.kensartisan.com) prompted the opening of **Ken's Artisan Pizza** (✉ 304 SE 28th Ave. ☎ 503/517–9951) in the Laurelhurst neighborhood in 2006. The wood-fired oven at the heart of the restaurant delivers a modern take on Neapolitan pies, with memorably chewy crusts and the perfect ratio of toppings.

PORTLAND BREWS

Portland is the proclaimed beer capital of the world, affectionately deemed "Beervana" and "Munich on the Willamette," boasting 35 craft breweries operating within city limits.

(above) A sample of brews from Widmer Gasthaus. (opposite page, top) Attendees at the North American Organic Brewers Festival. (opposite page, bottom) Brewers at work at the Upright Brewing Co.

That's more than any other city in the world. Bumper stickers across town toast to Brewtopia with catchy slogans: Just Brew It and SNOBs (Supporters of Native Oregon Beer). Besides a notoriously misty climate conducive to the brewpub culture, the region is fertile with the essential ingredients that are needed to make high-quality beer, and is surrounded by the largest hop-growing regions in the United States. Fourteen varieties of hops are grown in the nearby Willamette Valley, and Oregon is overall the second-largest hop-growing state in the country.

The Portland metro area triumphs as the largest craft brewing market in the nation. The granddaddy breweries BridgePort Brewing Company and Widmer Brothers Brewing are still landmark institutions—but the future tastes hoppy good with the new generation of brewers emerging.–by Kerry Newberry

ON TAP

Bailey's Taproom (⊠ *213 Southwest Broadway* ☎ *503/295–1004* ⊕ *www. baileystaproom.com*), in downtown Portland, is a shrine to artisan beer featuring 20 constantly rotating taps of hard-to-find craft ales and lagers, spotlighting Oregon breweries. The beers change so frequently that the Tap Room sends out Twitter and blog posts for devotees to follow.

LOCAL BREWERIES

Whether you're thirsty for a pale ale or an over-the-top stout, Portland breweries will tap it. Bountiful throughout the city, it is close to impossible to pick favorites. But if we had to—here are some of our top picks ranging from traditional to avant-garde.

BridgePort Brewpub + Bakery (✉ *1313 NW Marshall St.* ☎ *503/241–3612* ⊕ *www.bridgeportbrew.com*): Visit the oldest microbrewery in Portland, a beautiful brick-and-ivy building that is listed on the National Register of Historic Places. Their heritage beer, Blue Heron, was first brewed in 1987 and honors Portland's official city bird. Brewery tours are free and take place on Saturday at 1, 3, and 5 PM.

Widmer Brothers Brewing Company (✉ *929 N. Russell St.* ☎ *503/281–2437* ⊕ *www.widmer.com*): Founded in 1984, this is Oregon's largest brewery, and their Hefeweizen is still the top-selling craft beer in the state. Brewery tours take place on Friday at 3 PM and Saturday at 11 AM and noon.

Hopworks Urban Brewery "HUB" (✉ *2944 SE Powell Blvd.* ☎ *503/232–4677* ⊕ *www.hopworksbeer.com*): In addition to brewing only organic beer, the brewery is powered with 100% renewable energy. Pint picks include the Organic Survival "Seven-Grain" Stout, finished with the iconic Stumptown Hairbender espresso and their namesake Organic Hopworks IPA, a Northwest classic. Brewery tours, which cost $5, take place on Saturday at 11 AM and 3 PM.

Beer geeks must visit two cult favorites, **Hair of the Dog Brewing Co.** (✉ *61 SE Yamhill St.* ☎ *503/232–6585* ⊕ *www. hairofthedog.com*), known for unusual and bottle-conditioned beers that improve with age, similar to wine; and **Upright Brewing Co.** (✉ *240 N. Broadway, Suite 2* ☎ *503/735–5337* ⊕ *www.uprightbrewing.com*), specializing in farmhouse-inspired beers with a Pacific Northwest twist. Both breweries can accommodate tours, but only with advance scheduling. Tasting fees apply and vary.

BEER FESTIVALS

Festivals that celebrate the city's most beloved beverage are quite common in Portland. **The North American Organic Brewers Festival** (⊕ *www. naobf.org*) kicks off summer in Portland the last weekend in June, pledging to "save the planet one beer at a time." This ode to sustainability spotlights beers and ciders made with organic ingredients from across the globe. July marks the start of **Oregon Craft Beer Month** (⊕ *www. oregoncraftbeermonth. com*) with more than 120 beer events throughout the state. The beertastic climax is the **Oregon Brewers Festival** (⊕ *www. oregonbrewfest.com*), one of the nation's longest-running craft-beer festivals, held the last full weekend in July on the banks of the Willamette River. This sun-soaked celebration features more than 80 craft breweries, live music, and Mount Hood as the backdrop. Portland pays tribute to the world's most legendary brewing styles at the **Portland International Beer Festival** (⊕ *www. seattlebeerfest.com*) in mid-July.

PORTLAND'S MUSIC SCENE

Maybe it has something to do with all of Portland's notorious rain. Maybe the wealth of nearby natural scenery is the source of inspiration. Or perhaps the combination of raw, organic vegan food and locally brewed, super-hopped IPAs gives Portlanders that extra edge. Whatever the reason, Portland's musicians rock.

(above) Joan as Policewoman at Doug Fir. (opposite page, top) Nathan Junior and M. Ward performing in Portland. (opposite page, bottom) Sunny Day Real Estate at Crystal Ballroom

The city features a wealth of homegrown talent, thanks in part to the array of fresh-faced twentysomethings moving into town every day with guitars slung over their shoulders and creative ideas circling in their minds. Well, they don't all have guitars; there are also saxophones, cellos, djembe drums, Moog synthesizers, and laptops.

It's not simply the number of outstanding musicians that makes Portland unique, but their eclecticism. It's a city where stray-far-from-the crowd individualism and a highly cooperative sense of community are prized in equal measure, and the local scene reflects that: talented, idiosyncratic musicians making all genres of music together. *–by Matt Graham*

FAMOUS LOCALS

The Decemberists: Dubbed "hyperliterate prog rock" by Stephen Colbert. **Elliot Smith:** Performed at the Oscars when Portland native Gus Van Sant featured him in the soundtrack for *Good Will Hunting*. **M. Ward:** Recently garnered attention working with Zooey Deschanel in *She & Him.* **The Shins:** Rocking out in the Pacific Northwest since bringing their jangly brand of alt-rock to Portland in 2002.

2

VENUES

Whether you're interested in listening to a singer-songwriter tell it like it is as you sip Stumptown Coffee, getting down and dirty in a rocking dive bar, or simply dancing the night away to electronic trance beats, Portland's got you covered. Here are our top places to listen to live tunes. (⇨ *Also see the Live Music section in Nightlife.*)

Crystal Ballroom. Restored by the McMenamin brothers, this ballroom transformed into one of Portland's most interesting music venues. Home to shows by nationally touring acts as well as locals, the spring-loaded ballroom floor makes dancing extra fun. ✉ *1332 W. Burnside St., Downtown* ☎ *503/225–0047.*

Doug Fir. This intimate music venue with a Northwest log-cabin theme and crystal-clear acoustics also doubles as a bar and restaurant. Acts performing at the Doug Fir tend to be of acoustic guitar, folk, and Americana variety. ✉ *830 E. Burnside St.,* ☎ *503/231–9663.*

Hawthorne Theatre. Bang your head! While Portland is becoming recognized for indie-folk, this city was one of the original hotbeds of grunge music. The Hawthorne Theatre keeps that tradition alive as one of the best local rock venues. Their amps go to 11. ✉ *3862 SE Hawthorne Blvd., East of Willamette River* ☎ *503/233–7100.*

FESTIVALS

The **Bite of Oregon** (✉ *Waterfront Park, Downtown* ☎ *503/248–0600* ⊕ *www.biteoforegon.com*) in early August features the best of local food and wine, with eclectic live entertainment.

Last Thursday (✉ *NE Alberta St., East of Willamette River* ⊕ *www.lastthursdaypdx.ning.com*) is a tremendous block party that occurs on—you guessed it—the last Thursday of every month throughout the spring and summer. Street vendors, performance artists, and musicians let their freak flags fly.

MusicfestNW (✉ *various locations* ⊕ *www.musicfestnw.com*), Portland's largest music festival, brings four days of music featuring dozens of artists. Attendees can buy tickets to each show individually, or purchase a wristband for unlimited access to all venues.

The second-largest blues festival in the country (and the biggest on the Left Coast), the four-day **Waterfront Blues Festival** (✉ *Waterfront Park* ☎ *503/973–3378* ⊕ *www.waterfrontbluesfest.com*), has been drawing big names in blues and big crowds over the July 4 weekend since 1987.

PEDALING PORTLAND

Bicycling is a cultural phenomenon in Portland—possibly the most beloved mode of transportation in the city. Besides the sheer numbers of cyclists you see on roads and pathways, you'll find well-marked bike lanes and signs reminding motorists to yield to cyclists.

(above) Biking from Portland to Cascade Locks along the Historic Columbia River Highway. (opposite page, top) Biking the Steel Bridge Path.

There are more than 300 mi of bicycle boulevards, lanes, and off-street paths in Portland. Accessible maps, specialized tours, parking capacity (including lockers and sheltered racks downtown), and bicycle-only traffic signals at confusing intersections make biking in the city easy. Cyclists can find the best routes by following green direction-and-distance signs that point the way around town, and the corresponding white dots on the street surface.

Educators, advocates, riding groups, businesses, and the city government are working toward making Portland even more bike-friendly and safe. An intended 950-plus mi of bike paths are to be added over the next two decades. –by Sarah Cypher

BIKING COMMUNITY

Portland bikers gather on the last Friday of every month to ride in **Critical Mass** (⊕ www.rosecitycriticalmass.org), an event meant to publicize bicycles as a powerful alternative to cars. Several bike co-ops in the city are devoted to providing used bikes at decent prices, as well as to teaching bike maintenance and the economic and environmental benefits of becoming a two-wheel commuter.

ROUTES

If you're a social rider, group rides set out from several local shops. Check the events pages of **Bike Gallery** (⊕ *www.bikegallery.com*), **River City Bicycles** (⊕ *www.rivercitybicycles.com*), and **Fat Tire Farm** (⊕ *www.fattirefarm.com*).

Bike paths on both sides of the **Willamette River** continue south of downtown, so you can easily make a mild, several-mile loop through Waterfront Park by crossing the Steel, Hawthorne, or Sellwood bridges to get from one side to the other.

Leif Erikson Drive is an 11-mi off-road ride through Northwest Portland's Forest Park, accessible from the serene west end of Northwest Thurman Street. Leif's wide, double-track trail is popular with runners and mountain bikers, winding through a 5,000-acre city park far from the noise and distraction of neighborhood traffic. Its dense canopy occasionally gives way to river views. To reach the trailhead, bike up steep Thurman Street or shuttle there via TriMet Bus 15.

Bicycling **Sauvie Island**'s 12-mi loop is a rare treat. Situated near the mouth of the Willamette River and Columbia Slough, the island is entirely rural farmland. Besides the main loop, it also offers out-and-back jaunts to beaches and pristine wetlands. To get to Sauvie Island from Portland, you can brave the 10-mi ride in the wide bike lane of U.S. 30 or shuttle your bike there via TriMet Bus 17.

The **Columbia Historic Highway** begins 17 mi east of Portland on U.S. 84 and rolls almost 90 mi along the Columbia River Gorge. This National Scenic Area will take you past a series of thundering waterfalls towards sporty Hood River, Oregon. You can shorten the route by turning around after the awe-inspiring river view at Mile 12, or after a breathtaking descent to Multnomah Falls at Mile 18. Many riders begin and end at McMenamins Edgefield, a comfortable resort where anyone (not just guests) can get a warm shower, cold beer, and good meal. Reach the Edgefield by bike or shuttle there via TriMet's Bus 77.

WHERE TO RENT

Bikes can be rented at several places in the city. Rentals typically run from $20 to $50 per day with cheaper weekly rates from $75 to $150. Bike helmets are generally included in the cost of rental.
CityBikes Workers Cooperative (✉ *734 SE Ankeny St., East of Willamette River* ☎ *503/239–6951*) rents hybrid bikes good for casual city riding.
Fat Tire Farm (✉ *2714 NW Thurman St., West of Downtown* ☎ *503/222–3276*) rentsmountain bikes, greatfor treks in Forest Park.
Waterfront Bicycle Rentals (✉ *315 SW Montgomery St., Suite 3, Downtown* ☎ *503/227–1719*) is convenient for jaunts along the Willamette.

BIKING RESOURCE

For more information on bike routes and resources in and around Portland, visit the **Department of Transportation** (⊕ *www.portlandonline.com/transportation*). You can download maps, or order "Bike There," a glossy detailed bicycle map of the metropolitan area.

PORTLAND'S PARKS

The variety of Portland's parks ensures that there's something for just about everyone, from the world's smallest park (Mill Ends) to one of the largest urban natural areas in the country (Forest Park).

(above) Peninsula Park and Rose Garden. (opposite page, top) Governor Tom McCall Waterfront Park. (opposite page, bottom) Forest Park.

Portland aspired to be a city of parks starting in 1852. Those first parks (now known as the Plaza Blocks and South Park Blocks) were designed to help residents enjoy the simple things in life, and to steer them away from those darker ones that tempted good Portlanders (ahem, beer). These days, more than 12,000 acres of parks and open spaces in more than 250 locations house six public gardens, 204 parks, five golf courses, and thousands of acres of urban forest.

True to the city's nicknames, Rose City or City of Roses, the fragrant favorite is found at many of the area's parks. There is no one official reason for the city's moniker, but many suggested ones. The first known reference was in 1888 at an Episcopal Church convention. And though the first Rose Festival was held in 1907, the city did not officially take the nickname until 2003.
–by Crystal Wood

'TIS A WEE PARK

No one can say that Portlanders don't have a sense of humor, because there is no other way to explain how **Mill Ends Park**—the world's smallest city park, according to Guinness World Records—has survived since 1948. What started out as a hole where a light pole was supposed to go became the darling of Dick Fagan, a local journalist whose office overlooked it. Visit the hole—we mean park—at SW Naito Parkway and Taylor Street.

The following parks are our top picks. After each listing, the ⟨ specifies who will especially enjoy the park. Washington Park and its gardens are not listed here; please see ⇨ Exploring in Washington Park for those listings.

Cathedral Park. Whether it's the view of the imposing and stunning Gothic St. John's Bridge or the historic significance of Lewis and Clark having camped here in 1806, this park is divine. Though there's no church, the park gets its name from the picturesque arches supporting the bridge. It's rumored that the ghost of a young girl haunts the bridge, and that may be true, but if you're told that it was designed by the same man who envisioned the Golden Gate Bridge, that's just a popular misconception. Dog lovers, or those who aren't, should take note of the off-leash area. ⊠ *N. Edison St. and Pittsburg Ave., east of the Willamette* ⊙ *5* AM–*midnight* ⟨ *Good for: Bridge Buffs, Dog Lovers, Ghost Hunters, History Lovers.*

Council Crest Park. The second-highest point in Portland, at 1,073 feet, is a superb spot to watch sunsets and sunrises. If you visit on a weekday, there are far fewer folks than on the busy weekends. Along with great views of the Portland metro area, a clear day also affords views of the surrounding peaks—Mt. Hood, Mt. St. Helens, Mt. Adams, Mt. Jefferson, and Mt. Rainier. A bronze

fountain depicting a mother and child has been erected in the park twice; first in the 1950s and the second in the 1990s. The peaceful piece was stolen in the 1980s, uncovered in a narcotics bust ten years later, and then returned to the park. ⊠ *3400 Council Crest Dr., West of Downtown* ⊙ *5* AM–*midnight, closed to cars after 9* PM ⟨ *Good for: Picnickers, View Seekers.*

Forest Park. One of the nation's largest urban wildernesses (5,000 acres), this city-owned, car-free park, has more than 50 species of birds and mammals and more than 70 mi of trails. Running the length of the park is the 24½-mi Wildwood Trail, which extends into Washington Park. The 11-mi Leif Erikson Drive, which picks up from the end of Northwest Thurman Street, is a popular place to jog or ride a mountain bike. The **Portland Audubon Society** (⊠ *5151 NW Cornell Rd.* ☎ *503/292–6855* ⊕ *www.audobonportland. org*) supplies free maps and sponsors a flock of bird-related activities, including guided bird-watching events. There's a hospital for injured and orphaned birds as well as a gift shop stocked with books and feeders. ⊠ *Past Nob Hill in Northwest District* ☎ *503/823–7529* ⊕ *www.forestparkconservancy. org* ⊙ *Daily dawn–dusk* ⟨ *Good for: Hikers, Nature Lovers, Photographers, Bird-watchers, Mountain Bikers.*

Fodor'sChoice ★ Governor Tom McCall Waterfront Park. Named for a former governor revered for his statewide land-use planning initiatives, this park stretches north along the Willamette River for about a mile to Burnside Street. Broad and grassy, Waterfront Park's got a fine ground-level view of downtown Portland's bridges and skyline. Once an expressway, it's now the site for many events, among them the Rose Festival, classical and blues concerts, Cinco de Mayo, and the Oregon Brewers Festival. The arching jets of water at the **Salmon Street Fountain** change configuration every few hours, and are a favorite cooling-off spot during the dog days of summer. ⊠ *SW Naito Pkwy. (Front Ave.), from south of Hawthorne Bridge to Burnside Bridge, Downtown ⛲ Good For: Families, Bikers, Walkers, Runners.*

Fodor'sChoice ★ Laurelhurst Park. Completed in 1914, resplendent Laurelhurst Park is evocative of another time, and gives you the urge to don a parasol. It's no wonder that it was the first park to be put on the National Register of Historic Places. Take a stroll around the large spring-fed pond (granted, a bit murky with algae) and keep an eye out for blue heron, the city's official bird. On the south side of this 26-acre park is one of the busiest basketball courts in town. Though the park is always beautiful, it is especially so in fall. ⊠ *SE 39th Ave. and Stark St., East of Willamette River ⛲ 5 AM–10:30 PM ⛲ Good for: Basketballers, Dog Lovers, Anglers, Picnickers, Runners, Nappers, Lovers, Volleyballers, Horseshoe Players.*

Marquam Nature Park. Itching to get a hike in but no time to get out of Portland? Just minutes from downtown are 176 acres of greenery and 5 mi of trails to explore. No playgrounds or dog parks here, just peace and quiet. Maps of trails that range from 1 to 3.5 mi are available at the shelter at the base of the trails or on the Friends of Marquam Park Web site. ⊠ *SW Marquam St. and Sam Jackson Park Rd., West of Downtown ⊕ www.fnmp.org ⛲ 5 AM–midnight ⛲ Good for: Nature Lovers, Hikers, Solitude Seekers.*

Mt. Tabor Park. A playground on top of a volcano cinder cone? Yup, that's here. The cinders, or glassy rock fragments, unearthed in the park's construction,

2

were used to surface the respite's roads; the ones leading to the top are closed to cars, but popular with cyclists. They're also popular with cruisers—each August there's an old-fashioned soapbox derby. Picnic tables and tennis, basketball, and volleyball courts make Mt. Tabor Park perfection. ⊠ *SE 60th and Salmon Sts., East of Willamette River* ☉ *5 AM–midnight* ♿ *Good for: Families, Picnickers, Dog Lovers, Geologists, Walkers, Cyclists, Sunset Seekers.*

Fodor's Choice ★ **Oaks Bottom Wild Refuge.** Bring your binoculars, because birds are plentiful here; more than 400 species have been spotted, including hawks, quail, pintails, mallards, coots, woodpeckers, kestrels, widgeons, hummingbirds, and the sedately beautiful blue heron. The 140-acre refuge is a floodplain wetland—rare because it is in the heart of the city. The hiking isn't too strenuous, but wear sturdy shoes, as it can get muddy; part of the park is on top of a landfill layered with soil. ⊠ *SE 7th and Sellwood Ave., east of the Willamette* ☉ *5 AM–midnight* ♿ *Good for: Bird-watchers, Hikers, Cyclists.*

Fodor's Choice ★ **Peninsula Park & Rose Garden.** The "City of Roses" moniker started here, at this park that harks back to another time. The city's oldest (1909) public rose garden (and the only sunken one) houses almost nine thousand plantings and 65 varieties of roses. The daunting task of deadheading all these flowers is covered in classes taught to volunteers twice a season. The bandstand is a historic landmark, and the last of its kind in the city. There's also a 100-year-old fountain, playground, wading pool, tennis and volleyball courts, and picnic tables. ⊠ *700 N. Rosa Parks Way, east of the Willamette* ☉ *5 AM–midnight* ♿ *Good for: Botanists, Gardeners, Runners, Picnickers, Romantics.*

Sellwood Park. Sixteen acres of tall old pines make a visit here purely relaxing.

A paved path circles the park and most of the action—ballpark, pool, football field, playground, and tennis court. Sellwood also sports a terrific location; Oaks Bottom Refuge, Oaks Amusement Park, and the Willamette River are nearby, and the Sellwood neighborhood has charming shops and restaurants, convenient for a takeout picnic. ⊠ *SE 7th Ave. and Miller St., east of the Willamette* ☉ *5 AM–midnight* ♿ *Good for: Families, Walkers, Runners, Picnickers.*

Tryon Creek State Natural Area. Portland is chock-full of parks, but this is the only state park within city limits. And at 670 acres, there's plenty of room for all its admirers. The area was logged starting in the 1880s, and the natural regrowth has produced red alder, Douglas fir, big leaf maple, and western red cedar, giving home to more than 50 bird species. The eastern edge has a paved trail, in addition to 14 mi of trails for bikes, hikers, and horses. Before heading to the trails, stop by the nature center to check out the exhibits and topographical relief map. ⊠ *SW Boones Ferry Rd. and Terwilliger Blvd., West of Downtown* ☎ *503/636–4398* ⊕ *www.tryonfriends. org* ☉ *Daily 7 AM–8 PM, Nature Center 9–4* ♿ *Good for: Cyclists, Bird-watchers, Walkers, Hikers.*

(opposite) Sellwood Park. (bottom) Laurelhurst Park

PORTLAND PLANNER

Getting Here

Air Travel. It takes about 5 hours to fly nonstop to Portland from New York, 4 hours from Chicago, and 2½ hours from Los Angeles. Flying from Seattle to Portland takes just under an hour; flying from Portland to Vancouver takes an hour and 15 minutes. **Portland International Airport** (PDX) (☎ 877/739–4636 ⊕ www.flypdx.com) is a sleek, modern airport with service to many national and international destinations. **TriMet's Red Line MAX light rail** (☎ 503/238–7433 ⊕ www.trimet.org) leaves the airport for downtown about every 15 minutes. Trains arrive at and depart from just outside the passenger terminal near the south baggage claim. The trip takes about 35 minutes, and the fare is $2.30. By taxi, the trip downtown takes about 30 minutes and costs about $35.

Train Travel. Amtrak (☎ 800/872–7245) has daily service to Union Station from the Midwest and California. The *Cascades* runs between Seattle and Vancouver and between Seattle, Portland, and Eugene. The trip from Seattle to Portland takes 3½ hours and costs $28–$44. The *Empire Builder* travels between Portland and Spokane (7 hours, $75). From Portland to Eugene it's a 3-hour trip; the cost is $21–$35.

Getting Around

Bike Travel. It's tough to find a more bike-friendly city in America. Visitors are impressed by the facilities available for bicyclists—more than 300 mi of bike lanes, paths, and boulevards. ⇨ *See Pedaling Portland.*

Car Travel. I–5 enters Portland from the north and south. I–84, the city's major eastern approach, terminates in Portland. U.S. 26 and U.S. 30 are primary east–west thoroughfares. Bypass routes are I–205, which links I–5 and I–84 before crossing the Columbia River into Washington, and I–405, which arcs around western downtown.

From the airport to downtown, take I–205 south to westbound I–84. Drive west over the Willamette River and take the City Center exit. If going to the airport, take I–84 east to I–205 north; follow I–205 to the airport exit.

Traffic on I–5 north and south of downtown and on I–84 and I–205 east of downtown is heavy between 6 AM and 9 AM and between 4 and 8 PM. Four-lane U.S. 26 west of downtown can be bumper-to-bumper any time of day going to or from downtown.

Most city-center streets are one-way only, and SW 5th and 6th avenues between Burnside and SW Madison are limited to bus traffic.

Though there are several options, parking in downtown Portland can be tricky and expensive. If you require more than several hours, your most affordable and accessible option is to park in one of seven city-owned "Smart Park" lots.

Rates range from $1.50 per hour (short-term parking, four hours or less) to $3–$5 per hour (long-term parking, weekdays 5 AM–6 PM), with a $15 daily maximum; rates are lower weekends and evenings. Participating merchants will validate tickets and cover the first two hours of parking when you spend at least $25 in their stores. There are numerous privately owned lots around the city as well; fees for those vary.

Street parking is metered only, and requires you to visibly display a sticker on the inside of your curbside window. The meters that dispense the stickers take coins or credit cards. Metered spaces are mostly available for 90 minutes to three hours; parking tickets for exceeding the limit are regularly issued. Once you get out of downtown and into residential areas, there's plenty of nonmetered street parking available.

Car-rental rates in Portland begin at $30 a day and $138 a week, not including the 17% Multnomah County tax if you rent in this county, which includes the airport. All major agencies are represented.

Taxi Travel. Taxi fare is $2.50 at flag drop plus $2.30 per mi for one person. Each additional passenger pays $1. Cabs cruise the city streets, or you can phone for one.

Contacts Broadway Cab (☎ 503/227–1234). **New Rose City Cab** (☎ 503/282–7707). **Portland Taxi Company** (☎ 503/256–5400). **Radio Cab** (☎ 503/227–1212).

TriMet/MAX Travel. TriMet operates an extensive system of buses, streetcars, and light rail trains. The Central City streetcar line runs between Legacy Good Samaritan Hospital in Nob Hill, the Pearl District, downtown, and Portland State University. To Nob Hill it travels along 10th Avenue and then on NW Northrup; from Nob Hill it runs along NW Lovejoy and then on 11th Avenue. Trains stop every few blocks. Buses can operate as frequently as every five minutes or only once an hour.

Metropolitan Area Express, or MAX light rail, links the eastern and western Portland suburbs with downtown, Washington Park and the Oregon Zoo, the Lloyd Center district, the convention center, and the Rose Quarter. From downtown, trains operate daily 5:30 AM–1 AM and run about every 10 minutes Monday–Saturday and every 15 minutes on Sunday and holidays.

Bus, MAX, and streetcar fare is $2 for one or two zones, which covers most places you'll go, and $2.30 for three zones, which includes all of the city's outlying areas. A "Fareless Square" extends through downtown from I–405 to the Willamette River, and from NW Irving to the South Waterfront area, and includes the Lloyd Center stop across the river. The free area applies to MAX light rail and Portland Streetcar only. To qualify, your entire trip must stop and start in the fareless area.

Day passes for unlimited system-wide travel cost $4.75. Three-day, weekly, and monthly passes are available. As you board the bus, the driver will hand you a transfer ticket good for one to two hours on all buses and MAX trains. Be sure to hold on to it whether you're transferring or not; it also serves as proof that you have paid for your ride. Bikes are allowed in designated areas on MAX trains, and there are bike racks on the front of all buses.

Contacts TriMet/MAX (☎ 503/238–7433 ⊕ www.trimet.org).

Tour Options

Boat Tours. Portland Spirit (☎ 503/224–3900 or 800/224-3901 ⊕ www.portlandspirit.com) has a variety of tours on multiple types of marine craft. **Willamette Jetboat Excursions** (☎ 888/538–2628 or 503/231–1532 ⊕ www.willamettejet.com) offers whirling, swirling one- and two-hour tours along the Willamette River that include an up-close visit to the falls at Oregon City.

Trolley Tours. The **Willamette Shore Trolley** (☎ 503/697–7436 ⊕ www.oregonelectricrailway.org) provides scenic round-trips between suburban Lake Oswego and downtown, along the west shore of the Willamette River. The 6-mi route, which the trolley makes in 45 minutes, passes over trestles and through Elk Rock Tunnel along one of the most scenic stretches of the river.

Walking Tours. For a guided tour packed with information, the variety of options from **Portland Walking Tours** (☎ 503/774–4522 ⊕ www.portlandwalkingtours.com) ensures something for all touring tastes.

VISITOR INFORMATION

Contacts Travel Portland Information Center (✉ 701 SW 6th Ave., Pioneer Courthouse Sq. ☎ 503/275–8355 or 877/678–5263 ⊕ www.travelportland.com).

PORTLAND PLANNER

When to Go

Portland's mild climate is best from June through September. Hotels are often filled in July and August, so it's important to book reservations in advance. Spring and fall are also excellent times to visit. The weather usually remains quite good, and the prices for accommodations, transportation, and tours can be lower (and the crowds much smaller) in the most popular destinations. In winter, snow is uncommon in the city but abundant in the nearby mountains, making the region a skier's dream.

Average daytime summer highs are in the 70s; winter temperatures are generally in the 40s. Rainfall varies greatly from one locale to another. In the coastal mountains, for example, 160 inches of rain fall annually, creating temperate rain forests. Portland has an average of only 36 inches of rainfall a year—less than New York, Chicago, or Miami. In winter, however, the rain may never seem to end. More than 75% of Portland's annual precipitation occurs from October through March.

Forecasts National Weather Service (⊕ www. wrh.noaa.gov). Weather Channel (⊕ www.weather. com).

About the Restaurants

Lovers of ethnic foods have their pick of Chinese, French, Indian, Peruvian, Italian, Japanese, Polish, Middle Eastern, Tex-Mex, Thai, and Vietnamese specialties. Most of the city's trendier restaurants and reliable classics are concentrated in Nob Hill, the Pearl District, and downtown. A smattering of cuisines can also be found on the east side of town as well, near Fremont, Hawthorne Boulevard, Sandy Boulevard, and Alberta Street.

Compared to other major cities, Portland restaurants aren't open quite as late, and it's unusual to see many diners after 11 PM even on weekends, though there are a handful of restaurants and popular bars that do serve late. Many diners dress casually for even higher-end establishments; jeans are acceptable almost everywhere.

About the Hotels

The hotels near the city center and on the riverfront are appealing for their proximity to Portland's attractions. MAX light rail is within easy walking distance of most properties. Additional accommodations clustered near the Convention Center and the airport are almost all chain hotels that tend to be less expensive than those found downtown. Several beautiful bed-and-breakfasts are in the northwest and northeast residential neighborhoods.

Most of Portland's luxury hotels can be booked for under $250 per night. If you are willing to stay outside the downtown area, you can easily find a room in a suburban chain hotel for well under $100 per night. Before booking your stay, visit ⊕ www.travelportland.com to check out "Portland Perks" packages.

WHAT IT COSTS IN U.S. DOLLARS

	¢	$	$$	$$$	$$$$
Restaurants	under $10	$10–$16	$17–$23	$24–$30	over $30
Hotels	under $100	$100–$150	$151–$200	$201–$250	over $250

Restaurant prices are per person, for a main course at dinner. Hotel prices are for two people in a standard double room in high season, excluding tax.

2

Updated by
Janna Mock-
Lopez and
Crystal Wood

What distinguishes Portland from the rest of America's cityscapes? Or for that matter, from the rest of the world's urban destinations? In a Northwest nutshell: everything. For some, it's the wealth of cultural offerings and never-ending culinary choices; for others, it's Portland's proximity to the ocean and mountains, or simply the beauty of having all these attributes in one place.

Strolling through downtown or in one of Portland's numerous neighborhoods, you discover an unmistakable vibrancy to this city—one that is created by the clean air, the wealth of trees, and a blend of historic and modern architecture. Portland's various nicknames—Rose City, Bridgetown, Beervana, Brewtopia—tell its story in a nutshell as well.

Portland has a thriving cultural community, with ballet, opera, symphonies, theater, and art exhibitions both minor and major in scope. Portland also has long been considered a hub for indie music. Hundreds of bands flock to become part of the creative flow of alternative, jazz, blues, and rock that dominate the nightclub scene seven nights a week. Factor in an outrageous number of independent brewpubs and coffee shops—with snowboarding, windsurfing, or camping within an hour's drive—and it's easy to see why so many young people take advantage of Portland's eclectic indoor and outdoor offerings.

For people on a slower pace, there are strolls through never-ending parks, dimmed dining rooms for savoring innovative regional cuisine, and gorgeous cruises along the Willamette River aboard the *Portland Spirit*. Families can explore first-rate museums and parks, including the Children's Museum, the Oregon Museum of Science and Industry, and Oaks Park. At most libraries, parks, and recreational facilities, expect to find hands-on activities, music, story times, plays, and special performances for children. Many restaurants in and around Portland are family-friendly, and with immediate access to the MAX light rail and streetcars, toting kids around is easy.

GREAT ITINERARIES

IF YOU HAVE 1 DAY
Spend the morning exploring downtown. Visit the **Portland Art Museum** or the **Oregon History Center**, stop by the historic **First Congregational Church** and Pioneer Courthouse Square, and take a stroll along the **Park Blocks** or **Waterfront Park**. Eat lunch and do a little shopping along **Northwest 23rd Avenue** or at **Powell's Books** in the early afternoon, and be sure to get a look at the beautiful historic homes in **Nob Hill**. From there, drive up into the northwest hills by the **Pittock Mansion**, and finish off the afternoon at the **Japanese Garden** and the **International Test Rose Garden** in Washington Park. If you still have energy, head across the river for dinner on **Hawthorne Boulevard**; then drive up to **Mt. Tabor Park** for Portland's best sunset.

IF YOU HAVE 3 DAYS
On your first day, follow the itinerary above, but stay on the west side for dinner, and take your evening stroll in **Waterfront Park**. On your second morning, visit the **Lan Su Chinese Garden** in Old Town, and then head across the river to the **Sellwood District** for lunch and antiquing. Stop by the **Crystal Springs Rhododendron Garden**, then head up to the **Hawthorne District** in the afternoon. Wander through the Hawthorne and Belmont neighborhoods for a couple of hours, stop by **Laurelhurst Park**, and take a picnic dinner up to **Mt. Tabor Park**. In the evening, catch a movie at the **Bagdad Theatre**, or get a beer at one of the **east-side brewpubs**. On Day 3, take a morning hike in **Hoyt Arboretum** or **Forest Park**, then spend your afternoon exploring shops and galleries in the **Pearl District** and on **northeast Alberta Street**. Drive out to **the Grotto**, and then eat dinner at the **Kennedy School** or one of the other McMenamins brewpubs.

EXPLORING PORTLAND

One of the greatest things about Portland is that there's so much to explore. This city rightfully boasts that there's something for everyone. What makes discovering Portland's treasures even more enticing is that its attractions, transportation options, and events are all relatively accessible and affordable.

DOWNTOWN

Portland has one of the most attractive, inviting downtown centers in the United States. It's clean, compact, and filled with parks, plazas, and fountains. Architecture fans find plenty to admire in its mix of old and new. Hotels, shops, museums, restaurants, and entertainment can all be found here, and much of the downtown area is part of the TriMet transit system's Fareless Square, within which you can ride the light rail or the Portland Streetcar for free.

Numbers in the margin correspond to numbers on the Downtown map.

WHAT'S FREE (OR CHEAPER) WHEN

Children's Museum: Free from 4–8 PM the first Friday of each month.

Crystal Springs Rhododendron Garden: Free the day after Labor Day through February.

Oregon Historical Society: Two free children for each adult the third Sunday of each month.

Oregon Museum of Science and Industry: $2 admission the first Sunday of each month.

Oregon Zoo: $4 admission the second Tuesday of each month.

Portland Art Museum: Free from 5–8 PM the fourth Friday of each month.

World Forestry Discovery Center Museum: $2 admission the first Wednesday of each month.

TOP ATTRACTIONS

② **Central Library.** The elegant, etched-graphite central staircase and elaborate ceiling ornamentation make this no ordinary library. With a gallery space on the second floor and famous literary names engraved on the walls, this building is well worth a walk around. ⊠ *801 SW 10th Ave., Downtown* ☎ *503/988–5123* ☉ *Mon. and Thurs.–Sat. 10–6, Tues. and Wed. 10–8, Sun. noon–5.*

⑩ **Keller Auditorium.** Home base for the Portland Opera, the former Civic Auditorium also hosts traveling musicals and other theatrical extravaganzas. The building itself, part of the Portland Center for the Performing Arts, is not particularly distinctive, but the **Ira Keller Fountain,** a series of 18-foot-high stone waterfalls across from the front entrance, is worth a look. ⊠ *SW 3rd Ave. and Clay St., Downtown* ☎ *503/274–6560* ⊕ *www.pcpa.com.*

⑦ **Old Church.** This building erected in 1882 is a prime example of Carpenter Gothic architecture. Tall spires and original stained-glass windows enhance its exterior of rough-cut lumber. The acoustically resonant church hosts free classical concerts at noon each Wednesday. If you're lucky, you'll get to hear one of the few operating Hook and Hastings tracker pipe organs. ⊠ *1422 SW 11th Ave., Downtown* ☎ *503/222–2031* ⊕ *www.oldchurch.org* ☉ *Weekdays 11–3.*

⑤ **Oregon Historical Society.** Impressive eight-story-high trompe l'oeil murals of Lewis and Clark and the Oregon Trail cover two sides of this downtown museum, which follows the state's story from prehistoric times to the present. A pair of 9,000-year-old sagebrush sandals, a covered wagon, and an early chainsaw are displayed inside "Oregon My Oregon," a permanent exhibit that provides a comprehensive overview of the state's past. Other spaces host large traveling exhibits and changing regional shows. The center's research library is open to the public Thursday through Saturday; its bookstore is a good source for maps and publications on Pacific Northwest history. Every month the Oregon Historical Society has a day on which kids are admitted for free. Check the

Downtown

KEY

—O— *Max Light Rail*
- ← - *Streetcar*
········· *Bus*
o‾o *Bike only*

GOVERNOR TOM McCALL
WATERFRONT PARK

Willamette River

TO
CHILDREN'S
MUSEUM

0 _____ 1/4 mile
0 _____ 1/4 kilometer

Web site for dates. ✉ *1200 SW Park Ave., Downtown* ☎ *503/222–1741* ⊕ *www.ohs.org* 🎫*$11* ⊙ *Tues.–Sat. 10–5, Sun. noon–5.*

① Pioneer Courthouse Square. In many ways the living room, public heart, and commercial soul of downtown, Pioneer Square is not entirely square, rather an amphitheater-like brick piazza. Special seasonal, charitable, and festival-oriented events often take place in this premier people-watching venue. On Sunday **vintage trolley cars** (☎ *503/323–7363*) run from the MAX station here to Lloyd Center, with free service every half hour between noon and 6 PM. Call to check on the current schedule. You can pick up maps and literature about the city and the state here at the **Portland/Oregon Information Center** (☎ *503/275–8355* ⊕ *www. travelportland.com* ⊙ *Weekdays 8:30–5:30, Sat. 10–4*) . Directly across the street is one of downtown Portland's most familiar landmarks, the classically sedate **Pioneer Courthouse.** Built in 1869, it's the oldest public building in the Pacific Northwest. ✉ *701 SW 6th Ave., Downtown.*

⑥ Portland Art Museum. The treasures at the Pacific Northwest's oldest arts
Fodor's Choice facility span 35 centuries of Asian, European, and American art. A high
★ point is the Center for Native American Art, with regional and contemporary art from more than 200 tribes. The **Jubitz Center for Modern and Contemporary Art** contains six floors devoted entirely to modern art, with the changing selection chosen from more than 400 pieces in the museum's permanent collection. The film center presents the annual Portland International Film Festival in February and the Northwest Film Festival in early November. Also, take a moment to linger in the peaceful outdoor sculpture garden. Kids under 18 are admitted free. ✉ *1219 SW Park Ave., Downtown* ☎ *503/226–2811, 503/221–1156 film schedule* ⊕ *www.portlandartmuseum.org* 🎫*$12* ⊙ *Tues., Wed., and Sat. 10–5, Thurs. and Fri. 10–8, Sun. noon–5.*

⑨ Portland Farmers Market. On Saturday from March through mid-December, local farmers, bakers, chefs, and entertainers converge at the South Park Blocks near the PSU campus for Oregon's largest open-air farmer's market. It's a great place to sample the regional bounty and to witness the local-food obsession that's revolutionized Portland's culinary scene. There's also a Wednesday market between Southwest Salmon and Southwest Main. ✉ *South Park Blocks at SW Park Ave. and Montgomery St., Downtown* ☎ *503/241–0032* ⊕ *www.portlandfarmersmarket. org* ⊙ *Mar.–mid-Dec., Sat. 8:30–2; May–Oct., Wed. 10–2.*

WORTH NOTING

⑫ Chapman and Lownsdale squares. During the 1920s these parks were segregated by sex: Chapman, between Madison and Main streets, was reserved for women, and Lownsdale, between Main and Salmon streets, was for men. The elk statue on Main Street, which separates the parks, was given to the city by David Thompson, mayor from 1879 to 1882. It recalls the elk that grazed in the area in the 1850s.

⑭ City Hall. Portland's four-story, granite-faced City Hall, which was completed in 1895, is an example of the Renaissance Revival style popular in the late 19th century. Italian influences can be seen in the porch, the pink scagliola (faux marble) columns, the cornice embellishments, and other details. Much beauty was restored when the building was

Pioneer Square, Downtown

renovated in the late 1990s. The ornate interior—with intricate scroll-work, decorative tile, a sunny atrium, and art exhibits—provides a fine shortcut between Southwest 4th and 5th avenues. ✉ *1221 SW 4th Ave., Downtown* ☎ *503/823–4000* ⊙ *Weekdays 8–5.*

❹ First Congregational Church. This Venetian Gothic church, modeled after Boston's Old South Church, was completed in 1895, and you still can hear its original bell, purchased in 1871, ringing from its 175-foot tower. The church provided much of the land on which the Portland Center for the Performing Arts was built. If the front doors are locked, knock on the office door for entrance. ✉ *1126 SW Park Ave., Downtown* ☎ *503/228–7219* ⊕ *www.uccportland.org* ⊙ *Weekdays 9–2.*

⓭ Justice Center. This modern building houses the jail, county courts, and police support offices. Visitors are welcome to browse the **Police Museum** (☎ *503/823–0019* ✉ *Free* ⊙ *Tues.–Fri. 10–3*) on the 16th floor, which has uniforms, guns, and badges worn by the Portland Police Bureau. Motorcycles and a jail cell can also be explored. Photo ID is required to enter the main building. ✉ *1111 SW 2nd Ave., Downtown* ⊕ *www.portlandpolicemuseum.com.*

⓯ Portland Building. *Portlandia,* the second-largest hammered-copper statue in the world, surpassed only by the Statue of Liberty, kneels on the second-story balcony of one of the first postmodern buildings in the United States. Built in 1982, and architect Michael Graves's first major design commission, this 15-story office building is buff-color, with brown-and-blue trim and exterior decorative touches. A huge fiber-glass mold of Portlandia's face is exhibited in the second-floor Public Art Gallery, which provides a good overview of Portland's 1% for Art

CLOSE UP

Top Festivals

SPRING
Every May, McCall Waterfront Park fills with live entertainment, rides, and food for **Cinco de Mayo Fiesta**, one of the largest of its kind in America.

SUMMER
In early August, support the Special Olympics while stuffing your face with delectable foods at **Bite of Oregon**. The largest gathering of independent brewers means lots of beer and beer lovers the last weekend of July for **Oregon Brewers Festival**. More than 50 organic beers and ciders are enjoyed with live entertainment in June at **North American Organic Brewers Festival**. In June, lovers of rare and obscure beers can try more than 100 at the **Portland International Beer Festival**. From the pet parade to the Pride Parade, **Portland Pride Festival and Parade** in June is never dull. Now more than 100 years old, the **Portland Rose Festival** in

June has two parades, carnival, fireworks, and dragon boat races. Help stock the local food bank and listen to top headliners from around the nation each July at the **Waterfront Blues Festival**, the largest blues festival west of the Mississippi.

WINTER
The holiday spirit is vibrant at **Festival of Lights**, with 500,000 lights and the Pacific Northwest's largest choral gathering. In the heart of downtown, **Holiday Ale Festival** helps chase away the chill of a long winter's night. The top short films, features, and documentaries from the Northwest are chosen by prominent filmmakers and critics each November at the **Northwest Film and Video Festival**. For more than 30 years film lovers have enjoyed the **Portland International Film Festival**, featuring works from throughout the world each February.

Program, and the hundreds of works on display throughout the city. ✉ *1120 SW 5th Ave., Downtown* ☉ *Weekdays 8–6.*

❸ Portland Center for the Performing Arts. The "old building" and the hub of activity here is the **Arlene Schnitzer Concert Hall,** host to the Oregon Symphony, musical events of many genres, and lectures. Across Main Street, but still part of the center, is the 292-seat **Delores Winningstad Theatre,** used for plays and special performances. Its stage design and dimensions are based on those of an Elizabethan-era stage. The 916-seat **Newmark Theatre** is also part of the complex. ✉ *SW Broadway and SW Main St., Downtown* ☎ *503/274–6560* ⊕ *www.pcpa.com* ☉ *Free tours Wed. at 11 AM, Sat. every ½ hr 11–1.*

❽ Portland State University. The state's only university in a major metropolitan area takes advantage of downtown's South Park Blocks to provide trees and greenery for its 15,000 students. The compact campus, between Market Street and I–405, spreads west from the Park Blocks to 12th Avenue and east to 5th Avenue. Seven schools offer undergraduate, masters, and doctoral degrees. ✉ *Park Ave. and Market St., Downtown* ☎ *503/725–3000* ⊕ *www.pdx.edu.*

⓫ Yamhill National Historic District. Trains glide by many examples of 19th-century cast-iron architecture on the MAX line between the Skidmore and Yamhill stations, where the streets are closed to cars. Take a moment at the Yamhill station to glance around at these old buildings, which have intricate rooflines and facades. Nearby, on Southwest Naito Parkway at Taylor Street, is **Mill Ends Park,** which sits in the middle of a traffic island. This patch of whimsy, at 24 inches in diameter, has been recognized by *Guinness World Records* as the world's smallest official city park. ⊠ *Between SW Naito Pkwy. and SW 3rd Ave. and SW Morrison and SW Taylor Sts., Downtown.*

PEARL DISTRICT AND OLD TOWN/CHINATOWN

The Old Town National Historic District, commonly called Old Town/ Chinatown, is where Portland was born. The 20-square-block section, bounded by Oak Street to the south and Everett Street to the north, includes buildings of varying ages and architectural styles. Before it was renovated, this was skid row. Vestiges of it remain in parts of Chinatown; older buildings are slowly being remodeled, and over the last several years the immediate area has experienced a surge in development. MAX serves the area with a stop at the Old Town/Chinatown station.

Bordering Old Town to the northwest is the Pearl District. Formerly a warehouse area along the railroad yards, the Pearl District is the fastest-growing part of Portland. Mid-rise residential lofts have sprouted on almost every block, and boutiques, outdoor retailers, galleries, and trendy restaurants border the streets. The Portland Streetcar passes through here on its way from Nob Hill to downtown and Portland State University, with stops at two new, ecologically themed city parks.

Numbers in the margin correspond to numbers on the Pearl District and Old Town/Chinatown map.

TOP ATTRACTIONS

3 **Japanese-American Historical Plaza.** Take a moment to study the evocative figures cast into the bronze columns at the plaza's entrance; they show Japanese and Japanese-Americans before, during, and after World War II—living daily life, fighting in battle for the United States, and marching off to internment camps. Simple blocks of granite carved with haiku poems describing the war experience powerfully evoke this dark episode in American history. ⊠ *NW Naito Pkwy. and Davis St., in Waterfront Park, Old Town/Chinatown.*

4 **Lan Su Chinese Garden.** In a twist on the Joni Mitchell song, the city of
Fodor's Choice   Portland and private donors took down a parking lot and unpaved
★   paradise when they created this wonderland near the Pearl District and Old Town/Chinatown. It's the largest Suzhou-style garden outside China, with a large lake, bridged and covered walkways, koi- and water lily–filled ponds, rocks, bamboo, statues, waterfalls, and courtyards. A team of 60 artisans and designers from China literally left no stone unturned—500 tons of stone were brought here from Suzhou—in their efforts to give the windows, roof tiles, gateways, including a "moongate," and other architectural aspects of the garden some specific meaning or purpose. Also on the premises are a gift shop and a two-story teahouse overlooking the lake and garden. ⊠ *239 NW Everett, Old*

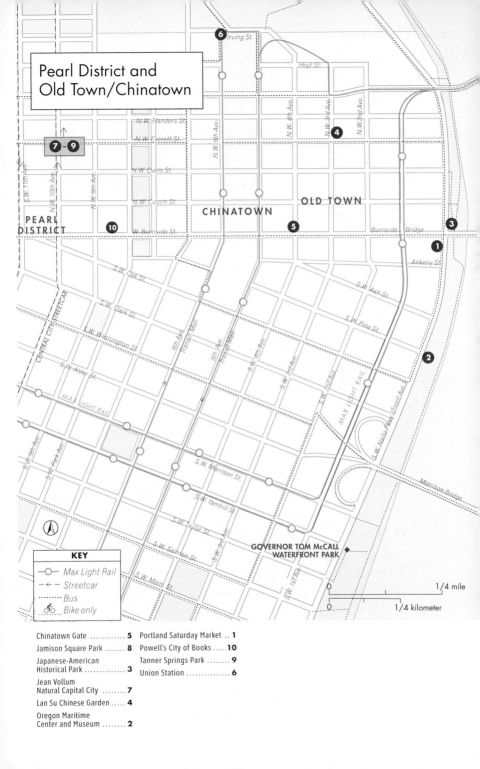

Pearl District and Old Town/Chinatown

Town/Chinatown ☎ *503/228–8131* ⊕ *www.lansugarden.org* ⊠ *$8.50*
⊙ *Nov.–Mar., daily 10–5; Apr.–Oct., daily 10–6.*

② **Oregon Maritime Museum.** Local model makers created most of this
☺ museum's models of ships that once plied the Columbia River. Contained within the stern-wheeler steamship *Portland*, this small museum
provides an excellent overview of Oregon's maritime history with
artifacts and memorabilia. The Portland was the last steam-powered
stern-wheeler built in the United States. ⊠ *On steamship at end of SW
Pine St., in Waterfront Park, Old Town/Chinatown* ☎ *503/224–7724*
⊕ *www.oregonmaritimemuseum.org* ⊠ *$5* ⊙ *Wed.–Sat. 11–4, Sun.
12:30–4:30.*

① **Portland Saturday Market.** On weekends from March to Christmas, the
☺ west side of the Burnside Bridge and the Skidmore Fountain area has
Fodor's Choice North America's largest open-air handicraft market. If you're looking
★ for jewelry, yard art, housewares, and decorative goods made from
every material under the sun, then there's an amazing collection of
talented works on display here. Entertainers and food and produce
booths add to the festive feel. If taking the MAX train to the market,
get off at the Skidmore Fountain stop. ⊠ *Waterfront Park and Ankeny
Park, both at SW Naito Pkwy and SW Ankeny, Old Town/Chinatown*
☎ *503/222–6072* ⊕ *www.saturdaymarket.org* ⊙ *Mar.–Dec., Sat. 10–5,
Sun. 11–4:30.*

⑩ **Powell's City of Books.** The largest independent bookstore in the world,
Fodor's Choice with more than 1.5 million new and used books, this Portland land-
★ mark can easily consume several hours. It's so big it has its own map
available at the info kiosks, and rooms are color-coded according to
the types of books, so you can find your way out again. Be sure to look
for the pillar bearing signatures of prominent sci-fi authors who have
passed through the store—the scrawls are protected by a jagged length
of Plexiglas. At the very least, stop into Powell's for a peek or grab a
cup of coffee at the adjoining branch of World Cup Coffee. ⊠ *1005
W. Burnside St., Pearl District* ☎ *503/228–4651* ⊕ *www.powells.com*
⊙ *Daily 9 AM–11 PM.*

WORTH NOTING

⑤ **Chinatown Gate.** Recognizable by its 5 roofs, 64 dragons, and 2 huge
lions, the Chinatown Gate is the official entrance to the Chinatown District. During the 1890s Portland had the second-largest Chinese community in the United States. Today's Chinatown has shrunk to a handful
of blocks with a few shops, grocery stores, and so-so restaurants (there
are better places for Chinese food outside the district). ⊠ *NW 4th Ave.
and Burnside St., Old Town/Chinatown.*

⑧ **Jamison Square Park.** This gently terraced park surrounded by tony Pearl
District lofts contains a soothing fountain that mimics nature. Rising
water gushes over a stack of basalt blocks, gradually fills the open plaza,
and then subsides. Colorful 30-foot tiki totems by pop artist Kenny
Scharf stand along the park's west edge. Take the streetcar to Jamison
Square. ⊠ *NW 10th Ave. and Lovejoy St., Pearl District.*

Lan Su Chinese Garden, Old Town/Chinatown

7 Jean Vollum Natural Capital Center. Known to most locals as the Ecotrust Building, this building has a handful of organic and environment-friendly businesses and other retail outlets, including Hot Lips Pizza, World Cup Coffee, Laughing Planet Café, and Patagonia (selling outdoor clothes). Built in 1895 and purchased by Ecotrust in 1998, the former warehouse has been adapted to serve as a landmark in sustainable, "green" building practices. Grab a "field guide" in the lobby, and take the self-guided tour of the building, which begins with the original "remnant wall" on the west side of the parking lot, proceeds throughout the building, and ends on the "eco-roof," a grassy rooftop with a great view of the Pearl District. ⊠ *721 NW 9th Ave., Pearl District* ☎ *503/227–6225* ⊕ *www.ecotrust.org/ncc* ☒ *Free* ⊙ *Weekdays 7–6; ground-floor businesses also evenings and weekends.*

9 Tanner Springs Park. Tanner Creek, which once flowed through the area, lends its name to Portland's newest park, created in 2005. Today this creek flows underground, and this quiet, man-made wetland and spring with alder groves was built in the middle of the Pearl District as a reminder of what the area was once like. ⊠ *NW 10th Ave. and Marshall St., Pearl District.*

6 Union Station. You can always find your way to Union Station by heading toward the huge neon GO BY TRAIN sign that looms high above the building. The vast lobby area, with high ceilings and marble floors, is worth a brief visit if you hold any nostalgia for the heyday of train travel in the United States. Amtrak trains stop here. ⊠ *800 NW 6th Ave., Old Town/Chinatown.*

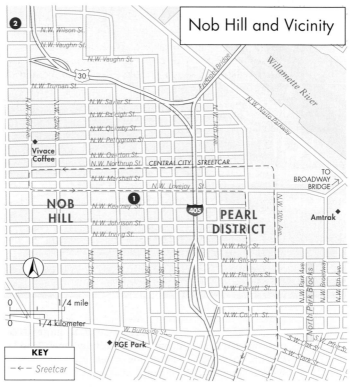

NOB HILL AND VICINITY

The showiest example of Portland's urban chic is Northwest 23rd Avenue—sometimes referred to with varying degrees of affection as "trendy-third"—a 20-block thoroughfare that cuts north–south through the neighborhood known as Nob Hill. Fashionable since the 1880s and still filled with Victorian houses, the neighborhood is a mixed-use cornucopia of Old Portland charm and New Portland hip. With its cafés, restaurants, galleries, and boutiques, it's a great place to stroll, shop, and people-watch. More restaurants, shops, and nightspots can be found on Northwest 21st Avenue, a few blocks away. The Portland Streetcar runs from Legacy Good Samaritan Hospital in Nob Hill, through the Pearl District on 10th and 11th avenues, connects with MAX light rail near Pioneer Courthouse Square downtown, and then continues on to Portland State University and RiverPlace on the Willamette River.

Numbers in the margin correspond to numbers on the Nob Hill and Vicinity map.

2 **Clear Creek Distillery.** The distillery keeps such a low profile that it's practically invisible. But ring the bell and someone will unlock the wrought-iron gate and let you into a dim, quiet tasting room where you can sample Clear Creek's world-famous Oregon apple and pear brandies and grappas. ✉ *2389 NW Wilson, Nob Hill* ☎ *503/248-9470* ⊕ *www.clearcreekdistillery.com* ⊙ *Mon.–Sat. 9–5.*

❶ The 3D Center of Art and Photography. Half gallery and half museum, this center devoted to three-dimensional imagery exhibits photographs best viewed through red-and-blue glasses, in addition to artifacts on the history of stereoscopic art. A collection of rare Nazi-era stereo-cards is displayed next to View-Masters and 3-D snapshot cameras. A three-dimensional rendering of famous classical paintings is one of the many changing 3-D slide shows you might see in the backroom Stereo Theatre. ✉ *1928 NW Lovejoy St., Nob Hill* ☎ *503/227-6667* ⊕ *www.3dcenter.us* 💲 *$5* ⊙ *Thurs.–Sat. 11–5, Sun. 1–5; also 1st Thurs. of month 6 PM–9 PM.*

NEED A BREAK?

Vivace Coffee (✉ *1400 NW 23rd Ave.* ☎ *503/228-3667*) is inside Petty-grove House, a restored Victorian gingerbread house built in 1892 that was once the home of Francis Pettygrove, the man who named Portland after winning a coin toss. Today it's a creperie and coffeehouse with colorful walls and comfortable chairs.

WASHINGTON PARK

The best way to get to Washington Park is via MAX light rail, which travels through a tunnel deep beneath the city's West Hills. Be sure to check out the Washington Park station, the deepest (260 feet) transit station in North America. Graphics on the walls depict life in the Portland area during the past 16.5 million years. There's also a core sample of the bedrock taken from the mountain displayed along the walls. Elevators to the surface put visitors in the parking lot for the Oregon Zoo, the World Forestry Center Discovery Museum, and the Children's Museum.

Numbers in the margin correspond to numbers on the Washington Park and Forest Park map.

TOP ATTRACTIONS

❸ Children's Museum. Colorful sights and sounds offer a feast of sensations for kids of all ages where hands-on play is the order of the day. Visit nationally touring exhibits, catch a story time, a sing-along, or a puppet show in the Play It Again theater, create sculptures in the clay studio, splash hands in the waterworks display, or make a creation from junk in the Garage. To reach the museum's complex, take the Zoo exit off U.S. 26, or take MAX light rail to Washington Park station. ✉ *4015 SW Canyon Rd., Washington Park* ☎ *503/223-6500* ⊕ *www.portlandcm. org* 💲 *$8* ⊙ *Mar.–Aug., daily 9–5; Sept.-Feb., Tues.–Sun. 9–5.*

❹ Hoyt Arboretum. Ten miles of trails wind through the arboretum, which has more than 1,000 species of plants and one of the nation's largest collections of coniferous trees; pick up trail maps at the visitor center. Also here are the Winter Garden and a memorial to veterans of the Vietnam War. ✉ *4000 SW Fairview Blvd., Washington Park* ☎ *503/865-8733* ⊕ *www.hoytarboretum.org* 💲 *Free* ⊙ *Arboretum daily dawn–dusk, visitor center Mon.–Fri. 9–4, Sat. 9–3.*

⑤ International Rose Test Garden. Despite the name, these grounds are not an
Fodor's Choice experimental greenhouse laboratory, but rather three terraced gardens,
★ set on 4 acres, where 10,000 bushes and 400 varieties of roses grow.
The flowers, many of them new varieties, are at their peak in June,
July, September, and October. From the gardens you can see highly
photogenic views of the downtown skyline and, on fine days, the Fuji-
shaped slopes of Mt. Hood, 50 mi to the east. Summer concerts take
place in the garden's amphitheater. Take MAX light rail to Washington
Park station, and transfer to Bus No. 63 or Washington Park Shuttle.
⊠ *400 SW Kingston Ave., Washington Park* ☎ *503/823–3636* ⊕ *www.
rosegardenstore.org* ✉ *Free* ☉ *Daily dawn–dusk.*

⑥ Japanese Garden. The most authentic Japanese garden outside Japan
Fodor's Choice takes up 5½ acres of Washington Park above the International Rose
★ Test Garden. This serene spot, designed by a Japanese landscape master,
represents five separate garden styles: Strolling Pond Garden, Tea Garden, Natural Garden, Sand and Stone Garden, and Flat Garden. The
Tea House was built in Japan and reconstructed here. The west side of
the Pavilion has a majestic view of Portland and Mt. Hood. Take MAX
light rail to Washington Park station, and transfer to Bus No. 63 or the
Washington Park Shuttle. ⊠ *611 SW Kingston Ave., Washington Park*
☎ *503/223–1321* ⊕ *www.japanesegarden.com* ✉ *$9.50* ☉ *Oct.–Mar.,
Mon. noon–4, Tues.–Sun. 10–4; Apr.–Sept., Mon. noon–7, Tues.–Sun.
10–7.*

WORTH NOTING

⑦ Oregon Holocaust Memorial. This memorial to those who perished during
the Holocaust bears the names of surviving families who live in Oregon and Southwest Washington. A bronzed baby shoe, a doll, broken
spectacles, and other strewn possessions await notice on the cobbled
courtyard. Soil and ash from six Nazi concentration camps is interred
beneath the black granite wall. Take MAX light rail to Washington Park
station, and transfer to Bus No. 63 or Washington Park Shuttle. ⊠ *SW
Wright Ave. and Park Pl., Washington Park* ☎ *503/245–2733* ⊕ *www.
ohrconline.org* ✉ *Free* ☉ *Daily dawn–dusk.*

① Oregon Zoo. This beautiful animal park in the West Hills is famous for
♲ its Asian elephants. Major exhibits include an African section with rhi-
nos, hippos, zebras, and giraffes. Steller Cove, a state-of-the-art aquatic
exhibit, has two Steller sea lions and a family of sea otters. Other exhibits include polar bears, chimpanzees, an Alaska Tundra exhibit with
wolves and grizzly bears, a penguin house, and habitats for beavers,
otters, and reptiles native to the west side of the Cascade Range. In
summer a 4-mi round-trip narrow-gauge train operates from the zoo,
chugging through the woods to a station near the International Rose
Test Garden and the Japanese Garden. Take the MAX light rail to the
Washington Park station. ⊠ *4001 SW Canyon Rd., Washington Park*
☎ *503/226–1561* ⊕ *www.oregonzoo.org* ✉ *$10.50, $4 2nd Tues. of
month* ☉ *Mid-Apr.–mid-Sept., daily 8–6; mid-Sept.–mid Apr., daily 9–4.*

⑧ Pittock Mansion. Henry Pittock, the founder and publisher of the *Oregonian* newspaper, built this 22-room, castlelike mansion, which combines
French Renaissance and Victorian styles. The opulent manor, built in

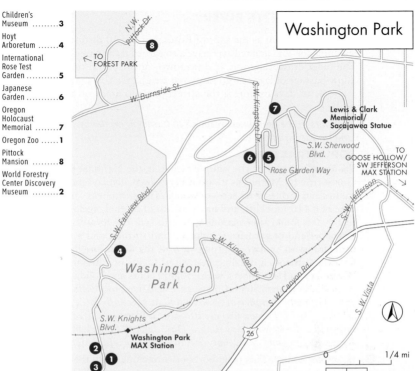

Washington Park

TO
FOREST PARK

N.W. Pittock Dr.

W. Burnside St.

S.W. Kingston Dr.

Lewis & Clark
Memorial/
Sacajawea Statue

S.W. Sherwood
Blvd.

TO
GOOSE HOLLOW/
SW JEFFERSON
MAX STATION

Rose Garden Way

S.W. Jefferson

S.W. Fairview Blvd.

S.W. Kingston Dr.

S.W. Canyon Rd.

S.W. Vista

Washington
Park

S.W. Knights
Blvd.

Washington Park
MAX Station

26

0   1/4 mi

0   1/4 km

2

1914, is filled with art and antiques. The 46-acre grounds, north of Washington Park and 1,000 feet above the city, have superb views of the skyline, rivers, and the Cascade Range. There's a teahouse and a small hiking trail. ✉ *3229 NW Pittock Dr., from W. Burnside St. heading west, turn right on NW Barnes Rd. and follow signs, north of Washington Park* ☎ *503/823–3623* ⊕ *www.pittockmansion.com* ✉ *$8* ⊙ *July–Aug., daily 10–4; Sept.–Dec. and Feb.–June, daily 11–4.*

② **World Forestry Discovery Center Museum.** Visitors will find interactive and multimedia exhibits that teach forest sustainability. A white-water raft ride, smoke-jumper training simulator, and Timberjack tree harvester all provide different perspectives on Pacific Northwest forests. On the second floor the forests of the world are explored in various travel settings. A canopy lift ride hoists visitors to the 50-foot ceiling to look at a Douglas fir. A $2 parking fee is collected upon entry. Or take MAX light rail to the Washington Park station. ✉ *4033 SW Canyon Rd., Washington Park* ☎ *503/228–1367* ⊕ *www.worldforestry.org* ✉ *$8* ⊙ *Daily 10–5.*

EAST OF THE WILLAMETTE RIVER

Portland is known as the City of Roses, but the 10 distinctive bridges spanning the Willamette River have also earned it the name Bridgetown. The older drawbridges, near downtown, open several times a day to allow passage of large cargo ships and freighters. You can easily spend a couple of days exploring the attractions and areas on the east side of the river.

Numbers in the margin correspond to numbers on the East of the Willamette River map.

TOP ATTRACTIONS

8 The Grotto. Owned by the Catholic Church, the National Sanctuary of Our Sorrowful Mother, as it's officially known, displays more than 100 statues and shrines in 62 acres of woods. The grotto was carved into the base of a 110-foot cliff, and has a replica of Michelangelo's *Pietà*. The real treat is found after ascending the cliff face via elevator, as you enter a wonderland of gardens, sculptures, and shrines, and a glass-walled cathedral with an awe-inspiring view of the Columbia River and the Cascades. There's a dazzling Festival of Lights at Christmastime (late November and December), with 250,000 lights and holiday concerts in the 600-seat chapel. Sunday masses are held here, too. ⊠ *8840 NE Skidmore St., main entrance at Sandy Blvd. at NE 85th Ave., near airport* ☎ *503/254-7371* ⊕ *www.thegrotto.org* ⌑ *Plaza level free; elevator to upper level $4* ☉ *Mid-May–Labor Day, daily 9–8:30; Labor Day–late Nov. and Feb.–mid-May, daily 9–5:30; late Nov.–Jan., daily 9–4.*

3 Hawthorne District. This neighborhood stretching from the foot of Mt.
Fodor's Choice   Tabor to 30th Avenue attracts a more college-age, bohemian crowd than
★   downtown or Nob Hill. With many bookstores, coffeehouses, taverns, restaurants, antiques stores, and boutiques filling the streets, it's easy to spend a few hours wandering here. ⊠ *SE Hawthorne Blvd. between 30th and 42nd Aves., Hawthorne District.*

1 Oregon Museum of Science and Industry (OMSI). Hundreds of hands-on
☾   exhibits draw families to this interactive science museum, which also has an Omnimax theater and the Northwest's largest planetarium. The many permanent and touring exhibits are loaded with enough hands-on play for kids to fill a whole day exploring robotics, ecology, rockets, computers, animation, and outer space. Moored in the Willamette as part of the museum is a 240-foot submarine, the USS *Blueback,* which can be toured for an extra charge. ⊠ *1945 SE Water Ave. south of Hawthorne Bridge, on Willamette River* ☎ *503/797-4000 or 800/955-6674* ⊕ *www.omsi.edu* ⌑ *Full package $21, museum $12, planetarium $5.75, Omnimax $8.50, submarine $5.75* ☉ *Mid-June–Labor Day, daily 9:30–7; Labor Day–mid-June, daily 9:30–5:30.*

2 Vera Katz Eastbank Esplanade. A stroll along this 1½-mi pedestrian and
Fodor's Choice   cycling path across from downtown is one of the best ways to expe-
★   rience the Willamette River and Portland's bridges close-up. Built in 2001, the esplanade runs along the east bank of the Willamette River between the Hawthorne and Steele bridges, and features a 1,200-foot walkway that floats atop the river, a boat dock, and public art.

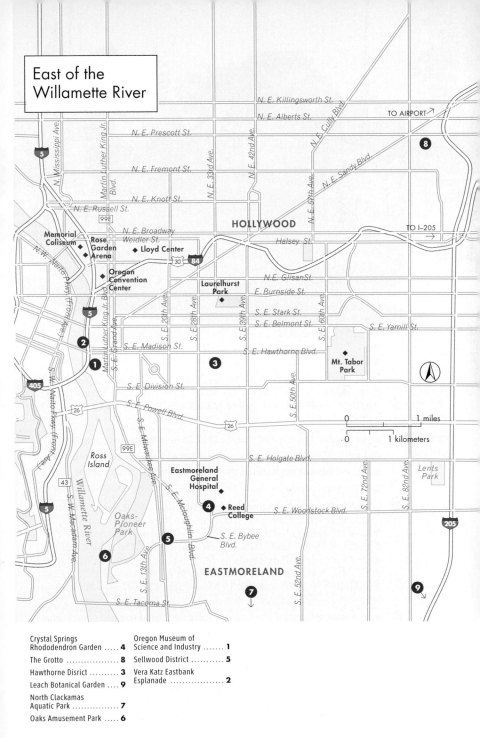

East of the Willamette River

HOLLYWOOD

EASTMORELAND

N. E. Killingsworth St.
N. E. Alberts St.
TO AIRPORT →
N. E. Prescott St.
N. E. Fremont St.
N. E. Knott St.
N. E. Russell St.
99E
N. E. Broadway
Weidler St.
Halsey St.
TO I-205 →
Memorial Coliseum
Rose Garden Arena
Lloyd Center
30 84
Oregon Convention Center
Laurelhurst Park
N.E. Glisan St.
E. Burnside St.
S. E. Stark St.
S. E. Belmont St.
S. E. Yamill St.
S. E. Madison St.
Mt. Tabor Park
S. E. Hawthorne Blvd.
S. E. Division St.
S. E. Powell Blvd.
26
0   1 miles
0   1 kilometers
99E
Ross Island
S. E. Holgate Blvd.
Lents Park
Eastmoreland General Hospital
Reed College
S. E. Woodstock Blvd.
205
43
Oaks-Pioneer Park
S. E. Bybee Blvd.
Willamette River
S. E. Tacoma St.

N. E. Sandy Blvd.
N. E. Cully Blvd.
N. E. 42nd Ave.
N. E. 33rd Ave.
N. E. 57th Ave.
S. E. 20th Ave.
S. E. 28th Ave.
S. E. 39th Ave.
S. E. 60th Ave.
S. E. 50th Ave.
S. E. 72nd Ave.
S. E. 82nd Ave.
S. E. 52nd Ave.
S. E. Milwaukee Ave.
S. E. McLoughlin Blvd.
S. E. 13th Ave.
S. W. Macadam Ave.
N. W. Naito Pkwy. (Front Ave.)
N. W. Naito Pkwy. (Front Ave.)
Martin Luther King Jr. Blvd.
Martin Luther King Jr. Blvd.
N. E. Mississippi Ave.
S. E. Grand Ave.
5
405
26
5

Portland Rose Festival parade

Pedestrian crossings on both bridges link the esplanade to Waterfront Park, making a 3-mi loop. Take MAX light rail to the Rose Quarter station. ✉ *Parking at east end of Hawthorne Bridge, between Madison and Salmon Sts.*

NEED A BREAK?
At the Bagdad Theatre and Pub (✉ *3702 SE Hawthorne Blvd., Hawthorne District* ☎ *503/236–9234*) you can buy a pint of beer, a slice of pizza, and watch a movie in a large classic theater complete with dining tables.

WORTH NOTING

4 Crystal Springs Rhododendron Garden. For much of the year, this 7-acre retreat near Reed College is frequented mainly by bird-watchers and those who want a restful stroll. But starting in April, thousands of rhododendron bushes and azaleas burst into flower. The peak blooming season for these woody shrubs is May; by late June the show is over. ✉ *SE 28th Ave., west side, 1 block north of Woodstock Blvd., Eastmoreland* ☎ *503/771–8386* ✉ *$3 Mar.–Labor Day, Thurs.–Mon. 10–6; otherwise free* ☉ *Daily dawn–dusk.*

9 Leach Botanical Garden. The Leaches were dedicated to plants and fauna. In her professional life, Lilla Leach was an accomplished botanist responsible for discovering five new species of plants, including the *Kalmiopsis leachiana,* which can be found in this garden. Trails wind up and around the property, giving ample opportunities to stop and admire the 2,000 special hybrids and cultivars. Unless there's a school tour, it's quiet and serene, which is perfect, since the Leaches originally called their property Sleepy Hollow. If you want to take some of the garden home with you, check out the plant table and troughs outside the gift shop. The gardening library has over 1,110 books in the circulating collection. Check ahead for a schedule of classes and guided tours. ✉ *6704 SE 122nd Ave., East of Willamette River* ☎ *503/823–9503* ⊕ *www.leachgarden.org* ⊘ *Tues.—Sat. 9–4, Sun. 1–4.*

❼ **North Clackamas Aquatic Park.** If you're visiting Portland with kids and
⤴ looking for a great way to cool off—especially on one of Portland's hot July or August days—check out this 45,000-square-foot, all-indoor attraction, whose main pool has 4-foot waves and three super slides. There's also a 25-yard-long lap pool, a wading pool, an adults-only hot whirlpool, and a café. Children under age 8 must be accompanied by someone 13 or older. ✉ *7300 SE Harmony Rd., Milwaukie* ☎ *503/557–7873* ⊕ *www.clackamas.us/ncprd/aquatic* 💲 *$9.99* ⊘ *Open swim mid-June–Labor Day, weekdays noon–4 and 7–9, weekends 12–7; Labor Day–mid-June, Sat. noon–7, Sun. noon–5.*

North Mississippi Avenue. Four blocks of old storefronts reinvented as cafés, collectives, shops, and music venues along this north Portland street showcase the indie spirit of the city's do-it-yourselfers and creative types. Bioswale planter boxes, found-object fences, and café tables built from old doors are some of the innovations you'll see around this hip new district. At the hub of it all is the ReBuilding Center, an outlet for recycled building supplies that has cob (clay-and-straw) trees and benches built into the facade. Take MAX light rail to the Albina/Mississippi station. ✉ *Between N. Fremont and Shaver Sts., off N. Interstate Ave.*

Northeast Alberta Street. Quirky handicrafts by local artists are for sale inside the galleries, studios, coffeehouses, restaurants, and boutiques lining this street in the northeast Portland neighborhood. It's a fascinating place to witness the intersection of cultures and lifestyles in a growing city. Shops unveil new exhibits during an evening event called the Last Thursday Art Walk. The Alberta Street Fair in September showcases the area with arts-and-crafts displays and street performances. ✉ *Between Martin Luther King Jr. Blvd. and 30th Ave., Alberta Arts District.*

❻ **Oaks Amusement Park.** There's a small-town charm to this park that has
⤴ bumper cars, thrill rides, and roller-skating year-round. A 360-degree-loop roller coaster and other high-velocity, gravity-defying contraptions border the midway, along with a carousel and Ferris wheel. The skating rink, built in 1905, is the oldest continuously operating one in the United States, and features a working Wurlitzer organ. There are outdoor concerts in summer. ✉ *7805 SE Oaks Park Way; from SE Tacoma St. on east side of Sellwood Bridge, take SE 6th Ave. north and SE Spokane west, Sellwood* ☎ *503/233–5777* ⊕ *www.oakspark.com* 💲 *Park free, multiride bracelets $11.75–$14.75, individual-ride tickets $2.25* ⊘ *Mid-June–Labor Day, Tues.–Thurs. noon–9, Fri. and Sat. noon–10, Sun. noon–7; late-Apr.–mid-June and Labor Day–Oct., weekends noon–7; late-Mar.–late-Apr., weekends noon–5.*

❺ **Sellwood District.** The pleasant neighborhood that begins east of the Sellwood Bridge was once a separate town. Annexed by Portland in the 1890s, it retains a modest charm. On weekends the antiques stores along 13th Avenue do a brisk business. Each store is identified by a plaque that tells the date of construction and the original purpose of the building. More antiques stores, specialty shops, and restaurants are near the intersection of Milwaukie and Bybee. ⊠ *SE 13th Ave. between Malden and Clatsop Sts., Sellwood.*

WHERE TO EAT

DOWNTOWN

Use the coordinate (✛ 1:B2) at the end of each listing to locate a site on the corresponding "Where to Eat in Downtown Portland" map.

Finding a fabulous place to dine downtown is almost as easy as closing your eyes and pointing on the map. One thing visitors appreciate about lunch downtown is the plethora of food carts lining the streets. Smells of Greek, Russian, Japanese, Lebanese, and Mexican food permeate the air as the noon hour approaches. Lines of workers hover around the makeshift kitchen trailers, waiting to get their fill of the inexpensive and authentic selection of food. (⇨ *See Portland Eats feature for more about food carts.*)

$ ✕ **Al-Amir.** After moving beyond this Middle Eastern restaurant's small
MIDDLE EASTERN front bar, you pass through an elaborately large and ornate gateway into a dark, stylish dining room. Choose between excellent broiled kebabs, falafel, hummus, tabbouleh, and baba ghanoush. There's live music and belly dancing on Friday and Saturday. ⊠ *223 SW Stark St., Downtown* ☎ *503/274–0010* ⊕ *www.alamirportland.com* ⊟ *AE, D, MC, V* ⊘ *No lunch weekends.* ✛ *1:E4*

¢ ✕ **Bijou Cafe.** This spacious, sunny restaurant with high ceilings has some
AMERICAN of the best breakfasts in town, and they're served all day: French-style crepes and oyster hash are both popular, as are fabulous pancakes and French toast. At lunch the breakfast dishes are joined by burgers, sandwiches, and soups. ⊠ *132 SW 3rd Ave., Downtown* ☎ *503/222–3187* ⊟ *MC, V* ⊘ *No dinner.* ✛ *1:E4*

$ ✕ **Bo's Asian Bistro.** Combining the trend toward tapas and chic cocktails,
ASIAN this hotel bar brings both to delicious heights. The stylish dark walls accented by colorful modern art create a sleek setting in which to sip a specialty martini made with some esoteric liqueur. ⊠ *Hotel Lucia, 400 SW Broadway, Downtown* ☎ *503/222–2688* ⊕ *www.bobistro.com* ⊟ *AE, DC, MC, V* ⊘ *Closed Sun.* ✛ *1:D4*

$$ ✕ **Carafe.** Straightforward French favorites and proximity to the Keller
FRENCH Auditorium make this quaint bistro a popular choice. Confit of albacore tuna niçoise served with heirloom tomatoes, haricots verts, and hard-boiled egg, as well as crispy duck leg confit with seasonal offerings, are a few of the dishes here. If you're in the mood for lighter fare, there are also plenty of pastas, sandwiches, and soups. Call ahead, especially if there's a show going on at the Keller. ⊠ *200 SW Market St.,Downtown* ☎ *503/248–0004* ⊕ *www.carafebistro.com* ⊟ *AE, DC, MC, V* ⊘ *Closed Sun.* ✛ *1:D6*

$ ✕ **Clyde Common.** If you want to experience "community," then this
CONTINENTAL bustling, contemporary spot is for you. Visitors from all walks of

BEST BETS FOR PORTLAND DINING

Fodor's writers and editors have selected their favorite restaurants by price, cuisine, and experience in the lists below. In the first column, Fodor's Choice properties represent the "best of the best" in every price category. You can also search by neighborhood for excellent eats—just peruse our reviews on the following pages.

Fodor's Choice ★

Andina, $$$, p. 74
El Gaucho, $$$$, p. 68
50 Plates, $$, p. 76
Genoa, $$$$, p. 85
Gracie's, $$$, p. 68
Higgins, $$$, p. 69
Le Bouchon, $$$, p. 76
Lemongrass, $, p. 88
Mother's Bistro, $, p. 70

By Price

¢

Bijou Café, p. 64
Pearl Bakery, p. 77
Pok Pok, p. 89
St. Honoré, p. 80

$

Alameda Brewhouse, p. 81
Bread and Ink, p. 82
Lemongrass, p. 88
Mother's Bistro, p. 70
Silk By Pho Van, p. 77

$$

50 Plates, p. 76
clarklewis, p. 84
Lauro Kitchen, p. 85
Pazzo, p. 72

$$$

Andina, p. 74
Gracie's, p. 68
Higgin's, p. 69
Le Bouchon, p. 76

$$$$

El Gaucho, p. 68
Genoa, p. 85
London Grill, p. 70

By Cuisine

AMERICAN

50 Plates, p. 76
clarklewis, p. 84
Gracie's, p. 68
Mother's Bistro, p. 70

ASIAN

BeWon, p. 78
Lemongrass, p. 88

Murata, p. 70
Typhoon!, p. 73

FRENCH

Higgin's, p. 69
Le Bouchon, p. 76

ITALIAN

Genoa, p. 85
Mama Mia Trattoria, p. 70
Pazzo, p. 72

SEAFOOD

Jake's Famous Crawfish, p. 69
Southpark Seafood Grill and Wine, p. 72

By Experience

BRUNCH

Meriwether's, p. 79
Mother's Bistro, p. 70
Original Pancake House, p. 92
Tin Shed, p. 91

CHILD-FRIENDLY

Belly Restaurant, p. 82
Kornblatt's, p. 78
McMenamins Kennedy School Courtyard Restaurant, p. 88
Pastini, p. 79
Vita Café, p. 91

GOOD FOR GROUPS

Doug Fir, p. 84
Lemongrass, p. 88
Rheinlander, p. 89
Serratto, p. 80

HAPPY HOUR

Bo's Asian Bistro, p. 64
50 Plates, p. 76
Oba!, p. 77
Saucebox, p. 72
23 Hoyt, p. 78

HOT SPOT

Andina, p. 74
Departure, p. 68
El Gaucho, p. 68
Portland City Grill, p. 72

LATE-NIGHT DINING

The Gilt Club, p. 76
Le Happy, p. 76
Lucy's Table, p. 78
Saucebox, p. 72

MOST ROMANTIC

Bluehour, p. 74
The Gilt Club, p. 76
Gracie's, p. 68

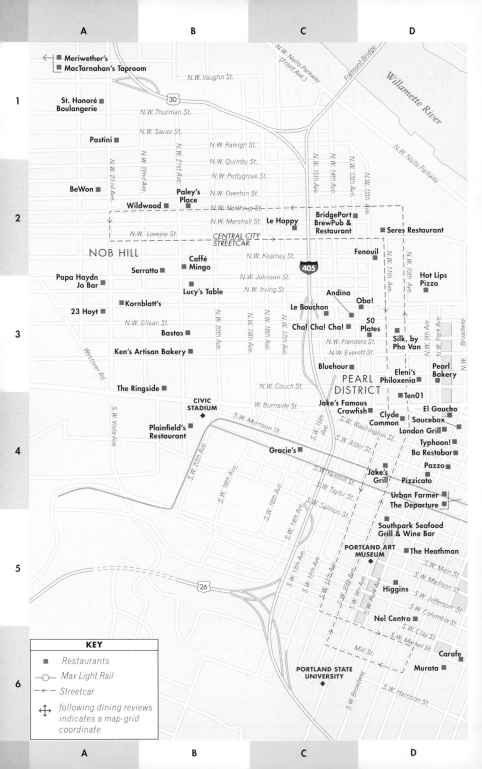

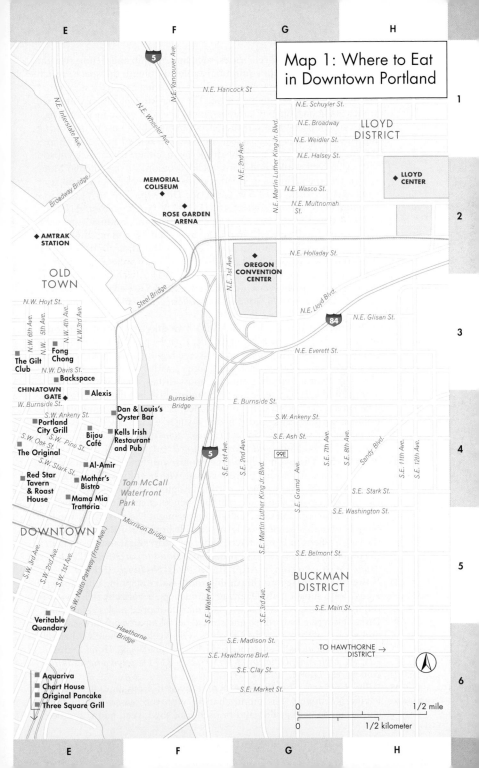

Map 1: Where to Eat in Downtown Portland

life—politicians, quasi-celebrities, socialites, the hip and trendy, straight and gay—eat here. Big communal tables dominate the space, which means you'll never know who you'll end up sitting next to or what interesting conversations you may have. The open kitchen allows you to see what's going on from any vantage point. The edgy menu includes frogs' legs, chicken livers, and sardines, accompanied by a host of interesting ingredients such as horseradish, nettles, and refried peanuts. There's no shortage of invention on the drink menu, either: try the Ace Gibson with Medoyeff vodka and house pickled onion, or the Anemic Mary with serrano chili and sun-dried tomato vodka, celery juice, and sour mix. ⊠ *Ace Hotel, 1014 SW Stark St., Downtown* ☏ *503/228–3333* ⊕ *www.clydecommon.com* ▭ *AE, D, MC, V* ⊘ *Closed Sun.* ✛ *1:D4*

$ ✕ **Dan & Louis's Oyster Bar.** Oysters at this Portland landmark near the
SEAFOOD   river come fried, stewed, or on the half shell. The clam chowder is tasty, but the crab stew is a rare treat. Combination dinners let you mix your fried favorites. The collection of steins, plates, and marine art has grown since the restaurant opened in 1907 to fill beams, nooks, crannies, and nearly every inch of wall. ⊠ *208 SW Ankeny St., Downtown* ☏ *503/227–5906* ⊕ *www.danandlouis.com* ▭ *AE, D, DC, MC, V.* ✛ *1:E4*

$ ✕ **Departure.** If you want to sink into a swanky restaurant that could
JAPANESE   just as easily be in a much bigger city, then Departure is for you. The interior is over-the-top lush, and a scenic highlight for locals and visitors alike is the outdoor rooftop lounge, with gorgeous views of the city. The food is artfully prepared; most dishes, such as the hamachi sashimi and calamari tempura come in smallish but flavorful portions. The fried ginger ice cream, for instance, is served with panko breadcrumbs, sesame seeds, and powdered sugar. ⊠ *525 SW Morrison St., Downtown* ☏ *503/802–5370* ⊕ *www.departureportland.com* ▭ *AE, MC, V* ⊘ *Closed Sun. and Mon. No lunch* ✛ *1:D4.*

$$$$ ✕ **El Gaucho.** Three dimly lit dining rooms with blue walls and striped
STEAK   upholstery are an inviting place for those with healthy wallets. The spe-
Fodor'sChoice   cialty here is 28-day, dry-aged, certified Angus beef, but chops, ribs, and
★   chicken entrées are also cooked in the open kitchen. The chateaubriand for two is carved tableside. Seafood lovers might want to try the tomato fennel bouillabaisse. Service is impeccable at this Seattle transplant in the elegant Benson Hotel. Each night live Latin guitar music serenades the dinner guests. ⊠ *319 SW Broadway, Downtown* ☏ *503/227–8794* ⊕ *www.elgaucho.com* ▭ *AE, DC, MC, V* ⊘ *No lunch.* ✛ *1:D4*

$$$ ✕ **Gracie's.** Stepping into this dining room is like stepping into a presti-
AMERICAN   gious 1940s supper club. Dazzling chandeliers, beautifully rich floor-to-
Fodor'sChoice   ceiling draperies, velvet couches, and marble-topped tables exude class.
★   Dishes like grilled swordfish and stuffed pork loin are perfectly seasoned and served with seasonal vegetables. On weekends there's a brunch menu that includes fresh fruit, waffles, and omelets. ⊠ *Hotel DeLuxe, 729 SW 15th Ave., Downtown* ☏ *503/222–2171* ⊕ *www.graciesdining. com* ▭ *AE, D, MC, V* ✛ *1:C4.*

$$ ✕ **The Heathman.** Chef Philippe Boulot revels in fresh ingredients of the
CONTINENTAL   Pacific Northwest. His menu changes with the season and includes entrées made with grilled and braised fish, fowl, veal, lamb, and beef.

El Gaucho, Downtown

Among the chef's Northwest specialties are a delightful Dungeness crab, mango, and avocado salad and paella made with mussels, clams, shrimp, scallops, and chorizo. Equally creative choices are available for breakfast and lunch. The dining room, scented with wood smoke and adorned with Andy Warhol prints, is a favorite for special occasions. ⊠ *Heathman Hotel, 1001 SW Broadway, Downtown* ☎ *503/790–7752* ▭ *AE, D, DC, MC, V* ✛ *1:D5.*

$$
FRENCH
Fodor's Choice
★

✕ **Higgins.** Chef Greg Higgins, former executive chef at the Heathman Hotel, focuses on ingredients from the Pacific Northwest and on organically grown herbs and produce while incorporating traditional French cooking styles and other international influences into his menu. Start with a salad of warm beets, asparagus, and artichokes, or the country-style terrine of venison, chicken, and pork with dried sour cherries and a roasted-garlic mustard. Main courses, which change seasonally, might include dishes made with Alaskan spot prawns, halibut, duck, or pork loin. Vegetarian options are available. A bistro menu is available in the adjoining bar, where comfortable leather booths and tables provide an alternative to the main dining room. ⊠ *1239 SW Broadway, Downtown* ☎ *503/222–9070* ▭ *AE, D, DC, MC, V* ☉ *No lunch weekends* ✛ *1:D5.*

$$
SEAFOOD

✕ **Jake's Famous Crawfish.** Diners have been enjoying fresh Pacific Northwest seafood in Jake's warren of wood-paneled dining rooms for more than a century. The back bar came around Cape Horn during the 1880s, and the chandeliers hanging from the high ceilings date from 1881. The restaurant gained a national reputation in 1920, when crawfish was added to the menu. White-coated waiters take your order from an almost endless sheet of daily seafood specials year-round, but try to come during crawfish season (May–September), when you can sample the tasty crustacean in pie, cooked Creole style, or in a Cajun-style stew over rice. ✉ *401 SW 12th Ave., Downtown* ☎ *503/226–1419* ⊕ *www.* *mccormickandschmicks.com* ⊟ *AE, D, DC, MC, V* ☯ *No lunch Sun.* ✛ *1:D4.*

$$ ✕ **Jake's Grill.** Not to be confused with the Jake's of seafood fame,
AMERICAN although they do share the same owners, this eatery in the Governor Hotel has more turf than surf. Steaks and the Sunday brunch are popular draws. Private booths with green velvet curtains make for a cozy, intimate dinner. The bar is famous for its Bloody Marys. ✉ *611 SW 10th Ave., Downtown* ☎ *503/220–1850* ⊕ *www.mccormickandschmicks. com* ⊟ *AE, D, DC, MC, V* ✛ *1:D4.*

$ ✕ **Kells Irish Restaurant and Pub.** Step into cool, dark Kells for a pint of
IRISH Guinness and such authentic pub fare as fish-and-chips, Guinness stew, shepherd's pie, and Irish soda bread. Burgers and vegetarian sandwiches round out the bar menu, and there's breakfast on weekends. Live Irish musicians play every night of the week. Be sure to ask the bartender how all those folded-up dollar bills got stuck to the ceiling. ✉ *112 SW 2nd Ave.,Downtown* ☎ *503/227–4057* ⊕ *www.kellsirish.com* ⊟ *AE, D, MC, V* ✛ *1:E4.*

$$$$ ✕ **London Grill.** The plush, dimly lit dining room in the historic Benson
CONTINENTAL Hotel serves classic dishes made with fresh, seasonal local ingredients. Try the cedar-smoked salmon with juniper-berry sauce. With one of the longest wine lists around and a good chance of live jazz guitar or piano music, this is a place to truly indulge. Breakfast is also available. Jackets are encouraged, but not required, for men. ✉ *309 SW Broadway, Downtown* ☎ *503/295–4110* ⊟ *AE, D, DC, MC, V* ✛ *1:D4.*

$ ✕ **Mama Mia Trattoria.** Warmth and comfort are the specialties at
ITALIAN Mama's, which is the place to come if you're in the mood for old-school Italian-American favorites like spaghetti with meatballs, lasagna, or potato gnocchi. Don't let the sultry red interior, sparkly chandeliers, and starched tablecloths fool you. This mildly boisterous place allows you to be more casual than it is (just like Mama), and the bar is open late into the night. ✉ *439 SW 2nd Ave., Downtown* ☎ *503/295–6464* ⊕ *www.mamamiatrattoria.com* ⊟ *AE, D, DC, MC, V* ☯ *No lunch weekends.* ✛ *1:E4.*

$ ✕ **Mother's Bistro.** The menu is loaded with home-style favorites—maca-
AMERICAN roni and cheese with extra ingredients of the day, soups, pierogi, matzo-
Fodor's Choice ball soup, pot roast, and meat loaf. For vegetarians there's a couscous
★ stew. The high ceilings in the well-lit dining room lend an air of spaciousness, but the tables are a bit close together. The bar is open late Friday and Saturday. ✉ *212 SW Stark St., Downtown* ☎ *503/464–1122* ⊕ *www.mothersbistro.com* ⊟ *AE, D, MC, V* ☯ *Closed Mon. No dinner Sun.* ✛ *1:E4.*

$$ ✕ **Murata.** Slip off your shoes and step inside one of the tatami rooms
JAPANESE at Murata, Portland's best Japanese restaurant. You can also pull up a chair at the corner sushi bar. So ordinary looking it barely stands out among the office towers near Keller Auditorium, the restaurant draws a crowd of locals, celebrities, and Japanese businesspeople who savor the sushi, sashimi, tempura, hamachi, and teriyaki. Grilled salmon cheeks stand out among many seafood specialties. ✉ *200 SW Market*

CLOSE UP

A Chef's Paradise

The quest for the most eco-friendly, farm-supporting methods has become an obsession among chefs who flock from all over the world to take advantage of the area's local abundance. Portland is perfectly poised to take the cooking universe by storm. First, compared to major metropolitan cities like New York, Chicago, and Los Angeles, real estate is somewhat affordable, which makes setting up shop a more obtainable reality for aspiring chefs.

Second, because of the urban growth boundary, city sprawl is kept to a minimum. Farmland is within miles, and therefore everyday deliveries of a broad spectrum of fruits and vegetables are achievable. Most chefs in Portland try to adhere to delivery from a distributor within a 100-mi radius. Not only does this make the menu offerings exciting and ever-changing, it requires chefs to come up with creative new dishes based on what's available for that month, that week,

or even that day. Many chefs indicate that it's the artistic challenge and constant change of ingredients that makes Portland seductive.

Also within a 100-mi radius of Portland are lush forests and the Pacific Ocean, where regional specialty ingredients, such as chanterelle mushrooms and wild-caught salmon, are in fresh supply. Walk into any one of Portland's most notable restaurants, and you'll find entire menus serving dishes exclusively made from regional ingredients. For desserts you're bound to discover the amazing selection of local fruits—Anjou pears, peaches, and blackberries—that turn up in pies, pastries, toppings, and cakes.

Exploration of creative cuisine infused by local ingredients isn't only reserved for fine dining. Scores of local bakeries (such as Ken's Artisan Bakery) and pizzerias (Hot Lips Pizza) have built their businesses around locally harvested, organic-based menu items as well.

St., Downtown ☎ *503/227–0080* ▭ *AE, MC, V* ☺ *Closed Sun. No lunch Sat.* ✛ *1:D6.*

$$
FRENCH
✕**Nel Centro.** With a menu and wine list deeply respectful of the Riviera, this elegantly modern restaurant oozes attitude. Breakfast, lunch, or dinner, the offerings are traditional and not too audacious. The split roast pork and rotisserie chicken are rightfully the entrees that diners talk to their fellow food lovers about. Cool evenings are just right for cozying up to the fire pits on the patio and make for a pleasant, though busy, happy hour. ⊠ *1408 SW 6th, Downtown* ☎ *503/484–1099* ⊕ *www.nelcentro.com* ▭ *AE, D, MC, V* ✛ *1:D5.*

$
AMERICAN
✕**The Original.** At this upscale diner-ish restaurant, one of the oddest foods in Portland can be ordered: a donut cheeseburger. It's made with a Voodoo glazed donut, and only available on the late night menu. Other specialties are more traditional—stroganoff, meat loaf, brisket, and burgers—but have an upscale twist, many with a Pacific Northwestern flair. The food, service, and vibe make this a restaurant that appeals to almost everyone. ⊠ *300 SW 6th Ave., Downtown* ☎ *503/546–2666* ⊕ *www.originaldinerant.com* ▭ *AE, D, MC, V* ✛ *1:E4.*

$$ ✕ **Pazzo.** The aromas of roasted garlic and wood smoke greet patrons
ITALIAN   of the bustling, street-level dining room of the Hotel Vintage Plaza.
Pazzo's menu relies on deceptively simple new Italian cuisine—creative
pastas, risottos, and grilled meats, fish, and poultry as well as antipasti
and appetizers. All the baked goods are made in the Pazzoria Bakery
& Cafe next door. The decor is a mix of dark wood, terra-cotta, and
dangling garlands of garlic. Breakfast is served daily. ✉ *627 SW Wash-
ington St., Downtown* ⊕ *www.pazzo.com* ☎ *503/228–1515* ▭ *AE, D,
DC, MC, V* ✛ *1:D4.*

¢   ✕ **Pizzicato.** This local chain serves pies and slices topped by inventive
PIZZA   combinations such as chanterelles, shiitakes, and portobellos; or andou-
ille sausage, shrimp, and smoked mozzarella. The menu also includes
large salads to share, antipasti, and panini. The restaurant interiors are
clean, bright, and modern. Beer and wine are available. There are 16
locations in the Portland metro area. ✉ *705 SW Alder St., Downtown*
☎ *503/226–1007* ✉ *505 NW 23rd Ave., Nob Hill* ☎ *503/242–0023*
⊕ *www.pizzicatopizza.com* ▭ *AE, D, DC, MC, V* ✛ *1:D4.*

$$$ ✕ **Portland City Grill.** On the 30th floor of the U.S. Bank Tower, Portland
AMERICAN   City Grill has one of the best views in town. You can sit at a window
table and enjoy the Portland skyline while eating fine steak and seafood
with an Asian flair; it's no wonder that this restaurant is a favorite hot
spot. The adjoining bar and lounge has comfortable armchairs all along
its windowed walls, which are the first to get snatched up during the
extremely popular happy hour each day. ✉ *111 SW 5th Ave., Downtown* ☎ *503/450–0030* ⊕ *www.portlandcitygrill.com* ▭ *AE, D, MC, V*
☻ *No lunch weekends* ✛ *1:E4.*

$$ ✕ **Red Star Tavern & Roast House.** Cooked in a wood-burning oven,
AMERICAN   smoker, rotisserie, or grill, the cuisine at Red Star can best be described
as American comfort food inspired by the bounty of the Pacific North-
west. Spit-roasted chicken, maple-fired baby back ribs with a brown-
ale glaze, charred salmon, and crayfish étouffée (seasonal) are some
of the better entrées. The wine list includes regional and international
vintages, and 10 microbrews are on tap. The spacious restaurant, adja-
cent to Hotel Monaco, has tufted leather booths, murals, and copper
accents. ✉ *503 SW Alder St., Downtown* ☎ *503/222–0005* ⊕ *www.
redstartavern.com* ▭ *AE, D, DC, MC, V* ✛ *1:E4.*

$ ✕ **Saucebox.** Creative pan-Asian cuisine and many creative cocktails
ASIAN   draw the crowds to this popular restaurant and nightspot near the big
downtown hotels. Inside the long and narrow space, with closely spaced
tables draped with white cloths, Alexis Rockman's impressive and col-
orful 24-foot painting *Evolution* spans the wall over your head, and
mirrored walls meet your gaze at eye level. The menu includes Korean
baby back ribs, Vietnamese pork tenderloin, and Indonesian roasted
Javanese salmon. An excellent late-night menu is served after 10 PM.
✉ *214 SW Broadway, Downtown* ☎ *503/241–3393* ⊕ *www.saucebox.
com* ▭ *AE, DC, MC, V* ☻ *No lunch* ✛ *1:D4.*

$$ ✕ **Southpark Seafood Grill & Wine Bar.** Wood-fired seafood is served in
SEAFOOD   this comfortable, art deco–tinged room with two bars. Chef Broc Wil-
lis's Northwest-influenced menu includes wild king salmon with baked
gnocchi, as well as Oregon-raised Carlton Farms rib eye. There's a

wide selection of fresh Pacific Northwest oysters, and fine regional wines are available by the glass. Some of the desserts are baked to order. ⊠ *901 SW Salmon St., Downtown* ☎ *503/326–1300* ⊕ *www. southparkseafood.com* ⊟ *AE, D, MC, V* ✛ *1:D5.*

$$ ✕ **Typhoon!** A Buddha statue with burning incense watches over diners **THAI** at this popular restaurant in the Lucia Hotel. Come enjoy the excellent food in a large, modern dining room filled with colorful art and sleek red booths. The spicy chicken or shrimp with crispy basil, the curry and noodle dishes, and the vegetarian spring and salad rolls are standouts. As for tea, 25 varieties are available, from $4 a pot to $10 for some of the world's rarest. ⊠ *410 SW Broadway, Downtown* ☎ *503/224–8285* ⊕ *www.typhoonrestaurants.com* ⊟ *AE, D, DC, MC, V* ✛ *1:D4.*

$$$$ ✕ **Urban Farmer.** In the atrium of the upscale hotel the Nines, you'll **AMERICAN** discover why this restaurant calls itself a modern steak house. Making much use of organic and sustainable ingredients, the dishes here are presented with flair in glass canning jars and mini cast-iron skillets. The focus is understandably on its steaks (choose from corn-fed or grass-fed), but there are also interesting alternatives, such as slow-braised lamb flavored with apricot, and roasted Alaskan halibut served with fried green tomatoes. Leave room for moonshine whiskey or the banana-cream pie served with coffee ice cream. ⊠ *525 SW Morrison St., Downtown* ☎ *503/222–4900* ⊕ *www.urbanfarmerrestaurant.com* ⊟ *AE, MC, V* ✛ *1:D4.*

$$$ ✕ **Veritable Quandary.** There are so many delicious options at this long-**AMERICAN** standing local favorite: the tantalizing French toast and revered chocolate soufflé pair well with the beautiful outdoor patio, where you're surrounded by roses, fuchsias, and hanging begonia baskets. The menu emphasizes fresh, flavorful produce and seafood; prices are reasonable for the quality, and the wine list is one of the best in town. ⊠ *1220 SW 1st Ave., Downtown* ☎ *503/227–7342* ⊕ *www.veritablequandary.com* ⊟ *AE, D, DC, MC, V* ✛ *1:E5.*

PEARL DISTRICT AND OLD TOWN/CHINATOWN

The Pearl District, once full of worn, empty warehouses and little more than a reminder of Portland's industrial past, is now the city's most bustling destination for arts and dining. Many of the warehouses have been refurbished into hot spots in which to gather for drinks and food. On any given day or night, visitors can comb the scene for a perfectly selected glass of wine or a lush designer cocktail. Within this small area are global selections of Greek, French, Italian, Peruvian, Japanese, and more. Restaurants here tend to be slightly more upscale, though there are plenty of casual bakeries, coffee shops, and places to grab sandwiches. Keep in mind that the city's gallery walk event, held the first Thursday of every month, keeps restaurants jammed on that night.

$ ✕ **Alexis.** The Mediterranean furnishings here consist only of white walls **GREEK** and basic furnishings, but the authentic Greek flavor keeps the crowds coming for *kalamarakia* (deep-fried squid served with *tzatziki,* a yogurt dip), *horiatiki* (a Greek salad with feta cheese and kalamata olives), and other traditional dishes. If you have trouble making up your mind, the

Mother's Bistro, Downtown

gigantic Alexis platter includes a little of everything. ✉ *215 W. Burn-side St., Old Town* ☎ *503/224–8577* ⊕ *www.alexisfoods.com* ▭ *AE, D, MC, V* ⊗ *Closed Sun.* ✛ *1:E4*

$$$
PERUVIAN
Fodor's Choice
★

✕ **Andina.** Portland's sleekest, trendiest, and most brightly colored restaurant gives an artful presentation to designer and traditional Peruvian cuisine. Asian and Spanish flavors are the main influences here, and they're evident in an extensive seafood menu that includes five kinds of ceviche, grilled octopus, and pan-seared scallops with white and black quinoa. There are also entrées with poultry, beef, and lamb. A late-night bar offers sangria, small plates, and cocktails; downstairs, a shrine-like wine shop hosts private multicourse meals. Live music Sunday through Saturday. ✉ *1314 NW Glisan St., Pearl District* ☎ *503/228–9535* ⊕ *www.andinarestaurant.com* ▭ *AE, D, MC, V.* ✛ *1:C3*

¢
CAFÉ

✕ **Backspace.** Taking "eclectic" to a new level, Backspace is an Internet café, LAN gaming center, art gallery, concert venue, vegan nosh stop, and coffee shop all rolled in one. In between checking e-mail or marathon rounds of Halo, you can select a focused, freshly brewed cup of Stumptown coffee paired with a Voodoo donut. There are also lots of sandwiches, such as roasted red pepper hummus or the club vegan, with veggie turkey and ham, red onions, and herbed faux mayonnaise. There's also a great selection of healthy soups, salads, and entrees, including soy tacos with grilled mushrooms or a curry rice bowl. ✉ *115 NW 5th Ave., Old Town* ☎ *503/248–2900* ⊕ *www.backspace.bz* ▭ *AE, MC, V.* ✛ *1:E3*

$$$
MEDITERRANEAN

✕ **Bluehour.** At this vast, towering restaurant the waitstaff is as sophisticated as the white tablecloths and floor-to-ceiling curtains. The menu changes daily, based on available ingredients and the chef's whims.

Four-course prix-fixe menus are available for lunch and dinner. Ongoing appetizers to try are the "20 greens" salad and sea scallops wrapped in applewood-smoked bacon with celery-root puree. Top the meal off with a bittersweet chocolate chestnut torte with honey cream. ⊠ *250 NW 13th Ave., Pearl District* ☎ *503/226–3394* ⊕ *www.bluehouronline. com* ⊟ *AE, D, MC, V.* ✛ *1:C3*

¢   ✕ **BridgePort BrewPub & Restaurant.** The hops- and ivy-covered, century-

AMERICAN   old industrial building seems out of place among its newer, posher fashion- and furniture-focused neighbors, but once inside you'll be clear about the business here: frothy pints of BridgePort's ale, brewed on the premises. The India Pale Ale is a specialty, but a good option for the indecisive is the seven-glass sampler that might also include Old Knucklehead, the brewery's barley wine–style ale. Seafood, chicken, steak, pastas, salads, and small plates are served for lunch and dinner, as well as pub favorites. In summer the flower-festooned loading dock is transformed into a beer garden. ⊠ *1313 NW Marshall St., Pearl District* ☎ *503/241–3612* ⊕ *www.bridgeportbrew.com* ⊟ *MC, V.* ✛ *1:C2*

$$ ✕ **Caffé Mingo.** Straightforward, flavorful, and fresh is what you'll find

ITALIAN   at this restaurant with some of the best pizza around. There are also fish and chicken entrées, as well as nightly soup and pasta specials. Don't miss out on the rich chocolate mousse with fresh berries and cream for dessert. ⊠ *807 NW 21st Ave., Pearl District* ☎ *503/226–4646* ⊕ *www. barmingonw.com* ⊟ *AE, DC, MC, V* ◔ *No lunch.* ✛ *1:B2*

¢   ✕ **Cha! Cha! Cha! Taqueria** Burritos and tacos are so tasty at this lively

MEXICAN   taqueria that if it weren't always shoehorned with customers, patrons would probably get up and dance. Part of a local chain, Cha! Cha! Cha! takes cuisine you'd expect to find on a taco truck in L.A. or southern Mexico and puts it on a plate in the Pearl. The extensive menu includes *machaca* (a burrito with shredded beef, sautéed vegetables, scrambled eggs, and Spanish rice) and fish tacos filled with fresh pollack. ⊠ *1208 NW Glisan St., Pearl District* ☎ *503/221–2111* ⊟ *AE, D, MC, V.* ✛ *1:C3*

$ ✕ **Eleni's Philoxenia.** This upscale version of its sister restaurant in Sell-

GREEK   wood offers an extensive menu of Mediterranean specialties. The chef's personal favorite is the *kalatsounia* (spinach, fresh dill, and green onions rolled inside phyllo dough). Other surprising standouts are the *lahano salata* (thinly sliced cabbage and shaved fennel, toasted almonds, and lemon paprika dressing) and the *makaronia me kima* (ground beef simmered with peppers, onion, tomatoes, zucchini, and garlic served over spaghetti). ⊠ *112 NW 9th Ave., Pearl District* ☎ *503/227–2158* ⊕ *www.elenisrestaurant.com* ⊟ *AE, D, MC, V* ◔ *Closed Sun. and Mon. No lunch.* ✛ *1:D3*

$$$ ✕ **Fenouil.** The large stone fireplace, expansive bar, bistro menu, and

FRENCH   widely revered spring-onion soup are a few of the reasons patrons keep coming back to this warm and elegant two-story restaurant. Notable entrée choices vary by season, but two reliable crowd pleasers are the grilled Kobe sirloin and the wood-fired duck breast with Armagnac-soaked prunes. There's live music on Friday nights. At the end of each month the chef creates an all-inclusive "regional dinner" that explores foods from a unique culinary region. ⊠ *900 NW 11th Ave., Pearl*

District ☎ *503/525–2225* ⊕ *www.fenouilinthepearl.com* ▭ *AE, DC, MC, V.* ✛ *1:D2*

$$
AMERICAN
Fodor's Choice
★

✕ **50 Plates.** You wish you had more room to try everything here, where everything seems designed to put Mom's tried-and-true favorites to the test. Evoking regional cuisine from all 50 states, the restaurant creates fresh culinary interpretations. The delightful "silver dollar sammies" include sweet and spicy Carolina pulled pork on a sweet potato roll and a smoked portobello rendition with butter lettuce, fried green tomatoes, and herbed goat cheese. There's also a crowd-pleasing succotash whose components vary depending upon the availability of locally harvested ingredients. The rich desserts include dark-chocolate fudge cake served with homemade brown-sugar ice cream, and bananas Foster. ⊠ *333 NW 13th Ave., Pearl District* ☎ *503/228–5050* ⊕ *www.50plates.com* ▭ *AE, MC, V.* ✛ *1:D3*

¢
CHINESE

✕ **Fong Chong.** Some people believe that this rundown restaurant serves the best dim sum in town, and that includes the dumplings filled with shrimp, pork, or vegetables, accompanied by plenty of different sauces. If you haven't eaten dim sum before, just take a seat: the food is brought to you on carts, and you pick what you want as it comes by; your ticket will be stamped based on the cost of the individual dish (ask if you aren't sure how this works). ⊠ *301 NW 4th Ave., Chinatown* ☎ *503/228–6868* ▭ *AE, MC, V.* ✛ *1:E3*

$$
CONTINENTAL

✕ **The Gilt Club.** Cascading gold curtains, ornate showpiece chandeliers, and high-back booths complement a swanky rich-red dining room. The food is equally lush, with buttercup pumpkin gnocchi topped with an Oregon venison ragu, and a truffle, red quinoa, and goat cheese custard with roasted autumn baby vegetables. The drink menu is loaded with flavor-embellished drinks such as Tracy's First Love, with vodka, cucumber, basil, and lime. ⊠ *306 NW Broadway, Pearl District* ☎ *503/222–4458* ⊕ *www.giltclub.com* ▭ *AE, MC, V* ☽ *Closed Sun.* ✛ *1:E3.*

¢
PIZZA

✕ **Hot Lips Pizza.** A favorite of Portland's pizza lovers, Hot Lips bakes organic and regional ingredients into creative pizzas, available whole or by the slice. Seasonal variations might feature apples, squash, wild mushrooms, and blue cheese. It also has soups, salads, and sandwiches. Beverages include house-made berry sodas, a large rack of wines, and microbrew six-packs. Dine inside the Ecotrust building, outside on the "eco-roof," or take it all across the street for an impromptu picnic in Jamison Square. This is one of five different citywide locations. ⊠ *721 NW 9th Ave., Pearl District* ☎ *503/595–2342* ⊕ *www.hotlipspizza.com* ▭ *AE, D, MC, V* ✛ *1:D3.*

$$
FRENCH
Fodor's Choice
★

✕ **Le Bouchon.** A warm, jovial waitstaff makes Francophiles feel right at home at this bistro in the Pearl District, which serves classic examples of the cuisine for lunch and dinner. Duck confit, truffle chicken, bouillabaisse, and escargots are all cooked with aplomb by chef Claude Musquin. And for dessert, chocolate mousse is a must-try. ⊠ *517 NW 14th Ave., Pearl District* ☎ *503/248–2193* ⊕ *www.bouchon-portland.com* ▭ *AE, MC, V* ☽ *Closed Sun. and Mon.* ✛ *1:C3*

$
FRENCH

✕ **Le Happy.** This tiny crepe-maker outside the hubbub of the Pearl District can serve as a romantic dinner-date spot or just a cozy place to enjoy a drink and a snack. You can get sweet crepes with fruit, cheese, and cream or savory ones with meats and cheeses; in addition, the dinner menu is rounded out with steaks and salads. It's a classy joint, but not without a sense of humor: Le Trash Blanc is a bacon-and-cheddar crepe served with a can of Pabst. ✉ *1011 NW 16th Ave., Pearl District* ☎ *503/226–1258* ✆ *www.lehappy.com* ▭ *MC, V* ☾ *Closed Sun. No lunch.* ✛ *1:C2.*

$$$ ✕ **Oba!** Many come to Oba! for the upscale bar scene, but this Pearl
LATIN AMERICAN   District salsa hangout also serves excellent Latin American cuisine, including coconut prawns, roasted vegetable enchiladas and tamales, and other seafood, chicken, pork, and duck dishes. The bar is open late Friday and Saturday. ✉ *555 NW 12th Ave., Pearl District* ☎ *503/228–6161* ✆ *www.obarestaurant.com* ▭ *AE, D, DC, MC, V* ☾ *No lunch* ✛ *1:D3.*

¢   ✕ **Pearl Bakery.** A light breakfast or lunch can be had at this popular
CAFÉ   spot, which is known for its excellent fresh breads and sandwiches. The cakes, cookies, croissants, and Danish are some of the best in the city. ✉ *102 NW 9th Ave., Pearl District* ☎ *503/827–0910* ✆ *www. pearlbakery.com* ▭ *MC, V* ☾ *No dinner* ✛ *1:D3.*

$$ ✕ **Seres Restaurant.** Tantalizing organic dishes of the East meet the sty-
CHINESE   listic panache of the West at this highly polished establishment. Beauty is in the details, from stainless-steel chopsticks to delicate orchids; it's also present in the artful twists of traditional favorites, such as crispy prawns with honeyed walnuts or spicy sesame beef served with sweet sauce and topped with roasted sesame seeds. ✉ *1105 NW Lovejoy St., Pearl District* ☎ *971/222–7327* ✆ *www.seresrestaurant.com* ▭ *AE, MC, V* ✛ *1:D2.*

$ ✕ **Silk, by Pho Van.** This spacious, minimalist restaurant is the newer and
VIETNAMESE   trendier of the two Pho Van locations in Portland—the less expensive twin is on the far-east side, on 82nd Avenue. A big bowl of pho (noodle soup) is delicious, enough to fill you up, and costs only $8 or $9. The friendly waitstaff will help you work your way through the menu, and can make suggestions to give you the best sampling of Vietnamese cuisine. ✉ *1012 NW Glisan St., Pearl District* ☎ *503/248–2172* ✆ *www. phovanrestaurant.com* ▭ *AE, D, MC, V* ☾ *Closed Sun.* ✉ *1919 SE 82nd Ave.* ☎ *503/788–5244.* ✛ *1:D3*

$$$ ✕ **Ten01.** Soft light, endless ceilings, and clean architectural lines make
AMERICAN   for a very chic dining room at Ten01. Indulge in practically plucked-off-the-farm entrées upstairs or dozens of available small plates downstairs. Save room for the signature chocolate-peanut-butter bread pudding served with malted-milk ice cream and peanut-butter caramel. The wine list is among the city's best. ✉ *1001 NW Couch St., Pearl District* ☎ *503/226–3463* ✆ *www.ten-01.com* ▭ *AE, DC, MC, V* ✛ *1:D4.*

NOB HILL AND VICINITY

Head northwest to sample the broadest scope of this city's food scene. From the finest of the fine (Paley's Place, Wildwood, Papa Haydn, and Hoyt 23) to the come-as-you-are casual (McMenamins Blue Moon, Pizza Schmizza, and Rose's Deli), there's something for everyone within a handful of blocks. Most restaurants in the Nob Hill area are open for lunch and dinner and on weekends; reservations are recommended for the higher-end establishments. This neighborhood draws an eclectic crowd: progressives and conservatives, lifetime residents and recent transplants, wealthy as well as struggling students. There are numerous retail shops and galleries in the neighborhood to help you work up an appetite before or after your meal.

$$$ ✕ **23 Hoyt.** From the prominent antler chandelier to the owner's private
CONTINENTAL   collection of contemporary art on walls and in glass cases, an eclectic mix of fun in a chic, contemporary setting is what this place is about. The restaurant has received national accolades for its interpretation of Northwest cuisine. Choices, which change seasonally, may include a mixed-grill dish with juniper-rubbed quail, rabbit sausage, and smoky bacon; or a Moroccan couscous with Alaskan halibut, manila clams, squid, and sea scallops. If it's available, don't miss the strudel made with crispy phyllo layered with poached pears and caramel custard. In a savory twist, it's served with black-pepper ice cream. ⊠ *529 NW 23rd Ave., Nob Hill* ☎ *503/445–7400* ⊕ *www.23hoyt.com* ⊟ *AE, MC, V* ⊙ *Closed Sun. and Mon. No lunch.* ✛ *1:A3*

$$$ ✕ **Bastas.** In a converted Tastee-Freez, this arty bistro serves dishes from
ITALIAN   all over Italy. The walls are painted with Italian earth tones, and a small side garden provides alfresco dining in good weather. The menu includes scaloppine, grilled lamb, and creative seafood and pasta dishes. ⊠ *410 NW 21st Ave., Nob Hill* ☎ *503/274–1572* ⊕ *www.bastastrattoria.com* ⊟ *AE, MC, V* ⊙ *No lunch.* ✛ *1:B3*

$$ ✕ **BeWon.** Named for the favorite secret garden of ancient Korean
KOREAN   royalty, BeWon prepares a tasty Korean feast. An array of traditional Korean side dishes, presented in an elegant assembly of little white bowls, accompanies such entrées as stir-fried seafood, simmered meat and fish, rice and soup dishes, and kimchi (spicy fermented cabbage). To really experience the cuisine, there's *han jung shik,* a traditional seven-course prix-fixe dinner available with or without wine pairings. ⊠ *1203 NW 23rd Ave., Nob Hill* ☎ *503/464–9222* ⊕ *www.bewonrestaurant. com* ⊟ *AE, D, MC, V* ⊙ *No lunch weekends, closed Sun.* ✛ *1:A2*

¢   ✕ **Ken's Artisan Bakery.** Golden crusts are the trademark of Ken's rustic
CAFÉ   breads, croissants, tarts, and puff pastries, good for breakfast, lunch, and light evening meals. Sandwiches, barbecue pulled pork, and croque monsieur are served on thick slabs of freshly baked bread, and local berries fill the flaky pastries. And if the dozen tables inside the vibrant blue bakery are crammed (they usually are), you can sit outside at one of the sidewalk tables. On Monday nights they serve pizza, and the bakery stays open to 9 PM. ⊠ *338 NW 21st Ave. Nob Hill* ☎ *503/248–2202* ⊕ *www.kensartisan.com* ⊟ *MC, V* ⊙ *No dinner Tues.–Sun.* ✛ *1:B3.*

¢   ✕ **Kornblatt's.** This kosher deli and bagel bakery evokes a 1950s diner.
AMERICAN   Thick sandwiches are made with fresh bread and lean fresh-cooked meats, and the tender home-smoked salmon and pickled herring are simply mouthwatering. For breakfast, try the poached eggs with spicy corned-beef hash, blintzes, or potato latkes. ⊠ *628 NW 23rd Ave., Nob Hill* ☎ *503/242–0055* ⊟ *AE, MC, V* ✛ *1:A3.*

$$ ✕ **Lucy's Table.** In this regal purple and gold corner bistro, chef Michael
CONTINENTAL   Conklin creates Northwest cuisine with a mix of Italian and French

accents. The seasonal menu includes lamb, steak, pork, and seafood dishes. For dessert try the *boca negra*, chocolate cake with Frangelico whipped cream, and cherries poached with port and walnut Florentine. Valet parking is available Wednesday–Saturday. ⊠ *706 NW 21st Ave., Nob Hill* ☎ *503/226–6126* ⊕ *www.lucystable.com* ▭ *AE, DC, MC, V* ☺ *Closed Sun. No lunch.* ✛ *1:B3*

$
AMERICAN
✕ **MacTarnahan's Taproom.** The copper beer-making equipment at the door tips you off to the specialty of the house: beer. This restaurant in the Northwest industrial district is part of a 27,000-sq-ft brewery complex. Start with a tasting platter of seven different beers. The haystack baby back ribs with garlic-rosemary fries are popular, and the fish-and-chips use a batter made with Mac's signature ale. Asparagus-artichoke lasagna is a good vegetarian option. You can enjoy it all on the patio overlooking the landscaped grounds. ⊠ *2730 NW 31st Ave., off NW Yeon St., Nob Hill* ☎ *503/228–5269* ⊕ *www.macsbeer.com* ▭ *AE, DC, MC, V* ✛ *1:A1.*

$$$
CONTINENTAL
✕ **Meriwether's.** A fabulous garden patio adorns this quaint, higher-end—yet unpretentious—restaurant. The outdoor seating area is covered and heated, so during cooler months you can still enjoy Tuscan seafood stew or celery-root ravioli while basking in the garden, where something is always in bloom. Dishes are prepared with fruits and vegetables harvested from Meriwether's own farm, 20 minutes away. The always-changing dessert menu features tasty seasonal treats. ⊠ *2601 NW Vaughn, Nob Hill* ☎ *503/228–1250* ⊕ *www.meriwethersnw.com* ▭ *AE, D, MC, V* ✛ *1:A1.*

$$$
FRENCH
✕ **Paley's Place.** This charming bistro serves French cuisine Pacific Northwest–style. Among the entrées are halibut poached in olive oil and a grilled Laughing Stock Farm pork chop served with polenta. A vegetarian selection is also available. There are two dining rooms and a classy bar. In warmer months there's outdoor seating on the front porch and back patio. ⊠ *1204 NW 21st Ave., Nob Hill* ☎ *503/243–2403* ⊕ *www. paleysplace.net* ▭ *AE, MC, V* ☺ *No lunch* ✛ *1:B2.*

$$
AMERICAN
✕ **Papa Haydn/Jo Bar.** Many patrons come to this bistro just for the luscious desserts or for the popular Sunday brunch (reservations essential). Favorite dinner choices include pan-seared scallops, dinner salads, and grilled flatiron steak. Wood-fired, rotisserie-cooked meat, fish, and poultry dishes plus pastas and pizza are available next door at the jazzy Jo Bar. ⊠ *701 NW 23rd Ave., Nob Hill* ☎ *503/228–7317 Papa Haydn, 503/222–0048 Jo Bar* ⊕ *www.papahaydn.com* ▭ *AE, MC, V* ✛ *1:A3.*

¢
ITALIAN
✕ **Pastini.** It's hard to go wrong with anything at this classy Italian bistro, which has more than two dozen pasta dishes under $10. Rigatoni *zuccati* comes in a light cream sauce with butternut squash, wild mushrooms, and spinach; *linguini misto mare* is a seafood linguine in white wine. It also has panini, antipasti, and dinner salads. Open for lunch and dinner, Pastini is part of a local chain. There's often a crowd, but from this location you can browse the shops while waiting for a table. ⊠ *1506 NW 23rd Ave., Nob Hill* ☎ *503/595–1205* ⊕ *www. pastini.com* ⌚ *Reservations not accepted* ▭ *AE, DC, MC, V* ☺ *No lunch Sun.* ✛ *1:A1.*

$$$$ ✕**Plainfield's Restaurant.** Portland's finest Indian food is served in an ele-
INDIAN gant Victorian house. The tomato-coconut soup with fried curry leaves
and the vegetarian and vegan dishes are highlights. Appetizers include
the authentic Bombay *bhel* (puffed rice and crispy noodles) salad with
tamarind dressing and the *dahi wadi* (crispy fried lentil savory donuts
in a spicy yogurt sauce). Meat and seafood specialties include lobster
in brown onion sauce and tandoori lamb. ⊠ *852 SW 21st Ave., one
block south of Burnside, close to Nob Hill* ☎ *503/223–2995* ⊕ *www.
plainfields.com* ⊟ *AE, D, DC, MC, V* ⊘ *No lunch* ✛ *1:B4.*

$$$ ✕**The Ringside.** This Portland institution has been famous for its beef
AMERICAN for more than 50 years. Dine in cozy booths on rib eye, prime rib, and
New York strip, which come in regular- or king-size cuts. Seafood lov-
ers will find plenty of choices: a chilled seafood platter with an 8-ounce
lobster tail, Dungeness crab, oysters, jumbo prawns, and Oregon bay
shrimp. The onion rings, made with the local Walla Walla sweets vari-
ety, are equally renowned. ⊠ *2165 NW Burnside St., close to Nob
Hill* ☎ *503/223–1513* ⊕ *www.ringsidesteakhouse.com* ⊟ *AE, D, MC,
V* ⊘ *No lunch* ✛ *1:B3.*

$ ✕**Serratto.** Good for a date night, business meeting, or even a casual
CONTINENTAL outing with a friend, this open, spacious dining room comes with warm
service, a knowledgeable staff, and a solid menu. Pasta is made from
scratch and artfully prepared. Good options include the ravioli filled
with butternut squash and goat cheese, served in a white wine-sage
cream sauce with toasted hazelnuts, and the cavatelli with Dungeness
crab, sunchokes, fennel, onions, and kale in a lemon-tomato-fennel
broth. Equally tantalizing entrées include lamb shank with mascar-
pone polenta and a tomato-fennel-rosemary ragout or grilled pork loin
with roasted shallot applesauce. Top off the meal with the bittersweet
chocolate cobbler, served warm with vanilla-bean gelato. ⊠ *2112 NW
Kearney St., Nob Hill* ☎ *503/221–1195* ⊕ *www.serratto.com* ⊟ *AE,
MC, V* ✛ *1:B2.*

¢ ✕**St. Honoré Boulangerie.** Light meals and pastries are available at this
CAFÉ authentic French bakery, named for the patron saint of bakers. Start
the day off with a plain or chocolate croissant, or café au lait. For
lunch and dinner there's quiche, savory puff pastries and tarts, croque-
monsieur, and a variety of fresh salads. Or simply unwind from shop-
ping with a glass of wine and a luscious dessert at one of the sidewalk
café tables. ⊠ *2335 NW Thurman St., Nob Hill* ☎ *503/445–4342*
⊕ *www.sainthonorebakery.com* ⊟ *MC, V* ✛ *1:A1.*

$$$ ✕**Wildwood.** The busy center bar, stainless-steel open kitchen, and
CONTINENTAL blond-wood chairs set the tone at this restaurant serving fresh Pacific
Northwest cuisine. Chef Dustin Clark's entrées include dishes made
with lamb, pork loin, chicken, steak, and seafood. An obsession with
sustainable, fresh ingredients means that that menu changes often, and
that there's always a broad vegetarian selection. Wildwood also has
a family-style Sunday supper menu with selections for two or more
people. ⊠ *1221 NW 21st Ave., Nob Hill* ☎ *503/248–9663* ⊕ *www.
wildwoodrestaurant.com* ⊟ *AE, MC, V* ⊘ *No lunch Sun.* ✛ *1:B2.*

EAST OF THE WILLAMETTE RIVER

Use the coordinate (✛ 2:B2) at the end of each listing to locate a site on the corresponding "Where to Eat East of the Willamette River" map. A whole new food movement is sprouting up east of the river, just outside downtown Portland. As restaurants become more daring and inventive, they are also finding less-predictable locations. One benefit of dining outside of downtown is that parking is less expensive and easier to find. Getting from place to place, though, takes more time, as these establishments are not necessarily concentrated in any one area. But with some of Portland's most sought-after dining spots—such as Genoa, Pok Pok, clarklewis—on the east side, a little research will go a long way toward uncovering amazing new flavors.

$ ✕ **Alameda Brewhouse.** The spacious room—with light wood, high ceilings, and lots of stainless steel—feels chic while still managing to remain friendly and casual. Many people come for the excellent microbrews made here, but the food's worth a look, too; this is no boring pub grub. With creative pasta dishes such as mushroom-artichoke linguine, salmon gyros, tuna tacos, and delicious burgers, it's clear that this restaurant has as much thought going into its menu and ingredients as it does into its brewing. ✉ *4675 NE Fremont St., Alameda* ☎ *503/460–9025* ⊕ *www.alamedabrewhouse.com* ▭ *AE, DC, MC, V* ✛ *2:F2.*

AMERICAN

$$ ✕ **Apizza Scholls.** You will pay more for this pizza, but the crispy yet chewy crust—the end result of 24-hour fermentation—is worth it. Slow fermentation with a minimum of yeast produces acidity, which gives it a creamy, textured flavor. Dough is made daily then topped with whole fresh cheeses and a small amount of meats to spotlight the richness of the crust and sauce flavorings. ✉ *4741 SE Hawthorne Blvd., Hawthorne District* ☎ *503/233–1286* ⊕ *www.apizzascholls.com* ▭ *MC, V* ☽ *No lunch* ✛ *2:F4.*

ITALIAN

$ ✕ **Beaker and Flask.** Inspired by *The Gentleman's Companion*, an influential cocktail manual published in 1946, the sassily named cocktails here are modern twists on classics. For instance, there's the rum-based Sal's Minion, served over coconut-water ice cubes, or the Chimney Sweep, a concoction of ouzo, blended scotch, and Ramazzotti (an Italian bitters). Drink choices frequently change based on seasons and available ingredients. The food, equally chic and selectively prepared, often unites ingredients in unconventional ways, as in the macaroni and cheese with blood sausage and a herb-thyme crust or the maple-braised pork belly accompanied by creamed kale, squash, and apple relish. ✉ *720 SE Sandy Blvd., Buckman* ☎ *503/235–8180* ⊕ *www. beakerandflask.com* ▭ *MC, V* ☽ *Closed Sun.* ✛ *2:D4.*

CONTINENTAL

$$$$ ✕ **Beast.** This quintessential example of Portland's creative cuisine is in a nondescript red building with no signage. Inside, the seating is communal, at two large tables that seat 8 and 16. The frequently changing menus are prix-fixe, and you have the option of either three or five courses. The dishes that come from the open kitchen live up to the restaurant's name: there might be chicken and duck-liver mousse, wine and truffle-braised beef, or steak tartare with quail-egg toast. (Vegetarians may struggle to eat here.) There are two seatings per night; call

CONTINENTAL

ahead for times and the day's menus. ⊠ *5425 NE 30th Ave., Concordia* 🕾 *503/841–6968* ⊕ *www.beastpdx.com* ▭ MC, V ☉ *Closed Mon. and Tues. No dinner Sun.* ✛ *2:F3.*

$ ✕ **Belly Restaurant.** In this neighborhood restaurant people feel wel-
AMERICAN   comed, and can dine on an incredible meal made from sustainable ingredients. The name "Belly" is about showing up with an appetite big enough for the vast selection of small dishes—including potato and kale soup or pork meatballs—or the hearty three-course meals. Sunday brunches are also a hit: there's banana-bread French toast and a chance to build your own biscuit sandwich stuffed with eggs, bacon, sausage, and gravy. ⊠ *3500 NE Martin Luther King Jr. Blvd., Alameda* 🕾 *503/249–9764* ⊕ *www.bellyrestaurant.com* ▭ AE, D, DC, MC, V ☉ *Sun. brunch only. Closed Mon.* ✛ *2:D2.*

$$ ✕ **Bernie's Southern Bistro.** You definitely won't find finer soul food in
SOUTHERN   Portland. Made of fresh, organic ingredients, the healthy portions here are in a different realm from that of your garden-variety fried chicken. Other specialties include crisp fried green tomatoes, crawfish, and cat-fish, in addition to delectable collard greens and black-eyed peas. The inside of the restaurant is painted in warm orange, and the lush outdoor patio is a Portland favorite. ⊠ *2904 NE Alberta St., Alberta District* 🕾 *503/282–9864* ⊕ *www.berniesbistro.com* ▭ AE, D, MC, V ☉ *Closed Mon. No lunch* ✛ *2:E1.*

$ ✕ **Biwa.** Taking ramen to whole new heights is what this bustling, indus-
JAPANESE   trial restaurant with an open kitchen does best. Homemade noodles are the focal point of aromatic, flavorful soups enriched by accompa-niments such as sliced pork and grilled chicken. Also try the thicker udon noodles served in a soup made from dried fish and seaweed. A fitting sendoff for the filling, authentic meals here would be one of the many sakes. ⊠ *215 SE 9th Ave., Buckman* 🕾 *503/239–8830* ⊕ *www. biwarestaurant.com* ▭ MC, DC, V ☉ *No lunch* ✛ *2:D4.*

$ ✕ **Bread and Ink.** The old-fashioned elegance will strike you as soon as
AMERICAN   you walk in; the dining room, done in cream and forest green and with high ceilings, is not trendy in any way. The look's impressive, but it's mainly the earnest dedication to quality food that's made Bread and Ink a neighborhood landmark. Breakfast, a specialty, might include brioche French toast, smoked fish, and blintzes (they're legendary). Lunch and dinner yield good choices, including burgers, poached salmon, and crab cakes. ⊠ *3610 SE Hawthorne Blvd., Hawthorne District* 🕾 *503/239–4756* ⊕ *www.breadandinkcafe.com* ▭ AE, D, MC, V ✛ *2:E4.*

¢   ✕ **Broder.** Smells of freshly brewed coffee and wonderful breads greet
SWEDISH   you as you walk into this friendly Swedish restaurant. Broder is known for its excellent takes on breakfast: if you can't decide between the many tasty, home-cooked options on the menu, go with the Swedish Breakfast Bord. For only 10 bucks, you get the best of what's offered: depending on the day, that could include walnut toasts, smoked trout, ham, seasonal fruit, yogurt and honey, a soft-boiled egg, and some sort of brilliant cheese. The coffee cakes, pastries, and breads are delectable. Lunch and dinner include a variety of sandwiches and salads—and yes, they serve meatballs. ⊠ *2508 SE Clinton St., Clinton* 🕾 *503/736–3333* ⊕ *www.broderpdx.com* ▭ MC, V ✛ *2:E5.*

$$$
CONTINENTAL

✕**Castagna.** Enjoy the bouillabaisse or one of the inventive Mediterranean seafood entrées at this tranquil Hawthorne restaurant. The pan-seared scallops with mushrooms are the signature dish. Next door is the more casual **Cafe Castagna** (☎ *503/231–9959*), a bistro and bar open nightly, serving pizzas and other slightly less expensive, lighter fare. ⊠ *1752 SE Hawthorne Blvd., Hawthorne District* ☎ *503/231–7373* ⊕ *www.castagnarestaurant.com* ▭ *AE, D, DC, MC, V* ⊗ *Closed Sun.– Tues. No lunch* ✛ *2:D4.*

$$
CONTINENTAL

✕**clarklewis.** This cutting-edge restaurant, aka "darklewis" for its murky lighting, is making big waves for inventive farm-fresh meals served inside a former warehouse loading dock. Regional vegetables, seafood, and meat from local suppliers appear on a daily changing menu of pastas, entrées, and sides. Diners can order small, large, and family-style sizes, or let the chef decide with the fixed-price meal. Although the food is great, the lack of signage or a reception area can make your first visit feel a little like arriving at a party uninvited. ⊠ *1001 SE Water Ave., Buckman* ☎ *503/235–2294* ⊕ *www.clarklewispdx.com* ▭ *AE, MC, V* ⊗ *Closed Sun. No lunch weekends* ✛ *2:D4.*

¢
AMERICAN

✕**Doug Fir.** In what resembles a futuristic lumberjack hangout, the surroundings make use of brick and glass, and the walls and ceilings are made from wood logs. Add a menu of hearty, homey dishes, and you've got a fun, eclectic restaurant. The morning shift can go for the banana-hazelnut pancakes or egg scrambles, and lunch crowds will appreciate big hearty sandwiches that include a signature hamburger. For dinner, grandma's meat loaf with gravy or Diego's marionberry chicken are both good. Downstairs is a concert venue open seven nights a week that attracts lots of wannabe rockers who come to hang out, drink, and socialize. ⊠ *830 E. Burnside St., Buckman* ☎ *503/231–9663* ⊕ *www. dougfirlounge.com* ▭ *AE, MC, V* ✛ *2:D3.*

$
CONTINENTAL

✕**Equinox.** Locally grown organic produce, free-range meats, wild seafood, and cage-free chickens all come to the table at this fusiony neighborhood restaurant on North Mississippi Street. Renovated-garage chic and a pleasant outdoor patio create a casual atmosphere for enjoying unusual combinations of ingredients. Spicy *togorashi* chicken is roasted with sesame seeds, chilies, and orange peel, and topped with a ginger demi-glace. Vegetarian entrées might include tofu, spinach, and coconut-tomato-basil curry. An almond flan dessert is served in a towering martini glass. ⊠ *830 N. Shaver St., at N. Mississippi St., Albina* ☎ *503/460–3333* ⊕ *www.equinoxrestaurantpdx.com* ▭ *D, MC, V* ⊗ *Closed Mon. No dinner Sun.* ✛ *2:C2.*

$
SOUTHWESTERN

✕**Esparza's Tex-Mex Café.** Be prepared for south-of-the-border craziness at this beloved local eatery. Wild West kitsch festoons the walls, but it isn't any wilder than some of the entrées that emerge from chef-owner Joe Esparza's kitchen. Look for such creations as lean smoked-sirloin tacos—Esparza's is renowned for its smoked meats. ⊠ *2725 SE Ankeny St., at SE 28th Ave., near Laurelhurst* ☎ *503/234–7909* ⌆ *Reservations not accepted* ▭ *AE, D, MC, V* ✛ *2:E3.*

¢
CHINESE

✕**Fu Jin.** Although the place is a bit tattered, this family-run neighborhood restaurant consistently serves good wok-cooked favorites at reasonable prices. The fried tofu dishes and sesame-crusted shrimp are tasty. ✉ *3549 SE Hawthorne Blvd., Hawthorne District* ☎ *503/231–3753* 🖶 *D, MC, V* ⊗ *Closed Thurs.* ✛ *2:E4.*

$$$$
ITALIAN
Fodor'sChoice
★

✕ **Genoa.** Widely regarded as the finest restaurant in Portland, Genoa serves a five-course prix-fixe Italian menu that changes with the availability of ingredients and the season. Diners can chose from several entrées; the portions are hearty, thoughtfully crafted, and paired with some vibrant accompaniments such as sautéed brussels-sprout leaves or roasted root vegetables. As for the dining room, its dark antique furnishings, long curtains, and dangling light fixtures all help make it feel sophisticated. Seating is limited to under a few dozen diners, so service is excellent. ✉ *2822 SE Belmont St., near Hawthorne District* ☎ *503/238–1464* ⬦ *Reservations essential* ⊕ *www.genoarestaurant.com* 🖶 *AE, D, DC, MC, V* ⊗ *No lunch.* ✛ *2:E4.*

$
ITALIAN

✕ **Il Piatto.** On a quiet residential street, this laid-back trattoria and espresso house turns out inventive dishes and classic Italian favorites. A tasty sun-dried-tomato–pesto spread instead of butter accompanies the bread. Entrées include smoked salmon ravioli in a lemon cream sauce with capers and leeks. The vegetarian lasagna with grilled eggplant and zucchini, topped with pine nuts, is rich and satisfying. The extensive wine selection focuses on varieties from Tuscany. ✉ *2348 Ankeny St., near Laurelhurst* ☎ *503/236–4997* ⊕ *www.ilpiattopdx.com* 🖶 *DC, MC, V* ⊗ *No lunch Sat.–Mon.* ✛ *2:E4.*

¢
ITALIAN

✕ **Ken's Artisan Pizza.** Old wine barrels and hungry crowds surround the pizza prep area and its glowing, 700-degree wood-fired oven. Ken, also of Ken's Artisan Bakery & Café, prides himself on the use of fresh, organic ingredients for the dough, sauces, and toppings. Fans rave about the margherita pizza with arugula. Another favorite is the handpressed sausage and onion. Although there are some fun appetizers and salads, pizza is the star. ✉ *304 SE 28th Ave., Laurelhurst* ☎ *503/517–9951* ⊕ *www.kensartisan.com* 🖶 *MC, V* ⊗ *Closed Sun. and Mon. No lunch* ✛ *2:E4.*

$
CONTINENTAL

✕ **L'Astra Bistro.** Come as you are to this no-frills restaurant for a simple selection of Italian and French dishes: gnocchi with spinach, garlic sausage with lentils, and roasted duck are some unassuming favorites. Ice cream lovers will appreciate special flavors, which change daily. Ask for them if they're not on the menu. ✉ *22 NE 7th Ave., Kerns* ☎ *503/236–3896* ⊕ *www.lastrabistro.com* 🖶 *MC, V* ⊗ *No lunch* ✛ *2:E3.*

$$$
AMERICAN

✕ **Laurelhurst Market.** Vegetarians beware; it's all about the meat here. Even the liquor is infused with meat, and makes for some swell martinis. By day, the restaurant plays it low-key as a butcher shop and droolworthy deli, but at night it's a crowded and often loud steak house. All the meats served are hormone and antibiotic free, and from the pâtés, to the Andouille, to the two styles of pancetta, all are prepared inhouse. Come for a menu with no shortage of daring and ever-changing carnivorous variations. Be prepared for a well-earned but lengthy wait. ✉ *3155 E. Burnside, Kerns* ☎ *503-206-3097* ⊕ *www.laurelhurstmarket.com* 🖶 *AE, D, DC, MC, V* ✛ *2:E3.*

$$
MEDITERRANEAN

✕ **Lauro Kitchen.** The wide, inviting space, large windows, and exposed wooden beams set the mood for enjoying the action from an open kitchen, from which dishes like the seafood paella or the Greek-style

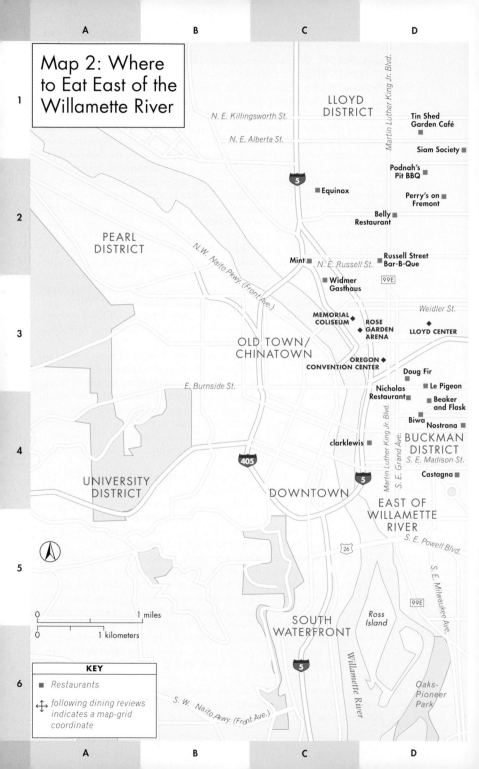

Map 2: Where to Eat East of the Willamette River

LLOYD DISTRICT

Martin Luther King Jr. Blvd.

N. E. Killingsworth St.

N. E. Alberta St.

Tin Shed Garden Café ■

Siam Society ■

Podnah's Pit BBQ ■

■ Equinox

Perry's on Fremont ■

Belly Restaurant ■

PEARL DISTRICT

N.W. Naito Pkwy. (Front Ave.)

Mint ■   N. E. Russell St.

Russell Street Bar-B-Que ■

99E

■ Widmer Gasthaus

Weidler St.

MEMORIAL COLISEUM ◆   ROSE GARDEN ARENA ◆

LLOYD CENTER ◆

OLD TOWN/ CHINATOWN

OREGON CONVENTION CENTER ◆

Doug Fir ■   ■ Le Pigeon

E. Burnside St.

Nicholas Restaurant ■

■ Beaker and Flask

Biwa ■   Nostrana ■

Martin Luther King Jr. Blvd.

S.E. Grand Ave.

BUCKMAN DISTRICT
S. E. Madison St.

clarklewis ■

UNIVERSITY DISTRICT

405

Castagna ■

5

DOWNTOWN

EAST OF WILLAMETTE RIVER

S. E. Powell Blvd.

26

S. E. Milwaukee Ave.

Ross Island

99E

SOUTH WATERFRONT

5

Willamette River

Oaks-Pioneer Park

S. W. Naito Pkwy. (Front Ave.)

0 ——— 1 miles
0 ——— 1 kilometers

KEY
■ Restaurants
⬌ following dining reviews indicates a map-grid coordinate

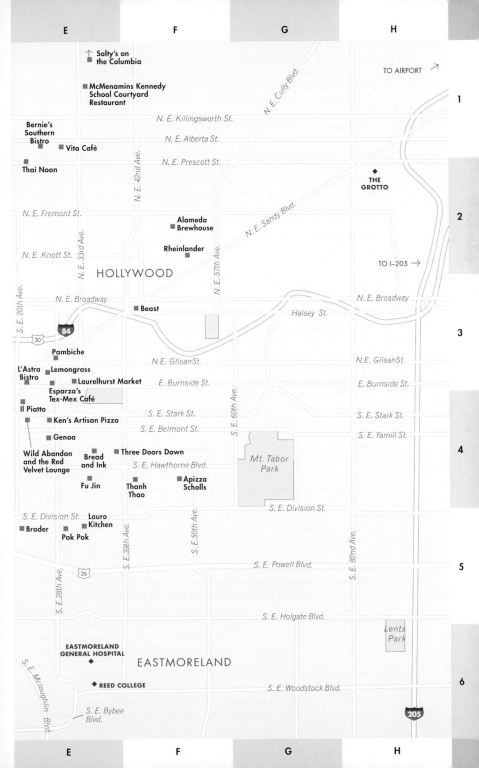

braised pork shoulder emerge. Complete your meal with a glass of scotch or brandy, or warm cherry bread pudding with pistachio caramel sauce. Since this place is usually busy, expect to wait for a table. ⊠ *3377 SE Division St., Richmond* ☎ *503/239-7000* ⊕ *www.laurokitchen.com* ⊟ *AE, DC, MC, V* ✛ *2:E5.*

$$$ **FRENCH** ✕ **Le Pigeon.** With exposed brick, bar seating, and an open kitchen, the atmosphere at this 42-seat restaurant is trendy, yet casual. And yes, pigeon, aka squab—cooked in red wine and served with liver crostini—is an entrée. Hardcore meat lovers might also appreciate the veal tongue appetizer. Aside from a changing menu, there are a few pasta and salad dishes as well. The wine menu is extensive, and they are open late. ⊠ *738 E. Burnside St., Buckman* ☎ *503/546-8796* ⏤ *Reservations essential* ⊕ *www.lepigeon.com* ⊟ *MC, V* ☺ *No lunch* ✛ *2:D3.*

$ **THAI** **Fodor's Choice** **★** ✕ **Lemongrass.** Set in an old house, this lovely, intimate establishment consistently serves tantalizing pad thai and a garlic basil chicken with sauce so delicious you wish you had a straw. Fresh flowers adorn the white-linen tablecloths. Dishes are cooked to order, and just about everything is delectable, including the chicken chili paste and peanut curry. ⊠ *1705 NE Couch St., Kerns* ☎ *503/231-5780* ⏤ *Reservations not accepted* ⊟ *No credit cards* ✛ *2:E3.*

$ **AMERICAN** ✕ **McMenamins Kennedy School Courtyard Restaurant.** Whether you are coming to the Kennedy School to stay at the hotel, to watch a movie, or just to enjoy dinner and drinks, the Courtyard Restaurant can add to your evening. The food, with old reliables like burgers, salads, and pizzas, fish-and-chips, pasta, prime rib, and beef stew, can satisfy most any appetite. Several standard McMenamins microbrews are always available, in addition to seasonal specialty brews. ⊠ *5736 NE 33rd Ave., near Alberta District* ☎ *503/288-2192* ⊕ *www.kennedyschool. com* ⊟ *AE, D, MC, V* ✛ *2:E1.*

$$ **CONTINENTAL** ✕ **Mint.** The owner of this cool, romantic restaurant also happens to be a top-notch bartender. Drinks made with maple syrup, nutmeg, and avocados are commonplace—and just as the beverages here are hard to categorize, so too are the menu items. Global flavors influence an evolving choice of interesting dishes like opah (a kind of fish) poached in coconut lemongrass sake, and sautéed rabbit loin with garlic mashed potatoes and wild-boar bacon. When you're done, slip next door to 820, the sister lounge to this suave establishment. ⊠ *816 N. Russell St., Eliot* ☎ *503/284-5518* ⊕ *www.mintrestaurant.com* ⊟ *AE, MC, V* ☺ *Closed Sun–Tues. No lunch* ✛ *2:C2.*

¢ **MIDDLE EASTERN** ✕ **Nicholas Restaurant.** In a small streetfront along an unimpressive stretch of Grand Avenue, this hidden gem serves some of the best Lebanese food in Portland, for prices that can't be beat. Everything from the fresh homemade pita to the hummus, falafel, baba ghanoush, and kebabs is delicious, and comes in enormous portions. No alcohol is served here. ⊠ *318 SE Grand Ave., near Burnside Bridge* ☎ *503/235-5123* ⊕ *www. nicholasrestaurant.com* ⊟ *No credit cards* ✛ *2:D4.*

$ **PIZZA** ✕ **Nostrana.** This well-liked restaurant delivers delicious pizzas and wood-grilled specialties (even desserts) from their signature oven. Between pies topped with roasted squash and smoked mozzarella to those sprinkled with radicchio and pancetta, the pizzas here would make mamma mia proud. Other tempting entrées are the fresh prawns and Satsuma oranges with white bean purée, and the Tuscan pork ribs with smashed celery root and spicy onion relish. ✉ *1401 SE Morrison St., Belmont* ☎ *503/234-2427* ⊕ *www.nostrana.com* ▭ *MC, V* ✛ *2:D4.*

$ ✕**Pambiche.** Locals know that you can drive by Pambiche any night of
CARIBBEAN the week and find it packed. With traditional Cuban fare (plantains, roast pork, mojitos, and Cuban espresso), it is no surprise why. If you have some time to wait for a table, you should stop by and make an evening of it at this hopping neighborhood hot spot. Don't miss out on the incredible desserts here; they are the sole reason why some people make the trip. Try the Selva Negra, a coconut chocolate cake filled with mango and other tropical fruit. ✉ *2811 NE Glisan St., near Laurelhurst* ☎ *503/233-0511* ⊕ *www.pambiche.com* ⊘ *Reservations not accepted* ▭ *D, MC, V* ✛ *2:E3.*

$$ ✕**Perry's on Fremont.** This diner, famous for burgers, chicken potpies,
AMERICAN and fish-and-chips, has gone a bit more upscale with the addition of pricier menu choices such as steak and salmon. Eat outside on the large patio among the flowers, and don't pass up one of the desserts. ✉ *2401 NE Fremont St., Alameda* ☎ *503/287-3655* ⊕ *www.perrysonfremont. com* ▭ *AE, D, MC, V* ⊗ *Closed Sun. and Mon. No lunch weekdays* ✛ *2:D2.*

$ ✕**Podnah's Pit BBQ.** This nondescript little storefront diner hardly even
SOUTHERN declares itself with outdoor signage—but don't be fooled—the Texas- and Carolina-style dishes at Podnah's are the stuff big boy barbecues are made of. Melt-in-your-mouth pulled pork, ribs, chicken, and lamb are all slow-smoked on hardwood and served up in a sassy vinegar-based sauce. ✉ *1469 NE Prescott St., Alberta District* ☎ *503/281-3700* ▭ *MC, V* ⊗ *Closed Mon.* ✛ *2:D2.*

¢ ✕**Pok Pok.** There's no shortage of culinary adventure here. The food
ASIAN resembles what street vendors in Thailand would make: charcoal-grilled game hen stuffed with lemongrass or shredded chicken and coconut milk (made in-house). Diners have options of sitting outside by heated lamps under tents, or down below in the dark, funky cave. Foods are unique blends of flavors and spices, such as the coconut and jackfruit ice cream served on a sweet bun with sticky rice, condensed milk, chocolate syrup, and peanuts. ✉ *3226 SE Division St., Richmond* ☎ *503/232-1387* ⊕ *www.pokpokpdx.com* ▭ *MC, V* ✛ *2:E5.*

$$ ✕**Rheinlander.** A strolling accordionist and singing servers entertain as
GERMAN patrons dine on authentic traditional German food, including sauerbra-ten, hasenpfeffer, schnitzel, sausage, and rotisserie chicken. **Gustav's,** the adjoining pub and grill, serves slightly less expensive entrées, including sausages, cabbage rolls, and German meatballs, in an equally festive and slightly more raucous environment. ✉ *5035 NE Sandy Blvd., Holly-wood* ☎ *503/288-5503* ⊕ *www.rheinlander.com* ▭ *AE, MC, V* ✛ *2:F2.*

$ ✕**Russell St. Bar-B-Que.** Pig bric-a-brac tips you off to the star specialty at
SOUTHERN this casual neighborhood joint, but there are also beef, poultry, seafood, and smoked tofu dishes available. A saucy pulled-pork sandwich and collard greens pairs well with a strawberry soda. ✉ *325 NE Russell St., off NE Martin Luther King Jr. Blvd., Eliot* ☎ *503/528-8224* ⊕ *www. russellstreetbbq.com* ▭ *AE, MC, V* ✛ *2:D2.*

Dragon boat races on the Willamette River

$$$
SEAFOOD
✗ **Salty's on the Columbia.** Pacific Northwest salmon (choose blackened or grilled, a half or full pound) is what this comfortable restaurant overlooking the Columbia River is known for. Blackberry-barbecue-glazed salmon highlights local ingredients. Loaded with prawns, oysters, crab, mussels, and clams, the seafood platter offers plenty of variety. The menu also includes chicken and steak. There are both a heated, covered deck and an uncovered deck for open-air dining. ⊠ *3839 NE Marine Dr., East Columbia* ☎ *503/288–4444* ⊕ *www.saltys.com* ▭ *AE, D, DC, MC, V* ✛ *2:E1.*

$
ASIAN
✗ **Siam Society.** Oversize red shutter doors, a beautiful outdoor patio surrounded by full plants and flowers, and a lush upstairs lounge create an inviting atmosphere. Expect large portions of dishes such as char-grilled steak with a red-wine reduction and sweet-potato fries lightly sprinkled with white-truffle oil. The banana-roasted pork is made by slow-cooking pork shoulder for five days while wrapped in banana leaves; it's served with grilled pineapple. Drinks not to be missed include a ginger-lime cosmo and jalapeño-pear kamikaze. ⊠ *2703 NE Alberta St., Alberta District* ☎ *503/922–3675* ⊕ *www.siamsociety.com* ▭ *MC, V* ✛ *2:D1.*

¢
THAI
✗ **Thai Noon.** The excellent traditional dishes here, including red, green, and yellow curry; stir-fries; and noodle dishes, are served in a vibrant orange dining room with only about 12 tables. You can choose the spiciness of your meal, but beware that although "medium" may be milder than "hot," it's still spicy. Thai iced tea is also transformed into a boozy cocktail in the adjoining bar and lounge. Try the fried banana split or the mango ice cream for dessert. ⊠ *2635 NE Alberta St., Alberta District* ☎ *503/282–2021* ⊕ *www.thainoon.com* ▭ *MC, V* ✛ *2:E1.*

¢ ✕ **Thanh Thao.** This busy Asian diner in the heart of Portland's bohe-
VIETNAMESE mian Hawthorne neighborhood has an extensive menu of Vietnamese
stir-fries, noodles, soups, and Thai favorites. Be prepared to wait for
and at your table: the place is often packed, and service is famously
slow. But the food and generous portions are worth the wait. ✉ *4005
SE Hawthorne Blvd., Hawthorne District* ☎ *503/238–6232* ⊟ *D, MC,
V* ⊙ *Closed Tues.* ✚ *2:F4.*

$$ ✕ **Three Doors Down.** Down a side street, this small Italian restaurant is
ITALIAN known for quality Italian food, with exquisite seafood dishes, skillful
pasta concoctions, and rich desserts. The intimate restaurant's reputa-
tion brings people back again and again, even though they might have
to wait on the sidewalk for close to an hour. You can call one hour
before you arrive to put your name on the list. ✉ *1429 SE 37th Ave.,
Hawthorne District* ☎ *503/236–6886* ⊕ *www.3doorsdowncafe.com*
⊟ *AE, D, MC, V* ⊙ *Closed Mon. No lunch* ✚ *2:E4.*

¢ ✕ **Tin Shed Garden Cafe.** This small restaurant is a popular breakfast
CAFÉ spot known for its shredded-potato cakes, biscuits and gravy, sweet-
potato cinnamon French toast, creative egg and tofu scrambles, and
breakfast burritos. The lunch and dinner menu has creative choices
like a creamy artichoke sandwich, and a chicken sandwich with bacon,
Gorgonzola, and apple, in addition to burgers, salads, and soups. A
comfortable outdoor patio doubles as a beer garden on warm spring
and summer evenings, and the adjacent community garden rounds
off the property with a peaceful sitting area. ✉ *1438 NE Alberta St.,
Alberta District* ☎ *503/288–6966* ⌦ *Reservations not accepted* ⊕ *www.
tinshedgardencafe.com* ⊟ *MC, V* ✚ *2:D1.*

¢ ✕ **Vita Cafe.** Vegan mac and cheese and vegetarian biscuits and gravy
VEGETARIAN are just a few of the old favorites with a new, meatless spin. This hip
restaurant along Alberta Street has a large menu with American, Mexi-
can, Asian, and Middle Eastern–inspired entrées, and both herbivores
and carnivores are sure to find something. There is also plenty of free-
range, organic meat to go around. Finish off your meal with a piece
of German chocolate cake or a peanut-butter fudge bar. ✉ *3023 NE
Alberta St., Alberta District* ☎ *503/335–8233* ⊕ *www.vita-cafe.com*
⊟ *MC, V* ✚ *2:E1.*

$ ✕ **Widmer Gasthaus.** This OLd World–style brewpub, part of the Wid-
GERMAN mer Brothers Brewery, is steps away from the MAX light-rail station
on North Interstate Avenue. Ale-dunked sausages, schnitzel, and sau-
erbraten go well with the signature hefeweizen and other German-style
beers that come from the handsome hardwood-and-brass bar. Chicken
potpie, steak, pastas, and burgers are also served, in addition to the
Widmer brothers' beloved beer cheese soup. ✉ *955 N. Russell St., at
N. Interstate Ave., Albina* ☎ *503/281–3333* ⊕ *www.widmer.com* ⊟ *AE,
D, MC, V* ✚ *2:C3.*

$ ✕ **Wild Abandon and the Red Velvet Lounge.** Inside this small, bohemian-
CONTINENTAL looking building, where the dominant color is deep red and the light
fixtures are multicolor glass, owner Michael Cox creates an inventive
Mediterranean-influenced menu that includes fresh seafood, pork, beef,
and pasta entrées. Vegetarian selections might be ziti, panfried tofu, or
polenta lasagna made with roasted eggplant, squash, and spinach. The

popular weekend brunch includes omelets, Benedict dishes, breakfast burritos, and vegan French toast. ✉ *2411 SE Belmont St., near Hawthorne District* ☎ *503/232–4458* ⊕ *www.wildabansonrestaurant.com* ▭ *AE, D, DC, MC, V* ✆ *Closed Tues.* ✛ *2:E4.*

WEST OF DOWNTOWN

Beyond downtown to the west are a handful of restaurants worth visiting. Without parking to worry about, the 5- to 15-minute drive will reward you with some delicious dining surprises, including pancakes, pizza, and some of the best tapas in Portland. Several establishments are right alongside the Willamette River, so there are also lovely views to be had. During the summer months, many offer deck seating. These seats are in high demand, but watching the boats sail by on a warm summer night while indulging in a round of tasty appetizers is totally worth the wait.

$$ ✕**Aquariva.** Choose from a vast selection of innovative Italian tapas—
ITALIAN such as the spinach gnocchi with morels and Oregon truffles—in one of the prime dining locations in Portland. Gaze out the windows at the Willamette River while sipping on a glass of Italian Syrah chosen from an impressive wine list. There are plenty of cushy couches to lounge in for happy hour, but if the weather's nice, head for the deck. ✉ *470 SW Hamilton Ct., South Waterfront* ☎ *503/802–5850* ⊕ *www.aquarivaportland.com* ▭ *AE, DC, MC, V* ✆ *No lunch weekends.* ✛ *1:E6*

$$ ✕**Chart House.** On a hill high above the Willamette River, the Chart
AMERICAN House has a stunning view of the city and the surrounding mountains from almost all of its tables. Prime rib is a specialty, but the seafood dishes, including coconut-crunchy shrimp deep-fried in tempura batter and the Cajun-spiced yellowfin ahi, are just as tempting. ✉ *5700 SW Terwilliger Blvd., Southwest Hills* ☎ *503/246–6963* ⊕ *www.charthouse.com* ▭ *AE, D, DC, MC, V* ✆ *No lunch weekends.* ✛ *1:E6*

¢ ✕**Original Pancake House.** The original of what's now a franchise with
AMERICAN more than 100 branches, this pancake house is the real deal. Faithful customers have been coming for close to 50 years to wait for a table at this bustling, cabinlike local landmark, and you can expect to find a contented crowd of locals and tourists alike from the time the place opens at 7 AM until afternoon. With pancakes starting at $7.25, it's not the cheapest place to get a stack, but with 20 varieties and some of the best waffles and crepes around, it's worth the trip. ✉ *8601 SW 24th Ave., Crestwood* ☎ *503/246–9007* ⊕ *www.originalpancakehouse.com* ✍ *Reservations not accepted* ▭ *No credit cards* ✆ *Closed Mon. and Tues. No dinner* ✛ *1:E6.*

$$ ✕**Three Square Grill.** Hidden within an old shopping plaza in the Hills-
AMERICAN dale neighborhood, you'll discover the best place in Portland to go on
⟳ Tuesdays: that's fried chicken and waffle night. Indulge in large servings of comfort food, including Louisiana-style bouillabaisse with shrimp, crab, oysters, and crawfish, as well as 21-day dry-aged New York steak with truffle butter. Dishes focus on organic ingredients, some of which came from the chef's own garden, and everything from the bread to

desserts is baked fresh daily. Weekend brunches and live music in the evening are a big hit at this kid-friendly place. ⊠ *6320 SW Capitol Hwy., Hillsdale* ☎ *503/244–4467* ⊕ *www.threesquare.com* ▭ *MC, V* ☽ *Closed Mon.* ⊹ *1:E6.*

WHERE TO STAY

DOWNTOWN

Use the coordinate (⊹ B2) at the end of each listing to locate a site on the corresponding "Where to Stay in Portland" map.

Staying downtown ensures that you'll have immediate access to just about everything Portland offers, including events, restaurants, cultural venues, shops, movie theaters, and more. Transportation options are abundant thanks to the MAX, bus lines, and taxis; in addition, many hotels offer shuttle service. Portland has clean streets and, overall, is considered relatively safe.

$$ ⛨ **Ace Hotel.** Designed to appeal to younger, budget-minded travelers who crave quality, this funky, bohemian property is in the center of downtown. Each room is uniquely adorned by original hand-painted wall art; in a few, you can find retro accessories like turntables (and record collections) and bathrooms with cast-iron tubs. In case you forgot your camera, there's even a photo booth in the lobby in which to capture your stay. The great Clyde Common restaurant is downstairs. **Pros:** unique lodging experience; original artwork in each room; free city bicycles available for guests. **Cons:** poor water pressure; rooms are noisy. ⊠ *1022 SW Stark St., Downtown* ☎ *503/228–2277* ⊕ *www. acehotel.com* ⤳ *79 rooms* ♿ *In-room: refrigerator, Wi-Fi. In-hotel: restaurant, laundry service, Wi-Fi hotspot, parking (fee), some pets allowed* ▭ *AE, D, DC, MC, V* ⊹ *C4.*

$$$ ⛨ **Avalon Hotel & Spa.** On the edge of Portland's progressive South Waterfront District and just a few minutes from downtown, this tranquil boutique property is sheltered among trees along the meandering Willamette River. Rooms range widely in size (from about 340 up to 1,030 sq ft), and they are all tastefully decorated with simple yet warm furnishings; most have a balcony. There are a full service spa and extensive fitness facility on-site. Aquariva, an Italian restaurant and wine bar on the premises, serves wonderful tapas and drinks. **Pros:** great river views; trails nearby for walking and jogging; breakfast served on each hotel floor. **Cons:** not in the center of downtown, spa tubs in the fitness facility are not coed; steep overnight parking fee. ⊠ *455 SW Hamilton Ct., Downtown* ☎ *503/802–5800 or 888/556–4402* ⊕ *www. avalonhotelandspa.com* ⤳ *99 rooms* ♿ *In-room: refrigerator (some), Wi-Fi. In-hotel: restaurant, room service, bar, gym, concierge, laundry service, Wi-Fi hotspot, parking (fee)* ▭ *AE, MC, V* ⎟◯⎟ *CP* ⊹ *D6.*

$$ ⛨ **Benson Hotel.** Portland's grandest hotel was built in 1912. The hand-carved Circassian walnut paneling from Russia and the Italian white-marble staircase are among the noteworthy design touches in the public areas. In the guest rooms expect to find small crystal chandeliers and

BEST BETS FOR PORTLAND LODGING

Fodor's offers a selective listing of quality lodging experiences in every price range, from the city's best budget beds to its most sophisticated luxury hotels. Here we've compiled our top recommendations by price and experience. The very best properties—in other words, those that provide a particularly remarkable experience in their price range—are designated in the listings with the Fodor's Choice logo.

Fodor's Choice ★

Heathman Hotel, $$$ p. 95
Hotel deLuxe, $$ p. 98
Lion and the Rose, $$ p. 105
McMenamins Kennedy School, $ p. 105
RiverPlace Hotel, $$$$ p. 102

By Price

¢

Monticello Motel, p. 106

$

Georgian House, p. 104
Inn @ Northrup Station, p. 103
Jupiter Hotel, p. 105
McMenamins Kennedy School, p. 105
Park Lane Suites and Inn, p. 102

$$

Aloft Portland Airport at Cascade Station, p. 108
Benson Hotel, p. 93
Hotel deLuxe, p. 98
Hotel Fifty, p. 98
Hotel Vintage Plaza, p. 99
Lion and the Rose, p. 105
Portland's White House, p. 106

$$$

Avalon Hotel & Spa, p. 93
Hotel Lucia, p. 99
Heathman Hotel, p. 95

$$$$

RiverPlace Hotel, p. 102

By Experience

BEST FOR KIDS

Marriott Residence Inn–Lloyd Center, p. 105
Shilo Inn Rose Garden, p. 107
Silver Cloud Inn, p. 103

BEST FOR ROMANCE

Hotel deLuxe, p. 98
Paramount, p. 101
RiverPlace Hotel, p. 102

BEST B&BS

Lion and the Rose, p. 105
Portland's White House, p. 106
Georgian House, p. 104

BEST LOCATION

The Nines, p. 101
RiverPlace Hotel, p. 102
Inn @ Northrup Station, p. 103

PET-FRIENDLY

Aloft Portland Airport at Cascade Station, p. 108
Hotel Monaco, p. 99
The Nines, p. 101
Hotel Lucia, p. 99
Mark Spencer, p. 101

BEST SERVICE

Benson Hotel, p. 93
Heathman Hotel, p. 95
Hotel Lucia, p. 99

BEST HOTEL BARS

Avalon Hotel & Spa, p. 93
Heathman Hotel, p. 95

BEST POOLS

Embassy Suites, p. 95
McMenamins Kennedy School, p. 105

TRENDIEST

Ace Hotel, p. 93
Hotel deLuxe, p. 98
Hotel Fifty, p. 98
Jupiter Hotel, p. 105

inlaid mahogany doors. Some even have the original ceilings. Extra touches include fully stocked private bars and bathrobes in every room. **Pros:** beautiful lobby; excellent location. **Cons:** hallways could use updating. ⊠ *309 SW Broadway, Downtown* ☎ *503/228–2000 or 888/523–6766* ⊕ *www.bensonhotel.com* ↗ *287 rooms* ♿ *In-room: refrigerator (some), dial-up, Wi-Fi. In-hotel: 2 restaurants, room service, bar, gym, concierge, laundry service, Wi-Fi hotspot, parking (fee)* ▭ *AE, D, DC, MC, V* ✦ *C4.*

2

$$ ⊡ **Courtyard by Marriott–Portland City Center.** Certified Gold LEED (Leadership in Energy and Design) for its energy efficiency, this 2009 hotel is one of just over a dozen U.S. hotels with this designation. The lobby, as welcoming as a living room, has individual kiosks rather than one big reception desk. The spacious rooms showcase local art and photography, and the bathrooms offer bins for recycling and water-saving toilets. The Original restaurant serves upscale twists on traditional diner-style fare. **Pros:** everything's new and environmentally conscious, great on-site restaurant. **Cons:** small gift shop; tubs available only in some rooms (on request). ⊠ *550 SW Oak St., Downtown* ☎ *503/505–5000* ⊕ *www.marriott.com* ↗ *256 rooms* ♿ *In-room: refrigerator, Wi-Fi. In-hotel: restaurant, room service, bar, gym, laundry service, Wi-Fi hotspot, parking (fee)* ▭ *AE, D, DC, MC, V* ✦ *D4.*

$$$ ⊡ **Embassy Suites.** The grand lobby welcomes you here, in the former Multnomah Hotel, built in 1912. The spacious two-room suites have large windows, sofa beds, and wet bars. The indoor pool curves around the lower level of the hotel. A cooked-to-order full breakfast and cocktail reception with light snacks are included in the rate. **Pros:** beautiful building; excellent location. **Cons:** snack reception is popcorn and nachos; no in-and-out privileges in self-park garage across the street. ⊠ *319 SW Pine St., Downtown* ☎ *503/279–9000 or 800/643–7892* ⊕ *www.embassyportland.com* ↗ *276 suites* ♿ *In-room: refrigerator, Wi-Fi. In-hotel: restaurant, lounge, pool, gym, laundry service, Wi-Fi hotspot, parking (fee)* ▭ *AE, D, DC, MC, V* ⏐◉⏐ *BP* ✦ *D4.*

$$ ⊡ **Governor Hotel.** With mahogany walls and a mural of Pacific Northwest Indians fishing at Celilo Falls, the clubby lobby of the distinctive Governor helps set the 1920s Arts and Crafts style that's followed throughout the hotel. Painted in soothing earth tones, the tasteful guest rooms have large windows, honor bars, and bathrobes. Some have whirlpool tubs, fireplaces, and balconies. Jake's Grill is on the property, the streetcar runs right out front, and the hotel is one block from MAX. **Pros:** large rooms; beautiful 1920s property; excellent restaurant. **Cons:** some rooms in need of updates; limited late-night room-service menu. ⊠ *614 SW 10th Ave., Downtown* ☎ *503/224–3400 or 800/554–3456* ⊕ *www.govenorhotel.com* ↗ *68 rooms, 32 suites* ♿ *In-room: refrigerator, dial-up, Wi-Fi. In-hotel: restaurant, room service, bar, concierge, laundry service, Wi-Fi hotspot, parking (fee)* ▭ *AE, D, DC, MC, V* ✦ *C4.*

$$$ ⊡ **Heathman Hotel.** The Heathman more than deserves its reputation

Fodor's Choice ★

for quality. From the teak-paneled lobby to the rosewood elevators (with Warhol prints hung at each landing) and marble fireplaces, this hotel exudes refinement. The guest rooms provide the latest in customized comfort: a bed menu allows you to choose from Tempurpedic,

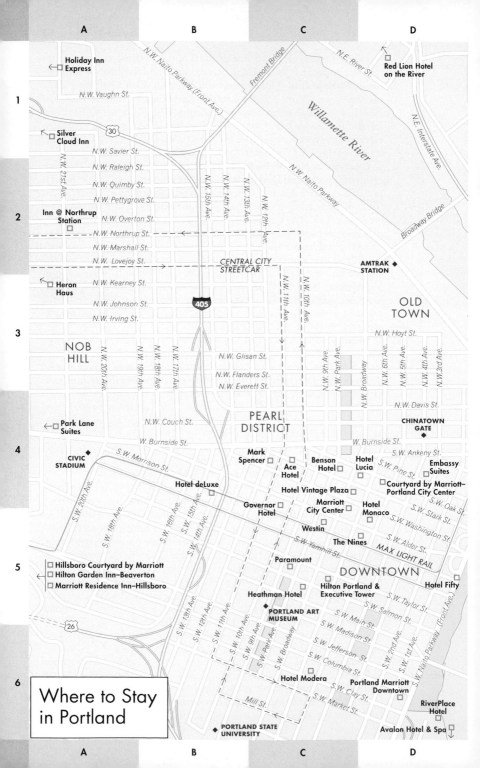

Where to Stay in Portland

A

Holiday Inn Express

Silver Cloud Inn

N.W. Vaughn St.

30

N.W. Savier St.
N.W. Raleigh St.
N.W. Quimby St.
N.W. Pettygrove St.

N.W. 21st Ave.

Inn @ Northrup Station

N.W. Overton St.
N.W. Northrup St.
N.W. Marshall St.
N.W. Lovejoy St.

Heron Haus

N.W. Kearney St.
N.W. Johnson St.
N.W. Irving St.

NOB HILL

N.W. 20th Ave.
N.W. 19th Ave.
N.W. 18th Ave.
N.W. 17th Ave.

Park Lane Suites

N.W. Couch St.
W. Burnside St.

CIVIC STADIUM

S.W. Morrison St.

S.W. 20th Ave.
S.W. 18th Ave.

Hotel deLuxe

S.W. 18th Ave.
S.W. 16th Ave.
S.W. 15th Ave.
S.W. 14th Ave.

Hillsboro Courtyard by Marriott
Hilton Garden Inn–Beaverton
Marriott Residence Inn–Hillsboro

26

S.W. 13th Ave.
S.W. 12th Ave.
S.W. 11th Ave.

B

N.W. Naito Parkway (Front Ave.)

Fremont Bridge

N.W. 15th Ave.
N.W. 14th Ave.
N.W. 13th Ave.
N.W. 12th Ave.

405

CENTRAL CITY STREETCAR

N.W. 11th Ave.

N.W. Glisan St.
N.W. Flanders St.
N.W. Everett St.

PEARL DISTRICT

Mark Spencer
Ace Hotel
Governor Hotel

Hotel Vintage Plaza

Westin

Paramount

Heathman Hotel

PORTLAND ART MUSEUM

S.W. 10th Ave.
S.W. 9th Ave.
S.W. Park Ave.
S.W. Broadway

Hotel Modera

Mill St.

PORTLAND STATE UNIVERSITY

C

N.E. River St.

Willamette River

N.W. Naito Parkway

AMTRAK STATION

OLD TOWN

N.W. Hoyt St.

N.W. 9th Ave.
N.W. Park Ave.
N.W. Broadway

CHINATOWN GATE

N.W. Davis St.

W. Burnside St.

S.W. Ankeny St.

Benson Hotel
Hotel Lucia

S.W. Pine St.

Marriott City Center
Hotel Monaco

S.W. Yamhill St.

The Nines

DOWNTOWN

Hilton Portland & Executive Tower

S.W. Taylor St.
S.W. Salmon St.

S.W. Main St.
S.W. Madison St.
S.W. Jefferson St.
S.W. Columbia St.
S.W. Clay St.
S.W. Market St.

Portland Marriott Downtown

D

Red Lion Hotel on the River

N.E. Interstate Ave.

Broadway Bridge

OLD TOWN

N.W. 6th Ave.
N.W. 5th Ave.
N.W. 4th Ave.
N.W. 3rd Ave.

Embassy Suites

Courtyard by Marriott–Portland City Center

S.W. Oak St.
S.W. Stark St.
S.W. Washington St.
S.W. Alder St.

MAX LIGHT RAIL

Hotel Fifty

S.W. 2nd Ave.
S.W. 1st Ave.
S.W. Naito Parkway (Front Ave.)

RiverPlace Hotel

Avalon Hotel & Spa

1
2
3
4
5
6

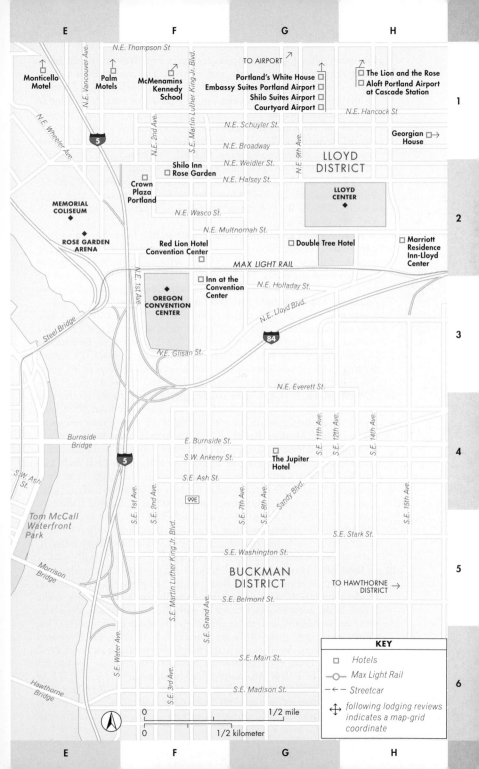

European pillowtop, or European featherbed mattresses, and the bathrooms have plenty of marble and mirrors. The second-floor mezzanine—showcasing local art (works change every few weeks) and a small library (primarily filled with the signed editions of notable Heathman guests)—overlooks the high-ceilinged Tea Court, a popular gathering spot in the evening. **Pros:** superior service; central location adjoining the Performing Arts Center; renowned on-site restaurant. **Cons:** small rooms; expensive parking. ⊠ *1001 SW Broadway, Downtown* ☎ *503/241–4100 or 800/551–0011* ⊕ *www.heathmanportland.com* ⇗ *117 rooms, 33 suites* ♿ *In-room: refrigerator, Internet, Wi-Fi. In-hotel: restaurant, 24 hour room service, bar, fitness suite, concierge, laundry service, Wi-Fi hotspot, parking (fee), pets allowed* ▭ *AE, D, DC, MC, V* ✛ *C5.*

$$ ⚏ **Hilton Portland & Executive Tower.** Together, two buildings comprise a gargantuan complex of luxuriously contemporary bedrooms, meeting rooms, two restaurants, and athletic center and gym, including two indoor swimming pools. The property is within walking distance of the Performing Arts Center, Pioneer Courthouse Square, the Portland Art Museum, and MAX light rail. **Pros:** nice workout facilities and indoor pools; prime downtown location near attractions and restaurants. **Cons:** sporadic downtown construction could mean noise and traffic; not for visitors looking for homier lodging. ⊠ *921 SW 6th Ave., Downtown* ☎ *503/226–1611 or 800/445–8667* ⊕ *www.hilton.com* ⇗ *773 rooms, 9 suites* ♿ *In-room: Internet. In-hotel: 2 restaurants, bars, pools, gym, Wi-Fi hotspot, parking (fee)* ▭ *AE, D, DC, MC, V* ✛ *C5.*

$$
Fodor'sChoice
★

⚏ **Hotel deLuxe.** If you long to be transported back to the Hollywood glamour of the 1940s, this place is perfect. The more than 400 black-and-white photographs on the corridor walls are arranged by cinematic themes (Music Masters, Rebels, Exiles, and Immigrants). If the standard King James Bible in the drawer doesn't ignite your spiritual flame, than choose from a selection of other texts found at the front desk, including Buddhist, Taoist, Catholic, and even Scientologist offerings. **Pros:** "pillow menu" and other extra touches lend an air of luxury; artistic vibe. **Cons:** older windows in building can be drafty at night; cold bathroom floors. ⊠ *729 SW 15th Ave., Downtown* ☎ *503/219–2094 or 866/895–2094* ⊕ *www.hoteldeluxeportland.com* ⇗ *130 rooms* ♿ *In-room: refrigerator, Wi-Fi. In-hotel: restaurant, room service, bar, Wi-Fi hotspot, parking (fee), some pets allowed* ▭ *AE, D, DC, MC, V* ⏐◉⏐ *CP* ✛ *B4.*

$$ ⚏ **Hotel Fifty.** This reasonable boutique property recently underwent a major renovation, and the final results are pleasing. The decor is modern and clean, with glass, stone, and marble floor accents in the lobby. In the guest rooms, decorated with chocolate browns, deep purples, and oak highlights, there are 42" wall-mounted plasma HDTVs, ample work space, top-of-the-line memory-foam beds, and oversized walk-in showers. Another star attraction is the riverfront location. **Pros:** comfortable beds; river location. **Cons:** no gift shop; no on-site fitness facility. ⊠ *50 SW Morrison St., Downtown* ☎ *503/221–0711 or 877/237–6775* 🖷 *503/484–1417* ⊕ *www.hotelfifty.com* ⇗ *140 rooms 1 suite* ♿ *In-room: refrigerator, Wi-Fi. In-hotel: restaurant, room service, bar, laundry service, Wi-Fi hotspot, parking (paid), some dogs allowed* ▭ *AE, D, DC, MC, V* ✛ *D5.*

2

$$$ ⬚ **Hotel Lucia.** Modern track lighting, black-and-white David Hume Kennerly celebrity photos, and comfy leather chairs adorn this nine-story boutique hotel in the heart of downtown—within walking distance of Nordstrom, Powell's, and the MAX line. The hotel's goal of "delivering calm" is accomplished in part through seven choices in pillows, stored customer profiles (so you automatically receive that same pillow next time), and Aveda soaps and lotions. The Pet Package comes with a special bed, set of dishes, treats, and bottled water. **Pros:** prime location; luxurious amenities; consistently good service. **Cons:** small rooms; limited shelf and storage space in the bathrooms; those with allergies should request a pet-free room. ⊠ *400 SW Broadway St., Downtown* ☎ *503/225–1717 or 877/225–1717* ⊕ *www.hotellucia.com* ⟋ *127 rooms, 16 suites* ⬥ *In-room: Wi-Fi. In-hotel: restaurant, room service, gym, laundry service, parking (fee), some pets allowed* ▤ *AE, D, DC, MC, V* ✛ *D4.*

$$$ ⬚ **Hotel Modera.** This boutique property, with contemporary furnishings and local artwork, is accessibly sophisticated. The well-appointed rooms are equipped with flat-screen TV, wireless phone, an iPod docking station, and a do-not-disturb switch that lights up a sign outside your room. The most distinguishing features are the outdoor firepits in the courtyard, where guests gather for warmth, cocktails, and conversation. **Pros:** large massage showerheads; individually bagged ice in hand-carved chests in every hall. **Cons:** rooms on the small side; located in the business district and far from restaurants and nightlife. ⊠ *515 SW Clay St., Downtown* ☎ *503/484–1084 or 877/484–1084* ⊕ *www. hotelmodera.com* ⟋ *168 rooms, 6 suites* ⬥ *In-room: refrigerator, Wi-Fi. In-hotel: restaurant, laundry service, Wi-Fi hotspot, parking (fee)* ▤ *AE, D, DC, MC, V* ✛ *C6.*

$$$ ⬚ **Hotel Monaco.** Constructed in 1912, this building originally served as Lipman Wolfe, an upscale downtown department store. In 1996 the historic building reopened as a 221-suite luxury boutique hotel, and in 2007 the new owners, the Kimpton Group, completed a major upgrade. A tall vestibule with a marble mosaic floor leads to the art-filled lobby, where guests gather by the fireplace for an early-evening glass of wine or a morning cup of coffee. Upholstered chairs, fringed ottomans, lots of patterns, and other appointments in the sitting areas will make you feel right at home (or wish you had one like this). Downstairs in the lobby is the full-service Dosha Spa, and adjacent is the Red Star Tavern restaurant. Pets of guests receive treat baskets and a bed and water bowl. **Pros:** newly renovated fitness center; bathrooms stocked with lots of amenities; historic building; free Starbucks coffee in the morning. **Cons:** can get chilly at night because of drafty windows; rooms on lower floors tend to be noisier. ⊠ *506 SW Washington St., Downtown* ☎ *503/222–0001 or 888/207–2201* ⊕ *www.portland-monaco. com* ⟋ *82 rooms, 137 suites* ⬥ *In-room: refrigerator, Wi-Fi. In-hotel: restaurant, 24-hr room service, gym, laundry service, Wi-Fi hotspot, parking (fee), some pets allowed* ▤ *AE, D, DC, MC, V* ✛ *D5.*

$$ ⬚ **Hotel Vintage Plaza.** This historic landmark takes its theme from the area's vineyards. Guests can fall asleep counting stars in top-floor rooms, where skylights and wall-to-wall conservatory-style windows are some

McMenamins Kennedy School

Hotel deLuxe

Heathman Hotel

2

of the special details. Hospitality suites have extra-large rooms with a full living area, and the deluxe rooms have a bar. All are appointed in warm colors and have cherrywood furnishings; some rooms have hot tubs. Complimentary wine is served in the evening, and an extensive collection of Oregon vintages is displayed in the tasting room. Two-story town-house suites are named after local wineries. **Pros:** beautiful decor; excellent complimentary wine selections; pet-friendly. **Cons:** those with allergies should ask for pet-free rooms; some street noise on the lower levels on the Washington Street side of the hotel. ⊠ *422 SW Broadway, Downtown* ☎ *503/228–1212 or 800/263–2305* ⊕ *www.vintageplaza. com* ⤳ *117 rooms, 21 suites* ⌂ *In-room: refrigerator, Wi-Fi. In-hotel: restaurant, room service, bar, gym, concierge, Wi-Fi hotspot, parking (fee), some pets allowed* ⊟ *AE, D, DC, MC, V* ✛ *C4.*

$$ ⛯ **Mark Spencer.** The Mark Spencer, near Portland's gay-bar district and Powell's City of Books, is one of the best values in town. The rooms are clean and comfortable, and all have full kitchens. The hotel, a major supporter of local arts, offers special packages that include tickets to the Artists Repertory Theatre, Portland Opera, Oregon Symphony, Portland Art Museum, and Center Stage. **Pros:** complimentary breakfast; afternoon tea and cookies, and a weekly local-wine tasting for all guests. **Cons:** some rooms could use updating; those with allergies should request a pet-free room. ⊠ *409 SW 11th Ave., Downtown* ☎ *503/224–3293 or 800/548–3934* ⊕ *www.markspencer.com* ⤳ *102 rooms* ⌂ *In-room: kitchen, Wi-Fi. In-hotel: laundry facilities, laundry service, Wi-Fi hotspot, pets allowed* ⊟ *AE, D, DC, MC, V* ¶⊙¶ *CP* ✛ *C4.*

$$ ⛯ **Marriott City Center.** Close to many restaurants and arts organizations, this 20-story stone-and-brick property has a grand staircase, maple paneling, and marble floors inside. The "plus" rooms have voice mail, large work desks, and coffeemakers. The MAX light rail is two blocks away. **Pros:** work-friendly rooms; great location. **Cons:** refrigerators available upon request only. ⊠ *520 SW Broadway, Downtown* ☎ *503/226–6300 or 800/228–9290* ⊕ *www.marriott.com* ⤳ *249 rooms, 10 suites* ⌂ *In-room: refrigerator, Wi-Fi. In-hotel: restaurant, room service, bar, gym, concierge, laundry service, Wi-Fi hotspot, parking (fee)* ⊟ *AE, D, DC, MC, V* ✛ *C4.*

$$$ ⛯ **The Nines.** If you're looking for a little of the cosmopolitan flair of New York or Chicago, or if you want to spot celebrities passing through town, then this is the place for you. The decor is very swanky in this former landmark department store, with abstract art in the lobby and hallways and furnishings in deep, rich tones of cream, turquoise, brown, and burgundy. Rooms are spacious and well appointed with iPod docking stations, 42″ flat-screen TVs, and DVD players. **Pros:** spacious bathrooms; excellent gym. **Cons:** rooms facing the atrium and overlooking the hotel's bar and restaurant can be noisy. ⊠ *525 SW Morrison St., Downtown* ☎ *503/222–9996 or 877/229–9995* ⊕ *www.thenines.com* ⤳ *331 rooms, 13 suites* ⌂ *In-room: refrigerator, DVD, Wi-Fi. In-hotel: 2 restaurants, room service, bar, gym, laundry service, Wi-Fi hotspot, parking (fee), some pets allowed* ⊟ *AE, D, DC, MC, V* ✛ *D5.*

$ ⛯ **Paramount.** This pale-stone, 15-story hotel is two blocks from Pioneer Square, MAX, and the Portland Art Museum. The cozy rooms are adorned with earth tones, plush dark-wood furnishings, and dried flowers, and some have outdoor balconies and whirlpool tubs. The grand suites also have wet bars and gas fireplaces. Dragonfish, an excellent Pan-Asian restaurant, is on the premises. Pros: beautiful granite bathrooms; in-room honor bars. Cons: small fitness facilities. ⊠ *808 SW Taylor St., Downtown* ☎ *503/223–9900* ⊕ *www.portlandparamount. com* ⮑ *154 rooms* ♿ *In-room: refrigerator, Wi-Fi. In-hotel: restaurant, room service, gym, concierge, laundry service, parking (fee)* ⊟ *AE, D, DC, MC, V* ✢ *C5*

$ 🛏 **Park Lane Suites and Inn.** A few blocks from Washington Park, Nob Hill, and downtown, this property is in a prime location, and consists of two buildings. Suites come with spacious, work-friendly living areas, and the kitchens come stocked with decent dishware, lots of cabinet space, and a full-size refrigerator, stovetop, microwave, and dishwasher. The standard rooms include flat-screen TVs. Pros: proximity to several of Portland's most prominent neighborhoods; expanded kitchen capacity. Cons: parking is free but limited; not enough soundproofing. ⊠ *809 SW King Ave., Downtown* ☎ *503/226–6288* ⊕ *www.parklanesuites. com* ⮑ *44 rooms* ♿ *In-room: kitchen, refrigerator, Internet, Wi-Fi. In-hotel: laundry facilities, laundry service, some pets allowed* ⊟ *AE, D, DC, MC, V* ✢ *A4*

$$ 🛏 **Portland Marriott Downtown.** The large rooms at this 16-floor, corporate-focused Marriott are decorated in off-whites; the best ones face east, with a view of the Willamette and the Cascades. All rooms have work desks, high-speed Internet access, and voice mail. Champions Lounge, filled with sports memorabilia, is a singles' hot spot on weekends. Pros: excellent waterfront location; six blocks from MAX light rail. Cons: no refrigerators or minibars; can get crowded. ⊠ *1401 SW Naito Pkwy., Downtown* ☎ *503/226–7600 or 800/228–9290* ⊕ *www.marriott.com* ⮑ *503 rooms, 6 suites* ♿ *In-room: dial-up, Wi-Fi. In-hotel: restaurant, room service, bar, pool, gym, laundry facilities, laundry service, airport shuttle (fee), parking (fee)* ⊟ *AE, D, DC, MC, V* ✢ *D6*

$$$$ 🛏 **RiverPlace Hotel.** All the guest rooms here have muted color schemes,
Fodor's Choice Craftsman-style desks, and ergonomic chairs, and more than a quarter
★ of them have amazing views of the river, marina, and skyline, as well as a landscaped courtyard. Extras include bathrobes, locally roasted coffee, Tazo tea in the room, and afternoon tea and cookies in the lobby. Pros: great location; wide selection of room options; great beds. Cons: no pool. ⊠ *1510 SW Harbor Way, Downtown* ☎ *503/228–3233 or 800/227–1333* ⊕ *www.riverplacehotel.com* ⮑ *39 rooms, 45 suites* ♿ *In-room: DVD, Wi-Fi. In-hotel: restaurant, room service, concierge, parking (fee)* ⊟ *AE, D, DC, MC, V* ✢ *D6.*

$$$ 🛏 **Westin.** This pale-stone European-style hotel combines luxury with convenience. Rooms here include entertainment-center armoires, work desks, plush beds covered with layers of down, and granite bathrooms with separate showers and tubs. Pioneer Square and MAX are two blocks away. The Daily Grill serves traditional American fare in upscale surroundings. Pros: prime downtown location; comfortable beds; well-equipped fitness center. Cons: no spa or sauna; limited room-service menu. ⊠ *750 SW Alder St., Downtown* ☎ *503/294–9000*

*or 888/625–5144 ⊕ www.westin.com ⤴ 205 rooms ♿ In-room: safe,
refrigerator, Internet, Wi-Fi. In-hotel: restaurant, room service, bar, gym,
concierge, laundry service, parking (fee) ⊟ AE, D, DC, MC, V ✢ C5.*

NOB HILL AND VICINITY

2

$$ ⊞ **Heron Haus.** This lovely, bright bed-and-breakfast is inside a stately,
100-year-old three-floor Tudor-style mansion near Forest Park. Special
features include a tulip-shaped bathtub in one room and a tiled, seven-
head antique shower in another. You can enjoy a relaxing afternoon
in the secluded sitting garden. All rooms have phones, work desks,
and fireplaces. **Pros:** modern amenities; fancy Continental breakfast
included; plenty of room to roam on huge property. **Cons:** in a residen-
tial neighborhood; not immediately near public transportation. ⊠ 2545
NW Westover Rd., Nob Hill ☎ 503/274–1846 ⊕ www.heronhaus.com
⤴ 6 rooms ♿ In-room: Wi-Fi. In-hotel: no elevator, Wi-Fi hotspot,
parking (no fee) ⊟ MC, V ❚❘❘❘ CP ✢ A3.

$ ⊞ **Holiday Inn Express.** Spacious, updated rooms are at this hotel on the
edge of Portland's trendy Northwest 23rd Avenue neighborhood. On-
site is an indoor pool, and a generous continental breakfast buffet is
included for guests. **Pros:** indoor pool; friendly service. **Cons:** close to a
highway. ⊠ 2333 NW Vaughn Ave., NW 23rd Ave. ☎ 503/484–1100 or
800/464–5329 ⊕ www.hiexpress.com ⤴ 90 rooms ♿ In-room: refriger-
ator, Internet, Wi-Fi. In-hotel: laundry facilities, laundry service ⊟ AE,
D, DC, MC, V ❚❘❘❘ CP ✢ A1.

$ ⊞ **Inn @ Northrup Station.** Bright colors, original artwork, retro designs,
and extremely luxurious suites fill this hotel in Nob Hill—it looks like
a stylish apartment building from the outside, with patios or balco-
nies adjoining most of the suites, and a garden terrace for all guests
to use. The striking colors and bold patterns found on bedspreads,
armchairs, pillows, and throughout the halls and lobby manage to be
charming, elegant, and fun, never falling into the kitsch that plagues
many places that strive for "retro" decor. All suites have full kitchens
or kitchenettes, two TVs, three phones, and large sitting areas. **Pros:**
roomy suites feel like home; great location that's close to the shopping
and dining on Northwest 21st Avenue. **Cons:** past guests have com-
mented on the lack of noise insulation. ⊠ 2025 NW Northrup St., Nob
Hill ☎ 503/224–0543 or 800/224–1180 ⊕ www.northrupstation.com
⤴ 70 suites ♿ In-room: kitchen. In-hotel: Wi-Fi hotspot, parking (no
fee) ⊟ AE, D, DC, MC, V ❚❘❘❘ CP ✢ A2.

$ ⊞ **Silver Cloud Inn.** Staying at the Silver Cloud, adjacent to lively North-
west 23rd Avenue, is a great alternative to being right downtown.
There's a broad selection of spacious, contemporary rooms—kings and
minisuites—with 42" HDTVs. During the week, select local-area shuttle
service is available. **Pros:** free parking; spacious rooms. **Cons:** no pool.
⊠ 2426 NW Vaughn St., Downtown ☎ 503/242–2400 or 800/205–
6939 ⊕ www.silvercloud.com ⤴ 82 rooms ♿ In-room: refrigerator,
microwave, Wi-Fi. In-hotel: laundry facilities, laundry service ⊟ AE,
D, DC, MC, V ❚❘❘❘ CP ✢ A1.

EAST OF THE WILLAMETTE RIVER

The area east of the Willamette is not nearly as condensed as downtown Portland, which means fewer interesting buildings. It's also a little harder to get around, though thanks to MAX and excellent bus service it's still doable. Properties tend to be older, with lower prices than downtown, and with more rooms free. The majority of chain hotels are clustered around the Oregon Convention Center; nearby is Lloyd Center mall, which has an ice-skating rink, movie theaters, and several levels of shops and restaurants. There are also a number of bed-and-breakfasts on this side of town, tucked away in historical neighborhoods like Irvington.

$$ ⊞ **Crowne Plaza Portland.** This sleek, modern hotel is close to the Rose Quarter, the Coliseum, and the convention center, and is within easy walking distance of Lloyd Center, the MAX line, and the Broadway Bridge leading to downtown. Given its attractive rooms and ample facilities, it's a reliable and convenient option for both business travelers and tourists. **Pros:** indoor pool; good selection of accommodations and room sizes. **Cons:** location near the Rose Quarter means traffic congestion during basketball games and concerts. ⊠ *1441 NE 2nd Ave., Lloyd District/Convention Center* ☎ *503/233–2401 or 877/777–2704* ⊕ *www.cpportland.com* ⌨ *241 rooms* ⅄ *In-room: refrigerator, Wi-Fi. In-hotel: restaurant, bar, pool, gym* ▭ *AE, D, DC, MC, V* ✛ *F2.*

$$ ⊞ **Doubletree Hotel.** This bustling, business hotel maintains a huge traffic in meetings and special events. The public areas are a tasteful mix of marble, rose-and-green carpet, and antique-style furnishings. The large rooms, many with balconies, have views of the mountains or the city center. The Lloyd Center and the MAX light-rail line are across the street; the Oregon Convention Center is a five-minute walk away. **Pros:** convenient location; nice views, access to shops. **Cons:** pool is outdoors; can be crowded. ⊠ *1000 NE Multnomah St., Lloyd District* ☎ *503/281–6111 or 800/222–8733* ⊕ *www.doubletree.com* ⌨ *476 rooms* ⅄ *In-room: Wi-Fi. In-hotel: 2 restaurants, room service, bar, pool, gym, concierge, laundry service, Wi-Fi hotspot, parking (fee)* ▭ *AE, D, DC, MC, V.*

$ ⊞ **Georgian House.** This redbrick Georgian colonial with neoclassical columns is on a quiet, tree-lined street in a historic neighborhood. The gardens in back can be enjoyed from one of the guest verandas or from the gazebo. The largest and sunniest of the guest rooms is the Lovejoy Suite, with a tile fireplace and brass canopy bed. **Pros:** warm hospitality; intimate environment; ample convenient parking. **Cons:** residential neighborhood; some rooms have shared bathrooms; no elevator. ⊠ *1828 NE Siskiyou St., Irvington* ☎ *503/281–2250 or 888/282–2250* ⊕ *www.thegeorgianhouse.com* ⌨ *2 rooms with shared bath, 2 suites* ⅄ *In-room: no phone, no TV (some)* ▭ *MC, V* ⍥ *BP* ✛ *H1.*

¢ ⊞ **Inn at the Convention Center.** Convenience is the big plus of this no-frills, independently run six-story hotel: it's directly across the street from the convention center, four blocks from Lloyd Center, and right along the MAX line. Rooms are simple and comfortable. **Pros:** right next to convention center; walking distance to Lloyd Center mall. **Cons:** not wheelchair-friendly; could use updates. ⊠ *420 NE Holladay St.,*

Lloyd District/Convention Center ☎ *503/233–6331* ⊕ *www.innatcc. com* ⤳ *97 rooms* ↺ *In-room: refrigerator (some), Wi-Fi. In-hotel: laundry facilities, laundry service, Wi-Fi hotspot, parking (no fee)* ═ *AE, D, DC, MC, V* ✛ *F3.*

$ ⬚ **The Jupiter Hotel.** The hip and adventurous, looking for a place to crash for the night, flock to this contemporary hotel, which provides easy access to downtown. Rooms come with iPod docking stations, modern furniture, down comforters and colorful shag pillows, and chalkboard doors you can write on. Also on-site are a hair salon, massage parlor, and the Doug Fir rock club. **Pros:** easy access to downtown; funky lodging; built-in nightlife. **Cons:** not to everyone's taste; not immediately near a lot of shops or restaurants; near a loud hot spot. ⊠ *800 E. Burnside, near Downtown* ☎ *503/230–9200 or 877/800– 0004* ⊕ *www.jupiterhotel.com* ⤳ *82 rooms, 1 suite* ↺ *In-room: Wi-Fi. In-hotel: restaurant, room service, bar, spa, Wi-Fi hotspot, parking (fee), some pets allowed* ═ *AE, D, DC, MC, V* ✛ *G4.*

$$ ⬚ **Lion and the Rose.** Oak and mahogany floors, original light fixtures,
Fodor's Choice antique silver, and a coffered dining-room ceiling set a tone of formal
★ elegance here, while the wonderfully friendly, accommodating, and knowledgeable innkeepers make sure that you feel perfectly at home. May through October a full breakfast is included; November through April breakfast is Continental. In a beautiful residential neighborhood, you're a block from the shops and restaurants that fill Northeast Broadway and within an easy walk of a free MAX ride downtown. Good last-minute rates are sometimes available; check the Web site. **Pros:** gorgeous house; top-notch service; afternoon tea available upon request. **Cons:** no elevator; fills up quickly (particularly in summer). ⊠ *1810 NE 15th Ave., Irvington* ☎ *503/287–9245 or 800/955–1647* ⊕ *www. lionrose.com* ⤳ *8 rooms* ↺ *In-room: Wi-Fi. In-hotel: no kids under 10* ═ *AE, D, DC, MC, V* ✛ *H1.*

$$ ⬚ **Marriott Residence Inn—Lloyd Center.** With large, fully equipped suites and a short walk both to the Lloyd Center and a MAX stop within the Fareless Square, this three-level apartment-style complex is perfect for extended-stay visitors or for tourists. Rooms come equipped with full kitchens and ample seating space, and many have wood-burning fireplaces. There's a large complimentary breakfast buffet each morning, and an hors d'oeuvres reception on weekday evenings. **Pros:** full kitchens; accessible location. **Cons:** pool is outdoors and closed during winter. ⊠ *1710 NE Multnomah St., Lloyd District* ☎ *503/288–1400 or 800/331–3131* ⊕ *www.residenceinn.com* ⤳ *168 rooms* ↺ *In-room: kitchen, Wi-Fi. In-hotel: bar, pool, gym, laundry facilities, Wi-Fi hotspot, parking (no fee), some pets allowed* ⦿ *BP* ✛ *H2.*

$ ⬚ **McMenamins Kennedy School.** In a renovated elementary school in
Fodor's Choice northeast Portland, the Kennedy School may well be one of the most
★ unusual hotels you'll ever encounter. With all the guest rooms occupying former classrooms, complete with the original chalkboards and cloakrooms, the McMenamin brothers have created a multiuse facility that is both luxurious and fantastical. Go to the Detention Bar for cigars and one of the only two TVs on-site; visit the Honors Bar for classical music and cocktails. **Pros:** funky and authentic Portland experience;

room rates include movie admission and use of the year-round outdoor soaking pool. **Cons:** no bathtubs (shower stalls only) in bathrooms; no TVs in rooms; no elevator. ⊠ *5736 NE 33rd Ave., near Alberta District* ☏ *503/249–3983* ⊕ *www.kennedyschool.com* ⤳ *35 rooms* ⅄ *In-room: no TV, Wi-Fi. In-hotel: restaurant, bars, Wi-Fi hotspot, parking (no fee)* ⊟ *AE, D, DC, MC, V* ❘⊙❘ *BP* ✥ *F1*

¢ ⛫ **Monticello Motel.** This is a smaller property with several accommodation options. Most of the one- and two-bedroom kitchen suites have cooking ranges with an oven, refrigerator, and microwave oven. Decor is standard motel fare, with floral bedspreads and dark-wood tables and chairs. It's close to freeway access, the MAX line, and buses. **Pros:** kitchen suites are well equipped. **Cons:** not immediately near shops and restaurants; little character; no elevator. ⊠ *4801 N. Interstate Ave., North Interstate* ☏ *503/285–6641* ⊕ *www.monticellomotel.com* ⤳ *9 rooms* ⅄ *In-room: refrigerator. In-hotel: Wi-Fi hotspot.* ✥ *E1*

¢ ⛫ **Palms Motel.** Clean, simple, and accessible to downtown, this property offers an affordable alternative to some of the larger chains. It's close to freeway access, the MAX line, and buses. The rooms, renovated in 2008–09, are equipped with free Wi-Fi, microwaves, and refrigerators. **Pros:** affordable; friendly and eager staff. **Cons:** no frills; not immediately near shops and restaurants. ⊠ *3801 N. Interstate Ave., North Interstate* ☏ *503/287–5788 or 800/620–9652* ⊕ *www.palmsmotel.com* ⤳ *55 rooms* ⅄ *In-room: refrigerator, Wi-Fi. In-hotel: Wi-Fi hotspot, parking (fee).* ✥ *E1*

$$ ⛫ **Portland's White House.** Hardwood floors with oriental rugs, chandeliers, antiques, and fountains create a warm and romantic mood at this elegant bed-and-breakfast in the historic Irvington District. The Greek Revival mansion was built in 1910, and is on the National Register of Historic Landmarks. Rooms have private baths, flat-screen TVs, and mahogany canopy or four-poster queen- and king-size beds. A full breakfast is included in the room rate, and the owners offer vegetarian or vegan options. Smoking and pets are not allowed, and there's no elevator. **Pros:** romantic; authentic historic Portland experience; excellent service. **Cons:** located in residential neighborhood; shops and restaurants several blocks away. ⊠ *1914 NE 22nd Ave., Irvington* ☏ *503/287–7131 or 800/272–7131* ⊕ *www.portlandswhitehouse.com* ⤳ *8 suites* ⅄ *In-room: dial-up, Wi-Fi. In-hotel: parking (free)* ⊟ *AE, D, MC, V* ❘⊙❘ *BP* ✥ *G1*

$ ⛫ **Red Lion Hotel–Convention Center.** Across the street from the convention center and adjacent to the MAX, this hotel is convenient for both business travelers and tourists. It provides a few more on-site amenities than some of the other hotels right by the convention center, which is reflected in its slightly higher rates. They do accept pets, so be sure to ask for a no-pet room if you're allergic. **Pros:** right next to convention center; walking distance to Lloyd Center mall; pet-friendly. **Cons:** pet-friendly; can be crowded. ⊠ *1021 NE Grand Ave., Lloyd District* ☏ *503/235–2100 or 800/343–1822* ⊕ *www.redlion.com* ⤳ *174 rooms* ⅄ *In-room: refrigerator, Wi-Fi. In-hotel: restaurant, room service, bar, gym, Wi-Fi hotspot, parking (fee), some pets allowed* ⊟ *AE, D, MC, V* ✥ *F2*

$ ⬚ **Shilo Inn Rose Garden.** This family-friendly hotel provides respectable
🐾   accommodations and great service. Some rooms have sofas, and all
the furnishings and amenities are up-to-date. It's a five-minute walk to
the MAX transit center, which has direct service to the airport. **Pros:**
recently remodeled property; spa and sauna on-site. **Cons:** no shuttle
service; off the beaten path from shops and restaurants. ✉ *1506 NE
2nd Ave., Lloyd District* ☎ *503/736–6300 or 800/222–2244* ⊕ *www.
shiloinns.com* ➩ *44 rooms* ♿ *In-room: refrigerator, Wi-Fi. In-hotel:
spa, no elevator, laundry service, Wi-Fi hotspot, parking (paid), some
pets allowed* ⊟ *AE, D, DC, MC, V* ❄⊙❄ *CP* ✚ *F2.*

WEST OF DOWNTOWN

Once you start heading west, beyond Nob Hill and the West Hills, Portland begins to blur into the suburbs of Beaverton and Hillsboro. Several
larger companies, including Nike and Intel, are headquartered here, so
there are lots of lodging options, mostly larger chains. Weekdays tend
to be busier, with lower rates on weekends.

Getting to and from the city from these outlying areas requires a drive
on Highway 26, which is heavily congested during commute times. A
great alternative to driving is taking the MAX. There are numerous stations throughout Hillsboro and Beaverton, and travel time is less than
30 minutes to downtown by MAX.

$ ⬚ **Hillsboro Courtyard by Marriott.** This hotel provides easy access to shop-
ping and restaurants in Hillsboro, as well as access onto U.S. 26 toward
Portland. With large, comfortable rooms, it's perfect for business travelers, or for tourists who don't mind being several miles from downtown
Portland. **Pros:** nice indoor pool; free shuttle service to MAX light-rail
station. **Cons:** about 10 mi from downtown. ✉ *3050 NW Stucki Pl.,
Hillsboro* ☎ *503/690–1800 or 800/321–2211* ⊕ *www.marriott.com*
➩ *149 rooms, 6 suites* ♿ *In-room: Wi-Fi. In-hotel: restaurant, room
service, bar, pool, gym, laundry facilities, laundry service, Wi-Fi hotspot*
⊟ *AE, D, DC, MC, V* ✚ *A5.*

$$ ⬚ **Hilton Garden Inn–Beaverton.** This four-level Hilton in suburban Bea-
verton brings a much-needed lodging option to Portland's west side.
The property offers bright rooms with plush carpeting, work desks,
and microwaves. It's right off U.S. 26. **Pros:** good value for money,
nice indoor pool and whirlpool. **Cons:** not immediately near public
transportation; far from shopping and restaurants. ✉ *15520 NW Gate-
way Ct., Beaverton* ☎ *503/439–1717 or 800/445–8667* ⊕ *www.hilton.
com* ➩ *150 rooms* ♿ *In-room: refrigerator, Wi-Fi. In-hotel: restaurant,
room service, bar, pool, Wi-Fi hotspot, parking (no fee)* ⊟ *AE, D, DC,
MC, V* ✚ *A5.*

$ ⬚ **Marriott Residence Inn–Hillsboro.** Near the west side's many high-tech
offices and factories, this all-suites hotel is popular with people relocat-
ing to Portland and perfect for extended stays. It's within walking dis-
tance of several restaurants, a shopping center, and a multiplex theater.
The homey suites, some with fireplaces, have full kitchens. **Pros:** full
kitchens; free Wi-Fi; on-site market open 24 hours. **Cons:** a distance
from downtown Portland. ✉ *18855 NW Tanasbourne Dr., Hillsboro*

☎ *503/531–3200 or 800/331–3131* ⊕ *www.marriott.com* ⤶ *122 suites* ♿ *In-room: VCR (some), kitchen, Wi-Fi. In-hotel: tennis court, pool, gym, no elevator, laundry facilities, laundry service, Wi-Fi hotspot, parking (no fee), some pets allowed* ▭ *AE, D, DC, MC, V* ⦿|*BP.*

PORTLAND INTERNATIONAL AIRPORT AREA

If you're flying in and out for a quick business trip, then staying by the airport may be a good idea. The lodging options here are only the larger chains. The airport is about a 20- to 25-minute drive away from downtown Portland.

Generally speaking, there's not much here in terms of noteworthy beauty, culture, restaurants, shops, or attractions—with the possible exception of Cascade Station, a newer mixed-use development for retail, lodging, and commercial office space. Cascade Station offers the convenience of several restaurants and larger chain stores, including IKEA and Best Buy. For all other attractions and nightlife, you'll have to travel into the city or to a neighboring town.

$$ 🏨 **Aloft Portland Airport at Cascade Station.** High-end vibrant design, sophisticated amenities, and fresh new concepts in a hotel experience make the first Aloft in Oregon a standout amid airport travel mediocrity. The ceilings are nine feet high, windows are oversized, and even the bathroom offers natural light with full-length frosted-glass panels surrounding walk-in showers. Other features include touch-screen kiosks for choosing your room, getting your key, and printing your departing flight's boarding pass. Dogs are not only welcomed, they're treated like royalty by receiving their own bed, toys, treats, and food bowl. Make time to relax in the re:mix lounge, which flows into the WXYZ bar, where there's a pool table and four-panel LCD TV "screenwall" for watching sports. **Pros:** lots of high-tech amenities; welcoming social areas; unique, spacious rooms; near IKEA. **Cons:** airport location; no sit-down restaurant. ✉ *9920 NE Cascades Pkwy., Airport* ☎ *503/200– 5678* ⊕ *www.starwoodhotels.com/alofthotels* ⤶ *136 rooms* ♿ *In-room: refrigerator, Wi-Fi. In-hotel: bar, pool, gym, laundry facilities, laundry service, Wi-Fi hotspot, parking (free), some pets allowed* ▭ *AE, D, DC, MC, V* ⊹ *H1.*

¢ 🏨 **Courtyard Airport.** This six-story Marriott inn is designed for business travelers. Rooms are brightly decorated in royal blue and gold tones and have sitting areas and work desks. It's ¾ mi east of I–205 and 3 mi east of the airport. **Pros:** reliable service and amenities; work-friendly. **Cons:** airport location. ✉ *11550 NE Airport Way, Airport* ☎ *503/252–3200 or 800/321–2211* ⊕ *www.courtyard.com* ⤶ *150 rooms, 10 suites* ♿ *In-room: Wi-Fi. In-hotel: restaurant, room service, bar, pool, gym, laundry facilities, laundry service, Wi-Fi hotspot, parking (no fee)* ▭ *AE, D, DC, MC, V* ⊹ *G1.*

$ 🏨 **Embassy Suites Portland Airport.** Suites in this eight-story atrium hotel have beige walls and blond-wood furnishings. The lobby has a waterfall and koi pond. All suites come with separate bedrooms and living areas with sleeper sofas. It's on the MAX airport light-rail line. **Pros:** spacious suites; full breakfast included; free cocktails at happy hour. **Cons:**

airport location. ⌧ *7900 NE 82nd Ave., Airport* ☎ *503/460–3000*
⊕ *www.portlandairport.embassysuites.com* ↝ *251 suites* ♿ *In-room:
refrigerator. In-hotel: restaurant, room service, pool, gym, concierge,
laundry service, airport shuttle, Wi-Fi hotspot, parking (no fee)* ⊟ *AE,
D, DC, MC, V* ⊺⊙⎪*BP* ✣ *G1.*

$ ⊡ **Red Lion Hotel on the River.** The rooms in this four-story hotel, on the
Columbia River, have balconies and good views of the river and Vancouver, Washington. Public areas glitter with brass and bright lights that
accentuate the greenery and the burgundy, green, and rose color scheme.
Pros: river location; views from room balconies; close to the Jantzen
Beach shopping center. **Cons:** pool is outdoors. ⌧ *909 N. Hayden Island
Dr., east of I–5's Jantzen Beach exit, Jantzen Beach* ☎ *503/283–4466
or 800/733–5466* ⊕ *www.redlion.com* ↝ *320 rooms, 24 suites* ♿ *In-
room: Wi-Fi. In-hotel: 2 restaurants, room service, bar, tennis court,
pool, gym, laundry facilities, laundry service, Wi-Fi hotspot, parking
(no fee)* ⊟ *AE, D, DC, MC, V* ✣ *D1.*

$ ⊡ **Shilo Suites Airport.** Each room in this large, four-level all-suites inn is
bright, with floral-print bedspreads and drapes, and has a microwave,
wet bar, and two oversize beds. The indoor pool and hot tub are open
24 hours. **Pros:** large indoor pool; spacious rooms; free local calls. **Cons:**
airport location. ⌧ *11707 NE Airport Way, Airport* ☎ *503/252–7500
or 800/222–2244* ⊕ *www.shiloinns.com* ↝ *200 rooms* ♿ *In-room:
refrigerator. In-hotel: restaurant, room service, bar, pool, gym, laundry facilities, laundry service, airport shuttle, Wi-Fi hotspot, parking
(no fee)* ⊟ *AE, D, DC, MC, V* ⊺⊙⎪*CP* ✣ *G1.*

NIGHTLIFE AND THE ARTS

Portland is quite the creative town. Every night, performances by top-
ranked dance, theater, and musical talents take the stage somewhere
in the city. Expect to find never-ending choices for things to do, from
taking in true independent films, performance art, and plays to checking
out some of the Northwest's (and the country's) hottest musical groups
at one of the city's many nightclubs.

As for the fine-art scene, galleries abound in all four corners of Portland, and if you take the time and do a little research, you'll discover
extraordinarily creative blends of artistic techniques. Painted, recycled,
photographed, fired, fused, welded, or collaged—the scope and selection of art is one of the most notable attributes of what makes this city
so metropolitan and alive.

PUBLICATIONS

"A&E, The Arts and Entertainment Guide," published each Friday
in the *Oregonian* (⊕ *www.oregonlive.com*), contains listings of performers, productions, events, and club entertainment. *Willamette Week*
(⊕ *wweek.com*), published free each Wednesday and widely available
throughout the metropolitan area, contains similar, but hipper, listings. *Portland Family Magazine* (⊕ *www.portlandfamily.com*) is a
free monthly publication that has an excellent calendar of events for
recreational and educational opportunities for families. The *Portland*

CLOSE UP

Classic Cocktails

Classic cocktails are back with a vengeance chic enough to make James Bond proud, and they have a new twist: being infused with anything flavorful that grows under the sun. Throughout the Northwest, emphasis on freshness and sustainability has spilled over into the mixers, shakers, and blenders of creative mixologists. Avocados, cucumbers, chilies, green peppers, cilantro, nutmeg, rhubarb, and beets are some of the luminaries infusing tangy hints and boldness into rums, vodkas, and whiskeys. Regionally, drink swankiness and sophistication have reached soaring heights. The book *Hip Sips*, by Portland Mint/820 bartender and restaurateur Lucy Brennan is dedicated to this intoxicating topic, with more than 60 imaginative recipes to choose from.

Mercury (⊕ *www.portlandmercury.com*) is another free entertainment publication distributed each Wednesday. *Just Out* (⊕ *www.justout. com)*, the city's gay and lesbian newspaper, is published bimonthly.

NIGHTLIFE

Portland has become something of a base for young rock bands, which perform in dance clubs scattered throughout the metropolitan area. Good jazz groups perform nightly in clubs and bars. Top-name musicians and performers in every genre regularly appear at the city's larger venues. (⇨ *Also see Portland's Music Scene feature, and Portland Brews.*)

BARS AND LOUNGES

From chic to cheap, cool to cultish, Portland's diverse bars and lounges blanket the town. The best way to experience some of the city's hottest spots is to check out the happy-hour menus found at almost all of Portland's bars; they offer excellent deals on both food and drinks.

DOWNTOWN

Many of the best bars and lounges in Portland are found in its restaurants.

At the elegant **Heathman Hotel** (⊠ *1001 SW Broadway* ☎ *503/241–4100*) you can sit in the marble bar or the wood-paneled Tea Court.

Huber's Cafe (⊠ *411 SW 3rd Ave.* ☎ *503/228–5686*), the city's oldest restaurant, is notable for its Spanish coffee and old-fashioned feel.

The young and eclectic crowd at the **Lotus Cardroom and Cafe** (⊠ *932 SW 3rd Ave.* ☎ *503/227–6185*) comes to drink and play pool or foosball.

The **Rialto** (⊠ *529 SW 4th Ave.* ☎ *503/228–7605*) is a large, dark bar with several pool tables and enthusiastic players as well as some of the best Bloody Marys in town.

Saucebox (⊠ *214 SW Broadway* ☎ *503/241–3393*) attracts a sophisticated crowd that enjoys colorful cocktails and trendy DJ music Wednesday–Saturday evenings.

PORTLAND TOP 5 NIGHTLIFE TIPS

■ Become immersed in an Oregon Symphony classical or pops concert at the Arlene Schnitzer Concert Hall; enjoy a postsymphony glass of wine at a nearby restaurant bar afterward.

■ Cruise for brews at dozens of local microbreweries, brewpubs, and pub theaters.

■ Catch an internationally known jazz band or discover a new blues group at one of Portland's many live-music venues.

■ Go to a First Thursday event in the Pearl District or a Last Thursday showing in Alberta and soak up the local visual-arts scene.

■ Sip a designer cocktail made with fresh ingredients—from run-of-the-mill juices and mixers to chilies, nutmeg, and even rhubarb—at any one of the trendy downtown bars.

With more than 120 choices, **Southpark** (⊠ *901 SW Salmon St.* ☏ *503/ 326–1300*) is a perfect spot for a postsymphony glass of wine.

At **Veritable Quandary** (⊠ *1220 SW 1st Ave.* ☏ *503/227–7342*), next to the river, you can sit on the cozy, tree-filled outdoor patio or in the glass atrium.

PEARL DISTRICT AND OLD TOWN/CHINATOWN

The modern bar at **Bluehour** (⊠ *250 NW 13th Ave., Pearl District* ☏ *503/226–3394*) draws a chic crowd for specialty cocktails such as the Bluehour Breeze (house-infused grapefruit vodka with a splash of cranberry).

Henry's 12th Street Tavern (⊠ *10 NW 12th Ave., Pearl District* ☏ *503/227– 5320*) has more than 100 beers on draft, plasma-screen TVs, and a bil-liards room in a building that was once Henry Weinhard's brewery.

At **Oba!** (⊠ *555 NW 12th Ave., Pearl District* ☏ *503/228–6161*), plush tans and reds with lime-green backlit walls create a backdrop for South American salsa.

NOB HILL AND VICINITY

Boisterous **Gypsy** (⊠ *625 NW 21st Ave., Nob Hill* ☏ *503/796–1859*) has 1950s-era furnishings.

Young hipsters pack **Muu-Muu's** (⊠ *612 NW 21st Ave., Nob Hill* ☏ *503/ 223–8169*) on weekend nights.

21st Avenue Bar & Grill (⊠ *721 NW 21st Ave., Nob Hill* ☏ *503/222– 4121*) open until 2:30 AM, has a patio and outdoor bar.

An upscale martini-loving crowd chills at **Wildwood** (⊠ *1221 NW 21st Ave., Nob Hill* ☏ *503/248–9663*).

EAST OF WILLAMETTE RIVER

Artsy, hip east-siders, not to be mistaken for the jet-setters down-town, hang and drink martinis and wine at the minimalist **Aalto Lounge** (⊠ *3356 SE Belmont St.* ☏ *503/235–6041*).

One of the few bars on Northeast Alberta Street, **Bink's** (✉ *2715 NE Alberta St.* ☎ *503/493–4430*) is a small, friendly neighborhood spot with cozy seats around a fireplace, a pool table, and a good jukebox. It serves only beer and wine.

Green lanterns glow on the curvy bar as hip patrons sip mojitos or other mixed drinks at the no-smoking hot spot **820** (✉ *820 N. Russell St.* ☎ *503/284–5518*).

A laid-back beer-drinking crowd fills the **Horse Brass Pub** (✉ *4534 SE Belmont St.* ☎ *503/232–2202*), as good an English-style pub as you will find this side of the Atlantic, with more than 50 beers on tap.

The open, airy **Imbibe** (✉ *2229 SE Hawthorne Blvd.* ☎ *503/239–4002*) serves up creative cocktails, such as its namesake, the Imbibe Infusion—a thyme-and-ginger-infused vodka and strawberry martini with a touch of lemon.

Noble Rot (✉ *1111 E. Burnside St., 4th fl.* ☎ *503/233–1999*) is a chic east-side wine bar with excellent food and red-leather booths.

Swift Lounge (✉ *1932 NE Broadway* ☎ *503/288–3333*), a popular tapas bar, draws a cocktail-sipping crowd of hipsters at night.

BREWPUBS, MICROBREWERIES, AND PUB THEATERS
Dozens of small breweries operating in the metropolitan area produce pale ales, bitters, bocks, barley wines, and stouts. Some have attached pub operations, where you can sample a foaming pint of house ale. "Pub theaters," former neighborhood movie houses where patrons enjoy food, suds, and recent theatrical releases, are part of the micro-brewery phenomenon. Many are branches of McMenamins, a locally owned chain of bars, restaurants, nightclubs, and hotels, and some of these pubs can be found in restored historic buildings. (⇨ *Also see our Portland Brews feature.*)

The **Bagdad Theater and Pub** (✉ *3702 SE Hawthorne Blvd., Hawthorne District* ☎ *503/236–9234*) screens second-run Hollywood films and serves McMenamins ales and Pizzacato Pizza.

The first McMenamins brewpub, the **Barley Mill Pub** (✉ *1629 SE Hawthorne Blvd., Hawthorne District* ☎ *503/231–1492*), is filled with Grateful Dead memorabilia and concert posters. It's a fun place for families.

BridgePort BrewPub & Restaurant (✉ *1313 NW Marshall St., Pearl District* ☎ *503/241–7179*), Port-

PUB THEATERS

Sipping a pint of local brew is one of Oregon's favorite pastimes, but Portlanders have taken this a step further with so-called pub theaters—movie theaters showing second-run, classic, or cult films for $3 or so that let you buy a pitcher of good locally brewed beer and a slice of pizza to enjoy while watching. The McMenamin brothers are largely to thank for this phenomenon, being the masterminds behind such popular spots as the Bagdad Theater, the Mission Theater, and the St. John's Pub. In addition, unaffiliated establishments like the Laurelhurst Theater and the Clinton Street Theater have managed to get in on the action as well.

Last Thursday Art Walk on Alberta Street

land's oldest microbrewery, prepares hand-tossed pizza (⇨ *Where to Eat*) to accompany its ales.

Inside an old warehouse with high ceilings and rustic wood tables, the **Lucky Labrador Brew Pub** (✉ *915 SE Hawthorne Blvd.* ☎ *503/236–3555*) serves handcrafted ales and pub food both in the brewery and on the patio, where your four-legged friends are welcome to join you.

First opened in 1987, the **Mission Theater** (✉ *1624 NW Glisan St., Nob Hill* ☎ *503/223–4527*) was the first McMenamins brew theater. It shows recent Hollywood offerings.

Ringlers (✉ *1332 W. Burnside St., Downtown* ☎ *503/225–0627*) occupies the first floor of the building that houses the famous Crystal Ballroom (⇨ *Dancing*).

Ringlers Annex (✉ *1223 SW Stark St., Downtown* ☎ *503/525–0520*), one block east of Ringlers, is a pie-shaped corner pub where you can puff a cigar while drinking beer, port, or a single-malt scotch.

In a former church, the **St. John's Pub** (✉ *8203 N. Ivanhoe, East of Willamette River* ☎ *503/283–8520*) includes a beer garden and a movie theater.

Tugboat Brewery (✉ *711 SW Ankeny St., Downtown* ☎ *503/226–2508*) is a small, cozy brewpub with books and games, picnic tables, and experimental jazz several nights a week.

Widmer Brewing and Gasthaus (✉ *955 N. Russell St., North Portland, near Fremont Bridge* ☎ *503/281–3333*) brews German-style beers and has a full menu; you can tour the adjacent brewery Friday and Saturday.

COFFEEHOUSES AND TEAHOUSES

Coffee is to Portland as tea is to England. For Portlanders, sipping a cup of coffee is a right, a ritual, and a pastime that occurs no matter the time of day or night. There's no shortage of cafés in which to park and read, reflect, or rejuvenate for the long day or night of exploration ahead.

DOWNTOWN

Serving quite possibly the best coffee around, **Stumptown Coffee Roasters** (✉ *128 SW 3rd Ave., Downtown* ☎ *503/295–6144*) has three local cafés, where its beans are roasted daily on vintage cast-iron equipment for a consistent, fresh flavor.

NOB HILL AND VICINITY

Anna Bannanas (✉ *1214 NW 21st Ave., Nob Hill* ☎ *503/274–2559*) serves great espresso and coffee, veggie sandwiches, soup, and smoothies. There's outdoor seating out front.

One of the more highly trafficked locales in the Portland coffee scene, **World Cup Coffee and Tea** (✉ *1740 NW Glisan St., Nob Hill* ☎ *503/228–4152*), sells excellent organic coffee and espresso in Nob Hill, as well as at its store in the Pearl District at the Ecotrust building and at Powell's City of Books on Burnside.

EAST OF WILLAMETTE RIVER

Common Grounds (✉ *4321 SE Hawthorne Blvd., East of Willamette River* ☎ *503/236–4835*) has plush couches and serves desserts plus sandwiches and soup.

Palio Coffee and Dessert House (✉ *1996 SE Ladd St., East of Willamette River* ☎ *503/232–9412*), in the middle of peaceful residential Ladd's Addition, has delicious desserts and espresso, and is open later than many coffee shops in the area.

Post-collegiate sippers lounge on sofas and overstuffed chairs at **Pied Cow** (✉ *3244 SE Belmont St., East of Willamette River* ☎ *503/230–4866*), a laid-back alternative to the more yuppified establishments.

Rimsky Korsakoffee House (✉ *707 SE 12th Ave., East of Willamette River* ☎ *503/232–2640*), one of the city's first coffeehouses, is still one of the best, especially when it comes to desserts.

Stumptown Coffee Roasters (✉ *4525 SE Division St.* ☎ *503/230–7702* ✉ *3356 SE Belmont St.* ☎ *503/232–8889*) has two cafés on the east side. At the original site (SE Division), organic beans are still roasted daily. At the Stumptown Annex, the newer branch next door, patrons can participate in "cuppings" (tastings) daily at 3 PM.

With soft music and the sound of running water in the background, the **Tao of Tea** (✉ *3430 SE Belmont St., East of Willamette River* ☎ *503/736–0119*) serves vegetarian snacks and sweets as well as more than 80 loose-leaf teas.

DANCING

A couple of cocktails and some good music are all that's needed to shake your groove thing at Portland's hot spots for dancing. Clubs feature both live bands and DJs spinning the latest in dance-floor favorites.

Part 1950s diner, part log cabin, the **Doug Fir** (✉ *830 E. Burnside St., East of Willamette River* ☎ *503/231–9663*) hosts DJs and live rock shows from up-and-coming bands seven nights a week.

Tuesday through Saturday, the funky, Moroccan-style **Fez Ballroom** (✉ *316 SW 11th St., Downtown* ☎ *503/221–7262*) draws a dancing crowd.

McMenamins Crystal Ballroom (✉ *1332 W. Burnside St., Downtown* ☎ *503/225–0047*) is a famous Portland dance hall that dates from 1914. Rudolph Valentino danced the tango here in 1923, and you may feel like doing the same once you step out onto the 7,500-sq-ft "elastic" floor (it's built on ball bearings) and feel it bouncing beneath your feet. Bands perform everything from swing to hillbilly rock nightly except Monday.

GAY AND LESBIAN CLUBS

Portland's gay community has a decent selection of places to mingle, dance, and drink; several of these nightspots are open into the wee hours, until 4 AM or so.

Part of the same disco-bar-restaurant complex as the Fez Ballroom, **Boxxes** (✉ *1035 SW Stark St., Downtown* ☎ *503/226–4171*) has multiple video screens that display everything from music to messages from would-be dates.

Attracting mostly gay men, **C.C. Slaughters** (✉ *219 NW Davis Ave., Old Town* ☎ *503/248–9135*) bar has a restaurant and a dance floor that's crowded on weekend nights; weeknights bring karaoke and country dancing.

Egyptian Room (✉ *3701 SE Division St., East of Willamette River* ☎ *503/236–8689*), Portland's lesbian bar-disco, has pool tables, video poker, and a medium-size dance floor.

Open till 4 AM, **Embers** (✉ *11 NW Broadway Ave., Old Town* ☎ *503/222–3082*) is a popular after-hours place to dance; the club hosts occasional drag shows and theme nights.

Fox and Hounds (✉ *217 NW 2nd Ave., Old Town* ☎ *503/243–5530*) is popular with both gay men and lesbians. A full menu is served in the evenings, and the place is packed for Sunday brunch.

Scandals (✉ *1125 SW Stark St., Downtown* ☎ *503/227–5887*) has plate-glass windows with a view of Stark Street and the city's streetcars. At this low-key place there's a small dance floor, video poker, and a pool table, and the bar serves light food noon to closing.

LIVE MUSIC

Perhaps one of Portland's greatest attributes is the quality selection of live music—especially jazz and blues—that's available seven nights a week. Clubs are full most nights with faithful followers who go to see and hear some of the most talented musicians take the stage and command the crowds with awesome performances. (⇨ *Also see Portland's Music Scene feature.*)

BLUES, FOLK,
AND ROCK

The **Aladdin Theater** (✉ *3017 SE Milwaukie Ave., East of Willamette River* ☎ *503/234–9694*), in an old movie theater, is one of the best music venues in town. It serves microbrews and pizza.

Berbati's Pan (✉ *10 SW 3rd Ave.*, *Old Town* ☎ *503/226–2122*), on the edge of Old Town, has dancing and live music, everything from big band and swing to acid jazz, rock, and R&B.

The **Candlelight Room** (✉ *2032 SW 5th Ave.*, *Downtown* ☎ *503/222–3378*) presents blues nightly.

Dublin Pub (✉ *6821 SW Beaverton–Hillsdale Hwy.*, *west of Downtown* ☎ *503/297–2889*), on the west side, pours more than 50 beers on tap and hosts Irish bands and rock groups.

Kells Irish Restaurant & Pub (✉ *112 SW 2nd Ave.*, *Old Town* ☎ *503/227–4057*) serves terrific Irish food and presents Celtic music nightly.

Locals crowd the **Laurelthirst Public House** (✉ *2958 NE Glisan St.*, *East of Willamette River* ☎ *503/232–1504*) to eat tasty food, sit in cozy red booths, and listen to folk, jazz, country, or bluegrass music on its tiny stage. There are pool tables in an adjoining room.

The down-to-earth **Produce Row Cafe** (✉ *204 SE Oak St.*, *East of Willamette River* ☎ *503/232–8355*) has a huge beer list, a great beer garden, and live bluegrass, folk, and acoustic music most nights of the week.

COUNTRY AND WESTERN

Duke's (✉ *14601 SE Division St.*, *East of Willamette River* ☎ *503/760–1400*) books occasional country and country-rock performers and hosts nightly DJ dancing to country music.

Not your ordinary truck stop, the Ponderosa Lounge at **Jubitz Truck Stop** (✉ *10350 N. Vancouver Way*, *East of Willamette River* ☎ *503/345–0300*) presents live country music and dancing Thursday through Saturday.

JAZZ

Upstairs at the **Blue Monk** (✉ *3341 SE Belmont St.*, *East of Willamette River* ☎ *503/595–0575*) local artists' works are on display and patrons nosh on large plates of pasta and salads; the live-jazz venue downstairs displays jazz memorabilia and photos.

Dubbed one of the world's "top 100 places to hear jazz" by *Down-Beat*, **Jimmy Mak's** (✉ *300 SW 10th*, *Pearl District* ☎ *503/295–6542*) also serves Greek and Middle Eastern dishes and has a basement lounge outfitted with two pool tables and an Internet jukebox.

THE ARTS

The conundrum of delving into Portland's art scene won't be *if* you can find something to do—it will be *what* to do when you discover there's almost too much to choose from. For a city of this size, there is truly an impressive—and accessible—scope of talent from visual artists, performance artists, and musicians. The arts are alive, with outdoor sculptural works strewn around the city, ongoing festivals, and premieres of traveling Broadway shows. Top-name international acts, such as Bruce Springsteen, the Rolling Stones, Paul McCartney, and Billy Joel, regularly include Portland in their worldwide stops.

TICKETS

Most Portland-based performing-arts groups have their own box-office numbers; *see individual listings.*

For tickets to most events, call **Ticketmaster** (☎ *800/745–3000* ⊕ *www. ticketmaster.com*). Tickets are also available from **TicketsWest** (☎ *503/ 224–8499* ⊕ *www.ticketswest.com*).

During the summer half-price tickets for almost any event are available the day of the show at Ticket Central in the **Visitor Information and Services Center** (✉ *Pioneer Courthouse Sq., Downtown* ☎ *503/275–8358 after 10* AM), open Monday–Saturday 9–4:30. This is an outlet for tickets from Ticketmaster and TicketsWest. Credit cards are accepted, but you must buy tickets in person.

PERFORMANCE VENUES

The **Agnes Flanagan Chapel at Lewis & Clark College** (✉ *615 SW Palatine Hill Rd., west of downtown*) hosts some smaller concerts.

The 2,776-seat **Arlene Schnitzer Concert Hall** (✉ *Portland Center for the Performing Arts, SW Broadway and Main St., Downtown* ☎ *503/274–6560*), built in 1928 in an Italian rococo revival style, hosts rock stars, choral groups, lectures, and concerts by the Oregon Symphony and others.

Downtown, the **First Baptist Church** (✉ *1425 SW 20th Ave., Downtown*) occasionally hosts more intimate concerts and performances.

With 3,000 seats and outstanding acoustics, **Keller Auditorium** (✉ *222 SW Clay St., Downtown* ☎ *503/274–6560*) hosts performances by the Portland Opera and Portland Ballet, as well as country and rock concerts and touring shows.

Memorial Coliseum (✉ *1 Center Ct., Rose Quarter, East of Willamette River* ☎ *503/235–8771* ⊕ *www.rosequarter.com*), a 12,000-seat venue on the MAX light-rail line, books rock groups, touring shows, the Ringling Brothers circus, ice-skating extravaganzas, and sporting events.

PGE Park (✉ *1844 SW Morrison St., Nob Hill* ☎ *503/553–5400* ⊕ *www. pgepark.com*) is home to the Portland Beavers Triple-A baseball team and the Portland Timbers soccer team. The 20,000-seat stadium also hosts concerts and other sporting events. No parking is available at the park; MAX light rail is the most convenient option. Your game ticket entitles you to a free round-trip.

Portland Center for the Performing Arts (✉ *1111 SW Broadway, Downtown* ☎ *503/274–6560* ⊕ *www.pcpa.com*) hosts opera, ballet, rock shows, symphony performances, lectures, and Broadway musicals in its three venues (⇨ *Downtown in Exploring Portland*).

Reed College's Kaul Auditorium (✉ *3203 SE Woodstock Blvd., East of Willamette River*) hosts the Portland Baroque Orchestra, among other groups.

The 21,000-seat **Rose Garden** (✉ *1 Center Ct., Broadway and N. Interstate Ave., East of Willamette River* ☎ *503/235–8771* ⊕ *www. rosequarter.com*) is home to the Portland Trail Blazers basketball team and the site of other sporting events and rock concerts. The arena is on the MAX light-rail line.

The **Roseland Theater** (✉ *8 NW 6th Ave., Old Town/Chinatown* ☎ *503/ 224–2038*), which holds 1,400 people, primarily stages rock and blues shows.

CLASSICAL MUSIC

CHAMBER MUSIC   **Chamber Music Northwest** (✉ *522 SW 5th Ave., Suite 725, Downtown* ☎ *503/294–6400* ⊕ *www.cnmw.org*) presents some of the most sought-after soloists, chamber musicians, and recording artists from the Portland area and abroad for a five-week summer concert series; performances take place at Reed College and the Catlin Gabel School.

OPERA   **Portland Opera** (✉ *222 SW Clay St.* ☎ *503/241–1802 or 866/739–6737* ⊕ *www.portlandopera.org*) and its orchestra and chorus stage five productions annually at the Keller Auditorium.

ORCHESTRAS   The **Oregon Symphony** (✉ *923 SW Washington* ☎ *503/228–1353 or 800/228–7343* ⊕ *www.orsymphony.org*), established in 1896, is Portland's largest classical group—and one of the largest orchestras in the country. Its season officially starts in September and ends in May, but throughout the summer the orchestra and its smaller ensembles can be seen at Waterfront Park and Washington Park for special outdoor summer performances. It also presents more than 40 classical, pop, children's, and family concerts each year at the Arlene Schnitzer Concert Hall.

☺   The **Metropolitan Youth Symphony** (✉ *4800 SW Macadam St., Suite 105* ☎ *503/239–4566* ⊕ *www.playmys.org*) performs family-friendly concerts throughout the year at various Portland venues, including the Arlene Schnitzer Concert Hall.

The **Portland Baroque Orchestra** (☎ *503/222–6000* ⊕ *www.pbo.org*) performs works on period instruments in a season that runs October to April. Performances are held at various venues, including Reed College's Kaul Auditorium, the Agnes Flanagan Chapel at Lewis & Clark College, and the First Baptist Church.

DANCE

Body Vox (☎ *503/229–0627* ⊕ *www.bodyvox.com*) performs energetic contemporary dance–theater works at several locations in Portland.

Do Jump! Extremely Physical Theater (✉ *1515 SE 37th Ave.* ☎ *503/231–1232* ⊕ *www.dojump.org*) showcases its creative acrobatic work at the Echo Theatre near Hawthorne.

Oregon Ballet Theatre (✉ *818 SE 6th Ave.* ☎ *503/222–5538 or 888/922–5538* ⊕ *www.obt.org*) produces five classical and contemporary works a year, including a much-loved holiday *Nutcracker*. Most performances are at Keller Auditorium.

Since its founding in 1997, **White Bird Dance** (✉ *5620 SW Edgemont Pl.* ☎ *503/245–1600* ⊕ *www.whitebird.org*) has been dedicated to bringing exciting dance performances to Portland from around the world.

FILM

Cinema 21 (✉ *616 NW 21st Ave., Nob Hill* ☎ *503/223–4515*) an art-movie house in Nob Hill, hosts the annual gay and lesbian film festival.

Cinemagic (✉ *2021 SE Hawthorne Blvd., East of Willamette River* ☎ *503/231–7919*) shows progressive and cult films.

An over-80-year-old landmark, and another host of the annual gay and lesbian film festival, the **Hollywood Theatre** (✉ *4122 NE Sandy Blvd.,*

East of Willamette River ☎*503/281–4215*) shows everything from obscure foreign art films to old American classics and second-run Hollywood hits, and hosts an annual Academy Awards viewing party.

The **Laurelhurst Theater** (✉*2735 E. Burnside, East of Willamette River* ☎*503/232–5511*) is a beautiful theater and pub showing excellent second-run features and cult classics for only $3.

Not-to-be-missed Portland landmarks when it comes to movie-viewing, the **McMenamins theaters and brewpubs** offer beer, pizza, and inexpensive tickets to second-run blockbusters in uniquely renovated buildings that avoid any hint of corporate streamlining. The **Bagdad Theater** (✉*3702 SE Hawthorne Blvd., East of Willamette River* ☎*503/236–9234*) is a local favorite. The **Kennedy School** (✉*5736 NE 33rd St., East of Willamette River* ☎*503/249–3983*) theater is in a renovated elementary school that also contains a bed-and-breakfast and a restaurant. The **Mission Theater** (✉*1624 NW Glisan, Nob Hill* ☎*503/223–4527*) has a popular "Burger, Beer and a Movie" night.

The **Northwest Film Center** (✉*1219 SW Park Ave., Downtown* ☎*503/221–1156* ⊕*www.nwfilm.org*), a branch of the Portland Art Museum, screens art films, documentaries, and independent features and presents the three-week Portland International Film Festival in February and March. Films are shown at the Whitsell Auditorium, next to the museum.

THEATER

Artists Repertory Theatre (✉*1516 SW Alder St., Downtown* ☎*503/241–1278* ⊕*www.artistsrep.org*) stages seven productions a year—regional premieres, occasional commissioned works, and classics.

Imago Theatre (✉*17 SE 8th Ave., East of Willamette River* ☎*503/231–9581* ⊕*www.imagotheatre.com*), considered by some to be Portland's most outstanding innovative theater company, specializes in movement-based work for both young and old.

Ⓒ **Oregon Children's Theatre** (☎*503/228–9571* ⊕*www.octc.org*) puts on three or four shows a year at major venues throughout the city for school groups and families.

Portland Center Stage (✉*Gerding Theater at the Armory, 128 NW 1st Ave., Downtown* ☎*503/445–3700* ⊕*www.pcs.org*) produces contemporary and classical works between October and April.

Ⓒ **Tears of Joy Puppet Theater** (☎*503/248–0557* ⊕*www.tojt.org*) stages five children's productions a year at different locations in town.

SHOPPING

One of Portland's greatest attributes is its neighborhoods' dynamic spectrum of retail and specialty shops. The Pearl District is known for chic interior design and high-end clothing boutiques. Trek over to the Hawthorne area and you'll discover wonderful stores for handmade jewelry, clothing, and books. The Northwest has some funky shops for housewares, clothing, and jewelry, while in the Northeast there are fabulous galleries and crafts. Downtown has a blend of it all, as well as bigger options, including the Pioneer Place Mall and department stores such as Nordstrom and Macy's.

No Portland shopping experience would be complete without a visit to the nation's largest open-air market, Saturday Market, where an array of talented artists converge to peddle handcrafted wares beyond your wildest do-it-yourself dreams. It's also open Sunday.

Portland merchants are generally open Monday to Saturday between 9 or 10 AM and 6 PM, and on Sunday noon to 6. Most shops in downtown's Pioneer Place, the east side's Lloyd Center, and the outlying malls are open until 9 PM Monday to Saturday and until 6 PM on Sunday.

SHOPPING AREAS

Portland's main shopping area is **downtown,** between Southwest 2nd and 10th avenues and between Southwest Stark and Morrison streets. The major department stores are scattered over several blocks near Pioneer Courthouse Square. Northeast **Broadway** between 10th and 21st avenues is lined with boutiques and specialty shops. **Nob Hill,** north of downtown along Northwest 21st and 23rd avenues, has eclectic clothing, gift, book, and food shops. Most of the city's fine-art galleries are concentrated in the booming **Pearl District,** north from Burnside Street to Marshall Street between Northwest 8th and 15th avenues, along with furniture and design stores. **Sellwood,** 5 mi from the city center, south on Naito Parkway and east across the Sellwood Bridge, has more than 50 antiques and collectibles shops along southeast 13th Avenue, plus specialty shops and outlet stores for sporting goods. You can find the larger antiques stores near the intersection of Milwaukie Avenue and Bybee. **Hawthorne Boulevard** between 30th and 42nd avenues has a selection of alternative bookstores, coffeehouses, antiques stores, and boutiques.

FLEA MARKETS

Fodor's Choice ★ The open-air **Portland Saturday Market** (⊠ *Burnside Bridge, underneath west end, Old Town* ☎ *503/222–6072* ⊕ *www.saturdaymarket.org*), open on weekends (including Sunday, despite the name), is a favorite place to experience the people of Portland and also find one-of-a-kind, unique handcrafted home, garden, and gift items.

MALLS AND DEPARTMENT STORES

DOWNTOWN

Shopping downtown is not only fun, it's also easy, thanks to easy transportation access and proximity to many of Portland's hotels. Locally based favorites Nike and Columbia Sportswear both have major stores downtown; REI has one in the Pearl District (⇨ *Outdoor Sports, below*)

Macy's at Meier & Frank Square (⊠ *621 SW 5th Ave., Downtown* ☎ *503/223–0512*), until 2005 the main location of the local Meier & Frank chain, has five floors of general merchandise.

Seattle-based **Nordstrom** (⊠ *701 SW Broadway, Downtown* ☎ *503/224–6666*) sells fine-quality apparel and accessories and has a large footwear department. Bargain lovers should head for the **Nordstrom Rack**

Portland Saturday Market

(⊠ *245 SW Morrison St., Downtown* ☎ *503/299–1815*) outlet across from Pioneer Place Mall.

Pioneer Place (⊠ *700 SW 5th Ave., Downtown* ☎ *503/228–5800*) has more than 80 upscale specialty shops (including April Cornell, Coach, J. Crew, Godiva, and Fossil) in a three-story, glass-roof atrium setting. You can find good, inexpensive ethnic foods from more than a dozen vendors in the Cascades Food Court in the basement. Paradise Bakery is known for fresh home-baked breads and delicious chocolate-chip cookies; Suki Hana has some yummy soups and noodle dishes.

Saks Fifth Avenue (⊠ *850 SW 5th Ave., Downtown* ☎ *503/226–3200*) has two floors of men's and women's clothing, jewelry, and other merchandise.

BEYOND DOWNTOWN

Once you venture outside of downtown, you can find several major malls and outlets in which to shop 'til you drop. Both Woodburn (30 mi south of Portland) and Troutdale (20 mi east) have outlet malls with dozens of discount name-brand clothing stores.

EAST OF THE WILLAMETTE RIVER

Clackamas Town Center (⊠ *Sunnyside Rd. at I–205 Exit 14, East of Willamette River* ☎ *503/653–6913*) has four major department stores, including Nordstrom and Macy's, as well as more than 180 shops. Discount stores are nearby.

Lloyd Center (⊠ *NE Multnomah St. at NE 9th Ave., East of Willamette River* ☎ *503/282–2511*), on the MAX light-rail line, has more than 170 shops (including Nordstrom, Sears, and Macy's), an international food court, a multiscreen cinema, and an ice-skating pavilion. The mall is within walking distance of Northeast Broadway, which has many specialty shops, boutiques, and restaurants.

WEST OF DOWNTOWN

Bridgeport Village (✉ *SW Boones Ferry Rd., at SW Lower Boones Ferry Rd., off I–5, Exit 290, west of Downtown* ☎ *503/968–8940*), an outdoor mall, has tall buckets full of handheld yellow umbrellas on hand throughout the property in case it rains. Visit the movie-theater complex, eat at one of over a dozen restaurants such as P.F. Chang's or Zao Noodle bar, or visit major shops that include Tommy Bahama and Crate & Barrel.

South of Portland, the **Streets of Tanasbourne** (✉ *NW 194th at Cornell Rd., off U.S. 26, Hillsboro* ☎ *503/533–0561*) has 52 choices of high-end specialty shops, including Clogs 'n' More, Abercrombie & Fitch, and White House/Black Market.

Washington Square (✉ *9585 SW Washington Sq. Rd., at SW Hall Blvd. and Hwy. 217, Tigard* ☎ *503/639–8860*) contains five major department stores, including Macy's and Sears; a food court; and more than 140 specialty shops. Discount and electronics stores are nearby.

The **Water Tower** (✉ *5331 SW Macadam Ave., west of downtown*), in the John's Landing neighborhood on the Willamette River, is a pleasant mall, with Pier 1 Imports and several restaurants.

SPECIALTY STORES

Portland's specialty stores are as varied and authentic as the city itself. Residents applaud and encourage locally made quirky goods, so stores offering these creative wares are abundant. Discover all the innovative approaches to household items, art, jewelry, and clothing for a fun afternoon.

ANTIQUES

Moreland House (✉ *826 NW 23rd Ave., Nob Hill* ☎ *503/222–0197*) has eclectic antiques and gifts, with a notable selection of dog collectibles, old printing-press type, and fresco tiles.

Shogun's Gallery (✉ *1111 NW 23rd Ave., Nob Hill* ☎ *503/224–0328*) specializes in Japanese and Chinese furniture, especially the lightweight wooden Japanese cabinets known as *tansu*. Also here are chairs, tea tables, altar tables, armoires, ikebana baskets (originally for flower arrangements), and Chinese wooden picnic boxes, most at least 100 years old and at reasonable prices.

Stars Antique Mall (✉ *7027 SE Milwaukie Ave., East of Willamette River* ☎ *503/235–5990* ⊕ *starsantique.com*), Portland's largest antiques mall, has two stores across the street from each other in the Sellwood-Moreland neighborhood. Since it rents its space to about 300 antiques dealers; you might find anything from low-end 1950s kitsch to high-end treasures.

ART DEALERS AND GALLERIES

EVENTS **First Thursday** (☎ *503/295–4979* ⊕ *www.firstthursdayportland.com*) gives art appreciators a chance to check out new exhibits while enjoying music and wine. Typically, the galleries are open in the evening, but hours vary depending on the gallery. Find out what galleries are participating on the Web site.

The Alberta Arts District hosts a **Last Thursday Arts Walk** (☎ *503/972–2206* ⊕ *www.artonalberta.org*) each month.

Many galleries in the **Pearl District** (⊕ *www.firstthursday.org*) host First Thursday events.

GALLERIES **Butters Gallery, Ltd.** (✉ *520 NW Davis, Pearl District* ☎ *503/248–9378*) has monthly exhibits of the works of nationally known and local artists in its Pearl District space.

Exit 21 Gallery (✉ *1502 SE 21st, East of Willamette River* ☎ *503/867–8495*) has wall-mounted and floor-standing sculptures made from reclaimed materials as well as hand-knitted apparel. They are recognized for supporting local artists and showcasing an eclectic blend of works, with a wide range of prices.

The **Laura Russo Gallery** (✉ *805 NW 21st Ave., Nob Hill* ☎ *503/226–2754*) displays contemporary Northwest work of all styles, including landscapes and abstract expressionism.

Emphasizing sustainable and fair trade practices, the **Onda Gallery** (✉ *2215 NE Alberta St., East of Willamette River* ☎ *503/493–1909*) is a collective of Northwestern and Latin American artists. Gift items are also for sale.

Pulliam/Deffenbaugh Gallery (✉ *929 NW Flanders St., Pearl District* ☎ *503/228–6665*) generally shows contemporary abstract and expressionistic works by Pacific Northwest artists.

Quintana's Galleries of Native American Art (✉ *120 NW 9th Ave., Pearl District* ☎ *503/223–1729 or 800/321–1729*) focuses on Pacific Northwest Coast, Navajo, and Hopi art and jewelry, along with photogravures by Edward Curtis.

Talisman Gallery (✉ *1476 NE Alberta St., East of Willamette River* ☎ *503/284–8800* ⊕ *talismangallery.com*) showcases two artists each month—they may include local painters and sculptors.

Twist (✉ *30 NW 23rd Pl., Nob Hill* ☎ *503/224–0334* ✉ *Pioneer Pl., Downtown* ☎ *503/222–3137*) has a huge space in Nob Hill and a smaller shop downtown. In Nob Hill are contemporary American ceramics, glass, furniture, sculpture, and handcrafted jewelry; downtown carries an assortment of objects, often with a pop, whimsical touch.

BOOKS

Annie Bloom's (✉ *7834 SW Capital Hwy., west of Downtown* ☎ *503/246–0053* ⊕ *www.annieblooms.com*), a local favorite, has a friendly, knowledgeable staff and great selections of children's books, remainders, Judaica, and fun greeting cards.

PORTLAND TOP 5 SHOPPING TIPS

■ Munch on a fresh-out-of-the-fryer elephant-ear pastry while perusing aisles of handmade wares at Portland's Saturday Market.

■ Scout for something totally fun and funky at one of Northwest 23rd Avenue's boutique gift shops.

■ Leisurely rifle through racks of clothes at some of Portland's more notable secondhand stores, such as Buffalo Exchange downtown and Red Light in Hawthorne.

■ Visit Columbia Sportswear downtown to see just how surprisingly fashionable clothing options for every type of outdoor condition can be.

■ Saunter through Powell's City of Books and see what treasures are in its rare-books section.

Broadway Books (⊠ *1714 NE Broadway, East of Willamette River* ☎ *503/284–1726* ⊕ *www.broadwaybooks.net*) is a fabulous independent bookstore with books on all subjects, including the Pacific Northwest and Judaica.

In Other Words (⊠ *3734 SE Hawthorne Blvd., East of Willamette River* ☎ *503/232–6003*) is a nonprofit bookstore that carries feminist literature and hosts feminist events and readings.

New Renaissance Bookshop (⊠ *1338 NW 23rd Ave., Nob Hill* ☎ *503/224–4929*), between Overton and Pettygrove, is dedicated to New Age and metaphysical books and tapes.

Fodor's Choice ★ **Powell's City of Books** (⊠ *1005 W. Burnside St., Downtown* ☎ *503/228–4651* ⊕ *www.powells.com*), the largest retail store of used and new books in the world (with more than 1.5 million volumes), covers an entire city block on the edge of the Pearl District. It also carries rare and collectible books. There are also three branches in the Portland International Airport.

Powell's for Cooks and Gardeners (⊠ *3747 Hawthorne Blvd., East of Willamette River* ☎ *503/235–3802*), on the east side, has a small adjoining grocery.

CLOTHING

Clogs 'n' More (⊠ *717 SW Alder St., Downtown* ☎ *503/279–9358* ⊠ *3439 SE Hawthorne, East of Willamette River* ☎ *503/232–7007*), with locations on the west and east sides of the city, carries quality clogs and other shoes.

Eight Women (⊠ *3614 SE Hawthorne Blvd., East of Willamette River* ☎ *503/236–8878*) is a tiny boutique "for mother and child," with baby clothes, women's nightgowns, jewelry, and handbags.

Hanna Andersson sells high-quality, comfortable clothing for children and families from their **retail store** (⊠ *327 NW 10th Ave., Nob Hill* ☎ *503/321–5275*) , next to the company's corporate office, as well as through their **outlet store** (⊠ *7 Monroe Pkwy., Lake Oswego* ☎ *503/697–1953*) in Oswego Towne Square, south of Portland.

Imelda's Designer Shoes (⊠ *3426 SE Hawthorne Blvd., East of Willamette River* ☎ *503/233–7476*) is an upscale boutique with funky, fun shoes for women with flair.

Magpie (⊠ *520 SW 9th St., Downtown* ☎ *503/220–0920*) sells funky retro garb that dates from the '50s through the '80s. Lots of jewelry, shoes, dresses, coats, and even rhinestone tiaras can be found here.

Portland's best store for fine men's and women's clothing, **Mario's** (⊠ *833 SW Morrison St., Downtown* ☎ *503/227–3477*) carries designer lines by Prada, Dolce & Gabbana, Etro, and Loro Piana—among others.

Niketown (⊠ *930 SW 6th Ave., Downtown* ☎ *503/221–6453*), Nike's flagship retail store, has the latest and greatest in swoosh-adorned products. The high-tech setting has athlete profiles, photos, and interactive displays.

Portland Nike Factory Store (⊠ *2650 NE Martin Luther King Jr. Blvd., East of Willamette River* ☎ *503/281–5901*) sells products that have been on the market six months or more.

Portland Outdoor Store (⊠ *304 SW 3rd Ave., Downtown* ☎ *503/222–1051*) stubbornly resists all that is trendy, both in clothes and decor, but if you want authentic western gear—saddles, Stetsons, boots, or cowboy shirts—head here.

Portland Pendleton Shop (⊠ *SW 4th Ave. and Salmon St., Downtown* ☎ *503/242–0037*) stocks clothing by the famous local apparel maker.

Tumbleweed (⊠ *1804 NE Alberta St., East of Willamette River* ☎ *503/335–3100*) carries fun and stylish designer clothing you might describe as "country chic," for the woman who likes to wear flirty feminine dresses with cowboy boots. There's also unique baby and toddler clothing in their children's shop next door.

Zelda's Shoe Bar (⊠ *633 NW 23rd Ave., Nob Hill* ☎ *503/226–0363*), two connected boutiques in Nob Hill, carry a sophisticated, highly eclectic line of women's clothes, accessories, and shoes.

GIFTS

Babik's (⊠ *738 NW 23rd Ave., Nob Hill* ☎ *503/248–1771*) carries an enormous selection of handwoven rugs from Turkey, all made from handspun wool and all-natural dyes.

The **Backyard Bird Shop** (⊠ *8960 SE Sunnyside Rd., Clackamas* ☎ *503/496–0908*) has everything for the bird lover: bird feeders, birdhouses, a huge supply of bird seed, and quality bird-theme gifts ranging from wind chimes to stuffed animals.

Christmas at the Zoo (⊠ *118 NW 23rd Ave., Nob Hill* ☎ *503/223–4048 or*

DID YOU KNOW?

Portland artists are known for their innovation when it comes to creating work reflective of the region. One such artist, Brian Mock (⊕ www.brianmock.com), creates curvaceous women's figures and jumping salmon nearly 7 feet tall by welding recycled nuts, bolts, forks, and hinges. Curious onlookers are left to ponder what better fate might have met Aunt Thelma's toaster other than the dumpster. Mock's work is represented by two area galleries: Exit 21 and Onda galleries.

800/223–5886) is crammed year-round with decorated trees, and has Portland's best selection of European hand-blown glass ornaments and plush animals.

In addition to offering the best eat-in or take-out soups, salads, and desserts, **Elephants Delicatessen** (✉ *111 NW 22nd Ave., Nob Hill* ☎ *503/299–6304)* has a vast gourmet food, cooking utensils, and household section. **La Bottega de Mamma Ro** (✉ *940 NW 23rd Ave., Nob Hill* ☎ *503/241–4960)* carries Italian tabletop and home accessories, including a colorful line of dishes and cloth for tablecloths and napkins.

Made in Oregon (☎ *866/257–0938)*, which sells books, smoked salmon, local wines, Pendleton woolen goods, carvings made of myrtle wood, and other products made in the state, has shops at Portland International Airport, the Lloyd Center, Washington Square, and Clackamas Town Center.

Even without getting a nod from Oprah in her magazine, **Moonstruck** (✉ *526 NW 23rd Ave., Nob Hill* ☎ *503/542–3400)*, would still be known as a chocolatier extraordinaire. Just a couple of the rich confections might sustain you if you're nibbling—water is available for palate cleansing in between treats—but whether you're just grazing or boxing some up for the road, try the Ocumarian Truffle, chocolate laced with chili pepper; the unusual kick of sweetness and warmth is worth experiencing.

Pastaworks (✉ *3735 SE Hawthorne Blvd., East of Willamette River* ☎ *503/232–1010)* sells cookware, fancy deli foods, organic produce, beer, wine, and pasta.

At **Stella's on 21st** (✉ *1108 NW 21st Ave., Nob Hill* ☎ *503/295–5930)* there are eccentric, colorful, and artsy items for the home, including lamps, candles, and decorations, as well as jewelry.

JEWELRY

Carl Greve (✉ *640 SW Broadway St., Downtown* ☎ *503/223–7121)*, in business since 1922, carries exclusive designer lines of fine jewelry, such as Mikimoto pearls, and has the state's only Tiffany boutique. The second floor is reserved for china, stemware, and housewares.

Maloy's Jewelry Workshop (✉ *717 SW 10th Ave., Downtown* ☎ *503/223–4720)* specializes in fine antique pieces, including some from the 18th century. Rare and vintage designs fill the sparkling glass cases.

Real Mother Goose (✉ *901 SW Yamhill St., Downtown* ☎ *503/223–9510)* sells mostly handcrafted, unique artistic pieces. One patron favorite: dangling earrings that incorporate copper wire wrapped around brilliant, colored glass.

MUSIC

Classical Millennium (✉ *3144 E. Burnside St., East of Willamette River* ☎ *503/231–8909)* has the best selection of classical CDs in Oregon.

Music Millennium Northwest (✉ *3158 E. Burnside St., East of Willamette River* ☎ *503/231–8926)* stocks a huge selection of music in every possible category, including local punk groups.

OUTDOOR SUPPLIES

Andy and Bax (✉ *324 SE Grand Ave.*, *East of Willamette River* ☎ *503/234–7538*) is an Army Navy/outdoors store that has good prices on camo gear, rafting supplies, and just about everything else.

Columbia Sportswear (✉ *911 SW Broadway, Downtown* ☎ *503/226–6800* ⊕ *www.columbia.com*), a local legend and global force in recreational outdoor wear, is especially strong in fashionable jackets, pants, and durable shoes.

Next Adventure Sports (✉ *426 SE Grand Ave.*, *East of Willamette River* ☎ *503/233–0706*) carries new and used sporting goods, including camping gear, snowboards, kayaks, and mountaineering supplies.

REI (✉ *1405 NW Johnson St.*, *Pearl District* ☎ *503/221–1938* ⊕ *www. rei.com*) carries clothes and accessories for hiking, biking, camping, fishing, bicycling, or just about any other outdoor activity you can possibly imagine.

PERFUME

Aveda Lifestyle Store and Spa (✉ *500 SW 5th Ave.*, *Downtown* ☎ *503/248–0615*) sells the flower- and herb-based Aveda line of scents and skin-care products.

Perfume House (✉ *3328 SE Hawthorne Blvd.*, *East of Willamette River* ☎ *503/234–5375*) carries hundreds of brand-name fragrances for women and men.

TOYS

Finnegan's Toys and Gifts (✉ *922 SW Yamhill St.*, *Downtown* ☎ *503/221–0306*), downtown Portland's largest toy store, stocks artistic, creative, educational, and other types of toys.

Kids at Heart (✉ *3445 SE Hawthorne Blvd.*, *East of Willamette River* ☎ *503/231–2954*) is a small, colorful toy store on Hawthorne with toys, models, and stuffed animals for kids of all ages.

Thinker Toys (✉ *7784 SW Capitol Hwy.*, *West of Downtown* ☎ *503/245–3936*), which bills itself as Portland's "most hands-on store," offers puppets, games, educational toys, and a large wooden playhouse that kids can hang out in.

SPORTS AND THE OUTDOORS

Portlanders definitely gravitate to the outdoors, and they're well acclimated to the elements year-round—including winter's wind, rain, and cold. Once the sun starts to shine in spring and into summer, the city fills with hikers, joggers, and mountain bikers, who flock to Portland's hundreds of miles of parks, paths, and trails. The Willamette and Columbia rivers are used for boating and water sports—though it's not easy to rent any kind of boat for casual use. Locals also have access to a playground for fishing, camping, skiing, and snowboarding all the way through June, thanks to the proximity of Mt. Hood.

As for competitive sports, Portland is home to several minor-league teams, including the Winterhawks (hockey), Beavers (baseball), and Timbers (soccer). Big-sports fervor is reserved for Trail Blazers

Runners crossing the Hawthorne Bridge

basketball games, held at the Rose Garden arena on the east side of the river. The Portland Visitors' Association, known as Travel Portland, provides information on sports events and outdoor activities in the city.

PARTICIPANT SPORTS

If there's something recreational to be done outdoors, Portlanders will find a way to do it. Because of the many parks, rivers, streams, mountains, and beaches within reach of the city, this region is a playground.

BICYCLING
⇨ *For information on biking, please see the Pedaling Portland feature.*

FISHING
The Columbia and Willamette rivers are major sportfishing streams, with opportunities for angling virtually year-round. Though salmon can still be caught here, runs have been greatly reduced in both rivers in recent years, and the Willamette River is still plagued by pollution. Nevertheless, the Willamette still offers prime fishing for bass, channel catfish, sturgeon, crappies, perch, panfish, and crayfish. It's also a good stream for winter steelhead. June is the top shad month, with some of the best fishing occurring below Willamette Falls at Oregon City. The Columbia River is known for its salmon, sturgeon, walleye, and smelt. The Sandy and Clackamas rivers, near Mt. Hood, are smaller waterways popular with local anglers.

OUTFITTERS Outfitters throughout Portland operate guide services. Few outfitters rent equipment, though, so bring your own or be prepared to buy. **Northwest Flyfishing Outfitters** (✉ *10910 NE Halsey St., East of Willamette*

PORTLAND TOP 5 OUTDOOR TIPS

■ Cheer on the Portland Trail Blazers when they're home playing a basketball game at the Rose Garden.

■ Ski down a Mt. Hood Meadows slope on a crisp, clear, early spring morning—less than an hour's drive away from the city.

■ Rent a bicycle and pedal down Portland's many bike-friendly roads and pathways, or on the Esplanade alongside the Willamette River, in what has been called the number one cycling city in the United States.

■ Hike up and around Mt. Tabor and be rewarded with an awesome view of downtown Portland.

■ Hang out at PGE Park on a warm summer night, hot dog and beer in hand, and watch a Portland Timbers soccer game.

River ☎ *503/252–1529 or 888/292–1137)* specializes in all things fly-fishing, including tackle, rentals, and guided outings.

You can find a broad selection of fishing gear, including rods, reels, and fishing licenses, at **Stewart Fly Shop** (✉ *23830 NE Halsey St., East of Willamette River* ☎ *503/666–2471)*.

REGULATIONS Local sport shops are the best sources of information on current fishing hot spots, which change from year to year. Detailed fishing regulations are available from the **Oregon Department of Fish and Wildlife** (✉ *17330 SE Evelyn St., Clackamas* ☎ *503/947–6000* ⊕ *www.dfw.state.or.us)*.

GOLF

There are several public and top-class golf courses within Portland and just outside the city where you can practice your putt or test your swing. Even in the wet months, Portlanders still golf—and you can bet the first clear day after a wet spell will mean courses fill up with those who have so faithfully waited for the sun. Depending upon the time of year, it's not a bad idea to call ahead and verify wait times.

Broadmoor Golf Course (✉ *3509 NE Columbia Blvd., East of Willamette River* ☎ *503/281–1337)* is an 18-hole, par-72 course where the greens fee runs $24 and an optional cart costs $14 per rider.

At the 18-hole, par-72 **Colwood National Golf Club** (✉ *7313 NE Columbia Blvd., East of Willamette River* ☎ *503/254–5515)*, the greens fee is $29–$33, plus $26 for an optional cart.

Eastmoreland Golf Course (✉ *2425 SE Bybee Blvd., East of Willamette River* ☎ *503/775–2900)* has a highly regarded 18-hole, 72-par course close to the Rhododendron Gardens, Crystal Springs Lake, and Reed College. The greens fee is $15–$37, plus $28 for an optional cart.

Glendoveer Golf Course (✉ *14015 NE Glisan St., East of Willamette River* ☎ *503/253–7507)* has two 18-hole courses, one par-71 and one par-73, and a covered driving range. The greens fee runs $18–$34; carts are $13 for 9 holes, $26 for 18 holes.

Heron Lakes Golf Course (✉ *3500 N. Victory Blvd., west of airport, off N. Marine Dr.* ☎ *503/289–1818)* consists of two 18-hole, par-72 courses:

the Great Blue, generally acknowledged to be the most difficult links in the greater Portland area; and the Greenback. The greens fee at the Green, as it's locally known, is $26–$37, while the fee at the Blue runs $30–$42. An optional cart at either course costs $26.

Pumpkin Ridge Golf Club (✉ *12930 NW Old Pumpkin Ridge Rd., North Plains* ☎ *503/647–4747 or 888/594–4653* ⊕ *www.pumpkinridge.com*) has 36 holes, with the 18-hole Ghost Creek par-71 course open to the public. According to *Golf Digest*, Ghost Creek is one of the best public courses in the nation. Pumpkin Ridge hosted the U.S. Women's Open in 1997 and in 2003. The greens fee is $150; the cart fee is $16.

Rose City Golf Course (✉ *2200 NE 71st Ave., East of Willamette River* ☎ *503/253–4744*) has one 18-hole, par-72 course. Greens fees are $28–$35; carts are $26 for 18 holes.

ICE-SKATING

Ice Chalet at Lloyd Center (✉ *Multnomah St. and NE 9th Ave., East of Willamette River* ☎ *503/288–6073*) is a large rink in the middle of the mall and has open skating and skate rentals ($9 admission includes skate rental). The indoor rinks are open year-round.

SKIING

With fairly easy access to decent skiing nearly eight months out of the year, it's no wonder that skiers love Portland. There are several ski resorts on Mt. Hood, less than an hour's drive away, including Ski Bowl, Mt. Hood Meadows, and Timberline Lodge.

Mountain Shop (✉ *628 NE Broadway, East of Willamette River* ☎ *503/288–6768*) rents skis and equipment. **REI** (✉ *1405 NW Johnson St., Pearl District* ☎ *503/221–1938*) can fill all your ski-equipment rental needs.

SWIMMING

Swimming and sunbathing season in Portland is brief: in summer temperatures are never too hot for too long, while most of the waters—including lakes, rivers, and the Pacific Ocean—remain cold. On those few hot and sunny days, though, locals and visitors flock to these watering holes to cool off and splash around.

Blue Lake Regional Park (✉ *20500 NE Marine Dr., Troutdale* ☎ *503/797–1850*) has a swimming beach that's packed on hot summer days. You can also fish and rent small boats here. This is a great place for a hike on the surrounding trails or for a picnic.

If you feel like tanning au naturel, drive about a half hour northwest of downtown to **Sauvie Island,** a wildlife refuge with a secluded beach-front that's popular with (and legal for) nude sunbathers. If the sky is clear, you'll get a spectacular view from the riverbank of three Cascade peaks—Hood, St. Helens, and Adams. Huge oceangoing vessels cruise by on their way to and from the Port of Portland. To get here, take U.S. 30 north to Sauvie Island bridge, turn right, and follow Reeder Road until you hit gravel. Look for the Collins Beach signs. There's plenty of parking, but a permit is required. You can buy it ($3.50 for a one-day permit, $11 for an annual permit) at the Cracker Barrel country store just over the bridge on the left side of the road.

TENNIS

Portland Parks and Recreation (☎ *503/823–7529* ⊕ *www.portlandonline. com/parks*) operates more than 100 outdoor tennis courts (many with night lighting) at Washington Park, Grant Park, and many other locations. The courts are open on a first-come, first-served basis year-round, but you can reserve one, starting in March, for play May to September.

The **Portland Tennis Center** (✉ *324 NE 12th Ave., just south of I–84* ☎ *503/823–3189*) operates four indoor courts and eight lighted outdoor courts.

The **St. John's Racquet Center** (✉ *7519 N. Burlington Ave., East of Willamette River* ☎ *503/823–3629*) has three indoor courts.

SPECTATOR SPORTS

Since Portland isn't home to a large national football or baseball team, fans tend to show a lot of support for their city's only true professional team, the NBA's Portland Trail Blazers. Fans are also loyal in cheering on their minor-league teams: hockey, auto racing, baseball, and soccer events are well-attended by excited crowds.

BASKETBALL

The **Portland Trail Blazers** (✉ *Rose Garden, 1 Center Ct., East of Willamette River* ☎ *503/797–9617*) of the National Basketball Association play in the Rose Garden.

ICE HOCKEY

The **Portland Winter Hawks** (✉ *Memorial Coliseum, 300 N. Winning Way, East of Willamette River* ☎ *503/236–4295*) of the Western Hockey League play home games September to March at Memorial Coliseum and sometimes at the Rose Garden.

SOCCER

The **Portland Timbers** (✉ *PGE Park, 1844 SW Morrison St., Downtown* ☎ *503/553–5550 for Portland Timbers office, 503/553–5400 for PGE Park*), Portland's major-league soccer team, play at the downtown PGE Park from April through September.

The Willamette Valley and Wine Country

WORD OF MOUTH

"The heart of Oregon's wine country is quite a bit north of Eugene; better as a day trip from Portland if you could figure it out. A couple around Eugene that I know are worth a visit are King Estates and Silvan Ridge."

—beachbum

WELCOME TO THE WILLAMETTE VALLEY AND WINE COUNTRY

TOP REASONS TO GO

★ **Swirl and sip.** Each region in the Willamette Valley offers some of the finest vintages and dining experiences found anywhere.

★ **Soar through the air.** Newberg's hot-air balloons will give you a bird's-eye view of Yamhill's wine country.

★ **Run rapids.** Feel the bouncing exhilaration and the cold spray of white-water rafting on the wild, winding McKenzie River outside Eugene.

★ **Walk on the wild side.** The Jackson Bottom Nature Preserve gives walkers a chance to view otters, beavers, herons, and eagles.

★ **Back the Beavers or Ducks.** Nothing gets the blood pumping like an Oregon State Beaver or University of Oregon Ducks football game.

1 **North Willamette Valley.** Most visitors begin their journey into wine country here, an area rich with upscale dining, shopping, the arts, and wineries. Close to Portland, North Willamette's communities provide all the amenities of urban life with a whole lot less concrete. Wine enthusiasts will relish the excellent vineyards in Beaverton, Hillsboro, and Forest Grove.

2 **Yamhill County.** This part of the state has undergone a renaissance in the last 20 years, as the world has beaten a path to its door, seeking the perfect Pinot. Many of Willamette's highest-rated wineries are here. There are gorgeous inns, wine bars, and unforgettable restaurants providing a complete vacation experience.

3 **Mid-Willamette Valley.** Agriculture is the mainstay of this region; its roadsides are dotted with fruit and veggie stands, and towns boast farmers' markets. Its flat terrain is ideal for bicycle trips and hikes. The state capitol is Salem, and Oregon State University is in Corvallis.

4 **South Willamette Valley.** Here visitors soak in natural hot springs, hike in dense forest, run the rapids, or cheer on the Oregon Ducks. Eugene has a friendly, youthful vibe, which is enhanced by the natural splendor of the region.

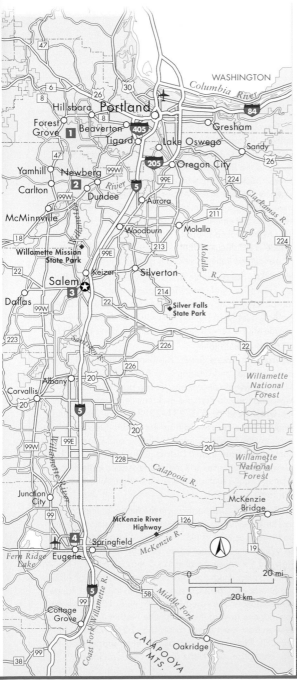

GETTING ORIENTED

3

The Willamette Valley is a fertile mix of urban, rural, and wild, stretching from Portland at the north to Cottage Grove at the south. It is bordered by the Cascade Range to the east and the Coast Range to the west. The Calapooya Mountains border it to the south and the mighty Columbia River runs along the north. Running north and south, Interstate 5 connects communities throughout the valley. In the mid-1800s, the Willamette Valley was the destination of emigrants on the Oregon Trail, and today is home to about two-thirds of the state's population. The Willamette Valley is 150 mi long and up to 60 miwide, which makes it Oregon's largest wine-growing region.

WILLAMETTE VALLEY AND WINE COUNTRY PLANNER

When to Go

July to October are the best times to wander the country roads in the Willamette Valley, exploring the grounds of its many wineries. Fall itself is spectacular, with leaves at their colorful peak in late October. Winters are usually mild, but they can be relentlessly overcast and downright rainy. Visitors not disturbed by dampness or chill will find excellent deals on lodging. In the spring rains continue, but the wildflowers begin to bloom, which pays off at the many gardens and nature parks throughout the valley.

Look high in the sky for evidence of the colorful **Tigard Festival of Balloons** in June—hot-air balloons soar above the town throughout the weekend. Wine lovers flock to McMinnville to sample fine regional vintages in late July and early August during the **International Pinot Noir Celebration.** Eugene hosts the world-class **Oregon Bach Festival,** 19 summer days of classical music performances. In late August and early September the **Oregon State Fair** (☎ 503/947–3247 ⊕ www.oregonstateparks.org) in Salem has 8,000 things to do, see, and taste, ranging from carnival rides, top-name concert performances, animals, carnival-style games, and bodacious rides.

Getting Here and Around

Air Travel. Portland's airport is an hour's drive east of the northern Willamette Valley; The **Aloha Express Airport Shuttle** (☎ 503/356–8848 ⊕ www.alohaexpressshuttle. com) and the **Beaverton Airporter** (☎ 503/760–6565 ⊕ www.beavertonairporter.com) provide shuttle service. **Eugene's Mahlon Sweet Airport** (☎ 541/682–5544 ⊕ www.flyeug.com) is more convenient if you're exploring the region's southern end. It's served by Delta, Horizon, and United/United Express. The flight from Portland to Eugene is 40 minutes. There are smaller airports scattered throughout the valley for private aircraft.

Rental cars are available at the Eugene airport from Budget, Enterprise, and Hertz. Taxis and airport shuttles will transport you to downtown Eugene for about $22. **Omni Shuttle** (☎ 541/461–7959 ⊕ www.omnishuttle.us) will provide shuttle service to and from the Eugene airport from anywhere in Oregon.

Bus Travel. In Forest Grove, Hillsboro, Beaverton, Tigard, Lake Oswego, and Oregon City, **TriMet** (☎ 503/238–7433 ⊕ www.trimet.org) bus service provides frequent transportation into Portland and between these communities. **Greyhound** (☎ 800/231–2222 ⊕ www.greyhound. com) provides bus service from Portland to Newberg, McMinnville, Salem, Corvallis, Albany, and Eugene. Many of the **Lane Transit District** (LTD) (☎ 541/687–5555 ⊕ www.ltd.org) buses will make a few stops to the outskirts of Lane County, such as McKenzie Bridge. All buses have bike racks.

Car Travel. I–5 runs north–south the length of the Willamette Valley. Many Willamette Valley attractions lie not too far east or west of I–5. Highway 22 travels west from the Willamette National Forest through Salem to the coast. Highway 99 travels parallel to I–5 through much of the Willamette Valley. Highway 34 leaves I–5 just south of Albany and heads west, past Corvallis and into the Coast Range, where it follows the Alsea River. Highway 126 heads east from Eugene toward the Willamette National Forest; it travels west from town to the coast. U.S. 20 travels west from Corvallis. Rental cars are available from Budget (Beaverton), Enterprise, and Hertz (both Beaverton, Salem).

About the Restaurants

The buzzwords associated with fine dining in this region are *sustainable, farm-to-table,* and *local.* Fresh salmon, Dungeness crab, mussels, shrimp, and oysters are harvested just a couple of hours away on the Oregon Coast. Lamb, pork, and beef are local and plentiful, and seasonal game appears on many menus. Desserts made with local blueberries, huckleberries, raspberries, and marionberries should not be missed. But what really sets the offerings apart are the splendid local wines that receive worldwide acclaim.

Restaurants in the Willamette Valley are low-key and unpretentious. Expensive doesn't necessarily mean better, and locals have a pretty good nose for good value. Reasonably priced Mexican, Indian, Japanese, and Italian do very well. Food carts in the cities are a growing phenomenon. But there's still nothing like a great, sit-down meal at a cozy bistro for some fresh fish or lamb, washed down with a stellar Pinot Noir.

About the Hotels

One of the great pleasures of touring the Willamette Valley is the incredible selection of small, ornate bed-and-breakfast hotels sprinkled throughout Oregon's wine country. In the summer and fall they can fill up quickly, as visitors come from around the world to enjoy wine tastings at the hundreds of large and small wineries. Many of these have exquisite restaurants right on the premises, with home-baked goods available day and night. There are plenty of larger properties located closer to urban areas and shopping centers, including upscale resorts with expansive spas, as well as national chains that are perfect for folks who just need a place to lay their heads.

WHAT IT COSTS IN U.S. DOLLARS

	¢	$	$$	$$$	$$$$
Restaurants	under $10	$10–$16	$17–$23	$24–$30	over $30
Hotels		under $100	$100–$150	$151–$200	$201–$250	over $250

Restaurant prices are per person, for a main course at dinner. Hotel prices are for two people in a standard double room in high season, excluding tax.

Tour Options

Oregon Wine Tours and **EcoTours of Oregon** provide informative, guided outings across the Willamette Valley wine country.

Contacts EcoTours of Oregon (☎ 503/245–1428 or 888/868–7733 ⊕ www. ecotours-of-oregon.com). **Oregon Wine Tours** (☎ 503/681–9463 ⊕ www. orwinetours.com).

VISITOR INFORMATION

Contacts Chehalem Valley Chamber of Commerce (Newberg, Dundee, and St. Paul) (✉ 415 E. Sheridan ☎ 503/538–2014 ⊕ www. chehalemvalley.org). **Oregon Wine Country/ Willamette Valley Visitors Association** (✉ 553 NW Harrison Blvd., Corvallis ☎ 866/548–5018 ⊕ www.oregonwinecountry. org). **Travel Lane County** (Eugene, Cascades, and Coast) (✉ 754 Olive St., Eugene ☎ 541/343–6335 or 800/547–5445 ⊕ www.travellanecounty. org). **Washington County Visitors Association** (Beaverton, Forest Grove, Hillsboro, Tigard, and Tualatin) (✉ 11000 SW Stratus St., Suite 170, Beaverton ☎ 503/644–5555 ⊕ www. visitwashingtoncountyoregon. com). **Yamhill Valley Visitors Association** (☎ 503/883–7770 ⊕ www.yamhillvalley.org).

3

Updated by
John Doerper
and Deston S.
Nokes

The Willamette (pronounced "wil-*lam*-it") Valley has become a wine lovers' Shangri-la, particularly in the northern Yamhill and Washington counties. An entire tourism industry has sprung up between Interstate 5 and the Oregon Coast, encompassing small hotels and inns, cozy restaurants, and casual wine bars.

The valley divides two mountain ranges (the Cascades and Coast), and contains more than 200 wineries. The huge wine region is made up of six subappellations: Chehalem Mountains, Ribbon Ridge, Dundee Hills, Yamhill-Carlton, Eola-Amity Hills, and McMinnville. (⇨ *See the Wine feature on p. 158 for tours by AVA.*) With its incredibly rich soil perfect for growing Pinot Noir, Pinot Gris, Chardonnay, and Riesling, the valley has received worldwide acclaim for its vintages. The region's farms are famous for producing quality fruits, vegetables, and cheeses that are savored in area restaurants. During spring and summer there are many roadside stands dotting the country lanes, and farmers' markets appear in most of the valley's towns. Also delicious are the locally raised lamb, pork, and beef. The valley also is a huge exporter of plants and flowers for nurseries, with a large number of farms growing ornamental trees, bulbs, and plants.

The valley definitely has an artsy, expressive, and fun side, with its wine and beer festivals, theater, music, crafts, and even ballooning. Many folks are serious runners and bicyclists, particularly in Corvallis and Eugene, so pay attention while driving.

The entire state is riveted by the collegiate rivalry between the Willamette Valley–based Oregon State Beavers in Corvallis and University of Oregon Ducks in Eugene. In these towns businesses think nothing of closing for the home football games, and getting a ticket to the "civil war" game between the two is a feat in itself.

NORTH WILLAMETTE VALLEY

Just outside Portland the suburban areas of Beaverton, Tigard, Hillsboro, and Forest Grove have gorgeous wineries, wetlands, rivers, and nature preserves. In the shadow of Nike headquarters, the area has a wealth of golfing, bicycling, and trails for running and hiking. From its wetlands to the residential neighborhoods, it's not unusual to spot red-tail hawks, beavers, and ducks on your route. Shopping, fine dining, and proximity to Portland make this a great area in which to begin your exploration of the Willamette Valley and the wine country.

3

EN
ROUTE

Vineyard and Valley Scenic Tour. Oregon's newest driving route, the Vineyard and Valley Scenic Tour Route, is a 50-mi drive through the lush Tualatin Valley, which runs between the city of Sherwood to the southern part of the valley and the Swiss-settled Helvetia at the northern end. The rural driving route showcases much of Washington County's agricultural bounty, including 17 of the county's 21 wineries and several farms (some with stands offering seasonal fresh produce and/or U-pick), along with pioneer and historic sites, wildlife refuges, and scenic viewpoints of the Cascade Mountains. For more information, contact the **Washington County Visitors Association** (☎ *503/644–5555* ⊕ *www. visitwashingtoncountyoregon.com*).

BEAVERTON

10 mi southwest of Portland.

Named for its location in the midst of a large network of beaver dams, Beaverton has itself become a network of residential neighborhoods, shopping areas, and business parks spanning 15 square mi. Once a small town surrounded by thriving Washington County farm fields, Beaverton today has well over 75,000 residents, and is the fifth-largest community in Oregon. Just 10 mi from Portland, it is considered Portland's long-expanding, affluent suburb to the west. The roots of Oregon's Silicon Forest are in Beaverton, with some of the state's largest high-tech employers contributing to the town's popularity. Among Beaverton's high-profile employers are Adidas and Nike, whose famous world-headquarters campus is regularly visited by celebrities. The town has more than 100 parks spread over 1,000 acres. There is an extensive system of hiking trails and bike paths, as well as numerous public and private golf courses and tennis courts.

GETTING HERE

Beaverton is just 21 mi from Portland International Airport. The **Aloha Express Airport Shuttle** (☎ *503/356–8848* ⊕ *www.alohaexpressshuttle.com*) and the **Beaverton Airporter** (☎ *503/760–6565* ⊕ *www.beavertonairporter. com*) provide shuttle service.

Beaverton borders U.S. 26 to the north, linking the community to west Portland and the Oregon Coast. Highway 217 intersects Beaverton and links it with I–5. The only thing holding you back from driving to the wine country from downtown is the commuter and shopping traffic. MAX light rail connects Beaverton with Portland and Hillsboro, and

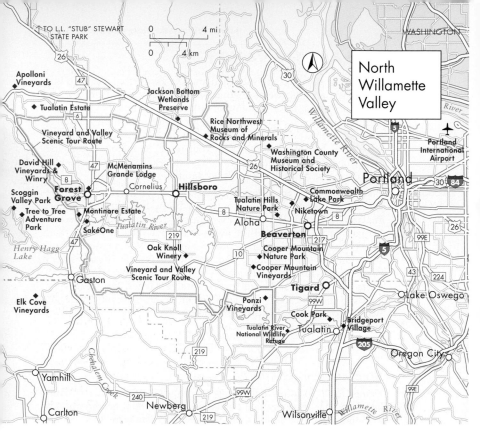

there is bus service to the neighboring cities of Tigard, Tualatin, and Lake Oswego.

VISITOR INFORMATION
Washington County Visitors Association (✉ *11000 SW Stratus St., Suite 170, Beaverton* ☎ *503/644–5555* ⊕ *www.visitwashingtoncountyoregon. com*)

EXPLORING

Beaverton Farmers Market. Oregon's largest all-agricultural market boasts one of the largest selections of nursery stock in the region. The market has been recognized as one of the best farmers' markets on the West Coast. In 2008 the Beaverton Farmers Market celebrated 20 years of bringing quality fruits, berries, vegetables, flowers, meats, and baked goods to the public. Live entertainment and family activities are featured each week. ✉ *12455 SW 5th St., Beaverton* ☎ *503/643–5345* ⊕ *www.beavertonfarmersmarket.com* ☉ *May–Oct., Sat. 8–1:30; mid-June–Aug., Wed. 3–6*

WINERIES

Cooper Mountain Vineyards. This vineyard prides itself on creating wines made from organic grapes. It uses natural preparations, rather than man-made chemicals, to enhance its vines by repairing and building its soils to help provide ideal growing conditions. It features Pinot Noir, Pinot Gris, Chardonnay, Pinot Blanc, and Malbec. One interesting tidbit is that this 121-acre vineyard is situated on an extinct volcano. ✉ *9480 SW Grabhorn Rd., Beaverton* ☎ *503/649–0027* ⊕ *www. coopermountainwine.com)*

Fodor's Choice
★
Ponzi Vineyards. Completed in 2008, the new Ponzi Vineyards winery is a sustainable, four-level gravity-flow facility on one of the Chehalem Mountains' slopes. Its gravity-flow process eliminates unnecessary use of forceful pumps or pressure to move the wine from one stage to the next. The Ponzi family also launched the BridgePort Brewing Company in 1984, and runs a wine bar and restaurant in Dundee *(⇨ Dundee Bistro in Dundee).* The winery is open daily 10–5. ✉ *14665 SW Winery La., Beaverton* ☎ *503/628–1227* ⊕ *www.ponziwines.com.*

3

WHERE TO EAT

$
AMERICAN
Fodor's Choice
★
✗ **Café Murrayhill.** You don't have to journey downtown to enjoy artful cuisine. The breakfasts here are inventive and hearty, with an assortment of Benedicts. Sandwiches are stellar, and dinners range from simple roasted turkey to pan-seared sea scallops over risotto. Try the buttery, grilled mahi mahi with lobster ravioli. It also serves a nice selection of Northwest wines. ✉ *14500 Murray-Scholls Dr., Beaverton* ☎ *503/590–6030* ⊕ *www.cafemurrayhill.com* ▭ *AE, D, MC, V.*

$$
CONTINENTAL
✗ **Decarli.** Showcasing the state's considerable bounty of seasonal ingredients, chef Paul Decarli's culinary style draws on his Swiss/Italian-American roots. He creates food that is at once sophisticated and rustic. Working alongside his wife Jan, Decarli presents an authentically local, delicious experience. ✉ *4545 SW Watson Ave., Beaverton* ☎ *503/641–3223* ⊕ *www.decarlirestaurant.com* ▭ *AE, D, MC, V* ☻ *No lunch. Closed Mon.*

$$
SEAFOOD
✗ **McCormick's Fish House & Bar.** The neighborhood feeling of this restaurant belies its association with the national chain. Try creative seasonal preparations such as macadamia nut–crusted Alaskan halibut with mango beurre blanc or salmon baked on a cedar plank. Mounted fish are displayed on the ceiling of the rusty-brown main dining room. The restaurant is popular as a fine night out and is open late—until 11 weeknights, until midnight weekends. ✉ *9945 SW Beaverton–Hillsdale Hwy., Beaverton* ☎ *503/643–1322* ⊕ *www.mccormickandschmicks. com* ▭ *AE, D, DC, MC, V* ☻ *No lunch Sun.*

SHOPPING

Washington Square. One of the largest retail centers in the state has 170 nationally recognized retail shops, including high-end retailers such as Coach, and five anchor department stores, including Macy's, Dick's Sporting Goods, and the largest Nordstrom in Oregon. In addition to a food court and several eateries, the mall also houses local favorite Newport Bay seafood restaurant, as well as the only Cheesecake Factory in the state. ✉ *9585 SW Washington Square Rd., Beaverton* ☎ *503/639–8860* ⊕ *www.shopwashingtonsquare.com* ☻ *Mon.–Sat. 10–9, Sun. 10–7.*

SPORTS AND THE OUTDOORS

RECREATIONAL AREAS

Commonwealth Lake Park. This park has 22 acres of athletic fields, play equipment for rent, trails, wetlands, and a 3-acre fishing lake. It's a great place to hang out with the ducks. ⊠ *SW Huntington Ave. and SW Foothills Dr., Beaverton* ☎ *503/645–6433* ⊕ *www.thprd.org/parks.*

Cooper Mountain Nature Park. Opened in summer 2009, this park features spectacular views of the Chehalem Mountains and the Tualatin Valley. It has 3 mi of trails (including one loop that is wheelchair accessible) with varying difficulty through the mountain's three distinct habitats—orest, prairie, and oak woodlands. Gardens at the nature center showcase native and drought-tolerant plants, and hikers will have the opportunity to experience the native trees and wildflowers and rare animal species, such as the northern red-legged frog and the western gray squirrel. ⊠ *18892 SW Kemmer Rd., Beaverton* ☎ *503/797–1850* ⊕ *www.oregonmetro.gov/index.cfm/go/by.web/id=16016.*

Tualatin Hills Nature Park. A real forest oasis in the middle of Oregon's Silicon Valley has creeks, ponds, fir trees, and red cedars. The 222-acre urban wilderness has, appropriately, beavers, as well as great blue herons and dozens of other bird species. There are several trails, some with boardwalks, picnic areas, restrooms, and two paved trails. To reach the park, take the MAX light rail to the Merlo Road station or take Buses 57 or 62. No dogs are allowed. ⊠ *15655 SW Millikan Blvd., Beaverton* ☎ *503/629–6350* ⊕ *www.thprd.com/parks/thnp.cfm.*

GOLF

RedTail Golf Course. Named after the red-tailed hawks that nest in the surrounding trees, this 18-hole course has been renovated and upgraded to championship status. RedTail is a challenge for golfers of all levels. Rolling hills, picturesque water hazards and tree-lined fairways make play a joy. RedTail holds a course rating of 74.4 and a slope of 136. It also has a large club fitting and demo facility, and offers private or group instruction. ⊠ *8200 SW Scholls Ferry Rd., Beaverton* ☎ *503/646–5166* ⊕ *www.golfredtail.com* ⛳ *18 holes: $42 Fri.–Sun., $33 Mon.–Thurs.*

Reserve Vineyards & Golf. The Reserve's North and South courses deliver diverse experiences in one location. The South Course (designed by John Fought) has trees and terrain that are pure Willamette Valley in character, whereas the North Course (designed by Bob Cupp) evokes a sense of playing among Oregon's coastal dunes. Golf Digest just proclaimed it one of the state's best courses. The club's Vintage Room features Northwest-inspired cuisine and fine wines from notable local vineyards: Lange Winery, J. Albin, and Oak Knoll. Its deck provides gorgeous sunset views in the summer, and its Summer Music Series features many of the Northwest's most talented jazz musicians. ⊠ *4805 SW 229th Ave., Aloha* ☎ *503/649–8191* ⊕ *www.reservegolf.com* ⛳ *18 holes: $30–$59.*

HILLSBORO

10 mi west of Beaverton on Hwy. 8.

Hillsboro offers a wealth of eclectic shops, preserves, restaurants, and proximity to the valley's fine wineries. In the past 20 years Hillsboro has experienced rapid growth associated with the Silicon Forest, where high-tech business found ample sprawling room. Several of Intel's industrial campuses are in Hillsboro, as are the facilities of other leading electronics manufacturers. Businesses related to the town's original agricultural roots remain a significant part of Hillsboro's culture and economy. Alpaca ranches, nurseries, berry farms, nut and fruit orchards, and numerous wineries are among the area's most active agricultural businesses.

GETTING HERE

Hillsboro is about a 45-minute drive west from Portland International Airport. The **Aloha Express Airport Shuttle** (☎ *503/356-8848* ⊕ *www. alohaexpressshuttle.com*) and the **Beaverton Airporter** (☎ *503/760-6565* ⊕ *www.beavertonairporter.com*) provide shuttle service.

From downtown Portland it's a short, 20-minute car ride, or visitors can ride the MAX light rail. The TriMet Bus Service connects to the MAX light rail in Hillsboro, with connections to Beaverton, Aloha, and other commercial areas.

VISITOR INFORMATION

Washington County Visitors Association (✉ *11000 SW Stratus St., Suite 170, Beaverton* ☎ *503/644–5555* ⊕ *www.visitwashingtoncountyoregon.com*)

EXPLORING

Hillsboro Saturday Market. Fresh local produce—some from booths, some from the backs of trucks—as well as local arts and crafts are all here. Live music is played throughout the day, and it's just a block from the light-rail line. ✉ *Main St. between 1st and 2nd Aves., and along 2nd Ave. between Main and Lincoln Sts., Hillsboro* ☎ *503/844–6685* ⊕ *www.hillsboromarkets.org* ⊗ *May–Oct., Sat. 8–1:30.*

⟳ **Rice Northwest Museum of Rocks and Minerals.** In 1938 Richard and Helen Rice began collecting beach agates. Over the years they developed one of the largest private mineral collections in the United States. The most popular item here is the Alma Rose rhodochrosite, a 4-inch red crystal. The museum (in a ranch-style home) also has petrified wood from all over the world and a gallery of Northwest minerals—including specimens of rare crystallized gold. ✉ *26385 NW Groveland Dr., Hillsboro* ☎ *503/647–2418* ⊕ *www.ricenorthwestmuseum.org* 🖃 *$7* ⊗ *Wed.–Sun. 1–5.*

Washington County Museum and Historical Society. Catch a glimpse of history through exhibits on early pioneers and the Tualatin Indians. Exhibits rotate, usually with a hands-on display geared toward children. ✉ *17677 NW Springville Rd., Hillsboro* ☎ *503/645–5353* ⊕ *www. washingtoncountymuseum.org* 🖃 *$3; free on Mon.* ⊗ *Mon.–Sat. 10–4.*

WINERIES

Oak Knoll. This is one of the closest wineries to Portland, but once you're on the property, you're a world away, with views of the surrounding Chehalem mountain ridge. Its tastings offer a selection of Oak Knoll wines, some of which are only available at the winery. Oak Knoll is lauded for its Pinot Noir, Chardonnay, Riesling, and Pinot Gris. It also produces an unoaked Chardonnay, a slightly sweet, spätlese-styled Riesling, and a Native American varietal, Niagara. The vineyard's large manicured lawn is ideal for picnics or a wine-tour lunch stop. ⊠ *29700 SW Burkhalter Rd., Hillsboro* ☎ *503/648–8198 or 800/625–5665* ⊕ *www.oakknollwinery.com* ⊙ *Weekdays 11–6, weekends 11–5.*

WHERE TO EAT

$ ✕ **Chennai Masala.** Whether it's a creamy, zesty lamb korma or a garlic-
INDIAN   topped slab of nan, this Indian eatery hits the spicy spot. If you're brave, try the Channa Masala, an incredibly hot chickpea curry. There are plenty of vegetarian and kids' options, too. ⊠ *2088 NW Stucki Ave., Hillsboro* ☎ *503/531–9500* ⊕ *www.chennaimasala.net* ▭ *MC, V* ⊙ *Closed Mon.*

$ ✕ **Mazatlan Mexican Restaurant.** Though it's hidden away in a small
MEXICAN   shopping mall, this spot feels like a small village inside, with stunning murals and ceramic wall furnishings. Try the Mazatlan Dinner, a house specialty with sirloin, a chile relleno, and an enchilada, or *arroz con camarones,* prawns sautéed with vegetables. Save room for the flan or the *sopapillas* (fried dough). The kids' menu is a good value. ⊠ *20413 SW TV Hwy., Aloha* ⊕ *www.mazatlanmexicanrestaurant.com* ☎ *503/591–9536* ▭ *AE, D, MC, V.*

$ ✕ **Syun Izakaya.** This Japanese restaurant has a large assortment of sushi
JAPANESE   and sashimi, soups, and salads. It also has wonderful grilled and fried meats and vegetables, and a vast sake selection. The tempura is a must. During happy hour (between 5 and 6 PM) there are lots of small plates for $5–$7. The chicken nuggets are a hit with the kids. ⊠ *209 NE Lincoln St., Hillsboro* ☎ *503/640–3131* ▭ *MC, V* ⊙ *No lunch Sun.*

NIGHTLIFE AND THE ARTS

Venetian Theatre and Bistro. An Italian restaurant, wine bar, performing-arts venue, and movie theater all in one. In a historic theater in downtown Hillsboro, the Venetian Theatre and Bistro is home to a local theater company, Bag & Baggage Productions, and also hosts concerts and live lounge entertainment, all in addition to being a second-run movie theater. The wine bar offers a vast selection of wines from Oregon, Washington, California, and across the globe. ⊠ *253 E. Main St., Hillsboro* ☎ *503/693–3953* ⊕ *www.venetiantheatre.com.*

SPORTS AND THE OUTDOORS

RECREATIONAL   **Jackson Bottom Wetlands Preserve.** Several miles of trails in this 710-acre
AREAS   floodplain and woods are home to thousands of ducks and geese, deer, otters, beavers, herons, and eagles. Walking trails allow birders and other animal watchers to explore the wetlands for a chance to catch a glimpse of indigenous and migrating creatures in their own habitats. The **Educational Center** has several hands-on exhibits, as well as a real bald eagle's nest that was rescued from the wild, and completely preserved (and sanitized) for public display. There's also an exhibit hall with hands-on activities and a gift shop. No dogs or bicycles are allowed. ⊠ *2600 SW Hillsboro Hwy., Hillsboro* ☎ *503/681–6206* ⊕ *www.jacksonbottom.org* ▭ *$2 suggested donation* ⊙ *Mon.–Sun. 10–4.*

⟳   **L.L. "Stub" Stewart State Park.** This 1,654-acre, full-service park has hiking, biking, and horseback riding trails for day use or overnight camping. There are full hookup sites, tent sites, small cabins, and even a horse camp. Lush rolling hills, forests, and deep canyons are terrific for

David Hill Vineyards and Winery, Forest Grove

bird-watching, wildflower walks, and other relaxing pursuits. ✉ *30380 NW Hwy. 47, Buxton* ☎ *503/324–0606* ⊕ *www.oregonstateparks.org.*

FOREST GROVE

6 mi west of Hillsboro on Hwy. 8.

This small town is surrounded by stands of Douglas firs and giant sequoia, including the largest giant sequoia in the state. There are nearby wetlands, birding, the Hagg Lake Recreation Area, a new out-door adventure park, and numerous wineries and tasting rooms. To get to the wineries, head south from Forest Grove on Highway 47 and watch for the blue road signs between Forest Grove, Gaston, and Yamhill.

GETTING HERE

Forest Grove is about an hour's drive west from Portland International Airport. The **Aloha Express Airport Shuttle** (☎ *503/356–8848* ⊕ *www. alohaexpressshuttle.com*) and the **Beaverton Airporter** (☎ *503/760–6565* ⊕ *www.beavertonairporter.com*) provide shuttle service.

From downtown Portland it's a short 35-minute car ride with only one traffic light during the entire trip. TriMet Bus Service provides bus service to and from Forest Grove every 15 minutes, connecting to the MAX light rail 6 mi east in Hillsboro, which continues into Portland. Buses travel to Cornelius, Hillsboro, Aloha, and Beaverton.

VISITOR INFORMATION

Forest Grove Chamber of Commerce (✉ *2417 Pacific Ave., Forest Grove* ☎ *503/357–3006* ⊕ *www.fgchamber.org*).

EXPLORING

Pacific University. With 1,800 students, this shady campus provides a respite from wine tasting and other outdoor recreation. It was founded in 1849, making it one of the oldest educational institutions in the western United States. Concerts and special events are held in McCready Hall in the Taylor-Meade Performing Arts Center. ⊠ *2043 College Way, Forest Grove* ☎ *503/357–6151* ⊕ *www.pacificu.edu.*

WINERIES

Apolloni Vineyards. At the north end of the Willamette Valley, this winery produces premium Pinot Noir, Pinot Gris, and Pinot Blanc grapes, specializing in traditional Pinot Noir and Italian-style wines. The white wines Alfredo Apollini makes are dry, fruity, crisp, and clean. The Pinot Noir is made in a traditional Oregon style, bringing the best of Old and New World winemaking. Alfredo uses only French oak barrels to craft a supple, elegant Pinot Noir. ⊠ *14135 NW Timmerman Rd., Forest Grove* ☎ *503/330–5946* ⊕ *www.apolloni.com* ⊗ *Fri.–Sun. noon–5.*

David Hill Vineyards and Winery. The David Hill Winery has splendid views of the Tualatin Valley from one of Oregon's oldest winery sites. It produces Pinot Noir, Chardonnay, Gewürztraminer, Merlot, Tempranillo, Pinot Gris, Riesling, Sauvignon Blanc, and several Rhône blends. They're well made and pleasant, especially the eclectic blends called Farmhouse Red and Farmhouse White and the estate Pinot Gris. Private tastings are only for groups of 8 to 20 people. ⊠ *46350 NW David Hill Rd., Forest Grove* ☎ *503/992–8545* ⊕ *www.davidhillwinery.com* ⊗ *Daily 5:30–7.*

Elk Cove Vineyard. Founded in 1974 by Pat and Joe Campbell, Elk Cove Vineyards is another older, well-established Oregon winery, with 600 acres on four separate vineyard sites. The winery's focus is on Willamette Valley Pinot Noir, Pinot Gris, and Pinot Blanc. ⊠ *27751 NW Olson Rd., Gaston* ☎ *503/985–7760 or 877/355–2683* ⊕ *www.elkcove. com* 🖃 *$5* ⊗ *Daily 10–5.*

Montinore Estate. Locals chuckle at visitors who try to show off their French savvy when they pronounce "Montinore." The estate, originally a ranch, was established by a tycoon who'd made his money in the Montana mines before he retired to Oregon; he decided to call his estate "Montana in Oregon." Montinore has 232 acres of vineyards, and its wines reflect their high-quality soil and fruit. Highlights include a crisp Gewürztraminer, a light Müller-Thurgau, an off-dry Riesling, a lush Pinot Noir, and a refreshing Pinot Gris that's a perfect partner for Northwest seafood. It also has a Pinot Noir Port. The tasting-room staff is among the friendliest and most knowledgeable in Oregon wine country. ⊠ *3663 SW Dilley Rd., Forest Grove* ☎ *503/359–5012* ⊕ *www. montinore.com* ⊗ *Daily 11–5.*

SakéOne. The world's only American-owned and -operated sakéry resides in Oregon. After SakéOne's founders realized that the country's best water supply for Saké was the Pacific Northwest, they built their brewery in Forest Grove in 1997. Its free tours are a great way to develop an appreciation for fine Saké and learn the importance of each ingredient. ⊠ *820 Elm St., Forest Grove* ☎ *503/357–7056 or 800/550–7253* ⊕ *www.sakeone.com* ☏ *Flights $3–$10* ☉ *Daily 11–5.*

Tualatin Estate Vineyards. Established in 1973, Tualatin Estate's 200-acre vineyard has produced world-renowned wines, including winning Best of Show for both the red and white categories at the London International Wine Competition in the same year. It offers Pinot Noir, Chardonnay, Gewürztraminer, and semisparkling Muscat. ⊠ *10850 NW Seavey Rd., Forest Grove* ☎ *503/357–5005* ⊕ *www.tualatinestate.com* ☉ *Mar.–Dec., weekends noon–5.*

WHERE TO STAY

⊞ **McMenamins Grand Lodge.** On 13 acres of pastoral countryside, this converted Masonic rest home has accommodations that run from bunk-bed rooms to a three-room fireplace suite. Its sturdy 1922 brick buildings also include pubs that serve several McMenamins draft beers. Rooms are furnished with period antiques such as oak nightstands and porcelain sinks. In the Compass Room Theater, feature films are screened nightly; kids accompanied by a guardian are permitted at the early show. Often, there's live music, too. **Pros:** relaxed, friendly brewpub atmosphere. **Cons:** not as refined as some tourists would like. ⊠ *3505 Pacific Ave., Forest Grove* ☎ *503/992–9533 or 877/992–9533* ⊕ *www.thegrandlodge.com* ⤳ *77 rooms* ⚬ *In-hotel: 2 restaurants, bars, spa, golf* ☐ *AE, D, DC, MC, V.*

SPORTS AND THE OUTDOORS

RECREATIONAL AREAS **Scoggin Valley Park and Henry Hagg Lake.** This beautiful area in the Coast Range foothills has a 15-mi-long hiking trail that surrounds the lake. Bird-watching is best in spring. Recreational activities include fishing, boating, waterskiing, picnicking, and hiking, and a 10½-mi, well-marked bicycle lane parallels the park's perimeter road. There's even a disc golf course. ⊠ *Scoggin Valley Rd., Gaston* ☎ *503/359–5732* ⊕ *www.co.washington.or.us* ☏ *$5* ☉ *Mar.–Nov., daily sunrise–sunset.*

Tree to Tree Adventure Park. This is the first public aerial adventure park in the Pacific Northwest—and only the second of its kind in the United States. The park, which opened in June 2010, welcomes explorers of all ages to test their agility on 40 courses, featuring zip lines, ropes, and tunnels. The courses range from beginner to extreme, with certified and trained instructors providing guidance to adventurers. The park has a course for children and shorter adults less than 5-feet tall. Harnesses and helmets are provided, and no open-toed shoes are allowed. ⊠ *2975 SW Nelson Rd., Gaston* ☎ *503/357–0109* ⊕ *www.treetotreeadventurepark. com* ☏ *$30 half course, $39 full course* ☉ *Weekdays 10–4, weekends 10–4:30.*

TIGARD

10 mi southwest of Portland, 5 mi south of Beaverton.

This Portland suburb has made great strides in attracting visitors with its festivals and shopping options. Its old downtown Main Street is enjoying a rebirth with antiques shops, espresso bars, and fashionable

Tigard Festival of Balloons 2010

eateries. Its shopping center, Bridgeport Village, is a magnet for excellent dining, boutique shopping, and movies.

GETTING HERE

Tigard is about 20 mi southwest of Portland International Airport driving on I–84 and I–5. The **Aloha Express Airport Shuttle** (☎ *503/356–8848* ⊕ *www.alohaexpressshuttle.com*) and the **Beaverton Airporter** (☎ *503/760–6565* ⊕ *www.beavertonairporter.com*) provide shuttle service.

Sitting on 99W, Tigard also is the gateway to the Oregon wine country, just 17 mi from the small town of Dundee. Tigard has frequent TriMet bus service into Portland and the neighboring communities of Beaverton, Lake Oswego and Tualatin. It also is 40 mi north of Salem on I–5.

VISITOR INFORMATION

Tigard Area Chamber of Commerce (✉ *12345 SW Main St., Tigard* ☎ *503/639–1656* ⊕ *www.tigardchamber.org*)

EXPLORING

Tualatin River Wildlife Refuge. The Tualatin River National Wildlife Refuge is located in Sherwood (about 12 mi south of downtown Portland). It is a sanctuary for indigenous and migrating birds, waterfowl, and mammals. As one of only a handful of national urban refuges in the United States, it has restored much of the natural landscape common to western Oregon prior to human settlement. The refuge is home to nearly 200 species of birds, 50 species of mammals, 25 species of reptiles and amphibians, and a variety of insects, fish, and plants. It features an interpretive center, a gift shop, photography blinds, and restrooms.

This restoration has attracted animals back to the area in great numbers, and with a keen eye, birders and animal watchers can catch a glimpse of these creatures year-round. In May the refuge holds its Migratory Songbird Festival. ✉ *19255 SW Pacific Hwy., Sherwood* ☎ *503/625–5945* 🌐 *wwwxfws.gov/tualatinriver.com.*

TIGARD FESTIVAL OF BALLOONS

In late June, activity at Cook Park reaches a fever pitch with the three-day hot-air balloon festival, which draws more than 20,000 people to enjoy dozens of hot-air balloons and events morning, noon, and night. (🌐 *www.tigardballoon.org*).

WHERE TO EAT AND STAY

$ ITALIAN ✕ **Café Allegro.** In the heart of Old Town Tigard, Café Allegro serves authentic Italian cuisine in a cozy bistro setting. The rustic decor provides a funky backdrop to tasty fresh salads, hearty pasta dishes and pizzas, and a variety of desserts. The Greek fettuccine is a tantalizing choice, and the small football-size meat calzone is a mighty plunge into decadence. ✉ *12386 SW Main St., Tigard* ☎ *503/684–0130* 🌐 *www.cafeallegrotigard.com* ▭ *AE, D, MC, V* ⊗ *No lunch Sun.*

¢ MEXICAN Fodor's Choice ★ ✕ **Sanchez Taqueria.** It may not look like much from the outside, but the Mexican food at this simple family restaurant has no peer. From its mole and crispy *sopes* (corn cakes) to its carnita enchiladas, the food is fresh and sumptuously authentic. Wash it all down with a cup of *orchata*, a drink made of rice, milk, and cinnamon. ✉ *13050 SW Pacific Hwy., Tigard* ☎ *503/684–2838* ▭ *MC, V.*

$ **The Grand Hotel at Bridgeport.** This independent hotel, opened in 2009, offers luxurious business-class accommodations and amenities, including a free, chef-prepared breakfast. Extremely attractive and comfortable, this property is steps away from tax-free shopping at Bridgeport Village, one of Oregon's premier shopping, dining, and entertainment centers. Built as a green hotel from the ground up, 124 rooms are dedicated to earth-friendly, sustainable practices, which include energy-efficient appliances and light bulbs, as well as recycling bins in all guest rooms and public areas. Each oversized room and suite comes with leather furniture in the living-room area and a desk. **Pros:** next to great shopping and dining. **Cons:** in a shopping center. ✉ *7265 SW Hazel Fern Rd., Tigard* ☎ *503/968–5757 or 866/968–5757* 🌐 *grandhotel-bridgeport.com* *124 rooms* *In-room: Wi-Fi, refrigerator. In-hotel: Pool, spa, gym, parking* ▭ *AE, MC, V* *BP.*

NIGHTLIFE AND THE ARTS

Broadway Rose Theatre Company. This professional musical theater company has earned rave reviews for its productions, ranging from new to well-known musicals. Performances have included *A Chorus Line*, *The King and I*, and *Honky Tonk Angels*, and kids' productions, such as *Aladdin*. Its summer performances are held in the Deb Fennell Auditorium. Other performances are held at the Broadway Rose New Stage Theatre. ✉ *Box office: 12850 SW Grant Ave., Tigard* ☎ *503/620–5262* 🌐 *www.broadwayrose.com* ⊗ *Mon–Fri., 10–6.*

SHOPPING

Bridgeport Village. This complex diverts more cars off Interstate 5 than any other site in the Willamette Valley. With 500,000 square feet of upscale shops, boutiques, eateries, and a luxury spa, the outdoor mall is a magnet for residents and visitors. It also has the largest multiscreen cinema in the state, including an IMAX theater. ⊠ *7455 SW Bridgeport Rd., Tigard* ☎ *503/968–8940* ⊕ *www.bridgeport-village.com.*

Stash Tea & Catalog Retail Store. Daily tea tastings are a welcome change of pace at this nationally recognized tea producer. An exclusive retail store showcases a large selection of its bagged and loose-leaf teas. It also sells seasonal and rare varieties, as well as artful gifts and teapots for tea lovers. ⊠ *7250 SW Durham Rd., Tigard* ☎ *503/603–9905* ⊕ *www. bridgeport-village.com* ⊘ *Tues.–Fri. 10–6, Sat. and Sun. 10–4.*

SPORTS AND THE OUTDOORS

RECREATIONAL AREAS   **Cook Park.** On the banks of the Tualatin River, this 79-acre park is where suburbanites gather to enjoy a variety of team sports. The park has horseshoe pits, a fishing dock, small boat ramp, picnic shelters, and several walking trails and bike paths. Wildlife includes great blue herons and river otters. Cook Park is located south of Durham Road at the end of 92nd Avenue near Tigard High School. ⊠ *17005 SW 92nd Ave., Tigard* ☎ *503/718–2641.*

BOATING   **Tualatin River.** The Tualatin River is a slow, meandering river, with fantastic opportunities for paddlers who are new to the sport, as well those who are experienced. With several launch points along the river, paddlers can plan to set out on the river independently, or as part of a planned expedition with the **Tualatin Riverkeepers** (☎ *503/620–7507* ⊕ *www.tualatinriverkeepers.org*).

YAMHILL COUNTY

Yamhill County, at the northern end of the Willamette Valley, has a fortunate confluence of perfect soils, a benign climate, and talented winemakers who craft world-class vintages. In recent years several new wineries have been built in Yamhill County's hills, as well as its flatlands. While vineyards flourished in the northern Willamette Valley in the 19th century, viticulture didn't arrive in Yamhill County until the 1960s and 1970s, with such pioneers as Dick Erath (Erath Vineyards Winery), David and Ginny Adelsheim (Adelsheim Vineyard), and David and Diana Lett (The Eyrie Vineyards). The focus of much of the county's enthusiasm lies in the Red Hills of Dundee, where the farming towns of Newberg, Dundee, Yamhill, and Carlton have made room for upscale bed-and-breakfasts, spas, wine bars, and tourists seeking that perfect swirl and sip.

The Yamhill County wineries are only a short drive from Portland, and the roads, especially Route 99W and Route 18, definitely can be crowded on weekends—that's because these roads link suburban Portland communities to the popular Oregon Coast.

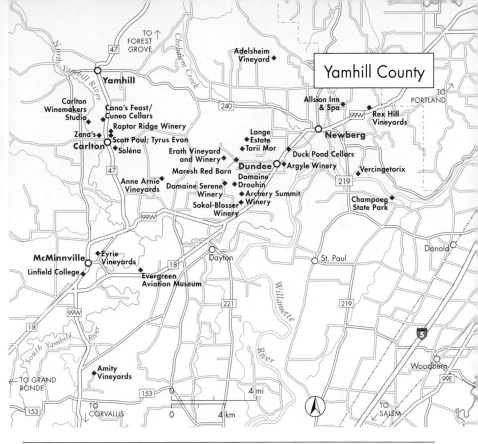

Yamhill County

TO FOREST GROVE

Adelsheim Vineyard ◆

TO PORTLAND

Yamhill

Carlton Winemakers Studio

Cana's Feast/ Cuneo Cellars

Raptor Ridge Winery

Zena's ◆

Scott Paul; Tyrus Evan

Soléna

Carlton

Allison Inn & Spa

Rex Hill Vineyards

Lange ◆ Estate
◆ Torii Mor

Newberg

Erath Vineyard and Winery ◆

Maresh Red Barn

Duck Pond Cellars

Dundee ◆ Argyle Winery

Vercingetorix

Domaine ◆ Drouhin

Anne Arnie Vineyards

Domaine Serene Winery

◆ Archery Summit Winery

Champoeg State Park

Sokol-Blosser Winery

McMinnville

Eyrie Vineyards

Linfield College

Dayton

St. Paul

Donald

Evergreen Aviation Museum

Amity Vineyards

TO GRAND RONDE

TO CORVALLIS

Willamette River

North Yamhill River
Chehalem Creek
South Yamhill River

Woodburn

TO SALEM

4 mi

4 km

NEWBERG

15 mi west of Tigard, 24 mi south of Portland on Hwy. 99W.

Newberg sits in the Chehalem Valley, known as one of Oregon's most fertile wine-growing locations, and is called the Gateway to Oregon Wine Country. Many of Newberg's early settlers were Quakers from the Midwest, who founded the school that has become George Fox University, an accredited four-year institution. Newberg's most famous resident, likewise a Quaker, was Herbert Hoover, the 31st president of the United States. For about five years during his adolescence, he lived with an aunt and uncle at the Hoover-Minthorn House, now a museum listed on the National Register of Historic Places. Now the town is on the map for the nearby wineries, fine dining establishments, and a spacious, spectacular resort, the Allison. St. Paul, a historic town with a population of about 325, is about 8 mi south of Newberg, and every July holds a professional rodeo.

GETTING HERE

Newberg is just under an hour's drive from Portland International Airport; **Caravan Airport Transportation** (☎ *541/994–9645* ⊕ *www. caravanairporttransportation.com*) provides shuttle service. The best way to visit Newberg and the Yamhill County vineyards is by car. Sitting

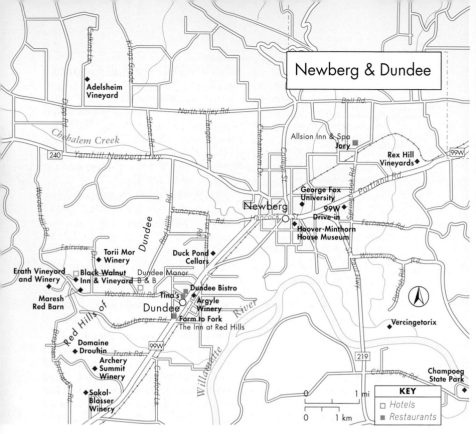

Newberg & Dundee

Adelsheim Vineyard

Chehalem Creek

North Valley Rd.

Bell Rd.

240

Yamhill–Newberg Hwy.

Allsion Inn & Spa
Jory

Rex Hill
Vineyards

99W

George Fox
University

Portland Rd.

Newberg

Sunnycrest Rd.

Hancock St.

99W
Drive-in

Fernwood Rd.

Hoover-Minthorn
House Museum

Dundee

Torii Mor
Winery

Duck Pond
Cellars

Fairview

Erath Vineyard
and Winery

Black Walnut
Inn & Vineyard

Dundee Manor

B & B

Wilsonville Rd.

Maresh
Red Barn

Worden Hill Rd.

Tina's

Dundee Bistro

Dundee

Niederberger Rd.

Argyle
Winery

Farm to Fork
The Inn at Red Hills

Willamette River

Vercingetorix

Red Hills of

99W

Domaine
Drouhin

Trunk Rd.

Archery
Summit
Winery

219

Crawford Rd.

Champoeg Rd.

Champoeg
State Park

Sokol-
Blosser
Winery

0   1 mi

0   1 km

KEY

□ Hotels
■ Restaurants

on Highway 99W, Newberg is 15 mi outside Tigard and 90 minutes from Lincoln City, on the Oregon Coast.

Yamhill County Transit Area (YCTA) (☎ *503/472–0457 ext. 122* ⊕ *www.yctransitarea.org*) provides bus service for Yamhill County, with links to Hillsboro/MAX, Sherwood/TriMet, and Salem/SAMT. Greyhound provides bus service to McMinnville.

VISITOR INFORMATION
Chehalem Valley Chamber of Commerce (Newberg, Dundee, and St. Paul) (✉ *415 E. Sheridan, Newberg* ☎ *503/538–2014* ⊕ *www.chehalemvalley.org*)

EXPLORING
Champoeg State Park. Pronounced "sham-*poo*-ee," this 615-acre state park on the south bank of the Willamette River is on the site of a Hudson's Bay Company trading post, granary, and warehouse that was built in 1813. This was the seat of the first provisional government in the Northwest. The settlement was abandoned after a catastrophic flood in 1861, then rebuilt and abandoned again after the flood of 1890. The park's wide-open spaces, groves of oak and fir, modern visitor center, museum, and historic buildings provide vivid insight into pioneer life. Tepees and wagons are displayed here, and there are 10 mi of hiking and cycle trails.

Robert Newell was among the inaugural American settlers in the Willamette Valley and helped establish the town of Champoeg; a replica of his 1844 home, now the **Newell House Museum** (✉ *8089 Champoeg Rd. NE, St. Paul* ☎ *503/678–5537* ⊕ *www.newellhouse.com* 💲 *$4 adults, $3 seniors, $2 children* ☉ *Mar.–Oct., Fri.–Sun. 1–5*), was built inside the park grounds in 1959 and paid for by the Oregon State Society Daughters of the American Revolution. The first floor is furnished with 1860s antiques. Pioneer quilts and a collection of gowns worn by the wives of Oregon governors at inaugurations are displayed on the second floor. There's also a pioneer jail and schoolhouse.

Also on park grounds is the historic **Pioneer Mother's Memorial Log Cabin** (✉ *8035 Champoeg Rd. NE, St. Paul* ☎ *503/633–2237* 💲 *$4 adults, $3 seniors, $2 children* ☉ *Mar.–Oct., Fri.–Sun. 1–5*), with pioneer artifacts from the Oregon Trail era. ✉ *8239 Champoeg Rd. NE, St. Paul* ☎ *800/551–6949* ⊕ *www.oregonstateparks.org* 💲 *$5 per vehicle.*

George Fox University. This 75-acre shady campus in a residential neighborhood was founded by the Quakers in 1884. Centennial Tower is surrounded by a campus quad and academic buildings, the library, and the student commons. Hess Creek Canyon cuts through the campus. ✉ *414 N. Meridian St., Newberg* ☎ *503/538–8383* ⊕ *www.georgefox.edu.*

Hoover-Minthorn House Museum. The boyhood home of President Herbert Hoover is the oldest and most significant of Newberg's original structures. Built in 1881, the preserved frame house still has many of its original furnishings. Outside is the woodshed that no doubt played an important role in shaping young "Bertie" Hoover's character. ✉ *115 S. River St., Newberg* ☎ *503/538–6629* ⊕ *www.nscda.org/museums/ oregon.htm* 💲 *$3* ☉ *Mar.–Nov., Wed.–Sun. 1–4; Dec. and Feb., weekends 1–4, closed Jan.*

WINERIES

Fodor's Choice ★ **Adelsheim Vineyard.** David Adelsheim is the knight in shining armor of the Oregon wine industry—tirelessly promoting Oregon wines abroad, and always willing to share the knowledge he has gained from his long viticultural experience. He and Ginny Adelsheim founded their pioneer winery in 1971. They make their wines from grapes picked on their 170 acres of estate vineyard, as well as from grapes they've purchased. Their Pinot Noir, Pinot Gris, Pinot Blanc, and Chardonnay all conform to the Adelsheim house style of rich, balanced fruit and long, clean finishes. ✉ *16800 NE Calkins Ln., Newberg* ☎ *503/538–3652* ⊕ *www.adelsheim.com* 💲 *$15* ☉ *Open July–Oct. daily 11–4; winter hours Wed.–Sun. 11–4, by appointment Mon-Tues.*

Rex Hill Vineyards. A few hundred feet off the busy highway, surrounded by conifers and overlooked by vineyards, Rex Hill seems to exist in a world of its own. The winery opened in 1982, after owners Paul Hart and Jan Jacobsen converted a former nut-drying facility. It produces first-class Pinot Noir, Pinot Gris, Chardonnay, Sauvignon Blanc, and Riesling from both estate-grown and purchased grapes. The tasting room has a massive fireplace, elegant antiques, and an absorbing collection of modern art. Another highlight is the beautifully landscaped garden, perfect for picnicking. ✉ *30835 N. Hwy. 99W, Newberg*

☎ *503/538–0666 or 800/739–4455* ⊕ *www.rexhill.com* ⊒ *$10* ⊙ *Daily 10–5; closed major holidays.*

Fodor'sChoice **Vercingetorix.** This small winery south of Newberg, which produces only ★ Pinot Gris and Pinot Noir, is part of Willamette Farms, a grower of hazelnuts, trees, and wine grapes. The crisp, fruity Pinot Gris is especially worth seeking out. The winery has a half mile of Willamette River frontage, so you can claim a picnic table and keep your eyes peeled for wildlife (beavers, deer, ducks, geese, or raptors). Picnic baskets are for sale in the tasting room. ✉ *800 NE Parrish Rd., Newberg* ☎ *503/538–9895* ⊕ *www.vxvineyard.com* ⊒ *Prices vary* ⊙ *Open weekends Memorial Day–Labor Day.*

WHERE TO EAT AND STAY

$$$ ✕ **Jory.** This exquisite restaurant is named after one of the soils in the **NEW AMERICAN** Oregon wine country. Here you can order grilled Muscovy duck over roasted grapes and watch it cook over a wood grill. Start off with butternut squash soup with shreds of fresh apple. Fish lovers will relish the saffron fettuccine in a tomato-fennel broth with bay scallops, prawns, and mussels. The dessert menu has orange-cardamom doughnuts accompanying a vanilla crème brûlée, and a brown-butter cake with hazelnut praline ice cream. Naturally, the restaurant has an expansive wine list. ✉ *2525 Allison La., Newberg* ☎ *503/554–2525* ⊕ *www. theallison.com* ⊟ *AE, D, DC MC, V* ⊙ *No lunch Sun.*

$$$$ ⊡ **The Allison Inn & Spa.** The new Allison (opened in Sept. 2009) provides a luxurious, relaxing base for exploring the region's 200 wineries. The attention to detail in its materials, art, grounds, and amenities is impressive. It's a great retreat for both locals and travelers. Each bright, comfortable room includes a gas fireplace, which is perfect for a misty day; original works of art, a soaking tub, impressive furnishings, bay-window seats, and views of the wine country from the terrace or balcony. The massive copper-coil curtain at the entrance to Allison's 15,000-square-foot spa conveys its opulence as a place to enjoy wines, a pinot pedicure, or mimosa massage in one of its 12 treatment rooms. The property lives up it its nickname, "the living room of the Willamette Valley." **Pros:** outstanding on-site restaurant, excellent gym and spa facilities, located in the middle of wine country. **Cons:** not many nearby off-property activities other than wine tasting. ✉ *2525 Allison La., Newberg* ☎ *503/554–2525* ⊕ *www.theallison.com* ⇗ *65 rooms, 20 suites* ⌂ *In-room: bar, refrigerator, Wi-Fi. In-hotel: restaurant, pool, gym* ⊟ *AE, D, DC, MC, V.*

NIGHTLIFE AND THE ARTS

99W Drive-in. Ted Francis built this drive-in in 1953, and operated it until his death at 98; the business is now run by his grandson. The first film begins at dusk. ✉ *Hwy. 99W (Portland Rd.), just west of Springbrook Rd. intersection, Newberg* ☎ *503/538–2738* ⊕ *www.99w.com* ⊒ *$7 per person, $11 minimum vehicle charge* ⊙ *Fri.–Sun.*

SPORTS AND THE OUTDOORS

BALLOONING Hot-air balloon rides are nothing less than a spectacular, breathtaking thrill—particularly over Oregon's beautiful Yamhill County. **Vista Balloon Adventures** (☎ *503/625–7385 or 800/622–2309* ⊕ *www.*

vistaballoon.com) launches several balloons daily from Sportsman Airpark. Flown by FAA-licensed pilots, they rise about 1,500 feet, and its pilots often can steer the craft down to skim the water, and up to view hawk's nests. A brunch is included afterwards.

DUNDEE

3 mi southwest of Newberg on Hwy. 99 W.

Dundee used to be known for growing the lion's share (more than 90%) of the U.S. hazelnut crop. Today it's better known for the numerous quaint and elegant wine bars, bed-and-breakfast inns and restaurants that are products of its wine tourism. Exploring the area's wineries is an experience you won't want to miss.

3

GETTING HERE

Dundee is just under an hour's drive from Portland International Airport; **Caravan Airport Transportation** (🕿 *541/994–9645* ⊕ *www. caravanairporttransportation.com*) provides shuttle service.

What used to be a pleasant drive through quaint Dundee on Highway 99W now can be a traffic hassle, as it serves as the main artery from Lincoln City to suburban Portland. Others will enjoy wandering along the 25 mi of Highway 18 between Dundee and Grande Ronde, in the Coast Range, which goes through the heart of the Yamhill Valley wine country.

Yamhill County Transit Area (YCTA) (🕿 *503/472–0457 ext. 122* ⊕ *www. yctransitarea.org*) provides bus service for Yamhill County, with links to Hillsboro/MAX, Sherwood/TriMet, and Salem/SAMT.

VISITOR INFORMATION

Chehalem Valley Chamber of Commerce (Newberg, Dundee, and St. Paul) (✉ *415 E. Sheridan, Newberg* 🕿 *503/538–2014* ⊕ *www.chehalemvalley.org*)

WINERIES

Fodor's Choice **Archery Summit Winery.** Gary and Nancy Andrus, the owners of Pine
★ Ridge winery in Napa Valley, started Archery Summit in the early 1990s; the first crush was in 1995. Because they believed that great wines are made in the vineyard, they adopted such innovative techniques as narrow spacing and vertical trellis systems, which give the fruit a great concentration of flavors. In addition, they did extensive clone research to develop the best possible vines for their more than 100 acres of estate vineyards. The Andruses focus on Pinot Noir, making their wines in a gravity-flow winery for the gentlest handling, and aging them in traditional caves—a rarity in Oregon—in French oak barrels. ✉ *18599 NE Archery Summit Rd., Dundee* 🕿 *503/864–4300* ⊕ *www. archerysummit.com* 🎟 *$15* ⊙ *Open daily.*

Argyle Winery. A beautiful establishment, Argyle has its tasting room in a Victorian farmhouse set amid gorgeous gardens. The winery is tucked into a former hazelnut processing plant—which explains the Nuthouse label on its reserve wines. Since Argyle opened in 1987, it has consistently produced sparkling wines that are crisp on the palate, with an aromatic, lingering finish and bubbles that seem to last forever. And these sparklers cost about a third of their counterparts from California.

The winery also produces Chardonnay, dry Riesling, Pinot Gris, and Pinot Noir. ⊠ *691 Hwy. 99W, Dundee* ☎ *503/538–8520 or 888/427–4953* ⊕ *www.argylewinery.com* ⊠ *Prices vary* ☉ *Open daily 11–5.*

Fodor's Choice ★ **Domaine Drouhin Oregon.** When the French winery magnate Robert Drouhin ("the Sebastiani of France") planted a vineyard and built a winery in the Red Hills of Dundee back in 1987, he set local oenophiles abuzz. Be forewarned, though: this is one winery where you're expected to buy some wine if you tour, and the wines are not cheap. Ninety acres of the 225-acre estate had been planted. The hillside setting was selected to take advantage of the natural coolness of the earth and to establish a gravity-flow winery. A visit is well worth planning for, however, because the tasting includes Drouhin wines from both Oregon and France, allowing you to compare the two. ⊠ *6750 NE Breyman Orchards Rd., Dundee* ☎ *503/864–2700* ⊕ *www.domainedrouhin.com* ⊠ *$10* ☉ *Open Wed.–Sun. Tours by appointment only.*

Duck Pond Cellars. Fronted by gardens north of Route 99W, Duck Pond is one of the region's jewels. Doug and Jo Ann Fries planted the vineyards in 1986 and opened the winery in 1993. They concentrate on estate-grown Willamette Valley Pinot Gris, Pinot Noir, and Chardonnay, but also make Cabernet Sauvignon and Merlot from grapes grown in Washington's Columbia Valley, where they have pioneered vineyard plantings on the Wahluke Slope above the Columbia River. The Duck Pond tasting room has a market that sells food and gifts, and the picnic area is a floral delight. ⊠ *23145 Hwy. 99W, Dundee* ☎ *503/538–3199 or 800/437–3213* ⊕ *www.duckpondcellars.com* ⊠ *Some tasting complimentary, others $2 taste, $5 flight* ☉ *Oct.–April, daily 11–5; May–Sept., daily 10–5.*

Erath Vineyards Winery. One of Oregon's pioneer wineries, Erath Vineyards opened more than a quarter century ago. Its owner and winemaker, Dick Erath, focused on producing distinctive Pinot Noir from grapes he'd been growing in the Red Hills since 1972—as well as full-flavored Pinot Gris, Pinot Blanc, Chardonnay, Cabernet Sauvignon, Riesling, and late-harvest Gewürztraminer. The wines were both excellent and reasonably priced. In 2006 the winery was sold to Washington State's giant conglomerate Ste. Michelle Wine Estate. The tasting room is in the middle of the vineyards, high in the hills, with views in nearly every direction: the hazelnut trees that covered the slopes not so long ago have been replaced with vines. The tasting-room terrace, which overlooks the winery and the hills, is a choice spot for picnicking. Crabtree Park, next to the winery, is a good place to stretch your legs after a tasting. ⊠ *9009 NE Worden Hill Rd., Dundee* ☎ *503/538–3318* ⊕ *www.erath.com* ⊠ *$10* ☉ *Open daily 11–5.*

Maresh Red Barn. When Jim and Loie Maresh planted two acres of vines in 1970, theirs became the fifth vineyard in Oregon and the first on Worden Hill Road. The quality of their grapes was so high that some of the Dundee Hills' best and most famous wineries soon sought them out. When the wine industry boomed in the 1980s, the Mareshes decided they might as well enjoy some wine from their renowned grapes. They transformed their old barn into a tasting room, where you can taste and purchase exceptional Chardonnay, Pinot Noir, Pinot Gris, and Sauvignon Blanc. ✉ *9325 NW Worden Hill Rd., Dundee* ☎ *503/537–1098* ⊕ *www.vineyardretreat.com* 🍷 *$5* ☉ *Open Wed.–Sun. 11–5 and by appointment. Closed Jan.–Feb.*

Sokol Blosser. Sokol Blosser is one of Yamhill County's oldest wineries (it was established in 1977), and it makes consistently excellent wines and sells them at reasonable prices. Set on a gently sloping south-facing hillside and surrounded by vineyards, lush lawns, and shade trees, it's a splendid place to learn about wine. A demonstration vineyard with several rows of vines contains the main grape varieties and shows what happens to them as the seasons unfold. ✉ *5000 Sokol Blosser La., 3 mi west of Dundee off Hwy. 99 W, Dundee* ☎ *503/864–2282 or 800/582–6668* 🍷 *Tasting room $5–$15* ⊕ *www.sokolblosser.com* ☉ *Open daily 10–4.*

Torii Mor Winery. Torii Mor, established in 1993, makes small quantities of handcrafted Pinot Noir, Pinot Gris, and Chardonnay. The tasting room is in Torii Mor's Olson Vineyard, one of Yamhill County's oldest vineyards, with an amazing setting amid Japanese gardens with breathtaking views of the Willamette Valley. The owners, who love things Japanese, named their winery after the distinctive Japanese gate of Shinto religious significance; they added a Scandinavian mor, signifying "earth," to create an east-west combo: "earth gate." Jacques Tardy, a native of Nuits Saint Georges, in Burgundy, France, is the current winemaker. Under his guidance Torii Mor wines have become more Burgundian in style. ✉ *18325 NE Fairview Dr., Dundee* ☎ *800/839–5004* ⊕ *www.toriimorwinery.com* 🍷 *$10* ☉ *Open daily 11–5.*

WHERE TO EAT AND STAY

$ | CONTEMPORARY
✕ **Dundee Bistro.** This highly regarded 80-seat restaurant run by the Ponzi wine family uses Northwest organic foods such as Draper Valley chicken and locally produced wines, fruits, vegetables, nuts, mushrooms, fish, and meats. Vaulted ceilings provide an open feeling inside, warmed by abundant fresh flowers and the works of local Oregon artists. ✉ *100-A SW 7th St., Dundee* ☎ *503/554–1650* ⊕ *www.dundeebistro.com* 🍴 *AE, DC, MC, V.*

$$ | NEW AMERICAN
✕ **Farm to Fork.** The restaurant serves breakfast, lunch, dinner, and a Sunday brunch. Its deli offers a wide selection of Oregon and international cheeses, charcuterie, and fresh salads from the kitchen. Its farm, located in the Chehalem Mountains AVA at de Lancellotti Family Vineyard, grows fruits, vegetables, herbs, and lavender for the restaurant. Request a custom picnic basket for a day of wine tasting, bike riding, hiking, or trail riding. Tastings in the Press Wine Bar are offered on the property, many from smaller, hard-to-find wineries. ✉ *1410 N. Hwy. 99 W, Dundee* ☎ *503/538–7970; wine bar 503/538–7989* ⊕ *www.www.innatredhills.com/farm_to_fork.html* 🍴 *AE, D, DC, MC, V.*

$$$ | FRENCH | Fodor's Choice ★
✕ **Tina's.** Chef–proprietors Tina and David Bergen bring a powerful one-two punch to this Dundee favorite that often lures Portlanders away from their own restaurant scene. The couple shares cooking duties—Tina does the baking and is often on hand to greet you—and David brings his experience as a former caterer and employee of nearby Sokol Blosser Winery to the table, ensuring that you have the right glass of

Continued on page 168

The Willamette Valley is Oregon's premier wine region. With a milder climate than any growing area in California, cool-climate grapes like Pinot Noir and Pinot Gris thrive here, and are being transformed into world-class wines.

There may be fewer and smaller wineries than in Napa, but the experience is often more intimate. The winemaker himself may even pour you wine.

Touring is easy, as most wineries are well marked, and have tasting rooms with regular hours. Whether you're taking a day trip from Portland, or staying for a couple of days, here's how to get the most out of your sipping experience.

By Dave Sandage and John Doerper

Above and right, Willamette Valley

Wine Tasting *in the* *Willamette* *Valley*

OREGON'S WINES: THEN AND NOW

Rex Hill Vineyards

THE EARLY YEARS

The French made wine first—French Canadians, that is. In the 1830s, retired fur trappers from the Hudson's Bay Company started to colonize the Willamette Valley and planted grapes on the south-facing buttes. They were followed by American settlers who made wine.

Although wine-making in the region-languished after these early efforts, it never quite vanished. A few wineries hung on, producing wines mainly for Oregonians of European descent.

It wasn't until the 1970s that the state's wine industry finally took off. Only after a group of young California winemakers started making vinifera wines in the Umpqua and Willamette Valleys and gained international acclaim for them, did Oregon's wines really take hold.

WINEMAKING TODAY

Today, Oregon's wine industry is racing ahead. Here the most prolific white and red grapes are Pinot Gris and Pinot Noir, respectively. Other prominent varietals include Riesling, Gewürztraminer, Viognier, Chardonnay, Carbernet Franc, and Syrah.

The wine industry in Oregon is still largely dominated by family and boutique wineries that pay close attention to quality and are often keen to experiment. That makes traveling and tasting at the source an always-interesting experience.

OREGON CERTIFIED SUSTAINABLE WINE

The latest trend in Oregon winemaking is a dedication to responsible grape growing and winemaking. When you see the Oregon Certified Sustainable Wine (OCSW) logo on the back of a wine bottle, it means the winery ensures accountable agricultural and winemaking practices (in conjunction with agencies such as USDA Organic, Demeter Biodynamic, the Food Alliance, Salmon-Safe, and Low Input Viticulture and Enology) through independent third-party certification. For more information on Oregon Certified Sustainable wines and participating wineries, check ⊕ www.ocsw.org.

WINE TASTING PRIMER

Ordering and tasting wine—whether at a winery, bar, or restaurant—is easy once you master a few simple steps.

LOOK AND NOTE
Hold your glass by the stem and look at the wine in the glass. Note its color, depth, and clarity.

For whites, is it greenish, yellow, or gold? For reds, is it purplish, ruby, or garnet? Is the wine's color pale or deep? Is the liquid clear or cloudy?

SWIRL AND SNIFF
Swirl the wine gently in the glass to intensify the scents, then sniff over the rim of the glass. What do you smell? Try to identify aromas like:

- **Fruits**—citrus, peaches, berries, figs, melon

- **Flowers**—orange blossoms, honey, perfume

- **Spices**—baking spices, pungent, herbal notes

- **Vegetables**—fresh or cooked, herbal notes

- **Minerals**—earth, steely notes, wet stones

- **Dairy**—butter, cream, cheese, yogurt

- **Oak**—toast, vanilla, coconut, tobacco

- **Animal**—leathery, meaty notes

Are there any unpleasant notes, like mildew or wet dog, that might indicate that the wine is "off?"

SIP AND SAVOR
Prime your palate with a sip, swishing the wine in your mouth. Then spit in a bucket or swallow.

Take another sip and think about the wine's attributes. Sweetness is detected on the tip of the tongue, acidity on the sides of the tongue, and tannins (a mouth-drying sensation) on the gums. Consider the body—does the wine feel light in the mouth, or is there a rich sensation? Are the flavors consistent with the aromas? If you like the wine, try to pinpoint what you like about it, and vice versa if you don't like it.

Take time to savor the wine as you're sipping it—the tasting experience may seem a bit scientific, but the end goal is your enjoyment.

WINE TOURING AND TASTING

Wine tasting at Argyle and Rex Hill

WHEN TO GO

In high season (June through October) and on weekends and holidays during much of the year, wine-country roads can be busy and tasting rooms are often crowded. If you prefer a more intimate tasting experience, plan your visit for a weekday.

To avoid the frustration of a fruitless drive, confirm in advance that wineries of interest will be open when you plan to visit.

Choose a designated driver for the day: Willamette wine-country roads are often narrow and curvy, and you may be sharing the road with bicyclists and wildlife as well as other wine tourists.

IN THE TASTING ROOM

Tasting rooms are designed to introduce newcomers to the pleasures of wine and to the wines made at the winery. At popular wineries you'll sometimes have to pay for your tasting, anything from a nominal $2 fee to $30 and up for a tasting that might include a glass you can take home. This fee is often deducted if you buy wine before leaving.

WHAT'S AN AVA?

AVAs (American Viticultural Areas) are geographic winegrowing regions that vaguely reflect the French concept of terroir, or "sense of place." The vineyards within a given AVA have similar characteristics such as climate, soil types, and/or elevation, which impart shared characteristics to the wines made from grapes grown in that area. AVAs are strictly geographic boundaries distinct from city or county designations. AVAs can also be subdivided into sub-AVAs; each of the AVAs mentioned here is actually part of the larger Willamette Valley AVA.

Each taste consists of an ounce or two. Feel free to pour whatever you don't finish into one of the dump buckets on the bar. If you like, rinse your glass between pours with a little water. Remember, those sips add up, so pace yourself. If you plan to visit several wineries, try just a few wines at each so you won't suffer from palate fatigue, when your mouth can no longer distinguish subtleties. It's also a good idea to bring a picnic lunch, which you can enjoy on the deck of a winery, taking in the surrounding wine country vistas.

FALL FOLIAGE

In autumn, Willamette Valley vineyards are particularly stunning as the leaves change color.

DAY TRIP FROM PORTLAND

With nearly 150 vineyards, the Chehalem Mountain and Ribbon Ridge AVAs offer widely varied soil types and diverse Pinot Noirs. The region is less than an hour away from Portland.

Ponzi Vineyards

CHEHALEM MOUNTAIN AND RIBBON RIDGE AVAS

❶ PONZI VINEYARDS

First planted in 1970, Ponzi has some of Oregon's oldest Pinot Noir vines. In addition to current releases, the tasting room sometimes offers older library wines. **Try:** *Arneis, a crisp Italian white varietal.*

- ✉ 14665 SW Winery La., Beaverton
- ☎ 503/628–1227
- 🌐 www.ponziwines.com

❷ REX HILL VINEYARDS

Before grapevines, the Willamette Valley was widely planted with fruits and nuts. Enjoy classic Oregon Pinot Noir in this tasting room built around an old fruit and nut drying facility. **Try:** *dark and spicy Dundee Hills Pinot Noir.*

- ✉ 30835 N. Hwy. 99W, Newberg
- ☎ 800/739–4455
- 🌐 www.rexhill.com

❸ VERCINGETORIX (VX) VINEYARD

This 10-acre vineyard sits in the middle of a 210-acre farm near the Willamette River. The tasting room is in one of the barns; a relaxed, friendly atmosphere for sampling. **Try:** *crisp and refreshing Pinot Blanc.*

- ✉ 8000 N.E. Parrish Rd., Newberg
- ☎ 503/538–9895
- 🌐 www.vxvineyard.com

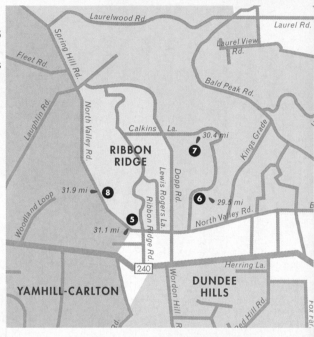

❹ FOX FARM VINEYARDS TASTING ROOM

In addition to offering their own wines, this multi-winery tasting room in downtown Newberg features samples from several small local producers. The menu changes periodically.

- ✉ 602 E. First St., Newberg
- ☎ 503/538–8466
- 🌐 www.foxfarmvineyards.com

❺ UTOPIA VINEYARD

The tasting room at this small Oregon winery is quite intimate—you'll likely be served by the winemaker himself. **Try:** *light and slightly sweet Rosé.*

- ✉ 17445 N.E. Ribbon Ridge Rd., Newberg
- ☎ 503/298–7841
- 🌐 www.utopiawine.com

Vercingetorix (VX) Vineyard

Adelsheim Vineyard

Rex Hill

Pinot Gris grapes

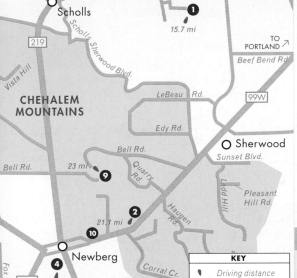

KEY

🍷 Driving distance
00 mi from Portland

❽ ARAMENTA CELLARS

A small, family-run operation that offers tastings in its winery, built on the foundation of an old barn. The on-site vineyard grows primarily Pinot Noir and Chardonnay. **Try:** *smooth and structured Tillie Claret.*

✉ 17979 N.E. Lewis Rogers La., Newberg

☎ 503/538–7230

🌐 www.aramentacellars.com

STOP FOR A BITE

❾ JORY RESTAURANT

Located within the luxurious Allison Inn and Spa, Jory serves creative dishes that highlight the bounty of the Willamette Valley.

✉ 2525 Allison La., Newberg

☎ 503/554–2526

🌐 www.theallison.com

❿ SUBTERRA

Casual fine dining in a wine cellar atmosphere underneath the Dark Horse wine bar. The menu features global cuisine and a good selection of local wines.

✉ 1505 Portland Rd., Newberg

☎ 503/538–6060

🌐 www.subterrarestaurant.com

❻ ADELSHEIM VINEYARD

One of Oregon's older Pinot Noir producers, Adelsheim has just opened a new tasting room inside its modern winery, with friendly, knowledgeable employees. **Try:** *dark and smoky Elizabeth's Reserve Pinot Noir.*

✉ 16800 N.E. Calkins La., Newberg

☎ 503/538–3652

🌐 www.adelsheim.com

❼ BERGSTROM WINERY

A beautiful tasting room, but the real high point here is the classic Oregon Pinot Noir sourced from several of its estate vineyards as well as other local sites. **Try:** *earthy Bergstrom Pinot Noir.*

✉ 18215 N.E. Calkins La., Newberg

☎ 503/554–0468

🌐 www.bergstromwines. com

TWO DAYS IN WINE COUNTRY

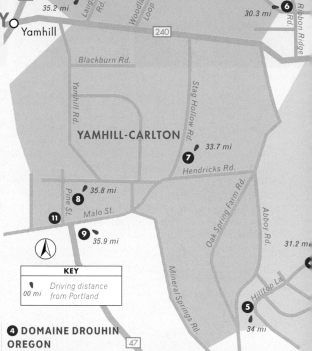

DAY 1

DUNDEE HILLS AVA

The Dundee Hills AVA is home to some of Oregon's best known Pinot Noir producers. Start your tour in the town of Dundee, about 30 miles southwest of Portland, then drive up into the red hills and enjoy the valley views from many wineries.

❶ ARGYLE WINERY

If you don't want to drive off the beaten path, this winery is right on Highway 99W in Dundee. They specialize in sparkling wines, but also make very nice still wines. **Try:** *crisp Brut Rosé.*

✉ 691 Hwy. 99 W, Dundee
☎ 503/538–8520
🌐 www.argylewinery.com

❷ PONZI WINE BAR

This tasting room close to Argyle has a huge selection of local wines. It's a good choice for those who want to sample a large selection side-by-side. **Try:** *bright and fruity Ponzi Pinot Gris.*

✉ 100 S.W. 7th St., Dundee
☎ 503/554–1500
🌐 www.ponziwinebar.com

❸ ARCHERY SUMMIT

An Oregon Pinot Noir pioneer, Archery Summit features memorable wines and equally pleasing views. Call in advance to schedule a tour of the winery and aging caves. **Try:** *dark and rich Premier Cuvée Pinot Noir.*

✉ 18599 NE Archery Summit Rd., Dayton
☎ 503/864–4300
🌐 www.archerysummit.com

❹ DOMAINE DROUHIN OREGON

Started in the late 1980s by the Drouhin family of Burgundy fame, this winery makes notable Oregon Pinot Noir, as well as Chardonnay. **Try:** *smooth and earthy Willamette Valley Pinot Noir.*

✉ 6750 Breyman Orchards Rd., Dayton
☎ 503/864–2700
🌐 www.domainedrouhin.com

❺ VISTA HILLS VINEYARD

The so-called Treehouse is arguably the most stunning tasting room in Oregon. Sample wine made from estate fruit on a deck that overlooks the vineyards of the Dundee Hills. **Try:** *fruity Treehouse Pinot Noir.*

✉ 6475 N.E. Hilltop La., Dayton
☎ 503/864–3200
🌐 www.vistahillsvineyard.com

DAY 2

YAMHILL-CARLTON AVA

To the west of the Dundee Hills AVA is the horseshoe-shaped Yamhill-Carlton AVA. Vineyards here are found on the slopes that surround the towns of Yamhill and Carlton. Carlton has become a center of wine tourism, and you could easily spend a day visiting tasting rooms in town.

❻ PENNER-ASH WINE CELLARS

This state-of-the-art winery and tasting room is atop a hill with an excellent view of the valley below. **Try:** *smooth and dark Shea Vineyard Pinot Noir.*

✉ 15771 N.E. Ribbon Ridge Rd., Newberg
☎ 503/554–5545
🌐 www.pennerash.com

Penner-Ash Wine Cellars

Ponzi Wine Bar

STOP FOR A BITE

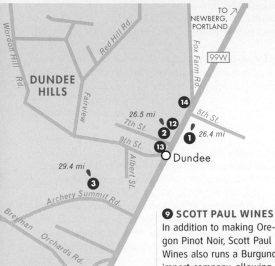

TO ↗
NEWBERG,
PORTLAND

99W

Wordon Hill Rd.

Red Hill Rd.

Fox Farm Rd.

**DUNDEE
HILLS**

Fairview

26.5 mi

7th St.

9th St.

5th St.

⑭

⑫

② ❶ 26.4 mi

⑬

Albert St.

29.4 mi

○ Dundee

❸

Archery Summit Rd.

Breyman

Orchards Rd.

❼ LEMELSON VINEYARDS
Although it specializes in single-vineyard Pinot Noir, Lemelson also makes several crisp white wines. The deck overlooking the vineyards is perfect for picnics. **Try:** *crisp and fruity Riesling.*
✉ 12020 N.E. Stag Hollow Rd., Carlton
☎ 503/852-6619
⊕ www.lemelsonvineyards.com

❽ TYRUS EVAN WINE
Well-known winemaker Ken Wright's second label features big reds. The tasting room is in the historic Carlton train station. **Try:** *bold and spicy Del Rio Claret.*
✉ 120 N. Pine St., Carlton
☎ 503/852-7070
⊕ www.tyrusevanwine.com

❾ SCOTT PAUL WINES
In addition to making Oregon Pinot Noir, Scott Paul Wines also runs a Burgundy import company, allowing you to taste locally grown Pinot Noir alongside some of the best Burgundies.
Try: *structured and elegant La Paulée Pinot Noir.*
✉ 128 S. Pine St., Carlton
☎ 503/852-7300
⊕ www.scottpaul.com

❿ LENNÉ ESTATE
Lenné specializes in highly regarded Pinot Noir, although it's often pouring a couple of non-Pinot wines from other wineries as well. The tasting room in a small stone building overlooks the vineyards.
Try: *complex and earthy Estate Pinot Noir.*
✉ 18760 Laughlin Rd., Yamhill
☎ 503/956-2256
⊕ www.lenneestate.com

⑪ THE HORSERADISH WINE AND CHEESE BAR
Located in downtown Carlton, The Horseradish offers a wide selection of local wines as well as cheese from around the world. The sandwiches and small plates make for a great quick lunch.
✉ 211 W. Main St., Carlton
☎ 503/852-6656
⊕ www.thehorseradish.com

⑫ DUNDEE BISTRO
A favorite of winemakers, Dundee Bistro serves seasonal local ingredients paired with Willamette Valley wines. Enjoy outdoor seating, or watch chefs work in the open kitchen inside.
✉ 100-A S.W. 7th St., Dundee
☎ 503/554-1650
⊕ www.dundeebistro.com

⑬ TINA'S
The warm and intimate Tina's features dishes made with seasonal ingredients, organic vegetables, and free-range meats. Stop by for lunch Tuesday–Friday, or nightly dinner.
✉ 760 Hwy. 99 W, Dundee
☎ 503/538-8880
⊕ www.tinasdundee.com

⑭ RED HILLS PROVINCIAL DINING
French and Italian fare made with fresh ingredients from the Willamette Valley. It has an extensive wine list with local and global selections.
✉ 276 N. Hwy. 99 W, Dundee
☎ 503/538-8224
⊕ www.redhills-dining.com

wine to match your course. Fish and game vie for attention on the country-French menu: entrées might include grilled Oregon salmon or Alaskan halibut, or a braised rabbit, local lamb, or tenderloin. Avail yourself of any special soups, particularly if there's corn chowder in the house. A lunch menu includes soup, sandwiches, and Tina's grilled hamburger, made with free-range beef. Service is as intimate and laid-back as the interior. A double fireplace divides the dining room, with heavy glass brick shrouded by bushes on the highway side, so you're not bothered by the traffic on Highway 99. ⊠ *760 Hwy. 99W, Dundee* 🕾 *503/538–8880* ⊕ *www.tinasdundee.com* ⊟ *AE, D, MC, V* ⊘ *No lunch Sat.–Mon.*

$$$$ ⊡ **Black Walnut Inn and Vineyard.** Located in the heart of Oregon wine country, the inn takes its inspiration from old Tuscan villas. It is filled with modern art, amenities, antiques, and the works of local artisans. It has six suites in the main house and three in the carriage house. The inn works with local farms to bring in fresh Northwest ingredients to provide unique, tasty breakfasts. Selections include salmon Benedict, vanilla custard French toast, and fruit parfait. **Pros:** comfortable, inventive breakfasts, in the middle of wine country. **Cons:** far from other activities other than wine tasting. ⊠ *9600 NE Worden Hill Rd., Dundee* 🕾 *866/429–4114* ⊕ *www.blackwalnut-inn.com* ↝ *9 suites* ⚇ *In-room: a/c, DVD (some). In-hotel: Wi-Fi* ⊟ *AE, MC, V* ⦵*BP.*

$$$ ⊡ **Dundee Manor Bed and Breakfast.** This 1908-built traditional bed-
Fodor'sChoice   and-breakfast features expansive grounds, a perfect location, and trea-
★   sures and collectibles that add intrigue to each themed room: African, Asian, European, and North American. Visitors are greeted with Pinot Noir, chocolate, and afternoon appetizers. Its garden has gazebos with views of Mt. Hood, Mt. Jefferson, and Mt. Bachelor. Breakfasts are fresh, plentiful, and delicious, using local ingredients. There are fire pits, croquet, horseshoes, golf chipping, boccie ball, and 38 different places to sit and ponder your good fortune. Its concierge service will book tee times, fine-dining reservations, massages, and private vineyard tours. **Pros:** terrific amenities, lots of activities, attentive staff. **Cons:** few rooms. ⊠ *8380 NE Worden Hill Rd., Dundee* 🕾 *503/554–1945 or 888/262–1133* ⊕ *www.dundeemanor.com* ↝ *4 rooms* ⚇ *In-room: Wi-Fi* ⊟ *AE, MC, V* ⦵*BP.*

$$ ⊡ **The Inn at Red Hills.** This is about as local as it gets. From the materials in the building, the wines it serves, and the ingredients in the kitchen, the Inn at Red Hills works to be sustainable and to use Oregon's bounty. Located in downtown Dundee, the inn has 20 spacious, comfortable rooms, each with its own layout and impressive wine-country views. Wide-screen televisions and huge bathrooms add to the amenities. **Pros:** modern and upscale. **Cons:** located in the town rather than the country. ⊠ *1410 N. Hwy. 99W, Dundee* 🕾 *503/538–7666* ⊕ *www.innatredhills. com* ↝ *20 rooms* ⚇ *In-room: a/c, Wi-Fi* ⊟ *AE, D, DC, MC, V.*

YAMHILL-CARLTON

14 mi west of Dundee.

The small towns of Carlton and Yamhill are neatly combed benchlands and hillsides, an AVA established in 2004, and home to some of the finest Pinot Noir vineyards in the world. The area is a gorgeous quilt of nurseries, grain fields, and orchards. Come here for the wine tasting, and not much else.

GETTING HERE

Having your own car is the best way to explore this rural region of Yamhill County, located a little more than an hour's drive from Portland International Airport. The towns of Yamhill and Carlton are about an hour's drive from downtown Portland, traveling through Tigard, to Newberg and west on Highway 240.

Yamhill County Transit Area (YCTA) (☎ *503/472–0457 ext. 122* ⊕ *www. yctransitarea.org*) provides bus service for Yamhill County, with links to Hillsboro/MAX, Sherwood/TriMet, and Salem/SAMT.

VISITOR INFORMATION

Yamhill Valley Visitors Association (☎ *503/883–7770* ⊕ *www.yamhillvalley. org*).

WINERIES

Anne Amie Vineyards. Early wine country adopters Fred and Mary Benoit established this namesake hilltop winery in 1979. Since the winery changed hands in 1999, it has been concentrating on Pinot Blanc, Pinot Gris, and Pinot Noir, but still makes a dry Riesling. Both the winery and the picnic area have spectacular views across the hills and valleys of Yamhill County. ✉ *6580 NE Mineral Springs Rd., McMinnville* ☎ *503/864–2991* ⊕ *www.anneamie.com* ✉ *$5–$10* ☽ *Open Mar.– Dec., daily 10–5; Jan.–Feb., Fri.–Sun. or by appointment.*

Cana's Feast/Cuneo Cellars. This outfit got its start in 1993, when Gino and Pam Cuneo bought a winery in the Eola Hills. In 2001 they moved Cuneo Cellars into a new winery, a Tuscan-inspired building north of Carlton on Route 47, outside of McMinnville. There the olive trees they've planted on the grounds are thriving. As the setting suggests, the winery works with some Italian grape varietals, such as Nebbiolo and Sangiovese. They also produce Cabernet Franc, Cabernet Sauvignon, Pinot Noir, Barbera, Primitivo, and Syrah. A boccie-ball court is a popular winemaker hangout, and a picnic area invites visitors to linger. In summer the winery offers weekend lunches and chef's supper on Friday and Saturday. ✉ *750 Lincoln St., Carlton* ☎ *503/852–0002* ⊕ *canasfeastwinery.com* ✉ *$10, includes 6 wines* ☽ *Open daily 11–5; Sun. brunch 11–3.*

Carlton Winemakers Studio. Oregon's first cooperative winery was specifically designed to house multiple small premium wine producers. This gravity-flow winery has up-to-date winemaking equipment as well as multiple cellars for storing the different makers' wines. You can taste and purchase bottles from the different member wineries: Andrew Rich, Hamacher Wines, Ayoub Wines, Brittan Vineyards, Carlton Wine, Lazy River Vinex, and Wahle Vineyards and Cellars. The emphasis is on

Pinot Noir, but more than a dozen other types of wines are poured, from Cabernet Franc to Gewürztraminer to Mourvèdre. From spring to autumn, the studio holds winemakers' dinners on Wednesdays. Reservations are essential. ⊠ *801 N. Scott St., Carlton* ☎ *503/852–6100* ⊕ *www.winemakersstudio.com* ⊠ *$3 and up* ⚘ *Wed. winemaker dinner reservations essential* ☉ *Open Feb.–Dec., daily 11–5.*

Raptor Ridge Winery. High up in the Chehalem Mountains, the raptors who fly over these vineyards (red-tail hawks, sharp-shinned hawks, and kestrels) give this small winery its name. Because the ridge intercepts the sea breeze, it's often foggy here. The fog cools the vineyards and imparts subtle, highly desirable flavors to the grapes, making for first-rate Pinot Noir, Pinot Gris, and Chardonnay wines. This remained true even after the winery moved from the ridge to a new facility in downtown Carlton in autumn 2007, because the grapes still come from the old vineyards. The winery produces small lots of handcrafted wines, aging them in French oak barrels. An unusual touch is the synchronizing of racking with the full moon, to "help bring out natural flavors and delicate aromas of Willamette Valley grapes" (though whether this timing accomplishes that end is dubious). In addition to employing its own crops, Raptor Ridge buys grapes from five different vineyards in the northern Willamette Valley. ⊠ *103 Monroe St., Carlton* ☎ *503/887–5595, tasting room appointments 503/367–4263* ⊕ *www.raptoridge.com* ☉ *Fri.–Sat. 11–4.*

Scott Paul Tasting Room and Winery. Pinot noir fans, listen up: this small spot in the center of Carlton is an outstanding Pinot Noir resource. It not only makes Pinot Noir from local grapes, but it also imports and sells Pinot Noirs from Burgundy. The three Pinot Noirs made from local grapes are Audrey, the finest wine of the vintage, La Paulée, a selection of the best lots of each vintage, and Cuvée Martha Pirrie, a fruit-forward, silky wine meant to be drunk young. All are splendid examples of the wines that can be made from this great, challenging grape. The tasting room, a quaint redbrick building, is across the street from the winery. Winery tours are by appointment only. Wine seminars are offered in the evenings. ⊠ *128 S. Pine St., Carlton* ☎ *503/852–7300* ⊕ *www.scottpaul.com* ⊠ *$10* ☉ *Open Wed.–Sun. 11–4.*

Soléna. This small winery originated in the passion of two seasoned Yamhill County oenologists. Laurent Montalieu was the winemaker at WillaKenzie Estate; Danielle Andrus Montalieu ran her family's Archery Summit winery. The two got married in 2002, opened a winery of their own that same year, and had a daughter in 2003, and they named both the winery and the daughter Soléna. Visit the tasting room and the cellar to sample Cabernet Sauvignon, Merlot, Pinot Gris, Pinot Noir, Syrah, and Zinfandel from the bottle and the barrel. ⊠ *213 S. Pine St., Carlton* ☎ *503/852–0082* ⊕ *www.solenaestate.com* ⊠ *$5* ☉ *Open Wed.–Sun. 12–5.*

Tyrus Evan Tasting Room. Carlton's former train depot is now the tasting room for Ken Wright's warm-climate label, Tyrus Evan. These wines are quite different from the Ken Wright pinots: they are warm-climate varieties like Cabernet Franc, Malbec, Syrah, and red Bordeaux blends,

Carlton Winemakers Studio

from grapes Wright buys from vineyards in eastern Washington and southern Oregon. The tasting room pours some Ken Wright wines alongside, as well as wines of other warm-climate producers. You can also pick up cheeses and other picnic supplies. ✉ *120 N. Pine St., Carlton* ☎ *503/852–7010* ⊗ *Open Fri.–Sat. 11–6, Sun.–Thurs. 11–5.*

Zenas Tasting Room. Encouraged by Carlton's growth spurt, Klamath Valley Vineyards decided to open this tasting room, although the winery itself is in Klamath Falls. The big, powerful flavors in the red wines are reminiscent of those in California vintages, especially those of the Cabernet Franc and Merlot. For a white, try the Riesling made from local grapes. ✉ *407 W. Main St., Carlton* ☎ *503/852–3000* ⊕ *www. zenaswines.com* ✎ *$10* ⊗ *Open Sat.–Sun. 12–5.*

MCMINNVILLE

11 mi south of Yamhill on Hwy. 99 W.

The Yamhill County seat, McMinnville lies in the center of Oregon's thriving wine industry. There is a larger concentration of wineries in Yamhill County than in any other area of the state, and the vineyards in the McMinnville area produce the most award-winning wines. Among the varieties are Chardonnay, Pinot Noir, and Pinot Gris. Most of the wineries in the area offer tours and tastings. McMinnville's downtown area, with a pleasantly disproportionate number of bookstores and art galleries for its size, is well worth exploring; many of the historic district buildings, erected 1890–1915, are still standing, and are remarkably well maintained.

GETTING HERE

McMinnville is a little more than an hour's drive from downtown Portland; **Caravan Airport Transportation** (☎ *541/994–9645* ⊕ *www. caravanairporttransportation.com*) provides shuttle service. McMinnville is just 70 minutes from Lincoln City on the Oregon Coast, and 27 mi west of Salem.

Yamhill County Transit Area (YCTA) (☎ *503/472–0457 ext. 122* ⊕ *www. yctransitarea.org*) provides bus service for Yamhill County, with links to Hillsboro/MAX, Sherwood/TriMet, and Salem/SAMT. Caravan Airport Transportation provides shuttle service to Portland International Airport.

VISITOR INFORMATION

McMinnville Chamber of Commerce (✉ *417 NW Adams St., McMinnville* ☎ *503/472–6196* ⊕ *www.mcminnville.org*)

EXPLORING

Ⓒ **Evergreen Aviation Museum.** The claim to fame here is the Howard
Fodor's Choice Hughes' *Spruce Goose*, on permanent display. If you can take your eyes
★ off the *Spruce Goose* there are also more than 45 historic planes and replicas here from the early years of flight and World War II, as well as the postwar and modern eras. IMAX shows are on Friday and Saturday nights. There's a museum store and café—the Spruce Goose Café, of course—and there are ongoing educational programs and special events. ✉ *500 NE Michael King Smith Way, McMinnville* ☎ *503/434–4180* ⊕ *www.sprucegoose.org* ⬚ *$20* ⓞ *Daily 9–5, closed holidays.*

Linfield College. A perennial football powerhouse in NCAA Division III, this is Oregon's second-oldest college (founded in 1849). Linfield hosts the **International Pinot Noir Celebration** (☎ *503/883–2200* ⊕ *www. ipnc.org*) for one week at the end of July. ✉ *900 SE Baker St., McMinnville* ⊕ *www.linfield.edu.*

NEED A BREAK? **Serendipity Ice Cream** provides a true, old-fashioned ice-cream parlor experience. Try a sundae, and take home some cookies made from scratch. The parlor is located in the historic Cook's Hotel, built in 1886. (✉ *502 NE 3rd St., McMinnville* ☎ *503/474–9189* ⊕ *serendipityicecream.com*)

WINERIES

Amity Vineyards. Its original tasting area was the back of a 1952 Ford pickup. Its Gamay noir label notes that the wine gives "more enjoyment to hamburgers [and] fried chicken." And the winery's current architecture still includes a trailer affectionately referred to as the "mobile chateau," already on the property when winemaker Myron Redford purchased the winery in 1974. These modest and whimsical touches underscore what seems to be Redford's philosophy: take your winemaking a lot more seriously than you take yourself. Taste the Pinot Blanc for Redford's take on the grape, and also linger in the tasting room to sample the Pinot Noir and the Gewürztraminer, among other varieties. Chocolates made with Amity's Pinot Noir and other products are available for sale. ✉ *18150 Amity Vineyards Rd. SE, Amity* ☎ *503/835–2362* ⊕ *www.amityvineyards.com* ⓞ *Oct.–May, daily noon–5; June–Sept., daily 11–5.*

Domaine Serene. In Dundee's Red Hills, this is a world-class five-level winery and a well-regarded producer of Oregon Pinot Noir, as well as Chardonnay and Syrah. ✉ *6555 NE Hilltop La., Dayton* ☎ *503/864–4600* ⊕ *www.domaineserene.com* ☼ *Wed.–Sun. 11–4.*

WHERE TO EAT AND STAY

$$$
CONTEMPORARY
✕ **Joel Palmer House.** Joel Palmer was an Oregon pioneer, and his 1857 home in Dayton is now on the National Register of Historic Places. There are three small dining rooms, each seating about 15 people. The chef specializes in wild-mushroom dishes; a popular starter is Heidi's three-mushroom tart. Entrées include rib eye au poivre, rack of lamb, breast of duckling, and coq au vin; desserts include apricot-walnut bread pudding and crème brûlée. Or, if you really, really like mushrooms, have your entire table order Jack's Mushroom Madness Menu, a five-course extravaganza for $75.00 per person. ✉ *600 Ferry St., Dayton* ☎ *503/864–2995* ⊕ *www.joelpalmerhouse.com* ▭ *AE, D, DC, MC, V* ☼ *Closed Sun. and Mon. No Lunch.*

$$$
ITALIAN
✕ **Nick's Italian Cafe.** Famed for serving Oregon's wine country enthusiasts, this fine-dining venue is a destination for a special evening or lunch. Modestly furnished but with a voluminous wine cellar, Nick's serves spirited and simple food, reflecting the owner's northern Italian heritage. A five-course prix-fixe menu changes nightly for $65. À la carte options are also available. ✉ *521 NE 3rd St., McMinnville* ☎ *503/434–4471* ⚇ *Reservations essential* ▭ *AE, MC, V* ⊕ *www.nicksitaliancafe.com.*

¢
⌂ **Hotel Oregon.** Built in 1905, this historic facility—the former Elberton Hotel—was rescued from decay by the McMenamins chain, renovated in 1998, and reopened the following year. It is a four-story brick structure, and its rooms have tall ceilings and high windows. The hotel is outfitted in late-Victorian furnishings, but its defining design element is its art. The hotel is whimsically decorated by McMenamins' artists: around every corner, even in the elevator, you'll find art—sometimes serene, often bizarre—as well as photos and sayings scribbled on the walls. The Oregon has a first-floor pub serving three meals a day, a rooftop bar with an impressive view of Yamhill County, and a cellar wine bar, resembling a dark speakeasy, that serves only area vintages. **Pros:** inexpensive, casual yet lively. **Cons:** those seeking upscale ambiance should look elsewhere. ✉ *310 NE Evans St., McMinnville* ☎ *503/472–8427 or 888/472–8427* ⊕ *www.mcmenamins.com* ⊅ *42 rooms* ⚐ *In-hotel: Wi-Fi, restaurant, 2 bars* ▭ *AE, D, DC, MC, V.*

$
Fodor's Choice
★
⌂ **Mattey House Bed & Breakfast.** Built in 1982 by English immigrant Joseph Mattey, a local butcher, this Queen Anne Victorian mansion—on the National Register of Historic Places—has several cheerful areas that define it. Downstairs is a cozy living room jammed with antiques, dual dining areas—a parlor with white wicker and a dining room with elegant furniture—and a porch with a swing. The four upstairs rooms are whimsically named after locally grown grape varieties—Riesling, Chardonnay, Pinot Noir, and Blanc de Blancs—and are decorated in keeping with the character of those wines: the Chardonnay Room, for instance, has tall windows and crisp white furnishings, and the Pinot Noir has dark-wood pieces and reddish wine accents. A small balcony off the

upstairs landing is perfect for sipping a glass of wine on a cool Yamhill Valley evening. A fine full breakfast might include poached pears with raspberry sauce, frittatas, and Dutch-apple pancakes. Or your hosts will have pastry and hot coffee available before you set off. **Pros:** refined bed-and-breakfast atmosphere. **Cons:** not many modern amenities in the rooms. ⊠ *10221 NE Mattey La., off Hwy. 99W, ¼ mi south of Lafayette, McMinnville* ☎ *503/434–5058* ⊕ *www.matteyhouse.com* ⇨ *4 rooms* ⚫ *In-room: no phone* ☰ *AE, MC, V* ⎮⊙⎮ *BP.*

NIGHTLIFE AND THE ARTS

Spirit Mountain Casino and Lodge. Located 24 mi southwest of McMinnville on Highway 18, this is a popular casino owned and operated by the Confederated Tribes of the Grande Ronde Community of Oregon. The 90,000-square-foot casino has more than a thousand slots, as well as poker and blackjack tables, roulette, craps, Pai Gow poker, keno, bingo, and off-track betting. Big-name comedians and rock and country musicians perform in the 1,700-seat concert hall, and there's an arcade for the kids. There's complimentary shuttle service from Portland and Salem. Dining options include an all-you-can-eat buffet, a deli, and a café. ⊠ *27100 SW Hwy. 18, Grande Ronde* ☎ *503/879–3764 or 888/668–7366* ⊕ *www.spirit-mountain.com.*

MID-WILLAMETTE VALLEY

While most of the wineries are concentrated in Washington and Yamhill counties, there are several finds in the Mid-Willamette Valley that are worth extending a wine enthusiast's journey. There are also flower, hops, berries, and seed gardens scattered throughout Salem, Albany, and Corvallis. The huge number of company stores concentrated on Interstate 5 will have you thinking about some new Nikes, and Oregon State University will have you wearing orange and black long after Halloween is over. Be aware that many communities in this region are little more than wide spots in the road. In these tiny towns you might find only a gas station, a grocery store, a church or two, and a school. Watch out for any School Crossing signs: Oregon strictly enforces its speed-limit laws.

SALEM

24 mi from McMinnville, south on Hwy. 99W and east on Hwy. 22, and 45 mi south of Portland on I–5.

Salem has a rich pioneer history, but before that it was the home of the Calapooia Indians, who called it Chemeketa, which means "place of rest." Salem is said to have been renamed by missionaries. Although trappers and farmers preceded them in the Willamette Valley, the Methodist missionaries had come in 1834 to minister to Native Americans, and they are credited with the founding of Salem. In 1842 they established the first academic institution west of the Rockies, which is now known as Willamette University. Salem became the capital when Oregon achieved statehood in 1859 (Oregon City was the capital of the Oregon Territory). Salem serves as the seat to Marion County as well

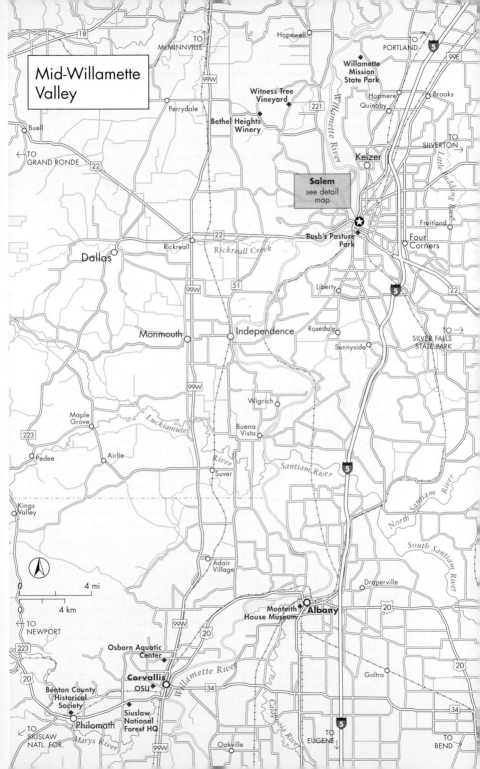

Mid-Willamette Valley

TO McMINNVILLE

TO PORTLAND

Hopewell

Willamette Mission State Park

Witness Tree Vineyard

Hopmere
Quinaby

Brooks

Perrydale

Bethel Heights Winery

TO SILVERTON

Buell

TO GRAND RONDE

Keizer

Salem
see detail map

Bush's Pasture Park

Fruitland

Four Corners

Dallas

Rickreall

Rickreall Creek

Liberty

Rosedale

SILVER FALLS STATE PARK

Monmouth

Independence

Sunnyside

TO

Maple Grove

Pedee

Airlie

Wigrich

Buena Vista

Suver

Kings Valley

Luckiamute River

Santiam River

North Santiam River

South Santiam River

Adair Village

Draperville

4 mi

4 km

Monteith House Museum

Albany

TO NEWPORT

Osborn Aquatic Center

Corvallis
OSU

Willamette River

Goltra

Benton County Historical Society

Siuslaw National Forest HQ

Philomath

TO SIUSLAW NATL. FOR.

Marys River

Calapooia River

Oakville

TO EUGENE

TO BEND

as the home of the state fairgrounds. Government ranks as a major industry here, while the city's setting in the heart of the fertile Willamette Valley stimulates rich agricultural and food-processing industries. More than a dozen wineries are in or near Salem. The main attractions in Salem are west of I–5 in and around the Capitol Mall.

GETTING HERE

Salem is located on I–5 with easy access to Portland, Albany, and Eugene. **Hut Portland Airport Shuttle** (☎ *503/364–4444* ⊕ *www.portlandairportshuttle.com*) provides transportation to Portland International Airport, which is located 1 hour and 15 minutes away. Salem's McNary Field no longer has commercial airline service, but serves general aviation aircraft.

Bus transportation throughout Salem is provided by **Cherriot's** (⊕ *www.cherriots.org*). Amtrak operates regularly, and its train station is located at 500 13th Street SE.

VISITOR INFORMATION

Salem Convention & Visitors Center (✉ *1313 Mill St. SE* ☎ *503/581–4325 or 800/874–7012* ⊕ *www.travelsalem.com*)

EXPLORING

Numbers in the margin correspond to the Salem map.

WHAT TO SEE

❺ **Bush's Pasture Park.** These 105 acres of rolling lawn and formal English gardens include the remarkably well-preserved Bush House, an 1878 Italianate mansion at the park's far-western boundary. It has 10 marble fireplaces and virtually all of its original furnishings. The house and gardens are on the National Register of Historic Places. Bush Barn Art Center, behind the house, exhibits the work of Northwest artists and has a sales gallery. ✉ *600 Mission St. SE* ☎ *503/363–4714* ⊕ *www.salemart.org* 🖾 *$4* ☉ *Mar. and Apr., Tues.–Sun. 1–4; May–Sept., Tues.–Sun. 12–5; Oct.–Dec., Tues.–Sun. 1–4; Jan., Feb. call for times.*

❶ **Elsinore Theatre.** This flamboyant Tudor Gothic vaudeville house opened on May 28, 1926, with Edgar Bergen in attendance. Clark Gable (who lived in Silverton) and Gregory Peck performed on stage. The theater was designed to look like a castle, with a false-stone front, chandeliers, ironwork, and stained-glass windows. It's now a lively performing arts center with a busy schedule of bookings, and there are concerts on its Wurlitzer pipe organ. Group Tours for $3.00 per person can be arranged. ✉ *170 High St. SE* ☎ *503/375–3574* ⊕ *www.elsinoretheatre.com.*

❹ **Mission Mill Village.** The **Thomas Kay Woolen Mill Museum** complex (circa 1889), complete with working waterwheels and millstream, looks as if the workers have just stepped away for a lunch break. Teasel gigging, napper flock bins, and the patented Furber double-acting napper are but a few of the machines and processes on display. The **Jason Lee House**, the **John D. Boon Home**, and the **Methodist Parsonage** are also part of the village. There is nothing grandiose about these early pioneer homes, the oldest frame structures in the Northwest, but they reveal a great deal about domestic life in the wilds of Oregon in the 1840s. The adjacent **Marion County Historical Society Museum** (☎ *503/364–2128*)

displays pioneer and Calapooia Indian artifacts. ⊠ *Museum complex, 1313 Mill St. SE* ☎ *503/585–7012* ⊕ *www.missionmill.org* ☺ *$6, includes tour* ☼ *Daily 10–5* ☞ *Guided tours of houses and woolen mill museum are given when possible.*

❻ Mount Angel Abbey. On a 300-foot-high butte, this Benedictine monastery was founded in 1882. It's the site of one of two American buildings designed by Finnish architect Alvar Aalto. A masterpiece of serene and thoughtful design, Aalto's library opened its doors in 1970, and has become a place of pilgrimage for students and aficionados of modern architecture. ⊠ *18 mi from Salem, east on Hwy. 213, and north on Hwy. 214* ☎ *503/845–3030* ⊕ *www.mountangelabbey.org* ☺ *Free.*

❷ Oregon Capitol. A brightly gilded bronze statue of the *Oregon Pioneer* stands atop the 140-foot-high Capitol dome, looking north across the Capitol Mall. Built in 1939 with blocks of gray Vermont marble, Oregon's Capitol has an elegant yet austere neoclassical feel. East and west wings were added in 1978. Relief sculptures and deft historical murals soften the interior. Tours of the rotunda, the House and Senate chambers, and the governor's office leave from the information center under the dome. ⊠ *900 Court St.* ☎ *503/986–1388* ⊕ *www.leg.state. or.us* ☺ *Free* ☼ *Weekdays 8–5.*

Oregon Capitol building in Salem

❸ Willamette University. Behind the Capitol, across State Street but half a world away, are the brick buildings and grounds of Willamette University, the oldest college in the West. Founded in 1842, Willamette has long been a breeding ground for aspiring politicians. **Hatfield Library,** built in 1986 on the banks of Mill Stream, is a handsome brick-and-glass building with a striking campanile; tall, prim **Waller Hall,** built in 1867, is one of the oldest buildings in the Pacific Northwest. ✉ *Information desk, Putnam University Center, Mill St.* ☎ *503/370–6300* ⊕ *www.willamette.edu* ⊘ *Weekdays 8–5.*

WINERIES

Bethel Heights Vineyard. The tasting room has one of the most glorious panoramic views of any winery in the state; its terrace and picnic area overlook the surrounding vineyards, the valley below, and Mount Jefferson in the distance. Founded in 1977, Bethel Heights was one of the first vineyards planted in the Eola Hills region of the Willamette Valley. It produces Pinot Noir, Chardonnay, Pinot Blanc, and Pinot Gris. ✉ *6060 Bethel Heights Rd. NW* ☎ *503/581–2262* ⊕ *www. bethelheights.com* 🖃 *$5, refundable with purchase* ⊘ *Varies by season.*

Witness Tree Vineyard. Named for the ancient oak that towers over the vineyard (it was originally used as a surveyor's landmark in 1854), this winery produces premium Pinot Noir made entirely from grapes grown on its 100-acre estate nestled in the Eola Hills northwest of Salem. Witness Tree Vineyard also produces limited quantities of estate Chardonnay, Viognier, Pinot Blanc, Dolcetto, and a sweet dessert wine called Sweet Signé. Tours are conducted frequently. ✉ *7111 Spring Valley Rd.*

NW ☎ 503/585–7874 ⊕ www.witnesstreevineyard.com ⊙ Summer: Tues.–Sun. 11-5; weekends year-round.

WHERE TO EAT AND STAY

$$
AMERICAN
✕**Bentley's Grill.** Located in the Grand Hotel in Salem, this steak and seafood eatery strives to serve ingredients from the Northwest, whether it's Oregon bay shrimp, Rogue Valley bleu cheese, Oregon hazelnuts, or local beef. Its menu also has occasional wild game entrées. Rounding out its menu are selections from its pizza oven. ⊠ *201 Liberty St. SE* ☎ *503/779–1660* ⊕ *bentleysgrill.com* ▭ *AE, DC, MC, V.*

$$
ITALIAN
Fodor's Choice
★
✕**DaVinci.** Salem politicos flock to this two-story downtown restaurant for Italian-inspired dishes cooked in a wood-burning oven. No shortcuts are taken in the preparation, so don't come if you're in a rush. But if you're in the mood to linger over seafood and fresh pasta that's made on the premises, this may be your place. The wine list is one of the most extensive in the Northwest; the staff is courteous and extremely professional. There's wine tasting and live jazz Thursdays at 6 PM. ⊠ *180 High St.* ☎ *503/399–1413* ⊕ *www.davincisofsalem.com* ▭ *AE, DC, MC, V* ⊙ *No lunch.*

🛏 **Grand Hotel in Salem.** Formerly known as the Phoenix Grand Hotel, this property serves as the headquarters hotel for the new Salem Conference Center in downtown Salem. It's centrally located, a convenient base for trips to nearby parks, shopping, and wineries. The rooms are large, with comfortable, luxurious furnishings. It's restaurant, Bentley's Grill, is a local favorite. **Pros:** spacious rooms, centrally located. **Cons:** located on the street. ⊠ *201 Liberty St. SE, Salem* ☎ *503/540–7800 or 877/540–7800* ⊕ *www.GrandHotelSalem.com* ⇲ *143 rooms, 50 suites* ♿ *In-Room: refrigerator, Internet. In-hotel: restaurant, Wi-Fi, pool, gym* ▭ *AE, D, DC, MC, V.*

🛏 **Oregon Garden Resort.** Located 13 mi northeast of Salem, this luxurious property neighbors the Oregon Garden. The rooms are bright, roomy, and tastefully decorated. Rates include a full breakfast and admission to the Oregon Garden. The hotel is great for weddings, meetings and romantic getaways. Each room has a fireplace and a private, landscaped patio or balcony. The resort has a full-service spa, an outdoor pool, and free parking. Some pet-friendly rooms are available. **Pros:** gorgeous grounds, luxurious rooms, plenty of amenities. **Cons:** outside of town, away from other activities. ⊠ *895 W. Main St., Silverton* ☎ *503/874–2500 or 800/966–6490* ⊕ *www.oregongardenresort.com* ⇲ *143 rooms, 50 suites* ♿ *In-Room: a/c, refrigerator, Internet. In-hotel: restaurant, spa, pool, parking* ▭ *AE, D, DC, MC, V* ⦿*BP.*

SHOPPING

Reed Opera House. Located in downtown Salem, this 1869 opera house now contains a compelling collection of locally owned stores, shops, restaurants, bars, and bakeries. Its Trinity Ballroom hosts special events and celebrations. ⊠ *189 Liberty St. NE* ☎ *503/391–4481* ⊕ *www.reedoperahouse.com.*

Woodburn Company Stores. Located 18 mi north of Salem on Interstate 5 are more than 100 brand-name outlet stores, including Nike, Calvin Klein, Bose, Gymboree, OshKosh B'Gosh, Ann Taylor, Levi's, Chico's,

Fossil, Liz Claiborne, Polo, and Columbia Sportswear, and plenty of places to eat. Chances are that someone in your traveling party would enjoy burning an hour or three perusing famous outlet stores. ⊠ *1001 Arney Rd., Woodburn* ☎ *503/981–1900 or 888/664–7467* ⊕ *www. shop-woodburn.com* ⊙ *Mon.–Sat. 10–8, Sun. 10–7.*

SPORTS AND THE OUTDOORS

RECREATIONAL   **Silver Falls State Park.** Hidden amid old-growth Douglas firs in the foot-
AREAS   hills of the Cascades, Silver Falls is the largest state park in Oregon (8,700 acres). South Falls, roaring over the lip of a mossy basalt bowl into a deep pool 177 feet below, is the main attraction here, but 13 other waterfalls—half of them more than 100 feet high—are accessible to hikers. The best time to visit is in the fall, when vine maples blaze with brilliant color, or early spring, when the forest floor is carpeted with trilliums and yellow violets. There are picnic facilities and a day lodge; in winter you can cross-country ski. Camping facilities include 52 year-round electrical $24; 45 tent (tent sites closed Oct. 31–Apr. 1) $19; group tent (3 areas) $71; horse camp $19–$58; 14 cabins $39. ⊠ *20024 Silver Falls Hwy. SE, Sublimity* ☎ *503/873–8681 or 800/551–6949* ⊕ *www.oregonstateparks.org* ⊠ *$5 per vehicle* ⊙ *Daily dawn–dusk.*

Willamette Mission State Park. Along pastoral lowlands by the Willamette River, this serene park holds the largest black cottonwood tree in the United States. A thick-barked behemoth by a small pond, the 265-year-old tree has upraised arms that bring to mind J. R. R. Tolkien's fictional Ents. Site of Reverend Jason Lee's 1834 pioneer mission, the park also offers quiet strolling and picnicking in an old orchard and along the river. The Wheatland Ferry, at the north end of the park, began carrying covered wagons across the Willamette in 1844, using pulleys. ⊠ *Wheatland Rd., 8 mi north of Salem, I–5 Exit 263* ☎ *503/393–1172 or 800/551–6949* ⊕ *www.oregonstateparks.org* ⊠ *Day use $5* ⊙ *Daily 8–dusk.*

ALBANY

20 mi from Salem, south on I–5 and west on U.S. 20.

Known as the grass-seed capital of the world, Albany has some of the most historic buildings in Oregon. Some 700 buildings, scattered over a 100-block area in three districts, include every major architectural style in the United States since 1850. The area is listed on the National Register of Historic Places. Eight covered bridges can also be seen on a half-hour drive from Albany.

GETTING HERE

Albany is located on Interstate 5 with easy access to Portland, Salem, and Eugene. Portland International Airport is located 1 hour, 40 minutes away, and the Eugene airport is 1 hour away to the south. Several shuttle services are available from both airports.

Albany Transit System provides two routes for intercity travel. The Linn-Benton loop system provides for transportation between Albany and Corvallis. Albany is a destination stop for Amtrak railroad.

VISITOR INFORMATION
Albany Visitors Association (✉ *250 Broadalbin SW, #110* ☎ *541/928–0911 or 800/526–2256* ⊕ *www.albanyvisitors.com*).

EXPLORING
Monteith House Museum. The first frame house in Albany was Monteith House, built in 1849. Now a museum, restored and filled with period furnishings and historic photos, it is widely thought to be the most authentic restoration of a Pacific Northwest pioneer-era home. ✉ *518 2nd Ave. SW* ☎ *800/526–2256* ⊕ *www.albanyvisitors.com* 📄 *Donation* ⊙ *Mid-June–mid-Sept., Wed.–Sat. noon–4; mid-Sept.–mid-June, by appointment.*

WHERE TO EAT

$$ × **Sybaris.** This fine bistro in Albany's historic downtown strives to
ECLECTIC ensure that most of the menu's ingredients, including the lamb, eggs,
Fodor'sChoice and vegetables, are raised within 10 mi. Even the huckleberries in the ice
★ cream are gathered in secret locations by their mushroom picker. With a monthly rotating menu—which can be viewed online—it serves upscale, flavorful cuisine at reasonable prices. ✉ *442 1st Ave. W.* ☎ *541/928–8157* ⊕ *www.sybarisbistro.com* ⊙ *Closed Sun. and Mon. No lunch* ⊟ *AE, D, DC, MC, V.*

$ × **Novak's Hungarian.** Since 1984, the Novak family has been a delight-
HUNGARIAN ful fixture in Albany's dining scene. From Hungarian hash and eggs in the morning to chicken paprika served over homemade Hungarian pearl noodles, you can't go wrong in this establishment. There's a huge assortment of desserts as well. On Sunday they serve brunch. ✉ *2306 Heritage Way SE* ☎ *541/967–9488* ⊕ *www.novakshungarian. com* ⊟ *AE, D, MC, V.*

CORVALLIS

10 mi southwest of Albany on U.S. 20.

To some, Corvallis is a brief stopping place along the way to Salem or Portland. To others, it's a small town that gives you a chance to escape the bigger cities. Driving the area's economy are a growing engineering and high-tech industry, a burgeoning wine industry, and more traditional local agricultural crops, such as grass and legume seeds. Corvallis is home to Oregon State University and its Beavers. It offers plenty of outdoor activities as well as scenic attractions, from covered bridges to wineries and gardens.

GETTING HERE
Corvallis Transit System (CTS) operates eight bus routes throughout the city. **Hut Shuttle** (☎ *503/364–4444* ⊕ *www.portlandairportshuttle. com*) provides transportation between Corvallis and the Portland airport, located 1 hour, 53 minutes away. **OmniShuttle** (☎ *541/461–7959* ⊕ *www.omnishuttle.us*) provides transportation between Corvallis and the Eugene airport, 50 minutes away. Corvallis Municipal Airport is a public airport 4 mi south of the city.

VISITOR INFORMATION

Corvallis Tourism (⊠ *553 NW Harrison* ☎ *541/757–1544 or 800/334–8118* ⊕ *www.visitcorvallis.com*)

EXPLORING

Benton County Historical Society and Museum. The artifact collection of 66,000 items features local themes ranging from logging and technology to the arts. The museum also has artifacts of Camp Adair, which was a World War II military cantonment, and Philomath College, a United Brethren College that now houses the museum. ⊠ *1101 Main St., Philomath* ☎ *541/929–6230* ⊕ *www.bentoncountymuseum.org* ⊙ *Tues.–Sat. 10–4:30.*

Oregon State University. It's a thrill to be on campus on game day, as students are a sea of orange and black cheering on their beloved Beavers. This 400-acre campus, west of the city center, was established as a land-grant institution in 1868. OSU has more than 22,000 students, many of them studying the university's nationally recognized programs in conservation biology, agricultural sciences, nuclear engineering, forestry, fisheries and wildlife management, community health, pharmacy, and zoology. ⊠ *15th and Jefferson Sts.* ☎ *541/737–1000* ⊕ *oregonstate.edu.*

WHERE TO EAT AND STAY

$ ✕ **Gathering Together Farm.** When spring arrives, it means that the organic

NEW AMERICAN   farmers outside of Philomath are serving their bounty. Fresh vegetables,

Fodor'sChoice   pizzas, local lamb, pork, and halibut are frequent menu highlights.

★   Local wines and tempting desserts make the evening perfect. It also serves lunch four days a week and breakfast on Saturday. ⊠ *25159 Grange Hall Rd., Philomath* ☎ *541/929–4270* ⚑ *reservations essential* ⊟ *MC, V* ⊙ *Closed Mon. and Oct.–Mar. No dinner Sat.–Wed. No lunch Sun.*

$ ⊡ **Salbasgeon Suites & Conference Center.** Rooms here are spacious, clean, and equipped with new furnishings, although it doesn't shake the chain hotel feel. What's nice is its proximity to Oregon State University, Hewlett-Packard, movie theatres, and fine dining. **Pros:** close to Corvallis sights, in-hotel activities. **Cons:** suites seem a little cramped; bland and corporate. ⊠ *1730 NW 9th St., Corvallis* ☎ *541/753–4320 or 800/965–8808* ⊕ *www.salbasgeon.com* ↘ *95 rooms* ⚐ *In-room: refrigerator, a/c. In-hotel: restaurant, bar, pool, gym, laundry facilities, Wi-Fi* ❙⊙❙ *BP* ⊟ *AE, D, MC, V.*

SPORTS AND THE OUTDOORS

RECREATIONAL   **Siuslaw National Forest.** The highest point in the Coast Range (4,097

AREAS   feet), Mary's Peak offers panoramic views of the Cascades, the Wil-

Fodor'sChoice   lamette Valley, and the rest of the Coast Range. On a clear day you

★   can see as far as the Pacific Ocean. There are several picnicking areas, more than 10 mi of hiking trails, and a small campground. There are stands of noble fir and alpine meadows. The forest, just 2 mi from Corvallis, includes the Oregon Dunes National Recreation Area and the Cape Perpetua Interpretive Center. People usually access the Forest using one of several major highways: Highways 26, 6, and 18 all access the north central coast; Highways 20 and 34 access Newport and the central coast; Highway 126 accesses Florence and the north

Shimanek Bridge over Thomas Creek in Scio

part of the Oregon Dunes; and Highway 38 accesses Reedsport and the southern section of the Oregon Dunes. ✉ *4077 SW Research Way, Corvallis* ☎ *541/750–7000* ⊕ *www.fs.fed.us/r6/siuslaw* ✉ *Free* ☉ *Daily dawn–dusk.*

SWIMMING **Osborn Aquatic Center.** This is not the site of your ordinary lap pool. There are waterslides, a water channel, water cannons, and floor geysers. The indoor lap pool is open all year. ✉ *1940 NW Highland Dr.* ☎ *541/766–7946* ⊕ *www.ci.corvallis.or.us* ✉ *$4* ☉ *June–Sept.*

SOUTH WILLAMETTE VALLEY

Lane County rests at the southern end of the Willamette Valley. It encompasses Eugene, Springfield, Drain, McKenzie Bridge, and Cottage Grove to the south. There are plenty of wineries to enjoy, but visitors can also sprinkle their sipping fun with some white-water rafting, deep-woods hiking, and cheering on the Oregon Ducks. To the west lies the Oregon Dunes Recreation Area and to the east the beautiful Central Oregon communities of Sisters, Bend, and Redmond.

EUGENE

63 mi south of Corvallis on I–5.

Eugene was founded in 1846, when Eugene Skinner staked the first federal land-grant claim for pioneers. Eugene is consistently given high marks for its "livability." As the home of the University of Oregon, a large student and former-student population lends Eugene a youthful

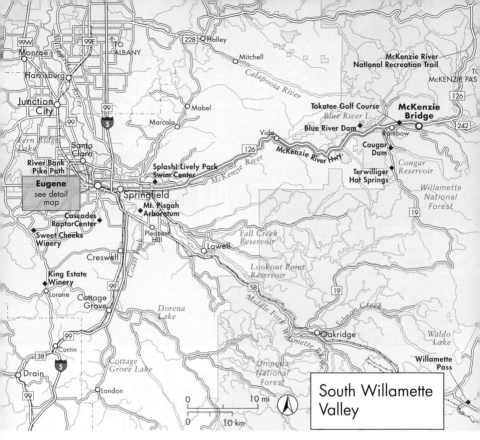

South Willamette Valley

vitality and countercultural edge. Full of parks and oriented to the outdoors, Eugene is a place where bike paths are used, pedestrians *always* have the right-of-way, and joggers are so plentiful that the city is known as the Running Capital of the World. Shopping and commercial streets surround the Eugene Hilton and the Hult Center for the Performing Arts, the two most prominent downtown buildings. During football season you can count on the University of Oregon Ducks being the primary topic of most conversations.

GETTING HERE

Eugene's airport has rental cars, cabs, and shuttles that make the 15-minute trip to Eugene's city center. By train, Amtrak stops in the heart of downtown. Getting around Lane County's communities is easy with **Lane Transit District** (LTD) (☎ 541/687–5555 ⊕ *www.ltd.org*) public transportation. Eugene is very bicycle-friendly.

VISITOR INFORMATION

Eugene, Cascades & Coast Adventure Center (✉ *3312 Gateway St., Springfield* ☎ *541/484–5307* ⊕ *www.travellanecounty.org*).

Numbers in the margin correspond to the Eugene map.

EXPLORING

② Alton Baker Park. Named after the Eugene *Register-Guard* newspaper's publisher, Alton Baker Park is the site of many community events. Live music is performed in summer. There's fine hiking and biking at Alton Baker on the banks of the Willamette River. A footpath along the river runs the length of the park. Also worth seeing is the Whilamut Natural Area, an open space with 13 "talking stones," each with an inscription. Also, there is an excellent dog section. ✉ *Centennial Blvd. east of Ferry St. Bridge, Eugene* ☎ *541/484–5307 or 541/682–2000* ⊕ *www.eugene-or.gov* ☉ *Daily 6 AM–11 PM.*

⑤ Cascades Raptor Center. This birds-of-prey nature center and hospital has over 30 species of birds. This is a great outing for kids, where they can learn what owls eat, why and where birds migrate. Some of its full-time residents include turkey vultures, bald eagles, owls, hawks, falcons, and kites. ✉ *32275 Fox Hollow Rd., Eugene* ☎ *541/485–1320* ⊕ *www.eRaptors.org* ✉ *$7* ☉ *Apr.–Oct., 10–6; closed Mon.*

③ Eugene Saturday Market. Every Saturday between April and November local craftspeople, farmers, and chefs provide cheap eats and nifty arts and crafts at this outdoor market. It's the oldest weekly open-air crafts festival in the United States. There are more than 200 booths, food, and live entertainment every Saturday. No pets are allowed. ✉ *8th Ave. and Oak St., Eugene* ☎ *541/686–8885* ⊕ *www.eugenesaturdaymarket.org* ✉ *Free* ☉ *Apr.–mid-Nov., Sat. 10–5.*

④ 5th Street Public Market. A former chicken-processing plant is the site of this popular shopping mall, filled with small crafts, art, and gifts stores. Dining includes sit-down restaurants, decadent bakeries, and the international diversity of the second-floor food esplanade. ✉ *5th Ave. and High St., Eugene* ☎ *541/484–0383* ⊕ *www.5stmarket.com* ☉ *Shops Mon.–Sat. 10–7, Sun. 11–5.*

⑥ George E. Owen Memorial Rose Garden. Three thousand roses bloom June–September at this 9-acre garden west of Skinner Butte Park, along the Willamette River. Magnolia, cherry, and oak trees dot the grounds. ✉ *300 N. Jefferson St., Eugene* ☎ *541/682–4833* ⊕ *www.downtowneugene.com* ✉ *Free* ☉ *Daily 6 AM–11 PM.*

⑦ Lane County Historical Museum. Collections dating from the 1840s to the present are in a 14,000-square-foot building. Exhibits include period rooms, vehicles, early trades, the Oregon Trail, and early settlement, historic photographs, and memorabilia from decades past. Exhibits change often. ✉ *740 W. 13th Ave., Eugene* ☎ *541/682–4242* ⊕ *www.lanecountyhistoricalsociety.org* ✉ *$3* ☉ *Tues.–Sat. 10–4.*

⑨ Mount Pisgah Arboretum. This beautiful nature preserve near southeast Eugene includes extensive all-weather trails, educational programs for all ages, and facilities for special events. Its visitor center holds workshops, and features native amphibian and reptile terraria; microscopes for exploring tiny seeds, bugs, feathers, and snakeskins; "touch me" exhibits; reference books; and a working viewable beehive. ⊠ *34901 Frank Parrish Rd., Eugene* ☎ *541/747–3817* ⊕ *www.mountpisgaharboretum. org* ⊠ *Donation suggested, $2 parking* ☉ *Daily, dawn to dusk.*

① **Science Factory.** Formerly the Willamette Science and Technology Center (WISTEC), and still known to locals by its former name, Eugene's imaginative, hands-on museum assembles rotating exhibits designed for curious young minds. The adjacent **planetarium**, one of the largest in the Pacific Northwest, presents star shows and entertainment events. ⊠ *2300 Leo Harris Pkwy., Eugene* ☎ *541/682–7888 museum, 541/461–8227 planetarium* ⊕ *www.sciencefactory.org* ⊠ *$7 for both science hall and planetarium, $4 each* ☉ *Wed.–Sun. 10–4. Closed Oregon Ducks home football games and major holidays.*

❽ **University of Oregon.** The true heart of Eugene lies southeast of the city center at its university. Several fine old buildings can be seen on the 250-acre campus; **Deady Hall,** built in 1876, is the oldest. More than 400 varieties of trees grace the bucolic grounds, along with outdoor sculptures that include *The Pioneer* and *The Pioneer Mother.* The two bronze figures by Alexander Phimster Proctor were dedicated to the men and women who settled the Oregon Territory and less than a generation later founded the university.

Eugene's two best museums are affiliated with the university. The **Jordan Schnitzer Museum of Art** (⊠ *1430 Johnson La.* ☎ *541/346–3027* ⊕ *www.uoma.uoregon.edu* ⊠ *$5* ☉ *Tues.–Sun. 11–5*), next to the library, underwent a major renovation and expansion, nearly doubling its size. It includes galleries featuring American, European, Korean, Chinese, and Japanese art. Relics of a more local nature are on display at the **University of Oregon Museum of Natural History** (⊠ *1680 E. 15th Ave.* ☎ *541/346–3024* ⊕ *www.natural-history.uoregon.edu* ⊠ *$3* ☉ *Wed.–Sun. 11–5*), devoted to Pacific Northwest anthropology and the natural sciences. Its highlights include the fossil collection of Thomas Condon, Oregon's first geologist, and a pair of 9,000-year-old sagebrush sandals. *Agate St. and Franklin Blvd.* ⊕ *www.uoregon.edu*

WINERIES

King Estate Winery. This certified organic estate is committed to producing world-class Pinot Gris and Pinot Noir. The visitors center offers complimentary wine tasting, extensive flight selections, and production tours. ⊠ *80854 Territorial Rd., Eugene* ☎ *541/942–9874 or 800/884–4441* ⊕ *www.kingestate.com* ⊠ *$7* ☉ *Daily 11–9, tours on the hour noon–5.*

Sweet Cheeks Winery. This estate vineyard lies on a prime sloping hillside in the heart of the Willamette Valley appellation. It also supplies grapes to several award-winning wineries. It has free Friday-night tastings with cheese pairings. Check the Web site for special dinners and events. ⊠ *27007 Briggs Hill Rd., Eugene* ☎ *541/349–9463 or 877/309–9463* ⊕ *www.sweetcheekswinery.com* ☉ *Daily noon–6; Fri.-night twilight tastings with cheese pairings 6–9.*

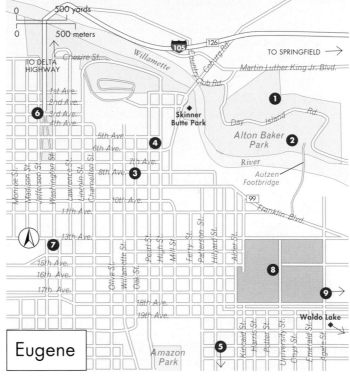

Eugene

3

WHERE TO EAT

$$$

NEW AMERICAN

✗ **Adam's Sustainable Table.** Serving delicious seasonal Northwest cuisine with an organic menu of local produce, meats, and sustainable seafood, Adam's works to obtain food from farms, ranches, and mills within a 75-mi radius, most within 25 mi to keep its ingredients as local as possible. Its most requested dish is the pasture-raised chicken picatta, and its produce is so fresh it will bring tears to your eyes. Adam's is a recipient of 10 *Wine Spectator* awards. ⌧ *30 E. Broadway, Eugene* ☎ *541/344–6948* ⊕ *www.adamsplacerestaurant.com* ▤ *AE, MC, V* ☉ *No lunch. Closed Sun. and Mon.*

$$

ITALIAN

✗ **Excelsior Café.** The expert cuisine enhances the appealing European elegance of this restaurant, bar, and bistro-style café across from the University of Oregon. The chef uses only fresh local produce, but Excelsior is best known for its authentic Italian cuisine, such as a delectable osso bucco Milanese and house-made artisan pasta. The menu changes according to the season, but staples include delicious salads and soups, gnocchi, grilled chicken, broiled salmon, and sandwiches. The dining room, shaded by blossoming cherry trees in the spring, has a quiet, understated feel. There's outdoor seating on the patio. Serves breakfast and Sunday brunch. ⌧ *754 E. 13th Ave., Eugene* ☎ *541/342–6963 or 800/321–6963* ⊕ *www.excelsiorinn.com* ▤ *AE, D, DC, MC, V.*

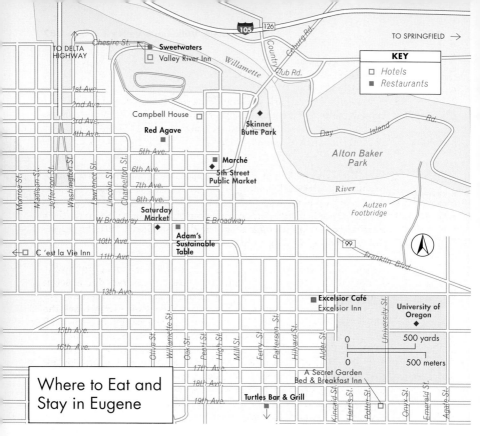

TO SPRINGFIELD →

KEY

☐ Hotels
■ Restaurants

Where to Eat and
Stay in Eugene

$$$ ✗**Marché.** The name translates into "market," meaning that this
FRENCH   renowned Eugene restaurant works with a dozen local farmers to bring
the freshest, most organic local food to the table. Specialties include
salmon, halibut, sturgeon, and beef tenderloin, braised pork shoulders,
and outstanding local oysters. It has an extensive wine list with an
emphasis on Oregon and France. There's also a Sunday brunch. ⊠ 296
E. 5th Ave., Eugene ☎ *541/342–3612* ⊕ *www.marcheprovisions.com*
▭ *AE, D, MC, V.*

$$ ✗**Red Agave.** Two local women managed to establish this cozy, roman-
SOUTHWESTERN   tic restaurant in an old building that at one point was a refuse dump,
Fodor's Choice   and the result is a hard-to-categorize winner that has Mexican and
★   Latino influences. Menu items might include sesame-crusted salmon
with chipotle barbecue glaze, which you can consider washing down
with a tamarind margarita. Flans, like much of the menu, are seasonal;
try the Kahlua flan or the orange flan with chocolate in the middle.
⊠ *454 Willamette St., Eugene* ☎ *541/683–2206* ⊕ *redagave.net* ▭ *AE,*
D, DC, MC, V ⊗ *Closed Sun. No lunch.*

$$ ✗**Sweetwaters.** The dining room at the Valley River Inn, which overlooks
AMERICAN   the Willamette at water level, specializes in Pacific Northwest cuisine.
Try the salmon with Szechuan peppercorn crust and cranberry vinai-
grette or the grilled beef fillet with Oregon blue-cheese crust. There is a
bar area outside, as well as a deck for open-air dining. Sunday brunch

and a kids' menu are available, too. ⊠ *1000 Valley River Way, Eugene* ☎ *541/687–0123* ⊕ *www.valleyriverinn/sweetwaters.com* ⊟ *AE, D, DC, MC, V.*

$ ✕ **Turtles Bar & Grill.** Parking around this spot is scarce, and there aren't
SOUTHERN   enough tables, but the food is worth the obstacles. The barbecue entrées, particularly the pulled-pork sandwich, are tasty, and the staff is friendly. ⊠ *2692 Willamette St., Eugene* ☎ *541/465–9038* ⊟ *AE, D, DC, MC, V.*

WHERE TO STAY

$ ⊞ **Campbell House.** Built in 1892 on the east side of Skinner Butte, Campbell House is one of the oldest structures in Eugene. Restored with fastidious care, the luxurious bed-and-breakfast is surrounded by an acre of landscaped grounds. The parlor, library, and dining rooms have their original hardwood floors and curved-glass windows. Differing architectural details, building angles, and furnishings (a mixture of century-old antiques and reproductions) lend each of the rooms a distinctive personality. Suites have Jacuzzis. The room rates include a full breakfast including fresh-baked pastries. The house now serves dinner seven nights a week, with a prix-fixe offering or à la carte. **Pros:** classic architecture, comfortable rooms, well-kept grounds. **Cons:** rooms lack the amenities of nearby hotels. ⊠ *252 Pearl St., Eugene* ☎ *541/343–1119 or 800/264–2519* ⊕ *www.campbellhouse.com* ⋙ *12 rooms, 7 suites, 1 cottage* ♿ *In-room: DVD (some), Wi-Fi* ⊟ *AE, D, MC, V.*

$ ⊞ **C'est la Vie Inn.** Listed on the National Register of Historic Places,
Fodor's Choice   the restored 1891 Queen Anne Victorian bed-and-breakfast has been
★   updated to provide Old World comfort with modern-day amenities. The inn serves as an excellent hub for enjoying Eugene, as it is close to downtown shops, restaurants, galleries, and bicycle paths. The Hult Center for the Performing Arts and the University of Oregon campus are also within walking distance. Each guest room is luxurious and romantic, with private bath and individual cooling/heating controls. The parlor and dining rooms are ornately decorated in period furnishings, and the inn offers concierge services for dry cleaning, theater tickets, and restaurant reservations. **Pros:** outstanding service and value. **Cons:** few rooms. ⊠ *1006 Taylor St., Eugene* ☎ *866/302–3014 or 541/302–3014* ⊕ *www.cestlavieinn.com* ⋙ *3 rooms, 1 suite* ♿ *In-room: DVD, Wi-Fi* ⊟ *AE, MC, V.*

$$ ⊞ **Excelsior Inn.** This small hotel manifests a quiet sophistication com-
Fodor's Choice   mensurate with lodgings found in quaint European villages. Crisply
★   detailed, with cherrywood doors and moldings, it has rooms furnished in a refreshingly understated manner, each with a marble-and-tile bath and some with fireplaces. The rates include a delicious breakfast. The ground-level Excelsior Café is one of Eugene's best restaurants. **Pros:** romantic accommodations, excellent service and restaurant. **Cons:** formal in a casual town. ⊠ *754 E. 13th Ave., Eugene* ☎ *541/342–6963 or 800/321–6963* ⊕ *www.excelsiorinn.com* ⋙ *14 rooms* ♿ *In-room: a/c, Wi-Fi. In-hotel: restaurant, parking* ⊟ *AE, D, DC, MC, V* ◎⛛ *BP.*

$$ ⊞ **A Secret Garden Bed & Breakfast Inn.** This intimate bed-and-breakfast mansion is the former home of the Baker family, owners of the distinguished newspaper, the Eugene *Register-Guard*. The nightly rate includes a breakfast of fresh fruits, juice, granola, breads, and a hot egg.

Fresh produce from Hey Bayles! Farm at the Eugene Saturday Market

Coffee and tea stations are located throughout the inn. The spacious lobby offers comfortable seating areas for conversation and reading, as does a nook on the second floor. Its dining room can seat up to 40, and is an ideal choice for small meetings, private parties, receptions, and weddings. It's the perfect place to hang your hat while enjoying local events, such as the annual Oregon Bach Festival, wine tastings at nearby King Estates, or golf at Bandon Dunes on the Oregon coast. **Pros:** pretty rooms. **Cons:** quiet and formal. ⊠ *1910 University St., Eugene* ☎ *541/484–6755 or 888/484–6755* ⊕ *secretgardenbbinn.com* ↘ *8 rooms, 2 suites* ⚴ *In-room: DVD, refrigerator, Wi-Fi* ⊟ *AE, MC, V* ⚭ *BP.*

$ ⬚ **Valley River Inn.** At this inn on the banks of the Willamette River, some rooms have an outdoor patio or balcony, some have river or pool views, and concierge rooms have access to a private lounge. The location is splendid, and current renovation should elevate the hotel's appearance to match its surroundings. The inn's restaurant is the popular Sweetwaters. It also provides bicycles to help guests get out and about. **Pros:** river location, amenities, great restaurant. **Cons:** basic room decor. ⊠ *1000 Valley River Way, Eugene* ☎ *541/687–0123 or 800/543–8266* ⊕ *www. valleyriverinn.com* ↘ *257 rooms* ⚴ *In-hotel: restaurant, bar, Wi-Fi, pool, gym, laundry service, parking* ⊟ *AE, D, DC, MC, V.*

NIGHTLIFE AND THE ARTS

Hult Center for the Performing Arts. This is the locus of Eugene's cultural life. Renowned for the quality of its acoustics, the center has two theaters that are home to Eugene's symphony and opera. ⊠ *1 Eugene Cen-*

ter, at 7th Ave. and Willamette St., Eugene ☎ *541/682–5087* ⊕ *www. hultcenter.org.*

In May and August the **John G. Shedd Institute for the Arts** (☎ *541/434– 7000 tickets; 541/687–6526* ⊕ *www.ofam.org*) presents concerts at the Hult Center and in parks around Eugene.

Conductor Helmuth Rilling leads the internationally known **Oregon Bach Festival** (☎ *541/682–5000 for tickets; 800/457–1486 for information* ⊕ *www.bachfest.uoregon.edu*) every summer. Concerts, chamber music, and social events—held mainly in Eugene at the Hult Center and the University of Oregon School of Music but also in Corvallis and Florence—are part of this 19-day event.

SHOPPING

Tourists coming to the Willamette Valley, especially to Eugene, can't escape without experiencing the **5th Street Public Market** in downtown Eugene. There are plenty of small crafts shops, and the food mall offers many cuisines, including vegetarian, pizza, and seafood.

Valley River Center (✉ *Delta Hwy. and Valley River Dr., Eugene* ☎ *541/ 683–5511*) is the largest shopping center between Portland and San Francisco. There are five department stores, including Meier & Frank and JCPenney, plus 130 specialty shops and a food court.

SPORTS AND THE OUTDOORS

RECREATIONAL AREAS
Ⓒ
Skinner Butte Park. Rising from the south bank of the Willamette River, this park provides the best views of any of the city's parks; it also has the greatest historic cachet, since it was here that Eugene Skinner staked the claim that put Eugene on the map. Children can scale a replica of Skinner Butte, uncover fossils, and cool off under a rain circle. Skinner Butte Loop leads to the top of Skinner Butte, from which Spencer Butte, 4 mi to the south, can be seen. The two main trails to the top of Skinner Butte traverse a sometimes difficult terrain through a mixed-conifer forest. ✉ *2nd Ave. and High St., Eugene* ☎ *541/682–5521* ⊕ *www.eugene-or. gov/parks* 🎟 *Free* ☉ *Daily 10* AM*–midnight.*

Ⓒ
Splash! Lively Park Swim Center. This indoor water park has wave surfing and a waterslide. There are family, lap, and kids' pools; as well as a spa, concessions, playground, park, and picnic shelters. ✉ *6100 Thurston Rd., Springfield* ☎ *541/747–9283* ⊕ *www.willamalane.org* 🎟 *$6.25* ☉ *Mon., Wed., Sun., 1–7:30; Tues. and Thur. 1–5; Fri. and Sat. 1–9.*

OFF THE BEATEN PATH
Waldo Lake. Nestled in old-growth forest, Waldo Lake is famed as a remarkably clean and pristine body of water. The lake is accessible only after a short hike, so bring comfortable shoes. ✉ *From Eugene, take Hwy. 58 to Oakridge and continue toward Willamette Pass; follow signs north to Waldo Lake.*

BIKING AND JOGGING
The **River Bank Bike Path,** originating in Alton Baker Park on the Willamette's north bank, is a level and leisurely introduction to Eugene's topography. It's one of 120 mi of trails in the area. **Prefontaine Trail,** used by area runners, travels through level fields and forests for 1½ mi.

SKIING
Willamette Pass (✉ *Hwy. 58, 69 mi southeast of Eugene* ☎ *541/345–7669 or 800/444–5030*), 6,666 feet high in the Cascade Range, packs an annual average snowfall of 300 inches atop 29 runs. The vertical drop is

1,563 feet. Four triple chairs and one double chair service the downhill ski areas, and 13 mi of Nordic trails lace the pass. Facilities here include a ski shop; day care; a bar and restaurant; and Nordic and downhill rentals, repairs, and instruction.

MCKENZIE BRIDGE

58 mi east of Eugene on Hwy. 126.

On the beautiful McKenzie River, lakes, waterfalls, and covered bridges surround the town of McKenzie Bridge and wilderness trails in the Cascades. Fishing, skiing, backpacking, and rafting are among the most popular activities in the area.

GETTING HERE

McKenzie Bridge is about an hour from Eugene, on Highway 126. It is just 38 mi from Hoodoo Ski Area, but its proximity can be deceiving if the snow is heavy. Bend also is close at 64 mi to the east.

VISITOR INFORMATION

Lane County Convention and Visitors Association (⌧ *754 Olive St., Eugene* ☎ *541/343–6335 or 800/547–5445* ⊕ *www.visitlanecounty.org*).

EXPLORING

McKenzie River Highway. Highway 126, as it heads east from Eugene, is known as the McKenzie River Highway. Following the curves of the river, it passes grazing lands, fruit and nut orchards, and the small riverside hamlets of the McKenzie Valley. From the highway you can glimpse the bouncing, bubbling, blue-green McKenzie River, one of Oregon's top fishing, boating, and white-water rafting spots, against a backdrop of densely forested mountains, splashing waterfalls, and jet-black lava beds. The small town of McKenzie Bridge marks the end of the McKenzie River Highway and the beginning of the 26-mi McKenzie River National Recreation Trail, which heads north through the Willamette National Forest along portions of the Old Santiam Wagon Road.

OFF THE BEATEN PATH

McKenzie Pass. Just beyond McKenzie Bridge, Highway 242 begins a steep, 22-mi eastward climb to McKenzie Pass in the Cascade Range. The scenic highway, which passes through the Mt. Washington Wilderness Area and continues to the town of Sisters (⇨ *Central Oregon*), is generally closed October to June because of heavy snow. Novice motorists take note, this is not a drive for the timid: it's a challenging exercise in negotiating tight curves at quickly fluctuating, often slow speeds—the skid marks on virtually every turn attest to hasty braking—so take it slow, and don't be intimidated by cars on your tail itching to take the turns more quickly.

WHERE TO EAT AND STAY

¢

AMERICAN

✕ **Takoda's Restaurant.** This restaurant has a full breakfast menu, burgers, great soups, a salad bar, pizza, and daily specials. In addition, a video game room keeps kids happy. ⌧ *91806 Mill Creek Rd, Milepost 47.5 McKenzie Hwy., Blue River* ☎ *541/822–1153* ▭ *AE, MC, V* ⊗ *Daily 8–8.*

$

🛏 **Belknap Hot Springs Resort.** As the name implies, this resort is all about getting into hot water—willingly. On the site of mineral springs 54 mi east of Eugene, Belknap Hot Springs is adjacent to two hot pools and acres of lush gardens. Stay in the beautiful lodge or campground on the McKenzie River. The Belknap Grill serves burgers and sandwiches. **Pros:** hot springs, wooded location. **Cons:** 14-day cancellation policy, two-night minimum on weekends. ✉ *59296 Belknap Springs Rd., McKenzie Bridge* ☎ *541/822–3512* ⊕ *www.belknaphotsprings.com* ↗ *19 rooms, 7 cabins, 39 RV sites, 13 tent sites* ⊟ *D, MC, V* ⍾ *BP.*

$$ ☎ **Eagle Rock Lodge.** This historic bed-and-breakfast on the McKenzie River is luxurious and cozy for a lodge located in the woods. Rooms have wood, quilts, and antiques, providing a romantic, relaxing atmosphere. The lodge specializes in weddings, retreats, and just great living. Guided fishing and rafting trips can be arranged. Their bodacious breakfasts include homemade pastries, fruits and vegetables, sausage patties, vegetable frittata, and roasted potatoes. Don't forget to pour on the house-made roasted pepper sauce. **Pros:** great location, comfortable atmosphere. **Cons:** a distance from nonoutdoor activities. ✉ *49198 McKenzie Hwy., Vida* ☎ *541/822–3630 or 888/773–4333* ⊕ *www.eaglerocklodge.com* ↗ *8 rooms* ☖ *In-room: refrigerator (some)* ⊟ *MC, V* ⍾ *BP.*

$$ ☎ **Holiday Farm Resort.** Originally built in 1910, the Holiday Farm served for many years as a stagecoach stop, and later a favorite stopover for President Herbert Hoover. Its 13 cottages are on or near the McKenzie River banks and can accommodate between 2 and 14 occupants. The Holiday Farm Restaurant is just a short walk from most cabins. A great feature of the property is the walking trails leading to the McKenzie River and to nearby ponds for fishing or relaxing. Five of the cabins are pet-friendly. There is a lounge and meeting room on the property. Golf, fishing, and rafting are nearby. **Pros:** great place for relaxation and outdoor activities. **Cons:** far from town. ✉ *54455 McKenzie River Dr., Blue River* ☎ *541/822–3725* ⊕ *www.holidayfarmresort.com* ↗ *13 cottages* ☖ *In-room: kitchens, Wi-Fi,* ⊟ *AE, MC, V* ⍾ *BP, MAP, FAP.*

SPORTS AND THE OUTDOORS

RECREATIONAL AREAS **Blue River Dam and Lake.** A 1,240-acre reservoir in the Willamette National Forest has miles of forested shoreline. From May through September, boats are launched from ramps at Saddle Dam and Lookout Creek. Recreational activities include fishing, swimming, waterskiing, and camping at Mona Campground. ✉ *Forest Rd. 15 in Willamette National Forest* ☎ *541/822–3381* ⊟ *Free* ⊙ *June–Sept., daily.*

Cougar Dam and Lake. Four miles outside of McKenzie Bridge is the highest embankment dam ever built by the Army Corps of Engineers—452 feet above the streambed. The resulting reservoir, on the South Fork McKenzie River, covers 1,280 acres. The public recreation areas are in the Willamette National Forest. A fish hatchery is in the vicinity. You can visit the dam year-round, but the campgrounds are open only from May to September. ✉ *Forest Rd. 19 in Willamette National Forest* ☎ *541/822–3381* ⊟ *Free* ⊙ *June–Sept., daily; most areas closed rest of yr.*

Terwilliger Hot Springs (Cougar Hot Springs). An hour and 20 minutes east of Eugene near Highway 126, take a short hike to a natural hot-springs area. Hot-springs aficionados will find Terwilliger to be rustic, which many regard as an advantage. The pools are in a forest of old-growth firs and cedars. No camping. ✉ *5 mi east of Blue River McKenzie Bridge (Aufderheide Scenic Byway), McKenzie Bridge* ☎ *541/822–3799* ⊕ *www.hoodoo.com/Willamette_National_Forest/South_Fork_Area/ Terwilliger_Hot_Springs.htm* ✎ *$5 day use only.*

Willamette National Forest. Stretching 110 mi along the western slopes of the Cascade Range, this forest boasts boundless recreation opportunities, including camping, hiking, boating, ATV riding, and winter sports. It extends from the Mt. Jefferson area east of Salem to the Calapooya Mountains northeast of Roseburg, encompassing 1,675,407 acres. ☎ *541/225-6300* ⊕ *www.fs.fed.us/r6/willamette/index.html.*

GOLF   **Tokatee Golf Club.** Ranked one of the best golf courses in Oregon by *Golf Digest*, this 18-hole beauty is tucked away near the McKenzie River with views of the Three Sisters Mountains, native ponds, and streams. *Tokatee* is a Chinook word meaning "a place of restful beauty." It offers a practice range, carts, lessons, rentals, a coffee shop and snack bar, and Wi-Fi. ✉ *54947 McKenzie Highway, McKenzie Bridge* ☎ *541/822–3220 or 800/452–6376* ⊕ *www.tokatee.com* ✎ *18 holes $42; 9 holes $24.*

WHITE-WATER   **High Country Expeditions.** Raft the white waters of the McKenzie River
RAFTING   on a guided full- or half-day tour. You'll bounce through rapids,
Fodor'sChoice   admire old-growth forest, and watch osprey and blue herons fish-
★   ing. The outfit provides life jackets, splash gear, wet suits, booties (if
☾   requested), boating equipment, paddling instructions, river safety talk, a three-course riverside meal, and shuttle service back to your vehicle. ✉ *Belknap Hot Springs Resort, 59296 Belknap Springs Rd., McKenzie Bridge* ☎ *541/822–8288 or 888/461–7238* ⚲ *reservations and deposit required* ⊕ *www.highcountryexpeditions.com* ✎ *Full day $90.00, half day $60.00.*

The Oregon Coast

WORD OF MOUTH

"I think the south coast, between Port Orford and Brookings, is the most dramatic. Might have something to do with the fact that it's also the most isolated."

—passerbye

WELCOME TO THE OREGON COAST

TOP REASONS TO GO

★ **A beach for everyone.** The Oregon Coast has breathtaking beaches, from romantic, bluffy stretches perfect for linking fingers with loved ones to creature-teeming tide pools great for exploring with kids.

★ **Blow a glass float.** Glass artisan shops dot the coastline, where you can craft your own colorful creations.

★ **Ride the dunes.** Whether you're a screaming dune buggy passenger or an ATV daredevil, southern Oregon's mountainous sand dunes are thrilling.

★ **Par a hole.** Oregon's golf Shangri-la, Bandon Dunes, has four beach courses of pure bliss.

★ **Wine and dine.** You don't have to spend a lot to enjoy fresh seafood, rich microbrews, and local wines. There are delicious coastal eateries for every budget.

1 **North Coast.** The north coast is the primary getaway for Portland and Vancouver residents. Its lighthouse-dotted shoreline stretches from the mouth of the Columbia River at Oregon's far northwestern corner south to Pacific City. The 90-mile region includes the revitalized working community of Astoria, the vacation town of Seaside, the art-fueled and refined Cannon Beach, the well-photographed Manzanita Beach, the dairy paradise of Tillamook, and Pacific City, where a colorful fleet of dories dots the wide, deep beach.

2 **Central Coast.** The 75-mi stretch from Lincoln City to Florence offers whale-watching, incomparable seafood, shell-covered beaches, candy confections, and close-up views of undersea life. At the north end, in Lincoln City, visitors can indulge in gaming, shopping, golfing, and

beachcombing. The harbor town of Depoe Bay is a center for whale-watching, and nearby Newport offers a stellar aquarium and science center. It's also home to one of Oregon's largest fishing fleets. Yachats is a true vacation community, where the only demands are to relax and enjoy. Visitors will want to check in at the Sea Lion Caves in Florence, and enjoy crabbing, shopping, or riding the Oregon dunes.

3 **South Coast.** From the heart of Oregon dunes country in Reedsport to the southernmost Oregon town of Brookings, riding, hiking, and even surfing along the 134-mi south coast is a rollicking thrill. North Bend and Coos Bay are centers for timber, commercial fishing, and commerce. There's also clamming, gaming, sport fishing, and plenty of shopping. Bandon offers a wealth of golfing, camping, lighthouse gazing, and cranberries. Port Orford has gorgeous beach landscapes and windsailing, while Gold Beach, farther south, bathes in sunshine, and gives its visitors a chance to rip up the Rogue River on a jet boat. At Oregon's farthest southwestern corner is Brookings—the "Banana Belt" of the Oregon Coast.

GETTING ORIENTED

Oregon's coastline begins in the north in the town of Astoria, which lies at the mouth of the Columbia River on the Washington state line. It is a 363-mi drive south along U.S. Highway 101 to reach the small town of Brookings at Oregon's southwestern corner, just 6 mi from the California border. The Oregon Coast is bordered by the Pacific Ocean on the left and by the Coast Range on the right. Farther east across the Coast Range is the Willamette Valley, which includes the larger Oregon communities of Portland, Salem, Corvallis, and Eugene.

THE OREGON COAST PLANNER

When to Go

December through June are generally rainy months, but once the fair weather comes coastal Oregon is one of the most gorgeous, greenest places on earth. July through September offer wonderful, dry days for beachgoers.

Even with the rain, coastal winter and spring do have quite a following. Many hotels are perfectly situated for storm watching, and provide a romantic proposition. Think of a toasty fire, sweet music, a smooth Oregon Pinot, and your loved one, settled in to watch the waves dance upon a jagged rocky stage.

If you're looking for one time of year to experience what friendly frivolity can be found on the coast, check out the **Cannon Beach Sandcastle Contest** in May—if you can find a room or a parking spot. The **Newport Seafood and Wine Festival** occurs the last full weekend in February, and calls itself the premier seafood and wine event of the West Coast. Dozens of wineries are represented at this expansive celebration, which also features myriad crafts and eateries. In Bandon each October, the **Cranberry Festival** comprises a fair and parade.

Getting Here and Around

Air Travel. The north coast is accessible from **Astoria Regional Airport** (AST) (☎ 800/860–4093 or 503/325–4521), which has daily flights from Portland on SeaPort Airlines. The central coast has daily flights into **Newport Municipal Airport** (ONP) (☎ 800/424–3655 or 541/867–3655) on SeaPort Airlines. The south coast has flights from its new **Southwest Oregon Regional Airport** (OTH) (☎ 541/756–8531) in North Bend to Portland and San Francisco on United Express. Taxis are available at all airports; Hertz car rental is at the Astoria and Southwest airports.

Portland's airport is roughly 100 mi away from both Astoria and Lincoln City, and the drive takes about two hours; Newport is 150 mi and a three-hour drive away. **PDX Shuttle Portland** (☎ 503/740-9485 ⊕ pdxshuttleportland.com) provides service from Portland's airport to the coast for around $200. **OmniShuttle** (☎ 800/741-5097) provides shuttle service from Eugene airport to the coast. The fare to Yachats is $135. It is more economical to rent a car.

Bus Travel. Greyhound (☎ 800/231–2222 ⊕ www.greyhound.com) serves Coos Bay, Newport, Toledo, and Waldport, connecting them with Corvallis, Salem, and Portland. **Sunset Empire Transportation** (☎ 503/861-7433 ⊕ www.ridethebus.org) travels between Portland and Astoria Monday, Wednesday, and Friday, and serves the north coast cities of Astoria, Warrenton, Hammond, Gearhart, Seaside, and Cannon Beach. **Porter Stage Lines** (☎ 541/269–7183) connects the Florence and Coos Bay area with Eugene.

Car Travel. Driving the coast is one of the singular pleasures of visiting Oregon. Car-rental agencies are available in the coast's larger towns; a branch of Enterprise is in Newport, Hertz is at the airports. U.S. 101 runs the length of the coast, sometimes turning inland for a few miles. The highway enters coastal Oregon from Washington State at Astoria and from California near Brookings. U.S. 30 heads west from Portland to Astoria. U.S. 20 travels west from Corvallis to Newport. Highway 126 winds west to the coast from Eugene. Highway 42 leads west from Roseburg toward Coos Bay.

About the Restaurants

Deciding which restaurant has the best clam chowder is just one of the culinary fact-finding expeditions you can embark upon along the Oregon Coast. Chefs here take full advantage of the wealth of sturgeon, chinook, steelhead, and trout found in coastal rivers. Fresh mussels, shrimp, and oyster shooters are also standard fare in many establishments. Newport's bounty is its Dungeness crab. When razor clams are in season, they appear as a succulent addition to restaurant menus throughout the state. Also popular are desserts made from Oregon's wealth of blueberries, marionberries, and huckleberries.

Away from the upscale resorts, most restaurants tend to be low-key and affordable. There are many hearty pizza establishments, and tasty fish-and-chips are easy to come by. In addition, Oregon Coast restaurants proudly serve reds and whites from Willamette Valley wineries and rich ales from local or on-site breweries.

About the Hotels

The Oregon Coast offers a pleasant variety of properties for visitors who either wish to wallow in luxury, stay at a beachside golf course, watch storms through picture windows, or take river-running fishing trips. There are plenty of chains in the area, as well as an eclectic assortment of properties: fascinating bed-and-breakfasts hosted by friendly folks with stories to tell, properties perched on cliffs, and hotels set in the midst of wilderness and hiking trails.

Properties in Seaside and Lincoln City fill up fast in the summer, so book in advance. Between June and October hotel rates nudge up for many properties, but with some research you'll find plenty that keep their rates fairly steady throughout the year. Many will require a minimum two-night stay on a summer weekend.

WHAT IT COSTS IN U.S. DOLLARS

	¢	$	$$	$$$	$$$$
Restaurants	under $10	$10–$16	$17–$23	$24–$30	over $30
Hotels		under $100	$101–$150	$151–$200	$201–$250	over $250

Restaurant prices are per person, for a main course at dinner. Hotel prices are for two people in a standard double room in high season, excluding tax.

Tour Options

Marine Discovery Tours (✉ Newport ☎ 800/903–2628) conducts a sealife cruise. The 65-foot excursion boat *Discovery*, with inside seating for 49 people and two viewing levels, departs throughout the day. Its public cruise season is March–October, while reserved group tours are welcome throughout the year.

NorthWest EcoExcursions (✉ Depoe Bay ☎ 541/765–2598 ⊕ www.nwecoexcursions.com) has kayaking, hiking, and whale-watching tours at various levels of difficulty. Its guides are experienced naturalists, with backgrounds in park-ranger service and education.

VISITOR INFORMATION

Central Oregon Coast Association (✉ 137 NE 1st St.Newport, ☎ 503/265–2064 or 800/767–2064 ⊕ www.coastvisitor.com). **Eugene, Cascades & Coast Adventure Center** (✉ 3312 Gateway St., Springfield ☎ 541/484–5307 ⊕ www.travellanecounty.org). **Oregon Coast Visitors Association** (✉ 137 NE 1st St., Newport ☎ 541/574–2679 or 888/628–2101 ⊕ www.visittheoregoncoast.com).

EXPLORING OREGON'S BEST BEACHES

Oregon's 300 mi of public coastline is the backdrop for thrills, serenity, rejuvenation, and romance. From yawning expanses of sand dotted with beach chairs to tiny patches bounded by surf-shaped cliffs, they're yours to explore.

(above) Surfing the Oregon Coast. (opposite page, top) Oregon Dunes National Recreation Area. (opposite page, bottom) Cannon Beach Sandcastle Contest

Most awe-inspiring are the massive rock formations just offshore in the northern and southern sections of the coast, breaking up the Pacific horizon. Beaches along the north coast, from Astoria to Pacific City, are perfect for romantic strolls on the sands. The central coast beaches, from Lincoln City to Florence, are long and wide, providing perfect conditions for sunbathers, children, clam diggers, horseback riders, and surfers. The southern-coast beaches from Reedsport to Brookings are less populated, ideal for getting away from it all.

In late July and August, the climate is kind to sun worshipers. During the shoulder months, keep layers of clothing handy for the unpredictable temperature swings. Winter can be downright blustery, but plenty of beachfront hotels cater to visitors who enjoy bundling up to walk along the wet, wind-whipped surf.

–by Deston S. Nokes

GLASS FLOATS: FINDERS KEEPERS

Since 1997, between mid-October and Memorial Day, more than 2,000 hand-crafted glass floats made by local artists have been hidden along Lincoln City's 7.5 mi public beach. If you happen to come upon one, call ☎ 800/452–2151 to register it, and find out which artist made it. While antique glass floats are extremely rare, these new versions make great souvenirs.

FODOR'S CHOICE BEACHES

Cannon Beach. In the shadow of glorious **Haystack Rock,** this beach is wide, flat, and perfect for bird-watching, exploring tide pools, building sandcastles, and romantic walks in the sea mist. Each June the city holds a **sandcastle contest,** drawing artists and thousands of visitors. The rest of the year the beach is far less populated. The beachfront town is a cultural destination featuring much of Oregon's finest dining, lodging, and boutique shopping.

Pacific City. This beach is postcard perfect, with its colorful fleet of dories sitting on the sand. Dozens of them lie tilted in between early-morning fishing excursions to catch lingcod, surfperch, and rockfish. Like Cannon Beach, this town also has a huge (less famous) Haystack Rock that provides the perfect scenic backdrop for horseback riders, beachcombers, and people with shovels chasing sand-covered clams. With safe beach breaks that are ideal for beginners and larger peaks a bit to the south, this is a great spot for surfers. Storm watchers love Pacific City, where winds exceeding 75 mi per hour twist Sitka spruce, and tides deposit driftwood and logs on the beach. Most stay inside to watch, but there are plenty of bold (or crazy) folks who enjoy the blast in their faces.

Samuel H. Boardman State Scenic Corridor. It doesn't get any wilder than this— or more spectacular. The 12-mi strip of forested, rugged coastline is dotted with smaller sand beaches, some more accessible than others. Here visitors will find the amazing **Arch Rock** and **Natural Bridges** and can hike 27 mi of the **Oregon Coast Trail.** Beach highlights include **Whaleshead Beach, Secret Beach,** and **Thunder Rock Cove,** where you might spot migrating gray whales. From the 345-foot-high **Thomas Creek Bridge** you can take a moderately difficult hike down to admire the gorgeous, jagged rocks off **China Beach.**

Winchester Bay. One reason the Pacific Northwest isn't known for its amusement parks is because nature hurls more thrills than any rattling contraption could ever provide. This certainly is true at **Oregon Dunes National Recreation Area.** Here riders of all-terrain vehicles (ATVs) will encounter some of the most radical slips, dips, hills, and chills in the nation. It is the largest expanse of coastal sand dunes in North America, extending for 40 mis, from Florence to Coos Bay. More than 1.5 million people visit the dunes each year. For those who just want to swim, relax, and marvel at the amazing expanse of dunes against the ocean, there are spaces off-limits to motorized vehicles. Overlooking the beach is the gorgeous **Umpqua River Lighthouse.**

4

Updated by
Deston S.
Nokes

The Oregon Coast truly epitomizes the finest in Pacific Northwest living. Thanks to its friendly seaside towns, outstanding fresh seafood, and cozy wine bars sprinkled among small hotels and resorts, visitors have the region's finest choices for sightseeing, dining, and lodging. But the true draw here is the beaches, where nature lovers will delight at their first site of a migrating whale or a baby harbor seal sitting on a rock.

Oregon's coastline is open to all; not a grain of its 300 mi of white-sand beaches is privately owned. The coast's large and small communities are linked by U.S. Highway 101, which runs the length of the state. It winds past sea-tortured rocks, brooding headlands, hidden beaches, historic lighthouses, and tiny ports. This is one of the most picturesque driving routes in the country, and should not be missed. Embracing it is the vast, gunmetal-gray Pacific Ocean, which presents a range of moods with the seasons. On summer evenings it might be glassy and reflective of a romantic sunset. In winter the ocean might throw a thrilling tantrum for storm watchers sitting snug and safe in a beachfront cabin.

Active visitors can indulge in thrills from racing up a sand dune in a buggy to making par at Bandon Dunes, one of the nation's finest golf experiences. Bicyclists can pedal along misty coastline vistas, cruising past historic lighthouses. Boaters can explore south coast rivers on jet boats, or shoot a rapid on a raft. If the weather turns, indoor venues such as the Oregon Coast Aquarium capture the imagination.

Shoppers will be equally engaged perusing fine-art galleries in Toledo or Cannon Beach; for more quirky shopping fun, giggle in the souvenir shops of Seaside or Lincoln City while eating fistfuls of caramel corn or chewing saltwater taffy.

NORTH COAST

Every winter Astoria celebrates fisherman poets: hardworking men and women who bare their souls as to what makes their relationship to Oregon's north-coast waters so magical. It's easy to understand their inspiration, whether in the incredibly tempestuous ocean or the romantic beaches. Throw in Victorian homes, tony art galleries, and memorable wine bars and restaurants, and you have yourself one heck of a vacation. This is the primary beach playground for residents of Portland. What distinguishes the region historically from other areas of the Oregon Coast are its forts, its graveyard of shipwrecks, Lewis and Clark's early visit, and a town—Astoria—that is closer in design and misty temperament to San Francisco than any other in the West. It has more amazing cheese, quality ales, and fine-dining venues than any other coastal town.

ASTORIA

96 mi northwest of Portland on U.S. 30.

The mighty Columbia River meets the Pacific at Astoria, the oldest city west of the Rockies. It is named for John Jacob Astor, owner of the Pacific Fur Company, whose members arrived in 1811 and established Fort Astoria. In its early days Astoria was a placid amalgamation of small town and hardworking port city. With rivers rich with salmon, the city relied on its fishing and canning industries. Settlers built sprawling Victorian houses on the flanks of Coxcomb Hill; many of the homes have since been restored and are no less splendid as bed-and-breakfast inns. In recent years the city itself has awakened with a greater variety of trendy dining and lodging options, staking its claim as a destination resort town. But it retains the soul of a fisherman's town, celebrated each February during its Fisher Poets Gathering.

GETTING HERE

Astoria is about a two-hour drive from Portland on U.S. Highway 30. It's also accessible from Washington on U.S. Highway 101. SeaPort Airlines offers an air shuttle between Portland and Seattle and Astoria's airport. The airport is 7 mi from downtown Astoria, with taxi service and car rental available. **Sunset Empire** (☎ *503/861-7433* ⊕ *www.ridethebus. org*) buses connect Portland with the northern coastal cities of Astoria, Warrenton, Hammond, Gearhart, Seaside, and Cannon Beach.

VISITOR INFORMATION

Astoria–Warrenton Area Chamber of Commerce (✉ *111 W. Marine Dr., Astoria* ☎ *503/325-6311 or 800/875-6807* ⊕ *www.oldoregon.com*).

EXPLORING

Astoria Column. For the best view of the city, the Coast Range, volcanic Mt. Helens and the Pacific Ocean, scamper up the 164 spiral stairs to the top of the Astoria Column. When you get to the top, you can throw a small wooden plane and watch it glide to earth; each year some 35,000 gliders are tossed. The 125-foot-high structure sits atop Coxcomb Hill, and was patterned after Trajan's Column in Rome. There are little platforms to rest on if you get winded, or, if you don't want to climb, the column's 500 feet of artwork, depicting important Pacific Northwest historical milestones, are well worth study. ✉ *From U.S. 30 downtown take 16th St. south 1 mi to top of Coxcomb Hill, Astoria*

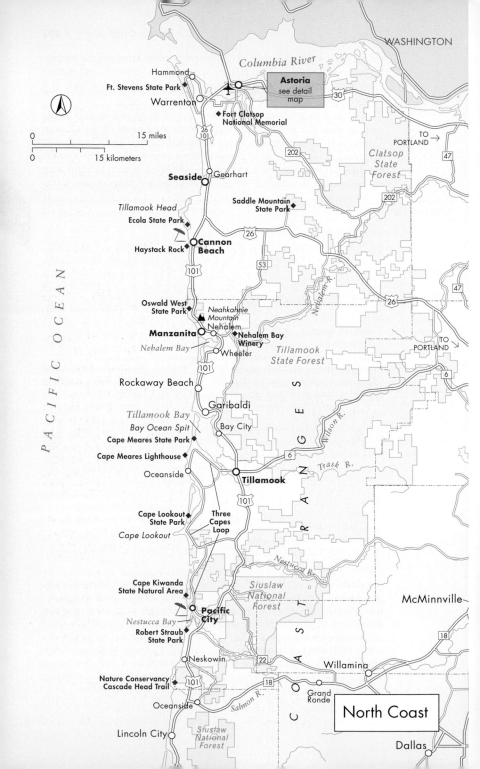

WASHINGTON

Columbia River

Hammond

Ft. Stevens State Park

Warrenton

Astoria
see detail
map

30

TO
PORTLAND →

47

Fort Clatsop
National Memorial

26
101

202

*Clatsop
State
Forest*

202

Seaside Gearhart

Saddle Mountain
State Park

Tillamook Head

Ecola State Park

26

Haystack Rock **Cannon
Beach**

101

53

Nehalem R.

47

26

Oswald West
State Park

*Neahkahnie
Mountain*
Nehalem

TO
PORTLAND →

6

Manzanita

Nehalem Bay
Winery

Nehalem Bay Wheeler

*Tillamook
State Forest*

101

Rockaway Beach

Wilson R.

Garibaldi

C O A S T   R A N G E S

Tillamook Bay
Bay Ocean Spit

Bay City

Cape Meares State Park

6

Trask R.

Cape Meares Lighthouse

Oceanside

Tillamook

101

Cape Lookout
State Park

Three
Capes
Loop

Cape Lookout

Nestucca R.

*Siuslaw
National
Forest*

McMinnville

Cape Kiwanda
State Natural Area

**Pacific
City**

Nestucca Bay

Robert Straub
State Park

C O A S T

18

Neskowin

22

Willamina

Nature Conservancy
Cascade Head Trail

101

18

Grand
Ronde

Dallas

Oceanside

Salmon R.

North Coast

Lincoln City

*Siuslaw
National
Forest*

PACIFIC OCEAN

0 — 15 miles
0 — 15 kilometers

N

☎ *503/325-2963* ⊕ *www.astoriacolumn.org* ✉ *$1 per car donation* ⊙ *Daily 9-dusk.*

Fodor'sChoice **Columbia River Maritime Museum.** One of Oregon's best coastal attractions
★ illuminates the maritime history of the Pacific Northwest and provides
☪ visitors with a sense of the perils of guiding ships into the mouth of the
Columbia River. Guests can experience what it was to pilot a tugboat
and participate in a Coast Guard rescue on the Columbia River Bar.
There's the actual bridge of a WWII-era U.S. Navy destroyer, the U.S.
Coast Guard lightship *Columbia,* and a 44-foot Coast Guard motor life-
boat. A captivating exhibit displays the personal belongings of some of
the ill-fated passengers of the 2,000 ships that have foundered here since
1811. ⊠ *1792 Marine Dr., Astoria* ☎ *503/325-2323* ⊕ *www.crmm.org*
✉ *$10* ⊙ *Daily 9:30-5.*

Flavel House. The Queen Anne Victorian-style mansion helps visitors
imagine what life was like for the wealthy in late-19th-century Astoria.
It rests on parklike grounds covering an entire city block, and is listed
on the National Register of Historic Places. Completely restored, its
three-story octagon tower is an area landmark. It was built for George
Flavel, an influential Columbia River Bar pilot and businessman who
was one of the area's first millionaires. Visits start in the Carriage House
interpretive center. ⊠ *441 8th St., Astoria* ☎ *503/325-2203* ⊕ *www.*
cumtux.org ✉ *$5* ⊙ *May-Sept., daily 10-5; Oct.-Apr., daily 11-4.*

Fodor'sChoice **Fort Clatsop National Memorial.** See where the 30-member Lewis and
★ Clark Expedition endured a rain-soaked winter in 1905-06, hunting,
☪ gathering food, making salt, and trading with Clatsop, Chinook, and
Tillamook Indians. This memorial is a faithful replica of the log fort
depicted in Clark's journal. The park has evolved into a 3,000-acre,
forested wonderland, including an exhibit hall, gift shop, film, and
trails. Park rangers dress in period garb during the summer and perform
such early-19th-century tasks as making fire with flint and steel. Hikers will enjoy the 1.5-mi Netul Landing trail, or the 6.5-mi Fort to Sea
trail. ⊠ *Fort Clatsop Loop Rd. 5 mi south of Astoria* ☎ *503/861-2471*
⊕ *www.nps.gov/focl* ✉ *$3* ⊙ *Daily 9-5 (Summer 9-6).*

☪ **Fort Stevens State Park.** This earthen fort at Oregon's northwestern tip
was built during the Civil War to guard the Columbia River against
attack. None came until World War II, when a Japanese submarine
fired upon it. The fort still has cannons and an underground gun bat-
tery. The park has year-round camping, with full hook up sites and 15
yurts. There are also bike paths, boating, swimming, hiking trails, and
a short walk to a gorgeous, wide beach where the corroded skeleton of
the *Peter Iredale* pokes up through the sand. This century-old English
four-master shipwreck is a reminder of the nearly 2,000 vessels claimed
by these treacherous waters. ⊠ *Fort Stevens Hwy.* ☎ *503/861-2000 or*
800/551-6949 ⊕ *www.visitfortstevens.com* ✉ *$5 per vehicle* ⊙ *Mid-*
May-Sept., daily 10-6; Oct.-mid-May, daily 10-4.

Oregon Film Museum. Housed in the old Clatsop County Jail, this museum
celebrates Oregon's long history of filmmaking, and provides artifacts
from and displays about prior productions. The location is apt because
it was featured prominently in famous cult film *The Goonies.* The state's

4

film productions date back to 1908 for *The Fisherman's Bride*. Oregon has helped give birth to such classics as *The General, The Great Race, One Flew Over the Cuckoo's Nest, Paint Your Wagon, Animal House, Kindergarten Cop*, and *Twilight*, leading some to call the state Hollywood North. ⊠ *732 Duane St., Astoria* ☎ *503/325–2203* ⊕ *www. oregonfilmmuseum.com* ⌨ *$4* ⊙ *Daily 10–5.*

WHERE TO EAT

$$
SEAFOOD

✕ **Baked Alaska.** Chef Christopher Holen's enthusiastic banter and flying fingers remind one of a wizard conjuring up delectable small plates, including fresh brioche or mouthwatering Pacific sea scallops. Other signature dishes include applejack halibut, crab and mushrooms Sambuca carbonara, and hand-tossed sourdough pizzas. All entrées include an inventive chef's-choice side dish. Its namesake dessert, the Half-Baked Alaska, is not to be missed. Holen often holds cooking demonstrations in his neighboring cooking store, Mise en Place. ⊠ *1 12th St., Astoria* ☎ *503/325–7414* ⊕ *bakedak.com* ⊟ *AE, D, MC, V.*

¢
CAFÉ

✕ **Blue Scorcher Bakery Café.** "Joyful work, delicious food, and strong community," is this tasty café's rallying cry. It serves up everything from Huevos Scorcheros and organic, handcrafted breads to a variety of foods using local and organic ingredients. The offerings change with the seasons, but there's always a vegan or gluten-free option. This workers collective also has a Pie-of-the-Month Club. ⊠ *1493 Duane St., Astoria* ☎ *503/338–7473* ⊕ *www.bluescorcher.com* ⊟ *D, MC, V* ⊙ *No dinner.*

$$
NEW AMERICAN

✕ **Bridgewater Bistro.** Astoria's fine-dining entry has a broad range of selections, whether you want meat, fish, or vegetarian fare. Located next to the new Columbia Pier Hotel, the restaurant specializes in inventive shared plates, Spanish-inspired tapas as well as hearty meat, seafood, and vegetarian dishes. ⊠ *20 Basin St., Astoria* ☎ *503/325–6777* ⊕ *www. bridgewaterbistro.com* ⊟ *AE, D, MC, V.*

$$
SEAFOOD
Fodor'sChoice
★

✕ **Clemente's.** Serving possibly the best seafood on the Oregon Coast, chefs Gordon and Lisa Clement are making a significant critical and popular splash in Astoria. Grounded in Mediterranean cuisine from Italy and the Adriatic Coast, Clemente's inventive specials feature the freshest catches of that day. From succulent sea-bass salad to a hearty sturgeon sandwich—meals are dished up for reasonable prices. Dungeness crab cakes stuffed with crab rather than breading, and wild scallop fish-and-chips liven up a varied menu. Not interested in fish? Try the spaghetti with authentic meatballs. ⊠ *1198 Commercial St., Astoria* ☎ *503/325–1067* ⊕ *www.clementesrestaurant.com* ⊟ *AE, D, MC, V* ⊙ *No lunch Mon.*

$$
ECLECTIC

✕ **Columbian Cafe.** Locals love this unpretentious diner that defies categorization by offering inventive, fresh seafood and spicy vegetarian dishes, while it also cures and smokes its meat selections. Open for breakfast, lunch, and dinner, it serves simple food, such as crepes with broccoli, cheese, and homemade salsa for lunch; grilled salmon and pasta with a lemon-cream sauce for dinner. The restaurant isn't shy about its culinary prowess, claiming that the experience "will change your life." Dishes are served by a staff that usually includes owner/chef Uriah Hulsey. Come early; this place always draws a crowd. ⊠ *1114*

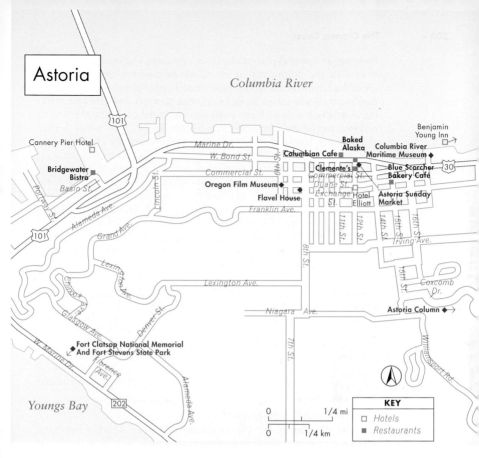

Astoria

Columbia River

Benjamin Young Inn

Cannery Pier Hotel

Baked Alaska

Columbian Cafe

Columbia River Maritime Museum

Marine Dr.

W. Bond St.

Bridgewater Bistro

Commercial St.

Clemente's

Blue Scorcher Bakery Cafe

Oregon Film Museum

Commercial St.

Duane St.

Basin St.

Flavel House

Exchange St.

Hotel Elliott

Astoria Sunday Market

Alameda Ave.

Franklin Ave.

Grand Ave.

Irving Ave.

Lexington Ave.

Lexington Ave.

Coxcomb Dr.

Niagara Ave.

Astoria Column

Fort Clatsop National Memorial And Fort Stevens State Park

W. Marine Dr.

Florence Ave.

Alameda Ave.

Youngs Bay

KEY	
□	*Hotels*
■	*Restaurants*

0 ———— 1/4 mi
0 ———— 1/4 km

Marine Dr., Astoria ☎ 503/325–2233 ⊕ *www.columbianvoodoo.com/ cafe* ▭ *No credit cards* ☉ *Closed Mon.–Tues.*

WHERE TO STAY

$ ☷ **Benjamin Young Inn.** On the National Register of Historic Places, this handsome 5,500-square-foot Queen Anne inn is surrounded by century-old gardens. Among the ornate original details are faux graining on frames and moldings, shutter blinds in windows, and Povey stained glass. The spacious guest rooms mix antiques with contemporary pieces, and have views of the Columbia River from their tall windows. City tennis courts are right next door. There's a two-night minimum on holiday and July, August, and September weekends. **Pros:** property has great character; large rooms with a river view; personable owner. **Cons:** not on the water. ✉ *3652 Duane St.*, Astoria ☎ 503/325–6172 or 800/201–1286 ⊕ *www.benjaminyounginn.com* ⇌ *3 rooms, 1 2-bedroom suite* ⚒ *In hotel: parking, Wi-Fi, refrigerator* ▭ *MC, V* ⦿| *BP.*

$$$ ☷ **Cannery Pier Hotel.** Every room has a gorgeous view of where the
Fodor's Choice mighty Columbia River meets the Pacific Ocean, and it's almost hyp-
★ notic to relax by a fire and watch the tugboats shepherding barges to and fro. Built upon century-old pilings, this captivating property is in the restored Union Fisherman's Cooperative Packing Company

building, an integral part of the town's history. The interior, however, is modern and bright, with a liberal use of glass and polished wood, including hardwood floors in the rooms. The property sits on the Astoria Riverwalk and on the trolley line, with gourmet dining within walking distance. But don't leave until you enjoy the complimentary wine and lox, served daily between 5 and 6 PM. Replica 1950s bicycles are available for use, and the hotel offers complimentary chauffeur service in a 1939 Buick, 1938 Packard, or 1945 Cadillac. **Pros:** amazing river views; great in-room amenities; nearby outstanding restaurants. **Cons:** no on site restaurant or room service. ⊠ *10 Basin St., Astoria* ☎ *503/325–4996 or 888/325–4996* ⊕ *www.cannerypierhotel.com* ↵ *46 rooms, 8 suites* ⚄ *In-room: refrigerator, DVD, Internet. In-hotel: gym, spa, some pets allowed, parking.* ═ *AE, D, MC, V* ⊣⊙⊢ *CP.*

$$ ⛨ **Hotel Elliott.** This upscale, five-story downtown hotel stands in the heart of Astoria's historic district. The property retains the elegance of yesteryear updated with modern comforts. On the rooftop you can relax in the garden and enjoy views of the Columbia River and the Victorian homes dotting the hillside. In your room you can warm your feet on the heated stone floors in the bathroom. Downstairs, you can sample fine wines in the Cabernet Room or enjoy a guilt-free cigar in the tucked-away Havana Room. **Pros:** captures the city's historic ambience beautifully; every effort made to infuse the rooms with upscale amenities; popular wine bar. **Cons:** some areas smell like cigar smoke; no on-site dining. ⊠ *357 12th St., Astoria* ☎ *877/378–1924* ⊕ *www.hotelelliott.com* ↵ *32 rooms* ⚄ *In-room: Internet, DVD. In-hotel: bar* ═ *AE, D, MC, V.*

NIGHTLIFE AND THE ARTS

Fisher Poets Gathering. For three days on the last weekend of February, the region's talented working fishermen open their souls by sharing their poetry to standing-room-only audiences in venues throughout Astoria. This collective affirmation of the romance and toil of the fishing trade attracts as many as 70 fishing and maritime industry people from near and far to share their original poems, stories and songs. ☎ *503/325–4972* ⊕ *www.clatsopcollege.com/fisherpoets.*

SHOPPING

Astoria Sunday Market. Every Sunday between May and October, the town closes three blocks of its 12th Street traffic so that more than 100 vendors can sell goods they've grown or made. There are booths and tables full of fresh fruits, vegetables, farm products, arts, crafts, and treats of all descriptions. ⊠ *12th and Commercial Sts., Astoria* ☎ *503/325–1010* ⊙ *May–Oct., Sun. 10–3.*

Josephson's. Here's your chance to visit one of the state's oldest commercial smokehouses, and one of the nation's premier mail-order specialty food companies. It uses alder wood for all processing, and specializes in Pacific Northwest chinook and coho salmon. You can buy mouthwatering selections of fish smoked on the premises, including hot smoked pepper or wine-maple salmon, as well as smoked halibut, sturgeon, tuna, oysters, mussels, scallops, and prawns by the pound or in sealed gift packs. ⊠ *106 Marine Dr., Astoria* ☎ *503/325–2190 or 800/772–3474* ⊕ *www.josephsons.com* ◩ *Free* ⊙ *Mon.–Sat. 9–6, Sun. 9–5:30.*

DID YOU KNOW?

For the best view of Astoria, the Coast Range, volcanic Mt. Helens, and the Pacific Ocean, climb the 164 spiral stairs to the top of the Astoria Column. Murals depicting Pacific Northwest history span 500 feet.

SEASIDE

12 mi south of Astoria on U.S. 101.

As a resort town, Seaside has spruced up its kitschy, arcade-filled reputation and now supports a bustling tourist trade, with hotels, condominiums, and restaurants lining a traditional promenade. It still has fun games and plenty of carny noise to appeal to young people, but it has added plenty of classy getaways for adults. Only 90 mi from Portland, Seaside is often crowded, so it's not the place to come if you crave solitude. Peak times include February, during the Trail's End Marathon; mid-March, when hordes of teenagers descend on the town during spring break; and July, when the annual Miss Oregon Pageant is in full swing. Just south of town, waves draw surfers to the Cove, a spot jealously guarded by locals.

GETTING HERE

Seaside is about an hour and a half's drive on U.S. Highway 26 from Portland, and 12 mi south of Astoria on U.S. Highway 101. **Sunset Empire** (☎ *503/861-7433* ⊕ *www.ridethebus.org*) buses connect Portland with the northern coastal cities of Astoria, Warrenton, Hammond, Gearhart, Seaside, and Cannon Beach.

VISITOR INFORMATION

Seaside Visitors Bureau (✉ *7 N. Roosevelt Ave., Seaside* ☎ *503/738-3097 or 888/306-2326* ⊕ *www.seasideor.com*).

WHERE TO EAT

$$
PIZZA

✕ **Angelina's Pizzeria & Café.** This friendly, busy pizzeria is perfect for those just a little bit tired of chowder. Whet your appetite with an antipasto salad of prosciutto, provolone, salami, pepperoni, artichoke hearts, roasted red peppers, and olives on a bed of spring greens. Then order a fine, homemade-dough pie, baked from a New York family pizza recipe. The Tuscan chicken with Alfredo sauce, garlic, and bacon is a popular choice. Whatever toppings you choose, it's simply the best pizza on the north coast. ✉ *300 S. Roosevelt, Seaside* ☎ *503/717–1230* ⊟ *AE, D, MC, V.*

$$
STEAKHOUSE

✕ **Girtle's Seafood & Steaks.** Huge portions at reasonable prices is the motto of this family-friendly eatery. Here you'll find juicy steaks, fresh local seafood, and plenty of homespun selections for kids. It also lays out a substantial, classic breakfast spread, and there are plenty of burgers and seafood selections for lunch. ✉ *311 Broadway, Seaside* ☎ *503/738–8417* ⊕ *www.girtles.com* ⊟ *AE, D, MC, V.*

$$
ITALIAN

✕ **Guido & Vito's Italian Cuisine.** In a sea of family-oriented fish restaurants sits this pleasant place cooking Italian food right. Be it a zesty Caesar, sausage and beef meatballs, or a belly-warming, mushroom-slathered veal Marsala, diners won't be disappointed. ✉ *604 Broadway, Seaside* ☎ *503/717–1229* ⊟ *D, MC, V.*

$
NEW AMERICA
Fodor's Choice
★

✕ **Yummy Wine Bar & Bistro.** Be adventurous and enjoy some of Seaside's best, most inventive cuisine, courtesy of Chef Corey Albert. Relaxed, colorful, and fun, this urban, artsy wine bar is a joy to the eye as well as the tummy. Enjoy flights of wine and dig in to ahi tuna tartar or crispy pot stickers. Move to an entrée of salmon steamed in a fresh clam tomato broth, or the pork medallions in a prune and white-wine cream sauce. Save room for wild Oregon berry sorbet or strawberry short-cake taken to whole new level of yum. Sorry, no kids allowed. ⊠ *831 Broadway, Seaside* ☎ *503/738–3100* ⊕ *www.yummywinebarbistro. com* ⊟ *AE, MC, V* ⊗ *Closed Tues. and Wed.*

WHERE TO STAY

$ 🏨 **Hillcrest Inn.** Friendliness, cleanliness, and convenience are bywords of the Hillcrest, which is only one block from both the beach and the convention center, and three blocks from the downtown area's restaurants and shops. You're welcome to use the picnic tables, lawn chairs, and even the barbecue on the grounds. **Pros:** affordable; near Seaside's beach and essentials. **Cons:** no frills except for Wi-Fi and laundry. ⊠ *118 N. Columbia St., Seaside* ☎ *503/738–6273 or 800/270–7659* ⤳ *19 rooms, 4 suites, 3 cottages, 1 house* ⚒ *In-room: kitchen (some), refrigerator, Wi-Fi. In-hotel: spa, laundry facilities* ⊟ *AE, D, MC, V.*

$$$$ 🏨 **Rivertide Suites.** Although it's not right on the beach, the Rivertide's
⟳ splendid accommodations are within walking distance of the town's best cuisine, shopping, and beach activities. This large, multilevel, family-friendly hotel is new in appearance, and has all the amenities of larger chains. Offering one- and two-bedroom suites and studios, Rivertide gives guests a choice among different packages to appeal to golfers, whale-watchers, or romantic couples. Breakfast is complimentary. **Pros:** new; clean; near plenty of shopping and boardwalk activities. **Cons:** it's on a city river instead of the beach; request a higher-floor room if you can. ⊠ *102 N. Holladay, Seaside* ☎ *503/436–2241 or 888/777–4047* ⊕ *www.rivertidesuites.com* ⤳ *45 rooms* ⚒ *In-room: Wi-Fi. In-hotel: pool, laundry facilities, some pets allowed* ⊟ *AE, D, MC, V* ⦿*BP.*

¢ 🏨 **Sandy Cove Inn.** Recently remodeled, this small boutique hotel is a fun, colorful place a block away from Seaside's promenade. Its themed rooms include names such as French Country, Wave, Boat, 1940s, Monopoly, Vintage Games, and Kids. There's also a Jacuzzi suite. Some rooms require a two-night minimum stay. Pets permitted in a couple of rooms for an extra charge. **Pros:** near surfing, the beach, and family restaurants. **Cons:** off the beach. ⊠ *241 Ave. U, Seaside* ☎ *503/738–7473* ⤳ *13 rooms, 2 suites* ⚒ *In-room: Refrigerator, Wi-Fi. In-hotel: laundry facilities, some pets allowed.* ⊟ *D, DC, MC, V.*

SHOPPING

Phillips Candy Kitchen. A trip to the beach isn't complete without buying a bag of saltwater taffy or caramel popcorn. It's fun to watch the staff wrestle with the taffy, pulling it about on a huge table like a candy-striped anaconda. (⊠ *217 Broadway, Seaside* ☎ *503/738–5402* ⊠ *Free* ⊗ *Winter daily 10–6:30; summer daily 10–9*).

SPORTS AND THE OUTDOORS

RECREATIONAL AREAS **Ecola State Park.** A playground of sea-sculpted rocks, sandy shoreline, green headlands, and panoramic views. Located 8 mi south of Seaside on U.S. 101, the park's main beach can be crowded in summer, but the **Indian Beach** area contains an often-deserted cove and explorable tidal pools. ☎ *503/436–2844 or 800/551–6949* ⊠*$3 per vehicle* ⊗ *Daily dawn–dusk.*

HIKING   **Saddle Mountain State Park.** It may be just a 2½-mi hike from the parking lot to the mountain's summit, but it's no walk in the park. Wear sturdy shoes, and be prepared for sections with steep upgrades. There's a zippy change in the altitude as you climb higher, but the wildflowers make it all worthwhile. The campground, 14 mi north of Seaside, has 10 primitive, first-come-first-served sites. ⊠ *Off U.S. 26, Seaside* ☎ *800/551–6949* 🖘 *$10 for overnight camping. Hiking is free* ☉ *Mar.–Nov., daily.*

Tillamook Head. A moderate 3.8-mi loop from U.S. 101, south of Seaside, brings you to a 900-foot-high viewing point, a great place to see the **Tillamook Rock Light Station,** which stands a mile or so off the coast. The lonely beacon, built in 1881 on a straight-sided rock, towers 41 feet above the ocean. Originally, keepers assigned to the rock spent three months on and two weeks off. But conditions proved extremely harsh as the cramped quarters, frequent storms, and foghorns blaring often caused tension. The trapped keepers were known to pass notes at dinner rather than speak to each other. One keeper was removed from his post after trying to kill the head keeper by putting ground glass in his food. In 1957 the lighthouse was abandoned. It had a brief reincarnation as a place to store urns with cremated remains, but its status remains uncertain. ⊕ *web.oregon.com/hiking/tillamook_head.cfm* 🖘 *$3 per vehicle* ☉ *Daily dawn–dusk*

CANNON BEACH

10 mi south of Seaside on U.S. 101.

Cannon Beach is a mellow, trendy place to enjoy art, wine, and fine dining, and to take in the sea air. Shops and galleries selling surfing gear, upscale clothing, local art, wine, coffee, and food line Hemlock Street, Cannon Beach's main thoroughfare. One of the most charming hamlets on the coast, the town has beachfront homes and hotels. On the downside, the Carmel of the Oregon coast can be more expensive and crowded than other towns along Highway 101.

Every May the town hosts the Cannon Beach Sandcastle Contest, for which thousands throng the beach to view imaginative and often startling works in this most transient of art forms.

GETTING HERE
Cannon Beach is about an hour and a half's drive from Portland on U.S. Highway 26, and 25 mi south of Astoria on U.S. Highway 101. **Sunset Empire** (☎ *503/861-7433* ⊕ *www.ridethebus.org*) buses connect Portland with the northern coastal cities of Astoria, Warrenton, Hammond, Gearhart, Seaside, and Cannon Beach.

VISITOR INFORMATION
Cannon Beach Chamber of Commerce (⊠ *207 N. Spruce St., Cannon Beach* ☎ *503/436-2623* ⊕ *www.cannonbeach.org*)

EXPLORING
Haystack Rock. Towering over the broad, sandy beach is a gorgeous, 235-foot-high dome that is one of the most-photographed natural wonders on the Oregon Coast. ⚠ **Please stay off the rock and enjoy the view from the beach. The rock is temptingly accessible during low tide, but the**

Coast Guard regularly airlifts stranded climbers from its precipitous sides, and falls have claimed numerous lives over the years.

EN
ROUTE
A portion of the Oregon Trail crosses the summit of **Neahkahnie Mountain**, just south of Cannon Beach. Cryptic carvings on the beach rocks below and old Native American legends of shipwrecked Europeans have sustained the belief that survivors of a sunken Spanish galleon buried a fortune in doubloons somewhere on the side of the 1,661-foot-high mountain. U.S. 101 climbs 700 feet above the Pacific, providing dramatic views and often hair-raising curves as it winds along the flank of the mountain. There's a moderate but steep 3-mi climb to the summit, gaining 900 feet of elevation.

WHERE TO EAT

$$$$
NEW AMERICAN
✕**EVOO.** School never tasted this good. EVOO Cooking School performs advanced feats of culinary education for large and small groups, set around seasonal or specific food themes. EVOO holds cooking demonstrations, or people can sign up for hands-on courses—both always based on what's local, in season, and tantalizing. They call them dinner shows for a reason: whether or not you remember how to duplicate these recipes at home, you'll have a great time sampling them there. The school also shares its recipes in a free online cookbook. ⊠ *188 S. Hemlock St., Cannon Beach* ☎ *503/436–8555* ⊕ *www.evoo.biz* ⊘ *Reservations required* ⊟ *AE, D, MC, V* ⊘ *Check Web site for class schedule.*

¢
CAFÉ
✕**Sleepy Monk.** In a region famous for its gourmet coffee, one small roaster brews a cup more memorable than any chain. Sleepy Monk attracts java aficionados on caffeine pilgrimages from near and far to sample it's specially roasted, certified organic, and fair trade beans. They are roasted without water, which adds unnecessary weight. Local, fresh pastries are stacked high and deep. If you're a coffee fan, this is your Shangri-la. It also opened a new restaurant on the premises, Irish Table. ⊠ *1235 S. Hemlock St., Cannon Beach* ☎ *503/436–2796* ⊕ *www.sleepymonkcoffee.com* ⊟ *MC, V* ⊘ *Closed Mon.–Thurs.*

$$
IRISH
✕**Irish Table.** This new restaurant has made a favorable splash into Cannon Beach's dining scene. Built adjacent to the Sleepy Monk café, it serves seasonal food with an Irish twist, such as potato kale soup and its heralded Irish stew. Other offerings include a perfect steak or delicate fresh halibut. Start with chicken-bacon chowder or the curried mussels. Soak up the sauce with slices of piping-hot soda bread. Naturally, there are plenty of libations, including Irish whiskey. It's a terrific stop for people seeking a little something different at the coast. ⊠ *1235 S. Hemlock St., Cannon Beach* ☎ *503/436–2796* ⊕ *www.sleepymonkcoffee. com* ⊟ *MC, V* C *Wed.*

$$$$
CONTINENTAL
Fodor's Choice
★
✕**Stephanie Inn.** As diners enjoy a romantic view of Haystack Rock, this upscale hotel's four-star dining room prepares a new menu nightly, crafting exquisite, four-course, prix-fixe dinners using fresh, local ingredients. Diners can expect dishes such as butternut squash risotto, cedar plank–roasted salmon, savory duck confit, and a lemon-curd tart with wild berry sauce. Naturally, it has an extensive regional and international wine list. The view, cuisine, and attentive service combine to make it one of the finest dining experiences in the Pacific Northwest. ⊠ *2740 S.*

Puffin Kite Festival, Cannon Beach

Pacific St., Cannon Beach ☎ *503/436–2221 or 800/633–3466* ⊕ *www. stephanie-inn.com* ⌂ *Reservations essential* ▬ *AE, D, DC, MC, V.*

WHERE TO STAY

$$$ ☝ **Arch Cape Inn and Retreat.** Between the artsy beach communities of Manzanita and Cannon Beach, this property lies along some of the most gorgeous stretch of coast in the region. It's perfect for those who want a little more of a getaway, putting some distance between themselves and the summer hordes. A three-course breakfast and nightly wine social are included in the room rate. No kids under 16 are permitted. **Pros:** elegant, distinctive rooms; fireplaces great in winter; most rooms have terrific ocean views. **Cons:** 200 yards from the beach. ✉ *31970 E. Ocean La., Cannon Beach* ☎ *503/436–2800* ⊕ *www.archcapeinn.com* ⤶ *10 rooms* ⌂ *In-room: refrigerators, DVD In-hotel: Wi-Fi, parking, some pets allowed* ▬ *AE, D, MC, V* ⑂ *BP.*

$$$$ ☝ **Ocean Lodge.** Designed to capture the feel of a 1940s beach resort, this lodge is perfect for special occasions and romantic getaways. Most rooms have oceanfront views, and all have open wood beams, gas fireplaces, and balconies or decks. A massive rock fireplace anchors the lobby, and there is a second fireplace in the second-floor library, with a large selection of games for the whole family. Other extras include an extensive book collection and DVD library. Bungalows across the street do not have ocean views but are large and private. **Pros:** beachfront location; spacious rooms; turndown service; and warm cookies delivered. **Cons:** one guest bemoaned the lack of privacy on the balcony. ✉ *2864 S. Pacific St., Cannon Beach* ☎ *503/436–2241 or 888/777–*

4047 ⊕ www.theoceanlodge.com ⤳ 45 rooms ♿ In hotel: beachfront, Wi-Fi, pool, laundry facility, some pets allowed ☰ AE, D, MC, V ⍩ CP.

$$$$
Fodor's Choice
★

☷ **Stephanie Inn.** One of the most beautiful views on the coast deserves one of the most splendid hotels. With a stunning view of Haystack Rock, the Stephanie Inn keeps its focus on romance, superior service, and luxurious rooms. Impeccably maintained, with country-style furnishings, fireplaces, large bathrooms with whirlpool tubs, and balconies, the rooms are so comfortable you may never want to leave. Generous country breakfasts are included in the room price, as are evening wine and hors d'oeuvres. The fresh-baked cookies in the lobby are a warm touch. No kids under 12 are permitted. Two-night minimum stays required during August or during weekends throughout the year. **Pros:** one of the finest romantic getaways in Oregon. **Cons:** expensive. ⊠ 2740 S. Pacific St., Cannon Beach 🕾 503/436–2221 or 800/633–3466 ⊕ www.stephanie-inn.com ⤳ 27 rooms, 14 suites ♿ In-room: A/C, safe, refrigerator, Internet, DVD. In-hotel: parking, spa ☰ AE, D, DC, MC, V ⍩ BP.

SHOPPING

Cannon Beach Art Galleries. The numerous art galleries that line Cannon Beach's Hemlock Street are an essential part of the town's spirit and beauty. A group of 10 galleries featuring beautifully innovative works in ceramic, bronze, photography, painting, and other mediums have collaborated to form the Cannon Beach Gallery Group. Through its Web site, it helps to promote exhibitions and special events for all 10 venues. *S. Hemlock St., Cannon Beach 97110 ⊕ www.cbgallerygroup.com).*

Cannon Beach Surf. If you're looking for lessons, surfboards, skateboards, boogie boards, or anything that rides the surf, this is a great place to start. Even if you're not inclined to get wet, the shop has all the clothing and accessories that come with the culture, such as freestyle watches, sunglasses, shorts, sandals, and shoes. But if you do plan to do some surfing at the Oregon Coast, you'll want to invest in one of their fine wet suits. (⊠ 1088 S. Hemlock St., Cannon Beach 🕾 503/436–0475).

MANZANITA

20 mi south of Cannon Beach on U.S. 101.

Manzanita is a secluded seaside community with only a few more than 500 full-time residents. It's on a sandy peninsula peppered with tufts of grass on the northwestern side of Nehalem Bay, a popular windsurfing destination. It is a tranquil small town, but its restaurants, galleries, and 18-hole golf course have increased its appeal to tourists.

GETTING HERE

Manzanita is in Tillamook County, a little under two hours from Portland on U.S. Highway 26. The town sits on Highway 101, about 40 mi south of Astoria and 27 mi north of Tillamook. The nearest airport is in Astoria. Tillamook County's bus, **The Wave** (🕾 503/815–8283 ⊕ www.tillamookbus.com), leaves from Portland's Union Station. The bus connects Manzanita, Tillamook, and Pacific City.

VISITOR INFORMATION

Oregon Coast Visitors Association (✉ *137 NE 1st St., Newport* ☎ *541/574–2679 or 888/628–2101* ⊕ *www.visittheoregoncoast.com*).

EXPLORING

Nehalem Bay Winery. Established in 1974, this winery is known for its Pinot Noir, Chardonnay, blackberry, and plum fruit wines. The winery also has a busy schedule of events, with concerts, barbecues, an occasional pig roast, children's activities, and a bluegrass festival the third week of August. ✉ *34965 Hwy. 53, Nehalem* ☎ *503/368–9463 or 888/368–9463* ⊕ *www.nehalembaywinery.com* ⊙ *Daily 9–6.*

WHERE TO EAT AND STAY

¢ ✕ **San Dune Pub.** What was once just a tavern is now a local magnet for

AMERICAN   bodacious burgers, sweet-potato fries, and, on Tuesdays, baby back ribs. With 17 beers on tap, live music, and a 50-inch screen for sports, it's a one-stop shop. Patio seating on nicer days is a bonus. ✉ *127 Laneda Ave., Manzanita* ☎ *503/368–5080* ⊕ *www.sandunepub.com* ▭ *MC, V* ⊙ *Closed Sun.*

$$ ⊡ **Inn at Manzanita.** This 1987 Scandinavian structure, filled with light-color woods, beams, and glass, is half a block from the beach. Shore pines on the property give upper-floor patios a tree house feel; all rooms have decks, and two have skylights. There are also three child-friendly rooms and a new penthouse suite. A nearby café serves breakfast, and area restaurants are nearby. In winter the inn is a great place for storm watching. There's a two-day minimum stay on weekends. **Pros:** wonderful ambience with a Japanese garden atmosphere; very light and clean. **Cons:** 20-day cancellation notice required. ✉ *67 Laneda Ave., Manzanita* ☎ *503/368–6754* ⊕ *www.innatmanzanita.com* ⌦ *13 rooms, penthouse* ♿ *In-room: no phone (some), kitchen (some), refrigerator* ▭ *AE, D, MC, V.*

SPORTS AND THE OUTDOORS

RECREATIONAL   **Oswald West State Park.** Adventurous travelers will enjoy a sojourn at

AREAS   one of the best-kept secrets on the Pacific coast, at the base of Neahkahnie Mountain. Park in one of the two lots on U.S. 101 and hike a ½-mi trail. There are several trails to the beach that lead to the Cape Falcon overlook or to the Oregon Coast Trail. The spectacular beach has caves and tidal pools. The trail to the summit (about 2 mi south of the parking lots marked only by a HIKERS sign) provides rewarding views of the surf, sand, forest, and mountain. Come in December or March and you might spot pods of gray whales. ✉ *Ecola Park Rd., Manzanita* ☎ *503/368–5943 or 800/551–6949* ⊕ *www.oregonstateparks.org* ⌦ *Free* ⊙ *Day use only, daily dawn–dusk.*

GOLFING   **Manzanita Golf Course.** This short, 9-hole course is a fun, coastal option for a quick, pleasant round. Designed by Ted Erickson, it offers tree-lined fairways, easy walking, and a 5th hole with a 60-foot drop to the fairway below. With only 280 yards from the back tees, it provides players with a great chance for an eagle. The course is open year-round, and has a full-service pro shop. The driving range is open May–September. Call for reservations, since many other vacationers have the same idea.

Lakeview Dr., Manzanita ☎ *503/368–5744* ⊕ *www.doormat.com/ mgc/mgc-1.htm* ▣ *$10-$20.*

WIND SPORTS Manzanita Beach is well known as a reliable summer windsurfing spot. Winds here typically range from 18 to 24 mph during the months of June through September, and offer world-class rides. Beginners will want to practice in nearby Nehalem Bay. There they can stand in the water several hundred feet from shore and learn water starts. Windsurfers always need to keep an eye on the outgoing tide, which produces strong currents. **Manzanita Bikes and Boards** (☎ *503/368-3337* ⊕ *www. manzanitabikesandboards.com*) has rentals.

TILLAMOOK

4

27 mi south of Manzanita on U.S. 101.

More than 100 inches of annual rainfall and the confluence of three rivers contribute to the lush green pastures around Tillamook, probably best known for its thriving dairy industry and cheese factory. The Tillamook County Cheese Factory ships about 40 million pounds of cheese around the world every year. Just south of town is the largest wooden structure in the world, one of two gigantic buildings constructed in 1942 by the U.S. Navy to shelter blimps that patrolled the Pacific Coast during World War II. Hangar A was destroyed by fire in 1992, and Hangar B was subsequently converted to the Tillamook Naval Air Station Museum.

The **Three Capes Loop** over Cape Meares, Cape Lookout, and Cape Kiwanda offers spectacular views of the ocean and coastline.

GETTING HERE

Tillamook is a 90-minute drive from Portland on U.S. Route 26 to Route 6. It sits on U.S. Highway 101 about 65 mi south of Astoria and 44 mi north of Lincoln City. Astoria's airport is the closest for air travel. Tillamook County's bus, **The Wave** (☎ *503/815–8283* ⊕ *www. tillamookbus.com*), leaves from Portland's Union Station. The bus connects Manzanita, Tillamook, and Pacific City.

VISITOR INFORMATION

Tillamook Chamber of Commerce (✉ *3705 U.S. 101N, Tillamook* ☎ *503/842– 7525* ⊕ *www.GoTillamook.com*).

EXPLORING

Latimer Quilt and Textile Center. Dedicated to the preservation, promotion, creation, and display of incredible works of fabric and woven art, spinners, weavers, beaders, and quilters are here working on projects. They may engage you in hands-on demonstrations. Rotating exhibits range from costumes, cloth dolls, crocheted items from the 1940s and 1950s, exquisite historical quilts dating from the early to mid-1800s, basketry, and weavings. ✉ *2105 Wilson River Loop Rd., Tillamook* ☎ *503/842– 8622* ⊕ *www.latimerquiltandtextile.com* ▣ *$3* ☉ *Apr.–Oct., Mon.–Sat. 10–5, Sun. 12–4; Nov.–Mar., Mon.–Sat. 10–4, closed Sun.*

Pioneer Museum. In Tillamook's 1905 county courthouse, the museum is an intriguing, old-fashioned hodgepodge of Native American, pioneer, logging, and natural history exhibits, along with antique vehicles and

DID YOU KNOW?

The Nature Conservancy Cascade Head Trail brings hikers to the grassy and treeless Cascade Head, a rare maritime prairie. There are magnificent views down to the Salmon River and east to the Coast Range. Coastal bluffs make this a popular hang gliding and kite-flying area.

military artifacts. ✉ *2106 2nd St., Tillamook* ☎ *503/842–4553* 🖱 *$4* ⏰ *Tues.–Sun. 10–4.*

Tillamook County Cheese Factory. More than 750,000 visitors annually journey to the largest cheese-making plant on the West Coast. Here the rich milk from the area's thousands of Holstein and brown Swiss cows becomes ice cream, butter, and cheddar and Monterey Jack cheeses. The product is heavenly—one of the true benefits of living in Oregon. Unfortunately the creamery's self-guided cheese-making tour is a letdown—fairly restrictive and lacking in personal interaction. Best cut to the chase and get to the cheese in the expansive store. There's also a selection of smoked meats and wonderful ice cream. Try the marionberry in a waffle cone. ✉ *4175 U.S. 101N, Tillamook* ☎ *503/815–1300* ⊕ *www.tillamookcheese.com* 🖱 *Free* ⏰ *Sept.–mid-June, daily 8–6; mid-June–Sept., daily 8–8.*

Tillamook Naval Air Station Museum. In the world's largest wooden structure, a former blimp hangar south of town displays one of the finest private collections of vintage aircraft from World War II. Its collection includes a P-38 Lightning, F4U-Corsair, P51-Mustang, PBY Catalina, SBD Dauntless dive-bomber, and an ME-109 Messerschmidt. The 20-story building is big enough to hold half a dozen football fields. ✉ *6030 Hangar Rd., Tillamook* ☎ *503/842–1130* ⊕ *www.tillamookair. com* 🖱 *$9* ⏰ *Daily 9–5.*

WHERE TO EAT AND STAY

$

ECLECTIC

✕ **Artspace.** You'll be surrounded by artwork as you enjoy homemade creations at Artspace in Bay City, 6 mi north of Tillamook. The menu may include garlic-grilled oysters, vegetarian dishes, and other specials, all beautifully presented, often with edible flowers. ✉ *9120 5th St., Bay City* ☎ *503/377–2782* ▭ *No credit cards* ⏰ *Closed Sat. No dinner.*

$$

SEAFOOD

✕ **Roseanna's.** Nine miles west of Tillamook in Oceanside, Roseanna's is in a rustic 1915 building on the beach opposite Three Arch Rock, a favorite resting spot for sea lions and puffins. The calm of the beach is complemented in the evening by candlelight and fresh flowers. Have halibut or salmon half a dozen ways, or the baked oysters or Gorgonzola seafood pasta. The evening's not complete without marionberry cobbler. ✉ *1490 Pacific Ave., Oceanside* ☎ *503/842–7351* 🖱 *Reservations not accepted* ▭ *MC, V.*

¢

🛏 **Hudson House.** The son of the original owner of this 1906 farmhouse was a photographer who captured the area's rough beauty on postcards. The larger suite is downstairs, with a parlor and private porch overlooking the Nestucca Valley. The more popular upstairs suite has a bedroom in the house's turret. The two guest rooms are under the high-gabled roof. The house has a wraparound porch from which you can enjoy a view of the surrounding woods. ✉ *37700 U.S. 101S, Cloverdale* ☎ *503/392–3533 or 888/835–3533* ⊕ *www.hudsonhouse.com* 🛏 *2 rooms, 2 suites* ⚙ *In-room: no phone, no TV, Internet* ▭ *MC, V* 🍽 *BP.*

SHOPPING

🐚 **Blue Heron French Cheese Company.** This special shop specializes in Brie—traditional, herb & garlic, pepper, and its flavorful smoked variety. You'll want to snag a wheel and some crackers for your trip along the coast. There's a free petting zoo for kids, a sit-down deli with fresh-baked bread, wine and cheese tastings, and a gift shop that carries wines and jams, mustards, and other products from Oregon. ⊠ *2001 Blue Heron Dr., Tillamook* ☎ *503/842–8281* ⊕ *www.blueheronoregon.com* ⊠ *Free* ☉ *Memorial Day–Labor Day, daily 8–8; Labor Day–Memorial Day, daily 8–6.*

PACIFIC CITY

24 mi south of Tillamook.

There's a lot to like about Pacific City, mostly that it's located three miles off Oregon's busy coastal Highway 101. That means fewer sputtering recreation vehicles or squeaking truck brakes breaking up the serenity of the sea. Also, there's no backup at the town's only traffic light—a blinking-red, four-way stop in the center of town. There's just the quiet, happy ambience of a town living the good life in the midst of extraordinary beauty. The dining venues and brewery are outstanding, and the lodging is stellar. Plus, the opportunities for recreation and tourism epitomize the best of the Oregon Coast. The beach at Pacific City is one of the few places in the state where fishing dories (flat-bottom boats with high, flaring sides) are launched directly into the surf instead of from harbors or docks.

GETTING HERE

Located between Tillamook and Lincoln City, the unincorporated village of Pacific City is off U.S. Highway 101 on the south end of the beautiful Three Capes Loop. It is a two-hour drive from Portland on U.S. Highway 26 to Route 6. From Salem, Pacific City is a 90-minute drive on Route 22. Tillamook County's bus, **The Wave** (☎ *503/815–8283* ⊕ *www.tillamookbus.com*), leaves from Portland's Union Station. The bus connects Manzanita, Tillamook, and Pacific City. The nearest airport is in Newport, 47 mi south.

VISITOR INFORMATION

Pacific City-Nestucca Valley Chamber of Commerce (☎ *503/392–4340 or 888/549–2632* ⊕ *www.PacificCity.com*).

WHERE TO EAT AND STAY

¢ ✕**Grateful Bread.** Open since 1991, this café uses the cod caught by
AMERICAN the local dories for its fish-and-chips. Everything it makes is fresh and from scratch. Its breads, pastries, breakfasts, and pizzas are simply perfect. ⊠ *34805 Brooten Rd., Pacific City* ☎ *503/965–7337* ▭ *MC, V* ☉ *Closed Tues. and Wed. No dinner.*

$$ ✕**Pelican Pub and Brewery.** This beer-lover's jewel stands on the ocean-
AMERICAN front by Haystack Rock. While its microbrewery has garnered national and international acclaim for its beers, the Pelican Pub has elevated the art of beer cuisine by listing beer pairings on its menu. Many of its fine entrées are infused with its beers, such as the linguine with fresh clams flavored with Kiwanda Cream Ale, and the Tsunami Stout brownie sundae. The pub periodically hosts Brewers Dinners—splendid affairs that have explored beer pairings with Scottish, Greek, Italian, and Belgian cooking. Kids love the gourmet pizzas and children's menu.

✉ *33180 Cape Kiwanda Dr., Pacific City* ☎ *503/965–7007* ⊕ *www. pelicanbrewery.com* ▭ *AE, D, MC, V.*

$$$ ✗ **Riverhouse.** On the Nestucca River, this is the area's best place for
SEAFOOD fresh crab, oysters, and filet mignon. It also has more casual fare, such
as sandwiches and salads. The interior has handmade redwood tables
and art pieces displayed by local artists. Best of all, it's famous through-
out the Pacific Northwest for its unmatched salad dressings, which
are available at popular grocery stores throughout the region. Its bleu
cheese flavor is so fine you'll make primitive sounds slurping it off your
lettuce. ✉ *34450 Brooten Rd., Pacific City* ☎ *503/965–6722* ▭ *MC, V.*

$$$$ ⊡ **Cottages at Cape Kiwanda.** For a five-star resort experience with a glo-
rious beach view, the Cottages at Cape Kiwanda has 18 units for rent
that can sleep four or six people. It's perfect for families or that beach
get-together with friends. Each dwelling has fine decor, the latest elec-
tronics, and kitchen gadgets for proper entertaining or preparing your
own feast. The concierge will help guests find the right trails or where
to buy a kite or rent a surfboard. There's a two-night minimum. **Pros:**
upscale; comfortable; and next to Pacific City eateries. **Cons:** there are
ownership opportunities, so there might be a sales pitch. ✉ *33000 Cape
Kiwanda Dr., Pacific City* ☎ *888/965–7001* ⊕ *www.kiwandacottages.
com* ⤳ *18 rooms* ⚒ *In-room: kitchen, refrigerator, DVD, Internet,
some pets allowed* ▭ *AE, D, MC, V.*

¢ ⊡ **Inn at Cape Kiwanda.** You won't find a weather-beaten beach cottage
here. Each of the 35 deluxe, fireplace-warmed rooms has a gorgeous
view of Haystack Rock. Along with top amenities in every room, a
workout facility, the Stimulus Espresso Café Coffee Shop, and pet-
friendly rooms are available. It's within walking distance of Pacific City
dining. **Pros:** great views; some pets are welcome; terrific restaurants
nearby. **Cons:** guests might get hit up with a sales pitch. ✉ *33105 Cape
Kiwanda Dr., Pacific City* ☎ *888/965–7001* ⊕ *www.innatcapekiwanda.
com* ⤳ *35 rooms* ⚒ *In-room: refrigerator, DVD. In-hotel: Wi-Fi, gym,
restaurant, some pets allowed.* ▭ *AE, D, MC, V.*

$$ ⊡ **Sandlake Country Inn.** Tucked into a bower of old roses on two acres,
this intimate bed-and-breakfast is in a farmhouse built of timbers that
washed ashore from a shipwreck in 1890. Listed in the Oregon Historic
Registry, it's filled with antiques. The Timbers Suite has a massive, king-
size wood canopy bed, wood-burning fireplace, and two-person jetted
tub; the Starlight Suite occupies four rooms on the second floor and
includes a canopy queen bed and double-sided fireplace. A complimentary four-course breakfast is delivered to the door. There's a two-night
minimum stay on weekends. **Pros:** comfortable stay; pretty property.
Cons: no pets. ✉ *8505 Galloway Rd., Pacific City* ☎ *503/965–6745 or
877/726–3525* ⊕ *www.sandlakecountryinn.com* ⤳ *1 room, 2 suites, 1
cottage* ⚒ *In-room: Wi-Fi, no phone (some)* ▭ *D, MC, V* ⊙ *BP.*

NIGHTLIFE AND THE ARTS

Twist. This fun and funky tasting lounge has been serving its twist-
top vintages since 2008. Sporting 1,000 vinyl records, customers can
choose what to spin while stretching out on the comfy furniture, or
they can go behind the sofa and play with the Atari game. Its wines
are made in Oregon's Yamhill wine country. ✉ *6425 Pacific Ave.,*

Three Capes Loop

Coastal views from the Three Capes Loop

The **Three Capes Loop**, a 35-mi byway off U.S. 101, is one of the coast's most thrilling driving experiences. The loop winds along the coast between Tillamook and Pacific City, passing three distinctive headlands—Cape Meares, Cape Lookout, and Cape Kiwanda. Bayocean Road heading west from Tillamook passes what was the thriving resort town of Bay Ocean. More than 30 years ago, Bay Ocean washed into the sea—houses, a bowling alley, everything—during a raging Pacific storm.

WHAT YOU'LL SEE
Cape Meares State Park is on the northern tip of the Three Capes Loop. The restored **Cape Meares Lighthouse,** built in 1890 and open to the public May toSeptember, provides a sweeping view over the cliff to the caves and sealion rookery on the rocks below. A many-trunked Sitka spruce known as the Octopus Tree grows near the lighthouse parking lot. ⊠ *Three Capes Loop, 10 mi west of Tillamook* ☎ *800/551–6949* ⊕ *www.*

oregonstateparks.org ✉ *Free* ⊙ *Park daily dawn–dusk. Lighthouse Apr.–Oct., daily 11–4.*

Cape Lookout State Park lies south of the beach towns of Oceanside and Netarts. A fairly easy 2-mi trail—marked on the highway as WILDLIFE VIEWING AREA—leads through giant spruces, western red cedars, and hemlocks, and ends with views of Cascade Head to the south and Cape Meares to the north. Wildflowers, more than 150 species of birds, and migrating whales passing by in early April make this trail a favorite with nature lovers. The park has a picnic area overlooking the sea and a year-round campground. ⊠ *Three Capes Loop, 8 mi south of Cape Meares, Oceanside* ☎ *800/551–6949* ⊕ *www. oregonstateparks.org* ✉ *Day use $5* ⊙ *Daily dawn–dusk.*

Huge waves pound the jagged sandstone cliffs and caves at **Cape Kiwanda State Natural Area**. The much-photographed, 235-foot-high **Haystack Rock** juts out of Nestucca Bay to the south. Surfers ride some of the longest waves on the coast, hang gliders soar above the shore, and beachcombers explore tidal pools and take in unparalleled ocean views. ⊠ *Three Capes Loop, 15 mi south of Cape Lookout, Pacific City* ☎ *800/551–6949* ⊕ *www. oregonstateparks.org* ✉ *Free* ⊙ *Daily sunrise–sunset.*

4

Pacific City ☎ *503/965–6887* ⊕ *www.twistwine.com* ☰ *AE, D, MC, V* ☽ *Closed weekdays.*

SPORTS AND THE OUTDOORS

RECREATIONAL
AREAS

Robert Straub State Park. A walk along the flat white-sand beach leads down to the mouth of the Nestucca River, considered by many to be the best fishing river on the north coast. ⊠ *West from main intersection in downtown Pacific City across Nestucca River, Pacific City* ☎ *800/551– 6949* ⊠ *Free* ☽ *Daily sunrise–sunset.*

OFF THE
BEATEN
PATH

Nature Conservancy Cascade Head Trail. This dense, green trail winds through a rain forest where 100-inch annual rainfalls nourish 250-year-old Sitka spruces, mosses, and ferns. Emerging from the forest, hikers come upon grassy and treeless Cascade Head, a rare maritime prairie. There are magnificent views down to the Salmon River and east to the Coast Range. Continuing along the headland, black-tailed deer often graze and turkey vultures soar in the strong winds. You need to be in fairly good shape for the first and steepest part of the hike, which can be done in about an hour. The 270-acre area has been named a United Nations Biosphere Reserve. Coastal bluffs also make this a popular hang-gliding and kite-flying area. ⊠ *Savage Rd., 6 mi south of Neskowin off U.S. 101, Pacific City* ☎ *503/230–1221* ⊕ *www.nature.org* ⊠ *Free* ☽ *Upper trail closed from Jan. to mid July.*

FISHING

Eagle Charters. Within three minutes of launching from the beach, customers can be fishing in a dory and catching rockfish right in front of Haystack Rock. Groups of up to five people can be accommodated, and families with children are welcome. Fishing and ecotourism trips last six hours except for halibut and tuna fishing, which are 10 to 12 hrs. ☎ *877/892–3679* ⊕ *www.eaglecharters.us* ☰ *MC, V.*

Haystack Fishing, Inc. Offering ocean fishing for salmon, bottom fish, halibut, and crab, Haystack Fishing targets lingcod larger than 10 lbs. After a day of fishing, they'll fillet your catch. These guided dory trips last between four and six hours and accommodate up to six people. Fishing tours are held between June and September. ☎ *503/965–7555 or 866/965–7555* ⊕ *www.haystackfishing.com* ☰ *MC, V.*

HORSEBACK
RIDING

Oregon Beach Rides. Saddle up for horseback rides that journey along the beach, up coastal trails, to Robert Straub State Park and Nestucca River. Reserved rides can last from one hour up to a full day. There's even a romantic sunset trot along the beach. ☎ *971/237–6653* ⊕ *www. oregonbeachrides.com* ⊠ *Reservations required* ☰ *AE, D, MC, V.*

SURFING

Kiwanda Surf Company Rentals. Cape Kiwanda is one of the most spectacular and scenic spots on the Oregon Coast, and Kiwanda Surf Company rents all the gear you need to experience it to the fullest. This small surf shack has plenty of boards and apparel, and it even rents kayaks for paddling in the Nestucca River. Rental rates are very reasonable. Surfboards are $30 for a full day; wet suit, booties, and hood $26 per day; and kayaks $50 per day. It has hourly rates and surfing instruction, too. ⊠ *6305 Pacific Ave., Pacific City* ☎ *503/965–3627* ⊕ *www. kiwandasurfco.com* ☽ *Daily 10–5* ☰ *MC, V.*

CENTRAL COAST

This is Oregon's coastal playland, drawing shoppers, kite flyers, deep-sea fishing enthusiasts, surfers, and dune-shredding daredevils. Lincoln City offers a wealth of shops devoted to antiques and knickknacks, and visitors can even blow their own glass float. Depoe Bay has the world's smallest harbor, and Newport is designated the Dungeness crab capitol of the world. The best barbecue is in Toledo, and Oregon Dunes National Recreation Area provides the best thrills. Even if you're not intent on making tracks in the sand, the dunes provide vast, unforgettable scenery.

LINCOLN CITY

4

16 mi south of Pacific City on U.S. 101; 78 mi west of Portland on Hwy. 99 W and Hwy. 18.

Lincoln City is a captivating destination for families and lovers who want to share some time laughing on the beach, poking their fingers in tide pools, and trying to harness wind-bucking kites. Once a series of small villages, Lincoln City is a sprawling town without a center. But the endless tourist amenities make up for a lack of a small coastal-town ambience. Clustered like barnacles on the offshore reefs are fast-food restaurants, gift shops, supermarkets, candy stores, antiques markets, dozens of motels and hotels, a factory-outlet mall, and a busy casino. Lincoln City is the most popular destination city on the Oregon Coast, but its only real geographic claim to fame is the 445-foot-long D River, stretching from its source in Devil's Lake to the Pacific; *Guinness World Records* lists the D as the world's shortest river.

GETTING HERE

Lincoln City is a two-hour drive from Portland. From Astoria, it's a 2½-hour drive along U.S. 101. **Lincoln Transit** buses connect riders with Newport, Siletz, Lincoln City, and Yachats. Newport has the nearest airport, 31 mi away.

VISITOR INFORMATION

Lincoln City Visitors Center (✉ *801 SW U.S. 101, 4th Floor, Lincoln City* ☎ *541/996–1274 or 800/452–2151* ⊕ *www.oregoncoast.org*).

WHERE TO EAT

¢ ✕ **Beach Dog Café.** Dang, these are good dogs, dressed in 16 different
AMERICAN ways. You'll find everything from Coney, Philly, and Kosher to Hot
Fodor's Choice Diggity. This family-owned joint has a galaxy of dog photos adorning
★ its walls. But its breakfasts have the morning crowds gathering. Roger and Sonja Seals offer a menu full of hearty potato dishes, scrambles, stuffed French toast, and incredible breakfast sandwiches. The apple potato pancake with sour cream and a Polish sausage is the keystone to any nutritious breakfast. ✉ *1266 SW 50th St., Lincoln City* ☎ *541/996–3647* ▭ *No credit cards* ⊙ *Closed Mon. No dinner.*

$$ ✕ **Blackfish Café.** Owner and chef Rob Pounding serves simple-but-
SEAFOOD succulent dishes that blend fresh ingredients from local fishermen and
Fodor's Choice gardeners. Before starting his own restaurant in 1999, Pounding was
★ the executive chef of acclaimed Salishan Lodge for 14 years, winning

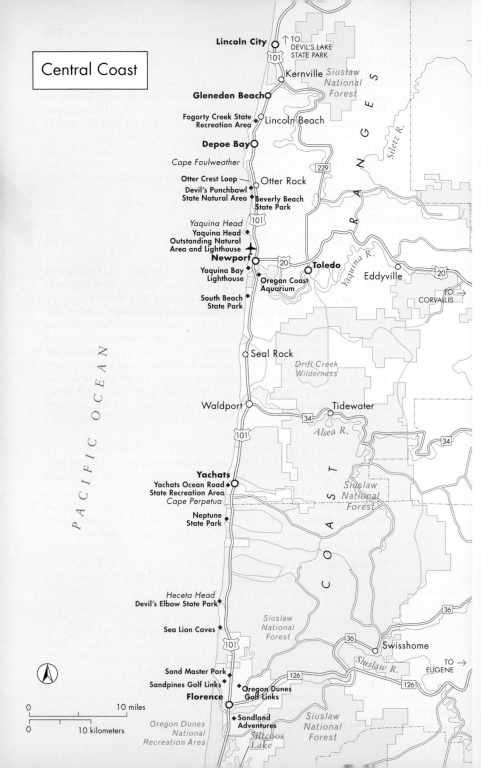

Central Coast

Lincoln City

↑ TO
DEVIL'S LAKE
STATE PARK

101

Kernville

*Siuslaw
National
Forest*

Gleneden Beach

Fogarty Creek State
Recreation Area ◆ Lincoln Beach

Depoe Bay

Cape Foulweather

229

Otter Crest Loop
Devil's Punchbowl
State Natural Area ◆ Otter Rock
Beverly Beach
State Park

Yaquina Head
Yaquina Head
Outstanding Natural
Area and Lighthouse

101

Newport

20

Toledo

Yaquina Bay
Lighthouse

Eddyville

20

Oregon Coast
Aquarium

Yaquina R.

Siletz R.

TO
CORVALLIS

South Beach
State Park

R A N G E S

Seal Rock

*Drift Creek
Wilderness*

Waldport

Tidewater

34

34

Alsea R.

101

C O A S T

Yachats
Yachats Ocean Road
State Recreation Area ◆
Cape Perpetua

*Siuslaw
National
Forest*

Neptune
State Park

Heceta Head
Devil's Elbow State Park

36

Sea Lion Caves

*Siuslaw
National
Forest*

36

Swisshome

101

Siuslaw R.

TO
EUGENE

Sand Master Park

126

Sandpines Golf Links
Florence

Oregon Dunes
Golf Links

126

Sandland
Adventures

*Siuslaw
National
Forest*

*Oregon Dunes
National
Recreation Area*

*Siltcoos
Lake*

P A C I F I C   O C E A N

0 ——— 10 miles

0 ——— 10 kilometers

top national culinary awards. His skillet-roasted, "ocean trolled" chinook salmon, basted with fennel lime butter, and Oregon blue-cheese potatoesare flavorful and perfect. The Blackfish Ding Dong dessert, with mixed-berry sauce and whipped cream, is the best way to finish a meal. ⊠ *2733 NW Hwy. 101,Lincoln City* ☎ *541/996–1007* ⊕ *www. blackfishcafe.com* ⚭ *Reservations recommended* ⊟ *AE, D, MC, V* ☾ *Closed Tues.*

$$$ ✕ **Culinary Center.** Whether she's conducting a small, hands-on class or
NEW AMERICAN orchestrating a full-blown cooking demonstration for dozens, executive chef Sharon Wiest loves sharing her passion for Pacific Northwest ingredients. Directly above the visitors' bureau, the Culinary Center is a wonderful stop for newcomers to the area. Guests can sign up to get their hands onto some food and learn, or they can sit back, sip wine, and enjoy learning what makes Oregon such a special place to dine. The center's schedule includes classes in oysters, pizza, sushi, tapas, Mexican, seafood, and even bacon. Chocolate-chip bacon-pecan cookie, anyone? ⊠ *801 SW Hwy 101, Suite 401, Lincoln City* ☎ *541/557–1125* ⊕ *www.oregoncoast.org/culinary/index.php* ⊟ *MC, V* ☾ *Closed Mon. No dinner.*

¢ ✕ **Rockfish Bakery.** The seed for this phenomenal bakery began when
CAFÉ Rob Pounding, owner and chef for Blackfish Café, couldn't find any hamburger buns that met his standards. Now his bakery publishes a weekly bread schedule so customers will know when to buy the freshest sourdough, olive ciabatta, rye, or brioche with raisins. It makes the coast's best cinnamon rolls, cookies, excellent pizza, hearty sandwiches, and a soup du jour from the nearby Blackfish Café. The Rockfish is a must for anyone who loves an upper-crust bakery. ⊠ *3026 NE Hwy. 101, Lincoln City* ☎ *541/996–1006* ⊕ *www.rockfishbakery.com* ⊟ *MC, V* ☾ *Closed Mon. and Tues. No dinner.*

WHERE TO STAY

$$$ ⊡ **Coho Oceanfront Lodge.** Set on a romantic cliff, the renovated Coho is
Fodor's Choice a perfect hybrid of family-friendly lodging and a quiet, intimate hideaway for couples. The expanded oceanfront property has 65 suites
★ and rooms—14 of them in a brand-new south wing, which is relegated to adults. The Coho also has a concierge service, and is particularly adept at recommending nearby trails, restaurants, and evening fun. If you want to stay in, its lobby has plenty of games, an expansive DVD collection, and a complimentary Continental breakfast daily. It even offers sand pails and kites to borrow for sandy fun. **Pros:** great value; family-friendly, concierge service; and shuttle to nearby casino. **Cons:** no restaurant. ⊠ *1635 NW Harbor Ave., Lincoln City* ☎ *541/994–3684* ⊕ *www.thecoholodge.com* ⇥ *33 studios, 32 suites* ⚬ *In-room: a/c, safe (some), kitchen (some), refrigerator (some), DVD, Wi-Fi. In-hotel: beachfront, parking, pool, fitness room* ⊟ *AE, D, MC, V* ⦿| *CP.*

¢ ⊡ **The Historic Anchor Inn.** This quirky bungalow might not be for everyone. But for those who appreciate a warm, spirited inn with a decidedly inventive and whimsical touch, this is a remarkable find. Started in the mid-1940s, it is the oldest hotel in Lincoln City. It's loaded with funky, fun treasures. The rooms are themed; check out the Web site for oodles of photos. Homemade breakfast is served between 9 and 10 AM, and dinner for groups and small parties can be arranged. **Pros:** a memorable, truly unique property with everything you need to explore Lincoln City. **Cons:** not on the beach, very quirky and rustic, which could be a pro too. ⊠ *4417 SW U.S. 101, Lincoln City* ☎ *541/996–3810* ⊕ *www. historicanchorinn.com* ⤙ *19 rooms* ♿ *In-hotel: Wi-Fi, restaurant, some pets allowed* ⊟ *MC, V* ⦿ *BP.*

$$$ ⊡ **Inn at Spanish Head.** Driving up to this luxury resort hotel, you'd think it might be small, but on further investigation you'll see that the property takes up the entire side of a bluff like a huge staircase. All of the bright, contemporary units have expansive ocean views, and guests will find tidal pools right outside the door. At this resort no two rooms are alike, Choose from one-bedroom suites, deluxe studios, or deluxe rooms. **Pros:** sweeping views of the ocean through floor-to-ceiling windows; restaurant on-site; easy beach access; great place to watch winter storms. **Cons:** pricey. ⊠ *4009 S. U.S. 101, Lincoln City* ☎ *541/996–2161 or 800/452–8127* ⊕ *www.spanishhead.com* ⤙ *78 rooms, 49 suites* ♿ *In-room: kitchen (some), Wi-Fi. In-hotel: beachfront, restaurant, room service, gym, pool* ⊟ *AE, D, DC, MC, V.*

NIGHTLIFE AND THE ARTS

Chinook Winds Casino Resort. Oregon's only beachfront casino has a great variety of slot machines, blackjack, poker, keno, and off-track betting. The Rogue River Steakhouse serves a great fillet and terrific appetizers. There's also the Siletz Bay Buffet, the Chinook Seafood Grill, a snack bar, and a lounge. An arcade will keep the kids busy while you are on the gambling floor. Big-name entertainers perform in the showroom. Players can take a break from the tables and enjoy a round of golf at the Chinook Winds Golf Resort next door. ⊠ *1777 NW 44th St., Lincoln City* ☎ *541/996–5825 or 888/244–6665* ⊘ *Daily, 24 hours* ⊟ *AE, D, MC, V.*

SHOPPING

Alder House II. The imaginative crafts folk at this studio turn molten glass into vases and bowls, which are available for sale. It is the oldest glass-blowing studio in the state. ⊠ *611 Immonen Rd., Lincoln City* ☎ *541/996–2483* ⊕ *www.alderhouse.com* ▱ *Free* ⊘ *Mid-Mar.–Nov., daily 10–5.*

Jennifer L. Sears Glass Art Studio. Blow a glass float or make a glorious glass starfish, heart, or fluted bowl of your own design. The studio's expert artisans will guide you every step of the way. It's a fun, memorable keepsake of the coast. ⊠ *4821 SE Hwy. 101, Lincoln City* ☎ *541/996–2569* ◿ *Call for an appointment* ⊕ *www.jennifersearsglassart.com* ▱ *$65 for a glass float* ⊘ *Wed.–Sun. 10–6.*

Lincoln City Surf Shop. Darn right they surf on the Oregon Coast. Maybe the surfers are dressed from head to toe in wet suits, but they're riding some tasty waves just the same. At Lincoln City's oldest surf shop there's equipment and apparel for purchase or rent. Lessons provide a great family activity, and rates include board, wet suits, hood, and booties. The shop also has a collection of kiteboards, skimboards, and skateboards. ⊠ *4792 SE Hwy. 101, Lincoln City* ☎ *541/996–7433* ⊕ *www. lcsurfshop.com* ⊘ *Summer, daily 9–7; winter, daily 10–5.*

Salishan Golf Resort, Gleneden Beach

SPORTS AND THE OUTDOORS

BOATING **Devil's Lake State Park.** Canoeing and kayaking are popular on this small lake, which is in turn popular with coots, loons, ducks, cormorants, bald eagles, and grebes. Visitors can sign up in advance for popular kayaking tours in the summer. It's the only Oregon Coast campground within the environs of a city. Hookups, tent sites, and yurts are available. ⊠ *1452 NE 6th St., Lincoln City* ☎ *541/994–2002 or 800/551–6649* ⊕ *www.oregonstateparks.org* ⊙ *Daily* ▭ *MC, V.*

GLENEDEN BEACH

7 mi south of Lincoln City on U.S. 101.

Gleneden Beach is primarily a resort town with Salishan, its most famous property, perching high above placid Siletz Bay. This expensive collection of guest rooms, vacation homes, condominiums, restaurants, golf fairways, tennis courts, and covered walkways blends into a forest preserve; if not for the signs, you'd scarcely be able to find it.

GETTING HERE

The closest airport to Gleneden Beach is in Newport, 23 mi south. Bus service to Newport is provided by **Lincoln County Transit Bus/Dail-A-Ride** (☎ *541/265–4900*). **Caravan Airport Transportation** (☎ *541/994–9645*) provides shuttle service to Portland International Airport for Lincoln City, Depoe Bay, and Newport.

VISITOR INFORMATION

Central Oregon Coast Association (⊠ *137 NE 1st St., Newport* ☎ *503/265–2064 or 800/767–2064* ⊕ *www.coastvisitor.com*).

EXPLORING

Lawrence Gallery at Salishan. The well-respected gallery has a well-informed staff that will guide you through the collections of work by Northwest artists, including paintings (pastels, oils, and watercolors), glassworks, bronze and metal, furniture, and ceramics and porcelain. ✉ *7755 N. U.S. 101, Gleneden Beach* ☎ *541/764–2318 or 800/764–2318* ⊕ *www.lawrencegallery.net* ☉ *Daily 10–5.*

WHERE TO EAT AND STAY

$$$$
STEAKHOUSE

✗ **Prime Steakhouse at Salishan.** If you're not on a budget, pull up a chair and slurp a bowl of Dungeness crab bisque, relish some oysters Rockefeller, and slice into a 28-day-aged steak or a mouth-watering seared scallop. It also serves game, lamb, and elegant desserts. The white-linen dining room has a gorgeous view of Siletz Bay and the private Salishan Spit, and there's a private dining room for those very special occasions. You could spend all evening perusing the wine list, as the resort's cellar has more than 17,000 bottles. ✉ *7760 N. U.S. 101, Gleneden Beach* ☎ *541/764–2371 or 800/452–2300* ⌂ *Reservations essential* ▭ *AE, D, DC, MC, V* ☉ *No lunch.*

$$
CONTINENTAL

✗ **Sidedoor Café.** This dining room, with a high ceiling, exposed beams, a fireplace, and many windows just under the eaves shares a former tile factory with the Eden Hall performance space. The menu changes constantly—fresh preparations have included mushroom-crusted rack of lamb and broiled swordfish with citrus-raspberry vinaigrette over coconut-ginger basmati rice. ✉ *6675 Gleneden Beach Loop Rd., Gleneden Beach* ☎ *541/764–3825* ▭ *AE, D, MC, V.*

$$

🛏 **BeachCombers Vacation Rentals.** This cluster of properties is right off the beach, and features spacious one-, two-, or three-bedroom accommodations, some with a hot tub or in-room Jacuzzi. The property is near a golf course, art galleries, shopping, and outstanding restaurants. **Pros:** very friendly; comfortable; near the beach. **Cons:** expect a rustic beach property, not a resort. ✉ *7045 NW Glen, Gleneden Beach* ☎ *541/764–2252 or 800/428–5533* ⊕ *www.beachcombershaven.com* ⟿ *14 homes* ⌂ *In-room: kitchen, DVD. In-hotel: Wi-Fi, beachfront, laundry service* ▭ *D, MC, V.*

$$$

🛏 **Salishan Lodge and Golf Resort.** Secluded and refined, this upscale property is located in a hillside forest preserve. Long revered as a luxury weekend away as well as a destination for tony corporate retreats, Salishan provides plenty of reasons to stay on the property. Its spa is outstanding and there are different dining venues perfect for brunch, a casual bite after golf, or a polished, white-linen dining experience. The rooms are spacious, comfortable, and toasty with wood-burning fireplaces. Each has a balcony and original artwork by Northwest artists. Its par-71 golf course, redesigned by Peter Jacobsen, is one of the coast's finest. **Pros:** very elegant; secluded resort with a terrific golf course;plenty of activities on the property. **Cons:** ocean views are few; some reviewers mentioned that service can be a bit lax. ✉ *7760 N. U.S. 101, Gleneden Beach* ☎ *541/764–3600 or 800/452–2300* ⊕ *www.salishan.com* ⟿ *205 rooms* ⌂ *In-room: refrigerator, Wi-Fi. In-hotel: 3 restaurants, room service, bar, golf course, tennis courts, pool, gym, beachfront, laundry service* ▭ *AE, D, DC, MC, V.*

SPORTS AND THE OUTDOORS

GOLF **Salishan Golf Resort.** Redesigned by Peter Jacobsen, this par-71 course is a year-round treat for hackers and aficionados alike. The front nine holes are surrounded by a forest of old-growth timber, while the back nine holes provide old-school, links-style play. It has an expansive pro shop with fine men's and women's sportswear, and a great bar and grill for relaxing after a "rough" day out on the links. It has rental clubs available, as well as lessons on its driving range and practice green. ⊠ *7760 N. U.S. 101, Gleneden Beach* ☎ *541/764–3600 or 800/452–2300* ⊕ *www.salishan.com* ✉ *$119 weekends, cart included.*

DEPOE BAY

5 mi south of Gleneden Beach on U.S. 101.

Depoe Bay calls itself the whale-watching capital of the world. The small town was founded in the 1920s and named in honor of Charles DePoe of the Siletz tribe, who was named for his employment at a U.S. Army depot in the late 1800s. With a narrow channel and deep water, its tiny harbor is also one of the most protected on the coast. It supports a thriving fleet of commercial- and charter-fishing boats. The Spouting Horn, a natural cleft in the basalt cliffs on the waterfront, blasts seawater skyward during heavy weather.

GETTING HERE

Depoe Bay is a short 12-mi drive north of Newport and its airport on U.S. Highway 101. **Lincoln Transit** provides bus service to Newport, Depoe Bay, Siletz, Lincoln City, and Yachats. Bus connections to Portland are accessible in Newport and are provided by **Greyhound** Newport and the **Valley Retriever** (☎ *541/265–2253* ⊕ *www.kokkola-bus.com/ValleyRetrieverBuslines.html*). **Caravan Airport Transportation** (☎ *541/994–9645*) provides shuttle service to Portland International Airport.

VISITOR INFORMATION

Depoe Bay Chamber of Commerce ⊠ *223 SW Hwy 101, Ste B, Depoe Bay* ☎ *541/765–2889* ⊕ *www.depoebaychamber.org.*

EXPLORING

EN ROUTE Five miles south of Depoe Bay off U.S. 101 (watch for signs), the **Otter Crest Loop,** another scenic byway, winds along the cliff tops. Only parts of the loop are open to motor vehicles, but you can drive to points midway from either end and turn around. The full loop is open to bikes and hiking. British explorer Captain James Cook named the 500-foot-high **Cape Foulweather,** at the south end of the loop, on a blustery March day in 1778. Backward-leaning shore pines lend mute witness to the 100-mph winds that still strafe this exposed spot. At the viewing point at the **Devil's Punchbowl,** 1 mi south of Cape Foulweather, you can peer down into a collapsed sandstone sea cave carved out by the powerful waters of the Pacific. About 100 feet to the north in the rocky tidal pools of the beach known as **Marine Gardens,** purple sea urchins and orange starfish can be seen at low tide. The Otter Crest Loop rejoins U.S. 101 about 4 mi south of Cape Foulweather near **Yaquina Head,** which has been designated an Outstanding Natural Area. Harbor seals, sea lions, cormorants, murres, puffins, and guillemots frolic in the water and on

4

the rocks below the gleaming, white tower of the **Yaquina Bay Lighthouse**, which was activated in 1873.

WHERE TO EAT AND STAY

$$

BISTRO

✕ **Café Bella Mar.** This charming, colorful bistro provides a fine selection of wines, local brews, tasty panini sandwiches, and flatbread pizzas. Owner Lauren Stenzel will be there to greet you, adorned with one of her famous hats. Try the hot artichoke dip. ⊠ *8 Bella Beach Dr., Depoe Bay* ☎ *541/764–4466w www.cafebellamar.com* ▭ *MC, V.*

$

SEAFOOD

✕ **Gracie's Sea Hag.** In 1963, Gracie Strom founded Gracie's Sea Hag Restaurant & Lounge, which specializes in fresh seafood, with an extensive buffet on Friday nights. Saturday the focus is prime rib with Yorkshire pudding. Several booths at the front of the restaurant have views of the "spouting horns" across the highway. The restaurant is kid-friendly, and there's an adjoining grown-up–friendly bar that gets hopping with live entertainment at night. ⊠ *58 U.S. 101, Depoe Bay* ☎ *541/765–2734* ▭ *AE, D, DC, MC, V.*

$$

⌷ **The Harbor Lights Inn.** This harbor-front bed-and-breakfast provides a dreamy setting for watching boats and relaxing in a quaint, quiet atmosphere. Nine rooms have fireplaces as well as balconies or patios. Breakfast is served between 8:30 and 10 AM. **Pros:** small, quiet, and pretty; great breakfasts. **Cons:** not on the beach. ⊠ *235 SE Bay View Ave., Depoe Bay* ☎ *541/765–2322 or 800/228–0448* ⊕ *www.theharborlightsinn.com* ⇲ *13 rooms* ⌕ *In-room: Wi-Fi, DVD. In-hotel: restaurant.* ▭ *AE, MC, V* ⏐⏐⏐*BP.*

SPORTS AND THE OUTDOORS

RECREATIONAL
AREAS

Fogarty Creek State Park. Bird-watching and viewing the tidal pools are the key draws here, but hiking and picnicking are also popular at this park 4 mi north of Depoe Bay on U.S. 101. Wooden footbridges arch through the forest. The beach is rimmed with cliffs. ⊠ *U.S. 101, Depoe Bay* ☎ *541/265–9278 or 800/551–6949* ⊕ *www.oregonstateparks.org* ▱ *Free* ◷ *Daily.*

OUTFITTERS

Coastal Outfitters provides kayak tours, rentals, and lessons for exploring area waters in Depoe Bay, Newport, and the Siletz River. Depending on the group and its ability, tours include whale-watching and cave exploring, Pacific Ocean tours, spotting blue heron and bald eagles up Beaver Creek, and a Yaquina Bay tour. Kayaks also can be rented by the day. ⊠ *104 NE Hwy. 101, Depoe Bay* ☎ *541/765–2776* ⊕ *coastaloutfitter. us* ▱ *$35 per day for one-person kayak, $50 per day for two-person kayak; tours are $70 per hour* ▭ *AE, MC, V.*

NEWPORT

12 mi south of Depoe Bay on U.S. 101.

Called the Dungeness crab capital of the world, Newport offers accessible beaches, a nationally renowned aquarium, a lively performing-arts center, and a local laid-back attitude. Newport exists on two levels: the highway above, threading its way through the community's main business district, and the old Bayfront along Yaquina Bay below (watch for signs on U.S. 101). With its high-masted fishing fleet, well-worn

Continued on page 237

WHALE-WATCHING
IN THE PACIFIC NORTHWEST

The thrill of seeing whales in the wild is, for many, one of the most enduring memories of a trip to the Pacific Northwest. In this part of the world, you'll generally spot two species—gray whales and killer "orca" whales.

About 20,000 grays migrate up the West Coast in spring and back down again in early winter (a smaller group of gray whales live off the Oregon coast all summer). From late spring through early autumn about 80 orcas inhabit Washington's Puget Sound and BC's Georgia Strait. Although far fewer in number, the orcas live in pods and travel in predictable patterns; therefore chances are high that you will see a pod on any given trip. Some operators claim sighting rates of 90 percent; others offer guaranteed sightings, meaning that you can repeat the tour free of charge until you spot a whale.

COMMON PACIFIC NORTHWEST SPECIES

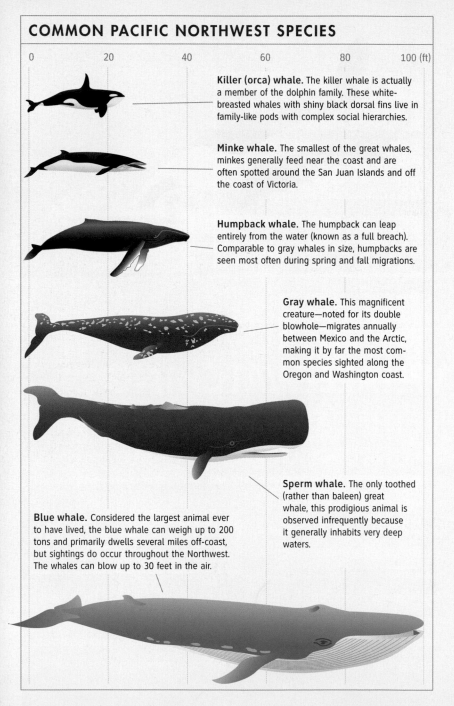

0   20   40   60   80   100 (ft)

Killer (orca) whale. The killer whale is actually a member of the dolphin family. These white-breasted whales with shiny black dorsal fins live in family-like pods with complex social hierarchies.

Minke whale. The smallest of the great whales, minkes generally feed near the coast and are often spotted around the San Juan Islands and off the coast of Victoria.

Humpback whale. The humpback can leap entirely from the water (known as a full breach). Comparable to gray whales in size, humpbacks are seen most often during spring and fall migrations.

Gray whale. This magnificent creature—noted for its double blowhole—migrates annually between Mexico and the Arctic, making it by far the most common species sighted along the Oregon and Washington coast.

Sperm whale. The only toothed (rather than baleen) great whale, this prodigious animal is observed infrequently because it generally inhabits very deep waters.

Blue whale. Considered the largest animal ever to have lived, the blue whale can weigh up to 200 tons and primarily dwells several miles off-coast, but sightings do occur throughout the Northwest. The whales can blow up to 30 feet in the air.

TAKING A TOUR

Spotting an orca in the Haro Strait between
British Columbia and Washington

CHOOSING YOUR BOAT

The type of boat you choose does not affect how close you can get to the whales. For the safety of whales and humans, government regulations require boats to stay at least 100 meters (328 feet) from the pods, though closer encounters are possible if whales approach a boat when its engine is off.

Motor Launches. These cruisers carry from 30 to more than 80 passengers. They are comfortable, with washrooms, protection from the elements, and even snack-and-drink concessions. They can be either glass-enclosed or open-air.

Zodiacs. Open inflatable boats, Zodiacs carry about 12 passengers. They are smaller and more agile than cruisers and offer both an exciting ride bouncing over the waves and an eye-level view of the whales. Passengers are supplied with warm, waterproof survival suits. Note: Zodiac tours are not recommended for people with back or neck problems, pregnant women, or small children.

Most companies have naturalists on board as guides, as well as hydrophones that, if you get close enough, allow you to listen to the whales singing and vocalizing. Although the focus is on whales, you also have a good chance of spotting marine birds, Dall's porpoises, dolphins, seals, and sea lions, as well as other marine life. And, naturally, there's the scenery of forested islands, distant mountains, and craggy coastline.

MOTION SICKNESS

Seasickness isn't usually a problem in the sheltered waters of Puget Sound and the Georgia Strait, but seas can get choppy off the Washington and Oregon coasts. If you're not a good sailor, it's wise to wear a seasickness band or take anti-nausea medication. Ginger candy often works, too.

THE OREGON AND WASHINGTON COAST

A full breach in open waters is a thrilling sight

WHEN TO GO

Mid-December through mid-January is the best time for viewing the southbound migration, with April through mid-June the peak period for the northbound return (when whales swim closer to shore). Throughout summer, several hundred gray whales remain in Oregon waters, often feeding within close view of land. Mornings are often the best time for viewing, as it's more commonly overcast at this time, which means less glare and calmer seas. Try to watch for vapor or water expelled from whales' spouts on the horizon.

WHAT IT COSTS

Trips are generally 2 hours and prices for adults range from $25 to $35.

RECOMMENDED OUTFITTERS

Depoe Bay, with its sheltered, deepwater harbor, is Oregon's whale-watching capital, and here you'll find several outfitters.

Dockside Charters (☎ 800/733–8915, ⊕ www. docksidedepoebay.com) and **Tradewind Charters** (☎ 800/445–8730, ⊕ www. tradewindscharters.com) have excellent reputations. Offering a twist on the theme, **Tillamook Air Tours** (☎ 503/842–1942, ⊕ www. tillamookairtours.com) offers gray-whale flightseeing tours along the coast in restored 1942 Stinson Reliant V-77 aircraft.

Along the Washington coast, several of the fishing-charter companies in Westport offer seasonal whale-watching cruises, including **Deep Sea Charters** (☎ 800/562–0151, ⊕ www.deepseacharters.

biz) and **Ocean Charters** (☎ 800/562–0105, ⊕ www. oceanchartersinc.com).

BEST VIEWING FROM SHORE

Washington: On Long Beach Peninsula, the North Head Lighthouse at the mouth of the Columbia River, makes an excellent perch for whale sightings. Westport, farther up the coast at the mouth of Grays Harbor, is another great spot.

Oregon Coast: You can spot gray whales all summer long and especially during the spring migration—excellent locales include Neahkanie Mountain Overlook near Manzanita, Cape Lookout State Park, the Whale Watching Center in Depoe Bay, Cape Perpetua Interpretive Center in Yachats, and Cape Blanco Lighthouse near Port Orford.

buildings, seafood markets, and art galleries and shops, Newport's Bayfront is an ideal place for an afternoon stroll. So many male sea lions in Yaquina Bay loiter near crab pots and bark from the waterfront piers that locals call the area the Bachelor Club. Visit the docks to buy fresh seafood or rent a kayak to explore the bay. In 2010 Newport was designated the National Oceanic and Atmospheric Administration's (NOAA) Pacific Marine Operations Center. That means that a new, $38 million, 5-acre facility (and a port for four ships), will open in May 2011.

GETTING HERE

Daily flights on SeaPort Airlines land at Newport Municipal Airport (ONP), just 5 mi from town. The city is served by **Greyhound**, **Valley Retriever** (☎ *541/265–2253* ⊕ *www.kokkola-bus.com/ValleyRetrieverBuslines. html*), and **Lincoln Transit** buses, connecting to Siletz, Lincoln City, Yachats, and Portland.

VISITOR INFORMATION

Greater Newport Chamber of Commerce (✉ *555 SW Coast Hwy., Newport* ☎ *503/265–8801 or 800/262–7844* ⊕ *www.newportchamber.org*).

EXPLORING

The Flying Dutchman Winery. Perched on a cliff, this small, family-owned winery enjoys one of the most spectacular locations on the Oregon Coast. It buys grapes from five Oregon vineyards, and brings them over the Coast Range to its salt-air environment for fermenting. Guests can enjoy its award-winning vintages in the cozy tasting room, or take a quick tour of the oak barrels next door with owner Dick Cutler. ✉ *915 First St., Otter Rock* ☎ *541/765–2553* ⊕ *www.dutchmanwinery.com* ⊘ *June–Sept., daily 11–6; Oct.–May, daily 11–5.*

Hatfield Marine Science Center. Interactive and interpretive exhibits at Oregon State University appeal to the kid in everyone. The star of the show is a large octopus in a touch tank near the entrance. She seems as interested in human visitors as they are in her; guided by a staff volunteer, you can sometimes reach in to stroke her suction-tipped tentacles. But more than just showcasing sea life, the center holds programs and classes that teach the importance of scientific research in managing and sustaining coastal and marine resources. ✉ *2030 S. Marine Science Dr., Newport* ☎ *541/867–0100* ⊕ *hmsc.oregonstate.edu* ✑ *Donation $5 per person or $20 per family* ⊘ *Memorial Day–Labor Day, daily 10–5; Labor Day–Memorial Day, Thurs.–Mon. 10–4.*

Fodor's Choice ★ **Oregon Coast Aquarium.** One of the true jewels of the Oregon Coast, this 4½-acre complex brings visitors face to face with the creatures living in offshore and near-shore Pacific marine habitats: Flirting, frolicking sea otters, colorful puffins, pulsating jellyfish, and even a 60-pound octopus. There's a hands-on interactive area for children, including tide pools perfect for "petting" sea anemones and urchins. The aquarium houses one of North America's largest seabird aviaries, including glowering turkey vultures. Permanent exhibits include Passages of the Deep, where visitors walk through a 200-foot underwater tunnel with 360-degree views of sharks, wolf eels, halibut, and a truly captivating array of sea life. Large coho salmon and sturgeon can be viewed in a naturalistic setting through a window wall 9-feet high and 20-feet wide.

The sherbet-colored nettles are hypnotizing. ⊠ *2820 SE Ferry Slip Rd., Newport* ☎ *541/867–3474* ⊕ *www.aquarium.org* ⊒ *$15.45* ⊙ *Summer, daily 9–6; winter, daily 10–5.*

Yaquina Bay Lighthouse. The state's oldest wooden lighthouse was only in commission for three years (1871–1874), because it was determined that it was built in the wrong location. Today the well-restored lighthouse with a candy-apple top shines a steady white light from dusk to dawn. Open to the public, it is thought to be the oldest structure in Newport, and the only Oregon lighthouse with living quarters attached. ⊠ *U.S. 101S, Newport* ☎ *541/867–7451* ⊕ *www.yaquinalights.org* ⊒ *Free* ⊙ *Memorial Day –Oct., daily 11–5; Oct.–Memorial Day, daily 12–4.*

⟳ **Yaquina Head Lighthouse.** The tallest lighthouse on the Oregon Coast has been blinking its beacon since its head keeper first walked up its 114 steps to light the wicks on the evening of August 20, 1873. Next to the 93-foot tower is an interpretive center. Bring your camera and call ahead for tour times. ⊠ *4 mi north of bridge in Newport, Newport* ☎ *541/574–3100* ⊕ *www.yaquinalights.org* ⊒ *$7 per car, 9 passengers or fewer* ⊙ *June–Labor Day, daily 9–4; Oct.–May, daily 12–4; closed Thanksgiving and Christmas.*

WHERE TO EAT

$
SEAFOOD
✕ **Mo's.** Started by Mohava Marie Niemi, Newport's crusty, big-hearted chain-smoking mother, Mo's has been delighting diners with its thick, creamy chowder since about 1950. Mo passed away in 1992 at the age of 79, but not before expanding beyond its original Newport location to Mo's Annex in Newport, Mo's West in Otter Rock, and Mo's in Lincoln City, Cannon Beach, and Florence. This coastal institution has consistently served great oysters, fish tacos, and other deep-water delicacies, along with down-home service. There's a kids menu, too, and burgers for the fish phobic. Mo's terrific fresh chowder and chowder base can be purchased online. ⊠ *622 SW Bay Blvd., Newport* ☎ *541/265–2979* w*ww.moschowder.com* ⊟ *AE, D, MC, V.*

¢
CAFÉ
✕ **Panini Bakery.** The owner, who operates this local favorite bakery and espresso bar, prides himself on hearty and home-roasted meats, hand-cut breads, and friendly service. The coffee's organic, the eggs free range, the orange juice fresh-squeezed, and just about everything is made from scratch. Take a seat inside, or, in good weather, streetside tables are a great place to view the Nye Beach scene. ⊠ *232 NW Coast Hwy., Newport* ☎ *541/265–5033* ⊟ *No credit cards* ⊙ *No dinner Wed.*

$
SEAFOOD
✕ **Quimby's.** This unpretentious little place hosts a busy, happy crowd on almost any given night. With lots of oak on the inside and gorgeous ocean views looking out, this restaurant proves that you don't have to spend much to get great food on the coast. Start with the coast's best clam chowder, loaded with deep-water clams, Yukon gold potatoes, onion, celery, and smoky bacon. The full bar has microbrews and regional fine wines. ⊠ *740 W. Olive St., Newport* ☎ *541/265–9919 or 866/784–6297* ⊕ *www.quimbysrestaurant.com* ⊟ *AE, D, DC, MC, V.*

$$$
SEAFOOD
✕ **Tables of Content.** The well-plotted prix-fixe menu at the restaurant of the outstanding Sylvia Beach Hotel changes nightly. Chances are that the main dish will be fresh local seafood, perhaps a moist grilled salmon fillet in a sauce Dijonnaise, served with sautéed vegetables,

fresh-baked breads, and rice pilaf; a decadent dessert is also included. The interior is functional and unadorned, with family-size tables, but be forewarned, dinners can be long, so young children may get restless. ✉ *267 NW Cliff St., from U.S. 101 head west on 3rd St., Newport* ☎ *541/265-5428* ⊕ *www.sylviabeachhotel.com* ⚓ *Reservations essential* ▤ *AE, D, MC, V.*

WHERE TO STAY

$ 🖫 **Sylvia Beach Hotel.** Make reservations far in advance for this 1913-vintage beachfront hotel, where reading, writing, and old conversation eclipse technological hotel-room isolation. Its antiques-filled rooms are named for famous writers. A pendulum swings over the bed in the Poe room. The Christie, Twain, Tolkien, Woolf, and Colette rooms are all notable; all have fireplaces, decks, and great ocean views. A well-stocked split-level upstairs library has decks, a fireplace, slumbering cats, and too-comfortable chairs. Complimentary mulled wine is served nightly at 10. **Pros:** unique; great place to disconnect. **Cons:** no Internet access. ✉ *267 NW Cliff St., Newport* ☎ *541/265-5428 or 888/795-8422* ⊕ *www.sylviabeachhotel.com* ⤳ *20 rooms* ⚭ *In-room: no phone. In-hotel: restaurant* ▤ *AE, MC, V* ⑩ *BP.*

$ 🖫 **The Whaler.** Located across the roadway from the coast, visitors enjoy wide views of the Pacific Ocean. Magnificent gray whales are often spotted offshore, and it's pleasant to watch the fishing boats leaving or returning to port. The Whaler is near the Newport Performing Arts Center and a short distance from Yaquina Bay, the Oregon Coast Aquarium, and the Newport Bayfront. **Pros:** great location; ocean views; roomy and clean. **Cons:** bland breakfast and rooms. ✉ *155 SW Elizabeth., Newport* ☎ *541/265-9261 or 800/433-9444* ⊕ *www.whalernewport. com* ⤳ *73 rooms* ⚭ *In-room: Internet, refrigerator. In-hotel: pool, spa, gym, laundry facilities* ▤ *AE, D, MC, V* ⑩ *CP.*

NIGHTLIFE AND THE ARTS

Newport Symphony Orchestra. The only year-round, professional symphony orchestra on the Oregon Coast plays at the 400-seat Newport Performing Arts Center, just a few steps away from the seashore in Nye Beach. Adam Flatt is the music director and conductor, and actor and narrator David Ogden Stiers serves as associate conductor. The orchestra performs a popular series of concerts in the Newport Performing Arts Center September through May, and special events in the summer, including its popular free community concert every July 4. *777 W. Olive St., Newport* ☎ *541/574-0614* ⊕ *newportsymphony.org.*

SPORTS AND THE OUTDOORS

RECREATIONAL AREAS **Beverly Beach State Park.** Seven miles north of Newport, this beachfront park extends from Yaquina Head, where you can see the lighthouse, to the headlands of Otter Rock. It's a great place to fly a kite, surf the waves, or hunt for fossils. The campground is well equipped, with a wind-protected picnic area and a yurt meeting hall. It has a campground with 53 full hookups ($26), 75 electrical ($26), 128 tent sites ($21), a hiker/biker camp ($6), and 21 yurts ($40). ✉ *U.S. 101, Newport* ☎ *541/265-9278 or 800/551-6949* ⊕ *www.oregonstateparks.org/* 🎫 *Free* ☉ *Daily.*

Devil's Punch Bowl State Natural Area. A rocky shoreline separates the day-use from the surf. It's a popular whale-watching site just 9 mi north of Newport, and has excellent tidal pools. ⊠ *9 mi north of Newport on U.S. 101, Newport* ☎ *541/265–9278* 🖼 *Free* ☉ *Daily.*

South Beach State Park. Fishing, crabbing, boating, windsurfing, hiking, and beachcombing are popular activities at this park. Kayaking tours are available for a fee. Pets welcome through September. A campground with Wi-Fi access has 228 electrical hookups ($27), 27 yurts ($40), group tent sites ($77), and a hiker/biker camp ($6). ⊠ *U.S. 101S, Newport* ☎ *541/867–4715 or 541/867–7451* ☉ *Daily.*

Yaquina Head Outstanding Natural Area. Thousands of birds—cormorants, gulls, common murres, pigeon guillemots—make their home just beyond shore on Pinnacle and Colony rocks, and nature trails wind through fields of sea grass and wildflowers, leading to spectacular views. There is also an interpretive center. ⊠ *750 NW Lighthouse Dr., Newport* ☎ *541/574–3100* ⊕ *www.yaquinalights.org* 🖼 *$7 per vehicle, 9 passengers or fewer* ☉ *Interpretive center open June–Labor Day, daily 9–4; Oct.–May, daily 10–4.*

TOLEDO

7 mi east of Newport on U.S. 20.

Once a rustic mill town, Toledo has reinvented itself as an enclave for painters, artisans, antiques, and the most amazing barbecue this side of Missouri. Landscape artists Ivan Kelly and Michael Gibbons reside here, as well as metal sculptor Sam Briseno, potter Jean Inglis, and contemporary artist Jon Zander. Just seven miles inland from the coast on the Yaquina River, it is the only inland coastal community with a deep-water channel. The Yaquina is fished for sturgeon, fall-run chinook, and steelhead.

GETTING HERE

Toledo is served by **Greyhound** to Corvallis and Newport. The Newport Municipal Airport is the closest airport, located 12 mi away.

VISITOR INFORMATION

Toledo Chamber of Commerce (⊠ *311 NE 1st St., Toledo* ☎ *541/336–3183* ⊕ *www.visittoledooregon.com*).

EXPLORING

Briseno Gallery. Sam Briseno's metal sculptures migrate from his Toledo studio and out into the town in the form of a heron-adorned bench. He also creates decorative wall pieces, furnishings, and commercial gates. ⊠ *357 NW 1st St.* ☎ *541/336–1256* ☉ *Mon.–Sat. 11–5.*

Ivan Kelly Studio. The Irish-born and raised landscape artist's work brought him to Oregon, where he and his wife built a studio in Toledo. His oil paintings are on display here. ⊠ *207 E. Graham St.* ☎ *541/336–1124* ⊕ *www.ivankelly.com* ☉ *Sat. 11–5, Sun. 1–5.*

Yaquina Pacific Railroad Historical Society. The enthusiastic conductor, Tom Chandler, will take you on a tour of the restored train that sits in the middle of town. The collection includes a gleaming 1922 Baldwin engine and the only restored mail car in the Pacific Northwest. It carried

Oregon Coast Aquarium, Newport

payroll, gold, silk, bees, and newly hatched chicks. ✉ *100 NW "A" St.* ☎ *541/336–5256* ⊕ *www.yaquinapacificrr.org* ⊠ *Free* ☉ *Tues.–Sat. 10–2.*

WHERE TO EAT

$ ✕**Pig Feathers.** "Everyone loves a great rack" is the rallying cry of the **SOUTHERN** best barbecue restaurant in the Pacific Northwest. Owner and chef **Fodor's Choice** Stu Miller's sauces and rubs transform mere wings, pulled pork, and **★** baby back ribs into tastes so rich and rare that they've brought grown men to tears. The OUCH, Slather, and Smokey Sweet sauces are available to purchase. ✉ *300 S. Main St., Toledo* ☎ *541/336–1833* ⊕ *www. pigfeathers.com* ▬ *D, MC, V.*

YACHATS

31 mi south of Toledo on U.S. 101.

The small town of Yachats (pronounced "yah-*hots*") is at the mouth of the Yachats River, and from its rocky shoreline, which includes the highest point on the Oregon coast, trails lead to beaches and dozens of tidal pools. A relaxed alternative to the more touristy communities to the north, Yachats has all the coastal pleasures: bed-and-breakfasts, good restaurants, deserted beaches, tidal pools, surf-pounded crags, fishing, and crabbing.

GETTING HERE

Yachats is 24 mi from Newport Municipal Airport, 84 mi from Eugene Airport, and 166 mi to Portland International Airport. **Lincoln Transit** provides bus service to Newport, Siletz, and Lincoln City. **Valley Retriever**

(☎ 541/265-2253 ⊕ www.kokkola-bus.com/ValleyRetrieverBuslines. html) and **Greyhound** bus connections to Corvallis are in Newport. The **Omni Shuttle** runs to the Eugene airport, and **Caravan Airport Transportation** runs shuttles to the Portland airport.

VISITOR INFORMATION

Yachats Visitors Center (✉ 241 U.S. 101 ☎ 541/547–3530 or 800/929–0477 ⊕ www.yachats.org).

WHERE TO EAT AND STAY

$$

SEAFOOD

✗ **Adobe Restaurant.** The extraordinary ocean views sometimes upstage the meal, but if you stick to the seafood, you'll be satisfied. The Baked Crab Pot is a rich, bubbling casserole filled with Dungeness crab and cheese in a shallot cream sauce. Its best dish is the Captain's Seafood Platter, heaped with prawns, scallops, grilled oysters, and razor clams. ✉ 1555 U.S. 101, Yachats ☎ 541/547–3141 ▬ AE, D, DC, MC, V.

$

SEAFOOD

Fodor'sChoice

★

✗ **The Drift Inn.** This restaurant is a terrific find, with the best fresh razor clams on the coast. Each night a musician plays to the crowd that sits below a ceiling full of umbrellas, with views of the Yachats River where it meets the ocean. Friday is open-mike night, and Saturday there's a dance rock band. Family-friendly and lively, the Drift Inn features fresh seafood, all-natural steaks, and other local meats and produce. The bar stools are usually crowded, and it has a great selection of Oregon craft brews and wines. ✉ 124 U.S. 10 N, Yachats ☎ 541/547–4477 ⊕ www. the-drift-inn.com ▬ MC, V.

$$$

Fodor'sChoice

★

▤ **Overleaf Lodge.** On a rocky shoreline at the north end of Yachats, the Overleaf Lodge is a romantic place to enjoy a spectacular sunset in splendid comfort. Its well-kept, spacious rooms have a variety of options, including fireplaces, corner nooks, and whirlpool tubs with ocean views. The adjacent coastal walk is populated with seals. Continental breakfast is provided. **Pros:** best hotel in one of the coast's best communities. **Cons:** no dining; small exercise room. ✉ 280 Overleaf Lodge La., Yachats ☎ 541/547–4880 ⊕ www.overleaflodge.com ⤴ 54 rooms and 4 suites ⌂ In-hotel: Wi-Fi, spa, gym, beachfront ▬ AE, D, MC, V ▭ CP.

SPORTS AND THE OUTDOORS

RECREATIONAL AREAS

Cape Perpetua. The highest lookout point on the Oregon Coast, Cape Perpetua towers 800 feet above the rocky shoreline. Named by Captain Cook on St. Perpetua's Day in 1778, the cape is part of a 2,700-acre scenic area popular with hikers, campers, beachcombers, and naturalists. General information and a map of 10 trails are available at the **Cape Perpetua Visitors Center,** on the east side of the highway, 2 mi south of Devil's Churn. The easy 1-mi **Giant Spruce Trail** passes through a fern-filled rain forest to an enormous 500-year-old Sitka spruce. Easier still is the marked Auto Tour; it begins about 2 mi north of the visitor center and winds through Siuslaw National Forest to the ¼-mi **Whispering Spruce Trail.** Views from the rustic rock shelter here extend 150 mi north and south, and 37 mi out to sea. The **Cape Perpetua Interpretive Center,** in the visitor center, has educational movies and exhibits about the natural forces that shaped Cape Perpetua. ✉ U.S. 101, 9 mi south of Yachats ☎ 541/547–3289 ▦ Parking fee $5 ☉ Daily 10–4.

Neptune State Park. Visitors will have fun searching for animals, watching the surf, or hunting for agates. The benches set above the beach on the cliff provide a great view of Cumming Creek. It's also a terrific spot for whale-watching. At low tide, beachcombers have access to a natural cave and tidal pools. ⊠ *U.S. 101 S, 3 mi south of Yachats, Yachats* ☎ *800/551–6949* ⊕ *www.oregonstateparks.org/park_126.php* ⊠ *Free* ⊙ *Daily.*

Yachats Ocean Road State Recreation Area. Drive this one-mi loop south of Yachats, and discover one of the most scenic viewpoints on the Oregon Coast. Park along the loop to see where the Yachats River meets the Pacific Ocean. There's fun to be had playing on the beach, poking around tide pools, and watching blowholes, summer sunsets, and whales spouting. ⊠ *U.S. 101 to Yachats Ocean Rd., Yachats* ☎ *541/997–3851 or 800/551–6949* ⊕ *www.oregonstateparks.org.*

FLORENCE

25 mi south of Yachats on U.S. 101, 64 mi west of Eugene on Hwy. 126.

Tourists and retirees have been flocking to Florence in ever-greater numbers in recent years. Its restored waterfront Old Town has restaurants, antiques stores, fish markets, and other diversions. But what really makes the town so appealing is its proximity to remarkable stretches of coastline. Seventy-five creeks and rivers empty into the Pacific Ocean in and around Florence, and the Siuslaw River flows right through town. When the numerous nearby lakes are added to the mix, it makes for one of the richest fishing areas in Oregon. Salmon, rainbow trout, bass, perch, crabs, and clams are among the water's treasures. Fishing boats and pleasure craft moor in Florence's harbor, forming a pleasant backdrop for the town's restored buildings. South of town, miles of white-sand dunes lend themselves to everything from solitary hikes to rides aboard all-terrain vehicles.

GETTING HERE
The closest airport is in Newport. **Eugene Porter Stage Lines** provides bus transportation from Florence to Eugene and Coos Bay.

VISITOR INFORMATION
Florence Area Chamber of Commerce (⊠ *290 U.S. 101* ☎ *541/997–3128* ⊕ *www.florencechamber.com*).

EXPLORING
Sea Lion Caves. In 1880 a sea captain named Cox rowed a small skiff into a fissure in a 300-foot-high sea cliff. Inside, he was startled to discover a vaulted chamber in the rock, 125 feet high and 2 acres in size. Hundreds of massive sea lions—the largest bulls weighing 2,000 pounds or more—covered every available surface. Cox's discovery would become one of the Oregon Coast's premier tourist attractions. An elevator near the cliff-top ticket office descends to the floor of the cavern, near sea level, where vast numbers of Steller's and California sea lions relax on rocks and swim about (their cute, fuzzy pups can be viewed from behind a wire fence). This is the only known hauling-out area and rookery for wild sea lions on the mainland in the Lower 48, and it's an awesome

sight and sound. In spring and summer the mammals usually stay on the rocky ledges outside the cave; in fall and winter they move inside. You'll also see several species of seabirds here, including migratory pigeon guillemots, cormorants, and three varieties of gulls. Gray whales are visible during their northern and southern migrations, October–December and March–May. The gift shop has amazing fudge—try the jalapeño. ✉ *91560 U.S. 101, 10 mi north of downtown Florence* ☏ *541/547–3111* 🖾 *$12* ⊙ *Daily 9–5* ⊕ *http://sealioncaves.com* ▭ *MC, V.*

Siuslaw Pioneer Museum. Built in an old schoolhouse, the museum displays the story of the Siuslaw River and its pioneers. It features photos and tangible treasures of home life, farming, fishing, lumbering, and transportation. The museum also features the Jensen Gallery of Historical Photos. ✉ *290 U.S. 101S, Florence* ☏ *541/997–7884* 🖾 *$3* ⊙ *Daily 12–4.*

NEED A BREAK?

Siuslaw River Coffee Roasters. This small, homey business serves cups of drip-on-demand coffee—you select the roast and they grind and brew it on the spot. Beans are roasted on-site, muffins and breads are freshly baked, and a view of the namesake river can be savored from the deck out back. ✉ *1240 Bay St., Florence* ☏ *541/997–3443* *wwww.coffeeoregon.com* ▭ *D, MC, V.*

WHERE TO EAT AND STAY

$$
SEAFOOD
✕ **Bridgewater Seafood Restaurant.** Freshly caught seafood—20 to 25 choices nightly—is the mainstay of this creaky-floored, Victorian-era restaurant in Florence's Old Town. Whether you opt for patio dining during summer or lounge seating in winter, the varied menu of pastas, burgers, and soups offers something for everyone. A live jazz band provides some foot-tapping fun. ✉ *1297 Bay St., Florence* ☏ *541/997–1133* ▭ *AE, D, MC, V.*

$
SEAFOOD
✕ **Waterfront Depot Restaurant and Bar.** The detailed chalkboard menu says it all: from the fresh, crab-encrusted halibut to Bill's Flaming Spanish Coffee, this is a place serious about fresh food and fine flavors. Located in the old Mapleton train station, it has a great view of the Siuslaw River and the Siuslaw River Bridge. In the summer diners can enjoy patio seating right at the water's edge and chomp on the nice variety of tapas plates. ✉ *1252 Bay St., Florence* ☏ *541/902–9100* ⊕ *www.thewaterfrontdepot.com* ▭ *D, MC, V.*

$$$
Fodor's Choice
★
🛏 **Heceta House.** On a windswept promontory, this unusual late-Victorian bed-and-breakfast surrounded by a white-picket fence is one of Oregon's most remarkable bed-and-breakfasts. Now owned by the U.S. Forest Service, it is managed by Steve and Michelle Bursey, certified executive chefs who prepare a seven-course breakfast (included in the room rate) each morning. The menu changes according to the season. Meals include herbs and produce out of the Lightstation garden and highlight the best of Oregon: artisan cheeses, sausages, produce, and Carol Korgan's pastries. The nicest of the simply furnished rooms is the Mariner's, with a private bath and an awe-inspiring view. Filled with period detailing and antiques, the common areas are warm and inviting. If you're lucky, you may hear Rue, the resident ghost, in the middle of

the night. **Pros:** you won't find any property quite like this—as though you were living in a novel. **Cons:** not within walking distance of the town or other activities. ✉ *92072 U.S. 101, Florence* ☎ *541/547–3696* ⊕ *www.hecetalighthouse.com* ↵ *6 rooms, 4 with bath* ▭ *D, MC, V* ⑂ *BP.*

$$ ⌂**River House Inn.** Located on the beautiful Siuslaw River, this property has terrific accommodations and is near quaint shops and restaurants in Florence's Old Town. Golfing, horseback riding. and sand dune activities are nearby. Most rooms have a stunning river view of boats and wildlife. **Pros:** Spacious; well decorated. **Cons:** Not located on the beach. ✉ *1202 Bay St., Florence* ☎ *541/997–3933 or 888/824-2750* ⊕ *www.riverhouseflorence.com* ↵ *40 rooms* ♿ *In-room: Wi-Fi, refrigerator* ▭ *AE, D, MC, V* ⑂ *CP.*

NIGHTLIFE AND THE ARTS

Three Rivers Casino and Hotel. This casino has 700 of the newest slots and video games. It also has table games, including roulette, craps, blackjack, no-limit Texas hold 'em, as well as keno and bingo. Five dining venues—from the refined to the casual—suit every taste. Nearby are beaches, shopping, fishing, and two popular golf courses. ✉ *5647 Highway 126, Florence* ☎ *541/997–7529 or 877/374–8378* ⊕ *www. threeriverscasino.com.*

SPORTS AND THE OUTDOORS

RECREATIONAL AREAS

Devil's Elbow State Park. A ½-mi trail from the beachside parking lot leads to **Heceta Head Lighthouse,** whose beacon, visible for more than 21 mi, is the most powerful on the Oregon Coast. ✉ *U.S. 101* ☎ *541/547–3416* ▭ *Day use $5, lighthouse tours free* ☉ *Lighthouse May–Oct., weekdays 11–1; Nov.–Feb. Park daily dawn–dusk.*

☺ Fodor's Choice ★

Oregon Dunes National Recreation Area. Open year-round, the Oregon Dunes National Recreation Area is the largest expanse of coastal sand dunes in North America, extending for 40 mi, from Florence to Coos Bay. The area contains some of the best ATV riding in the United States, with 5,930 acres of open sand and 6,140 acres with designated trails. More than 1.5 million people visit the dunes each year, and about 350,000 are ATV users, nearly half of them from outside Oregon. **Honeyman Memorial State Park,** 522 acres within the recreation area, is a base camp for dune-buggy enthusiasts, mountain bikers, hikers, boaters, horseback riders, and dogsledders (the sandy hills are an excellent training ground). It has 41 full sites $26; 121 electrical $26; 187 tent sites $21; hiker/biker sites $5; and yurts $39. The dunes are a vast playground for children, particularly the slopes surrounding cool **Cleawox Lake.** ✉ *Oregon Dunes National Recreation Area office, 855 U.S. 101, Reedsport* ☎ *541/271–6000* ▭ *Day use $5* ☉ *Daily dawn–dusk.*

☺ Fodor's Choice ★

Sandland Adventures. This has everything you need to get the whole family together for the ride of their lives. Start off with a heart-racing dune-buggy ride with a professional that will take you careening up, over, down, and around some of the steepest sand in the Oregon Dunes National Recreation Area. After you're done screaming and smiling, Sandland's park has bumper boats, a go-kart track, a miniature golf

Umpqua Sand Dunes in Oregon Dunes National Recreation Area

course, and a small railroad. ✉ *85366 Hwy. 101S* ☎ *541/997-8087* ⊕ *www.sandland.com.*

BOATING **Siltcoos River Canoe Trail.** Beginning at Siltcoos Lake, where cottages float on the water, this trail winds through thick rain forest, past towering sand dunes, emerging some 4 mi later at white-sand beaches and the blue waters of the Pacific, where seals and snowy plovers rest. The river is a Class I with no rapids, but there are a few trees to navigate and one very short portage around a small dam.

GOLF **Oregon Dunes Golf Links.** A favorite of locals year-round, Oregon Dunes
Fodor's Choice Golf Links is a straightforward 18 holes that reward great shots and
★ penalize the poor ones. You won't find many sand bunkers, because the narrow course is surrounded by sand dunes. Instead, you'll encounter fairways winding about dunes lined with ball-swallowing gorse, heather, shore pines, and native sea grasses. Pot bunkers guard small greens, and play can get pretty frisky if the frequent wind picks up. However, the course is well drained and playable—even under the wettest conditions. ✉ *3345 Munsel Lake Rd., Florence* ☎ *541/991–2744* ⊕ *www.oceandunesgolf.com* ✉ *Summer rates: 18 holes $42, 9 holes $25.*

Sandpines Golf Links. This Scottish Links-style course is playable year-round. Designed by Rees Jones, the outward nine is cut out of pine forest and near blue lakes; and the inward nine provides some undulating fun, with the rolling dunes at the forefront from tee to green. While challenging, the course is generous enough to provide a great day on the links for beginners and more polished players. Sandpines has a fully equipped practice area with a driving range, bunkers, and putting greens. When it opened in 1993, *Golf Digest* named it the Best New

Public Course in America. ✉ *1201 35th St., Florence* ☎ *800/971–4653* ⊕ *www.sandpines.com* 🖃 *Summer rates: 18 holes $79.*

HIKING   **Carl G. Washburne Memorial.** A trail from this park connects you to the Heceta Head Trail, which you can use to reach the Heceta Head Lighthouse. Its campground has 56 full hookups $26, 7 tent sites $21, hiker/biker sites $5, and 2 yurts $39. ✉ *93111 U.S. 101N, Florence* ☎ *541/547–3416* ⊕ *www.oregonstateparks.org.*

HORSEBACK   **C & M Stables.** Ride year-round along the Oregon Dunes National Rec-
RIDING   reation Area. The area is rich with marine life, including sea lions, whales, and coastal birds. Sharp-eyed riders also might spot bald eagles, red-tailed fox, and deer. Rides range from hour-long trots to half-day adventures. Children must be at least eight years old for the beach ride or six years old for the dune trail rides. There are also six overnight RV spaces. ✉ *90241 U.S. 101 N, Florence* ☎ *541/997–7540* ⊕ *www. oregonhorsebackriding.com* 🖃 *$40–$150* 🖃 *AE, D, MC, V* ☻ *Daily 10–5.*

SANDBOARD-   **Sand Master Park.** Everything you need to sandboard the park's private
ING   dunes is right here: Board rental, wax, eyewear, clothing, and instruc-tion. The staff is exceptionally helpful, and will get beginners off on their sandboarding adventure with enthusiasm. However, what must be surfed, must first be hiked up, and so on. ✉ *87542 U.S. 101N, Florence* ☎ *541/997–6006* ⊕ *www.sandmasterpark.com* ☻ *June–Sept. 10, daily 9–6:30; off-season, Mon.–Sat. 10–5, Sun. 11–5.*

SOUTH COAST

Outdoors enthusiasts will find a natural amusement park along this gorgeous stretch of coast from Reedsport to Brookings. Its northern portion has a continuation of the Oregon Dunes National Recreation Area, and is the location for its visitors' center. The Umpqua Discovery Center is a perfect trip with the kids, or just yourself, to learn about the region's history and animals. In Bandon golfers will find one of the most celebrated cluster of courses in the nation at Bandon Dunes—plus it just opened a new, fourth course, Old Macdonald. Lovers of lighthouses, sailing, fishing, crabbing, elk viewing, camping, and water sports will wonder why they didn't venture south sooner.

REEDSPORT

20 mi south of Florence on U.S. 101, 90 mi southwest of Eugene via I–5 and Hwy. 38.

The small town of Reedsport owes its existence to the Umpqua River, one of the state's great steelhead-fishing streams. Hikers will enjoy the picturesque, quiet hiking trails that wander through the forest, onto the dunes, and through the beach grass to the beaches. As in Florence to the north, there are plenty of ATV and dune-buggy riders on the dunes. The area is also a favorite of campers and nature lovers who watch herds of majestic elk in the Deer Creek Preserve.

GETTING HERE

From Reedsport, **Greyhound** bus lines provide limited service to Eugene. The nearest airport is 25 mi to the south in North Bend. Reedsport is 196 mi from Portland.

VISITOR INFORMATION

Reedsport/Winchester Bay Chamber of Commerce (✉ *855 Highway Ave., Reedsport* ☎ *541/271–3495 or 800/247–2155* ⊕ *www.reedsportcc.org*).

EXPLORING

Oregon Dunes National Recreation Area Visitors Center. The natural forces that created the towering sand dunes along this section of the Oregon Coast (⇨ *see the listing in Florence, above*) are explained in interpretive exhibits. The center, which also sells maps, books, and gifts, is a good place to pick up free literature on the area. ✉ *855 Highway Ave., south side of Umpqua River Bridge, Reedsport* ☎ *541/271–3611* 🖃 *Free* ☉ *June–Aug., daily 8–4:30; Sept.–May, weekdays 8–4:30.*

ↄ **Umpqua Discovery Center.** Exhibits at this waterfront location provide a good introduction to the Lower Umpqua estuary and surrounding region. One of two state-of-the-art wings focuses on cultural history; the other, on natural history, has an indoor simulated walking trail, which whisks you through four seasons. ✉ *409 Riverfront Way, Reedsport* ☎ *541/271–4816* ⊕ *www.umpquadiscoverycenter.com* 🖃 *Museum $8 adults, $6 ages 6–15, under 6 free* ☉ *June–Sept., daily 9–5; Oct.–May, daily 10–4.*

Umpqua Lighthouse Park. Some of the highest sand dunes in the country are found in this 50-acre park 6 mi south of Reedsport. The first **Umpqua River Lighthouse**, built on the dunes at the mouth of the Umpqua River in 1857, lasted only four years before it toppled over in a storm. It took local residents 33 years to build another one. The "new" lighthouse, built on a bluff overlooking the south side of Winchester Bay and operated by the U.S. Coast Guard, is still going strong, flashing a warning beacon out to sea every five seconds. The **Douglas County Coastal Visitors Center** adjacent to the lighthouse has a museum and can arrange lighthouse tours. ✉ *Umpqua Hwy., west side of U.S. 101, Reedsport* ☎ *541/271–4631* 🖃 *Donations suggested* ☉ *Lighthouse May–Sept., Wed.–Sat. 10–4, Sun. 1–4.*

EN ROUTE

A public pier at **Winchester Bay's Salmon Harbor**, 3¼ mi south of Reedsport, juts out over the bay and yields excellent results for crabbers and fishermen (especially those after rockfish). There's also a full-service marina with a fish market, **the Sportsmen's Cannery,** which serves a fresh seafood barbecue on weekends (from Memorial Day to Labor Day).

WHERE TO EAT AND STAY

$

PIZZA

✕ **Bedrocks on the Bay.** Outstanding pizza, sandwiches, and fresh fish-and-chips highlight this casual local restaurant on Winchester Bay's Salmon Harbor. Be sure and try the halibut fish-and-chips. It also serves breakfast. ✉ *105 Coho Point Loop, Winchester Bay* ☎ *541/271–2431* ⊕ *bedrocksrestaurants.com* ▭ *MC, V.*

¢

Anchor Bay Inn. In the center of Reedsport, this clean, inexpensive motel has hospitable service and easy access to the dunes. **Pros:** frugal choice. **Cons:** road noise. ✉ *1821 Winchester Ave.* ☎ *541/271–2149 or 800/767–1821* ⊕ *www.u-s-history.com/or/a/anchobin.htm* ↯ *21 rooms*

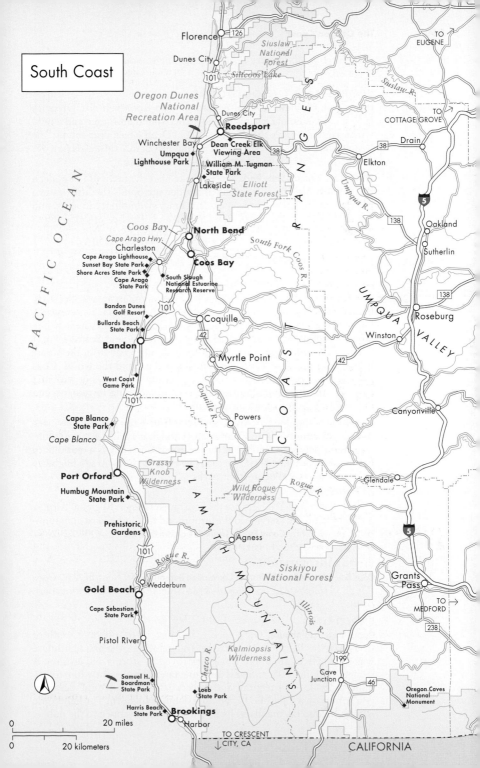

South Coast

Florence
126
Dunes City
Siuslaw
National
Forest
TO
EUGENE
101
Siltcoos Lake
Siuslaw R.
TO
COTTAGE GROVE

Oregon Dunes
National
Recreation Area
Dunes City
Reedsport
Dean Creek Elk
Viewing Area
38
38
Drain
Elkton
Winchester Bay
Umpqua
Lighthouse Park
William M. Tugman
State Park
Lakeside
Elliott
State Forest
Umpqua R.
138
5
Oakland
Sutherlin

PACIFIC OCEAN

Coos Bay
Cape Arago Hwy.
Charleston
North Bend
Cape Arago Lighthouse
Sunset Bay State Park
Shore Acres State Park
Coos Bay
Cape Arago
State Park
South Slough
National Estuarine
Research Reserve
South Fork Coos R.
138
Roseburg
Winston

Bandon Dunes
Golf Resort
Bullards Beach
State Park
101
Coquille
42
Myrtle Point
42
UMPQUA VALLEY
Bandon
Canyonville

West Coast
Game Park
101
Coquille R.
Powers
Cape Blanco
State Park
Cape Blanco
Glendale

Grassy
Knob
Wilderness
KLAMATH
Port Orford
Humbug Mountain
State Park
Wild Rogue
Wilderness
Rogue R.
5

Prehistoric
Gardens
101
Rogue R.
Agness
Siskiyou
National Forest
Grants
Pass
TO
MEDFORD

Gold Beach
Wedderburn
Cape Sebastian
State Park
Pistol River
MOUNTAINS
Illinois R.
238

Samuel H.
Boardman
State Park
Loeb
State Park
Kalmiopsis
Wilderness
Chetco R.
199
Cave
Junction
46
Oregon Caves
National
Monument

Harris Beach
State Park
Brookings
Harbor
TO CRESCENT
CITY, CA
CALIFORNIA

0
20 miles
0
20 kilometers

⟟ *In-hotel: pool, laundry facilities, some pets allowed* ▭ *AE, D, MC, V* ⍾⎮ *CP.*

SPORTS AND THE OUTDOORS

RECREATIONAL   **Dean Creek Elk Viewing Area.** A herd of wild Roosevelt elk, Oregon's
AREAS   largest land mammal, roams within sight. Abundant forage and a mild
⟲   winter climate enable the elk to remain at Dean Creek year-round. The
best viewing times are early morning and just before dusk. ⊠ *Hwy. 38,
3 mi east of Reedsport* ▤ *Free* ⊙ *Daily dawn–dusk.*

William M. Tugman State Park. On Eel Lake near the town of Lakeside, a
dense forest of spruce, cedar, fir, and alder surrounds the little-known
park. Recreational activities include fishing, swimming, canoeing, and
sailing. ⊠ *U.S. 101S, North Bend* ☎ *541/888–4902 or 800/551–6949*
⊕ *www.oregonstateparks.org* ▤ *$5 per vehicle day-use fee.*

BAY AREA: NORTH BEND AND COOS BAY

27 mi south of Reedsport on U.S. 101.

The North Bend–Charleston–Coos Bay metropolitan area, collectively
known as the Bay Area (population 25,000), is the gateway to reward-
ing recreational experiences. The town of Coos Bay lies next to the
largest natural harbor between San Francisco Bay and Seattle's Puget
Sound. A century ago, vast quantities of lumber cut from the Coast
Range were milled in Coos Bay and shipped around the world. Coos
Bay still has a reputation as a rough-and-ready port city, but with mill
closures and dwindling lumber reserves, it is looking to tourism and
other industries for economic growth.

To see the best of the Bay Area, head west from Coos Bay on Newmark
Avenue for about 7 mi to **Charleston.** Though it's a Bay Area community, this quiet fishing village at the mouth of Coos Bay is a world unto
itself. As it loops into town, the road becomes the Cape Arago Highway
and leads to several oceanfront parks.

GETTING HERE

Private and commercial jets use the Southwest Oregon Regional Airport
in North Bend. Bus service to the airport and to South Coast communities is provided by **Curry Public Transit's Coastal Express** (☎ *800/921–2871*
⊕ *www.currypublictransit.org*).

VISITOR INFORMATION

Coos Bay–North Bend Visitors & Convention Bureau (⊠ *50 Central Ave., Coos
Bay* ☎ *541/269–0215 or 800/824–8486* ⊕ *www.oregonadventurecoast.
com*).

EXPLORING

Cape Arago Lighthouse. On a rock island just 12 mi offshore south of
Coos Bay, this lighthouse has had several iterations; the first lighthouse
was built here in 1866, but it was destroyed by storms and erosion. A
second, built in 1908, suffered the same fate. The current white tower,
built in 1934, is 44 feet tall and towers 100 feet above the ocean. If
you're here on a foggy day, listen for its unique foghorn. The lighthouse
is connected to the mainland by a bridge. Neither is open to the public,

but there's an excellent spot to view this lonely guardian and much of the coastline. From U.S. 101, take Cape Arago Highway to Gregory Point, where it ends at a turnaround, and follow the short trail.

Coos County Historical Society Museum. The highlight here is a 1922 steam locomotive used in Coos County logging. On display are a formal 1900 parlor, a pioneer kitchen, and exhibits on Native American history, agriculture, and industry such as logging, shipping, and mining. ⊠ *1220 Sherman St., North Bend* ☎ *541/756–6320 or 541/756–4847* 🖃 *Free* ⊙ *Tues.–Sat. 10–4; Memorial Day–Labor Day, also Sun. 12–4.*

South Slough National Estuarine Research Reserve. The reserve's fragile ecosystem supports everything from algae to bald eagles and black bears. More than 300 species of birds have been sighted at the reserve, which has an interpretive center, guided walks (summer only), and nature trails that give you a chance to see things up close. ⊠ *Seven Devils Rd., 4 mi south of Charleston, Coos Bay* ☎ *541/888–5558* 🖃 *Free* ⊙ *Trails daily dawn–dusk, interpretive center daily 10–4:30.*

WHERE TO EAT AND STAY

$$
NEW AMERICAN

✕ **Blue Heron Bistro.** You'll find subtle preparations of local seafood, chicken, and homemade pasta at this busy bistro. There are no flat spots on the far-ranging menu; even the innovative soups and desserts are excellent. The skylit, tile-floor dining room seats about 70 amid natural wood and blue linen. The seating area outside has blue awnings and colorful Bavarian window boxes that add a festive touch. Eighteen microbrews are available. ⊠ *100 W. Commercial St., Coos Bay* ☎ *541/267–3933* 🖃 *D, MC, V* ⊙ *Closed Sun. Oct.–May.*

$$
SEAFOOD

✕ **Portside Restaurant.** The fish served at this restaurant overlooking the Charleston boat basin come straight to the kitchen from the dock outside. Try the steamed Dungeness crab with drawn butter. The nautical furnishings—vintage bayside photos, boat lamps, navigational aids, coiled rope—reinforce the view of the harbor through the restaurant's picture windows. ⊠ *8001 Kingfisher Rd.,Charleston* ☎ *541/888–5544* 🖃 *AE, MC, V.*

$$

🖭 **Coos Bay Manor.** Built in 1912 on a quiet residential street in Coos Bay, this 15-room Colonial Revival manor is listed on the National Register of Historic Places. Hardwood floors, detailed woodwork, high ceilings, and antiques and period reproductions offset the red-and-gold-flecked wallpaper. An unusual open balcony on the second floor leads to the large rooms. Innkeepers Jon and Felicia Noack serve a full breakfast (included in the rates), and are happy to fulfill dietary requests. Just let them know in advance. Kids and pets are welcome. **Pros:** very nicely kept and decorated. **Cons:** located in town, but only condos are on the beach. ⊠ *955 S. 5th St., Coos Bay* ☎ *541/269–1224 or 800/269–1224* ⊕ *www. coosbaymanor.com* ⇆ *5 rooms* ♿ *In-hotel: Wi-Fi* 🖃 *AE, MC, V* ⊙I *BP.*

NIGHTLIFE AND THE ARTS

The Mill Casino. This casino offers lively gaming, top-name touring entertainers, and a spacious hotel. The complex has a casino with more than 700 slots, craps, blackjack, poker, roulette, and bingo. Included in the property's five dining venues are a waterfront restaurant and a bakery.

✉ *3201 Tremont Ave., North Bend* ☏ *541/756–8800 or 800/953–4800* ⊕ *www.themillcasino.com* ▭ *AE, D, MC, V.*

SPORTS AND THE OUTDOORS

RECREATIONAL
AREAS

Cape Arago State Park. The distant barking of sea lions echoes in the air at a trio of coves connected by short but steep trails. The park overlooks the **Oregon Islands National Wildlife Refuge,** where offshore rocks, beaches, islands, and reefs provide breeding grounds for seabirds and marine mammals. ✉ *End of Cape Arago Hwy., 1 mi south of Shore Acres State Park* ☏ *866/888–6100* ▭ *Free* ☉ *Daily dawn–dusk. Trail closed Mar.–June* ⊕ *www.oregonstateparks.org.*

Shore Acres State Park. An observation building on a grassy bluff overlooking the Pacific marks the site that held the mansion of lumber baron Louis J. Simpson. The view over the rugged wave-smashed cliffs is splendid, but the real glory of Shore Acres lies a few hundred yards to the south, where an entrance gate leads into what was Simpson's private garden. Beautifully landscaped and meticulously maintained, the gardens incorporate formal English and Japanese designs. From March to mid-October the grounds are ablaze with blossoming daffodils, rhododendrons, azaleas, roses, and dahlias. In December the garden is decked out with a dazzling display of holiday lights. ✉ *10965 Cape Arago Hwy., 1 mi south of Sunset Bay State Park, Coos Bay* ☏ *866/888–6100* ▭ *$5 per vehicle day-use fee* ☉ *Daily 8–dusk.*

Sunset Bay State Park. A placid semicircular lagoon protected from the sea by overlapping fingers of rock and surrounded by reefs is one of the few places along the Oregon Coast where you can swim without worrying about the currents and undertows. Only the hardiest souls will want to brave the chilly water, however. ✉ *2 mi south of Charleston off Cape Arago Hwy., Coos Bay* ☏ *866/888–6100* ⊕ *www.oregonstateparks.org* ☉ *Daily dawn–dusk.*

BANDON

25 mi south of Coos Bay on U.S. 101.

Referred to by some who cherish its romantic lure as Bandon-by-the-Sea, Bandon is both a harbor town and a popular vacation spot. Bandon is famous for its cranberry products, its cheese factory, as well as its artists' colony, complete with galleries and shops. Two national wildlife refuges, Oregon Islands and Bandon Marsh, are within the city limits. The Bandon Dunes links-style course is a worldwide attraction, often ranked in the top three golf courses in the United States.

It may seem odd that tiny Bandon bills itself as Oregon's cranberry capital. But 10 mi north of town lie acres of bogs and irrigated fields where tons of the tart berries are harvested every year. Each October there's the Cranberry Festival, complete with a parade and a fair.

GETTING HERE

Bandon is 29 mi from the North Bend airport. Bus service is provided by **Curry Public Transit's Coastal Express** (☏ *800/921–2871* ⊕ *www.currypublictransit.org*), which travels the U.S. Hwy. 101 corridor from

Sunset Bay State Park, Coos Bay

Smith River, Calif., northward through Brookings, Gold Beach, Port Orford, Bandon, Coos Bay, and North Bend.

VISITOR INFORMATION
Bandon Chamber of Commerce (✉ *300 Second St., Bandon* ☎ *541/347–9616 www.bandon.com*).

EXPLORING
Bandon Historical Society Museum. In the old city hall building, this museum depicts the area's early history, including Native American artifacts, logging, fishing, cranberry farming, and the disastrous 1936 fire that destroyed the city. Its gift shop has books, knickknacks, jewelry, myrtle-wood, and other little treasures. ✉ *270 Fillmore St., Bandon* ☎ *541/347–2164* ⊕ *bandonhistoricalmuseum.org* 🎟 *$2* 🕐 *Mon.–Sat. 10–4.*

West Coast Game Park. The "walk-through safari" on 21 acres has free-roaming wildlife: 450 animals and 75 species, including lions, tigers, snow leopards, bears, chimps, cougars, and camels, make it one of the largest wild-animal petting parks in the United States. The big attractions here are the young animals: bear cubs, tiger cubs, whatever is suitable for actual handling. It is 7 mi south of Bandon on U.S. 101. ✉ *U.S. 101, Bandon* ☎ *541/347–3106* ⊕ *www.gameparksafari.com* 🎟 *$16* 🕐 *Mid-June–Labor Day, daily 9–5 (last admittance 4:30).*

WHERE TO EAT AND STAY
$$$

STEAK

Fodor'sChoice

★

✕**Lord Bennett's.** His lordship has a lot going for him: a cliff-top setting, a comfortable and spacious dining area, sunsets visible through picture windows overlooking Face Rock Beach, and occasional musical performers on weekends. The rich dishes include prawns sautéed with sherry and garlic and steaks topped with shiitake mushrooms. A Sunday brunch is served. ⊠ *1695 Beach Loop Rd., Bandon* ☎ *541/347–3663* ⊕ *www.lordbennett.com* ☐ *AE, D, MC, V* ☺ *No lunch Mon.–Thurs.*

$$$ ☝ **Bandon Dunes Golf Resort.** This golfing lodge provides a luxurious place
Fodor'sChoice to relax after a day on the links, with single rooms and four-bedroom
★ suites, many with beautiful views of the famous Bandon Dunes Golf Course. There are cottages available that are designed for a quartet of golfers. Each unit includes a gathering room with fireplace, outdoor patio area, and four separate bedrooms with a king bed and private bath. There are also other lodging options available throughout the vast resort property, and five different restaurant and lounge choices. **Pros:** if you're a golfer, this adds to an incredible overall experience; if not, you'll have a wonderful stay anyway. **Cons:** the weather can be coarse in the shoulder-season months. ⊠ *57744 Round Lake Dr., Bandon* ☎ *541/347–4380 or 800/345–6008* ⊕ *www.bandondunesgolf.com* ↝ *186 rooms* ☖ *In-hotel: Wi-Fi, gym, parking, room service* ☐ *AE, D, DC, MC, V.*

SPORTS AND THE OUTDOORS

RECREATIONAL **Bullards Beach State Park.** The octagonal **Coquille Lighthouse,** built
AREAS in 1896 and no longer in use, stands lonely sentinel at the mouth of the Coquille River. From the highway the 2-mi drive to reach it passes through the Bandon Marsh, a prime bird-watching and picnicking area. The beach beside the lighthouse is a good place to search for jasper, agate, and driftwood. Note: 104 full hookups, 81 electrical $24; 13 yurts $36; horse camp, 8 sites (3 single corrals, 3 double corrals, 2 four-space corrals) $19; hiker/biker camp $5. ⊠ *U.S. 101, 2 mi north of Bandon, Bandon* ☎ *800/551–6949; 541/347–3501 lighthouse* ☺ *Free* ☺ *Daily 9–5.*

GOLF **Bandon Dunes Golf Resort.** This playland for the nation's golfing elite is
Fodor'sChoice no stranger to well-heeled athletes flying in to North Bend on private
★ jets to play on the resort's four distinct courses, including the new Old Macdonald course, which opened in Spring 2010. The expectations at Bandon Dunes are that you will walk the course with a caddy—adding another refined, traditional touch. Greens fees range, according to season and other factors, $220 to $275 a round from May to October, $75 to $265 other months. Caddy fees are $55 for single bag, $110 double. ⊠ *57744 Round Lake Dr., Bandon* ☎ *541/347–4380 or 800/345–6008* ⊕ *www.bandondunesgolf.com* ☐ *AE, D, DC, MC, V.*

PORT ORFORD

30 mi south of Bandon on U.S. 101.

The westernmost incorporated city in the contiguous United States, Port Orford is surrounded by forests, rivers, lakes, and beaches. The jetty at Port Orford offers little protection from storms, so every night the fishing boats are lifted out and stored on the docks. Commercial fishing boats search for crab, tuna, snapper, and salmon in the waters out of Port Orford, and diving boats gather sea urchins for Japanese markets. Visitors can fish off the Port Orford Dock or the jetty for smelt, sardine, herring, lingcod, halibut, and perch. Dock Beach provides beach fishing. The area is a favorite spot for sport divers because of the near-shore, protected reef, and for whale-watchers in fall and early spring.

GETTING HERE

Port Orford is 56 mi from the North Bend airport. Bus service is provided by **Curry Public Transit's Coastal Express** (☎ *800/921–2871* ⊕ *www. currypublictransit.org*), which travels the U.S. 101 Corridor from Smith River, Calif., northward through Brookings, Gold Beach, Port Orford, Bandon, Coos Bay, and North Bend.

VISITOR INFORMATION

Port Orford Visitor's Center Information (✉ *Battle Rock Wayside, Port Orford* ☎ *541/332–4106* ⊕ *www.discoverportorford.com*).

EXPLORING

OFF THE BEATEN PATH

4

Prehistoric Gardens. As you round a bend between Port Orford and Gold Beach, you'll see one of those sights that make grown-ups groan and kids squeal with delight: a huge, open-jawed tyrannosaurus rex, with a green brontosaurus peering out from the forest beside it. Twenty-three life-size dinosaur replicas are on display. ✉ *36848 U.S. 101, Port Orford* ☎ *541/332–4463* ✍ *$9* ☉ *Summer, daily 9–6; winter, daily 9–5.*

WHERE TO STAY

$$ ⛺ **Floras Lake House by the Sea.** This cedar home rests beside freshwater Floras Lake, spring-fed and separated from the ocean by only a sand spit. It's a bit tricky to find. The owners run a windsurfing school on the lake. The interior of the house is light, airy, and comfortable, with picture windows, exposed beams, contemporary couches, and a woodstove. There are four rooms, two with fireplaces, and all have private deck entrances. Outside, there's a garden, with a sauna beside the lake. ✉ *92870 Boice Cope Rd., Langlois* ☎ *541/348–2573* ⊕ *www.floraslake. com* ⌨ *4 rooms* *In-room: no phone, no TV, Wi-Fi* ▬ *MC, V* ☉ *Closed Nov.–mid-Feb.* �‖ *BP.*

$ ⛺ **Home by the Sea.** One of the oldest bed-and-breakfasts in Oregon, this three-story shingle house is on a headland jutting into the Pacific. A nearby path leads down to the beach. Both guest rooms have views of the ocean, as does the lower-level solarium and breakfast room, a great spot for watching whales (October to May is the best time) and winter storms. ✉ *444 Jackson St., Port Orford* ☎ *541/332–2855* ⊕ *www. homebythesea.com* ⌨ *2 rooms* *In-room: Wi-Fi. In-hotel: laundry facilities* ▬ *MC, V* �‖ *BP.*

SPORTS AND THE OUTDOORS

RECREATIONAL AREAS

Cape Blanco State Park. The westernmost point in Oregon and perhaps the windiest—gusts clocked at speeds as high as 184 mph have twisted and battered the Sitka spruces along the 6-mi road from U.S. 101 to the **Cape Blanco Lighthouse.** The lighthouse, atop a 245-foot headland, has been in continuous use since 1870, longer than any other in Oregon. No one knows why the Spaniards sailing past these reddish bluffs in 1603 called them *blanco* (white). One theory is that the name refers to the fossilized shells that glint in the cliff face. Campsites at the 1,880-acre park are available on a first-come, first-served basis. Saturday-evening tours are available in summer, with a donation suggested. ✉ *Cape Blanco Rd., follow signs from U.S. 101, Sixes* ☎ *541/332–6774* ⊕ *www. oregonstateparks.org* 🚩 *Lighthouse tour $2. Park day use free* ☉ *Park daily dawn–dawn; lighthouse Apr.–Oct. 31, Tues.–Sun. 10–3:30.*

Humbug Mountain State Park. Six miles south of Port Orford, this park, especially popular with campers, usually has warm weather, thanks to the nearby mountains, which block the ocean breezes. Windsurfing and scuba diving are popular here. Hiking trails lead to the top of Humbug Mountain. The campground has 32 electrical ($20) and 62 tent sites ($17), and a hiker/biker camp ($5). Three electrical and four tent sites are accessible to the disabled. ✉ *U.S. 101, Port Orford* ☎ *541/332–6774 or 800/551–6949* ⊕ *www.oregonstateparks.org.*

GOLD BEACH

28 mi south of Port Orford on U.S. 101.

The fabled Rogue River is one of the few U.S. rivers to merit Wild and Scenic status from the federal government. From spring to late fall an estimated 50,000 visitors descend on the town to take one of the daily jet-boat excursions that roar upstream from Wedderburn, Gold Beach's sister city across the bay, into the Rogue River Wilderness Area. Black bears, otters, beavers, ospreys, egrets, and bald eagles are seen regularly on these trips.

Gold Beach is very much a seasonal town, thriving in summer and nearly deserted the rest of the year because of its remote location. It marks the entrance to Oregon's banana belt, where mild, California-like temperatures take the sting out of winter and encourage a blossoming trade in lilies and daffodils.

GETTING HERE

Gold Beach is 84 mi south of the North Bend airport. Bus service is provided by **Curry Public Transit's Coastal Express** (☎ *800/921–2871* ⊕ *www. currypublictransit.org*), which travels the US Hwy 101 corridor from Smith River, Calif., northward through Brookings, Gold Beach, Port Orford, Bandon, Coos Bay, and North Bend.

VISITOR INFORMATION

Gold Beach Visitors Center (✉ *94080 Shirley La., Gold Beach* ☎ *541/247–7526 or 800/525–2334* ⊕ *www.goldbeach.org*).

WHERE TO EAT AND STAY

$ | NEW AMERICAN | Fodor'sChoice | ★ ✕ **Rollin 'n Dough Bakery & Bistro.** Patti Joyce greets people like family in her kitchen. Not only does she create exquisite pastries, cheesecakes, and breads, but her Rollin 'n Dough Deli also carries imported cheeses, ethnic meats, and gourmet lunches. The bistro has table service for soups, salads, pasta dishes, specialty sandwiches, and desserts. It's a little tough to find, but worth seeking out: it's on the north bank of the Rogue River, across the street from Lex's Landing. ✉ *94257 N. Bank Rogue, Gold Beach* ☎ *541/247–4438* ▬ *D, MC, V* ✇ *Closed Mon. No dinner. Sporadic hours in winter.*

$$$$ | Fodor'sChoice | ★ 🛏 **Tu Tu' Tun Lodge.** Pronounced "too-*too*-tin," this well-known fishing resort is a slice of heaven on the Rogue River, 7 mi upriver from Gold Beach. Owner Kyle Ringer is intent on providing his guests with a singular Northwest experience. All the units in this small establishment have rustic elegance. Some have hot tubs, others have fireplaces, and a few have both; private decks overlook the river. Two deluxe rooms feature

outdoor soaking tubs with river views. Guided fishing trips and river activities here are popular, and nearby jet-boat excursions and world-class golf at Bandon Dunes are also draws. The restaurant (closed November to April) serves breakfast, lunch, and dinner; the last, open to outside guests (though reservations are hard to come by), consists of a five-course prix-fixe meal that changes nightly. **Pros:** warm, personable; beautiful and luxurious; delicious gourmet dining and wine tasting; activities to suit every taste. **Cons:** no TV; not well suited for young kids. ⊠ *96550 N. Bank Rogue, Gold Beach* ☎ *541/247–6664* ⊕ *www.tututun.com* ⇆ *16 rooms, 2 suites* ⚲ *In-room: no TV, Wi-Fi. In-hotel: restaurant, bar, golf course* ▭ *D, MC, V.*

SPORTS AND THE OUTDOORS

RECREATIONAL AREAS

Cape Sebastian State Park. The parking lots at this park are more than 200 feet above sea level. At the south parking vista you can see up to 43 mi north to Humbug Mountain. Looking south, you can see nearly 50 mi toward Crescent City, California, and the Point Saint George Lighthouse. A deep forest of Sitka spruce covers most of the park. There's a 1½-mi walking trail. Be warned: there's no drinking water. ⊠ *U.S. 101, Gold Beach* ☎ *541/469–2021 or 800/551–6949* ⊕ *www. oregonstateparks.org.*

BOATING

Jerry's Rogue Jets. These Rogue River jet boats operate in the most rugged section of the Wild and Scenic Rogue River, offering 64, 80, and 104-mi tours. Whether visitors choose a shorter, 6-hour lower Rogue scenic trip or an 8-hour white-water trip, folks will have a rollicking good time. Its largest vessels are 40-feet long and can hold 75 passengers. The smaller, white-water boats are 32-feet long and can hold 42 passengers. ⊠ *29985 Harbor Way, Gold Beach* ☎ *541/247–4571 or 800/451–3645* ⊕ *www. roguejets.com.*

FISHING

Five Star Charters. Fishing charter trips range from a 4-hour bottom-fish outing to a full-day salmon, steelhead, or halibut charter. They offer all the tackle needed, and customers don't even need experience—they'll take beginners and experts. The outfit has four riverboats, including two drift boats and two powerboats, as well as two ocean boats. They operate year-round. ⊠ *Port of Gold Beach, Gold Beach* ☎ *541/247–0217 or 888/301–6480* ⊕ *www.goldbeachadventures.com.*

BROOKINGS

27 mi south of Gold Beach on U.S. 101.

A startling 90% of the pot lilies grown in the United States come from a 500-acre area inland from Brookings. Mild temperatures along this coastal plain provide ideal conditions for flowering plants of all kinds— even a few palm trees, a rare sight in Oregon.

The town is equally famous as a commercial and sport-fishing port at the mouth of the turquoise-blue Chetco River. Salmon and steelhead weighing 20 pounds or more swim here.

EN ROUTE Between Gold Beach and Brookings, you'll cross Thomas Creek Bridge, the highest span in Oregon. Take advantage of the off-road coastal viewing points along the 10-mi-long Samuel H. Boardman State Park—especially in summer, when highway traffic becomes heavy and rubbernecking can be dangerous.

GETTING HERE

Brookings is 112 mi from the North Bend airport. Bus service is provided by **Curry Public Transit's Coastal Express** (☎ *800/921–2871* ⊕ *www. currypublictransit.org*), which travels the U.S. 101 Corridor from Smith River, Calif., northward through Brookings, Gold Beach, Port Orford, Bandon, Coos Bay, and North Bend.

VISITOR INFORMATION

Brookings Harbor Chamber of Commerce (✉ *16330 Lower Harbor Rd., Brookings* ☎ *541/469–3181 or 800/535–9469* ⊕ *www.brookingsor.com*).

EXPLORING

🅒 **Chetco Valley Historical Museum.** Inside a mid-19th-century stagecoach stop and trading post, this museum has some unusual items and is worth a brief visit. An iron casting that bears a likeness to Queen Elizabeth I has led to speculation that it was left during an undocumented landing on the Oregon coast by Sir Francis Drake. On a hill near the museum stands the **World Champion Cypress Tree,** 99 feet tall and with a 27-foot circumference. ✉ *5461 Museum Rd., Brookings* ☎ *541/469– 6651* 🖾 *$1 donation* ⊙ *Memorial Day–Labor Day, weekends noon–4.*

WHERE TO EAT AND STAY

$$

SEAFOOD

✕ **Sebastian's.** Fishing vessels docked in the adjacent boat basin and picture windows looking out to the sea lend a salty feel to this low-key restaurant. The daily seafood specials—usually halibut and salmon—are the best bets. For a real dinner splurge, dive into the steak and lobster for $72. ✉ *16011 Boat Basin Rd., Brookings* ☎ *541/469–6006* ⊟ *AE, D, MC, V* ⊙ *No lunch.*

$

🖾 **Portside Suites.** This all-suite hotel offers spacious rooms for business or relaxing and gazing at harbor ships. Although the Portside's local charm is somewhat diminished by the asphalt parking lot it sits in the middle of, it has pleasant harbor, ocean, or river views, and fireplaces and hot tubs in some rooms. There are meeting facilities for corporate guests. **Pros:** close to the harbor; spacious, clean rooms. **Cons:** surrounding grounds. ✉ *16219 Lower Harbor Rd., Brookings* ☎ *541/469–7100 or 866/767–8111* ⊕ *www.brookingsportsidesuites.com* 🗗 *12 suites* ⊛ *In-room: Wi-Fi. In-hotel: laundry facilities* ⊟ *AE, D, MC, V.*

SPORTS AND THE OUTDOORS

RECREATIONAL AREAS

Harris Beach State Park. Watch gray whales migrate in spring and winter. Bird Island, also called Goat Island, is a National Wildlife Sanctuary and a breeding site for rare birds. There is a campground with 36 full hookups, 50 electrical $26; 63 tent $20 (cable TV hookups for $1 in selected campsites in full or electric sites); 6 yurts $39; hiker/biker camp $5; and Wi-Fi. ✉ *U.S. 101, Brook-*

THE FAB 50

U.S. 101 between Port Orford and Brookings, often referred to as the "fabulous 50 mi," soars up green headlands, some of them hundreds of feet high, and past a seascape of cliffs and sea stacks. The ocean is bluer and clearer— though not appreciably warmer— than it is farther north, and the coastal countryside is dotted with farms, grazing cattle, and small rural communities.

ings ☎ *541/469–2021 or 800/551–6949* ⊕ *www.oregonstateparks.org* ▨ *Free* ⊙ *Daily.*

Loeb State Park. Fifty-three riverside campsites and some fine hiking trails, including one that leads to a hidden redwood grove, make up this park. There's also a grove of myrtlewood trees, which you'll find only in southwest Oregon and northern California. ✉ *North bank of Chetco River, 10 mi east of Brookings (follow signs from U.S. 101), Brookings* ☎ *541/469–2021 or 800/551–6949* ⚓ *Reservations not accepted* ▨ *Day use free, 48 electrical sites $20, 3 rustic cabins $39* ⊙ *Daily dawn–dusk* ⊕ *www.oregonstateparks.org.*

FISHING **Brookings Saltwater Fishing Trips.** From late September through March, Andy Martin runs salmon and steelhead trips on the Chetco and Rogue rivers, as well as guided ocean trips out of Brookings. A licensed U.S. Coast Guard captain, Andy knows the waters off Brookings, which is handy during the October ocean salmon season, when fish up to 50 pounds are caught off the mouth of the Chetco River. The outfit also runs trips for lingcod and steelhead in the winter. ✉ *Brookings* ☎ *541/813–1082* ⊕ *www.tidewindsportfishing.com.*

Tidewind Sportfishing. This Brookings charter company provides all the gear needed to catch bottom fish, salmon, shark, and even tuna. Because the Port of Brookings is in a cove, it provides calmer waters for fishing—especially with an earlier start. Cost includes use of fishing pole, bait and tackle, fillet service, and coffee, tea, or cocoa and snacks. Kids are welcome. Fishing license not included. Trips range from 5 to 8 hrs. ✉ *16368 Lower Harbor Rd., Brookings* ☎ *541/4690337* ⊕ *www. tidewindsportfishing.com.*

The Columbia River Gorge and Mt. Hood

WORD OF MOUTH

"Next stop was Bridal Veils, which was really neat. The sound and power of these falls is amazing. This was a really good little hike, short, but with some good inclines that helped work off the cupcake from the previous night."

—aggiegirl

WELCOME TO THE COLUMBIA RIVER GORGE AND MT. HOOD

TOP REASONS TO GO

★ **Waterfall walkabout.** Hikers will discover dozens of gorgeous cascades along the Historic Columbia River Highway and its adjoining trail network, including 620-foot Multnomah Falls.

★ **Outdoor rec mecca.** From kiteboarding the gorge to mountain biking the slopes of Mt. Hood, this is a region tailor-made for adventure junkies. Get the gear and the beta from outfitters in Hood River and Government Camp.

★ **Historico-luxe.** Grand and gaudy landmarks like McMenamins Edgefield, Timberline Lodge, and the Columbia Gorge Hotel are guest favorites and entries on the National Register of Historic Places.

★ **Suds-tacular.** Western Oregon is the national seat of craft brewing, and the Gorge/Hood area has its share of inviting taprooms, from Stevenson's tiny Walking Man Brewing to Full Sail's upbeat national headquarters in Hood River.

1 **Columbia River Gorge.** The dams of the early twentieth century transformed the Columbia River from the raging torrent that vexed Lewis and Clark in 1805 to the breathtaking, but comparatively docile waterway that hosts kiteboarders and windsurfers today. Auto visitors have been scoping out the gorge's picturesque bluffs and waterfalls for quite a while now—the road between Troutdale and The Dalles, on which construction began in 1913, was the country's first planned scenic highway.

2 **Mt Hood.** Visible from 100 mi away, Mt. Hood (or "the Mountain," as Portlanders often call it) is the kind of rock that commands respect. It's holy ground for mountaineers, about 10,000 of whom make a summit bid each year. Sightseers are often shocked by the summer snows, but skiers rejoice, keeping the mountain's resorts busy year-round. Mingle with laid-back powder hounds and other outdoorsy types in the hospitality villas of Welches and Government Camp.

WASHINGTON

0   20 mi

0   20 km

Columbia River Gorge
National Scenic Area

Columbia River

Hood
River
Mosier
Odell
Dee
The Dalles
84
Biggs
Junction
Wasco
97
197
Moro
35
Grass
Valley
Mt. Hood
97
Badger Creek
Wilderness
Government
Camp
Kent
Maupin
218
216
197
26
218
Warm Springs
Indian
Reservation
Warm Springs
Antelope
97
293
Deschutes River
Warm Springs
Madras
Lake
Simtustus
Lake Billy
Chinook
26
Ochoco
National
Forest
97
20
Prineville
26
Sisters
126
Redmond
20
97

GETTING ORIENTED

The mighty Columbia River flows west through the Cascade Range, past the Mt. Hood Wilderness area to Astoria. It is a natural border between Oregon and Washington to the north, and bridges link roads on both sides at Biggs Junction, The Dalles, Hood River, and Cascade Locks. The watery recreation corridor stretches from The Dalles in the east to the east Portland 'burbs. For most of that drive, snow-capped Mt. Hood looms to the southwest. Hood River drains the mountain's north side, emptying into the Columbia at its namesake town. Follow it upstream and you'll trade the warm, low-elevation climes of the gorge for the high country's tall pines and late-season snows. While it feels remote, the massive peak is just outside Portland. Look up from almost any neighborhood in town to see its white dome, just 60 mi east and accessible via U.S. 26 through Gresham.

5

THE COLUMBIA RIVER GORGE AND MT. HOOD PLANNER

When to Go

Winter weather in the Columbia Gorge and the Mt. Hood area is much more severe than in Portland and western Oregon. At times I–84 may be closed because of snow and ice. If you're planning a winter visit, be sure to carry plenty of warm clothes. High winds and single-digit temps are par for the course around 6,000 feet in January. Note that chains are a requirement for traveling over mountain passes.

Temperatures in the gorge are mild year-round, rarely dipping below 30 degrees in winter and hovering in the high 70s in midsummer. As throughout Oregon, however, elevation is often a more significant factor than season, and an hour-long drive to Mt. Hood's Timberline Lodge can reduce those midsummer temps by 20 to 30 degrees. Don't forget that the higher reaches of Mt. Hood retain snow as late as August.

In early fall, look for maple, tamarack, and aspen trees around the gorge, bursting with brilliant red and gold color. No matter the season, the basalt cliffs, the acres of lush forest, and that glorious expanse of water make the gorge worth visiting time and again.

About the Restaurants

A prominent locavore mentality pervades western Oregon generally, and low elevations around the gorge mean long growing seasons for dozens of local producers. Fresh foods grown, caught, and harvested in the Northwest dominate menus in gourmet restaurants around the gorge and Mt. Hood. Columbia River salmon is big, fruit orchards proliferate around Hood River, and the gorge nurtures a glut of excellent vineyards. Of course, beer culture is king across Oregon, and even the smallest towns around the region have their own lively brewpubs with casual American pub fare and tap after tap of craft ales. In keeping with the region's green and laid-back vibe, outdoor dining is big, Hood River's superb Stonehedge Gardens being the quintessential example.

About the Hotels

The hospitality industry is first-rate around the gorge and Mt. Hood, and the region's accommodations run the gamut from luxury hotels and sophisticated conference resorts to historic lodges, ski chalets, and cabin rentals. Cozy bed-and-breakfasts abound along the gorge, many of them historic structures overlooking the river. The slopes of Mt. Hood are spotted with smart ski resorts, and towns like Government Camp and Welches are long on rustic vacation rentals. The closer you are to Mt. Hood in any season, the earlier you'll want to reserve. With ski country working ever harder to attract summer patrons, Mt. Hood resorts like Timberline Lodge and Mt. Hood Skibowl offer some worthwhile seasonal specials.

WHAT IT COSTS IN U.S. DOLLARS					
	¢	$	$$	$$$	$$$$
Restaurants	under $10	$10–$16	$17–$23	$24–$30	over $30
Hotels		under $100	$100–$150	$151–$200	$201–$250	over $250

Restaurant prices are per person, for a main course at dinner. Hotel prices are for two people in a standard double room in high season, excluding tax.

Getting Here and Around

Air Travel. Portland International Airport (PDX)
(☎ 877/739–4636 ⊕ www.portofportland.com) is the only
nearby airport receiving commercial flights. Taxis out to Mt.
Hood or the gorge are not particularly practical, but you
can schedule a door-to-door shuttle with **Blue Star Transportation** (☎ 541/249–1837 ⊕ www.bluestarbus.com) or
Green Shuttle (☎ 541/252–4422 ⊕ www.greentrans.com)
Rates vary by destination, but a one-way trip to Hood River
runs $80–$90. If you're heading to Hood, ski resorts like
Mt. Hood Skibowl and Mt. Hood Meadows offer Portland
shuttles in season.

Bus Travel. Greyhound (☎ 800/454–2487 ⊕ www.
greyhound.com) provides service from Portland to Hood
River and The Dalles. Portland's eco-friendly **Greasebus**
(⊕ www.greasebus.com) runs seven days a week in winter
between a Portland donut shop and Mt. Hood Meadows Ski
Resort. On Thursdays, **Columbia Area Transit** (☎ 541/386–
4202 ⊕ community.gorge.net/hrctd) runs a fixed-route bus
between The Dalles and Portland via Hood River.

Car Travel. I–84 is the main east–west route into the Columbia River Gorge. U.S. 26, heading east from Portland and
northwest from Prineville, is the main route into the Mt.
Hood area. Portions of I–84 and U.S. 26 that pass through
the mountains pose winter-travel difficulties, though the
state plows these roadways regularly. The gorge is closed
frequently during harsh winters due to ice and mudslides.
Extreme winds can also make driving hazardous, and
potentially result in highway closures.

The Historic Columbia River Highway (U.S. 30) from Troutdale to just east of Oneonta Gorge passes Crown Point
State Park and Multnomah Falls. I–84/U.S. 30 continues
on to The Dalles. Highway 35 heads south from The Dalles
to the Mt. Hood area, intersecting with U.S. 26 at Government Camp. From Portland, the Columbia Gorge–Mt.
Hood Scenic Loop is the easiest way to see the gorge and
the mountain. Take I–84 east to Troutdale and follow U.S.
26 to Bennett Pass (near Timberline), where Highway 35
heads north to Hood River; then follow I–84 back to Portland. Or make the loop in reverse.

Major rental car agencies are available in Gresham (3 mi
west of Troutdale); Enterprise is also in Hood River and The
Dalles.

Local Agencies Apple City Rental Cars (✉ 3250 Bonneville Rd.,Hood River ☎ 541/386–5504).

Top Festivals

**Columbia Gorge Bluegrass
Festival.** One of the premier
bluegrass fests in the West
takes place in Stevenson,
Washington every fourth
weekend in July. **Mt. Hood
Festival of the Forest.** Local
bands and artists head to
the woods the second full
weekend in September for an
earthy gathering on 580 acres
of temperate rain forest in the
shadow of Mt. Hood.

Tour Options

Americas Hub World Tours
(☎ 800/673–3110 ⊕ www.
americashubworldtours.com)
offers waterfall and wine tours
through the gorge. **Eco Tours
of Oregon** (☎ 888/868–7733
⊕ www.ecotours-of-oregon.
com) combine naturalist-
led trips to the waterfalls
of the Historic Columbia
River Highway with loops
around Mt. Hood. **Explore
the Gorge** (☎ 800/899–5676
⊕ www.explorethegorge.com)
designs customized van and
bus tours of the gorge, Mt.
Hood, and the Hood River
Valley. **Martin's Gorge Tours**
(☎ 888/290–8687 ⊕ www.
martinsgorgetours.com) leads
wine tours and waterfall hikes.

**Columbia River Gorge Visi-
tors Association** (☎ 800/984–
6743 ⊕ www.crgva.org).
Oregon Tourism Commission
(☎ 800/547–7842 ⊕ www.
traveloregon.com).

Updated by
Brian Kevin

Volcanoes, lava flows, Ice Age floodwaters, and glaciers were nature's tools of choice when carving a breathtaking 80-mi landscape now called the Columbia River Gorge. Proof of human civilization here reaches back 31,000 years, and excavations near The Dalles have uncovered evidence that salmon fishing is a 10,000-year-old tradition in these parts. In 1805 Lewis and Clark discovered the Columbia River to be the only waterway that led to the Pacific. Their first expedition was a treacherous route through wild, plunging rapids, but their successful navigation set a new exodus in motion.

Today the towns are laid-back recreation hamlets whose residents harbor a fierce pride in their shared natural resources. Sightseers, hikers, and skiers have long found contentment in this robust region, officially labeled a National Scenic Area in 1986. They're joined these days by epicures trolling the Columbia's banks in search of gourmet cuisine, artisan hop houses, and top-shelf vino. Highlights of the Columbia River Gorge include Multnomah Falls, Bonneville Dam, and the rich orchard land of Hood River. Sailboaters, windsurfers, and kiteboarders take advantage of the blustery gorge winds in the summer, their colorful sails decorating the waterway like windswept confetti.

To the south of Hood River are all the alpine attractions of the 11,245-foot-high Mt. Hood. With more than two million people living just up the road in Portland, you'd think this mountain playground would be overrun, but it's still easy to find solitude in the 67,000-acre wilderness surrounding the peak. Some of the world's best skiers take advantage of the powder on Hood, and they stick around in summertime for ski conditions that are as close to year-round as anyplace in the country.

COLUMBIA RIVER GORGE

When glacial floods carved out most of the Columbia River Gorge at the end of the last Ice Age, they left behind massive, looming cliffs where the river bisects the Cascade mountain range. The size of the canyon and the wildly varying elevations make this small stretch of Oregon as ecologically diverse as anyplace in the state. In a few days along the gorge, you can mountain bike through dry canyons near The Dalles, hike through temperate rain forest in Oneonta Gorge, and take a woodland wildflower stroll just outside of Hood River. At night you'll be rewarded with historic lodging and good food in one of a half-dozen mellow river towns. The country's first National Scenic Area remains one of its most inviting.

TROUTDALE

16 mi east of Portland on I–84.

5

Troutdale is known for its great fishing spots, as well as antiques stores and the Columbia Gorge Premium Outlets. The city has a funky, walkable downtown, and it's the western terminus of the 22-mi-long **Historic Columbia River Highway**, U.S. 30 (also known as the Columbia River Scenic Highway and the Scenic Gorge Highway). In 1911, two years before work on the scenic road began, Troutdale became home to the Multnomah County Poor Farm, a massive Colonial Revival estate that housed Oregon's aged, indigent, and sick for most of the 20th century. After falling into disarray in the 1980s, the historic poor farm was reinvented in 1990 as the funky art resort McMenamins Edgefield, one of Troutdale's biggest draws today.

GETTING HERE

Troutdale is 16 mi east of downtown Portland on I–84, about a $40 cab ride from the airport. Reach Troutdale "the back way" by coming in from the east on U.S. 30, the Historic Columbia River Highway.

VISITOR INFORMATION

West Columbia Gorge Chamber of Commerce (✉ *226 W. Historic Columbia River Hwy., Troutdale* ☎ *503/669–7473* ⊕ *www.westcolumbia gorgechamber.com*).

WHERE TO EAT AND STAY

$$
NEW AMERICAN

✕ **Black Rabbit Restaurant & Bar.** Chef John Zenger's grilled rib-eye steak, old-fashioned roasted chicken, and Northwest cioppino are popular entrées at this McMenamins hotel restaurant. Vivid murals depicting the gorge's history enrich your view as you linger over dinner in a high-backed wooden booth. Enjoy an Edgefield wine or any one of five McMenamins brews (made on-site, approximately 50 yards away). Patio seating is available, with plenty of heaters to handle the unpredictable Oregon weather. Top off your meal with a homemade dessert and, wouldn't you know, a McMenamins home-roasted cup of coffee. ✉ *2126 SW Halsey St.* ☎ *503/492–3086* ⊕ *www.mcmenamins.com* ▭ *AE, D, MC, V.*

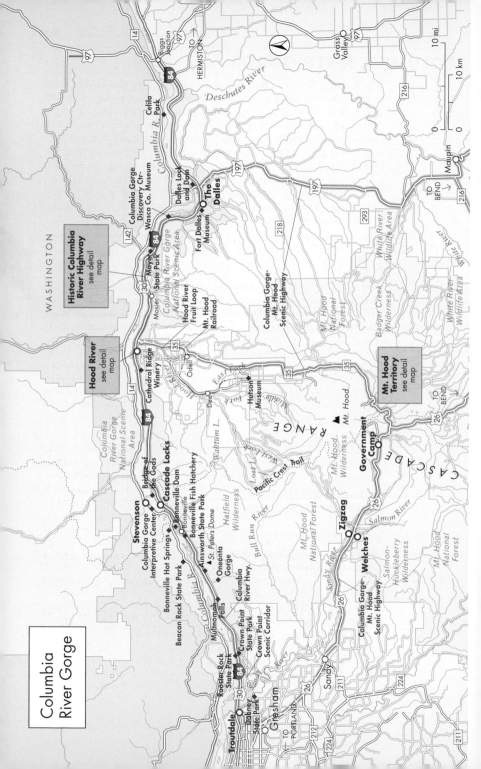

Columbia River Gorge

WASHINGTON

Deschutes River

Columbia R. Park

Biggs Junction

HERMISTON

TO HERMISTON

Grass Valley

Maupin

TO BEND

10 mi

10 km

Celilo Park

Columbia Gorge Discovery Ctr-Wasco Co. Museum

Dalles Lock and Dam

The Dalles

Fort Dalles Museum

Historic Columbia River Highway
see detail map

Mayer State Park

Mosier

Hood River Fruit Loop

Mt. Hood Railroad

Cathedral Ridge Winery

Hood River
see detail map

Columbia River National Scenic Area

Odell

Dee

Columbia Gorge-Mt. Hood Scenic Highway

Mt. Hood Territory
see detail map

Hutson Museum

Mt. Hood National Forest

Badger Creek Wilderness

White River Wildlife Area

White River

TO BEND

Mt. Hood

Mt. Hood Wilderness

C A S C A D E   R A N G E

Pacific Crest Trail

Wahtum L.

Lost Lake

Hood River

East Fork

Middle Fork

West Fork

Government Camp

Columbia Gorge National Scenic Area

Stevenson

Columbia Gorge Interpretive Center

Bridge of the Gods

Cascade Locks

Bonneville Hot Springs

Bonneville

Bonneville Fish Hatchery

Bonneville Dam

Beacon Rock State Park

St. Peters Dome

Ainsworth State Park

Oneonta Gorge

Hatfield Wilderness

Columbia River Hwy.

Multnomah Falls

Crown Point State Park

Crown Point Scenic Corridor

Rooster Rock State Park

Dabney State Park

Troutdale

Gresham

TO PORTLAND

PORTLAND

Sandy

Sandy River

Bull Run River

Salmon River

Zigzag

Welches

Columbia Gorge-Mt. Hood Scenic Highway

Mt. Hood National Forest

Salmon-Huckleberry Wilderness

Mt. Hood National Forest

¢ ⊡ **McMenamins Edgefield.** As you explore the grounds of this Georgian
Fodor'sChoice Revival manor, you'll feel as if you've entered a twisted European vil-
★ lage, filled with activity and offbeat beauty. McMenamins Edgefield is
what the Four Seasons would be if it were operated by dreamers and
Deadheads—which essentially describes Northwest brewers and hospitality innovators par excellence Mike and Brian McMenamin. On
this former poor farm, guests can wander through 74 acres of gardens,
murals, orchards, and vineyards with a drink in hand. Enjoy $3 movies
in the Power Station Theater, live music outdoors and in the winery, and
golf at one of two par-3 courses. There are three restaurants and nine
bars to choose from, with pool halls, distilleries, and tiny wine sheds
tucked away in unexpected places. Ruby's Spa offers an amplitude of
body treatments, and all guests have access to the outdoor soaking pool.
Edgefield is a western treasure, and even the most uptight vacationer
can't help but get swept up in Edgefield's mellow, bohemian vibe. Be
sure to make reservations ahead of time for the Black Rabbit restaurant
and Ruby's Spa. **Pros:** plenty of choices for eating and drinking; large
variety of rooms and prices to choose from. **Cons:** crowds can get large
at this busy place. ⊠ *2126 SW Halsey St.* ☎ *503/669–8610 or 800/669–
8610* ⊕ *www.mcmenamins.com* ↪ *114 rooms, 20 with private bath,
24 beds in men's/women's hostels* ⚹ *In-room: no phone, no TV, Wi-Fi.
In-hotel: 3 restaurants, bars, spa, parking (free)* ⊟ *AE, D, DC, MC, V.*

SHOPPING

Columbia Gorge Premium Outlets. Forty-five outlet stores, including Eddie
Bauer and Guess, will keep you looking sharp for your trip through the
gorge. Oregon's lack of a sales tax is a big draw for out-of-towners.
⊠ *450 NW 257th Way* ☎ *503/669–8060* ⊕ *www.premiumoutlets.com/
columbiagorge* ⊗ *Mon.–Sat. 10–8, Sun. 10–6.*

SPORTS AND THE OUTDOORS

RECREATIONAL **Rooster Rock State Park.** The most famous beach lining the Columbia
AREAS River is here, right below Crown Point. Three miles of sandy beaches,
panoramic cascades, and a large swimming area makes this a popular
spot. True naturists appreciate that one of Oregon's two designated
nude beaches is at the east end of Rooster Rock, and that it's not visible to conventional sunbathers. Rooster Rock is several miles east of
Troutdale, and it's accessible only via the interstate. ⊠ *I–84, 7 mi east
of Troutdale* ☎ *503/695–2261* ⊕ *www.oregonstateparks.org* ▣ *Day
use $5 per vehicle* ⊗ *Daily 7–dusk.*

FISHING Just east of town, the Sandy River is fed by Mt. Hood snowmelt, and
has a reputation as one of the state's best salmon and steelhead fisheries. **Jack's Snack N Tackle** can set you up with a license, bait, and tackle,
and they lead guided float trips throughout the year. ⊠ *1208 E. Historic
Columbia River Hwy.* ☎ *503/665–2257* ⊕ *www.jackssnackandtackle.
com* ▣ *Half-day trips $100, full-day trips $175* ⊗ *Feb.–mid-Oct., daily
8:30–5; mid-Oct.–Jan., Mon.–Sat. 7–5* ⊟ *MC, V.*

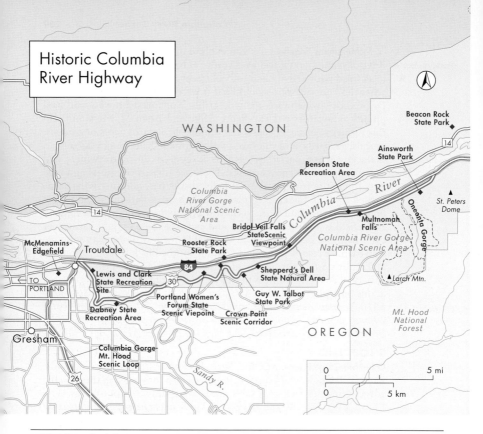

HISTORIC COLUMBIA RIVER HIGHWAY

U.S. 30, paralleling I–84 for 22 mi between Troutdale and interstate Exit 35.

The oldest scenic highway in the United States is a construction marvel that integrates asphalt path with cliff, river, and forest landscapes. Paralleling the interstate to the south of I–84, U.S. 30 climbs to forested riverside bluffs, passes half a dozen waterfalls, and provides access to hiking trails leading to still more falls and scenic overlooks. Completed in 1922, the serpentine highway was the first paved road in the gorge built expressly for automotive sightseers. The route is peppered with state parks. Eight of them are day-use only, with camping only available at Ainsworth State Park. Near The Dalles, an additional 15 mi of U.S. 30 are designated as part of the scenic byway, but the 22-mi western segment is the real draw.

GETTING HERE

U.S. 30 heads out of downtown Troutdale going east, and the route can be accessed from I–84 along the way, via Exit 22 near Corbett, Exit 28 near Bridal Veil Falls, Exit 31 at Multnomah Falls, and Exit 35, where it rejoins the interstate.

VISITOR INFORMATION

West Columbia Gorge Chamber of Commerce (✉ 226 W. *Historic Columbia River Hwy., Troutdale* ☎ 503/669–7473 ⊕ *www.westcolumbiagorge chamber.com*). **Multnomah Falls Visitor Center** (✉ *Exit 31 off I–84, 50000 Historic Columbia River Hwy., Bridal Veil* ☎ 503/695–2376 ⊕ *www. multnomahfallslodge.com* ⊙ *Daily 9–5*).

EXPLORING

Fodor'sChoice
★

Crown Point State Scenic Corridor. A few miles east of Troutdale on U.S. 30 is a 730-foot-high bluff with an unparalleled 30-mi view down the Columbia River Gorge. **Vista House,** the two-tier octagonal structure on the side of the cliff, opened its doors to visitors in 1916; the rotunda has displays about the gorge and the highway. Vista House's architect Edgar Lazarus was the brother of Emma Lazarus, author of the poem displayed at the base of the Statue of Liberty. ✉ *10 mi east of Troutdale on U.S. 30* ☎ *503/695–2261 or 800/551–6949* ⊕ *www. oregonstateparks.org* ➡ *Free* ⊙ *Daily.*

Multnomah Falls. Multnomah Falls, a 620-foot-high double-decker torrent, the second-highest year-round waterfall in the nation, is by far the most spectacular of the cataracts east of Troutdale. The scenic highway leads down to a parking lot; from there a paved path winds to a bridge over the lower falls. A much steeper trail climbs to a viewing point overlooking the upper falls. It's quite a hike to the top, but worth it to avoid the crowds that swarm Multnomah in every season. ✉ *Exit 31 off I–84, or 15 mi east of Troutdale on U.S. 30, Bridal Veil* ☎ *503/695–2376* ⊕ *www.multnomahfallslodge.com.*

WHERE TO EAT

$$
AMERICAN

✕ Multnomah Falls Lodge. Vaulted ceilings, stone fireplaces, and exquisite views of Multnomah Falls are complemented by wonderful service and an extensive menu at this restaurant, which is listed on the National Register of Historic Places. Consider the halibut fish-and-chips, the lemon- and herb-roasted wild salmon, or ancho chile and espresso-cured flatiron steak. Breakfast favorites include blueberry, buttermilk, or huckleberry pancakes. A particular pleaser for out-of-town guests, the champagne Sunday brunch is held 8–2. Try the brown sugar–glazed Salmon Multnomah. For a treat during warmer months, sit on the patio and get close to the falls without feeling a drop. ✉ *Exit 31 off I–84, 50000 Historic Columbia River Hwy., Bridal Veil* ☎ *503/695–2376* ⊕ *www. multnomahfallslodge.com* ▭ *AE, D, MC, V* ⊙ *Daily 8 AM–9 PM.*

SPORTS AND THE OUTDOORS

RECREATIONAL
AREAS

Ainsworth State Park. Trailheads in this hiker-friendly park lead 6 mi west to Multnomah Falls or eastward up the steep Nesmith Point Trail, showing off stellar views of the 350-foot St. Peter's Dome rock spire before continuing east to Cascade Locks. In the summer, rangers host occasional interpretive programs at an on-site amphitheater, and 49 forested campsites fill up on a first-come, first-served basis. ✉ *At exit 35 off I–84, 20 mi east of Troutdale on U.S. 30* ☎ *503/695–2301 or 800/551–6949* ⊕ *www.oregonstateparks.org* ➡ *Day use free; full hookups $20, tent sites $17* ⊙ *Mid-March–Oct.*

5

Dabney State Park. About 4 mi east of the Troutdale bridge, this state park has boating, hiking, and fishing. There's also a popular summer swimming hole and an 18-hole disc golf course. A boat ramp is open year-round. ⊠ *U.S. 30, 4 mi east of Troutdale* ☎ *800/551–6949* ⊕ *www. oregonstateparks.org* ⬛ *Day use $5 per vehicle* ⊙ *Daily dawn–dusk.*

Oneonta Gorge. Following the old highway east from Multnomah Falls, you come to a narrow, mossy cleft with walls hundreds of feet high. Oneonta Gorge is most enjoyable in summer, when you can walk up the streambed through the cool green canyon, where hundreds of plant species—some found nowhere else—flourish under the perennially moist conditions. At other times of the year, take the trail along the west side of the canyon. The clearly marked trailhead is 100 yards west of the gorge, on the south side of the road. The trail takes you to Oneonta Falls, about ½ mi up the stream, where it links with an extensive regional trail system exploring the region's bluffs and waterfalls. Bring boots or submersible sneakers—plus a strong pair of ankles—because the rocks are slippery. ⊠ *Exit 31 off I–84, 2 mi east of Multnomah Falls on U.S. 30* ☎ *503/308–1700* ⊕ *www.fs.fed.us/r6/columbia.*

CASCADE LOCKS

7 mi east of Oneonta Gorge on Historic Columbia River Hwy. and I–84, 30 mi east of Troutdale on I–84.

In pioneer days, boats needing to pass the bedeviling rapids near the town of Whiskey Flats had to portage around them. The locks that gave the town its new name were completed in 1896, allowing waterborne passage for the first time. In 1938 they were submerged beneath the new Lake Bonneville when the Bonneville Lock and Dam became one of the most massive Corps of Engineers projects to come out of the New Deal. The town of Cascade Locks hung on to its name, though. A historic stern wheeler still leads excursions from the town's port district, and the region's Native American tribes still practice traditional dip-net fishing near the current locks.

GETTING HERE

Reach Cascade Locks heading 45 mi east of Portland on I–84. If you're planning to come and go from Stevenson, Washington, carry cash for the $1 toll on the gorge-spanning Bridge of the Gods. The closest airport is Portland International, 40 mi east.

VISITOR INFORMATION

West Columbia Gorge Chamber of Commerce (⊠ *226 W. Historic Columbia River Hwy., Troutdale* ☎ *503/669–7473* ⊕ *www.westcolumbiagorge chamber.com*).

EXPLORING

Ⓒ **Bonneville Dam.** This is the first federal dam to span the Columbia, and was dedicated by President Franklin D. Roosevelt in 1937. Its generators (visible from a balcony during self-guided powerhouse tours) have a capacity of more than a million kilowatts, enough to supply power to more than 200,000 single-family homes. There is a modern visitor center on Bradford Island, complete with underwater windows where

Dog Mountain Trail, Columbia River Gorge National Scenic Area

gaggles of kids watch migrating salmon and steelhead as they struggle up fish ladders. The best viewing times are between April and October. In recent years the dwindling runs of wild Columbia salmon have made the dam a subject of much environmental controversy. ✉ *Bonneville Lock and Dam, U.S. Army Corps of Engineers, from I–84 take Exit 40, head northeast, and follow signs 1 mi to visitor center* ⊕ *www. nwp.usace.army.mil/op/b/home.asp* ☎ *541/374–8820* 🖾 *Free* ⊙ *Visitor center daily 9–5.*

🐾 **Bonneville Fish Hatchery.** Below Bonneville Dam, ponds teem with fingerling salmon, fat rainbow trout, and 6-foot-long sturgeon. The hatchery raises chinook and coho salmon; from mid-October to late November you can watch as staff members spawn the fish, beginning a new hatching cycle, or feed the trout with food pellets from a coin-operated machine. ✉ *70543 NE Herman Loop* ☎ *541/374–8393* 🖾 *Free* ⊙ *7:30–5 winter, 7:30–8 summer.*

Cascade Locks. This is the home port of the 600-passenger stern-wheeler *Columbia Gorge*, which churns upriver, then back again, on two-hour excursions through some of the Columbia River Gorge's most impressive scenery, mid-June to early October. The ship's captain will talk about the gorge's fascinating 40-million-year geology and about pioneering spirits and legends, such as Lewis and Clark, who once triumphed over this very same river. Group bookings and private rentals are available. ✉ *Cruises leave from Marine Park in Cascade Locks. Marine Park, 355 Wanapa St.* ☎ *541/224–3900 or 800/224–3901* ⊕ *www.portlandspirit.com* ✍ *Reservations essential* 🖾 *Prices vary* ⊙ *May–Oct.* ⊟ *AE, D, DC, MC, V.*

WHERE TO EAT

$ ✕ **Pacific Crest Pub.** A woodsy tavern with cedar-shake walls, historical
AMERICAN photos, and a stone fireplace provides hearty servings of starters, salads, and main courses, including on-site-smoked salmon chowder and oven-roasted chicken accompanied by house-specialty, sinus-destroying horseradish. If you like feta cheese with your pizzas, try the house favorite, the Greek "Pizza of the Gods." During warmer months, sit outside in the adjacent courtyard and take in mountain and river views while sipping one of a dozen or so featured microbrews, including Full Sail and Walking Man. ✉ *500 Wanapa St.* ☎ *541/374–9310* ▭ *D, MC, V* ⊙ *Closed Mon.*

SPORTS AND THE OUTDOORS

HIKING **Pacific Crest Trail.** Cascade Locks bustles with grubby thru-hikers refueling along the 2,650-mi Canada-to-Mexico Pacific Crest Trail. Check out a scenic and strenuous portion of it, heading south from the trailhead at Herman Creek Horse Camp, just east of town. The route heads up into the Cascades, showing off monster views of the gorge. Backpackers out for a longer trip will find idyllic campsites at Wahtum Lake, 14 mi south. ✉ *1 mi east of Cascade Locks off NW Forest Ln.* ☎ *541/308–1700* ⊕ *www.pcta.org.*

5

STEVENSON, WASHINGTON

Across the river from Cascade Locks via the Bridge of the Gods and 4 mi east on Hwy. 14.

So it's not quite Oregon, but with the Bridge of the Gods toll bridge spanning the Columbia River above the Bonneville Dam, Stevenson acts as a "twin city" to Cascade Locks. Tribal legends and the geologic record tell of the original Bridge of the Gods, a substantial landslide that occurred here sometime between AD 1000 and 1760, briefly linking the two sides of the gorge before the river swept away the debris. The landslide's steel namesake now leads to tiny Stevenson, where vacationers traverse the quiet Main Street, planning excursions to nearby Mt. Adams or Mt. St. Helens. Washington's Highway 14 runs through the middle of town, and since the cliffs on the Oregon side are more dramatic, driving this two-lane highway actually offers better views.

GETTING HERE

To get to Stevenson from the Oregon side of the gorge, cross the Columbia River at the Bridge of the Gods. Bring cash for the $1 toll. Stevenson proper is a mi east on Highway 14. The closest airport is Portland International, 43 mi east on the Oregon side of the river.

VISITOR INFORMATION

Skamania County Chamber of Commerce (✉ *167 NW Second Ave., Stevenson, WA* ☎ *509/427–8911* ⊕ *www.skamania.org*).

EXPLORING

Bridge of the Gods. For a magnificent vista 135 feet above the Columbia, as well as a speedy route between Oregon and Washington, $1 will pay your way over the grandly named bridge. Here also, hikers cross from Oregon to reach the Washington segment of the **Pacific Crest Trail,**

which picks up just west of the bridge. ⊕ *www.portofcascadelocks. org/bridge.htm.*

Ⓒ **Columbia Gorge Interpretive Center Museum.** A petroglyph whose eyes seem to look straight at you, "She Who Watches" or "Tsagaglalal" is the logo for this museum. Sitting among the dramatic basaltic cliffs on the north bank of the Columbia River Gorge, the museum explores the life of the gorge: its history, culture, architecture, legends, and much more. The younger crowd may enjoy the reenactment of the gorge's formation in the Creation Theatre. Or a 37-foot high fishwheel from the 19th century. Historians will appreciate studying the water route of the Lewis & Clark Expedition. There's also an eye-opening exhibit that examines current environmental impacts on the area. ⊠ *990 SW Rock Creek Dr., Stevenson, WA ✚ 1 mi east of Bridge of the Gods on Hwy. 14* ☎ *509/427–8211 or 800/991–2338* ⊕ *www.columbiagorge. org* ⊠ *$7* ☉ *Daily 10–5.*

NEED A BREAK? **Bahma Coffee Bar.** Funky and fun, '60s Haight-Ashbury meets Native American art, at *the* place in Stevenson for Wi-Fi (with purchase) and, of course, coffee. Or choose from grilled panini sandwiches, soups, fresh carrot juice, wine, sake, tea, and tasty homemade pastries. ⊠ *256 SW 2nd St., Hwy. 14* ☎ *509/427–8700* ⊕ *www.bahmacoffee.com* ☉ *Daily 7:30–4* ⊟ *MC, V.*

WHERE TO EAT AND STAY

$$$
NEW AMERICAN
✕ **The Cascade Room at Skamania Lodge.** Gaze at the perfect fusion of sky, river, and cliff scapes through the Cascade Room's expansive windows during an exquisite dining experience. Alder-plank potlatch salmon and oat-crusted trout stuffed with Northwest potatoes and herbs are signature dishes; also try the garlic sizzling shrimp and sautéed forest mushrooms. Melt-in-your-mouth chocolate soufflé and fresh mixed-berry cobbler are grand finales. Breakfast specialties include hazelnut pancakes and fresh berry crepes. A champagne brunch is offered on Sunday, and the seafood, salads, sushi, and pastas draw patrons from miles around. ⊠ *Skamania Lodge, 1131 SW Skamania Lodge Way* ☎ *509/427–7700* ⊟ *AE, D, DC, MC, V.*

$$$
AMERICAN
✕ **Pacific Crest Dining Room.** After a rejuvenating spa treatment or hike, the fresh healthy cuisine is a special treat. You can dine in the low light of the muted main room (metal pine-tree light fixtures are custom made) or in the adjoining lounge, its 12-foot high glass wall overlooking the manicured courtyard and the forest beyond. The pastry chef works through the night, ensuring fresh-baked breads and pastries by sunrise. Healthy never tasted so good, with crisp salads, Pacific Northwest fish (amazing ahi tuna!), Cascade-area beef, and gourmet vegetarian fare. Late afternoons, the lounge serves goodies such as hazelnut-crusted Brie and Walking Man beer-battered halibut and chips. ⊠ *Bonneville Hot Springs Resort, 1252 E. Cascade Dr., North Bonneville, WA* ☎ *509/427–9711* ⊕ *www.bonnevilleresort.com* ⊟ *AE, D, MC, V.*

$$$
🛏 **Bonneville Hot Springs Resort and Spa.** Enter an architectural wonderland of wood, iron, rock, and water, water everywhere. Owner Pete Cam and his sons built the resort to share their love of these historic mineral springs with the public, especially those seeking physical renewal. The

three-story lobby, with its suspended black iron trestle, Paul Bunyan-size river-rock fireplace, and floor-to-ceiling arched windows, is magnificent to behold. The unique redwood-paneled, 25-meter indoor lap pool is adjacent to an immaculate European spa, offering over 40 candlelit treatments (mineral baths, body wraps, massages). Rooms are spacious, with upscale furnishings. **Pros:** glorious grounds; impressive architectural detail; attentive and knowledgeable spa staff; the Pacific Crest Trail passes directly through the property. **Cons:** must reserve spa appointments separately from room reservations; the dull, boxy exterior belies what's inside. ✉ *1252 E. Cascade Dr., North Bonneville, WA* ☎ *509/427–7767 or 866/459–1678* ⊕ *www.bonnevilleresort.com* ⤴ *78 rooms* ♿ *In-room: a/c, Wi-Fi. In-hotel: restaurant, bar, pool, spa, parking (free)* ☰ *AE, D, MC, V.*

$$ ☖ **Skamania Lodge.** *Skamania*, the Chinook word for "swift water," ♻ overlooks exactly that with its 175 acres sitting to the north of the Columbia River Gorge. So big you need a map to get around, the Lodge impresses with Montana slate tiling, Native American artwork, an immense word-burning fireplace, and a multitude of windows that take in the surrounding forests and the gorge. Think of a modern conference hotel spliced with a national park lodge. Outstanding recreational facilities include an 18-hole, par-70 golf course, 3 winding hiking trails, a large indoor pool, and even a sand volleyball court. The accommodating staff will pack you a box lunch if you're going out to explore for the day. **Pros:** addresses the active guest as well as the kids; U.S. Forest Service has a kiosk in the lobby; well-suited to handle large events, conferences, weddings. **Cons:** costs can quickly multiply for a large family; can get crowded; sometimes there's a wait for table seating in the dining room. ✉ *1131 SW Skamania Lodge Way* ☎ *509/427–7700 or 800/221–7117* ⊕ *www.skamania.com* ⤴ *254 rooms* ♿ *In-room: a/c, Wi-Fi. In-hotel: restaurants, bars, golf course, tennis courts, pool, gym, spa, bicycles, Wi-Fi hotspot, parking (free), some pets allowed* ☰ *AE, D, DC, MC, V.*

NIGHTLIFE AND THE ARTS

Walking Man Brewing. Locals and tourists alike crowd this cozy brewery's sunshiny patio for creative pizzas and a dozen craft ales. After a couple of pints of the strong Homo Erectus IPA and Knuckle Dragger Pale Ale, you may go a little ape. The house country-rock band plays every Sunday night. ✉ *240 SW 1st St.* ☎ *509/427–5520* ⊕ *www.walkingmanbrewing.com* ⊗ *Closed Mon.–Tues.* ☰ *MC, V.*

SPORTS AND THE OUTDOORS

RECREATIONAL AREA **Beacon Rock State Park.** For several hundred years this 848-foot rock was a landmark for river travelers, including Native Americans, who recognized this point as the last rapids of the Columbia River. Lewis and Clark are thought to have been the first white men to see the volcanic remnant. Picnic atop old lava flows after hiking a 1-mi trail, steep but safe, which leads to tremendous views of the Columbia Gorge and the river. A round-trip hike takes 45–60 minutes. ✉ *Off Hwy. 14, 7 mi west of Bridge of the Gods, North Bonneville, WA* ☎ *509/427–8265 or 360/902–8844* ⊕ *www.parks.wa.gov* ☰ *Day use free.*

GOLF **Skamania Lodge Golf Course.** Several holes on the resort's forested, par-70
ⓒ course offer knockout views of the Columbia River Gorge, and there's
a full pro shop chock-full of Nike gear. On Sunday and Tuesday evenings, families can play on a scaled-down nine-hole course aimed at
wee-golfers, with free club rentals for kids. ⊠ *Skamania Lodge, 1131
SW Skamania Lodge Way* ☎ *509/427–2548 or 800/293–0418* ⊕ *www.
skamania.com* ▣ *Summer greens fees $85 full day, $55 after 3* PM*; off-
season rates vary month to month. Bigfoot family golf $25 for adults,
free for children* ▤ *AE, D, DC, MC, V.*

HOOD RIVER

17 mi east of Cascade Locks on I–84.

For years, the incessant easterly winds blowing through the town of
Hood River were nothing more than a nuisance. Then somebody bolted
a sail to a surfboard, waded into the fat part of the gorge, and a new
recreational craze was born. A fortuitous combination of factors—
mainly the reliable gale-force winds blowing against the current—has
made Hood River the self-proclaimed windsurfing capital of the world.
Especially in summer, this once-somnolent town swarms with colorful
"boardheads" from as far away as Europe and Australia.

Hood River's rich pioneer past is reflected in its downtown historic
district. The City of Hood River publishes a free self-guided walking
tour (available through the city government office or the Hood River
Chamber of Commerce) that will take you on a tour of more than 40
civic and commercial buildings dating from 1893 to the 1930s, some of
which are listed in the National Register of Historic Places.

GETTING HERE

Reach Hood River by driving 60 mi east of Portland on I-84, or if you're
coming from Mt. Hood, by heading north on Highway 35. The closest
airport is in Portland.

VISITOR INFORMATION

Hood River County Chamber of Commerce (⊠ *405 Portway Ave.* ☎ *541/386–
2000 or 800/366–3530* ⊕ *www.hoodriver.org*).

EXPLORING

Western Antique Aeroplane and Automobile Museum. Housed at Hood
River's tiny airport (general aviation only), the museum's meticulously
restored, propeller-driven planes are all still in flying condition. The
antique steam cars, Model Ts, and sleek Depression-era sedans are
road-worthy, too. Periodic car shows and an annual fly-in draw thousands of history nerds and spectators. ⊠ *1600 Museum Rd., off Hwy.
281, 2½ mi south of town* ☎ *541/308–1600* ⊕ *www.waamuseum.org*
▣ *$12* ⊙ *Daily 9–5.*

Fruit Loop. Either by car or bicycle, tour the quiet country highways of
Hood River Valley, whose vast orchards surround the river. You'll see
apples, pears, cherries, and peaches fertilized by volcanic soil, pure
glacier water, and a conducive harvesting climate. Along the 35 mi of
farms are a host of outlets for delicious baked goods, wines, flowers,
and nuts. Festive farm activities from April to November also give a

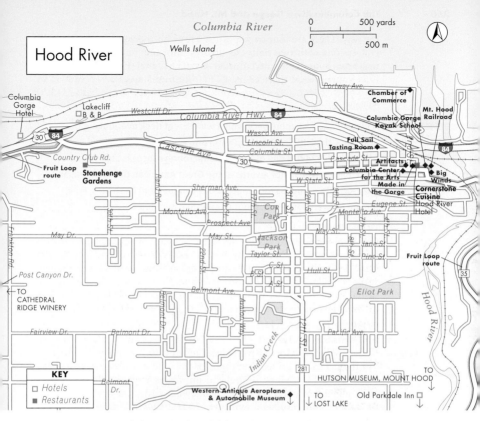

taste of the agricultural life. While on the loop, consider stopping at the town of **Parkdale** to lunch, shop, and snap a photo of Mt. Hood's north face. ⊠ *Rte. begins on Hwy. 35* ⊕ *www.hoodriverfruitloop.com.*

Hutson Museum. Situated on a 2-acre National Historic Site, exhibits feature Native American dolls, taxidermy, and a rare rock collection, which includes thousands of rough specimens, polished slabs, spheres, and eggs. More than 2,500 arrow and spear points, stone bowls, mortars, grinding tools, and specialized tools are prized for their regional geological and historical value. The Mt. Hood excursion train terminates at the museum. ⊠ *4967 Baseline Dr., Parkdale* ☎ *541/352–6808* 💷 *$1* ⊘ *Apr.–Oct.*

OFF THE
BEATEN
PATH

Lost Lake. One of the most-photographed sights in the Pacific Northwest, this lake's waters reflect towering Mt. Hood and the thick forests that line its shore. Cabins are available for overnight stays, and because no motorboats are allowed on Lost Lake, the area is blissfully quiet. ⊠ *Lost Lake Rd., take Hood River Hwy. south to town of Dee* ☎ *541/352–6002* 💷 *Day use $7.*

Mt. Hood Railroad. An efficient and relaxing way to survey Mt. Hood and the Hood River, this passenger and freight line was established in 1906. Chug alongside the Hood River through vast fruit orchards before climbing up steep forested canyons, glimpsing Mt. Hood along the way. There are four trip options: a four-hour excursion (serves light concessions with two daily departures, morning and afternoon), dinner, brunch, and a themed murder-mystery dinner. Exceptional service is as impressive as the scenery. ⊠ *110 Railroad Ave.* ☎ *541/386–3556 or 800/872–4661* ⊕ *www.mthoodrr.com* ⊟ *AE, D, V* ⎘ *$25–$70* ☾ *Apr.–Dec.*

NEED A BREAK?

A glass-walled microbrewery with a windswept deck overlooking the Columbia, the **Full Sail Tasting Room and Pub** (⊠ *506 Columbia St.* ☎ *541/386–2247*) is one of the great microbrew success stories in the West, having won major awards at the Great American Beer Festival and the World Beer Cup. Savory snack foods complement fresh ales. Free, on-site brewery tours last about twenty-five minutes.

WINERIES

Cathedral Ridge Winery. This six-acre vineyard was awarded Oregon Winery of the Year in 2007 by *Wine Press Northwest*, and in 2010 the same authority called it one of the region's best wine-country picnic spots. Popular varietals include Riesling, Pinot Gris, and Syrah. The tasting room is open 11 to 5 daily. ⊠ *4200 Post Canyon Dr.* ☎ *800/516–8710* ⊕ *www.cathedralridgewinery.com* ⎘ *Free* ☾ *Daily 11–5.*

WHERE TO EAT AND STAY

$
NEW AMERICAN

✕ **Cornerstone Cuisine.** A tapas menu and a selection of small vegetable dishes make the Hood River Hotel restaurant a popular lunch stop. Try the sea-salted grilled asparagus or the wild mushrooms with garlic and thyme. Chef Mark Whitehead impresses with simple dishes and fresh ingredients, and the covered sidewalk patio lets you keep an eye on comings and goings downtown. ⊠ *102 Oak St.* ☎ *541/386–1900* ⊕ *www.hoodriverhotel.com* ⊟ *AE, D, MC, V.*

$$$
NEW AMERICAN
Fodor's Choice
★

✕ **Stonehedge Gardens.** It's not just the cuisine that's out of this world, Stonehedge is of another time and place, surrounding you with 7 acres of lush English gardens that gracefully frame its multitude of stone terraces and trickling fountains. There's a *petanque* (bowling game) court for quick predinner activity, and music on Wednesday nights draws a full house of locals and visitors. Each of the four dining rooms in the restored 1898 home has a distinct personality, from cozy to verdant to elegant, but the tiered patio is where summer diners gather. Classics like steak Diane and filet mignon appeal to more traditional diners, while buffalo-style prawns and curry shiitake mushroom soup show off the kitchen's creative side. Just when you think your meal is complete, along comes the Flaming Bread Pudding. This restaurant is a Columbia Gorge institution. ⊠ *3405 Cascade Ave.* ☎ *541/386–3940* ⊕ *www.stonehedgegardens.com* ⊟ *AE, D, MC, V* ☾ *No lunch.*

$$$

🛏 **Columbia Gorge Hotel.** One selling point of this grande dame of gorge hotels is the view of a 208-foot-high waterfall. Rooms with plenty of wood, brass, and antiques overlook the impeccably landscaped formal gardens. While watching the sun set on the Columbia River, dine in the hotel's restaurant; selections include quinoa-stuffed sweet onion or a worthy cioppino. **Pros:** historic structure built by Columbia Gorge Highway visionary Simon Benson; unbeatable gorge views. **Cons:**

smallish rooms reflect their historic character. ⊠ *4000 Westcliff Dr.* ☎ *541/386–5566 or 800/345–1921* ⊕ *www.columbiagorgehotel.com* ⟁ *39 rooms* ♿ *In room: a/c, Wi-Fi. In-hotel: restaurant, bar* ═ *AE, D, DC, MC, V.*

$ ⬚ **Hood River Hotel.** Another Hood River hospitality gem found on the National Register of Historic Places. The restored building has a grand, Old West façade with antique-heavy interiors that feel more like a European inn. **Pros:** excellent downtown location; several available adventure packages; historic vibe. **Cons:** smallish rooms; no king-size beds. ⊠ *102 Oak St.* ☎ *541/386–1900* ⊕ *www.hoodriverhotel.com* ⟁ *41 rooms* ♿ *In-room: a/c, Wi-Fi, kitchen (some). In-hotel: restaurant, bar, some pets allowed.* ═ *AE, D, DC, MC, V.*

$$ ⬚ **Lakecliff Bed & Breakfast.** Perched on a cliff overlooking the Columbia Gorge, this beautiful 1908 summer home has long been a favorite spot for weddings. Designed by architect A.E. Doyle (who also created the Multnomah Falls Lodge), this 3-acre magical land of ferns, fir trees, and water is a stunner. There's a deck at the back of the house, fireplaces and river views in three of the rooms, great artwork throughout, and top-notch service, including hot coffee right outside your door in the morning. "Large, spoiling breakfasts," says owner Allyson Pate, referring to her poached pears, blueberry pancakes, and butterscotch pecan rolls. For summer, make reservations as far ahead as possible. **Pros:** glorious views; friendly and accommodating hosts; convenient-to-town location with a remote feel. **Cons:** no king-size beds; Wi-Fi in living room only, and a bit spotty. ⊠ *3820 Westcliff Dr.* ☎ *541/386–7000* ⊕ *www.lakecliffbnb.com* ⟁ *4 rooms* ♿ *In-room: no phone, no TV, no a/c. In-hotel: Wi-Fi.* ═ *MC, V.*

$ ⬚ **Old Parkdale Inn.** Tiny Parkdale is found along the Hood River Fruit Loop, and makes a fine base camp for tackling Hood River and Mt. Hood. This homey inn has queen beds and private baths in three rooms named for impressionist painters, plus a nice front porch looking out onto the town's quiet Main Street. Raid the attic for a trove of rainy-day books, puzzles, and games. **Pros:** beautiful gardens on-site; local/organic emphasis on breakfast ingredients; natural/organic linens. **Cons:** a bit removed from the amenities of Hood River. ⊠ *4932 Baseline Dr., Parkdale* ☎ *541/352–5551* ⊕ *www.hoodriverlodging.com* ⟁ *3 rooms* ♿ *In-room: DVD, Wi-Fi.* ═ *MC, V.*

NIGHTLIFE AND THE ARTS

☉ **Columbia Center for the Arts.** Half art museum, half theater, the center is home to professional and novice artists alike, both visual and theatrical. The successful blend of the decades-old Columbia Arts Stage Troupe (CAST) and the Columbia Art Galley happened by coincidence, when both realized they were looking for a home in 2003. Combining their efforts and fundraising, they renovated a 10,000-square-foot American Legion Hall and opened as one in 2005, calling themselves the Columbia Center for the Arts. ⊠ *215 Cascade Ave.* ☎ *541/387–8877* ⊕ *www.columbiaarts.org* ☉ *Gallery hrs Wed.–Sun. 11–5 and by appointment.*

WORD OF MOUTH

"The Hood River area win-
eries are all pretty close
together. You could hit them
all. However, there are many
more nearby. I suggest
checking out a wine tour like
this: www.hoodrivertours.
com/winetours." –LittleA

SHOPPING

Artifacts. "Good books and bad art" advertises this funky bookstore just off the downtown strip, and it doesn't disappoint. You'll find all the current bestsellers here, but the store also carries several shelves worth of DIY zines and anarcho-greenie manuals. A sizable segment of the shop is devoted to ironic novelty items, and the art is indeed paralyzingly bad. For a few dollars you can pick up a velvet Elvis or somebody's failed, conceptual-art school thesis. ⊠ *202 Cascade Ave.* ☎ *541/387–2482* ▭ *MC, V.*

Made in the Gorge. A downtown artists' co-op staffed by the artists themselves, Made in the Gorge is big on pottery, jewelry, and textile art. The hours are 10 to 7, but it's not uncommon to find a sign on the door when the artists have stepped out. ⊠ *108 Oak St.* ☎ *541/386–2830* ⊕ *www.madeinthegorge.com* ▭ *AE, D, MC, V.*

SPORTS AND THE OUTDOORS

⇨ *See the Adventures feature for more options.*

KAYAKING **Columbia Gorge Kayak School.** Whether you want to practice your Eskimo roll in the safety of a pool, run the Klickitat River in an inflatable kayak, or take a mellow midnight paddle, the gorge's premier kayak guides can arrange the trip. Book online, by phone, or at the Kayak Shed downtown. ⊠ *6 Oak St.* ☎ *541/806–4190* ⊕ *www.gorgekayaker.com* ⊠ *Lessons $40, flatwater and whitewater trips $60–$220 .*

WINDSURFING **Big Winds.** The retail hub for Hood River's windsurfing and kiteboarding culture also rents gear and provides windsurfing lessons for beginners. ⊠ *207 Front St.* ☎ *541/386–6086* ⊕ *www.bigwinds.com* ⊠ *Lessons and clinics $65–$250* ▭ *AE, D, MC, V .*

THE DALLES

20 mi east of Hood River on I–84.

The Dalles lies on a crescent bend of the Columbia River where it narrows and once spilled over a series of rapids, creating a flagstone effect. French voyagers christened it *dalle,* or "flagstone." The Dalles is the seat of Wasco County and the trading hub of north central Oregon. It gained fame early in the region's history as the town where the Oregon Trail branched, with some pioneers departing to travel over Mt. Hood on Barlow Road and the others continuing down the Columbia River. This may account for the small-town, Old West feeling that still permeates the area. Several historic Oregon moments as they relate to The Dalles' past are magnificently illustrated on eight murals painted by renowned Northwest artists, located downtown within short walking distance of one another.

GETTING HERE

The Dalles is best reached by car, 84 mi east of Portland or 126 mi west of Pendleton on I–84. The closest airport is Portland International.

VISITOR INFORMATION

The Dalles Area Chamber of Commerce (⊠ *404 W. 2nd St.* ☎ *541/296–2231* ⊕ *www.thedalleschamber.org*).

EXPLORING

♻ **Columbia Gorge Discovery Center–Wasco County Historical Museum.** Exhibits highlight the geological history of the Columbia Gorge, back 40 million years when volcanoes, landslides, and floods carved out the area. The museum focuses on 10,000 years of Native American life and exploration of the region by white settlers. ⊠ *5000 Discovery Dr.* ☎ *541/296–8600* ⊕ *www.gorgediscovery.org* ⊠ *$8* ☉ *Daily 9–5.*

The Dalles Lock and Dam. At this hydroelectric dam east of the Bonneville Dam, you can tour a visitor center with a surprisingly even-handed exhibit on differing views of Colombia River dams, with input from farmers, utility companies, environmentalists, and indigenous tribes. There's also a surreal live feed of salmon and sturgeon scaling the fish ladder. Call ahead for tours offered most weekends, photo ID required. ⊠ *Exit 87 (in summer) or Exit 88 other times off I–84, 2 mi east of The Dalles at Lake Celilo* ☎ *541/296–1181* ⊕ *www.nwp.usace.army.mil/op/d/thedalles.asp* ⊠ *Free* ☉ *Varied hrs throughout the year.*

Fort Dalles Museum. The 1856-vintage Fort Dalles Surgeon's Quarters is the site of the oldest history museum in Oregon. The museum's first visitors came through the doors in 1905. On display in authentic hand-hewn log buildings, originally part of a military base, are the personal effects of some of the region's settlers and a collection of early automobiles. The entrance fee gains you admission to the **Anderson Homestead** museum across the street, which also has pioneer artifacts. ⊠ *500 W. 15th St., at Garrison* ☎ *541/296–4547* ⊕ *www.fortdallesmuseum.org* ⊠ *$5* ☉ *Daily 10–4. Closed Nov.–Mar.*

Old St. Peter's Landmark. Built in 1897, this Gothic brick church has brilliant stained glass, hand-carved pews, marble altars, and an immense pipe organ. Steamboat captains once used the 176-foot steeple as a navigational benchmark. The landmark now functions as a nondenominational, nonprofit organization that is available for tours, weddings, and other private functions. ⊠ *3rd and Lincoln Sts.* ☎ *541/296–5686* ⊕ *www.oldstpeterslandmark.org* ⊠ *Free, donation suggested* ☉ *Feb.–Dec., Tues.–Fri. 11–3, weekends 1–3.*

WHERE TO EAT

$ ✕ **Baldwin Saloon.** The walls of this historic watering hole-turned-hip restaurant are a weirdly authentic mix of landscape art and early American oil-painting erotica. The immense menu likewise runs the gamut from pastas to seafood to burgers. Stop in at lunch for a bowl of the popular bouillabaisse, and make weekend reservations for a dinner set to music from the saloon's 1894 mahogany Schubert piano. ⊠ *205 Court St.* ☎ *541/296–5666* ⊕ *www.baldwinsaloon.com* ☉ *Closed Sun.* ⊟ *AE, D, MC, V.*

AMERICAN

$ ✕ **Petite Provence.** This popular downtown bistro/bakery/dessertery serves eggs, crepes, and croissants for breakfast; hot and cold sandwiches and salads for lunch, and fresh-baked pastries and breads (you can take a loaf home). The sparkling display case tempts with a goodly selection of napoleons, éclairs, tarts, mousses. ⊠ *408 E. 2nd St.* ☎ *541/506–0037* ⊕ *www.provence-portland.com* ⊟ *AE, MC, V.*

CAFÉ

5

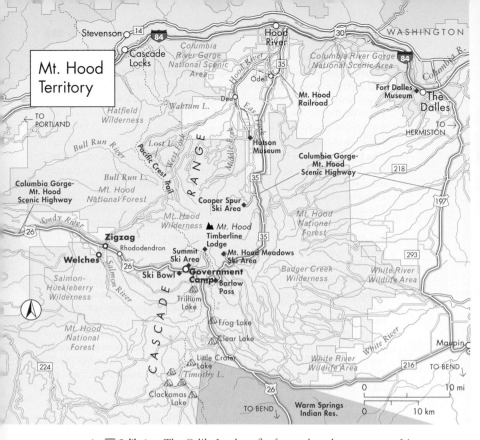

$
Fodor'sChoice
★

Celilo Inn. The Celilo Inn benefits from a knockout concept: It's a prototypical motor lodge gone high-design, with exterior-entry rooms and a '50s light-up motel sign that disguise the hotel's slick, boutique feel. The view doesn't hurt either, as Celilo is located on a high hill overlooking the Columbia, The Dalles Dam, and if you're in the right room, Mt. Hood. Flat-screen TVs, pillow-top mattresses, and smart decorating come standard, and the outdoor pool is mighty inviting during The Dalles' dry summers. **Pros:** sexy design; specializes in wine tours; bottles available on-site; complimentary espresso machine in lobby. **Cons:** not all rooms have views; those on the hotel's far end feel miles away from the front desk. ⊠ *3550 E. 2nd St.* ☎ *541/769–0001* ⊕ *www.celiloinn. com* ↝ *46 rooms* ⚬ *In-room: Wi-Fi. In hotel: gym, pool.* ▭ *AE, D, MC, V. Credit cards only.*

NIGHTLIFE AND THE ARTS

Rivertap Pub. Regional beers and wines are showcased at this hipster hangout with a feel like a friend's cool garage lair. Cocktails are also available, including the rare tap margarita, and the small menu appeals to a drinking crowd with nachos, hot wings, and fish tacos. Live music on Wednesday nights draws a crowd of slick young professionals. ⊠ *703 E. 2nd St.* ☎ *541/760–0059* ⊕ *www.rivertabpub.com* ☉ *Sun.–Thurs. 4–10, Sat.–Sun. noon–midnight* ▭ *AE, D, MC, V.*

SPORTS AND THE OUTDOORS

RECREATIONAL
AREAS

Celilo Park. Named for the falls that challenged spawning salmon here in the predam days, this favorite spot for windsurfers also has swimming, sailboarding, and fishing. It's 7 mi east of The Dalles. ⊠ *Exit 99 off I–84* ☎ *541/296–1181* ◫ *Free* ☉ *Daily.*

Mayer State Park. Views from atop the park's Rowena Crest bluff are knockout, especially during the March and April wildflower season. Recreational activities include swimming, boating, fishing, and picnicking. ⊠ *Exit 77 off I–84* ☎ *800/551–6949* ⊕ *www.prd.state.or.us* ◫ *Day use $5 per vehicle* ☉ *Daily.*

MT. HOOD

The Multnomah tribe call Mt. Hood "Wy'East," named, according to popular legend, for a jealous lover who once sparred over a woman with his rival, Klickitat. When their fighting caught the Great Spirit's attention, Wy'East and Klickitat were transformed into two angry, smoke-bellowing mountains—one became Washington's Mt. Adams, the other became Mt. Hood. Wy'East has mellowed out a bit since then, but the mountain is still technically an active volcano, and it's had very minor, lava-free eruptive events as recently as the mid-1800s. Today Mt. Hood is better known for the challenge it poses to climbers, its deep winter snows, and a dozen glaciers and snowfields that make skiing possible almost year-round. Resort towns and colorful hospitality villages are arranged in a semicircle around the mountain, full of ski bars and rental cabins that host hordes of fun-loving Portlanders each weekend. In every direction from the postcard-perfect peak, the million-acre Mt. Hood National Forest spreads out like a big green blanket, and 300,000 acres of that are designated wilderness. Mule deer, black bears, elk, and the occasional cougar share the space with humans who come to hike, camp, and fish in the Pacific Northwest's quintessential wild ecosystem.

AROUND THE MOUNTAIN

About 60 mi east of Portland on I–84 and U.S. 26, 65 mi from The Dalles, west on I–84 and south on Hwy. 35 and U.S. 26.

Majestically towering 11,245 feet above sea level, Mt. Hood is what remains of the original north wall and rim of a volatile crater. Although the peak no longer spews ash or fire, active steam vents can be spotted high on the mountain. The mountain took its modern moniker in 1792, when a crew of the British Royal Navy, the first recorded Caucasians sailing up the Columbia River, spotted it and named it after a famed British naval officer by the name of–you guessed it–Hood.

Mt. Hood offers the only year-round skiing in the lower 48 states, with three major ski areas and some 30 lifts, as well as extensive areas for cross-country skiing and snowboarding. Many of the ski runs turn into mountain-bike trails in summer. The mountain is also popular with climbers and hikers. In fact, some hikes follow parts of the Oregon Trail, and signs of the pioneers' passing are still evident.

GETTING HERE

From Portland, U.S. 26 heads west into the heart of Mt. Hood National Forest, while Highway 35 runs south from Hood River along the mountain's east face. The roads meet 60 mi east of Portland, near Government Camp, forming an oblong loop with I–84 and the Historic Columbia Gorge Highway. The closest airport is Portland International, 53 mi northwest of Government Camp. Ski resorts like Mt. Hood Skibowl and Mt. Hood Meadows offer Portland shuttles in season; call for timetables and pick-up and drop-off sites.

VISITOR INFORMATION

Mt. Hood Area Chamber of Commerce (✉ *24403 E. Welches Rd., Welches* ☎ *503/622–3017* ⊕ *www.mthood.org*). **Mt. Hood National Forest Headquarters** (✉ *16400 Champion Way, Sandy* ☎ *503/668–1700* ⊕ *www. fs.fed.us/r6/mthood*).

WHERE TO EAT AND STAY

$$$$

NEW AMERICAN

✕ **Cascade Dining Room.** If the wall of windows isn't coated with snow, you may get a good look at some of the neighboring peaks. Vaulted wooden beams and a wood-plank floor, handcrafted furniture, handwoven drapes, and a lion-size stone fireplace set the scene. The atmosphere is historic, but new in 2010 is executive chef Jason Stoller Smith, a former wine-country wunderkind whose resume includes orchestrating a salmon bake at the White House. The dinner menu's local/organic emphasis embraces, for example, Oregon lamb with fig compote and rabbit pasta with root veggies, featuring hares raised at nearby Nicky Farms. The daily Farmers Market Brunch is itself worth the drive up to Timberline, highlighting different seasonal ingredients and purveyors each week, from Dungeness crab to local hazelnuts to Oregon cherries. Pick up a few culinary tips from the chef demonstrations. ✉ *Timberline Rd., Timberline* ☎ *503/272–3104* ⊕ *www.timberlinelodge.com* ⌫ *Reservations essential* ☰ D, MC, V.

$$$

Fodor's Choice

★

☺

🏨 **Timberline Lodge.** The approach to Timberline Lodge builds excitement, an unforgettable 6-mi ascent that circles Mt. Hood. Now you see it, now you don't: The mountain teases you the whole way up, then quite unexpectedly, the Lodge materializes out of the mist and you momentarily forget about the snow-capped peak. It's no wonder that Stanley Kubrick used shots of the Lodge's exterior for the film *The Shining*. Built to complement the size and majesty of Mt. Hood, the massive structure was erected from timber and rock donated by the forests of the mountain itself. From 1936 to 1937 more than 500 men and women toiled, forging metal for furniture and fixtures, sculpting old telephone poles into beams and banisters, weaving, looming, sawing. But for once, the historical artifacts are not displayed behind a glass wall—they are the chairs you sit on, the doors you walk through, the floors you step on. You don't need to be a guest to appreciate Timberline. Check with the Forest Service desk in the front lobby for daily tours in summer. Enjoy the restaurants, snow sports, and hiking paths, or relax by the massive fireplace in the "headhouse," with its 96-foot stone chimney. Also, take in the marvelously detailed 22-minute film (located on the lower level) to learn about the building's genesis–it'll help you appreciate Timberline all the more. **Pros:** a thrill to stay on the

Mt. Hood

mountain itself; great proximity to all snow activity; plush featherbeds; amazing architecture throughout; fun dining places. **Cons:** rooms are small; no air-conditioning in summer; prepare yourself for carloads of tourists. ✉ *Timberline* ☎ *503/231–5400 or 800/547–1406* ⊕ *www. timberlinelodge.com* ⤳ *70 rooms, 10 with shared baths* ⟡ *In-room: no a/c, no phone (some), no TV (some). In-hotel: restaurant, 2 bars, pool, gym, parking (free), Wi-Fi hotspot.* ▭ *D, MC, V.*

SPORTS AND THE OUTDOORS
⇨ *See the Adventures feature for more options.*

Mt. Hood National Forest. The highest mountain in Oregon and the fourth-highest peak in the Cascades, "the Mountain" is a focal point of the 1.1-million-acre park, an all-season playground attracting more than 7 million visitors annually. Twenty miles southeast of Portland, it extends south from the Columbia River Gorge for more than 60 mi and includes 189,200 acres of designated wilderness. These woods are perfect for hikers, horseback riders, mountain climbers, and cyclists. Within the forest are more than 80 campgrounds and 50 lakes stocked with brown, rainbow, cutthroat, brook, and steelhead trout. The Sandy, Salmon, and other rivers are known for their fishing, rafting, canoeing, and swimming. Both forest and mountain are crossed by an extensive trail system for hikers, cyclists, and horseback riders. The **Pacific Crest Trail**, which begins in British Columbia and ends in Mexico, crosses at the 4,157-foot-high Barlow Pass. As with most other mountain destinations within Oregon, weather can be temperamental, and snow and ice may affect driving conditions as early as October and as late as June. Bring tire chains and warm clothes as a precaution.

Since this forest is close to the Portland metro area, campgrounds and trails are potentially crowded over the summer months, especially on weekends. If you're planning to camp, get info and permits from the **Mt. Hood National Forest Headquarters.** The National Forest manages more than 80 campgrounds in the area, including a string of neighboring campgrounds that rest on the south side of Mt. Hood: Trillium Lake, Still Creek, Timothy Lake, Little Crater Lake, Clackamas Lake, Summit Lake, Clear Lake, and Frog Lake. Each varies in what it offers and in price. The mountain is overflowing with day-use areas, and passes can be obtained for $5 to $7. There are also Mt. Hood National Forest maps with details about well-marked trails. From mid-November through April, all designated Winter Recreation Areas require a Sno-Park permit (*Single day $7, three-day permit $ 10, season $20*), available from the Forest Service and many local resorts and sporting goods stores.

GOVERNMENT CAMP

45 mi from The Dalles, south on Hwy. 35 and west on U.S. 26, 54 mi east of Portland on I–84 and U.S. 26.

Government Camp is an alpine resort village with a bohemian vibe and a fair number of hotels and restaurants. A bonanza of ski and mountain-biking trails converge at "Govy," and it's a convenient drive to Welches, which also has restaurants and lodging. Several of Mt. Hood's five ski resorts are just outside town, and the rest are a convenient drive away.

WHERE TO EAT AND STAY

¢
AMERICAN
✕ **Charlie's Mountain View.** Old and new ski swag plasters the walls, lift chairs function as furniture, and photos of famous (and locally famous) skiers and other memorabilia are as abundant as the menu selections. Open flame–grilled steaks and hamburgers are worthy here, and house specialties include creamy mushroom soup and chicken Caesar salad with dressing made from scratch. When they're in season, try the apple dumplings. Charlie's is a local institution for powder hounds, and the fun, divey bar in back stays busy with ski bums and other lively degenerates. Live music packs them in on Saturday nights from 9 to 1 AM. ✉ *88462 E. Government Camp Loop* ☎ *503/272–3333* ⊕ *www.charliesmountainview.com* ▭ *AE, D, MC, V.*

¢
AMERICAN
✕ **Huckleberry Inn.** Whether it's 2 AM or 2 PM, Huckleberry Inn welcomes you 24 hours a day with soups, milk shakes, burgers, sandwiches, and omelets. Well-known treats are made with huckleberries, and include pie, pancakes, tea, jelly, and vinaigrette salad dressing. ✉ *88611 E. Government Camp Loop* ☎ *503/272–3325* ⊕ *www.huckleberry-inn.com* ▭ *MC, V.*

$$
🏠 **Thunderhead Lodge.** Within walking distance of the Mt. Hood Ski Bowl (its night lights visible from your cabin), the condo units at the lodge are great jumping-off sites for many activities in the area: hiking, mountain biking, fishing, white-water rafting, and in winter, snow-boarding, sledding, and cross-county and downhill skiing. Room sizes and capacities vary according to your needs, and there's a rec room with foosball, a pool table, wet bar, and fireplace. A special treat: no

Continued on page 302

CHOOSE YOUR OWN ADVENTURE

Ride the wind, water, and snow—all in the same weekend and all within a 45-mile radius. In the Columbia River Gorge and Mt. Hood region, you can windsurf Hood River, white-water raft the glacially fed rivers that rush into the Columbia, or ski above timberline on Mt. Hood's austere Palmer Glacier, even in summer. Whatever your skill set, there's an adventure for you.

The windy, hip town of Hood River is anchored on one end by Mt. Hood, the state's highest mountain, and on the other by the Columbia River Gorge, an 80-mile-long and up to 4,000-foot-deep river canyon—the only sea-level route through the Cascade Mountain range. The Gorge is a unique wind corridor created by an opening in the Cascades. When the eastern Oregon desert heats up, cool wind is pulled into this cavity from the Pacific and Portland, turning Hood River into a playground for windsurfers and kite boarders.

When not riding wind, athletes head to the woods to spin on mountain bike trails near Post Canyon or Government Camp. On Mt. Hood, they ski the 11,242-foot glacial giant or hike the 92-mile base through forests thick with huckleberries, bear grass, and high-altitude wildflowers. It's one of the world's most oft-climbed mountains, second only to Mt. Fuji. Covered with snow year-round, it has 4,800 skiable acres and 8,300 vertical feet and is home to five ski resorts including Timberline, North America's only year-round ski destination.

by Jenie Skoy

Above, hiking up Munra Point in the Columbia River Gorge.

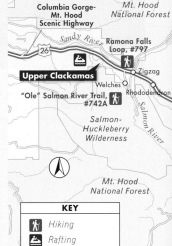

ADVENTURES AROUND THE COLUMBIA RIVER GORGE AND MT. HOOD

HIKING

The Columbia Gorge near Hood River is full of stunning waterfall hikes, while the area around Mt. Hood boasts superlative forest, lake, and high altitude paths. If you have time for just one hike, we recommend **Bald Mountain** from Top Spur Trailhead. You can tailor the hike to your skill level and time limit.

RAFTING

Three popular rafting rivers rule this area: the **Clackamas, the Deschutes,** and **the White Salmon.** Choose your route based on your skill level; the Deschutes is the most beginner friendly, the White Salmon the most intense.

WINDSPORTS

The Gorge has more than 30 launch areas for windsports. It's considered advanced terrain, but beginners can practice nearby in a protected cove called **the Hook.**

SKIING

Mt. Hood is a premier skiing destination, with resorts offering the country's largest night skiing course (**Mount Hood Ski Bowl**) and longest ski season (**Timberline**).

KEY

🏃	Hiking
🛶	Rafting
🏄	Windsports
⛷	Skiing
84	Scenic Highway

Top, a woman overlooks the Sandy Glacier from McNeil Point on Mt. Hood.

Bottom right, a hiker admires at Triple Falls in the Columbia River Gorge

Opposite left, Palmer Glacier, Mt. Hood, Timberline Lodge

Opposite right, rafting during the spring season.

Columbia River Gorge National Scenic Area

White Salmon River

Columbia River

White Salmon River

WASHINGTON

14

84

30

Hood River

Columbia Gorge-Mt. Hood Scenic Highway

35

Odell

Columbia River Gorge National Scenic Area

84

Columbia River

Columbia R.

Hood River

Mt. Hood Railroad

Dee

The Dalles

East Fork

TO HERMISTON

Wahtum L.

Lost L.

Parkdale

Middle Fork

Columbia Gorge-Mt. Hood Scenic Highway

218

197

West Fork

35

Pacific Crest Trail

Bull Run L.

Cooper Spur Trail, #600 B

Mt. Hood National Forest

CASCADE RANGE

Cooper Spur Ski Area

Mt. Hood Wilderness

Mt. Hood

Tamanawas Falls, Trail #650

Timberline Ski Area

Timberline Trail, #600

Timberline Lodge
Summit Ski Area

35

Government Camp

Mt. Hood Meadows Ski Area

Badger Creek Wilderness

White River Wildlife Area

Mirror Lake, Ski Bowl Trail #664

Trillium Lake, Trail #761

26

White River

Deschutes River

Timothy Lake, Trail #528

White River Wildlife Area

Maupin

Deschutes River

Timothy L.

26

216

Warm Springs Indian Res.

TO BEND

Bald Mountain

TO BEND

0   10 mi
0   10 km

HIKING

Hikers on trail bridge over Little North Santiam River in the Cascade Mountains.

The Columbia Gorge near Hood River is full of stunning waterfall hikes; on the other side of Mt. Hood trek through old growth forests, past lakes, and in high altitudes near the towns of Sandy, Welches, Zigzag, and Government Camp. For maps, visit **Mt. Hood National Forest Headquarters** in Sandy (☎ *503/668–1700*) or the **Zigzag Ranger Station** (☎ *503/622–3191* ⊕ *www.fs.fed. us/r6/mthood*), both on Highway 26. A NW Forest Pass for your vehicle is $5 per day; buy it at the Zigzag Ranger Station or at Zigzag Mountain Store (☎ *503/622–7681*) before you get to the trailhead.

OUTFITTERS

Cascade Huts (☎ 971/322–3638, ⊕ www.cascadehuts.com).
Julee's Gorge Tours and Guides (☎ 541/806–1075, ⊕ www.gorgetours.com).
Mt Hood Adventures (☎ 888/422–4776 ext. 5, ⊕ www.mthoodadventures.com).
Oregon Peak Adventures (☎ 877/965–5100, ⊕ www.oregonpeakadventures.com).

★ **Fodor's** Choice
BALD MOUNTAIN from Top Spur Trailhead
When to Go: August–October
Type: Alpine/Forest
Length: 2 mi to Bald Mountain Overlook; 11 mi to McNeil Point and the Muddy Fork of Sandy River
Duration: 1 hour; 4 hours if you make full hike
Difficulty: Moderate

Start with a breakfast of buttermilk pancakes and local berry compote at the **Zigzag Mountain Store** (☎ *503/622–7681*). Grab a map at the **Zigzag Ranger Station** (☎ *503/622–3191*) across the street, then set off on your way. Drive to the **Top Spur Trailhead,** which will take you to Bald Mountain. The trailhead is accessible via the Lolo Pass Road off Highway 26, a 12 mi drive from Zigzag.

The hike begins at the **Top Spur Cutoff Trail 765**. After climbing a half mile, you'll intersect the **Pacific Crest Trail 2000.** Follow this trail for a couple hundred feet to the right when you come to the intersection of four trails. Take the **Timberline Trail 600** to the immediate right of the large trail description sign.

TRAIL	When to Go	Type of Hike	Length	Duration	Difficulty
Trillium Lake, Trail #761* Hwy. 26, Milepost 56.7	Summer and Fall	Lake	2 mi	2 hours	Easy
"Ole" Salmon River Trail, #742 A Off Hwy. 26 to Welches	Year-round	Forest	5 mi	5 hours	Easy
Mirror Lake, Trail #664 Off Hwy. 26, 2 mi west of Government Camp	Summer and Fall	Lake	3 mi	3 hours	Easy to Moderate
Multnomah Falls, Trail #441 I-84, Exit 31	Summer and Fall	Waterfall	1.25 mi	1 hour	Easy to Moderate
Timothy Lake, Trail #528* Off Hwy. 26, on Skyline Rd. #42	Spring through Fall	Lake	14 mi	1–2 days	Moderate
Tamanawas Falls, Trail #650 Off Hwy. 35, 10 mi south of Parkdale	Summer and Fall	Waterfall	3.8 mi	4 hours	Moderate
Cooper Spur Trail, #600 B Hwy. 35 to the Cooper Spur Ski Area	Summer and Fall	Alpine (6,600 to 8,500 ft)	6.8 mi	1 day	Moderate to Difficult
Ramona Falls Loop, #797 Hwy. 26 to Zigzag, take the Lolo Pass	Spring through Fall	Alpine (2,500 to 3,500 ft)	7.5 mi	6 hours	Moderate to Difficult
Timberline Trail, #600 Timberline Lodge	Summer and Fall	Alpine (9,000 ft)	41 mi	3–5 days	Difficult

Bike Accessible

Follow Trail 600 for about 2/3 of a mile through forests of fir thick with huckleberries and thimbleberries. You'll also pass white, sun-facing avalanche lilies (that turn pink when pollinated by bees), Indian paintbrush, wild rhodies, clumps of bear grass, rare chocolate lilies (brown flowers wih yellow spots), and patches of snow still on the ground. Leave the forest behind to walk along a sunny ridge overlooking Sandy River below and a surprising view of snowy Mt. Hood at **Bald Mountain Overlook**, Trillium Lake in the distance. For the easy two mi roundtrip hike, turn around at the Bald Mountain Overlook. For longer hikes, continue along the ridge and through a Narnian-like forest and higher up around **McNeil Point** or onto a long loop that explores the canyon of the **Muddy Fork** of Sandy River.

You can mountain bike portions of the trail; it is mostly snow-free (except small patches) from July to October. The longer version of the hike involves river crossings, so go when water is lowest in August through the fall. In early summer, rivers are especially dangerous or impassable. Check with the Zigzag Ranger Station about trail conditions.

RAFTING

Look to the rivers that run into the Columbia for exhilarating white-water rafting, including one of the wildest rivers, Washington's Class III-V White Salmon River, filled with swift glacial melt from Mt. Adams. For something less intense, the Deschutes River is the most beginner friendly course, with mostly Class III to occasional Class IV rapids. A number of outfitters in the region have half-day trips tailored to novices.

The **Clackamas River**, a designated National Wild and Scenic River, is the most accessible from Portland. Originating in the state's Olallie Lake scenic area, it flows through old-growth forests of Douglas fir and around slow bends where you can get out and swim. After a day on the Clackamas, head to Bagby Hot Springs, just 10 minutes from the exit point of the Clackamas run. All commercial trips end on Labor Day.

The **Deschutes River** is Oregon's most popular rafting river: a sun-drenched ride through the desert with views of osprey, basalt (volcanic) rock formations, and endless sagebrush. It's also the warmest ride; in spring temperatures are in the 70s, and in summer they reach the 90s. The river originates in Little Lava Lake high in the Cascades and runs 250 miles through eastern Oregon before emptying into the Columbia. Don't miss the famous rapids Boxcar and Oak Springs. If you're going with a guide, ask to take the stretch that stops at the White River, where you can get out and play in the natural waterslides flowing into the main current.

Rafting the **White Salmon River** is a great way to cool-down on a hot day. The 40-degree springwater roars past basalt walls hanging with ferns, and through mossy, deciduous forests. It also drops the tallest commercially raftable waterfall in the nation: 14-foot Husum Falls. The river is intense; expect to pull your weight, helping your crew paddle through churning rapids as river guides prompt: "paddle right, paddle left, all paddle!" Toward the end, the ride mellows and drops into a sunny pine oak forest where nature lovers can enjoy wildlife along the designated National Wild and Scenic River. ■TIP→ For an intense challenge involving rock scrambling on portages and helping navigate your crew over ledge drops through in-your-face Class IV and V rapids, book a trip to the Farmlands section of the river. Previous rafting experience is required.

WHERE TO GO

When it's hot: White Salmon or the shady Clackamas rivers.
When it's cooler or overcast: the Deschutes.
For an adrenaline rush: White Salmon when water is highest in March through June.
For beginners: the Deschutes July through October.

Above, rafting the Sandy River Gorge.
Right, rafting and kayaking in Oregon.

RIVER	Best Time to Go	Length	Class	HUB entry point	Distance from Portland
Upper Clackamas	Mar.–July	6–13 mi	III to IV	12 mi south of Estacada at the Memaloose Log Gauging Station	45 mi
Deschutes	Mar.–Nov.	5–18 mi	III	Maupin, OR	100 mi
White Salmon	Mar.–Nov.	9 mi	III to V	White Salmon, WA	60 mi

PLANNING YOUR RAFTING TRIP

Rafting on the North Umpqua River

TOUR OPERATORS

Outfitters offer excursions as short as a half-day or as long as a seven-day overnight camping trip. They provide wetsuits, helmets, lifejackets, and booties.

All Star Rafting. Runs the Clackamas, Deschutes, and White Salmon rivers. On the Deschutes, request the popular Harpham Flats to Sandy Beach run. ☎ 800/909-7238 ⊕ www.asrk.com ✉ $50 half day, $70 full day, $575 5-day trip.

Blue Sky Outfitters. Runs six rivers, including the White Salmon. After the trip, a sirloin steak barbecue is served. ☎ 800/228-7238 ⊕ www.blueskyoutfitters.com ✉ $79-$92 full day.

High Desert. Runs eight rivers, including the Deschutes. A day trip includes a stop at White River to slide down the natural waterslides. Trips include a barbecue buffet lunch. ☎ 800/461-5823 ⊕ www.highdesertriver.com ✉ $50-$85 full day, $600 5-day trip.

River Drifters. Runs several rivers, including the Clackamas, Deschutes, and White Salmon. The company is one of the Northwest's original outfitters, with 28 years of experience. ☎ 800/972-0430 ⊕ www.riverdrifters.com ✉ $50-$90 full day, $345 3-day trip, $835 7-day trip.

Wet Planet. Runs the White Salmon, among others. Known for stellar guides who take rafters on a private two-mile stretch above the White Salmon. ☎ 877/390-9445 ⊕ www.wetplanetwhitewater.com ✉ $57-$95 full day, $1170 5-day trip.

Zollers. Runs the White Salmon. The third-generation family-run outfitter is great for trips with kids. ☎ 509/493-2641 ⊕ www.zooraft.com ✉ $55-$90 full day.

RAFT RENTALS

You can rent your own rafts if you run the Deschutes or the lower Clackamas, but don't try the White Salmon or the Upper Clackamas rivers without a guide unless you're an advanced whitewater rafter. All raft rentals come with paddles or oars and life jackets.

Deschutes River Adventures (☎ 800/723-8464 ⊕ www.800rafting.com).

Deschutes U-boat (☎ 541/395-2503 ⊕ www.deschutesuboat.com).

Ouzel Outfitters (☎ 800/788-7238 ⊕ www.oregonrafting.com).

River Trails (☎ 888/324-8837 ⊕ www.rivertrails.com).

Share a Raft (☎ 888/429-7238 ⊕ www.share-a-raft.com).

WINDSPORTS

Kiteboarding

The Columbia River Gorge is a mecca for windsports, with more than 30 launch areas. Experienced kiteboarders can launch their boards from the sandbar near the **Event Site** at the north end of the waterfront, at Exit 63 off I-84. Windsurfing and paddleboarding equipment are available there to rent. The river's considered advanced terrain, but beginners can take lessons and practice in a protected cove called **the Hook,** where there are no swells or barges. Take Exit 63 and drive to the westernmost point along the waterfront.

If you'd rather participate in the excitement of wind sports as a spectator, head to **Kite Beach** just west of the Event Site. Wear a windbreaker and bring binoculars, a camera with a telephoto lens, and a picnic lunch.

When summer heats up, wind may be flat for a few days at a time, ruling out wind sports. Check wind conditions at ⊕ *www.iwindsurf.com.*

TAKE SOME LESSONS

WINDSURFING

Big Winds (☎ *541/386–6086* ⊕ *www. bigwinds.com* ✉ *$65 for a 2-hour lesson and an hour of practice time).*
Brian's Windsurfing (☎ *541/386–1423* ⊕ *www.brianswindsurfing.com* ✉ *$85 for a 3-hour lesson).*

KITEBOARDING

Kiteboarding is a technical sport, and experts recommend at least a two-day class before hitting the sandbar with your kite. Kiteboards are rented only to IKO (International Kiteboarding Organization) members with Level 3 certification.
Kite the Gorge (☎ *541/490–9426* ⊕ *www.kitethegorge.com* ✉ *$85 basic flying skills, $285 for a 3-hour lesson, $570 for a 6-hour lesson, $1,140 for a 12-hour lesson).*
New Wind (☎ *541/387–2440* ⊕ *www. newwindkiteboarding.com* ✉ *$549 for 2-day lesson).*

PICK A WATER SPORT

Windsurfing. A surfing and sailing hybrid, you stand on a board, hold onto a sail that looks like an enormous dragonfly wing, and let the wind take you across the water. The single sail turns 360 degrees to catch wind, and to help you back up when you fall.

Kiteboarding. A more technical sport than windsurfing; imagine snowboarding on the water while being attached to a giant kite. The kite lifts you into the air so you feel the rush of 12 to 35 mph winds before landing back on the water.

Stand Up Paddleboarding (SUP). The trendy new sport doesn't require any wind. You'll paddle Huck Finn-like while standing on a long board in the calm waters near the Columbia. Think of it as vertical kayaking.

SKIING & SNOWBOARDING MT. HOOD

Above and below, snowboarding and skiing Timberline.

You'll see more than snow while skiing Oregon's glacial beauty, Mt. Hood. Runs take you next to basalt rock outcroppings and waterfalls rushing down faster than your skis can carry you. Skiing Mt. Hood is a study in juxtaposition, and there's no better example than **Timberline**, a place where even on 90-degree summer days you'll find plenty of cold snow to ride. It's North America's only year-round resort. Mt. Hood's four other ski resorts are **Cooper Spur, Mt. Hood Meadows, Mt. Hood Skibowl,** and **Summit Ski area** (a beginner's hill with one chair lift). Beginners can sign up for lessons at any of the resorts.

Snowboarding is welcome at all Mt. Hood ski resorts. Many snowshoeing and cross-country skiing trails crisscross the base of Mt. Hood, including Teacup Lake, Trillium Lake, and Mt. Hood Meadows Nordic facility.

KNOW YOUR SIGNS

On trail maps and the mountains, trails are rated and marked:

● Beginner   ◆ Advanced

■ Intermediate   ◆◆ Expert

PLANNING YOUR SKI TRIP

SKI RESORT	Skiable Acres	Longest Run	Vertical Drop	#of Trails & Lifts	Terrain Type ● ■ ◆◆◆			Adult Ticket
Cooper Spur Family-friendly runs and tubing center.	50	350 ft	350 ft	10/4	40%	40%	20%	$25
Mt. Hood Meadows Largest ski resort on Mt. Hood with only winter super pipe.	2,150	3 mi	2,777 ft	85/11	15%	50%	35%	$69
Mt. Hood Ski Bowl Most extreme skiing and snowboarding on Mt. Hood.	960	3 mi	1,500 ft	65/9	20%	40%	40%	$36–$44
Timberline Most vertical feet of any resort in the Northwest.	1,650	3.12 mi	3,690 ft	41/10	25%	50%	25%	$58

All resorts are open November through April. Timberline is open year round, the longest ski season in North America.

When to go: Northwest snow is crunchier than that in Utah, Colorado, or other surrounding states. In summer, it's like shaved ice—gliding down it feels like an odd mix between water and snow skiing. Stay on groomed runs for a smoother ride, and ski as early in the morning as possible when snow is firmer; snow becomes slushy by afternoon. On Timberline's summer snowfield, expect to be surrounded by dozens of teenage summer campers and training professional athletes.

What to wear: Even on hot days, there may be gusty wind on Palmer Glacier, so wear a windproof shell over a warm moisture-free garment, and bring something to cover your head. Sunglasses or shaded goggles are a must. Gloves with removable linings are best in summer. Some summer skiers wear tights with waterproof ski shorts over them, but traditional ski wear is appropriate for winter.

Deals: Many Hood River accommodations offer $39 lift tickets. Stay in the spacious two-story condos at **Collin's Lake Resort** (☎ 888/422–4776 ext. 1)

in Government Camp Sunday through Thursday and ski at Skibowl for free. (Requires a two-night stay. For each night you stay, you get two free passes to Skibowl.)

TOUR OPERATORS
Cascade Huts (☎ 971/322–3638 ⊕ www.cascadehuts.com).
Julee's Gorge Tours (☎ 541/806–1075 ⊕ www.gorgetours.com).
Mt Hood Adventures (☎ 888/422–4776 ext. 5 ⊕ www.mthoodadventures.com).
Oregon Peak Adventures (☎ 877/965–5100 ⊕ www.oregonpeakadventures.com).
EQUIPMENT RENTALS
Mountain Sports (☎ 503/622–3120).
Mountain Tracks Ski and Snowboard Shop (☎ 503/272–3380, ⊕ www.mtntracks.com).
Mt. Hood Adventures (☎ 888/422–4776 Ext. 5 ⊕ www.mthoodadventure.com).
Otto's Cross Country Ski Shop (☎ 503/668–5947).
Valian's Ski Shop (☎ 503/272–3525).
Winter Fox Shop/Meadowlark Ski and Sports (☎ 503/668–6500).

5

IN FOCUS CHOOSE YOUR OWN ADVENTURE

matter how cold, the outdoor pool is geothermally heated from underground. Note: this particular rental company, All Seasons Property Management, has many other properties as well, including pet-friendly facilities. Visit their Web site to find your ideal cabin. ⊠ *87577 E. Government Camp Loop* ☎ *503/622–1142* ⊕ *www.mthoodrent.com* ⤵ *10 units* ♿ *In-room: a/c, no phone, kitchen. In-hotel: pool, laundry facilities* ☰ *MC, V.*

SHOPPING

Govy General Store. Good thing this is a really nice grocery store, because it's the only one for miles around. Govy General stocks all the staples, plus a nice selection of gourmet treats like cheeses and chocolates. It's also a full-service liquor store and your one-stop shop for Mt. Hood sweatshirts, postcards, and other keepsake tchotchkes. Grab your Sno-Park permit here in winter. ⊠ *30521 E. Meldrum St.* ☎ *541/272–3107* ⊕ *www.govygeneralstore.com* ☽ *Daily 7* AM*–8* PM ☰ *AE, D, MC, V.*

SPORTS AND THE OUTDOORS
⇨ *See the Adventures feature for skiing options.*

WELCHES AND ZIGZAG

14 mi west of Government Camp on U.S. 26, 40 mi east of Portland, I–84 to U.S. 26.

One of a string of small communities known as the Villages at Mt. Hood, Welches' claim to fame is that it was the site of Oregon's first golf course, built at the base of Mt. Hood in 1928. Another golf course is still going strong today, and summer vacationers hover around both towns for access to basic services like gas, groceries, and dining. Others come to pull a few trout out of the scenic Zigzag River or to access trails and streams in the adjacent Salmon-Huckleberry Wilderness.

GETTING HERE

Most of Welches is found just off U.S. 26, often called the Mt. Hood Corridor here, about 45 mi east of Portland. On weekdays the **Mountain Express** (☎ *541/668–3466* ⊕ *www.thevillagesatmthood.com/mel-bus*) bus line links the villages along the corridor, connecting in Sandy with a commuter line to Portland.

VISITOR INFORMATION

Mt. Hood Area Chamber of Commerce (⊠ *24403 E. Welches Rd., Welches* ☎ *503/622–3017* ⊕ *www.mthood.org*).

WHERE TO EAT AND STAY

$$
NEW AMERICAN

✕ **Altitude.** The flagship restaurant at the Resort at the Mountain is a little schizophrenic, aiming for a sleek, modernist concept in a dining room that's filled with booths and bad hotel art. Don't let that stop you, though, as the kitchen steps it up with adventurous dishes like maple-fried quail and foie gras on a hazelnut waffle, plus you can still count on standards like grilled salmon and New York strip. There's an inexpensive kids' menu, and breakfast is also available. Ask to see the specialty cocktail menu in the small adjacent bar. ⊠ *68010 E. Fairway Ave., Welches* ☎ *503/622–2214* ⊕ *www.altituderestaurant.com* ☰ *AE, D, MC, V* ☽ *No lunch.*

$$ ✕ **The Rendezvous Grill & Tap Room.** "Serious food in a not-so-serious AMERICAN place" is the slogan of this upscale roadhouse, a locals' favorite for more than 15 years. For a landlocked joint, the 'Vous sure does a nice job with seafood, turning out appetizing plates of trout almondine, Willapa Bay oysters, Dungeness crab, and more. In the adjacent taproom, ask about the seasonal, house-infused vodkas. The bar's strong rhubarb liqueur is good enough to drink by the glass. ✉ *67149 E. Hwy. 26., Welches* 🕾 *503/622–6837* ⊕ *www.rendezvousgrill.net* ▭ *AE, D, MC, V.*

$ ⊡ **The Cabins Creekside at Welches.** Affordability, accessibility to recreational activities, and wonderful hosts make this a great lodging choice in the Mt. Hood area. Comfortable, large studio units that accommodate from one to four people have knotty-pine vaulted ceilings and log furnishings. As a bonus, full-size kitchens make cooking "at home" a breeze. Surrounding woods offer privacy, and owners Bob and Margaret Thurman have amassed an impressive collection of midcentury and pioneer-era bric-a-brac that they display throughout the property. Patios on each unit face the seasonal creek, and the cabins have lock-storage units large enough to hold bikes, skis, or snowboards. **Pros:** Family-run; quiet, off-highway location; anglers will benefit from the Thurmans' fly-fishing savvy. **Cons:** No dining within walking distance; no cabin-side parking. ✉ *25086 E. Welches Rd.* 🕾 *503/622–4275* ⊕ *www. mthoodcabins.com* ⤵ *10 cabins* ♿ *In-room: a/c, kitchen, DVD, Wi-Fi. In-hotel: laundry facilities* ▭ *AE, D, MC, V.*

$$$ ⊡ **Mt. Hood Vacation Rentals.** Doggedly determined to ensure a great time for the two and four-pawed vacationer alike, Mt. Hood Vacation Rentals welcomes the family pet into the great majority of its homes/ cabins/condos. Yet the properties are still on the upscale side, with fireplaces/woodburning stoves, hot tubs, river views, and full kitchens. The management service has been accommodating Mt. Hood visitors since 1991, carefully choosing properties that offer a true representation of a mountain home vacation spot with beauty as well as privacy. For families and groups, most rentals can accommodate 8 to 10 guests. **Pros:** knowledgeable, hospitable staff; gorgeous homes nestled throughout the Mt. Hood area, many secluded sites; family- and pet-friendly. **Cons:** bring your own shampoo and hair dryer; two-night minimum. ✉ *24403 E. Welches Rd* 🕾 *800/424–9168* ⊕ *www.mthoodrentals.com* ♿ *In-room: a/c (some) kitchen, DVD, Internet, Wi-Fi (some). In-hotel: laundry facilities, parking (free)* ▭ *D, MC, V.*

$$ ⊡ **The Resort at the Mountains.** Here in the highlands of Mt. Hood, the Cascades are seemingly close enough for golfers to hit with a long drive. You can croquet on the only court and lawn-bowling green in the Northwest or choose from plenty of nearby outdoor activities such as fly-fishing on the Salmon River, horseback riding, white-water rafting, and all snow-related sports. Treatments at the serene new spa include specialty massages for golfers and skiers. Accommodations run from double rooms to two-bedroom condos, and each of the sharp, contemporary rooms has a deck or patio overlooking the forest, courtyard, or fairway. Self-contained, the resort has its own golf shop (pros available for lessons), tennis courts, pool/Jacuzzi, gym, restaurants, bars, etc. Golf, skiing, and spa packages are available, as well as comprehensive

5

meeting and event facilities. **Pros:** every sport available; clean rooms; plenty of choices in room size. **Cons:** there will be crowds; may not appeal if a guest isn't a fan of golf; the gorgeous grounds seem more designed for golf carts than pedestrians. ⊠ *68010 E. Fairway Ave.* ☎ *503/622–3101 or 800/669–7666* ⊕ *www.theresort.com* ⤳ *158 rooms* ♿ *In-room: kitchen (some), Wi-Fi. In-hotel: 2 restaurants, bars, golf course, tennis courts, pool, gym, bicycles, laundry facilities, spa, Wi-Fi hotspot, some pets allowed (fee), parking (free)* ▭ *AE, D, MC, V.*

SPORTS AND THE OUTDOORS

RECREATIONAL AREAS **Salmon–Huckleberry Wildernss.** Named for the two main food groups of both black bears and frequent Mt. Hood restaurant diners, this sizeable wilderness area just south of Welches occupies the eroded foothills of the "Old Cascades," ancient mountains made mellow by time, water, and wind. Not surprisingly, trailside huckleberry picking is big here in late August and September. Inquire at the Zigzag Ranger Station for regulations and recommended trails. ⊠ *Mt. Hood National Forest Zigzag Ranger Station, 70220 E. Hwy. 26.* ☎ *503/622–3191* ⊙ *Daily 7:45–4:30.*

GOLF **The Courses.** The three nine-hole tracks at the Resort on the Mountain include the Pine Cone Nine, Oregon's oldest golf course, built on a rented hayfield in 1928. For families or more relaxed golfers, there's also an 18-hole putting course. Check the Web to review the club's dress code, or cover that tee with a collared shirt from the pro shop. ⊠ *68010 E. Fairway Ave.; follow signs south from U.S. 26 in Welches* ☎ *503/622–2216 or 800/669–7666* ⊕ *www.theresortcourses. com* 🖃 *Summer greens fees $81 weekday, $90 weekend for 27 holes; off-season rates vary month to month. Putting course $85 for adults, $5 for children.* ▭ *AE, D, MC, V.*

FISHING **The Fly Fishing Shop.** This heritage shop full of self-proclaimed "fish-aholics" has been peddling flies and guiding trips for three decades. Drop in to ask about the huge variety of customizable float trips, clinics, and by-the-hour walking trips for seasonal steelhead and salmon. Great nearby rivers include the glacial-fed Sandy and its tributary the Zigzag, closed to steelhead and salmon, but rich in native cuthroat. ⊠ *67296 E. U.S. 26* ☎ *503/622–4607 or 800/266–3971* ⊕ *www.flyfishusa.com* 🖃 *Half-day wade-fishing trips $120; half-day trout and steelhead classes $150.* ▭ *AE, D, MC, V.*

Central Oregon

WORD OF MOUTH

"There is a nice hike/walk from the Old Mill District in Bend. When it starts out it feels like it will be an urban walk but soon you are in the woods and walking along the Deschutes. I am sure if you park in the Old Mill area, someone can point out the trail to you."

—sunbum1944

WELCOME TO CENTRAL OREGON

TOP REASONS TO GO

★ **Become one with nature.**
Central Oregonians live on the flanks of the Cascade Range and are bracketed by rock formations, rivers, lakes, forests, ancient lava flows, and desert badlands. Bring your golf clubs, carabiners, snowboard, or camera, and explore deeper.

★ **Go on a Bend-er.**
Downtown Bend is lively and walkable, with a variety of appealing restaurants, galleries, and stores. Within a few blocks you can buy a painting, eat jambalaya, sample brandies, feed geese, and hear live music.

★ **Kick back at Sunriver.**
This family-oriented resort boasts bike paths, river trails, an airstrip, horse stables, tennis courts, a golf course, and several restaurants.

★ **Take down the craft brewing scene.** Nobody calls Bend "Munich on the Deschutes" yet, but it's home to eight breweries that make and pour distinctive, flavorful beers. Sisters and Redmond also have craft breweries.

1 West Central Oregon.
The western portion of central Oregon ranges from lush and green in the Cascades to dry and full of conifers down to the Deschutes River. It's the part with the ski areas, the high mountain lakes, most of the resorts, and the rushing waters. Conveniently, the region's largest town is Bend, and it straddles the forested west and the harshly beautiful east.

2 East Central Oregon.
East of the Deschutes River this land is marked by rugged buttes, tough junipers, and bristly sagebrush. It's a place that still hugs the frontier, with weathered barns, painted desert hills, a caldera holding two popular lakes, and some world-class rock climbing.

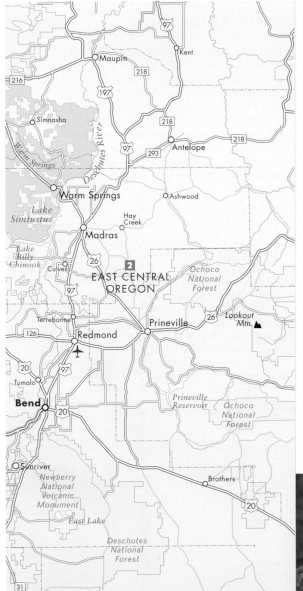

GETTING ORIENTED

Oregonians talk periodically about breaking the state into two pieces along the Cascade Range, but central Oregon provides a natural meeting place between the urban west side and the rural east side. It nestles neatly below the Columbia River Basin and is drained by the Deschutes River, which flows from south to north. Skiers and snowboarders flock to ski areas on the western edge, anglers head to the Deschutes, the Metolius, and the Cascade Lakes, and climbers, campers, rock hounds, and wanderers explore the arid landscapes on the east side. Bend, the largest town for more than 130 mi in any direction, sits roughly in the center of this region.

6

CENTRAL OREGON PLANNER

When to Go

Central Oregon is a popular destination year-round. Skiers and snowboarders come from mid-December through March, when the powder is deepest and driest. During this time, guests flock to the hotels and resorts along Century Drive, which leads from Bend to Mount Bachelor. In summer, when temperatures reach the upper 80s, travelers are more likely to spread throughout the region. But temperatures fall as the elevation rises, so take a jacket if you're heading out for an evening at the high lakes or Newberry Crater.

You'll pay a premium at the mountain resorts during ski season, and Sunriver and other family and golf resorts are busiest in summer. It's best to make reservations as far in advance as possible; six months in advance is not too early.

The **Sisters Rodeo** takes place in June, and Bend's **Pole, Pedal, Paddle**—a popular ski, bike, run, and kayak/canoe race—is in May. The **Sisters Folk Festival**, a celebration of American roots music, is in September. Bend celebrates the seasons with a **Fall Festival** in mid-September and **WinterFest** in February, featuring outdoor sports, ice carving, live music, beer, and wine.

About the Restaurants

The center of culinary ambition is in downtown Bend, where the industry remains strong after a brutal recession, but good-to-excellent restaurants also serve diners in Sisters, Redmond, Tumalo, Prineville, and the major resorts. Styles vary, but many hew to the Northwest preference for fresh foods grown, caught, and harvested in the region.

Central Oregon also has many down-home places and family-friendly brewpubs, and authentic Mexican restaurants have emerged to win faithful followings in Prineville, Redmond, Madras, and Bend.

About the Hotels

Central Oregon has lodging for every taste, from upscale resort lodges to an in-town brewpub village, eclectic bed-and-breakfasts, rustic western inns, and a range of independent and chain hotels and motels. If you're drawn to the rivers, stay in a rustic fishing cabin along the Metolius near Camp Sherman. If you came for the powder, you'll want a ski/snowboard condo at Mount Bachelor Village. A range of choices lines Century Drive between Bend and the mountain. If you're soaking up the atmosphere, you might favor downtown Bend's newest option, a sophisticated boutique inn called the Oxford Hotel, or Old St. Francis, the Catholic school-turned-brewpub village.

WHAT IT COSTS IN U.S. DOLLARS					
	¢	$	$$	$$$	$$$$
Restaurants	under $10	$10–$16	$17–$23	$24–$30	over $30
Hotels		under $100	$100–$150	$151–$200	$201–$250	over $250

Restaurant prices are per person, for a main course at dinner. Hotel prices are for two people in a standard double room in high season, excluding tax.

Getting Here and Around

Air Travel. Visitors fly into **Roberts Field-Redmond Municipal Airport** (RDM) (☎ *541/548–0646*), about 10 mi north of downtown Bend. Rental cars are available for pickup at the airport from several national agencies. The **Redmond Airport Shuttle** (☎ *541/382–1687 or 888/664–8449* ⊕ *www.redmondairportshuttle.net*) provides transportation throughout the region (reservations requested); a ride from the airport to downtown Bend costs about $33. Taxis are available at curbside, or can be summoned from the call-board inside the airport; a cab ride to Bend from the airport is about $40. Portland's airport is 160 mi northwest of Bend.

Bus Travel. Greyhound's (☎ *541/382–2151 or 800/231–2222* ⊕ *www.greyhound.com*) only service in central Oregon is a shuttle from Salem to Bend. The **Central Oregon Breeze** (☎ *541/389–7469 or 800/847–0157* ⊕ *www.cobreeze.com*), a regional carrier, runs one bus a day each way between Portland and Bend, with stops in Redmond and Madras. It also serves Prineville by reservation. **Cascades East Transit** (☎ *541/385–8680 or 866/385–8680* ⊕ *www.cascadeseasttransit.com*) is Bend's intercity bus service, and connects Redmond, Prineville, and Sisters. Trips require a reservation.

Car Travel. U.S. 20 heads west from Idaho and east from the coastal town of Newport into central Oregon. U.S. 26 goes southeast from Portland to Prineville, where it heads northeast into the Ochoco National Forest. U.S. 97 heads north from California and south from Washington to Bend. Highway 126 travels east from Eugene to Prineville; it connects with U.S. 20 heading south (to Bend) at Sisters. Major roads throughout central Oregon are well maintained and open throughout the winter season, although it's always advisable to have tire chains in the car. Some roads are closed by snow during winter, including Oregon 242. Check the **Oregon Department of Transportation's TripCheck** (⊕ *www.tripcheck.com*) or call **ODOT** (☎ *800/977–ODOT*).

Tour Options

Cog Wild (☎ *541/385–7002 or 866/610–4822* ⊕ *www.cogwild.com*) runs bicycle tours for people of all skill levels and interests.

Gadabout Serene Adventures (☎ *541/593–6200* ⊕ *www.gadaboutadventures.com*) runs bus tours for seniors and people who want to cruise comfortably to Newberry Crater, Fort Rock, Smith Rocks, the headwaters of the Metolius, and other central Oregon sites.

Sun Country Tours (☎ *541/382–6277 or 800/770–2161* ⊕ *www.suncountrytours.com*) is a longtime provider of raft and tube trips on central Oregon's waterways. Trips range from half days to two days.

Wanderlust Tours (☎ *541/389–8359 or 800/962–2862* ⊕ *www.wanderlusttours.com*) offers popular and family-friendly half-day excursions in Bend, Sisters, and Sunriver. Options include kayaking, hiking, snowshoeing, caving, and volcano exploring.

VISITOR INFORMATION

Central Oregon Visitors Association (✉ *661 SW Powerhouse Dr., Suite 1301, Bend* ☎ *541/389–8799 or 800/800–8334* ⊕ *www.covisitors.com*).

6

CENTRAL OREGON

Updated by
Mike Francis

After a day on the Sunriver bike paths, a first-time visitor from Germany shook her head. "This place is paradise," she declared. It's easy to see why she thought so. Central Oregon has snowfields so white they sharpen the edges of the mountains; canyons so deep and sudden as to induce vertigo; air so crisp that it fills the senses; water that ripples in mountain lakes so clear that boaters can see to the bottom, or rushes through turbulent rapids favored by rafters.

A region born of volcanic tumult is now a powerful lure for the adventurous, the beauty seeking, and even the urbane—which, in central Oregon, can be found all in the same person.

Bend has grown into a sophisticated city of 80,000-plus, a magnet for people retreating from larger, noisier urban centers. For most visitors it is the sunny face of central Oregon, a haven for hikers, athletes, and aesthetes, but with the charm and elegance of much larger cities.

From Bend it's easy to launch to the attractions that surround it. To the northwest, Camp Sherman is a stunning place to fish for rainbow trout or kokanee. The Smith Rocks formation to the north draws climbers and boulderers, and, to the south, Lava Lands and the Lava River Caves fascinate visitors more than 6,000 years after they were chiseled out of the earth. The Badlands Wilderness Study Area to the east draws hikers and horseback riders wanting to connect with the untamed landscape. Lake Billy Chinook to the north is a startling oasis, where summer visitors drift in houseboats beneath the high walls of the Deschutes River canyon. The Deschutes River itself carries rafters of all descriptions, from young families to solo adventurers.

The area's natural beauty has brought it a diverse cluster of resorts, whether situated on the shores of high mountain lakes or cradling golf courses of startling green. They dot the landscape from the dry terrain around Warm Springs to the high road to Mount Bachelor.

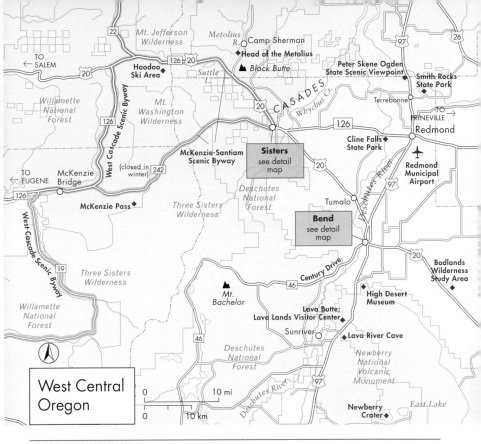

West Central
Oregon

0   10 mi

0   10 km

WEST CENTRAL OREGON

Sunshine, crisp pines, pure air, rushing waters, world-class skiing and
snowboarding at Mt. Bachelor, destination golf resorts, a touch of the
frontier West at Sisters, an air of sophistication in Bend—the forested side
of central Oregon serves up many recreational flavors. The area draws
young couples, seniors, families, athletes, and adventurers, all of whom
arrive with a certain sense of purpose, but also with an appreciation
for the natural world. Travelers will have no problem filling a week in
central Oregon's western half with memorable activities, from rafting to
enjoying a sensational meal.

BEND

160 mi from Portland, east and south on U.S. 26 and south on U.S. 97.

Bend, Oregon's largest city east of the Cascades, is emerging from a
boom-and-bust cycle, one that caused it to go from being the state's
fastest-growing city to the city with the nation's steepest fall in housing
prices. As banks have worked through their inventories of foreclosed
properties, the people of Bend have continued to enjoy the elements
that attracted all the attention in the first place: an enviable climate,

proximity to skiing, and a reputation as a playground and recreational escape. At times it seems that everybody in Bend is an athlete or a brewer, but it remains a tolerant, welcoming town, conscious of making a good first impression. Downtown Bend remains compact, vibrant, and walkable, and the Old Mill District draws shoppers from throughout the region. Chain stores and franchise restaurants have filled in along the approaches to town, especially along U.S. 20 and U.S. 97.

Neighboring Mt. Bachelor, though hardly a giant among the Cascades at 9,065 feet, is blessed by an advantage over its taller siblings—by virtue of its location, it's the first to get snowfall, and the last to see it go. Inland air collides with the Pacific's damp influence, creating skiing conditions immortalized in songs by local rock bands and raves from the ski press.

GETTING HERE AND AROUND
Portlanders arrive via car on U.S. 20 or U.S. 26, and folks from the mid-Willamette Valley cross the mountains on Oregon 126. Roberts Field–Redmond Municipal Airport, 14 mi to the north, is an efficient hub for air travelers, who can rent a car or take a shuttle or cab into town. **Greyhound** also serves the area with a shuttle from Salem. The **Central Oregon Breeze,** a privately operated regional carrier, runs daily between Portland and Bend, with stops in Redmond and Madras. Bend is served by a citywide bus system called **Cascades East Transit,** which also connects to Redmond, Sisters, Prineville, Madras, and Warm Springs. To take a Cascades East bus between cities in central Oregon, passengers must call to make a reservation.

If you're trying to head out of or into Bend on a major highway during the morning or 5 PM rush, especially on U.S. 97, you may hit congestion. Parking in downtown Bend is free for the first two hours, or park for free in the residential neighborhoods just west of downtown. In addition to the car-rental counters at the airport, Avis, Budget, Enterprise, and Hertz also have rental locations in Bend.

Contacts Cascades East Transit (☎ 541/385–8680 or 866/385–8680 ⊕ www. cascadeseasttransit.com). **Central Oregon Breeze** (☎ 541/389–7469 or 800/847–0157 ⊕ www.cobreeze.com). **Greyhound Bend** (✉ 1555 NENE Forbes Rd. ☎ 541/382–2151).

VISITOR INFORMATION
Bend Chamber of Commerce (✉ 777 NW Wall St. ☎ 541/382–3221 ⊕ www. bendchamber.org). **Central Oregon Visitors Association** (✉ 661 SW Powerhouse Drive., Ste. 1301, Bend ☎ 541389–8799 or 800/800–8334 ⊕ www. visitcentraloregon.com).

EXPLORING
Numbers in the margin correspond to numbers on the Bend map.

EN ROUTE

Century Drive. For 100 mi, this forest-highway loop beginning and ending in Bend meanders past dozens of high mountain lakes good for fishing, hiking, waterskiing, and camping in the summer months. (Much of the road is closed by snow during the colder months.) To find it, take Highway 46 for the first two-thirds of the trip, and then take U.S. 97 at LaPine to return to Bend.

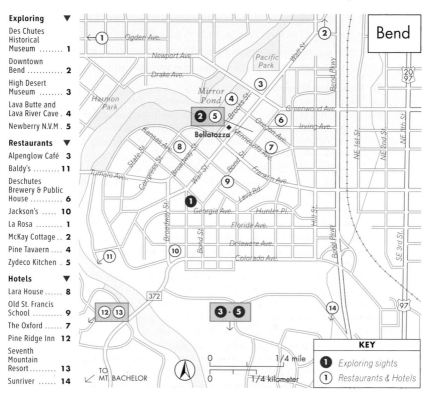

6

KEY

1 *Exploring sights*

① *Restaurants & Hotels*

---

❶   Des Chutes Historical Museum. A striking 1914 building constructed from
locally quarried volcanic tuff has Indian artifacts, historical photos of
the region, and a pioneer schoolroom from 1915. It's operated by the
Deschutes County Historical Society. Visit the 1915-era classroom and
imagine yourself a student when Bend was young and largely untamed.
✉ *129 NW Idaho Ave.* ☎ *541/389–1813* ⊕ *www.deschuteshistory.org*
💲 *$5* ☉ *Tues.–Sat. 10–4:30.*

❷   Downtown Bend. Bend's heart is an area of about nine blocks, centered on
Fodor's Choice Wall and Bond streets. Here you'll find boutique shops, fine restaurants,
★ and lively nightlife establishments, as well as a few traditional pharma-
cies, taverns, and hardware stores keeping it real. At its western edge,
downtown Bend slopes down to **Drake Park and Mirror Pond.** Thirteen
acres of manicured greensward and trees line the edge of the Deschutes,
attracting flocks of Canada geese and strollers from downtown. Note
the marker at the edge of Mirror Pond, where, in 1928, Socialist Labor
Party presidential candidate Frank Johns finished his campaign speech,
then plunged into the water to rescue two boys that had fallen in from
a nearby bridge. He drowned in the attempt. ✉ *Bounded on the west
by NW Brooks St. and Drake Park, NW Lava Rd on the east, NW
Franklin Ave. to the south, and NW Greenwood Ave. to the north.*
⊕ *www.downtownbend.org.*

A sleekly designed coffee shop with modernist blond-wood furnishings, **Bellatazza** (⌧ *869 NW Wall St., #100* ☎ *541/318-0606* ▭ *MC, V*) starts with morning jolts and pastries in the heart of downtown Bend, and continues serving into the night. Wireless Internet is available with purchase.

❸ High Desert Museum. The West was truly wild, and this combo museum/zoo proves it. Kids will love the up-close-and-personal encounters with gila monsters, snakes, porcupines, Ochoco the bobcat, and Snowshoe the lynx. Actors in costume take part in the Living History series, where you can chat with stagecoach drivers, boomtown widows, pioneers, and homesteaders. With 53,000 indoor square feet, a quarter-mile trail, and an additional 32,000 square feet of outdoor exhibits and live animal habitats, it's no wonder that the museum sells admission tickets that cover a two-day visit. ⌧ *59800 S. Hwy. 97, 7 mi south of Downtown Bend* ☎ *541/382-4754* ⊕ *www.highdesertmuseum.org* ⌫ *$15* ⊘ *Daily 9–5 May 1–Oct. 31, 10–4 other months.*

Fodor's Choice ★ ℃

❹ Lava Butte and Lava River Cave. On the north end of the Newberry National Volcanic Monument, the Lava Butte area has several large basalt lava flows as well as the 500-foot Lava Butte cinder cone—a coal-black, symmetrical mound thrust from the depths 7,000 years ago. The cone is now home to the recently expanded Lava Lands Visitor Center, which features a variety of interpretive exhibits covering the volcanic and early human history of the area. Lava River Cave is a 1-mi-long lava tube—a cave formed when molten lava drained from the channel, leaving a crust as a roof—that takes about 90 minutes to explore on your own. Lantern rental is $4. Enter by the tiny visitor center. ⌧ *58201 S. Hwy. 97* ☎ *541/593-2421* ⊕ *www.fs.fed.us/r6/centraloregon/newberrynvm/interest-lavabutte.shtml* ⌫ *$5 per vehicle* ⊘ *May–Oct., daily 9–5.*

❺ Newberry National Volcanic Monument. The last time Newberry Volcano blew its top was about 13 centuries ago. Paulina Peak, which is on an unpaved road at the south end of the national monument, has the best view into the crater and its two lakes, Paulina and East. Lava Butte and Lava River Cave are at the north end of the monument near the visitor center. You can also stay at rustic resorts on each lake. ⊕ *58201 S. Hwy. 97* ☎ *541/593-2421* ⊕ *www.fs.fed.us/r6/centraloregon/newberrynvm/index.shtml* ⌫ *$5 per vehicle* ⊘ *Late Apr.–mid-Oct., daily 9–5; Labor Day–Memorial Day, Wed.–Sun. 9–5.*

WHERE TO EAT

¢ ✕ Alpenglow Café. Locals will send you here for overstuffed breakfast
AMERICAN burritos, eggs Benedict, and buttermilk pancakes. The mandate for freshness dictates that no can openers are permitted in the kitchen. The good, strong coffee and fresh-squeezed orange juice are worthy companions to any meal. Order breakfast until closing (2 PM) or pick from tasty sandwiches and burgers. ⌧ *1133 NW Wall St, #100.* ☎ *541/383-7676* ⊕ *www.alpenglowcafe.com* ▭ *MC, V* ⊘ *No dinner.*

$ ✕ Baldy's Barbeque. With the arrival of Baldy's, Bend now has a top-
SOUTHERN notch, family-friendly barbecue joint with tender ribs, chicken, brisket, pulled pork, and even catfish. The space is humble, but Baldy's isn't gunning for raves from *Architectural Digest*; it invests instead in serving

Paulina and East lakes in Newberry National Volcanic Monument

up the tenderest, juiciest barbecue, seasoned with any of several house sauces. In warm weather, locals fill up the adjoining patio. ⊠ *235 SW Century Dr.* ☎ *541/385–7427* ⊕ *www.baldysbbq.com* ⊟ *MC, V.*

$ ✕ **Deschutes Brewery & Public House**. Bendites are fiercely loyal to their
AMERICAN   city's original brewpub, established in 1988. Not only does the Brewery bake its own bread and pizza dough (adding in its own malt), it makes its sausages, sauces, mustards, dressings, soups, etc. House favorites include sweet-and-spicy mac and cheese and fish-and-chips. Though the always-popular Black Butte Porter is a Public House classic, Deschutes brews a diverse lineup of craft beers, including such seasonals as Jubelale (Christmastime) and Twilight Ale (summer). It is almost always hopping, and you may find yourself waiting to be seated, as there are no reservations. However, time flies as you admire the quasi-medieval murals of peasants downing ale, watch the four TVs broadcasting sports, or people-watch the boisterous crowd while you wait. ⊠ *1044 NW Bond St.* ☎ *541/382–9242* ⊕ *www.deschutesbrewery. com* ⊟ *AE, MC, V.*

$ ✕ **Jackson's Corner**. This family-friendly community restaurant is housed
AMERICAN   in an unassuming two-story building tucked into a neighborhood outside downtown. The open, inviting space is a great place for casual gatherings, frequently with live music. The eclectic menu leans heavily on locally grown and organic dishes. It serves up cheesecake cups, mussels, pizza, fish, beef, and pork cutlets. ⊠ *845 NW Delaware Ave.* ☎ *541/647–2198* ⊟ *MC, V.*

$ ✕ **La Rosa**. Come for the Red Cactus Margarita—stay for the food. Voted
MEXICAN   Best Mexican Restaurant in Bend time and again, La Rosa offers classic Mexican combination plates, as well as gourmet lobster-tail enchiladas,

grilled prawns wrapped in apple-smoked bacon, and pork loin baked in banana leaves. There are plenty of vegetarian entrées offered as well. As one fan puts it, "La Rosa es la bomba!" Choose to dine indoors or on the heated patio. ✉ *2763 NW Crossing Dr.* ☎ *541/647–1624* ⊕ *www. larosabend.com* ▭ *AE, MC, V.*

$ ✕ **McKay Cottage.** This breakfast and lunch spot is housed in a 1916 pioneer cottage that was home to a former state senator. Locals relax throughout its cozy rooms and spill over onto the porch and patio below. The menu is long on comfort food, including fresh scones and sticky buns, and servers are friendly and attentive. On your way out, you can pick up baked goods and coffee drinks at the to-go bakery. ✉ *62910 O.B. Riley Rd.* ☎ *541/383–2697* ⊕ *www.themckaycottage. com* ▭ *MC, V* ⊗ *No dinner.*

AMERICAN

Fodor's Choice

★

$$ ✕ **Pine Tavern.** This restaurant, named for the Ponderosa pine tree growing through the back dining room, has been dishing up high-end meals in the heart of downtown Bend for more than 70 years. Its specialties are steaks and prime rib, especially Oregon Country Beef, which comes from hormone-free cattle raised on local ranches. Longtime regulars share the dining room with out-of-towners; in summertime, seek a spot on the patio, overlooking Mirror Pond and Drake Park. ✉ *967 NW Brooks St.* ☎ *541/382–5581* ▭ *MC, V.*

AMERICAN

$$ ✕ **Zydeco Kitchen & Cocktails.** A local secret no longer. The menu is mostly American—fillet medallions, chicken, and pasta—although there are jambalaya and redfish dishes, as you'd expect. The owners emphasize the preparation of fresh, organic foods. The blended menu of Northwest specialties and Cajun influences has made Zydeco a popular spot. The bar is trendy, but welcoming. In warm weather, ask to sit on the patio. Bonus: Kids eat free on Sundays. ✉ *919 NW Bond St.* ☎ *541/312–2899* ⊕ *www.zydeckokitchen.com* ▭ *MC, V* ⊗ *No lunch weekends.*

AMERICAN

OFF THE BEATEN PATH

Cowboy Dinner Tree Steakhouse. Seventy miles south of Sunriver you'll find an authentic campfire cook, and he's firing up a genuine taste of the Old West. Oregonians will tell you that the 30-ounce steak or whole chicken over an open flame, plus all the fixings, is more than worth the trip. Serving the "true cowboy cut," the Dinner Tree ensures that leftovers will be enjoyed for days. Don't expect to plug in your laptop: there's no electricity, nor is alcohol served, nor credit cards accepted. If you journey from afar, lodging is available in the rustic buckaroo bunkhouse. Plates are $23.50 per adult, $10.25 for kids 7–13; kids 6 and under free. ✉ *County Rd. 4–12/Forest Service Rd. 28, Silver Lake* ☎ *541/576–2426* ⊕ *www.cowboydinnertree.homestead.com* ⊗ *June–Oct., Thurs.–Sun. 4* PM*–8:30; Nov.–May, Fri.–Sun. 4–8:30* PM.

WHERE TO STAY

$$$$ ⊡ **Lara House Lodge.** Fully refurbished in pure Craftsman style, this six-suite bed-and-breakfast promises plenty of luxury. The kitchen gleams with modern appliances, and exposed dark-wood beams and wrought-iron appointments adorn the common rooms. An inviting fireplace is framed by artful tiles, and large-paned windows overlook Drake Park's Mirror Pond. From the Bachelor Suite on the main floor with private entrance to the spacious Summit Suite at the top, each of the six rooms exudes high style and warmth. The gourmet breakfast, served on the

Fodor's Choice

★

front porch or in the sunroom or great dining room, may consist of a crustless salmon rice torte, shortbread waffles, or herb-filled crepes. Try to arrive by 5 PM to enjoy the Northwest wine reception. **Pros:** clean lines and an uncluttered feel make a relaxing environment; park and town are a short walk away; wine and appetizer hour. **Cons:** no pets or kids. ✉ *640 NW Congress St. NW* ☎ *541/388–4064 or 800/766–4064* ⊕ *www.larahouse.com* ➷ *6 rooms* ♿ *In-room: a/c (central), no phone, refrigerator (some), Wi-Fi, DVD. In-hotel: parking (free) no guests younger than 18* ▭ *D, MC, V* ⍟ *BP.*

$ ⊡ **Old St. Francis School.** Not that you'd want to miss the rest of downtown Bend, but you could spend a charming weekend without leaving this delightful outpost of the McMenamin Brothers' regional hotel and brewpub empire. Old St. Francis is a restored 1936 Catholic schoolhouse converted to a destination village, with 19 classrooms that are now lodging rooms, a theater, and a pub. For a place that brews beer, bakes bread, shows movies, and exudes a laid-back charm, the property never lets you forget that it used to be a Catholic school. Enjoy the murals and the vintage photographs, and be sure to pick up the walking-tour primer, which explains why, for example, one mural depicts Catholic school kids releasing monarch butterflies. Old St. Francis also rents nearby cottages that sleep 2 to 10 people. **Pros:** a self-contained destination village, yet only footsteps from downtown Bend and Drake Park. **Cons:** no pets; few modern appliances. ✉ *700 NW Bond St.* ☎ *541/382–5174 or 877/661–4228* ⊕ *www.mcmenamins.com* ➷ *19 rooms* ♿ *In-room: a/c, Wi-Fi. In-hotel: room service, 3 bars, pool, spa, parking (free)* ▭ *AE, D, MC, V* ⍟ *EP.*

6

$$ ⊡ **The Oxford Hotel.** A new and notable arrival in downtown Bend is this attractive boutique hotel, which features appealing views, a workout room, complimentary bikes, and loaner iPods. A step into the sleek, high-ceilinged lobby tells you you've found a new kind of accommodation in central Oregon, with comfortably elegant guest rooms and a confidently assured restaurant and lounge called 10 Below. Pets are welcome, and are even offered proportionately sized pet beds. **Pros:** stylish; generous amenities; attentive concierge. **Cons:** property is wedged into a half block on the edge of downtown. ✉ *10 NW Minnesota Ave.* ☎ *877/440–8436* ⊕ *www.oxfordhotelbend.com* ➷ *59 suites* ♿ *In-room: a/c, safe, Wi-Fi., refrigerator, wet bar, kitchen (some), DVD players on request. In-hotel: restaurant, room service, bar, spa, loaner iPods, loaner bicycles, laundry facilities, Wi-Fi hotspot, parking (paid), some pets allowed* ▭ *AE, D, MC, V.*

$$ ⊡ **Pine Ridge Inn.** This immaculate two-floor hotel is surrounded by ponderosa pines and junipers. The friendly staff goes out of its way to accommodate—if you can't make it to the 5 PM wine social, they'll be happy to bring a glass to your room upon request. All rooms have fireplaces, with either decks or patios. The suites have full sitting areas, seven with Jacuzzis. Hot breakfasts come with a choice of entrées, as well as the usual Continental buffet spread of juices, pastries, and cereals. The turndown service comes with a special homemade goodie on the pillow. **Pros:** clean spacious rooms; wine socials; nightlight embedded on the stairs in the suites. **Cons:** the river view is also the highway view;

with 20 rooms, it has a less intimate feel than expected. ⊠ *1200 SW Century Dr.* ☎ *541/389–6137 or 800/600–4095* ⊕ *www.pineridgeinn. com* ⤴ *20 rooms* ⅗ *In-room: a/c, kitchens (some), DVD, refrigerator, Wi-Fi. In-hotel: Wi-Fi hotspot, parking (free)* ▭ *AE, D, MC, V* ⑩ *BP.*

$$ ⚏ **Seventh Mountain Resort.** Proud of the fact that it's "the closest accom-
⚙ modation to Mt. Bachelor" (approximately 14 mi away), this resort has been a host to central Oregon's year-round outdoor activities since 1972. Lodging is distributed among 20 three-story buildings on the banks of the Deschutes River, with white-water rafting and fishing right outside. Among the recreational facilities there's a miniature golf course in a former roller rink, which converts to an ice-skating rink in winter. For younger guests, Camp Ranger Kids Camp has activities for ages 4 to 11. Accommodations include standard bedrooms with a queen-size bed, deluxe bedrooms with private deck, and studios with fireplaces and full kitchens, as well as private 2- and 3-bedroom homes. Consider Seasons Restaurant, the resort's latest upscale dining spot, specializing in Pacific Northwest cuisine. **Pros:** kid-friendly; varied accommodations, some moderately priced; setting is terrific. **Cons:** golf course is not on-site, but ½ mi away; some guests have complained that service is uneven. ⊠ *18575 SW Century Dr., Deschutes National Forest* ☎ *541/382–8711 or 877/765–1501* ⊕ *www.seventhmountain.com* ⤴ *176 rooms* ⅗ *In-room: a/c, kitchen (most), refrigerator, DVD, Wi-Fi. In-hotel: 2 restau-rants, bar, tennis and basketball courts, pools, gym, spa, water sports, bicycles, children's programs (ages 4–11), laundry facilities, Wi-Fi hot-spot, parking (free)* ▭ *AE, D, MC, V* ⑩ *EP.*

$$$ ⚏ **Sunriver Resort.** Central Oregon's premier family playground con-
FodorsChoice tinues to draw locals and faraway visitors for, in many cases, annual
★ visits. They come because Sunriver encapsulates so many things that
⚙ are distinctive about central Oregon, from the views of the central Cascades to the highly canoeable and raftable waters of the Deschutes River, which flows directly through the resort. An extensive system of paved bike-and-pedestrian paths connects all corners of the 3,300-acre resort. There are three golf courses, including the renowned Crosswa-ter, 26 tennis courts, four swimming pools, and skiing at nearby Mt. Bachelor. If indoor fitness is more your style, check out Sage Springs Club. Lodging choices vary from vacation-house rentals to guestrooms in and around the lodge. Hundreds of houses on the property are avail-able for rent through real-estate brokerages separate from the hotel. For families, kids' programs are held at Fort Funnigan. Nature walks, raft trips, horseback excursions, bike tours, and night-sky observa-tion sessions will keep everyone engaged. **Pros:** many activities; much pampering; dog-friendly. **Con:** when visitors throng the shops, restau-rants, and bike paths, it can feel as if an entire city has relocated here. ⊠ *17600 Center Dr., Sunriver* ☎ *800/801–8765* ⊕ *www.sunriver-resort. com* ⤴ *205 units* ⅗ *In-room: a/c, kitchen (some), refrigerator, Wi-Fi. In-hotel: 4 restaurants, room service, bars, golf courses, tennis courts, pools, gym, spa, bicycles, water sports, children's programs (ages 3–12), Wi-Fi hotspot, laundry facilities, parking (free), pets allowed in some units (fee)* ▭ *AE, D, DC, MC, V* ⑩ *EP.*

Sunriver Resort

NIGHTLIFE AND THE ARTS

The Astro Lounge. Bend's take on a space-age cocktail haven comes complete with matte black–and-chrome industrial furnishings, a loft-style layout, and 25 specialty martinis. There's an Astrodiasiac martini for two—'nuff said. The bar connects to a bistro sharing the out-of-this-world motif. ✉ *147 NW Minnesota Ave.* ☎ *541/388–0116* ⊕ *www. astroloungebend.com.*

Bendistillery. Oregon may be synonymous with craft-brewed ales and Pinot Noir, but Bendistillery expands the alcoholic range by handcrafting small batches of spirits flavored with local herbs. Bend sits in the middle of one of the world's great juniper forests, making the juniper-infused Cascade Mountain gin a particular treat. This slick little tasting room stirs up bracing martinis and highballs incorporating Bendistillery's products, resulting in a perfect bar-crawl kickoff or classy, if sometimes noisy, nightcap. ✉ *850 NW Brooks St.* ☎ *541/318–0200* ⊕ *www.bendistillery.com.*

Les Schwab Amphitheater. Named for the Prineville tire tycoon, this open-air venue in the Old Mill District brings national music tours to Bend. ✉ *344 SW Shevlin Hixon Dr.* ☎ *541/322–9383* ⊕ *www.theoldmill.com/ live-events.*

SHOPPING

Azila Nora. Carrying high-end Asian furniture and whimsical keepsakes from around the world, this store is a visual treat. It's also the only Oregon distributor of a highly specialized line of handmade pottery from Zimbabwe called Penzo. ✉ *605 NW Newport Ave.* ☎ *541/389–6552* ⊕ *www.azilanora.com.*

Sparks Lake and Mt. Bachelor

Cowgirl Cash. A funky western outfitter also buys vintage boots and western apparel. You never know exactly what you'll find, but you can expect a fair share of leather, turquoise, silver, and, always, boots. It's a quirky and welcome addition to the downtown scene. ⊠ *924 NW Brooks St.* ☎ *541/815–8996* ⊕ *www.cowgirlcashbend.com.*

Dudley's BookShop Café. Bend's leading independent bookseller has used books, Wi-Fi, and interesting people who take part in everything from knitting circles to Italian language classes. ⊠ *135 NW Minnesota Ave.* ☎ *541/749–2010.*

Hot Box Betty. This fun, flashy shop sells high fashion for women and men, carrying DVF, Burning Torch, Frye Boots, and Isabelle Fiore bags. Visit the Hot Box if only to meet the delightful ladies running the store. ⊠ *903 NW Wall St.* ☎ *541/288–1189* ⊕ *www.hotboxbetty.com.*

Old Mill District. Bend was once the site of one of the world's largest sawmill operations, a sprawling industrial complex along the banks of the Deschutes. In recent years the abandoned shells of the old factory buildings have been transformed into an attractive shopping center, a project honored with national environmental awards. Bend's national chain retailers can be found here, along with restaurants, the Central Oregon Visitors Association, a 16-screen multiplex movie house, and the Les Schwab Amphitheater. Don't miss the famous Old Mill District rock chucks, the ground-hugging marmots who graze and hustle around the nearby rocks. ⊠ *520 SW Powerhouse Dr.* ☎ *541/312–0131* ⊕ *www. theoldmill.com* ⊘ *Closed Sun.*

Patagonia by Pandora's Backpack. A friendly and attentive staff sells sleek modern outdoor gear and clothing at a Patagonia concept store that's still independently owned. ⊠ *920 NW Bond St., Suite 101* ☎ *541/382–6694* ⊕ *www.pandorasbackpack.com.*

SPORTS AND THE OUTDOORS

RECREATIONAL AREAS

Deschutes National Forest. This 1.6-million-acre forest has 20 peaks higher than 7,000 feet, including three of Oregon's five highest mountains, more than 150 lakes, and 500 mi of streams. If you want to park your car at a trailhead, you'll need a Northwest Forest Pass. You'll also need day-use passes for boating and camping. ⊠ *1001 SW Emkay Dr.* ☎ *541/383–5300* ⊕ *www.fs.fed.us/r6/centraloregon/* ✑ *Park pass required: day-use pass $5* ☉ *Daily.*

BICYCLING

U.S. 97 north to the Crooked River Gorge, and Smith Rock provides bikers with memorable scenery and a good workout. **Sunriver** has 26 mi of paved bike paths.

SKIING

Many Nordic trails—more than 165 mi of them—wind through the **Deschutes National Forest** (☎ *541/383–5300*). Call for information about conditions.

6

⊙ **Mt. Bachelor** is one of the best alpine resort areas in the United States—60 percent of the downhill runs are rated expert. One of 10 lifts takes skiers all the way to the mountain's 9,065-foot summit. The vertical drop is 3,265 feet; the longest of the 70 runs is 2 mi. Facilities and services include equipment rental and repair, a ski school, and ski shop, Nordic skiing, weekly races, and day care; you can enjoy restaurants, bars, and six lodges. Other activities include cross-country skiing, a tubing park, sled-dog rides, snowshoeing, and in summer, hiking and chairlift rides. The 36 mi of trails at the **Mount Bachelor Nordic Center,** most of them near the base of the mountain, are intermediate.

During the offseason, the lift to the **Pine Marten Lodge** provides stunning views. Visitors can play disc golf on a downhill course that starts near the lodge. At the base of the mountain, take dry-land dog sled rides with four-time Iditarod musher Rachael Scdoris. ⊠ *Cascade Lakes Hwy.* ☎ *541/382–7888 or 800/829–2442* ⊕ *www.mtbachelor.com* ✑ *Lift tickets $59–$69 per day* ☉ *Nov.–May, daily 8–4, or as weather allows.*

SISTERS

18 mi northwest of Bend on U.S. 20.

If Sisters looks as if you've stumbled into the Old West, that's entirely by design. The town fathers—or perhaps we should say "sisters"—strictly enforce 1800s-style architecture. Rustic cabins border a llama ranch on the edge of town. Western storefronts give way to galleries, a bakery occupies the former general store, and the town blacksmith's home now has a flower shop. Although its population remains under 2,000, Sisters increasingly attracts visitors as well as urban runaways who appreciate its tranquillity and charm. If you're driving over from the Willamette Valley, note how the weather seems to change to sunshine

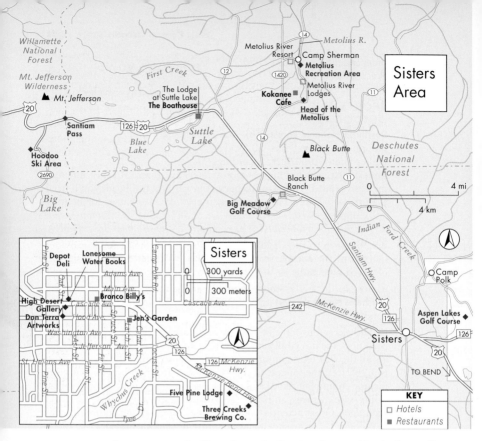

when you cross the Cascades at the Santiam Pass and begin descending toward the town.

Black Butte, a perfectly conical cinder cone, rises to the northwest. The Metolius River/Camp Sherman area to the west is a special find for fly-fishermen as well as springtime wildflower lovers.

GETTING HERE

Travelers from Portland and the west come to Sisters over the Santiam Pass on Oregon Highway 126. This is also the route for visitors who fly into Roberts Field–Redmond Municipal Airport; rent a car and drive 20 mi west. Those coming from Bend drive 20 mi northwest on U.S. 20. **Cascades East**, a regional bus carrier, runs routes between Sisters and Redmond by reservation.

Contacts **Cascades East Transit** (☎ 541/385–8680 or 866/385–8680 ⊕ www.cascadeseasttransit.com)

VISITOR INFORMATION

Sisters Chamber of Commerce (☎ 541/549–0251 ⊕ www.sisterscountry.com).

EXPLORING

Camp Sherman. Surrounded by groves of whispering yellow-bellied ponderosa pines, larch, fir, and cedars and miles of streamside forest trails, this small, peaceful resort community of 250 residents is part of a designated 86,000-acre conservation area. The area's beauty and natural resources are the big draw: the spring-fed Metolius River prominently glides through the community. In the early 1900s Sherman County wheat farmers escaped the dry summer heat by migrating here to fish and rest in the cool river environment. To help guide fellow farmers to the spot, devotees nailed a shoebox top with the name CAMP SHERMAN to a tree at a fork in the road. Several original buildings still stand from the homesteader days, including some cabins, a schoolhouse, and a tiny chapel. The "action" is at the Camp Sherman Store, adjacent to the post office. ⊠ *25451 Forest Service Rd., 10 mi northwest of Sisters on U.S. 20, 5 mi north on Hwy. 14.* ☎ *541/595-6711* ⊙ *Mon.–Sat., 9-5, Sun., 9–4* ⊕ *www.metoliusriver.com*

NEED A BREAK? In a rustic-looking former general store, Sisters Bakery (⊠ *251 E. Cascade St.* ☎ *541/549–0361* ⊕ *www.sisters-bakery.com*) turns out high-quality pastries, coffee, and doughnuts. Sunday through Thursday the Oven Schedule starts with croissants and biscuits by 7 AM, dumplings and scones by 8, power cookies by 8:30, pies by 9, and breads by 10:30.

WHERE TO EAT

$$$
AMERICAN ✗ **The Boathouse.** From a simple marina tackle shop comes a woodsy boathouse, replete with pine, Mexican tiling, Native American art, and water as far as the eye can see. Dishes are ambitious and zesty variations on such core elements as salmon, halibut, tenderloin, and pheasant. Many fine Northwest and California wines are available by the bottle or glass. Lovely food and the management's genuine joie de vivre give the Boathouse its unique flavor. ⊠ *The Lodge at Suttle Lake, 13300 U.S. Hwy. 20* ☎ *541/595–2628* ⊕ *www.thelodgeatsuttlelake. com* ▭ *AE, MC, V* ⊙ *Closed Tues. and Wed.*

$$
AMERICAN ✗ **Bronco Billy's.** Rustle up some good grub at this outrageous tip of the cowboy hat to the Wild West. Look up and find corral fences swinging from the ceiling. Look for the kitchen, and instead you'll find the "Ranch Grill." In Bronco Billy's General Store, find foods and dry goods. Whether you go for American (burgers, steaks, BBQ ribs), south-of-the-border (quesadillas, tacos), or even a Caesar salad, the portions are hefty and tasty to boot. Kids are welcome, but management requests you leave your horse outside. ⊠ *190 E. Cascade St.* ☎ *541/549–7427* ⊕ *www.broncobillysranchgrill.com* ▭ *D, MC, V.*

¢
AMERICAN ✗ **Depot Deli & Cafe.** A railroad theme prevails at this main-street deli. A miniature train circles above as the kitchen dishes out excellent, inexpensive sandwiches and burgers. Sit inside next to the rough-wood walls or out back on the deck. ⊠ *250 W. Cascade St.* ☎ *541/549–2572* ▭ *MC, V.*

$$$$
FRENCH
Fodor's Choice
★ ✗ **Jen's Garden.** This "garden" has grown to become the first world-class restaurant Sisters could claim in years. Jen's offers a three-course prix-fixe option as well as its traditional five-course meal. In keeping with the European custom of small servings, the courses are deliberately integrated so that the flavors complement each other. The menu changes every two weeks, with choices for each course; chanterelle-and-butternut-squash ravioli or New Zealand cockles/fennel/tomato/sausage broth, osso buco or berry-bread-pudding-stuffed roasted quail.

6

324 < **Central Oregon**

If you prefer, you can always order à la carte. ✉ *403 E. Hood Ave.* ☎ *541/549–2699* ⊕ *www.intimatecottagecuisine.com* ⚱ *Reservations essential* ▭ *MC, V* ⊗ *No lunch.*

$$$ ✕ **Kokanee Cafe.** The remarkable Kokanee draws diners from across
AMERICAN the mountains to sample dishes at this homey hideaway on the banks
Fodor'sChoice of the Metolius. Crab cakes, rolled into smallish balls buried inside a
★ crisscross of crisped vermicelli, are crunchy-succulent. Roast duck is enhanced by a sprinkling of organic chocolate bits; and wild salmon is just that when brushed with creamy potato and then heaped with calamari-corn salsa. As if brilliant appetizers, entrées and a fine wine list weren't enough, enjoy hand-cranked ice cream daily. ✉ *25545 SW Forest Service Rd., #1419, Camp Sherman* ☎ *541/595–6420* ⊕ *www. kokaneecafe.com* ▭ *MC, V* ⊗ *Closed Nov.–Apr. No lunch.*

WHERE TO STAY

$$$$ ⌂ **Black Butte Ranch.** Eight miles west of Sisters, Black Butte Ranch has gorgeous mountain views and landscaping to match, with biking and hiking paths meandering for miles around golf courses, ponds, and meadows. Window views throughout keep you in perpetual contact with the snowcapped mountains and pine forests that envelop the property. Horseback riding, swimming, and golf are dominant sports here. The Ranch is convenient to Smith Rock State Park, the Deschutes River, Mt. Bachelor, and the Hoodoo Ski Bowl. **Pros:** great for people who want to avoid a "big hotel" venue; resort amenities; natural setting. **Cons:** many properties don't have air-conditioning; some units haven't been updated for years. ✉ *12930 Hawks Beard* ☎ *541/595–6211 or 866/901–2961* ⊕ *www.blackbutteranch.com* ↪ *82 houses, 38 rooms* ⚸ *In-room: a/c (some), kitchen (most), refrigerator, DVD, Wi-Fi (some). In-hotel: 2 restaurants, 2 bars, golf courses, tennis courts, pools, gym, spa, bicycles, laundry facilities, children's programs (ages 10 and younger), Internet access, pets allowed (some units, with a fee)* ▭ *AE, D, DC, MC, V*⦿*EP.*

$$ ⌂ **Five Pine Lodge.** This new property looks like a forest lodge, but it's conveniently located on the eastern fringe of downtown Sisters. The luxury western-style resort features high-end furnishings hand built by Amish craftsmen, lots of dark wood, and warm tile. The rooms and the campus behind the lodge exude western, country charm. In front of the lodge, a brewpub, restaurant, spa, and movie theater share a parking area. **Pros:** top-quality craftsmanship; high-end fixtures, like the Kohler waterfall tubs. **Cons:** the lodge is only slightly set back from U.S. Highway 20, where traffic is sometimes quite heavy. ✉ *1021 Desperado Trail* ☎ *541/549–5900 or 866/974–5900* ⊕ *www.fivepinelodge.com* ↪ *8 rooms, 24 cabins* ⚸ *In-room: a/c, refrigerator, DVD, Wi-Fi. In-hotel: 2 restaurants, spa, gym, bicycles, pets allowed in some units(fee)* ▭ *AE, D, DC, MC, V.*

¢ ⌂ **The Lodge at Suttle Lake.** Built in the Grand Cascadian style, this 10,000
Fodor'sChoice square-foot lodge presides over the eastern side of Suttle Lake. Supersized
★ wooden architecture and whimsical charm characterize the main Great Room, which is often flooded with light beneath a sky-high ceiling. The 10 new lodge rooms are big on luxury, with fireplaces and glorious lake or forest views. The six exterior cabins vary in modern conveniences and size, and feature access to the high lake. For biking, hiking, boating, or

The Lodge at Suttle Lake

just relaxing, beautiful Suttle Lake is well situated, inviting quiet contemplation. **Pros:** peaceful setting; accessibility to varied sports in all seasons; variation in room and price. **Cons:** no air-conditioning in summer. ⊠ *13300 U.S. Hwy. 20 (also known as Oregon Highway 126, 13 mi northwest of Sisters)* ☎ *541/595–2628* ⊕ *www.thelodgeatsuttlelake.com* ➩ *10 rooms, 14 cabins* ⅃ *In-room: no a/c, kitchen (some), refrigerator (some), DVD, Wi-Fi (some). In-hotel: restaurant, bar, spa, water sports, Wi-Fi, parking (free), pets allowed in some units (fee)* ⊟ *AE, MC, V* ⍩ *EP.*

$ ⊡ **Metolius River Lodges.** Homespun cottages give you cozy river views, fireplaces, and woodsy interiors complemented by top-notch hospitality. Pick from studiolike fourplex lodges or freestanding lodges with kitchen and bedrooms. Big picture windows bring in the pine scenery and blue sky reflecting off the water. Of the cabins, the Salmonfly is the most popular; its large front deck overhangs the current. Make reservations well in advance, especially for summer. **Pros:** within walking distance of the river and the Camp Sherman store. **Cons:** few amenities. ⊠ *12390 SW Forest Service Rd., #1419* ☎ *800/595–6290 or 541/595–6290* ⊕ *www.metoliusriverlodges.com* ➩ *13 cabins* ⅃ *In-room: no phone, refrigerator, kitchen (some), no TV. In hotel: parking (free)* ⊟ *MC, V* ⍩ *EP.*

$$$ ⊡ **Metolius River Resort.** Each of the 12 individually owned cabins at this
Fodor's Choice resort has splendid views of the sparkling Metolius River, decks furnished with Adirondack chairs, a full kitchen, a fireplace—and are all in immaculate condition. Children are allowed, but management asks that they respect the resort's request to maintain a "peaceful and quiet area." And therein lies its beauty: the genuine get-away-from-it-all feel of a private residence nestled in ponderosa pines and aspen. Not to mention

that one of the best fly-fishing rivers in the Cascades flows right out-
side your window and a gourmet restaurant is mere steps away. ⚠ Make
sure to drive in north from Hwy. 20—other routes are dangerous or ill advised.
Pros: privacy; full view of the river; cabins that feel like home. **Cons:** no
additional people (even visitors) allowed; no cell-phone service. ✛ *Off
U.S. 20, northeast 10 mi from Sisters, turn north on Camp Sherman
Rd, stay to left at fork (1419), and then right at only stop sign.*✉ *25551
SW Forest Service Rd. #1419, Camp Sherman* ☎ *800/818–7688* ⊕ *www.
metoliusriverresort.com* ⤵ *12 cabins* ⚲ *In-room: no a/c, kitchen, DVD
(some), Wi-Fi. In-hotel: parking (free)* ▭ *MC, V* ¶⊙¶ *EP.*

NIGHTLIFE AND THE ARTS

Three Creeks Brewing Co. The brewery has its own amber ale and IPA,
but the seasonals are where it distinguishes itself. Look for the rye
at Three Creeks. ✉ *721 Desperado Ct.* ☎ *541/549–1963* ⊕ *www.
threecreeksbrewing.com* ⊗ *Closed Sun.*

SHOPPING

Don Terra Artworks. A newcomer on the Sisters scene, this gallery represents local artists and craftspeople. You'll find stone sculptures, pottery,
jewelry, glass, and paintings. ✉ *222 W. Hood Ave.* ☎ *541/549–1299*
⊕ *www.donterra.com.*

High Desert Gallery. More than a dozen central Oregon artists are showcased here at "the art and soul of central Oregon," a repository of
affordable contemporary art that includes precious metal jewelry, clay
jewelry, oil paintings, vases, and stained glass. ✉ *281 W. Cascade Ave.*
☎ *541/549–6250 or 866/549–6250* ⊕ *www.highdesertgallery.info*
⊗ *Open by appointment in fall and winter.*

Lonesome Water Books. This well-stocked independent bookstore does
considerable online business, but walk-in traffic is welcome. You can
find everything from $1 paperbacks to premium first editions. ✉ *221 W.
Cascade Ave., Suite C* ☎ *541/549–2203* ⊕ *www.lonesomewaterbooks.
com* ⊗ *Daily, 10–5:30.*

SPORTS AND THE OUTDOORS

RECREATIONAL
AREAS

Metolius Recreation Area. On the eastern slope of the Cascades and within
the 1.6-million-acre Deschutes National Forest, this bounty of recreational wilderness is drier and sunnier than the western side of the
mountains, giving way to bountiful natural history, outdoor activities,
and wildlife. Spectacular views of jagged, 10,000-foot snowcapped Cascade peaks—including Broken Top, the Three Sisters, and Mt. Jefferson,
the second-highest peak in Oregon—sprawl high above the basin of an
expansive evergreen valley carpeted by pine.

Five miles south of **Camp Sherman**, the dark and perfectly shaped cinder
cone of **Black Butte** rises 6,400 feet. At its base the **Metolius River** springs
forth. Witness the birth of this "instant" river by walking a paved ¼-mi
path embedded in ponderosa forest, eventually reaching a viewpoint with
the dramatic snow-covered peak of **Mt. Jefferson** on the horizon. At
this point, water gurgles to the ground's surface and pours into a wide
trickling creek cascading over moss-covered rocks. Within feet it funnels
outward, expanding its northerly flow; becomes a full-size river; and

meanders east alongside grassy banks and a dense pine forest to join the Deschutes River 35 mi downstream. In 1988 the 4,600-acre corridor of the Metolius was designated a National Wild and Scenic River, and in 2009 the state legislature designated the entire Metolius Basin Oregon's first "Area of Critical State Concern." Within the area and along the river, there are ample resources for camping, hiking, biking, swimming, and boating. Enjoy fly-fishing for rainbow, brown, and bull trout in perhaps the best spot within the Cascades. ⊠ *9 mi northwest of Sisters, off Hwy. 22* ⊕ *www.metoliusriver.com.*

FISHING   Fly-fishing the Metolius River attracts anglers who seek a challenge. A great fishing resource is the **Camp Sherman Store** (☏ *541/595–6711* ⊕ *www.campshermanstore.com*), which sells gear and provides information about where and how best to fish. For fishing guides, try **Fly and Field Outfitters** (☏ *541/389–7016* ⊕ *www.flyandfield.com*) out of Bend.

GOLF   **Aspen Lakes.** Golfers give high marks to this 18-hole bentgrass course designed by William Overdorf, which takes full advantage of the Sisters area's stunning vistas. ⊠ *16900 Aspen Lakes Dr.* ☏ *541/549–4653* ⊕ *www.aspenlakes.com.*

Big Meadow at Black Butte. This 18-hole course wins praise for its stunning views and the stately stands of firs that girdle the fairways. ⊠ *12930 Hawks Beard* ☏ *541/595–6211 or 866/901–2961* ⊕ *www.blackbutteranch.com.*

SKIING   On a 5,711-foot summit, **Hoodoo Ski Area** (⊠ *U.S. 20, 20 mi west of Sisters* ☏ *541/822–3799* ⊕ *www.hoodoo.com*) has 806 acres of ski-able terrain. With three quad lifts, one triple lift, one double lift, and 30 downhill runs, skiers of all levels will find suitable thrills. For tranquillity, upper and lower Nordic trails are surrounded by silence. At a 60,000-square-foot lodge at the mountain's base you can take in the view, grab bait, shop, or relax your weary feet. The ski area has kids' activities and child-care services available. Lift tickets range from $33 to $45 for adults, depending on time of day.

EAST CENTRAL OREGON

East of the Cascades, central Oregon changes to desert. The land is austere, covered mostly in sage and juniper, with a few hardy rivers and great extrusions of lava, which flowed or were blasted across the prehistoric landscape. In recent years resorts have emerged to draw west-side residents weary of the rain. They come over to bask in the sun and to soak up the feeling of the frontier, reinforced by ranches and resilient towns like Redmond and Prineville. They also come to fish and boat on the high lakes inside Newberry Crater and the man-made lakes near Culver and Prineville.

REDMOND

20 mi east of Sisters on Hwy. 126, 15 mi northeast of Bend on U.S. 97.

Redmond sits at the western end of Oregon's high desert, 4 mi from the Deschutes River and within minutes of several lakes. It is a place where

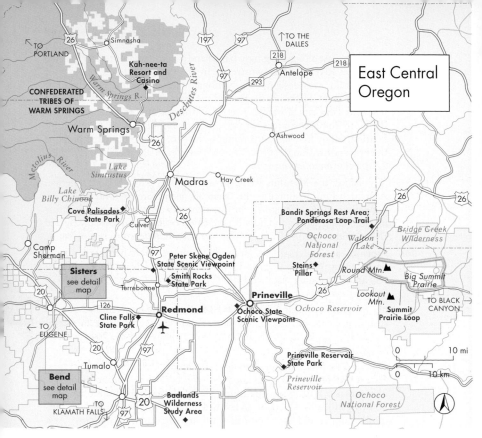

desert ranches meet runways, as it serves as the regional hub for air travel. Its compact, historic downtown has been girdled—some would say strangled—by one-way highway couplets that slingshot travelers north to Hood River and south to Bend and Sunriver. It is the town nearest to Eagle Crest Resortand Smith Rock, a magnet for rock climbers. As with Deschutes County, Redmond has experienced some of the most rapid growth in the state during the past 10 years, largely owing to a dry and mild climate and year-round downhill and cross-country skiing, fishing, hiking, mountain biking, and rock hounding. Still, this is no gentrified resort town à la Bend, as a stroll through downtown will attest. A few blocks of vintage buildings remain, but north–south traffic hustles through the city core, with most residents in neighborhoods strung out to the west. Centennial Park, a small-but-attractive open space with fountains and an expansive lawn, opened downtown in the summer of 2010.

GETTING HERE

A couple of highways—U.S. 97 and Oregon 126—cross in Redmond. Highway 97 carries travelers north and south to Washington and California, and Highway 126 runs between Sisters in the west to Prineville in the east. Taxis and the **Roberts Field–Redmond Airport Shuttle** ferry travelers to the Redmond Municipal Airport. Two bus lines, the **Central Oregon Breeze** and **Cascades East Transit**, serve Redmond. The Central

Cove Palisades State Park

Many people who drive through this part of north central Oregon are more intent on their distant destinations than on the arid landscape they're passing through. But venture down the two-lane roads to **Cove Palisades State Park**, a mini Grand Canyon of red-rock cliffs and gorges 14 mi west of small-town Madras. On a clear day a column of snowcapped Cascades peaks lines the horizon during the drive from town. Lake Billy Chinook, a glittering oasis amid the rocks, snakes through the park. It's formed by the Deschutes, Metolius, and Crooked rivers.

The park is accessible year-round, but high season is summertime, when families camp on the lakeshore and houseboats drift unhurriedly from cliff to cleft. The lake is renowned for its wildlife, from the lake's bull trout to turkey vultures that fill the sky with their cries. Nature lovers also flock to the park in February for the annual eagle watch.

The Crooked River Day Use Area is the most immediately accessible part of the park, a great place to cast a line into the water, launch a boat, or raid your picnic basket. Nearby is the Cove Palisades Marina, where you can rent boats, clean fish, and buy sandwiches and boat supplies, including kids' water toys.

In addition to 10 mi of hiking trails, Cove Palisades has a driving loop around its craggy rim. Near the Ship Rock formation, you may see petroglyphs carved into a boulder by indigenous people who moved through the area centuries ago.

A full-service campground has 85 full hookups, 89 electrical sites with water, and 91 tent sites, houseboats, and cabins. ⊠ *Off U.S. 97, 15 mi SW of Madras, 7300 Jordan Rd., Culver* ☎ *541/546–3412 or 800/551–6949* ⊕ *www.oregonstateparks.org* ☛ *Day use $5 per vehicle*

Oregon Breeze links Bend, Redmond, Madras and Portland, and Cascades East runs buses to and from Redmond and Madras, Prineville and Bend on demand. Passengers should call to ensure a ride.

Contacts Central Oregon Breeze (☎ *541/389–7469 or 800/847–0157* ⊕ *www.cobreeze.com*). **Cascades East Transit** (☎ *541/385–8680 or 866/385–8680* ⊕ *www.cascadeseasttransit.com*). **Redmond Airport Shuttle** (☎ *541/382–1687 or 888/664–8449* ⊕ *www.redmondairportshuttle.net*).

VISITOR INFORMATION
Redmond Chamber of Commerce and Convention and Visitors Bureau (⊠ *446 SW 7th St.* ☎ *541/923–5191* ⊕ *www.visitredmondoregon.com*).

EXPLORING
Peter Skene Ogden Wayside. Even the most seasoned traveler may develop vertigo peering from the cliff top into a 300-foot-deep river canyon. It is a view that gives insight into why Oregon's high desert looks the way it does, with sheer drops and austere landscapes. You'll want to take pictures, but hang on to your camera. ⊠ *U.S. 97 N, 10 mi north of Redmond* ☎ *541/548–7501.*

Petersen's Rock Gardens. Rasmus Petersen, a Danish immigrant who died in 1952, created this 4-acre garden about halfway between Redmond and Bend. All the petrified wood, agate, jasper, lava, and obsidian came from within an 85-mi radius of the garden, and was used to make miniature buildings and bridges, terraces, and towers. Among the structures are a micro–Statue of Liberty and five little castles up to 6 feet tall. The attraction includes a small museum and picnic tables. ⊠ *7930 SW 77th St.* ☏ *541/382–5574* 🖙 *$4.50* ⊙ *Daily 9–5.*

WHERE TO EAT AND STAY

$$$ ✕ **The Brickhouse Steak and Seafood.** The most elegant dining experience in Redmond is at the Brickhouse, a white-tablecloth and brick-wall place that specializes in steaks and chops, but also offers attractive plates of seafood, especially shellfish. The lighting is muted, but bright enough to let you see what you're eating. You can get lost in the list of cocktails and wines from Oregon and around the world. ⊠ *412 SW 6th St.* ☏ *541/526–1782* ⊕ *www.brickhouseredmond.com* 🖃 *MC, V* ⊙ *Closed Sun. and Mon. No lunch.*

$$ ✕ **Terrebonne Depot.** Finally, a Smith Rock restaurant that matches the
AMERICAN view. The Terrebonne offers an array of reasonably priced, tasty dishes. The kitchen plays it straight down the middle, with nicely seasoned steaks, salmon, chicken, and pork chops. You can also get lunch baskets to take with you on the climb. Service is friendly, and the menu is a cut above what you'd expect in this off-the-beaten-track location. The view allows you to reflect on the climb you've just made—or will inspire you to embark on one. ⊠ *400 NW Smith Rock Way* ☏ *541/548–5030* ⊕ *www.terrebonnedepot.com* 🖃 *MC, V* ⊙ *Closed Tues.*

$$ 🏨 **Eagle Crest Resort.** Eagle Crest is 5 mi west of Redmond, above the
Ⓒ canyon of the Deschutes River. In this high-desert area the grounds are covered with juniper and sagebrush, except for the lush golf course. Some rooms are vacation rentals, but others are clustered in a single building on the landscaped grounds, and some of the suites have gas fireplaces. The resort is on 1,700 acres. There are 10 mi of bike trails and a 2-mi hiking trail where you can fish in the river. **Pros:** a full-service resort; great for kids; pet-friendly. **Cons:** there can be crowds, kids, and pets. ⊠ *1522 Cline Falls Hwy* ☏ *800/682–4786* ⊕ *www.eagle-crest.com* 🖙 *100 rooms, 45 suites, 75 town houses* 🖧 *In-room: a/c, kitchen (some), refrigerator, DVD, Wi-Fi. In-hotel: 4 restaurants, bar, golf courses, tennis courts, pools, gym, spa, bicycles, children's programs (ages 3–12), free parking, Wi-Fi hotspot, some pets allowed.* 🖃 *AE, DC, MC, V* 🍴 *EP.*

SPORTS AND THE OUTDOORS

RECREATIONAL **Cline Falls State Park.** Picnicking, fishing, and bicycling are popular at this
AREAS nine-acre rest area commanding scenic views on the Deschutes River 5 mi west of Redmond. You'll feel free from civilization here. ⊠ *Hwy. 126, west of Redmond* ☏ *800/551–6949* ⊕ *www.oregonstateparks.org.*

ROCK **Smith Rock State Park.** Eight miles north of Redmond, this park is world
CLIMBING famous for rock climbing, with hundreds of routes of all levels of dif-
Fodor'sChoice ficulty. A network of trails serves both climbers and families dropping
★ in for the scenery. In addition to the stunning rock formations, the Crooked River, which helped shape these features, loops through the park You might spot golden eagles, prairie falcons, mule deer, river otters, and beavers. Due to the environmental sensitivity of the region,

Rock climbing in Smith Rock State Park

the animal leash law is strongly enforced. It can get quite hot in midsummer, so most prefer to climb in the spring and fall. ⊠ *Off U.S. 97, 9241 NE Crooked River Dr., Terrebonne* ☎ *541/548–7501 or 800/551–6949* ⊕ *www.oregonstateparks.org* 🗗 *Day use $5 per vehicle.*

Smith Rock Climbing Guides (☎ *541/788–6225* ⊕ *www.smithrockclimbingguides. com*) is run by professionals with emergency medical training. They take visitors to the Smith Rock formation for climbs of all levels of difficulty and supply all equipment. Guided climbs can run a half day or full day, and are priced according to the number of people in a group.

PRINEVILLE

17 mi east of Redmond on Hwy. 126.

Prineville is the oldest town in central Oregon, and the only incorporated city in Crook County. Tire entrepreneur Les Schwab founded his regional empire here, and it remains a key hub for the company. Recently, Facebook chose Prineville as the location for its new data center. Surrounded by verdant ranch lands and the purplish hills of the Ochoco National Forest, Prineville will likely interest you chiefly as a jumping-off point for some of the region's more secluded outdoor adventures. The area attracts thousands of anglers, boaters, sightseers, and rock hounds to its nearby streams, reservoirs, and mountains. Rimrocks nearly encircle Prineville, and geology nuts dig for free agates, limb casts, jasper, and thunder eggs. Downtown Prineville consists of a handful of small buildings along a quiet strip of Highway 26, dominated by the Crook County Courthouse, built in 1909. Shopping and dining opportunities are mostly on the basic side.

GETTING HERE

Travelers approaching Prineville from the west on Oregon 126 descend like a marble circling a funnel, dropping into a tidy grid of a town from a high desert plain. It's an unfailingly dramatic way to enter the seat of Crook County, dominated by the courthouse on Northeast Third Street, aka Highway 26, the main drag. Prineville is 20 mi east of Roberts Field–Redmond Municipal Airport. If you're coming to Prineville from the airport, it's easiest to rent a car and drive. However, two bus lines, **Central Oregon Breeze** and **Cascades East** run routes by appointment.

Contacts **Central Oregon Breeze** (☎ 541/389–7469 or 800/847–0157 ⊕ www. cobreeze.com). **Cascades East Transit** (☎ 541/385–8680 or 866/385–8680 ⊕ www.cascadeseasttransit.com).

VISITOR INFORMATION

Ochoco National Forest Headquarters and Prineville Ranger Station (⊠ 3160 NE 3rd St. ☎ 541/416–6500 ⊕ www.fs.fed.us/r6/centraloregon). **Prineville-Crook County Chamber of Commerce and Visitor Center** (⊠ 102 NW 2nd St. ☎ 541/447–6304 ⊕ www.visitprineville.com).

EXPLORING

Bowman Museum. A tough little stone building (it was a bank once, and banks out here needed to be tough) is the site of the museum of the Crook County Historical Society. The 1911 edifice is now on the National Register of Historic Places. Prominent are pioneer artifacts—agricultural implements, vintage mousetraps, firearms—that defined early Prineville. ⊠ 246 N. Main St. ☎ 541/447–3715 ⊕ www. bowmanmuseum.org ⌦ Free ⊘ Memorial Day–Labor Day, weekdays 10–5, weekends 11–4; Labor Day–Dec. and Feb.–Memorial Day, Tues.–Fri. 10–5, Sat. 11–4. Closed Jan.

EN
ROUTE

A 43-mi scenic route, the **Summit Prairie Loop** winds past Lookout Mountain, Round Mountain, Walton Lake, and Big Summit Prairie. The prairie abounds with trout-filled creeks and has one of the finest stands of ponderosa pines in the state; wild mustangs roam the area. The prairie can be glorious between late May and June, when wildflowers with evocative names like mule ears, wyethia, biscuit root, yellow bells, and desert shooting stars burst into bloom. ✛ Forest Service Rd. 22 east to Forest Service Rd. 30, which turns into Forest Service Rd. 3010, south, to Forest Service Rd. 42 heading west, which loops back to Forest Service Rd. 22 ☎ 541/416–6500.

Ochoco Viewpoint. About ½ mi west of Prineville is a truly fantastic scenic overlook that commands a sweeping view of the city and the hills, ridges, and buttes beyond. ⊠ ½ mi west of Prineville on U.S. Hwy. 126.

WHERE TO EAT AND STAY

$$ ✕ **Barney Prine's Steakhouse and Saloon.** Prineville has become home to a startlingly appealing restaurant and saloon named after the town's founder. It's a good place to get a filet mignon, pepper steak, T-bone, or other good cuts. Chicken, lamb, fish, elk, and veal also are on the menu. The waitstaff is cheerful and attentive, and the ambience is part frontier western, part contemporary. ⊠ 380 NE Main St. ☎ 541/447–3333 ⊕ www.barneyprines.com ▭ MC, V ⊘ Closed Mon. No lunch Sat.–Tues.

6

¢ ⟨T⟩ **Rustlers Inn.** From the old-style covered walkways to the large, antiques-furnished rooms, this motel is Old West all the way. Each room is decorated differently—if you call in advance, the managers will attempt to match your room furnishings to your personality. The Rustlers allows pets to stay for a one-time fee. **Pros:** Individually themed rooms; friendly management. **Cons:** Little street appeal, no restaurant. ⊠ *960 NW 3rd St. (U.S. 26)* ☎ *541/447–4185* ⊕ *www.rustlersinn.com* ⇨ *20 rooms* ⚙ *In-room: a/c, kitchen (some), refrigerator, DVD, Wi-Fi. In-hotel: free parking, some pets allowed.* ⊟ *AE, D, DC, MC, V.*

SPORTS AND THE OUTDOORS

RECREATIONAL **Ochoco National Forest.** Twenty-five miles east of the flat, juniper-dotted
AREAS countryside around Prineville, the landscape changes to forested ridges covered with tall ponderosa pines and Douglas firs. Sheltered by the diminutive Ochoco Mountains and with only about a foot of rain each year, the national forest, established in 1906 by President Theodore Roosevelt, manages to lay a blanket of green across the dry, high desert of central Oregon. This arid landscape—marked by deep canyons, towering volcanic plugs, and sharp ridges—goes largely unnoticed except for the annual influx of hunters during the fall. The Ochoco, part of the old Blue Mountain Forest Reserve, is a great place for camping, hiking, biking, and fishing in relative solitude. In its three wilderness areas—Mill Creek, Bridge Creek, and Black Canyon—it's possible to see elk, wild horses, eagles, and even cougars. ⊠ *Ranger Station 3160 NE 3rd St., U.S. 26* ☎ *541/416–6500* ◷ *Ranger station weekdays 7:30–4:30.*

The Oregon Badlands Wilderness. This 30,000-acre swath of Oregon's high desert was designated a national wilderness in 2009, following the long-time advocacy of Oregonians enamored by its harshly beautiful landscape riven by ancient lava flows and home to sage grouse, pronghorn antelope, and elk. Motorized vehicles are prohibited, but visitors can ride horses on designated trails and low-impact hikers are welcome. Bring a camera to capture the ancient lava flows, jagged rock formations, birds, and wildflowers. ⊠ *3050 NE 3rd St., U.S. 26* ☎ *541/416–6700.*

Prineville Reservoir State Park. Mountain streams flow out of the Ochoco Mountains and join together to create the Crooked River, which is dammed near Prineville. Bowman Dam on the river forms the park. Recreational activities include boating, swimming, fishing, hiking, and camping. ⊠ *19020 SE Parkland Dr.* ☎ *541/447–4363 or 800/452–5687* ⊕ *www.oregonstateparks.org* ⛺ *campgrounds $22 May 1–Sept. 30.*

FISHING It's a good idea to check the **Oregon Department of Fish and Wildlife**'s (⊕ *www.dfw.state.or.us/RR/index.asp*) weekly recreation report before you head out.

Ochoco Reservoir is stocked in the spring with fingerling trout, with holdover rainbows available throughout the year. As the weather warms through the summer, bass, crappie and bluegill are the leading species. ⊠ *7 mi east of Prineville on Highway 26* ☎ *541/447–1209* ⊕ *www. fs.fed.us/r6/centraloregon/recreation/fishing*

Some anglers return year after year to **Prineville Reservoir**, although temperatures can get uncomfortably hot and water levels relatively low by late summer. The reservoir is known for its bass, trout and crappie, with fly-fishing available on the Crooked River below Bowman Dam. ✉ *19020 SE Parkland Dr.* ☎ *541/447–4363 or 800/452–5687* ⊕ *www. oregonstateparks.org.*

GOLF Golfers with connections play **Brasada Canyons, at Brasada Ranch,** an 18-hole course designed by PGA golfer Peter Jacobsen and Jim Hardy. It is a private course, but open to visitors and guests of the ranch resort. ✉ *16986 SW Brasada Ranch Rd., Powell Butte* ☎ *866/976-8528* ⊕ *www.brasada.com.*

The public course at **Meadow Lakes** came into being when the city needed a place to treat wastewater in the late 1980s, and has blossomed into a well-regarded, 18-hole course that crosses the Crooked River. ✉ *300 SW Meadow Lakes Dr.* ☎ *541/447–7113* ⊕ *www.meadowlakesgc.com.*

HIKING Pick up maps at the Ochoco/Prineville Ranger Station for trails through the 5,400-acre **Bridge Creek Wilderness** and the demanding Black Canyon Trail (24 mi round-trip) in the **Black Canyon Wilderness.** The 1½-mi **Ponderosa Loop Trail** follows an old logging road through ponderosa pines growing on hills. In early summer wildflowers take over the open meadows. The trailhead begins at Bandit Springs Rest Area, 22 mi east of Prineville on U.S. 26. A 2½-mi, one-way trail winds through old-growth forest and mountain meadows to **Steins Pillar,** a giant lava column with panoramic views; be prepared for a workout on the trail's poorly maintained second half, and allow at least three hours for the hike. To get to the trailhead, drive east 9 mi from Prineville on U.S. 26, head north (to the left) for 6½ mi on Mill Creek Road (also signed as Forest Service Road 33), and head east (to the right) on Forest Service Road 500.

SKIING Two loops for cross-country skiers start at **Bandit Springs Rest Area,** 29 mi east of Prineville on U.S. 26. One loop is designed for beginners and the other for intermediate to advanced skiers. Both traverse the area near the Ochoco Divide and have great views. **Ochoco National Forest** headquarters has a handout on skiing trails, and can provide the required Sno-Park permits, which are also available from the **Department of Motor Vehicles** (✉ *Ochoco Plaza, 1595 E. 3rd St., Suite A-3, Prineville* ☎ *541/447-7855).*

Southern Oregon

WORD OF MOUTH

"I would suggest doing a daytime drive north on I-5 to Roseburg and go up along the Umpqua River to Crater Lake, then drive back to Ashland on whatever route you choose. Following the Umpqua is one of the most beautiful drives in the state. There are many stops along the way, short walks, and waterfalls just off the road."
—rolncathy

WELCOME TO SOUTHERN OREGON

TOP REASONS TO GO

★ **The other wine region.** The underrated Umpqua and Rogue River wine regions offer picturesque pastoral views and numerous tasting rooms. The warmer climate and varied terrain makes southern Oregon conducive to many more varietals than the more famous Willamette Valley.

★ **Oregon Shakespeare Festival.** This acclaimed festival draws drama lovers to Ashland nine months a year, and presents a wide variety of theater at three distinctive venues.

★ **Quaint towns.** Southern Oregon's own throwback to the Old West, Jacksonville abounds with well-preserved buildings and diverting eateries and bed-and-breakfasts. Ashland claims one of the prettiest downtowns in Oregon, with its hip cafés and urbane boutiques.

★ **Wild wonders.** Each fall more than 1 million waterfowl descend upon Klamath Basin National Wildlife Refuge Complex. The Rogue River is Oregon's white-water rafting capital.

1 Umpqua Valley. Known increasingly for its up-and-coming wineries, including Henry Estate and Abacela, this valley is home to historic Oakland, Roseburg and its family-friendly Wildlife Safari park, and the Umpqua River Scenic Byway, a particularly scenic route to Crater Lake.

2 Rogue Valley. This fertile, mild-temperature region that extends from Grants Pass southeast through Medford and down to Ashland takes in the most populous communities in the area—it's also the gateway for reaching Klamath Falls, to the east, and the remote but fascinating Oregon Caves National Monument to the southwest. The Oregon Shakespeare Festival and an abundance of historic buildings have turned Ashland into a hub of arts, culture, and fine bed-and-breakfasts. Grants Pass is the launch point for some of the best white-water rafting around, while Medford and historic Jacksonville are surrounded by vineyards and farms that produce some of the state's tastiest local edibles, from pears to Pinot Gris.

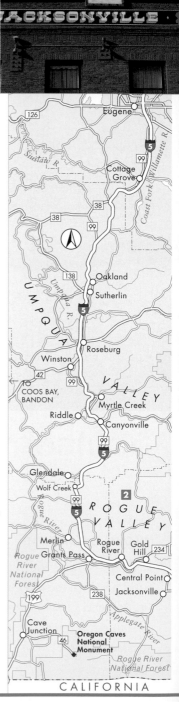

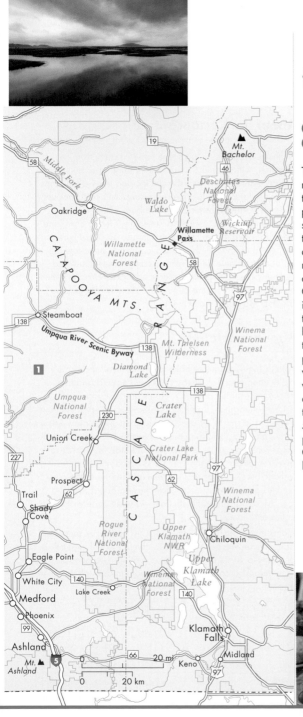

GETTING ORIENTED

To locals, southern Oregon refers to the southwestern third of the state, encompassing the Rogue and several other river valleys that lie between the Coast and Cascade mountain ranges, from a little north of Roseburg down to the California border. The area is due south of Eugene and the Willamette Valley, and has a similarly lush and fertile terrain that lends itself perfectly to agriculture and winemaking. Towns in the valleys, such as Ashland and Roseburg, have elevations ranging from about 500 to 2000 feet, while peaks to the east, in the Cascade Range, rise as high as 9,000 feet.

7

SOUTHERN OREGON PLANNER

When to Go

Southern Oregon's population centers, which all lie chiefly in the valleys, tend to be warmer and quite a bit sunnier than Eugene and Portland to the north, receiving almost no snow in winter and only 2 to 3 inches of rain per month. In summer, temperatures regularly climb into the 90s, but the low humidity makes for a generally comfortable climate. This makes most of the region quite pleasant to visit year-round, with spring and fall generally offering the best balance of sunny and mild weather.

The exception, during the colder months, are southern Oregon's mountainous areas to the east and west, which are covered with snow from fall through spring. Some of the roads leading from the Umpqua and Rogue valleys up to Crater Lake are closed because of snow from mid-October through June, making summer the prime time to visit.

Jacksonville hosts the world-class summer music **Britt Festivals**, and the **Oregon Shakespeare Festival** in Ashland lasts from February to October. Each February nature enthusiasts flock to the Klamath Basin for the **Bald Eagle Conference**, the nation's oldest birding festival.

About the Restaurants

Southern Oregon's dining scene varies greatly from region to region, with the more tourism-driven and upscale communities of Ashland and Jacksonville leading the way in terms of sophisticated farm-to-table restaurants, hip coffeehouses, and noteworthy bakeries and wine bars. Other larger towns in the valleys, including Roseburg, Grants Pass, and Medford, have grown in culinary stature and variety of late, while Klamath Falls and Cave Junction have few dining options of note. In the former communities you'll find chefs emphasizing Oregon-produced foods; Oregon wines, including many from the Rogue and Umpqua valleys, also find their way onto many menus.

About the Hotels

With its highly popular Shakespeare Festival and strategic location exactly halfway between Portland and San Francisco, Ashland has the region's greatest variety of distinctive lodgings, from the usual low- to mid-priced chain properties to plush bed-and-breakfasts set in restored Arts and Crafts and Victorian houses. Nearby Jacksonville also has several fine, upscale inns. Beyond that, in nearly every town in southern Oregon you'll find two or three interesting bed-and-breakfasts or small hotels, and in any of the communities along Interstate 5—including Roseburg, Grants Pass, Medford, and Klamath Falls—a wide variety of chain motels and hotels.

Rooms in this part of the state book up earliest in summer, especially on weekends. If you're coming to Ashland or Jacksonville, try to book at least a week or two ahead. Elsewhere, you can usually find a room in a suitable chain property on less than a day's notice.

WHAT IT COSTS IN U.S. DOLLARS

	¢	$	$$	$$$	$$$$
Restaurants	under $10	$10–$16	$17–$23	$24–$30	over $30
Hotels	under $100	$100–$150	$151–$200	$201–$250	over $250

Restaurant prices are per person, for a main course at dinner. Hotel prices are for two people in a standard double room in high season, excluding tax.

Getting Here and Around

Air Travel. Medford's **Rogue Valley International Airport (MFR)** (☎ 541/772-8068 ⊕ www.co.jackson.or.us) is the state's third-largest facility. Most national car rental branches are at the airport, with rates starting at $25 a day. A few taxi and shuttle companies provide transportation from the airport to other towns in the area; these are used mostly by locals, as a car is the only practical way to explore this mostly rural part of Oregon. The one exception is Ashland, in which many attractions, restaurants, and accommodations are within walking distance. **Cascade Airport Shuttle** (☎ 541/488-1998) offers door-to-door service from the airport to Ashland for about $30. Among taxi companies, Valley Cab (☎ 541/772-1818) serves the Rogue Valley region, with fares costing $3 base per trip, plus $2.50 per mile thereafter.

Roseburg is a 75-mi drive from Oregon's second-largest airport, in Eugene (EUG).Ashland is about 300 mi south of the state's largest airport, in Portland; and 350 mi north of San Francisco. Although it's often cheaper to fly into these larger airports than it is to Medford, what you lose in gas costs, time, and inconvenience may outweigh the savings.

Bus Travel. A half-dozen **Greyhound** (☎ 800/231-2222 ⊕ www.greyhound.com) buses a day connect Portland, Salem, Bend, and other northern points on the I-5 corridor to Grants Pass, Medford (southern Oregon's transportation hub), and Klamath Falls. Southern Oregon's one regional bus line, **Rogue Valley Transportation District** (☎ 541/734-9292 ⊕ www.rvtd.org), has service from Medford to Central Point, Jacksonville, and Ashland; however, this service is geared toward commuters and is unwieldy and impractical for short-term visitors, as buses run only during the day, run only once or twice an hour, and don't serve many of the region's key attractions.

Car Travel. Unquestionably, your best way to explore the region is by car, although most of Ashland's key attractions, hotels, and dining are downtown and within walking distance of one another. Interstate 5 runs north–south the length of the Umpqua and Rogue River valleys, linking Roseburg, Grants Pass, Medford, and Ashland. Many regional attractions lie not too far east or west of Interstate 5. Jacksonville is a short drive due west from Medford. Highway 138 winds scenically along the Umpqua River east of Roseburg to the less-visited northern end of Crater Lake National Park. Highway 140 leads from Medford east to Klamath Falls, which you can reach from Bend via U.S. 97.

Tour Options

You'll see some of Oregon's most magnificent scenery with **Hellgate Jetboat Excursions** (☎ 541/479-7204 or 800/648-4874 ⊕ www.hellgate.com), which depart from the Riverside Inn in Grants Pass. The 36-mi round-trip runs through Hellgate Canyon and takes 2 hours. There is also a 5-hour, 75-mi round-trip from Grants Pass to Grave Creek, with a stop for a meal on an open-air deck (cost of meal not included). Trips are available May through September.

Main Street Adventure Tours (☎ 541/482-9852 ⊕ www.southernoregonwinetours.com), based in Ashland, offers custom limo tours through the region's key wine regions, the Rogue, Applegate, Illinois, and Umpqua valleys. The company can also customize tours to Crater Lake, fly-fishing and skiing trips, and other activities and explorations throughout the region.

VISITOR INFORMATION

Southern Oregon Visitors Association (☎ 541/779-4691 ⊕ www.southernoregon.org).

7

Updated by Andrew Collins

Southern Oregon begins where the verdant lowlands of the Willamette Valley give way to a complex collision of mountains, rivers, and ravines. The intricate geography of the "Land of Umpqua," as the area around Roseburg is somewhat romantically known, signals that this is territory distinct from neighboring regions to the north, east, and west.

Wild rivers—the Rogue and the Umpqua are legendary for fishing and boating—and twisting mountain roads venture through the landscape that saw Oregon's most violent Indian wars and became the territory of a self-reliant breed. "Don't-Tread-on-Me" southern Oregonians see themselves as markedly different from fellow citizens of the Pacific Wonderland. In fact, several early-20th-century attempts to secede from Oregon and proclaim a "state of Jefferson" survive in local folklore and culture. That being said, Ashland and parts of the surrounding area have gradually become more progressive and urbane in recent decades, as wineries, art galleries, and hip restaurants have opened. The mix of folks from all different political, social, and stylistic bents is a big part of what makes southern Oregon so appealing.

Some locals refer to this sun-kissed, sometimes surprisingly hot landscape as the Mediterranean; others call it Oregon's banana belt. It's a climate built for slow-paced pursuits and a leisurely outlook on life, not to mention agriculture—the region's orchards, farms, and increasingly acclaimed vineyards have lately helped give southern Oregon cachet among food and wine aficionados. The restaurant scene has grown partly thanks to a pair of big cultural draws, Ashland's Oregon Shakespeare Festival and Jacksonville's open-air, picnic-friendly Britt Festivals concert series.

Roseburg, Medford, and Klamath Falls are also all popular bases for visiting iconic Crater Lake National Park (⇨ *see Chapter 8*), which lies at the region's eastern edge, about an hour or two away by car. Formed nearly 8,000 years ago by the cataclysmic eruption of Mt. Mazama, this stunningly clear-blue lake is North America's deepest.

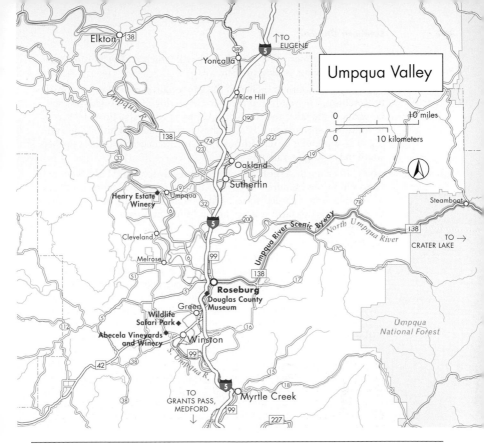

UMPQUA VALLEY

The northernmost part of southern Oregon, beginning about 40 mi south of Eugene and the Willamette Valley, the rural and sparsely populated Umpqua Valley is the gateway to this part of the state's sunny and relatively dry climate. As you drive down Interstate 5 you'll descend through twisting valleys and climb up over scenic highlands. In summer you can follow the dramatic Umpqua River Scenic Byway (Hwy. 138) east over the Cascades to access Crater Lake from the north—it's the prettiest route to the lake. Within the Umpqua Valley, attractions are relatively few, but this area has several excellent wineries, some of the best river fishing in the Northwest, and one of the region's top draws for animal lovers, the Wildlife Safari park.

ROSEBURG

73 mi south of Eugene on I–5.

Fishermen the world over hold the name Roseburg sacred. The timber town on the Umpqua River attracts anglers in search of a dozen popular fish species, including bass, brown and brook trout, and chinook, coho, and sockeye salmon. The native steelhead, which makes its run to the sea in the summer, is king of them all.

The north and south branches of the Umpqua River meet up just north of Roseburg. The roads that run parallel to this river provide spectacular views of the falls, and the North Umpqua route also provides access to trails, hot springs, and the Winchester fish ladder. White-water rafting is also popular here, although not to the degree that it is farther south in the Rogue Valley.

About 80 mi northwest of the northern gateway to Crater Lake National Park and in the Hundred Valleys of the Umpqua, Roseburg produces innovative, well-regarded wines. Wineries are sprouting up throughout the mild, gorgeous farm country around town, mostly within easy reach of Interstate 5.

GETTING HERE

Roseburg is the first large town you'll reach driving south from Eugene on Interstate 5. It's also a main access point into southern Oregon via Hwy. 138 if you're approaching from the east, either by way of Crater Lake or U.S. 97, which leads down from Bend. And from the Bandon–Coos Bay region of the Oregon Coast, windy but picturesque Hwy. 42 leads to just south of Roseburg. It's a 75-mi drive north to Eugene's airport, and a 95-mi drive south to Rogue Valley Airport in Medford. Attractions in the region are spread over a large area—a car is a must.

VISITOR INFORMATION

Roseburg Visitors & Convention Bureau (✉ *410 SE Spruce St.* ☎ *541/672–9731 or 800/444–9584* ⊕ *www.visitroseburg.com*).

EXPLORING

Douglas County Museum. One of the best county museums in the state surveys 8,000 years of human activity in the region. The fossil collection is worth a stop, as is the state's second-largest photo collection, numbering more than 24,000 images, some dating to the 1840s. ✉ *123 Museum Dr.* ☎ *541/957–7007* ⊕ *www.co.douglas.or.us/museum* ✉ *$5* ⊙ *Apr.–Sept., daily 10–5; Oct.–Mar., Mon.–Sat. 10–5*

Ⓒ **Wildlife Safari.** Come face-to-face with some 550 free-roaming animals
Fodor'sChoice at the 600-acre drive-through wildlife park. Inhabitants include alliga-
★ tors, bobcats, cougars, gibbons, lions, giraffes, grizzly bears, Tibetan yaks, cheetahs, Siberian tigers, and more than 70 additional species. There's also a petting zoo, a miniature train, and elephant rides. The admission price includes two same-day drive-throughs. This nonprofit zoological park is a respected research facility with full accreditation from the American Zoo and Aquarium Assocation, with a mission to conserve and protect endangered species through education and breeding programs. ✉ *1790 Safari Rd., Winston* ☎ *541/679–6761* ⊕ *www.wildlifesafari.net* ✉ *$18* ⊙ *Apr.–Sept., daily 9–6; Oct.–Mar., daily 10–5.*

WINERIES

Fodor'sChoice   **Abacela Vineyards and Winery.** The name derives from an archaic Span-
★ ish word meaning "to plant grapevines," and that's exactly what this winery's husband-wife team did not so very long ago. Abacela released its first wine in 1999, and has steadily established itself as one of the

Wine production in southern Oregon

state's most acclaimed producers—arguably the best outside the Willamette Valley. Hot-blooded Spanish Tempranillo is Abacela's pride and joy, though inky Malbec and torrid Sangiovese also highlight a repertoire heavy on Mediterranean varietals. ⊠ *12500 Lookingglass Rd.* ☎ *541/679–6642* ⊕ *www.abacela.com* ⊙ *Open daily 11–3.*

WHERE TO EAT AND STAY

$ | ✕ **The Mark V.** This cheery corner bar and grill in downtown Roseburg
AMERICAN | lends a bit of much-needed urbanity to this workaday downtown. Tall windows look onto the street from the plant-filled, warmly lighted dining room, where a friendly and easygoing staff serves both tapas-size and more substantial fare three meals a day. Try the blackened ahi tuna, clam chowder, and hefty steaks. ⊠ *563 SE Main St.* ☎ *541/229–6275* ⊟ *AE, D, MC, V.*

$$ | ✕ **Tolly's.** Most folks head to this sweetly nostalgic restaurant in the
AMERICAN | center of tiny and historic Oakland—18 mi north of Roseburg—for
Fodor's Choice | inexpensive lunch (including exceptionally good burgers) or to enjoy
★ | an old-fashioned soda or malt downstairs in the Victorian ice-cream parlor. On weekends, however, you can dine upstairs in the oak- and antiques-filled dining room on deftly prepared creative American cuisine. Try the wood-grilled salmon with a cremini-mustard sauce and herb polenta cake, or filet mignon sourced from Oregon's famed Carlton Farms ranch. There's also an excellent Sunday brunch. ⊠ *115 Locust St., Oakland* ☎ *541/459–3796* ⊕ *www.tollys-restaurant.com* ⊟ *AE, D, MC, V* ⊙ *No dinner Sun.–Thurs.*

$$$ | ⛳ **The Steamboat Inn.** Every fall a who's who of the world's top fly-fishermen
Fodor's Choice | converges here, high in the Cascades above the emerald North Umpqua
★ | River, in search of the 20-pound steelhead that haunt these waters; guide

344 < **Southern Oregon**

services are available, as are equipment rentals and sales. Others come simply to relax in the reading nooks or on the broad decks of the riverside guest cabins nestled below soaring fir trees and surrounded by verdant gardens. Lodging choices include riverside cabins, forest bungalows (some sleep up to six), and riverside suites; the bungalows and suites have kitchens. Make reservations well in advance, especially for a stay between July and October, the prime fishing months. The exceptionally good restaurant, which offers occasional winemaker and guest-chef dinners, caters primarily to guests, but also has a limited number of tables available by reservation. It's also open for breakfast and lunch to the general public. **Pros:** good option if en route to Crater Lake; access to some of the best fishing in the West; great escape. **Cons:** extremely far from civilization. ⊠ *42705 N. Umpqua Hwy., 38 mi east of Roseburg on Hwy. 138, near Steamboat Creek, Steamboat* ☎ *541/498–2230 or 800/840–8825* ⊕ *www.thesteamboatinn.com* ↝ *8 cabins, 5 cottages, 2 suites, 5 houses* ⚴ *In-room: no a/c, some refrigerators, no TV, Wi-Fi. In-hotel: restaurant, some pets allowed (paid)* ⊟ *MC, V.*

SPORTS AND THE OUTDOORS

FISHING You'll find some of the best river fishing in Oregon along the Umpqua, with smallmouth bass, shad, steelhead, salmon (coho, chinook, and sockeye), and sturgeon—the biggest reaching 10 feet in length—among the most prized catches. In addition to the Steamboat Inn, several outfitters in the region provide full guide services, which typically include all gear, boats, and expert leaders. There's good fishing in this region year-round, with sturgeon and steelhead at their best during the colder months, chinook and coho salmon thriving in the fall, and most other species prolific in spring and summer.

The **Oregon Angler** (☎ *800/428–8585* ⊕ *www.theoregonangler.com*), run by one of the state's most respected and knowledgeable guides, Todd Hannah, specializes in jet-boat and drift-boat fishing excursions along the famed "Umpqua Loop," an 18-mi span of river that's long been lauded for exceptional fishing. Full-day trips start at $175 per person.

Set along a 10-mi span of the upper Umpqua River near Elkton (about 35 mi north of Roseburg), **Big K Guest Ranch** (☎ *800/390–2445* ⊕ *www. big-k.com*) is a pastoral 2,500-acre guest ranch. The accommodations are geared primarily to groups and corporate retreats, but the ranch offers individual fishing packages starting at $350 per person, per day (meals and lodging included), with three- and four-night deals available at a better rate. Adventures include fly-fishing for smallmouth bass and summer steelhead, as well as spin-casting and drift-boat fishing.

RAFTING There's thrilling class-III and higher white-water rafting along the North Umpqua River, with several outfitters providing trips ranging from a few hours to a few days throughout the year.

Since 1987, **North Umpqua Outfitters** (☎ *888/454–9696* ⊕ *www.nuorafting. com*) has been a trusted provider of both half- and full-day rafting and kayaking trips along the frothy North Umpqua.

Oregon Ridge & River Excursions (☎ *888/454–9696* ⊕ *www.umpquarivers. com*) offers white-water rafting and kayaking throughout the Umpqua Basin. The company also has milder canoeing adventures on nearby lakes.

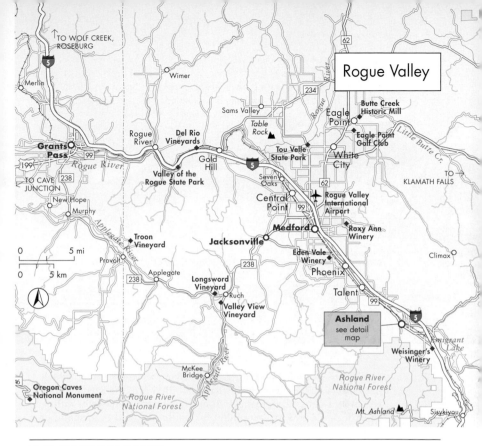

ROGUE VALLEY

Encompassing the broad, curving, southeasterly swath of towns from Grants Pass through Medford down to Ashland, the mild and sun-kissed Rogue Valley is southern Oregon's main population center, and also where you'll find the bulk of the region's lodging, dining, shopping, and recreation.

Interstate 5 cuts through the valley en route to northern California, but venture away from the main drag to see what makes this part of Oregon so special, including the superb—if underrated—wineries. With warmer temperatures, this area is conducive to many more varietals than the Willamette Valley—from reds like Syrah, Tempranillo, and Cabernet Sauvignon to increasingly well-known whites like Viognier and Pinot Gris. Foodies are drawn to the region's abundance of local food producers, from nationally acclaimed cheese makers and chocolatiers to farms growing juicy pears, blackberries, and cherries. Access to excellent food has helped turn the small but artsy city of Ashland into one of Oregon's top restaurant destinations, with nearby communities also growing in culinary cachet. Additionally, the area's reputation for performing arts, which manifests itself in the famed Oregon Shakespeare Festival in Ashland and Britt Music Festival in historic Jacksonville, continues to grow.

Kayaking Rainey Falls on the Rogue River

Flanked by 1.8-million-acre Rogue-Siskiyou National Forest, which has rangers' offices near Grants Pass and Medford, the Rogue Valley is a hub of outdoor recreation, from fishing and white-water rafting along its clear rivers to mountain-biking, hiking, and even skiing in the higher elevations—peaks in the Cascade Range, to the east, rise to nearly 10,000 feet. Klamath Falls lies technically a bit east of the Rogue Valley but shares the region's abundance of unspoiled wilderness and opportunities for getting in touch with nature.

GRANTS PASS

70 mi south of Roseburg on I–5.

It's the Climate! So says a confident 1950s vintage neon sign presiding over Josephine County's downtown. Grants Pass bills itself as Oregon's white-water capital: the Rogue River, preserved by Congress in 1968 as a National Wild and Scenic River, runs right through town. Downtown Grants Pass is a National Historic District, a stately little enclave of 19th-century brick storefronts housing folksy businesses harking back to the 1950s. It's all that white water, however, that compels most visitors—and not a few moviemakers (*The River Wild* and *Rooster Cogburn* were both filmed here). If the river alone doesn't serve up enough natural drama, the sheer rock walls of nearby Hellgate Canyon rise 250 feet.

GETTING HERE

Grants Pass is easily reached from elsewhere in the region via Interstate 5, and it's also where U.S. 199 cuts southwest toward Oregon Caves National Monument and, eventually, the northernmost section of California's coast (as well as the northern sections of Redwood National Park). Many visitors to the southern Oregon coastline backtrack inland up U.S. 199 to create a scenic loop drive, ultimately intersecting with Interstate 5 at Grants Pass. Medford's airport is a 30-mi drive away.

VISITOR INFORMATION

Grants Pass Visitors & Convention Bureau (⊠ *1995 N.W. Vine St.,* ☎ *541/476–5510* ⊕ *www.visitgrantspass.org*).

EXPLORING

Grants Pass Museum of Art. A city museum in Riverside Park displays classic and contemporary art, including the works of local artists. Sculpture and painting dominate, and the focus is on American and regional work. A first-Friday art night is a community rallying point. ⊠ *229 SW G St.* ☎ *541/479–3290* ⊕ *www.gpmusuem.com* ⧉ *Free* ☉ *Tues.–Sat. noon–4.*

WINERIES

Troon Vineyards. Few winemakers in southern Oregon have generated more buzz than Troon, whose swank tasting room and winery is patterned after a French country villa. Troon produces relatively small yields of exceptional wines more typical of Sonoma than Oregon (Zinfandel, Cabernet Sauvignon, and Syrah are the heavy hitters), but they've lately started planting less typical U.S. varietals, such as Primitivo, Roussanne, and Sangiovese. The winery is 14 mi southeast of downtown Grants Pass, in the northern edge of the Applegate Valley. ⊠ *1475 Kubli Rd.* ☎ *541/846–9900* ⊕ *www.troonvineyard.com.* ☉ *Jan., weekends 11–5; Feb.–late May and Oct.–Dec., daily 11–5; late May–Sept., daily 11–6.*

WHERE TO EAT AND STAY

$ ECLECTIC ✗ **Blondie's Bistro.** Sophisticated but affordable Blondie's serves globally inspired food and cocktails in a dapper downtown space with high ceilings and hardwood floors—the lone aesthetic drawback is the sometimes boisterous acoustics. The kitchen, however, prepares first-rate food, including an especially good list of starters, from Portuguese-style steamed clams with herbed sausage to a substantial Mediterranean antipasto platter. Cedar plank–grilled wild coho salmon and the innovative Kung Pao chicken spaghetti rank among the better main courses. Live bands perform some nights. ⊠ *226 SW G St.* ☎ *541/479–0420* ⊕ *www. blondiesbistro.com* ⊟ *AE, D, DC, MC, V.*

$ AMERICAN ✗ **Taprock Northwest Grill.** This cavernous family-friendly restaurant designed to resemble a Cascade mountain lodge lies on the southern edge of downtown, its dining room lined with tall windows overlooking the Rogue River. Expect hearty, reasonably priced fare that uses primarily regional ingredients, including such popular starters as pan-fried oysters and smoked chicken salad with candied Oregon hazelnuts. Burgers, sandwiches, and heftier main dishes like meatloaf and chicken potpie round out the menu. ⊠ *971 SE 6th St.* ☎ *541/955–5998* ▤ *AE, D, DC, MC, V.*

$ ⬚ **Lodge at Riverside.** The pool and many of the rooms of this airy, contemporary downtown hotel overlook the Rogue River as it passes through the southern end of downtown Grants Pass. The setting is far enough from the bustle for peace and quiet, but still an easy walk to several good restaurants. All but a few rooms have private balconies or patios, and all are furnished with stylish country house–inspired armoires, plush beds, and oil paintings; suites have river-rock fireplaces and Jacuzzi tubs. A complimentary evening wine reception and continental breakfast are served in the log cabin–style lobby, beneath its soaring cathedral ceiling, or on the shaded patio. **Pros:** central location; beautiful modern furnishings; set directly on the Rogue River. **Cons:** among the highest rates in town; no restaurant on-site. ⊠ *955 SE 7th St.* ☎ *541/955–0600 or 877/955–0600* ⊕ *www.thelodgeatriverside.com* ⏎ *29 rooms, 4 suites* ⚘ *In-room: a/c, Wi-Fi. In-hotel: pool* ▤ *AE, D, MC, V* ⍟ *CP.*

$$$ ⬚ **Weasku Inn.** Although posh in a country-chic sort of way, the ram-
Fodor's Choice bling Weasku Inn fits in perfectly with its piney surroundings—the ram-
★ bling timber-frame home overlooking the Rogue River was built as a vacation retreat in 1924, and has hosted the likes of Walt Disney, Clark Gable, and Carol Lombard. In 1998 the owners added 11 handsomely outfitted cabins and restored an original A-frame bungalow to create the boutique resort that today ranks among the most luxurious accommodations between Ashland and Eugene. Pacific Northwest–inspired art, handmade furnishings, and fabrics fill the accommodations, which range from smaller doubles in the main lodge to romantic Jacuzzi suites with deep tubs and separate slate-wall walk-in showers. Many units have private decks with rocking chairs overlooking the river. A complimentary wine reception is offered each night. **Pros:** set directly on the Rogue River; impeccably decorated; fireplaces in many rooms. **Cons:** it's a 10-minute drive east of downtown; among the highest rates in the region. ⊠ *5560 Rogue River Hwy.* ☎ *541/471–8000 or 800/493–2758* ⊕ *www.weaskuinn.com* ⏎ *5 rooms, 12 cabins* ⚘ *In-room: a/c, Wi-Fi* ▤ *AE, D, MC, V* ⍟ *CP.*

SPORTS AND THE OUTDOORS

RECREATIONAL **Rogue River and Siskiyou National Forests–Grants Pass.** In the Klam-
AREAS ath Mountains and the Coast Range of southwestern Oregon, the 1.8-million-acre forest contains the 35-mi-long Wild and Scenic section of the Rogue River, which races through the Wild Rogue Wilderness Area, and the Illinois and Chetco Wild and Scenic rivers, which run through the 180,000-acre Kalmiopsis Wilderness Area. Activities include white-water rafting, camping, and hiking, but many hiking areas require trail-park passes—check the Web site for details. ⊠ *Off U.S. 199* ☎ *541/858–2200* ⊕ *www.fs.fed.us/r6/rogue-siskiyou.*

Fodor's Choice **Valley of the Rogue State Park.** A 1¼-mi hiking trail follows the bank
★ of the Rogue, the river made famous by novelist and fisherman Zane Grey. A campground along 3 mi of shoreline has 88 full hookups ($24), 59 electrical ($24), 21 tent sites ($19), and 6 yurts ($36). There are picnic tables, walking trails, playgrounds, and restrooms. The park

is 12 mi east of downtown Grants Pass. *3792 N. River Rd., Gold Hill* ☎ *541/582–1118 or 800/551–6949* ⊕ *www.oregonstateparks.org* ⊙ *Daily.*

RAFTING
Fodor's Choice
★

More than a dozen outfitters guided white-water rafting trips along the Rogue River in and around Grants Pass. In fact, this stretch of class-III rapids ranks among the best in the West. The rafting season lasts from about July through September, and the stretch of river running south from Grants Pass, with some 80 frothy rapids, is exciting but not treacherous, making it ideal for novices, families, and others looking simply to give this enthralling activity a try.

Orange Torpedo Trips (☎ *541/479–5061 or 866/479–5061* ⊕ *www.orangetorpedo.com*) is one of the most reliable operators on the Rogue River, offering half-day to several-day trips, as well as relaxed dinner-and-wine float trips along a calmer stretch of river.

If you're up for an adventure that combines rafting with overnight accommodations, consider booking a trip with **Rogue River Raft Trips** (☎ *800/826–1963* ⊕ *www.rogueriverraft.com*).The rafting trips run along a 44-mi stretch of the Rogue River and last for four days and three nights, with options for both lodge and camping stays along the way.

MEDFORD

30 mi southeast of Grants Pass on I–5.

Medford is the professional, retail, trade, and service center for eight counties in southern Oregon and northern California. As such, it offers more professional and cultural venues than might be expected for a city of its size. The workaday downtown shows signs of gentrification and rejuvenation in recent years, and in the outskirts you'll find several major shopping centers and the famed fruit and gourmet-food mail-order company Harry & David.

Lodging tends to be cheaper in Medford than in nearby (and easily accessible) Ashland or Jacksonville, although fairly bland chain properties dominate the hotel landscape. But it's 71 mi southwest of Crater Lake and 80 mi northeast of the Oregon Caves, making it an affordable and convenient base for visiting either park.

GETTING HERE
Medford is in the heart of the Rogue Valley on I–5, and is home to the state's third-largest airport, Rogue Valley International. **Valley Cab** (☎ *541/772–1818*) serves the Rogue Valley region, with fares costing $3 base per trip, plus $2.50 per mile thereafter. Most attractions in Medford lie outside the downtown area, however, so a cab isn't an especially practical or cost-effective way to explore. Your best option is renting a car.

Medford is the main regional Greyhound hub.

VISITOR INFORMATION
Medford Visitors & Convention Bureau (✉ *101 E. 8th St.* ☎ *541/779–4847 or 800/469–6307* ⊕ *www.visitmedford.org*).

7

EXPLORING

Butte Creek Mill. This 1872 water-powered gristmill, which is 12 mi north of Medford, is listed in the National Historic Register and still produces whole-grain food products, which you can buy at the country store here. There's also a modest display of antiques. ✉ *402 Royal Ave. N., Eagle Point* ☎ *541/826–3531* ⊕ *www.buttecreekmill.com* ⊒ *Free* ☻ *Mon.–Sat. 9–5, Sun. 11–5.*

Crater Rock Museum. Jackson County's natural history and collections of the Roxy Ann Gem and Mineral Society are on display at this quirky museum in Central Point (6 mi northwest of Medford). Fossils, petrified wood, fluorescent rocks, and precious minerals from throughout Oregon and elsewhere in the West are included, plus works of glass by renowned artist Dale Chihuly. ✉ *2002 Scenic Ave., Central Point* ☎ *541/664–6081* ⊒ *$4* ☻ *Tues.–Sat. 10–4.*

WINERIES

EdenVale Winery. Four miles southwest of downtown Medford amid a bucolic patch of fruit orchards, this winery and tasting room, called the Rogue Valley Wine Center, adjoins a rather grand 19th-century white-clapboard farmhouse surrounded by flower beds and vegetable gardens. Inside the tasting room you can sample and buy not only EdenVale's noted reds and late-harvest whites but also other respected labels from vineyards throughout the region. ✉ *2310 Voorhies Rd.* ☎ *541/512–2955* ⊕ *www.edenvalewines.com.* ☻ *June–Aug., Mon.–Sat. 10–6, Sun. noon–4; Sept.–May, Mon.–Sat. 11–5, Sun. noon–4.*

WHERE TO EAT AND STAY

$$
AMERICAN

✗ **Porters Dining at the Depot.** Set in an opulent 1910 train station, Porters is a favorite spot for special-occasion meals or even just relaxed dinners on a wisteria-shaded patio. The menu features aged-beef steaks, pork tenderloin, rack of lamb, pastas, and fresh seafood. Leave room for the decadent desserts, including a rich bread pudding drizzled with Jack Daniels crème anglaise. The bar is a popular spot for drinks or, during the early- and late-evening happy hours, less expensive fare, such as prime-rib sandwiches and chicken satay with peanut-garlic sauce. ✉ *147 N. Front St.* ☎ *541/857–1910* ⊕ *www.porterstrainstation.com* ⊟ *AE, D, MC, V* ☻ *No lunch.*

$$
ECLECTIC
Fodor'sChoice
★

✗ **38 Central.** Set inside a handsomely restored 1910 downtown building, this casual yet smartly furnished bistro specializes in comfort-driven fare with notably urbane flourishes. The classic fish-and-chips, for instance, are prepared with fresh local lingcod and battered in a champagne sauce, while "grown up" mac and cheese comes with artisan cheddar and Parmesan cheeses and hardwood-smoked bacon. An oft-changing roster of starters, soups, salads, and sides (try haricots verts with shallots) are ideal for sharing. ✉ *38 N. Central Ave.* ☎ *541/776–0038* ⊕ *www.38oncentral. com* ⊟ *AE, D, MC, V* ☻ *No lunch Sat. No dinner Sun.*

$

▥ **Under the Greenwood Tree.** Regulars at this bed-and-breakfast between Medford and Jacksonville find themselves hard-pressed to decide what they like most: the luxurious and romantic rooms, the stunning 10-acre farm, or the hearty three-course country-style breakfasts. Gigantic old oaks hung with hammocks shade the inn, an 1860s farmhouse exuding

Bounty from Rogue River Creamery

genteel charm. There's a manicured 2-acre lawn and a creaky three-story barn for exploring; an outbuilding holds the buckboard wagon that brought the property's original homesteaders westward on the Oregon Trail. The interior is decorated in Renaissance splendor, and all rooms have private baths. Afternoon tea is served. **Pros:** stunning setting amid farm fields and overlooking the Cascades; breakfast will fill you up well into the late afternoon. **Cons:** a few miles southwest of downtown (but en route to Jacksonville); old-fashioned rooms won't appeal to modernists or minimalists. ⊠ *3045 Bellinger La.* ☎ *541/776–0000* ⊕ *www.greenwoodtree.com* ⊷ *4 rooms* ⚃ *In-room: a/c, no TV, Wi-Fi. In-hotel: bicycles.* ⊟ *AE, D, MC, V.*

NIGHTLIFE AND THE ARTS
The late Hollywood star Ginger Rogers retired to this area, and the restored **Craterian Ginger Rogers Theater** (⊠ *23 S. Central Ave.* ☎ *541/779–3000* ⊕ *www.craterian.org*), which was built in the Spanish Colonial style in 1924 as a vaudeville house, now presents concerts, ballets, plays, and touring shows.

SHOPPING
Famous for their holiday gift baskets, **Harry & David** (⊠ *1314 Center Dr.* ☎ *541/864–2278 or 877/322–8000* ⊕ *www.harryanddavid.com*) is based in Medford and offers hour-long tours of its huge facility on weekdays from 9:15 AM through 1:45 PM. The tours cost $5 per person, but the fee is refunded if you spend a minimum of $35 in the mammoth Harry & David store, great for snagging picnic supplies to carry with you on any winery tour.

Fodor'sChoice
★

Just a few miles up the road from Medford in the small and otherwise drab little town of Central Point, you'll find one of the nation's most respected cheese makers, **Rogue River Creamery** (✉ *311 N. Front St.* ☎ *541/664–1537 or 866/396–4704* ⊕ www.roguecreamery.com), which was started in 1935 by Italian immigrants. Current owners Cary Bryant and David Gremmels bought the company in 2002, and promptly won one of the highest honors for cheese making, the London World Cheese Award. You can purchase any of the company's stellar cheeses here, from Smokey Blue to a lavender-infused cheddar, and you can watch the production through a window on most days. There's a wine-tasting room that carries vintages by a few local vineyards; the best nearby place to enjoy a picnic is the small neighborhood park a few blocks north at Laurel and North 6th streets.

Fodor'sChoice
★

Next door to Rogue River Creamery, the artisan chocolatier **Lillie Belle Farms** (✉ *211 N. Front St.* ☎ *541/664–2815* ⊕ *www.lilliebellefarms. com*) handcrafts outstanding chocolates using local, often organic ingredients. A favorite treat is the Smokey Blue Cheese ganache made with Rogue River blue, but don't overlook the dark-chocolate–marionberry bonbons (made with organic marionberries grown on-site) or the delectable hazelnut chews. Most unusual, however, is the chocolate-covered bacon. Yes, you read that correctly—the bacon is coated in chipotle and brown sugar, hand-dipped in chocolate, and sprinkled with sea salt.

SPORTS AND THE OUTDOORS

RECREATIONAL AREAS

Rogue River and Siskiyou National Forests–Medford. Covering 1.8 million acres, this immense tract of wilderness woodland has fishing, swimming, hiking, and skiing. Motorized vehicles and equipment—even bicycles—are prohibited in the 113,000-acre Sky Lakes Wilderness, south of Crater Lake National Park. Its highest point is the 9,495-foot Mt. McLoughlin. Access to most of the forest is free, but there are fees at some trailheads—check the Web site for details. ✉ *I–5 to Exit 39, Hwy. 62 to Hwy. 140* ☎ *541/858–2200* ⊕ *www.fs.fed.us/r6/rogue-siskiyou.*

OFF THE BEATEN PATH

Rogue River Views. Nature lovers who want to see the Rogue River at its loveliest can take a side trip to the Avenue of the Boulders, Mill Creek Falls, and Barr Creek Falls, off Highway 62, near Prospect. Here the wild waters of the upper Rogue foam past volcanic boulders and the dense greenery of the Rogue River National Forest.

Ↄ

You'll find an impressive array of kids' games and recreation at **Rogue Valley Fun Center,** just off Exit 33 of Interstate 5 (about 5 mi north of Medford). Miniature golf, batting cages, a golf driving range, bumper boats, and go-karts are among the offerings, and there's also a video arcade and game room. ✉ *1A Peninger Rd., Central Point* ☎ *541/664–4263* ⊕ *www.rvfamilyfuncenter.com.*

TouVelle State Park. A popular spot for weddings and picnics, this day-use park has beautiful hiking trails that wind through a wildlife-viewing area. The park lies 9 mi north of downtown Medford, on the road leading to the Table Rock hiking trails. ✉ *Off I–5 to Table Rock Rd.* ☎ *541/582–1118 or 800/551–6949* ⊕ *www.oregonstateparks.org* ⧈ *Day use $5 per vehicle.*

FISHING   With close access to some of the best freshwater fishing venues in the Northwest, Medford has several companies that lead tours and provide gear. **Carson's Guide Service** (☎ *541/261–3279* ⊕ *carsonsguideservice. com*), based 22 mi north of Medford along Hwy. 62 (going toward Crater Lake), provides expert instruction and knowledge of many of the area's rivers, including the Rogue, Umpqua, Coquille, and Chetco, as well as several lakes. Steelhead, salmon, shad, and smallmouth bass are the most common catches.

GOLF   There are a number of public golf courses in Medford and in nearby surrounding towns. By far the most challenging and best-designed in the area is **Eagle Point Golf Club** (✉ *100 Eagle Point Dr., Eagle Point* ☎ *541/826–8225* ⊕ *eaglepointgolf.com; 7,099 yds; par 72; greens fee: $32–$50*), which is 10 mi northeast of Medford and was designed by legendary golf-course architect Robert Trent Jones Jr.

HIKING   One of the best venues for hiking in the Rogue Valley, **Table Rock** (✉ *Off*
Fodor's Choice   *Table Rock Rd., Central Point* ☎ *541/618–2200* ⊕ www.blm.gov) com-
★   prises a pair of monolithic rock formations that rise some 700 to 800 feet above the valley floor about 10 mi north of Medford and just a couple of miles north of TouVelle State Park. Operated by a partnership between the Bureau of Land Management and the Nature Conservancy, the Table Rock formations afford panoramic valley views from their summits. You reach Lower Table Rock by way of a moderately challenging 1.75-mi trail, and Upper Table Rock via a shorter (1.25-mi) and less steep route. The trailheads to these formations are a couple of miles apart—just follow the road signs from Table Rock Road, north of TouVelle State Park (reached from Exit 33 of Interstate 5).

RAFTING   Medford is close to a number of the region's great white-water rafting rivers, including the famed Rogue River. Both overnight and day trips are offered by several outfitters.

A popular outfitter for guided white-water rafting trips as well as fishing adventures (for salmon and steelhead) throughout the area, Medford's **Rogue Klamath River Adventures** (☎ *541/779–3708 or 800/231–0769,* ⊕ *www.rogueklamath.com*) also offers boating excursions on inflatable kayaks. The company visits a great variety of waterways, from gentle but scenic Class I rivers to wild and exciting Class V rapids.

JACKSONVILLE

5 mi west of Medford on Hwy. 238.

This perfectly preserved town founded in the frenzy of the 1851 gold rush has served as the backdrop for several Western flicks. It's easy to see why. Jacksonville is one of only eight towns corralled into the National Register of Historic Places lock, stock, and barrel. These days, living-history exhibits offering a glimpse of pioneer life and the world-renowned Britt Festivals of classical, jazz, and pop music are the draw, rather than gold. Trails winding up from the town's center lead to the festival amphitheater, mid-19th-century gardens, exotic madrona groves, and an intriguing pioneer cemetery.

GETTING HERE

Most visitors to Jacksonville come by way of Medford, 5 mi east, on Hwy. 238—it's a scenic drive over hilly farmland and past vineyards. Alternatively, you can reach the town coming the other way on Hwy. 238, driving southeast from Grants Pass. This similarly beautiful drive through the Applegate Valley takes about 45 minutes. **Valley Cab** (☎ *541/772–1818*) serves the Rogue Valley region, with fares costing $3 base per trip, plus $2.50 per mile thereafter. A cab ride from Medford's airport to Jacksonville costs about $20, and downtown Jacksonville can easily be explored on foot. However, if you plan on visiting any of the region's wineries and parks, you're better off renting a car.

VISITOR INFORMATION

Jacksonville Chamber of Commerce & Visitor Center (✉ *185 N. Oregon St.* ☎ *541/899–8118* ⊕ *www.jacksonvilleoregon.org*).

EXPLORING

Ⓒ **Jacksonville Cemetery.** A trip up the winding road—or, better yet, a hike via the old cart track marked Catholic access—leads to the resting place of the clans (the Britts, the Beekmans, and the Orths) that built Jacksonville. You'll also get a fascinating, if sometimes unattractive, view of the social dynamics of the Old West: older graves (the cemetery is still in use) are strictly segregated, Irish Catholics from Jews from Protestants. A somber granite plinth marks the pauper's field, where those who found themselves on the losing end of gold-rush economics entered eternity anonymously. The cemetery closes at sundown. ✉ *Oregon St.; follow direction signs from downtown.*

Fodor's Choice ★

Ⓒ **Jacksonville Museum.** Set inside the old Jackson County Courthouse, this repository of regional memorabilia has intriguing gold rush–era artifacts. The Jacksonville! Boomtown to Home Town exhibit lays out the area's history. Inside the 1920 Jackson County Jail, the Children's Museum has hands-on exhibits of pioneer life and a collection of antique toys, and is open by appointment. A special display highlights local resident Pinto Colvig, the original Bozo the Clown, who co-composed "Who's Afraid of the Big Bad Wolf?" and was the voice of a Munchkin, Goofy, both Sleepy and Grumpy, and many other animated film characters. ✉ *206 N. 5th St.* ☎ *541/899–8123* ⊕ *www.sohs. org* ▱ *$5 for both museums* ☉ *Wed.–Sun. 10–4.*

WINERIES

Valley View Vineyard. Perched on a bench in the scenic Applegate Valley, you can sample acclaimed Chardonnay, Viognier, Pinot Gris, Merlot, and Cabernet Sauvignon while soaking up some of the best views in southern Oregon. The valley's especially sunny, warm climate produces highly acclaimed vintages. Founded in the 1850s by pioneer Peter Britt, the vineyard was reestablished in 1972. A restored pole barn houses the winery and tasting room. ✉ *1000 Upper Applegate Rd., Ruch, 10 mi southwest of Jacksonville* ☎ *541/899–8468 or 800/781–9463* ⊕ *www. valleyviewwinery.com* ☉ *Daily 11–5.*

WHERE TO EAT AND STAY

$ ✕ **Back Porch BBQ.** For an excellent, midpriced alternative to Jackson-
SOUTHERN ville's several upscale eateries, head to this roadhouse-style clapboard
building six blocks northeast of the town's historic main drag. Authentic
central Texas–style barbecue is served here: char-grilled red-hot sausage,
slow-cooked pork ribs, chicken-fried steak, and ½-pound burgers, plus
a few dishes to remind you that you're in Oregon, including wild local
salmon baked with Cajun spices. ⊠ *605 N. 5th St.* ☎ *541/899–8821*
⊕ *www.backporchbbqinc.com* ⊟ *D, MC, V.*

$ ✕ **Bella Union.** Reliably good, if predictable, red-sauce Italian food is
ITALIAN the draw at this festive restaurant housed within an 1860s building on
historic California Street—exposed-brick walls, wood-plank floors, and
high ceilings give a sense of the building's age and character. The aroma
of traditional seafood fettuccini, ricotta-spinach ravioli, and pepperoni
pizzas fills the two noisy dining rooms. There's live music a few nights
a week, and in summer you can dine under ancient wisteria vines on a
breezy patio. ⊠ *170 W. California St.* ☎ *541/899–1770* ⊕ *www.bellau.
com* ⊟ *AE, D, DC, MC, V*

$$ ✕ **Gogi's.** Many visitors overlook this small, low-key restaurant just
ECLECTIC down the hill from Britt Gardens—it's a favorite of foodies and locals,
Fodor's Choice and word seems to be spreading about the artful presentation and inno-
★ vative style of chef-owner Gabriel Murphy's sophisticated international
cuisine. The menu changes regularly, but has featured a tower of roasted
beets and chèvre topped with toasted walnuts and a balsamic-truffle
reduction, followed by grilled pan-smoked pork chop atop a sweet-
potato pancake with haricots verts and an orange-zest compound but-
ter. The wine list is small but discerning. If you're in town on a Sunday,
do not miss the super brunch. ⊠ *235 W. Main St.* ☎ *541/899–8699*
⊕ *www.gogis.net* ⊛ *Reservations essential* ⊟ *MC, V* ☾ *Closed Mon.–
Tues. No lunch Wed.–Sat.*

$$ ⌑ **Jacksonville Inn.** The spotless period antiques and the host of well-chosen
amenities at this 1861-vintage inn evoke what the Wild West might have
been had Martha Stewart been in charge. In addition to the main building,
the inn includes four larger and more luxurious cottages with fireplaces
and saunas. One of the eight rooms in the main inn is named in honor
of ubiquitous Jacksonville founding father Peter Britt, while another, the
Blanchet Room, honors one of the area's earliest Catholic priests. All have
meticulous pioneer-period furnishings. Some rooms and cottages have
whirlpool tubs and double steam showers. Complimentary full breakfast
is served in the elegant restaurant, which also serves lunch and dinner
both to guests and nonguests (⇨ *see above*). The Jacksonville Mercantile
gourmet store and wine shop are on the ground floor. **Pros:** in heart of
downtown historic district; one of the town's most historically significant
buildings; very good restaurant on-site. **Cons:** rather old-fashioned decor
for some tastes. ⊠ *175 E. California St.* ☎ *541/899–1900 or 800/321–
9344* ⊕ *www.jacksonvilleinn.com* ⇄ *8 rooms, 4 cottages* ⌂ *In-room: a/c,
refrigerator, Wi-Fi. In-hotel: restaurant* ⊟ *D, MC, V* ⎰⌑ *BP.*

$ ⌑ **The McCully House Inn.** One of Jacksonville's six original homes, a gleam-
ing pale-gray Gothic Revival mansion built in 1860, McCully House
sits in the midst of a fragrant rose garden. The period-decorated rooms

and suites, one with a fireplace and all of them filled with antiques, are on the second floor and have private baths. One bedroom is furnished with its original bedstead, which was shipped around Cape Horn. The on-site Garden Bistro serves well-regarded American and continental cuisine, from gnocchi with baked chèvre to flatbread pizzas. The owners also operate the adjacent and more affordable 32-room Stage Lodge, as well as a few other rental cottages around town. **Pros:** centrally located; excellent restaurant; smart and contemporary furnishings. **Cons:** no TVs in rooms; adult ambience makes this a less than ideal choice for families with children. ⊠ *830 N. 5th St.* ☎ *541/899–2050 or 800/367–1942* ⊕ *www.mccullyhouseinn.com* ⚓ *3 rooms, 2 suites* ♨ *In-room: a/c, no TV, Internet. In-hotel: restaurant* ⊟ *AE, D, DC, MC, V* ⊺⊙⫙ *BP.*

$$
Fodor'sChoice
★
🖫 **TouVelle House B&B.** This six-room inn set inside a grand 1916 Craftsman-style home a few blocks north of Jacksonville's tiny commercial strip manages that tricky balance between exquisite and comfy. Museum-quality Arts and Crafts antiques fill the rooms, which include a common library, great room, and sunroom. Innkeepers Gary Renninger Balfour and Tim Balfour have filled the inn with welcoming touches, from CD players and down comforters in the understatedly elegant rooms to a DVD/TV with movie library, refrigerator, and guest computer in the common areas. During the warmer months you can slip into the pool or sauna for a bit of relaxation. **Pros:** situated on a gentle bluff surrounded by beautiful gardens; downtown dining is a 5-minute walk away; knowledgeable and friendly hosts. **Cons:** no TVs or phones in rooms. ⊠ *435 N. Oregon St.* ☎ *541/899–8938 or 800/846–8422* ⊕ *www.touvellehouse.com* ⚓ *6 rooms* ♨ *In-room: a/c, Wi-Fi. In-hotel: pool* ⊟ *D, MC, V* ⊺⊙⫙ *BP.*

NIGHTLIFE AND THE ARTS

Fodor'sChoice
★
Each summer some of the finest musicians in the world gather for the **Britt Festivals** (☎ *541/773–6077 or 800/882–7488* ⊕ *www.brittfest.org*), outdoor concerts and theater presentations lasting from mid-June to mid-September. Folk, country, pop, and classical performances are staged in an outdoor amphitheater, surrounded by gardens, on the estate of 19th-century photographer and painter Peter Britt. Tickets must be obtained well in advance for most performances, and those who want the best spaces on the lawn near the stage should show up early.

SHOPPING

Jacksonville's historic downtown has several engaging galleries, boutiques, and gift shops. It's best just to stroll along California Street and its cross streets to get a sense of the retail scene. Drop by the **Jacksonville Company** (⊠ *115 W. California St.* ☎ *541/899–8912 or 888/271–1047* ⊕ *www.jacksonvillecompany.com*) to browse the stylish selection of handbags, footwear, and women's apparel. MOTO Denim, Nicole Shoes, and Bernardo Footwear are among the top brands carried here. The **Jacksonville Barn Co.** (⊠ *150 S. Oregon St.* ☎ *541/702–0307* ⊕ *www.jacksonvillebarnco.com*) specializes in both antiques and contemporary home decor, from Victorian pieces that have come from many nearby estates to modern garden accessories and country-house furnishings. The racks of **Jacksonville Mercantile** (⊠ *120 E. California St.* ☎ *541/899–1047* ⊕ *www.jacksonvillebarnco.com*) abound with gourmet sauces, oils, vinegars, jams, and tapenades. Watch for Chukar chocolate-covered cherries from Seattle's Pike Place Market, and the shop's own private-label Merlot-wine jelly.

ASHLAND

20 mi southeast of Jacksonville and 14 mi southeast of Medford on I–5.

As you walk Ashland's twisting hillside streets, it seems like every house is a restored Victorian operating as an upscale bed-and-breakfast, though that's not quite all there is to this town: the Oregon Shakespeare Festival attracts thousands of theater lovers to the Rogue Valley every year, from mid-February to early November (though tourists don't start showing up en masse until June). That influx means that Ashland is more geared toward the arts, more eccentric, and more expensive than its size might suggest. The mix of well-heeled theater tourists, bohemian students from Southern Oregon University, and dramatic show folk imbues the town with some one-of-a-kind cultural frissons. The stage isn't the only show in town—skiing at Mt. Ashland and the town's reputation as a secluded getaway and growing culinary destination keep things hopping year-round.

GETTING HERE

Ashland is the first town you'll reach on Interstate 5 if driving north from California, and it's the southernmost community in this region. You can also get here from Klamath Falls by driving west on winding but dramatic Hwy. 66. **Cascade Airport Shuttle** (☎ *541/488–1998*) offers door-to-door service from the airport to Ashland for about $30. A car isn't necessary to explore downtown and to get among many of the inns and restaurants, but it is helpful if you're planning to venture farther afield or visit more than one town, which most visitors do.

VISITOR INFORMATION

Ashland Chamber of Commerce and Visitors Information Center (✉ *110 E. Main St.* ☎ *541/482–3486* ⊕ *www.ashlandchamber.com*).

EXPLORING

Fodors Choice ★ **Lithia Park.** The Elizabethan Theatre overlooks this park, a 93-acre jewel that is Ashland's physical and psychological anchor. The park is named for the town's mineral springs, which supply a water fountain by the band shell as well as a fountain on the town plaza—be warned that the slightly bubbly water has a strong and rather disagreeable taste. Whether thronged with colorful hippie folk and picnickers on a summer evening or buzzing with joggers and dog walkers in the morning, Lithia is a well-used, well-loved, and well-tended spot. On summer weekend mornings the park plays host to a '60s-ish artisans' market. Each June the Oregon Shakespeare Festival opens its outdoor season by hosting the Feast of Will in the park, with music, dancing, bagpipes, and food. Tickets (about $12) are available through the festival box office (☎ *541/482–4331*).

Schneider Museum of Art. At the edge of the Southern Oregon University campus, this museum includes a light-filled gallery devoted to special exhibits by Oregon, West Coast, and international artists. The permanent collection has grown considerably over the years, and includes

7

pre-Columbian ceramics and works by such notables as Alexander Calder, George Inness, and David Alfaro Siqueiros. Hallways and galleries throughout the rest of the 66,000-square-foot complex display many works by students and faculty. ⊠ *1250 Siskiyou Blvd.* ☎ *541/552–6245* ⊕ *www.sou.edu/sma* ⊘ *Mon.–Sat. 10–4* ⊒ *$5.*

NEED A BREAK?   **Zoey's Cafe** (⊠ **199 E. Main St.** ☎ **541/482–4794**) scores high marks for its creative, house-made ice cream in such enticing flavors as mountain blackberry and Rogue Valley pear. The fair-trade, organic beans used in the espresso drinks at **Noble Coffee Roasting** (⊠ **281 4th St.** ☎ **541/488–3288**) are among the best in town.

WINERIES

Weisinger's Winery. Although downtown Ashland has wine bars and tasting rooms, the only major winery of note here is Weisinger's, which set up shop in 1988 and is set a few miles south of town on a hilltop with broad views of the surrounding mountains. Specialties here include a Semillon-Chardonnay blend, a well-respected Viognier, and a rich Bordeaux blend called Petite Pompadour. ⊠ *3150 Siskiyou Blvd.* ☎ *541/488–5989 or 800/551–WINE* ⊕ *www.weisingers.com* ⊘ *May–Sept., daily 11–5; Oct.–Apr., Wed.–Sun. 11–5.*

WHERE TO EAT

$$$
ECLECTIC
Fodor's Choice
★

✕ **Amuse.** This locally celebrated restaurant features Northwest-driven French cuisine, infused with seasonal, organic meat and produce. Chef-owners Erik Brown and Jamie North prepare a daily-changing menu. You might sample wood-grilled white prawns with romesco sauce and fingerling potatoes, or truffle-roasted game hen with green beans and tarragon jus. Try your best to save room for the warm crepes filled with ricotta, honey, and local strawberries. ⊠ *15 N. 1st St.* ☎ *541/488–9000* ⊕ *www.amuserestaurant.com* ⌁ *Reservations essential* ⊟ *AE, D, MC, V* ⊘ *Closed Mon. and Tues. No lunch.*

$$
FRENCH

✕ **Chateaulin.** One of southern Oregon's most romantic restaurants is in an ivy-covered storefront a block from the Oregon Shakespeare Festival exhibit center, where it dispenses French food, local wine (there's a wine shop attached), and friendly, impeccable service with equal facility. This might be Ashland's most iconic restaurant, the fixed point in a hopping dining scene, where Shakespeare pilgrims return religiously year after year. The menu changes often, but mainstays include the pan-roasted rack of lamb rubbed with cocoa nibs and served with cream corn, a black-trumpet mushroom sauce, and braised spinach, accompanied by a bottle of Oregon Pinot Noir. But you have to begin with the escargots baked with garlic butter, parsley, and pernod. ⊠ *50 E. Main St.* ☎ *541/482–2264* ⊕ *www.chateaulin.com* ⌁ *Reservations essential* ⊟ *AE, D, MC, V* ⊘ *Closed Mon. Nov.–May. No lunch.*

¢
PIZZA

✕ **Creekside Pizza Bistro.** It's a little tricky to find this quirky pizza restaurant tucked down a flight of stairs beneath the North Main Street overpass, with a terrace overlooking gurgling Ashland Creek and a dining room filled with local artwork. The stone-baked pizzas here are both filling and delicious, topped with a wide variety of the usual and less obvious (caramelized yams, breaded eggplant) ingredients. There's

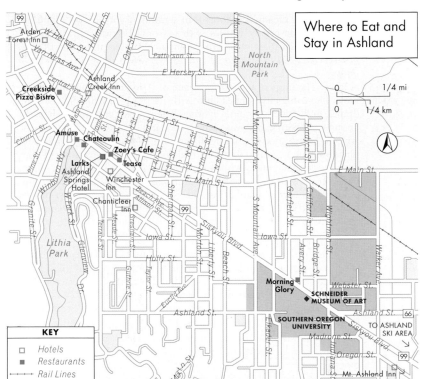

Where to Eat and Stay in Ashland

KEY

□ *Hotels*
■ *Restaurants*
┈┈ *Rail Lines*

also a terrific selection of Oregon beers on tap, and one of the more memorable desserts in town: a huge, hot, fresh-baked chocolate-chip-and-toffee cookie covered with melting vanilla ice cream and shaved chocolate. ⊠ 92½ N. Main St. ☎ 541/482–4131 ⊕ www.creeksidepizza. com ▭ D, MC, V.

$$$ ✕ **Larks**. In this restaurant off the lobby of the historic Ashland Springs
AMERICAN Hotel, owners Doug and Becky Neuman are putting their "farm to table" philosophy into practice. Larks pairs the freshest foods from local farms with great wines, artisan chocolate desserts, and drinks in a relaxing and soothing atmosphere. Modern interpretations of comfort food are the order of the day, with servings such as homemade meatloaf with mushroom gravy, Anniebelle's fried chicken, and maple-glazed pork chops with organic-apple compote and rosemary-roasted sweet potatoes. Dessert offerings include Dagoba chocolate sundaes, s'mores, and cheesecake of the day. The Sunday brunch is one of the best in town. ⊠ 212 E. Main St. ☎ 541/488–5558 ⊕ www.larksrestaurant.com ▭ AE, D, MC, V.

$ ✕ **Morning Glory**. Breakfast reaches new heights at this distinctive café
AMERICAN across the street from Southern Oregon University. In a blue Craftsman-
Fodor's Choice style bungalow, the café has eclectic furnishings and an attractive patio
★   space bounded by arbors. The extraordinarily good food emphasizes breakfast fare—omelets filled with crab, artichokes, Parmesan, and

smoked-garlic cream; Tandoori tofu scrambles with cherry-cranberry chutney; lemon-poppy waffles with seasonal berries; and cranberry-hazelnut French toast with lemon butter. No reservations; first-come, first-served. ⊠ *1149 Siskiyou Blvd.* ☎ *541/488–8636* ▭ *MC, V* ⊘ *No dinner.*

$ ✕ **Tease.** The hippest and most urbane of Ashland's restaurants, Tease
ECLECTIC   looks like a big-city supper club with its plush armchairs, sweeping drapes, and seductively dark lighting. The swank cocktails, such as the Spring Pearl with lemongrass-lime vodka and lychee fruit, live up to the vibe, as does the downright tantalizing cuisine—the menu is divided into tapas, nibbles, late-night items, and other categories geared toward sharing. Try the duck tacos with tomatillo and papaya salsas, goat-cheese panna cotta with chile–wild berry coulis, or the quail wrapped in prosciutto with curried lentil puree. The bar is a favorite for post-theater drinks. ⊠ *303 E. Main St.* ☎ *541/488–1458* ⊕ *www.teaseashland.com* ▭ *D, MC, V*

WHERE TO STAY

The Oregon Shakespeare Festival has stimulated one of the most extensive networks of bed-and-breakfasts in the country—more than 50 in all. High season for Ashland-area bed-and-breakfasts is between June and October. The **Ashland B&B Network** (☎ *800/944–0329* ⊕ *www.abbnet.com*) provides referrals to roughly 25 of the town's top inns.

$$ ⊡ **Arden Forest Inn.** Rooms at this mid-priced yet still handsomely furnished bed-and-breakfast are in either the 1890s main house or an adjacent carriage house (this is better if you're seeking privacy). The quiet property on a residential street is surrounded by meticulously designed gardens, with paths, decks, fountains, and statues making for an enchanting stroll in the morning after the extensive two-course breakfast (cinnamon-pecan pancakes are a specialty). Rooms have simple, rustic pine furnishings and wainscoting and an unfussy country-cottage ambience. **Pros:** stunning landscaping and gardens; good value. **Cons:** slightly longer walk (10 to 15 minutes) to downtown dining and theater. ⊠ *261 W. Hersey St.* ☎ *541/488–1496 or 800/460–3912* ⊕ *www.afinn.com* ⇆ *4 rooms, 1 suite* ⌂ *In-room: a/c, some kitchens, Internet. In-hotel: pool.* ▭ *MC, V* ℗ *BP.*

$$ ⊡ **Ashland Creek Inn.** Every one of the 10 plush suites in this converted mill has a geographic theme—the Normandy is outfitted with rustic country French prints and furniture, while Moroccan, Danish, and New Mexican motifs are among the designs in other units. Each sitting room–bedroom combo has its own entrance, either a full kitchen or kitchenette, and a deck just inches from burbling Ashland Creek. Privacy, space, high-concept elegance, and dynamite breakfasts served in an understated central dining room make this well-run place an alternative to up-close-and-personal traditional bed-and-breakfasts. Downtown shopping, Lithia Park, and the theaters are within an easy walk. **Pros:** exceptionally good breakfasts; peaceful but central location; enormous suites. **Cons:** among the higher rates in the region; limited common areas. ⊠ *70 Water St.* ☎ *541/482–3315* ⊕ *www.ashlandcreekinn.com* ⇆ *10 suites* ⌂ *In-room: a/c, some kitchens, Wi-Fi. In-hotel: some pets allowed (paid)* ▭ *MC, V* ℗ *BP.*

Ashland's Main Street

$$ **Ashland Springs Hotel.** Ashland's stately landmark hotel is a totally restored version of an original 1925 landmark hotel that towers seven stories over the center of downtown. The 70 rooms soothe with a preponderance of gentle fall colors and have work desks and flat-screen TVs. The unconventional decor—French-inspired botanical-print quilts and lampshades with leaf designs—makes for fascinating conversation in itself. The hotel offers theater, sports, and romance packages. A full range of soothing treatments is available at the hotel's adjacent Waterstone Spa. **Pros:** rich with history; upper floors have dazzling mountain views; the excellent Larks restaurant (⇨ *see above*) is on-site. **Cons:** Central location translates to some street noise and bustle; rooms are on the small side. ✉ *212 E. Main St.* ☎ *541/488–1700 or 888/795–4545* ⊕ *www. ashlandspringshotel.com* ⌨ *70 rooms* ⚘ *In-room: a/c, refrigerator, Wi-Fi. In-hotel: restaurant, room service, bar, spa.* ▭ *AE, D, DC, MC, V* ⭘❙ *CP.*

$$
Fodor'sChoice
★
 Chanticleer Inn. This courtly, 1920 Craftsman-style bed-and-breakfast is one of the most picturesque structures in this hilly and historic residential neighborhood just a few blocks south of the Shakespeare theaters and Main Street restaurants. Owners Ellen Campbell and Howie Wilcox have given the rooms a tasteful, contemporary flair with muted, nature-inspired colors and Arts and Crafts furnishings and patterns. You can relax in a fragrant butterfly garden, and in-room massage can be arranged by appointment. Breakfast here is a treat, served communally (although owners are happy to set up a small table in the garden in good weather, if you'd prefer some morning privacy while you dine) and consisting of two courses—almond-pear clafouti and shiitake-sherry frittatas are among the specialties. **Pros:** rooms all have expansive views of the Cascade Mountains; owners use only eco-friendly

products. **Cons:** it's intimate and homey, so fans of larger and more anonymous lodgings may prefer a bigger inn or hotel. ⊠ *120 Gresham St.* ☎ *541/482–1919 or 800/898–1950* ⊕ *www.ashland-bed-breakfast. com* ⇆ *6 rooms* ৬ *In-room: a/c, DVD, Wi-Fi. In-hotel: Some pets allowed (paid)* ⊟ *MC, V* ⦿ *BP.*

$$ ⊡ **The Winchester Inn.** This posh yet unpretentious inn is often booked well in advance, so plan ahead. Not only are the meals smashing, the location is smack-dab in the center of Ashland's hopping theater scene. The 11 rooms and 8 suites have character and restful charm—some have fireplaces, refrigerators, and wet bars, and private exterior entrances. Some rooms have a fireplace and refrigerator, with Wi-Fi throughout. Its restaurant relies upon locally grown produce, fresh fish and meats, including liberal use of herbs from its own garden. The breakfasts are works of art (and available to nonguests as well). **Pros:** the adjacent wine bar and restaurant serve very good international fare. **Cons:** among the more expensive lodgings in town. ⊠ *35 S. 2nd St.* ☎ *541/488–1113 or 800/972–4991* ⊕ *www.winchesterinn.com* ⇆ *11 rooms, 8 suites* ৬ *In-room: a/c, some refrigerators, some TVs, Wi-Fi. In-hotel: restaurant, bar* ⦿ *BP* ⊟ *AE, D, MC, V.*

NIGHTLIFE AND THE ARTS

With its presence of college students, theater types, and increasing numbers of tourists (many of them fans of local wine), Ashland has developed quite a festive nightlife scene. Much of the activity takes place at bars inside some of downtown's more reputable restaurants, such as Black Sheep and Creekside Pizza.

A good bet for local beers is **Standing Stone Brewing Company** (⊠ *101 Oak St.* ☎ *541/482–2448* ⊕ *www.standingstonebrewing.com*), which has live jazz on the patio and pours some excellent microbrews, including Milk & Honey Ale and Oatmeal Stout. The Nuevo Latino restaurant **Tabu** (⊠ *76 N. Pioneer St.* ☎ *541/482–3900* ⊕ *www.taburestaurant. com*) keeps busy with revelers into the later hours. Live comedy, reggae, salsa, and other entertainment takes place most Thursday through Saturday nights.

Fodor'sChoice
★

From mid-February to early November, more than 100,000 Bard-loving fans descend on Ashland for the **Oregon Shakespeare Festival** (⊠ *15 S. Pioneer St.* ☎ *541/482–4331* ⊕ *www.osfashland.org*), presented in three theaters. Its accomplished repertory company mounts some of the finest Shakespearean productions you're likely to see on this side of Stratford-upon-Avon—plus works by Ibsen, Williams, and contemporary playwrights. Between June and October plays are staged in the 1,200-seat Elizabethan Theatre, an atmospheric re-creation of the Fortune Theatre in London; the 600-seat Angus Bowmer Theatre, a state-of-the-art facility typically used for five different productions in a single season; and the 350-seat New Theater, which mostly hosts productions of new or experimental work. The festival generally operates close to capacity, so it's important to book ahead.

DID YOU KNOW?

Founded in 1935, the Oregon Shakespeare Festival is one of the oldest and largest professional non-profit theaters in the nation. The festival hosts more than 780 performances annually with an attendance of approximately 400,000.

SHOPPING

Downtown Ashland abounds with galleries and one-of-a-kind shops. A few miles' drive south of town you'll find **Dagoba Organic Chocolate** (✉ *1105 Benson St.* ☎ *866/608–6944* ⊕ *www.dagobachocolate.com*), the retail outlet of the company that produces those small, handsomely packed, superfine chocolate bars sold in fancy-food shops and groceries throughout the country. Although acquired by the Hershey Company in 2006, Dagoba was founded in Ashland, and its operation remains here, where a small retail shop sells its goods.

SPORTS AND THE OUTDOORS

OUTFITTERS The **Adventure Center** (✉ *40 N. Main St., Ashland* ☎ *541/488–2819 or 800/444–2819* ⊕ *www.raftingtours.com*) books outdoor expeditions in the Ashland region, including white-water rafting, fishing, and bike excursions.

RAFTING **Noah's River Adventures** (☎ *800/858–2811* ⊕ *www.noahsrafting.com*) is one of the most respected outfitters for white-water rafting and wilderness fishing trips in the region—the company can lead single- or multiple-day adventures along the mighty Rogue River as well as just across the border, in northern California, on the Salmon and Scott rivers.

SKIING **Mt. Ashland Ski Area.** This winter-sports playground in the Siskiyou Mountains is halfway between San Francisco and Portland. The ski runs get more than 300 inches of snow each year. There are 23 trails, virtually all of them intermediate and advanced, in addition to chute skiing in a glacial cirque called the bowl. Two triple and two double chairlifts accommodate a vertical drop of 1,150 feet; the longest of the runs is 1 mi. Facilities include rentals, repairs, instruction, a ski shop, a restaurant, and a bar. Anytime of year the drive up the twisting road to the ski area is incredibly scenic, affording views of 14,162-foot Mt. Shasta, some 90 mi south in California. ✉ *Mt. Ashland Access Rd., 18 mi southwest of downtown Ashland; follow signs 9 mi from I–5 Exit 6* ☎ *541/482–2897* ⊕ *www.mtashland.com* ⊠ *Lift ticket $39* ⊙ *Nov.–Apr., daily 9–4.*

KLAMATH FALLS

65 mi east of Ashland via Hwy. 66, 75 mi east of Medford via Hwy. 140.

Often overlooked by visitors to the region, the greater Klamath Falls area is one of the most beautiful parts of Oregon. The small if not especially engaging city of Klamath Falls stands at an elevation of 4,100 feet, on the southern shore of Upper Klamath Lake. The highest elevation in Klamath County is the peak of Mt. Scott, at 8,926 feet. There are more than 82 lakes and streams in Klamath County, including Upper Klamath Lake, which covers 133 square mi.

The Klamath Basin, with its six national wildlife refuges, hosts the largest wintering concentration of bald eagles in the contiguous United States and the largest concentration of migratory waterfowl on the continent. Each February nature enthusiasts from around the world flock here for the Bald Eagle Conference, the nation's oldest birding festival.

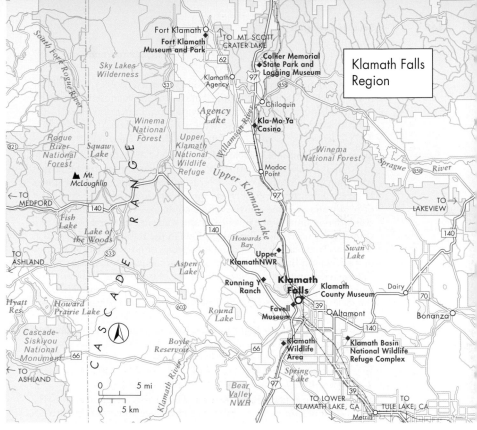

The Nature Conservancy has called the basin a western Everglades, because it is the largest wetland area west of the Mississippi. But humans have significantly damaged the ecosystem through farming and development. More than 25% of vertebrate species in the area are now endangered or threatened. Only 35 years ago about 6 million birds used the area every year, today that number is down to 2 to 3 million. Environmental organizations are working to reverse some of the damage.

GETTING HERE

Klamath Falls lies along U.S. 97, one of the Northwest's main north–south routes—it's a prime stop between Bend, 140 mi north, and Weed, California, about 70 mi south. You can also get here from the Rogue Valley, either by way of Hwy. 66 from Ashland or Hwy. 140 from Medford, which is home to the nearest airport (about a 90-min drive).

VISITOR INFORMATION

Klamath County Chamber of Commerce (✉ 205 Riverside Dr. ☎ 541/884–5193 ⊕ www.klamath.org).

EXPLORING

Favell Museum of Western Art and Native American Artifacts. More than 100,000 Native American artifacts, the works of 300 major contemporary Western artists, and the largest miniature-gun collection in the world are on display in a building made from local volcanic rock.

✉ *125 W. Main St.* ☎ *541/882–9996* ⊕ *www.favellmuseum.org* 🖼 *$7* ⊙ *Tues.–Sat. 10–5.*

Klamath County Museum. The anthropology, history, geology, and wildlife of the Klamath Basin are explained at this extensive museum set inside the city's historic armory building, with special attention given to the hardships faced by early white settlers. ✉ *1451 Main St.* ☎ *541/883–4208* ⊕ *www.co.klamath.or.us/museum* 🖼 *$5* ⊙ *Tues.–Sat. 9–5.*

Fodor's Choice
★

Klamath Basin National Wildlife Refuge Complex. As many as 1,000 bald eagles make Klamath Basin their rest stop, amounting to the largest wintering concentration of these birds in the contiguous United States. Located along the Pacific Flyway bird migration route, the vast acres of freshwater wetlands in the refuge complex—which comprises several different units, some in Oregon and some in California—serve as a stopover for nearly 1 million waterfowl in the fall. Any time of year is bird-watching season; more than 400 species of birds have been spotted in the Klamath Basin. It's best to begin your explorations at the refuge headquarters and visitor center, which are 24 mi south of Klamath Falls and 2 mi south of the California-Oregon border, in Tulelake. Here you can pick up maps and get advice on other sections of the reserve, including Klamath Marsh, Upper Klamath, and Bear Valley, which are all on the Oregon side. For a leisurely ramble by car, take the tour routes in the Lower Klamath and Tule Lake refuges. ✉ *4009 Hill Rd. (for refuge headquarters and visitor center), 24 mi south of Klamath Falls via U.S. 97 or Hwy. 39, Tulelake, CA* ☎ *530/667–2231* ⊕ *www.fws.gov/ klamathbasinrefuges* ⊙ *Weekdays 8–4:30, weekends 9–4.*

Senator George Baldwin Hotel Museum. The history of the region is the focus of guided tours and exhibits at this former hotel that the turn-of-the-20th-century politico Baldwin ran and where President Theodore Roosevelt once stayed. Some of the photographs on display were part of Senator Baldwin's daughter Maud's collection. In summer you can take a replica street trolley from here to the Klamath County Museum. ✉ *31 Main St.* ☎ *541/883–4207* ⊕ *www.co.klamath.or.us/museum/index.htm* 🖼 *$6 full tour* ⊙ *June–Sept., Wed.–Sat. 10–4, last tour at 2:30.*

WHERE TO EAT AND STAY

$$
AMERICAN

✕ **Basin Martini Bar.** Although the name of this swell-elegant storefront spot in the heart of the downtown historic district suggests an option for evening cocktails, Basin Martini Bar is best known for its reliably tasty dinner fare—New York strip steaks, burgers topped with Crater Lake blue cheese, and bacon-wrapped scallops are among the highlights. There's seating in a handful of comfy booths or at stools along the modern bar. The creative drinks are notable, too—consider the lemon-basil martini. ✉ *632 Main St.* ☎ *541/884–6264* ▭ *AE, D, DC, MC, V* ⊙ *No lunch.*

$$
FRENCH

✕ **Mr. B.'s Steakhouse.** The dark-wood dining room in this 1920s house suggests more formal pleasures, but maintains a relaxed mood. A talented French chef prepares tried-and-true classics like chicken Cordon Bleu, chateaubriand, shrimp scampi, veal dishes, and the house specialty, rack of lamb with rosemary and Dijon mustard. Fresh strawberry shortcake often appears on the menu, and there's a good wine list. It's in the

Running Y Ranch Resort

unappealing but convenient strip of motels and fast-food restaurants about 2 mi southeast of downtown. ✉ *3927 S. 6th St.* ☎ *541/883–8719* ⊕ *www.mrbssteaks.com* ☰ *AE, D, DC, MC, V* ⊗ *Closed Sun.–Mon. No lunch.*

$ 🖬 **Running Y Ranch Resort.** Golfers rave about the Arnold Palmer–designed course here, which winds its way through a juniper-and-ponderosa–shaded canyon overlooking Upper Klamath Lake. The resort consists of a main lodge and several town-house complexes, with hiking, biking, spa services, ATV rentals, outdoor ice-skating, swimming, horseback riding, sailing, fishing, and wildlife watching the prime activities. A concierge can help arrange a variety of excursions. Rooms in the lodge are spacious and modern; the two- to five-bedroom town houses and custom homes have numerous amenities (kitchens, decks, grills, outdoor hot tubs) and vary greatly in price according to size, with two-bedroom town houses starting at $230 per night in summer. The property has three restaurants, including an upscale steak house and lounge with bar food. **Pros:** the myriad activities are great for families and outdoorsy types; rates in lodge are quite reasonable. **Cons:** it's a 15-minute drive to town; those seeking an intimate hideaway won't find it here. ✉ *5500 Running Y Rd., 5 mi north of Klamath Falls* ☎ *541/850–5500 or 877/866–1266* ⊕ *www.runningy.com* ⟿ *82 rooms, 37 town houses* ⌂ *In-room: a/c, refrigerator, Internet. In-hotel: restaurants, bar, golf course, tennis courts, pools, gym, spa, water sports, bicycles, laundry service* ☰ *AE, D, DC, MC, V.*

Fodor's Choice
★
☺

$ 🖬 **Thompson's B&B.** Set in a contemporary residential neighborhood on a bluff high above Upper Lake Klamath, this low-keyed and reasonably priced bed-and-breakfast has four rooms with simple, modern furnishings. A full breakfast is served in the great room, with soaring windows overlooking the lake. Guests can come and go through a separate exterior entrance, which leads through a common room with a microwave and fridge stocked with drinks. Just down the hill, Moore Park has a marina, tennis courts, fishing, and hiking. **Pros:** great lake views from two rooms; relaxed alternative to downtown's uninteresting motel strip. **Cons:** cash only; a 10-minute drive from downtown; homey personality may not suit everybody. ⊠ *1420 Wild Plum Court* ☎ *541/882–7938* ⊕ *www.thompsonsbandb.com* ⇨ *4 rooms* ⛵ *In-room: a/c, Wi-Fi* ⊟ *No credit cards* ¶◎¶ *BP.*

NIGHTLIFE AND THE ARTS

On 9 acres along the Williamson River, **Kla-Mo-Ya Casino,** 22 mi north of Klamath Falls and 30 mi southeast of Crater Lake, has 380 slot machines, poker, blackjack, and a buffet restaurant and deli—it's open 24/7. The casino is owned by the Klamath, Modoc, and Yahooskin tribes. ⊠ *22 mi north of Klamath Falls on U.S. 97 at Crater Lake Junction, Chiloquin* ☎ *888/552–6692 www.klamoyacasino.com.*

The 700-seat **Ross Ragland Theater,** a 1939 art deco building, hosts performances of the Linkville Players local theater group, as well as traveling and local plays and musical performances. ⊠ *218 N. 7th St.,* ☎ *541/884–0651* ⊕ *www.rrtheater.org.*

SPORTS AND THE OUTDOORS

OUTFITTERS For advice, gear, clothing, books, and maps for hiking, birding, mountaineering, canoeing, camping, and fishing throughout the area, visit **The Ledge Outdoor Store** (⊠ *369 S. 6th St.* ☎ *541/882–5586* ⊕ *www. theledgeoutdoorstore.com*) in downtown Klamath Falls. This well-stocked store carries all kinds of equipment, and also offers guided fly-fishing trips.

RECREATIONAL AREAS **Winema National Forest.** Twelve miles north of Klamath Falls, the forest covers 2.3 million acres on the eastern slopes of the Cascades. It borders Crater Lake National Park. Hiking, camping, fishing, and boating are popular. In winter snowmobiling and cross-country skiing are available. ⊠ *U.S. 97* ☎ *541/883–6714* ⊕ *www.fs.fed.us/r6/frewin* ☉ *Daily; campgrounds and picnic areas Memorial Day–Labor Day.*

BOATING For a chance to enjoy the beauty of Klamath Lake while also observing the region's abundant birdlife, consider a trip led by **Birding & Boating** (☎ *541/885–5450* ⊕ *www.birdingandboating.com*), which offers guided sailing tours of the lake with expert guidance on spotting wildlife. Fishing trips are also offered, and you can also rent canoes or kayaks and paddle around the lake on your own.

FISHING **Roe Outfitters Flyway Shop** (⊠ *9349 U.S. 97 S.* ☎ *541/884–3825* ⊕ *www. roeoutfitters.com*) leads fishing and hunting trips on nearby lakes and rivers. Also offered are guided canoe and white-water rafting excursions.

GOLF The outstanding Arnold Palmer-designed 18-hole course at **Running Y Ranch** (⊠ *5115 Running Y Rd., 5 mi north of Klamath Falls* ☎ *541/850–5500 or 888/850–0275* ⊕ *www.runningy.com $50–$99 (discount for hotel guests,* 6,581 yards, par 72) delights golfers of all abilities. Ponderosa pines line the relatively short, undulating course, which is heavy on doglegs and has a number of holes in which water comes into play. There's also an 18-hole putting course that's ideal for honing your short game, and fun for families.

CAVE JUNCTION

30 mi southwest of Grants Pass via U.S. 199, 60 mi west of Jacksonville via Hwy. 238 and U.S. 199.

One of the least populated and most pristine parts of southern Oregon, the town of Cave Junction and the surrounding Illinois Valley attract outdoors enthusiasts of all kinds for hiking, backpacking, camping, fishing, and hunting. Expect rugged terrain and the chance to view some of the tallest Douglas fir trees in the state. Other than those passing through en route from Grants Pass to the northern California coast via U.S. 199, most visitors come here to visit the Oregon Caves National Monument, one of the world's only marble caves (formed by erosion from acidic rainwater). Sleepy Cave Junction makes an engaging little base camp, its main drag lined with a handful of quirky shops, short-order restaurants, and gas stations.

GETTING HERE

Cave Junction lies along U.S. 199, the main road leading from Grants Pass. You can also reach Cave Junction by heading west from Jacksonville on Hwy. 238 to U.S. 199. From Cave Junction, head east on Hwy. 46 to reach Oregon Caves National Monument. Cave Junction is a about a 75-minute drive southwest of Medford's regional airport. Alternatively, the small airport (served by United Airlines) in Crescent City, California, is the same distance.

VISITOR INFORMATION

Illinois Valley Chamber of Commerce (✉ *201 Caves Hwy., Cave Junction* ☎ *541/592-3326 or 541/592-4076* ⊕ *www.cavejunction.com*).

EXPLORING

Kerbyville Museum. Documenting area Native American and pioneer history, this museum is centered in an 1871 home on the National Register of Historic Places. You can investigate your pioneer and mining ancestors in the research library and see exhibits of taxidermy and antique dolls, as well as local Native American artifacts. ✉ *24195 Redwood Hwy.* ☎ *541/592-5252* 🖾 *$4* ☉ *Apr–Oct., Thurs.–Mon. 11–3; other times by appointment only.*

Oregon Caves National Monument. The "Marble Halls of Oregon," high in the verdant Siskiyou Mountains, have enchanted visitors since 1874. Huge stalagmites and stalactites, the Ghost Room, Paradise Lost, and the River Styx are part of a ½-mi subterranean tour that lasts about 90 minutes. The tour includes more than 200 stairs, and is not recommended for anyone who experiences difficulty walking or has respiratory or coronary problems. The temperature inside the cave is 44°F (7°C) year-round. Be sure to wear warm clothing and comfortable closed-toe walking shoes. Children over six must be at least 42 inches tall and pass a safety and ability test, because they cannot be carried.

7

✉ Hwy. 46, 20 mi southeast of Cave Junction ☎ 541/592–2100 🌐 www.nps.gov/orca 🎫 $8.50 🕒 Tours: late Mar.–late Nov., hours vary.

WINERIES

Bridgeview Vineyard and Winery. The producers of the increasingly well-distributed and reasonably priced Blue Moon wines (known especially for Riesling, Chardonnay, Pinot Gris, and Merlot), as well as more premium vintages such as Black Beauty Syrah and a very nice reserve Pinot Noir, established the winery in 1986, and—despite considerable skepticism from observers—have gone on to tremendous success. *✉ 4210 Holland Loop Rd. ☎ 541/592–4688 or 877/273–4843 🌐 www.bridgeviewwine.com 🕒 Daily 11–5.*

WHERE TO EAT AND STAY

¢ PIZZA **✕ Wild River Pizza Company & Brewery.** Cool your heels at the communal redwood picnic tables in this pizza parlor on the north end of Cave Junction. If you aren't in the mood for pizza, choose from fish-and-chips, chicken dishes, and sandwiches. There is also an all-you-can-eat buffet, and the restaurant's own seasonal brews, including an acclaimed Bohemian Pilsner, are on tap. *✉ 249 N. Redwood Hwy. ☎ 541/592–3556 ▭ D, MC, V.*

$ **Oregon Caves Chateau.** If you're looking for a quiet retreat in an unusual place, consider this six-story wood-frame lodge on the grounds of the national monument. Virtually unchanged since it was built in 1934, it has a rustic authenticity and steep gabled roofs. Rooms, all with their original furnishings, have canyon or waterfall views—the bare walls, old-fashioned radiators, and simple bedding are part of the charm. The dining room serves decent regional fare, using local wines, produce, and even buffalo from a nearby ranch. **Pros:** steps from national monument; historic and funky personality; wonderfully tranquil setting. **Cons:** no-frills rooms; no Internet or phones; location well out of the way if you aren't visiting the caves. *✉ 20000 Caves Hwy. ☎ 541/592–3400 or 877/245–9022 🌐 www.oregoncaveschateau.com ⇨ 23 rooms ♿ In-room: no phone, no a/c, no TV. In-hotel: restaurant ▭ MC, V 🕒 Closed mid-Oct.–mid May.*

$$ **Out 'n' About.** You sleep among the leaves in the tree houses of this extraordinary resort—the highest is 37 feet from the ground. One has an antique claw-foot bath; another has separate kids' quarters connected to the main room by a swinging bridge. Other units have stained-glass windows, sleeping lofts, and other quirky features. There is also an earth-bound cabin with a view of the old-growth forest. The least expensive units don't have bathrooms—guests use the common facilities, which also include a game area, fire pit, and common kitchen. **Pros:** kids love the Swiss Family Robinson atmosphere; it truly feels at one with the surrounding old-growth forest; amazingly quiet and peaceful. **Cons:** accommodations are extremely rustic; some units don't have bathrooms; two-night minimum during week and three-night minimum weekends during spring to fall. *✉ 300 Page Creek Rd. ☎ 541/592–2208 🌐 www.treehouses.com ⇨ 15 tree houses, 1 cabin ♿ In-room: no phone, kitchen (some), no TV, Wi-Fi (some). In-hotel: laundry facilities ▭ MC, V 🍴 BP in spring–fall, CP winter.*

Crater Lake
National Park

WORD OF MOUTH

"After arriving the evening before amidst fog and snow, we awoke to the incredible blue lake and fresh snow."
—photo by William A. McConnell, Fodors.com member

WELCOME TO CRATER LAKE NATIONAL PARK

TOP REASONS TO GO

★ **The lake.** Cruise inside the caldera basin and gaze into the extraordinary sapphire-blue water of the country's deepest lake.

★ **Native land.** Enjoy the rare luxury of interacting with totally unspoiled terrain.

★ **The night sky.** Billions of stars glisten in the pitch-black darkness of an unpolluted sky.

★ **Splendid hikes.** Accessible trails spool off the main roads and wind past colorful bursts of wildflowers and cascading waterfalls.

★ **Camping at its best.** Pitch a tent or pull up a motor home at Mazama Campground, a beautifully situated, guest-friendly, and well-maintained campground.

1 Crater Lake. The focal point of the park, this non-recreational, scenic destination is known for its deep blue hue.

2 Wizard Island. Visitors can take boat rides to this landmass protruding from the western section of Crater Lake; it's a great place for a hike or a picnic.

3 Mazama Village. This is your best bet for stocking up on snacks, beverages, and fuel in the park; it's about 5 mi from Rim Drive.

4 Cleetwood Cove Trail. The only safe, designated trail leading down to the lake's edge is on the rim's north side off Rim Drive.

GETTING ORIENTED

Crater Lake National Park covers 183,224 acres. In southern Oregon less than 100 mi from the California border, it's surrounded by several Cascade Range forests, including the Winema and Rogue River national forests. Of the nearby towns, Klamath Falls is closest, at 60 mi south of the park; Medford and Ashland, to the southwest, are approximately 80 mi and 90 mi from the lake, respectively. Bend is approximately 105 mi northeast (via seasonal Hwy. 138).

KEY	
🚹🚺	Ranger Station
⛰	Campground
🎋	Picnic Area
🍴	Restaurant
🏨	Lodge
🏃	Trailhead
🚻	Restrooms
⤳	Scenic Viewpoint
-----	Walking/Hiking Trails

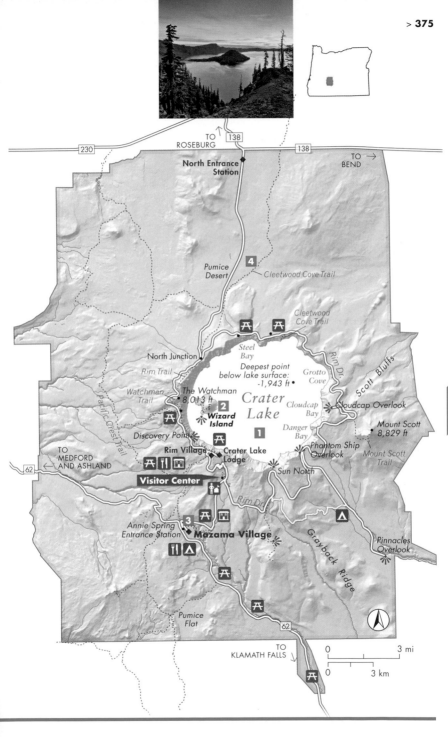

TO
ROSEBURG
[138]

[230]

[138]
TO →
BEND

**North Entrance
Station**

4

Pumice
Desert

Cleetwood Cove Trail

*Cleetwood
Cove Trail*

North Junction

*Steel
Bay*

Deepest point
below lake surface:
-1,943 ft •

*Grotto
Cove*

Scott Bluffs

8

Rim Trail

Rim Dr.

*Watchman
Trail*

The Watchman
8,013 ft

2
**Wizard
Island**

*Crater
Lake*

Cloudcap
Bay

Cloudcap Overlook

Mount Scott
8,829 ft

Pacific Crest Trail

Discovery Point

1

Danger
Bay

*Mount Scott
Trail*

Rim Village
Crater Lake
Lodge

Phantom Ship
Overlook

Sun Notch

TO
MEDFORD
AND ASHLAND
[62]

Visitor Center

Annie Spring
Entrance Station
3
Mazama Village

Graybeck Ridge

Pinnacles
Overlook

*Pumice
Flat*

[62]

TO
KLAMATH FALLS

0   3 mi

0   3 km

CRATER LAKE NATIONAL PARK PLANNER

When to Go

The park's high season is July and August. September and early October tend to draw smaller crowds. From October through most of May, most of the park closes due to heavy snowfall. The road is kept open just to the rim in winter, except during severe weather.

Getting Here and Around

Most of the park is only accessible from late June to early July through mid-October. The rest of the year, snow blocks all park roadways and entrances except Highway 62 and the access road to Rim Village from Mazama Village. Rim Drive is typically closed because of heavy snowfall from mid-October to mid-July, and you could encounter icy conditions any month of the year, particularly in early morning.

AVG. HIGH/LOW TEMPS.

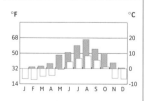

Flora and Fauna

Two primary types of fish swim beneath the surface of Crater Lake: kokanee salmon and rainbow trout. It's estimated that hundreds of thousands of kokanee inhabit the lake, but since boating and recreational access is so limited they elude many would-be sportsman. Kokanees average about 8 inches in length, but they can grow to nearly 18 inches. Rainbow trout are larger than the kokanee, but are less abundant in Crater Lake. Trout—including bull, eastern brook, rainbow, and German brown—swim in the park's many streams and rivers; they usually remain elusive, because these waterways flow through inaccessibly steep canyons.

Remote canyons shelter the park's elk and deer populations, which can sometimes be seen at dusk and dawn feeding at forest's edge. Black bears and pine martens—cousins of the short-tailed weasel—also call Crater Lake home. Birds such as hairy woodpeckers, California gulls, red-tailed hawks, and great horned owls are more commonly seen in summer in forests below the lake.

Good Reads

■ *Crater Lake National Park: A Global Treasure*, by former park rangers Ann and Myron Sutton, celebrates the park's first 100 years with stunning photography, charts, and drawings.

■ Ron Warfield's *A Guide to Crater Lake and the Mountain That Used to Be* gives a useful and lushly illustrated overview of Crater Lake's history and physical features.

■ The National Park Service uses Stephen Harris's *Fire Mountains of the West* in its ranger training; the detailed handbook covers Cascade Range geology.

■ *Wildflowers of the Olympics and Cascades*, by Charles Stewart, is an easy-to-use guide to the area's flora.

By Christine Vovakes

The pure, crystalline blue of Crater Lake astounds visitors at first sight. More than 5 mi wide and ringed by cliffs almost 2,000 feet high, the lake was created approximately 7,700 years ago, following Mt. Mazama's fiery explosion. Days after the eruption, the mountain collapsed on an underground chamber emptied of lava. Rain and snowmelt filled the caldera, creating a sapphire-blue lake so clear that sunlight penetrates to a depth of 400 feet (the lake's depth is 1,943 feet). Today it's both the clearest and deepest lake in the United States—and the seventh deepest in the world.

8

PARK ESSENTIALS

ACCESSIBILITY
All the overlooks along Rim Drive are accessible to those with impaired mobility, as are Crater Lake Lodge, the facilities at Rim Village, and Steel Information Center. A half-dozen accessible campsites are available at Mazama Campground.

ADMISSION FEES AND PERMITS
Admission to the park is $10 per vehicle, good for seven days. Backcountry campers and hikers must obtain a free wilderness permit at Rim Visitor Center or Steel Information Center for all overnight trips.

ADMISSION HOURS
Crater Lake National Park is open 24 hours a day year-round; however, snow closes most park roadways October through May and sometimes into early July. Lodging and dining facilities usually are open from late May to mid-October. The park is located in the Pacific Time Zone.

ATMS/BANKS
There's an ATM at the Mazama Camper Store near the park's Annie Spring entrance station. Look for banks in nearby towns.

CRATER LAKE IN ONE DAY

Begin at **Steel Information Center,** where interpretive displays and a short video introduce you to the story of the lake's formation and its unique characteristics. Then begin your circuit of the crater's rim by heading northeast on **Rim Drive,** allowing an hour to stop at over-looks—check out the Phantom Ship rock formation in the lake—before you reach the **Cleetwood Cove Trail** trailhead, the only safe and legal access to the lake. Hike down the trail to reach the dock, and hop aboard one of the **tour boats** for an almost-two-hour tour around the lake. If you have time, add on a trip to **Wizard Island** for a picnic lunch.

Back on Rim Drive, continue around the lake, stopping at the **Watchman Trail** for a short but steep hike to this peak above the rim, which affords not only a splendid view of the lake, but a broad vista of the surrounding southern Cascades. Wind up your visit at **Crater Lake Lodge**—allow time to wander the lobby of the 1915 structure perched on the rim. Dinner at the lodge restaurant, overlooking the lake and the Cascade sunset, caps the day.

CELL-PHONE RECEPTION

Cell-phone reception is unreliable in the park, although Verizon carries a reliably good signal along most of the Rim Drive and around Crater Lake Lodge. You'll find public telephones at Steel Information Center, Rim Village, Crater Lake Lodge, and the Mazama Village complex.

PARK CONTACT INFORMATION

Crater Lake National Park ✍ *P.O. Box 7, Crater Lake, OR 97604* ☎ *541/594–3000* ⊕ *www.nps.gov/crla.*

SCENIC DRIVE

Rim Drive. The 33-mi loop around the lake is the main scenic route, affording views of the lake and its cliffs from every conceivable angle. The drive alone takes up to two hours; frequent stops at overlooks and short hikes can easily stretch this to half a day. Be aware that Rim Drive is typically closed due to heavy snowfall from mid-October to mid-June, and icy conditions can be encountered any month of the year, particularly in early morning. ⊠ *Rim Dr. leads from Annie Spring entrance station to Rim Village, where the drive circles around the rim; it's about 7 mi from the entrance station to Rim Village. To get to Rim Dr. from the park's north entrance, access the north entrance road via either Hwy. 230 or Hwy. 138, and follow it for about 10 mi.*

WHAT TO SEE

For most visitors, the star attractions of Crater Lake are the lake itself and the breathtakingly situated Crater Lake Lodge. Other park highlights include the natural, unspoiled beauty of the forest and the geological marvels that you can access along the 33-mi Rim Drive.

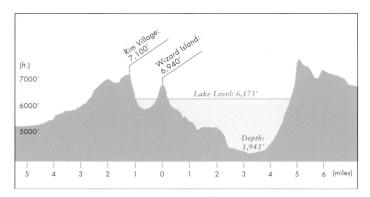

HISTORIC SITE

Fodor's Choice **Crater Lake Lodge.** First built in 1915, this classic log-and-stone structure
★ still boasts the original lodgepole-pine pillars, beams, and stone fireplaces.
The lobby, fondly referred to as the Great Hall, serves as a warm, welcoming gathering place, where you can play games, socialize with a cocktail, or gaze out of the many windows to view spectacular sunrises and
sunsets by a crackling fire. ⊠ *Rim Village, just east of Rim Visitor Center.*

SCENIC STOPS

Cloudcap Overlook. The highest road-access overlook on the Crater Lake
rim, Cloudcap has a westward view across the lake to Wizard Island
and an eastward view of Mt. Scott, the volcanic cone that is the park's
highest point, just 2 mi away. ⊠ *2 mi off Rim Dr., 13 mi northeast of
Steel Information Center.*

Discovery Point. This overlook marks the spot at which prospectors first
spied the lake in 1853. Wizard Island is just northeast, close to shore.
⊠ *Rim Dr., 1½ mi north of Rim Village.*

Mazama Village. In summer a campground, motor inn, amphitheater, gas
station, post office, and small store are open here. ⊠ *Mazama Village
Rd., off Hwy. 62, near Annie Spring entrance station* ☎ *541/594–2255
or 888/774–2728* ⊕ *www.nps.gov/crla* ☉ *June–Sept., daily 8–6.*

Phantom Ship Overlook. From this point you can get a close look at Phantom Ship, a rock formation that resembles a schooner with furled masts,
and looks ghostly in fog. ⊠ *Rim Dr., 7 mi northeast of Steel Information Center.*

Pinnacles Overlook. Ascending from the banks of Sand and Wheeler creeks,
unearthly spires of eroded ash resemble the peaks of fairy-tale castles. Once
upon a time, the road continued east to a former entrance. A path now
replaces the old road and follows the rim of Sand Creek (affording more
views of pinnacles) to where the entrance arch still stands. ⊠ *5 mi northeast
of Steel Information Center, then 2 mi east on Pinnacles Spur Rd.*

Sun Notch. It's a moderate ¼-mi hike through wildflowers and dry
meadow to this overlook, which has views of Crater Lake and Phantom
Ship. Mind the cliff edges. ⊠ *Rim Dr., 4.4 mi east of Steel Information
Center, east side of the lake.*

Wizard Island. To get here you've got to hike down Cleetwood Cove Trail (and back up upon your return) and board the tour boat (⇨ *Educational Offerings, below)* for a 1¾-hour ride. Bring a picnic. If you're in top shape, take the very strenuous 2-mi hike to Wizard Summit that leads to a path around the 90-foot deep crater at the top. A more moderate hike is the 1.8-mi trek on a rocky trail along the shore of the island. ✉ *Via Cleetwood Cove Trail to the Wizard Island dock* ☎ *541/594–2255 or 888/774–2728* ⊕ *www.craterlakelodges. com* ⊙ *Early July–mid-Sept., daily.*

VISITOR CENTERS

Rim Visitor Center. In summer you can obtain park information here, take a ranger-led tour, or stop into the nearby Sinnott Memorial, with a small museum and a 900-foot view down to the lake's surface. In winter, snowshoe walks are offered on weekends and holidays. The Rim Village Gift Store and cafeteria are the only services open in winter. ✉ *Rim Dr. on the south side of the lake, 7 mi north of Annie Spring entrance station* ☎ *541/594–3090* ⊕ *www.nps.gov/crla* ⊙ *Late May–late Sept., daily 9:30–4:30.*

Steel Information Center. The information center is part of the park's headquarters; you'll find restrooms and a first-aid station here. There's also a small post office and a shop that sells books, maps, and postcards. In the auditorium, an ongoing 18-minute film, *The Mirror of Heaven*, describes Crater Lake's formation. ✉ *Rim Dr., 4 mi north of Annie Spring entrance station* ☎ *541/594–3100* ⊕ *www.nps.gov/crla* ⊙ *Early May–early Nov., daily 9–5; early Nov.–early May, daily 10–4.*

SPORTS AND THE OUTDOORS

FISHING

Fishing is allowed in the lake, but you may find the experience frustrating—in such a massive body of water, the problem is finding the fish. Try your luck near the Cleetwood Cove boat dock, or take poles on the boat tour and fish off Wizard Island. Rainbow trout and kokanee salmon lurk in Crater Lake's aquamarine depths, and some grow to enormous sizes. You don't need a state fishing license, but to protect the lake's pristine waters, use only artificial bait as opposed to live worms. Private boats are prohibited on the lake.

HIKING

EASY

Castle Crest Wildflower Trail. The 1.4-mi creek-side loop in the upper part of Munson Valley is one of the park's flatter and less demanding hikes. Wildflowers burst into full bloom here in July. ✉ *Across the street from Steel Information Center parking lot, Rim Dr.*

Godfrey Glen Trail. This 1-mi loop trail is an easy stroll through an old-growth forest with canyon views. Its dirt path is accessible to wheelchairs with assistance. ⊠ *2.4 mi south of Steel Information Center.*

MODERATE

Annie Creek Canyon Trail. This somewhat strenuous 1.7-mi hike loops through a deep stream-cut canyon, providing views of the narrow cleft scarred by volcanic activity. This is a good spot to look for flowers and deer. ⊠ *Mazama Campground, Mazama Village Rd., near Annie Spring entrance station.*

SERIOUS SAFETY

There is only one safe way to reach Crater Lake's edge: the Cleetwood Cove Trail from the north rim. The rest of the inner caldera is steep and composed of loose gravel, basalt, and pumice—extremely dangerous, in other words. That's why all hiking and climbing are strictly prohibited inside the rim, and rangers will issue citations for violations.

Boundary Springs Trail. If you feel like sleuthing, take this moderate 5-mi round-trip hike to the headwaters of the Rogue River. The trail isn't always well marked, so a detailed trail guide is necessary. You'll see streams, forests, and wildflowers along the way before discovering Boundary Springs pouring out of the side of a low ridge. ⊠ *Pullout on Hwy. 230, near milepost 19, about 5 mi west of the junction with Hwy. 138.*

The Watchman Trail. This is the best short hike in the park. Though it's less than a mile each way, the trail climbs more than 400 feet—not counting the steps up to the actual lookout, which has great views of Wizard Island and the lake. ⊠ *Watchman Overlook, 3.8 mi northwest of Rim Village on Rim Dr., west side of the lake.*

DIFFICULT

Cleetwood Cove Trail. This strenuous 2.2-mi round-trip hike descends 700 feet down nearly vertical cliffs along the lake to the boat dock. ⊠ *Cleetwood Cove trailhead, Rim Dr., 11 mi north of Rim Village, north side of the lake.*

Fodor's Choice ★ **Mt. Scott Trail.** This 5-mi round-trip trail takes you to the park's highest point—the top of Mt. Scott, Mt. Mazama's oldest volcanic cone, at 8,929 feet. It will take the average hiker 90 minutes to make the steep uphill trek—and nearly 60 minutes to get down. The trail starts at an elevation of about 7,450 feet, so the climb is not extreme, but does get steep in spots. Views of the lake and the broad Klamath Basin are spectacular. ⊠ *14 mi east of Steel Information Center on Rim Dr., east side of the lake, across from the road to Cloudcap Overlook.*

Pacific Crest Trail. You can hike a portion of the Pacific Crest Trail, which extends from Mexico to Canada and winds through the park for 33 mi. For this prime backcountry experience, catch the trail off Highway 138 about a mile east of the north entrance road, where it heads toward the west rim of the lake and circles it for about 6 mi, then descends down Dutton Creek to the Mazama Village area. An online brochure offers further details. ⊠ *Pacific Crest Trail parking lot, north access road off Hwy. 138, 2 mi east of the Hwy. 138–north entrance road junction* ⊕ *www.nps.gov/crla/planyourvisit/upload/2010 PCT.pdf.*

EDUCATIONAL OFFERINGS

RANGER PROGRAMS

Boat Tours. The most extensively subscribed guided tours in Crater Lake are on the water, aboard launches that carry 49 passengers on a one-hour, 45-minute tour accompanied by a ranger. The boats circle the lake; two of the seven daily boats stop at Wizard Island, where you can get off and reboard a minimum of three hours later, or six hours later if you catch the morning boat. The first tour leaves the dock at 10 AM; the last departs at 3 PM. To get to the dock, you must hike down Cleetwood Cove Trail, a strenuous 1.1-mi walk that drops 700 feet; only those in excellent physical shape should attempt the hike. Bring adequate water with you. Purchase boat-tour tickets at the top of the trail. Restrooms are available at the top and bottom of the trail. ⊠ *Cleetwood Cove Trail, off Rim Dr., 10 mi north of Rim Village on the north side of the lake* ☎ *541/594–2255 or 888/774–2728* ⊕ *www.craterlakelodges.com* ☑ *$28; $38 with island drop-off* ☺ *Early July–mid-Sept., daily.*

Junior Ranger Program. Junior Ranger booklets and badges are available at Steel Information Center and Rim Visitor Center, and related activities are presented during the afternoon at the Rim Visitor Center from early July through Labor Day weekend. ☎ *541/594–3090.*

WHERE TO EAT

ABOUT THE RESTAURANTS

There are a few casual eateries and convenience stores within the park. For fantastic upscale dining on the caldera's rim, head to the Crater Lake Lodge.

IN THE PARK

$ ✕ **Annie Creek Restaurant.** It's family-style buffet dining here; pizza and
AMERICAN pasta, along with ham and roast beef, are the main features. Breakfast, lunch, and dinner are served. The outdoor seating area is surrounded by towering pine trees. ⊠ *Mazama Village Rd., near Annie Spring entrance station* ☎ *541/594–2255 Ext. 4533* ☐ *AE, D, MC, V* ☺ *Closed mid-Sept.–early June.*

$$$ ✕ **Dining Room at Crater Lake Lodge.** Virtually the only place where you can
AMERICAN dine well once you're in the park, the lodge emphasizes fresh, regional
Fodor'sChoice Northwest cuisine. The dining room is magnificent, with a large stone
★ fireplace and views of Crater Lake's clear blue waters. Breakfast and lunch are enjoyable here, but the evening menu is the main attraction, with tempting delights such as tarragon-infused wild Alaskan salmon, roasted duck with citrus-chili glaze, filet mignon with a mushroom-Merlot sauce, and roasted prime rib of bison. An extensive wine list tops off the gourmet experience. Book well ahead, as far as a week or two in advance for weekends. ⊠ *Crater Lake Lodge, Rim Village, east of Rim Visitor Center* ☎ *541/594–2255 Ext. 3217* ⚑ *Reservations essential* ☐ *AE, D, MC, V* ☺ *Closed mid-Oct.–mid-May.*

PICNIC AREAS **Rim Drive.** About a half-dozen picnic-area turnouts encircle the lake; all have good views, but they can get very windy. Most have pit toilets, and a few have fire grills, but none have running water. ⊠ *Rim Dr.*

Rim Village. This is the only park picnic area with running water. The tables are set behind the visitor center, and most have a view of the lake below. There are flush toilets inside the visitor center. ✉ *Rim Dr. on the south side of the lake, 7 mi north of Annie Spring entrance station.*

Wizard Island. The park's best picnic venue is on Wizard Island; pack a picnic lunch and book yourself on one of the early-morning boat-tour departures, reserving space on an afternoon return. There are no formal picnic areas and just pit toilets, but there are plenty of sunny, protected spots where you can have a quiet meal and appreciate the astounding scene that surrounds you. The island is accessible by boat tour only (⇨ *Educational Offerings, above*).

> **FAMILY PICKS**
>
> **Boat Tour.** Climb aboard for a close-up view of Crater Lake.
>
> **Annie Creek Restaurant.** Feast on a picnic at this eatery's outdoor seating area.
>
> **Crater Lake Lodge.** Tour this historic inn.

OUTSIDE THE PARK

¢ ✕**Beckie's Cafe.** You can get breakfast, lunch, or dinner at this rustic
AMERICAN roadhouse diner 15 mi from Crater Lake's southern entrance, but no one will fault you for skipping your veggies and plunging into dessert. For more than 80 years Beckie's homemade pies have been a must-have treat for travelers on their way to or from the park. Among the year-round selections, very berry and coconut cream are favorites; savor fresh peach or huckleberry when the fruit is in season. And don't forget to ask for à la mode! ✉ *Hwy. 62 at Union Creek, Prospect* ☎ *541/560–3563* ⊕ *www.unioncreekoregon.com/beckies/beckies.htm* ⊟ AE, D, MC, V.

WHERE TO STAY

ABOUT THE HOTELS

Crater Lake's summer season is relatively brief, and the park's main lodge is generally booked with guest reservations a year in advance. If you don't snag one, check availability as your trip approaches—cancellations are always possible. Outside the park are limited options in Prospect, and extensive choices in Klamath Falls, Roseburg, Medford, Ashland, and Bend.

ABOUT THE CAMPGROUNDS

Both tent campers and RV enthusiasts will enjoy the heavily wooded and well-equipped setting of Mazama Campground. Drinking water, showers, and laundry facilities help ensure that you don't have to rough it too much. Lost Creek Campground is much smaller, with minimal amenities and a more "rustic" Crater Lake experience.

IN THE PARK

$ ⌅ **The Cabins at Mazama Village.** In a wooded area 7 mi south of the lake, this complex is made up of several A-frame buildings. Most of the modest rooms have two queen beds and a private bath. These rooms fill up fast, so book early. A convenience store and gas station are nearby in the village. **Pros:** clean and well-kept facility. **Cons:** lots of traffic into adjacent campground, limited in-room amenities. ✉ *Mazama Village,* *near Annie Spring entrance station* ☎ *541/594–2255 or 888/774–2728* ⊕ *www.craterlakelodges.com* ↝ *40 rooms* ♿ *In-room: no a/c, no phone, no TV. In-hotel: laundry facilities* ▭ *AE, D, MC, V* ☉ *Closed mid-Oct.–late May.*

$$$ ⛄ **Crater Lake Lodge.** The period feel of this 1915 lodge on the caldera's rim is reflected in its lodgepole-pine columns, gleaming wood floors, and stone fireplaces in the common areas. With magnificent lake views, rooms at this popular spot are often booked a year in advance. Plan ahead, as this is the only "in-park" place to stay by the lake. **Pros:** ideal location for watching sunrise and sunset reflected on the lake. **Cons:** difficult to reserve rooms. ⊠ *Rim Village, east of Rim Visitor Center, 1 Lodge Loop Rd., Crater Lake* ☎ *541/594–2255 or 888/774–2728* ⊕ *www. craterlakelodges.com* ↝ *71 rooms* ♿ *In-room: no phone, no TV. In-hotel: restaurant* ▭ *AE, D, MC, V* ☉ *Closed mid-Oct.–late May.*

CAMPING 🏕 **Lost Creek Campground.** The small, remote sites here are available on a daily basis. In July and August arrive early to secure a spot. Lost Creek is for tent campers only; RVs must stay at Mazama. **Pros:** close to the fossil spires of Pinnacles Overlook. **Cons:** briefly open each summer; no reservations. ⊠ *3 mi south of Rim Rd. on Pinnacles Spur Rd. at Grayback Dr.* ☎ *541/594–3100* 🏕 *16 tent sites* ♿ *Flush toilets, drinking water, fire grates* ☉ *Closed early Oct.–mid-July.*

🏕 **Mazama Campground.** Crater Lake National Park's major visitor accommodation, aside from the famed lodge on the rim, is set well below the lake caldera in the pine and fir forest of the Cascades. Not far from the main access road (Highway 62), it offers convenience more than outdoor serenity—although adjacent hiking trails lead away from the roadside bustle. About half the spaces are pull-throughs, some with electricity; no hookups are available. The best tent spots are on some of the outer loops above Annie Creek Canyon. **Pros:** close to the Annie Spring and Pacific Crest trails. **Cons:** because it's popular, it's a noisy, crowded place during the busiest summer weeks. ⊠ *Mazama Village, near Annie Spring entrance station* ☎ *541/594–2255 or 888/774–2728* ⊕ *www.craterlakelodges.com* 🏕 *212 tent/RV sites* ♿ *Flush toilets, dump station, drinking water, guest laundry, showers, fire grates, public telephone* ▭ *AE, D, MC, V* ☉ *Mid-June–early Oct.*

OUTSIDE THE PARK

$$ ⛄ **Prospect Historic Hotel Bed and Breakfast.** Noted individuals such as Theodore Roosevelt, Zane Grey, Jack London, and William Jennings Bryan have stayed here (in rooms that now bear their names). Twenty-eight mi southwest of the park entrance on Highway 62, the main house has quaint, country-style guest accommodations. The historic Dinner House restaurant serves hearty pasta, chicken, and the signature prime rib special from May through October. Behind the main house are clean, economical, if rather basic motel units. **Pros:** three waterfalls within walking distance; beautiful, extensive grounds; motel units are very affordable. **Cons:** not much to do in tiny Prospect. ⊠ *391 Mill Creek Dr., Prospect* ☎ *541/560–3664 or 800/944–6490* ⊕ *www. prospecthotel.com* ↝ *10 main house rooms, 14 motel rooms* ♿ *In-room: refrigerator (some), Wi-Fi. In-hotel: Wi-Fi hotspot, some pets allowed* ▭ *D, DC, MC, V* ⛄❙ *BP.*

Eastern Oregon

WORD OF MOUTH

"Joseph is a cute artsy town that has bronze foundries that you can tour. There is also the Wallowa Lake Tramway that takes you up above the lake. The views and hikes up above are beautiful. This area is where many of the scenes from the movie *Homeward Bound* were filmed."

—BarbAnn

WELCOME TO EASTERN OREGON

TOP REASONS TO GO

★ **Wallowa wonder.** The usually snowcapped peaks of the Wallowa Range ornament one of the West's most overlooked alpine playgrounds, with Wallowa Lake resting at its base.

★ **Time travel.** See architecture from Oregon's mining-era heyday in Baker City's authentically restored downtown, where a short walking tour takes you past more than 100 historic buildings.

★ **For the birds.** Visit countless feathered friends at the ruggedly idyllic Malheur National Wildlife Refuge.

★ **Let 'er buck.** Pendleton's famous rodeo attracts 50,000 people every September, but the cowboy mystique sticks around all year.

★ **Canyon country.** Oregon doesn't get more remote than along the wild and scenic Owyhee River or among the fascinating formations at Leslie Gulch. Only serious adventurers need apply.

1 **East Gorge.** The high plains around Umatilla and Pendleton are the heart of Oregon's ranching and agricultural communities. "Let 'er Buck!" is the rallying cry at the hugely popular Pendleton Round-Up rodeo, a phrase that sets the tone for the whole region's rootin', tootin' vibe.

2 **Northeast Oregon.** The superlative Wallowa and Blue mountains dominate this corner of the state. The peaks that once presented formidable obstacles to Oregon Trail pioneers now attract bands of hikers, mountain bikers, and other adventure types. In former frontier towns like Joseph and Baker City, old-school ranchers and cowboys mingle with a swelling population of artists, craftsmen, and foodies.

3 **Southeast Oregon.** The sprawling, scrubby ranchlands of Oregon's high desert country have a beauty all their own, and give way when you least expect it to majestic river canyons and stunning vistas. Food and lodging can be scarce out here, but outdoor enthusiasts will be rewarded with great campsites, serene hot springs, and small-town hospitality.

GETTING ORIENTED

At its eastern end, Oregon begins in a high, sage-scented desert plateau that covers nearly two-thirds of the state's 96,000 square mi. To the north, the border with Washington follows the Colombia River, then stretches eastward across the Colombia River Plateau to meet the Snake River, itself forming much of the state's eastern border with Idaho. East-central Oregon is carved out by the forks and tributaries of the John Day River, the country's third-largest undammed waterway. Its north–south course to the Columbia marks an invisible line extending southward, separating eastern Oregon from central Oregon's high plateaus and Cascade foothills. To the south, the Nevada border is an invisible line slicing through a high, desolate country sometimes known as the Oregon outback.

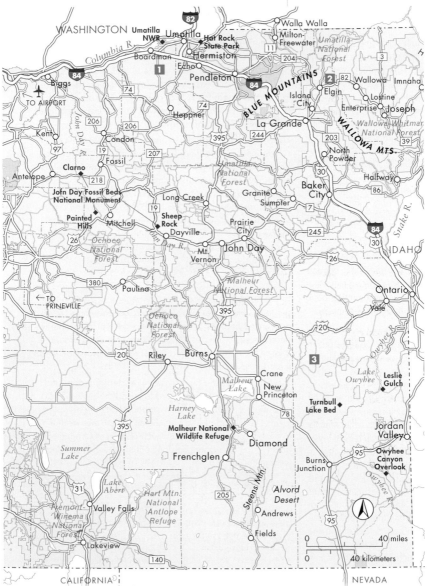

9

WASHINGTON

Columbia R.

Umatilla NWR
Umatilla
Hat Rock State Park
Boardman
Echo
Hermiston
Milton-Freewater
Walla Walla

Biggs
TO AIRPORT
Pendleton
Island City
Elgin
Wallowa
Imnaha
Lostine
Enterprise
Joseph

Heppner
La Grande
Wallowa-Whitman National Forest

Kent
Condon
North Powder

Antelope
Clarno
Fossil
Baker City
Halfway

John Day Fossil Beds National Monument
Long Creek
Granite
Sumpter

Painted Hills
Mitchell
Sheep Rock
Dayville
Prairie City

Ochoco National Forest
Mt. Vernon
John Day
IDAHO

Paulina
Malheur National Forest
Ontario
Vale

TO PRINEVILLE
Ochoco National Forest

Riley
Burns
Crane
Lake Owyhee
Leslie Gulch

New Princeton
Turnbull Lake Bed
Jordan Valley

Malheur Lake
Harney Lake
Diamond

Summer Lake
Malheur National Wildlife Refuge
Frenchglen
Burns Junction
Owyhee Canyon Overlook

Lake Abert
Hart Mtn. National Antlope Refuge
Steens Mtn.
Alvord Desert

Fremont-Winema National Forest
Valley Falls
Andrews

Lakeview
Fields
0 — 40 miles
0 — 40 kilometers

CALIFORNIA
NEVADA

EASTERN OREGON PLANNER

When to Go

Though skiers and snowboarders flock to the Blues and the Wallowas in winter, summer is eastern Oregon's primary travel season. It comes late in the state's northeast corner, where snow can remain in the mountains until July, and May flurries aren't uncommon at lower elevations. July and August are the best months for wildflowers in the high northeast, and they're also the only months when many remote-but-scenic Forest Service roads are guaranteed to be open. For visitors in the southeast, though, midsummer is often uncomfortably hot and dry, and avian action along the Pacific Flyway tends to peak around April and September.

Summer temps in northeast Oregon generally level out in the 80s around July and August. In midwinter, 20-degree days are the norm. The deserts of southeastern Oregon are a bit warmer. Midsummer sees highs in the upper 90s, while January and February can remain in the 40s in the low country. Bear in mind: Elevation varies greatly in eastern Oregon, and this can render seasonal averages pretty meaningless. It's not uncommon to gain or lose several thousand feet during the course of an hour's drive, and for much of the year this can mean the difference between flip-flops and snow boots.

About the Restaurants

Gourmet cuisine and chef-driven restaurants are rare on the eastern Oregon range, but it's not hard to find a tasty, authentic meal if you know where to look. Restaurants around the Wallowas, in particular, have a burgeoning local/organic ethos—locally grown produce abounds, farmers' markets are a big draw, and the rural county even has its own Slow Food chapter.

Elsewhere in the high desert, an entrenched ranching culture means big eating: farm-boy breakfasts and steak house after spur-jangling steak house. Generations of braceros have left their mark on the region's culinary scene as well, and excellent taquerias can be found in even the dustiest ranch towns. Pack a lunch if you're touring the southeasternmost corner of the state—towns are few and far between.

About the Hotels

Chain hotels are easy to find along the gorge and in bigger towns like Baker City and Burns, but elsewhere, small motels and bed-and-breakfasts are more typical. Properties described as "rustic" or "historic" aren't kidding around— a lot of the region's lodging hasn't seen a renovation since the Eisenhower administration.

Triple-digit rates are an anomaly in eastern Oregon, and you'd have to work pretty hard to spend more than $150 on a night's lodging. In summer, book early in no-stoplight towns like Diamond and Frenchglen, where the handful of available rooms fills up fast. Much of eastern Oregon shuts down in the off-season, so don't count on winter lodging without calling first.

WHAT IT COSTS IN U.S. DOLLARS

	¢	$	$$	$$$	$$$$
Restaurants	under $10	$10–$16	$17–$23	$24–$30	over $30
Hotels	under $100	$100–$150	$151–$200	$201–$250	over $250

Restaurant prices are per person, for a main course at dinner. Hotel prices are for two people in a standard double room in high season, excluding tax.

Getting Here and Around

Air Travel. Eastern Oregon Regional Airport at Pendleton (☎ 541/276–7754) receives daily flights from Portland and Seattle on SeaPort Airlines. Hertz Rental Caror **Elite Taxis** (☎ 541/276–8294) can get you into the city. Across the Washington border, **Tri-Cities Airport** (☎ 509/547–6352) is just 30 mi from Umatilla. Rental cars are available from most national agencies. Depending on where you're headed, check flights into Boise, ID (an hour from the eastern Oregon border), Spokane, WA (three hours from the northern border), and Elko, NV (three hours from the southern border).

Bus Travel. Many of the cities in eastern Oregon can be reached by **Greyhound** (☎ 800/231–2222 ⊕ www. greyhound.com) or by a smaller, regional bus line, but bear in mind that once you get there public transportation is usually not available, and not all cities have car-rental outlets. Also, most area bus routes operate only once or twice a day, and some don't run on weekends.

The major Greyhound route travels along I–84, passing through Pendleton, La Grande, Baker City, and Ontario. A bus operated by **Porter Stage Lines** (☎ 541/269–7183) runs daily from Ontario to Coos Bay on the coast, with stops at Burns, Vale, Bend, Eugene, and elsewhere. A shuttle bus called the **People Mover** (☎ 541/575–2370) runs round-trip on Mondays, Wednesdays, and Fridays between John Day and Bend, where it connects with the **Central Oregon Breeze** bus line to Portland.

Car Travel. The vast majority of travelers in eastern Oregon gets around by car. I–84 runs east along the Columbia River and dips down to Pendleton, La Grande, Baker City, and Ontario. U.S. 26 heads east from Prineville through the Ochoco National Forest, passing the three units of the John Day Fossil Beds. U.S. 20 travels southeast from Bend in central Oregon to Burns. U.S. 20 and U.S. 26 both head west into Oregon from Idaho.

In all these areas, equip yourself with chains for winter driving. Four-wheel drive is beneficial, if not essential, on a lot of eastern Oregon's designated Scenic Byways. Plan ahead for gas, since service stations can be few and far between. They often close early in small towns, and because drivers in Oregon can't legally pump their own gas, you'll be out of luck until morning.

Rental cars are available from Hertz at the Pendleton airport, and Sunray Auto in Ontario.

Local Agencies Sunray Auto Rentals (☎ 541/881–1383).

Top Festivals

Bronze, Blues & Brews. The title of Joseph's mid-August outdoor suds-fest pretty much says it all. (⊕ www. bronzebluesbrews.com). **Miner's Jubilee.** Baker City salutes its mining heritage on the third weekend of July with a rodeo, beer gardens, outdoor music, and the state championship gold-panning competition. (☎ 541/523–5855 ⊕ www.visitbaker. com). **Pendleton Round-Up.** This mid-September cowboy throwdown is the biggest one around. Saddle up for country music, flea markets, and plenty of bronc-ridin'. .

Tour Options

Hells Canyon Adventures (☎ 800/422–358 ⊕ www. hellscanyonadventures.com) leads full- and half-day jet-boat tours of the country's deepest gorge. **Jenkins Historical Tours** (☎ 888/493–2420 ⊕ www.roundbarn. net) are chatty, full-day van tours to the Steens Mountain and the Malheur National Wildlife Refuge areas. **Moffit Tours** (☎ 800/553–5222 ⊕ moffitbros.com) offer a weeklong bus tour of the Hells Canyon and Wallowa Mountain region.

VISITOR INFORMATION

Eastern Oregon Visitors Association (☎ 800/332–1843 ⊕ www.eova.com).

9

Updated by
Brian Kevin

Travel east from The Dalles, Bend, or any of the foothill communities blossoming in the shade of the Cascades, and you'll find a very different side of Oregon. The air is drier, clearer, often pungent with the smell of juniper. The vast landscape of sharply folded hills, wheat fields, and mountains shimmering in the distance evokes the mythic Old West. There is a lonely grandeur in eastern Oregon, a plain-spoken, independent spirit that can startle, surprise, and enthrall.

Much of eastern Oregon consists of national forest and wilderness, and the population runs the gamut from spur-janglin' cowboys to back-to-the-landers and urban expats. This is a world of ranches and rodeos, pickup trucks and country-western music. For the outdoor-adventure crowd, it's one of the West's last comparatively undiscovered playgrounds.

Some of the most important moments in Oregon's history took place in the towns of northeastern Oregon. The Oregon Trail passed through this corner of the state, winding through the Grande Ronde Valley between the Wallowa and Blue mountain ranges. The discovery of gold in the region in the 1860s sparked a second invasion of settlers, eventually leading to the displacement of the Native American Nez Perce and Paiute tribes. Pendleton, La Grande, and Baker City were all beneficiaries of the gold fever that swept through the area. Yet signs of even earlier times have survived, from the John Day Fossil Beds, with fragments of saber-toothed tigers, giant pigs, and three-toed horses, to Native American writings and artifacts hidden within canyon walls in Malheur County's Leslie Gulch.

Recreation and tourism are gaining a foothold in eastern Oregon today, but the region still sees only a fraction of the visitors that drop in on Mt. Hood or the coast each year. For off-the-beaten-path types, eastern Oregon's mountains and high desert country are as breathtaking as any landscape in the West, and you'd be pretty hard-pressed to get farther from the noise and distractions of city life.

EAST GORGE

Heading east along the interstate through the beige flats and monoculture croplands between Umatilla and Pendleton, you could be forgiven for supposing that the most interesting part of Oregon was behind you. But just off the beaten path in the East Gorge country are seasonal wetlands chock-full of avian wildlife, roadside relics of the Old West, and dusty frontier towns undergoing commercial rebirths. Parks like Hat Rock State Park offer boaters and anglers access to the vast Columbia River Gorge, one of the country's most impressive waterways. A few dozen miles away in Pendleton, one of the world's largest and oldest rodeos anchors a town with an unexpectedly hip dining and shopping scene. Look south and east to where the river plateau gives way to the forested foothills of the Blue Mountains—mule deer and bighorn sheep dot those hills in spots like the McKay Creek National Wildlife Refuge and Umatilla National Forest.

UMATILLA

180 mi east of Portland on I–84 and Hwy. 730; 40 mi northwest of Pendleton.

Umatilla is at the confluence of the Umatilla and Columbia rivers. It was founded in the mid-1800s as a trade and shipping center during the gold rush, and today is a center for fishing activities. Just east of Umatilla, Hat Rock State Park contains the unusual geological formation from which it gets its name. Farther upstream, McNary Dam generates extensive hydroelectric power and impounds a lake that extends from Umatilla to Richland, Washington, some 70 mi away. Umatilla is primarily a crossroads, but visitors crossing the Columbia here will appreciate the recreation opportunities along the massive river's banks.

GETTING HERE

Find Umatilla where I–82 crosses the Colombia River Gorge at the Washington-Oregon border. Commercial flights land at the Tri-Cities Airport in Pasco, Washington, 30 mi north on I–82, or in Pendleton's Eastern Oregon Regional Airport. From Portland, drive 165 mi east on I–84, then take a scenic, 15-mi shortcut along the gorge on Hwy. 730. It's a 40-mi trip from Pendleton, heading west on I–84, then cutting through Hermiston on Hwy. 395.

VISITOR INFORMATION

Umatilla Chamber of Commerce (⊠ *100 Cline Ave.* ☎ *541/922–4825* ⊕ *www. umatillachamber.com*).

WHERE TO EAT AND STAY

$ ✕ **Desert River Inn Restaurant.** "Homemade clam chowder every day" is the claim of this casual and family-friendly spot serving breakfast, lunch, and dinner. Prime rib is a favorite at night. With large booths and pastel walls, the room's atmosphere is family-restaurant generic, but a meal here is a satisfying addition to a day of exploring. ⊠ *705 Willamette Ave.* ☎ *541/922–1000 or 877/922–1500* ⊟ *AE, D, MC, V.*

AMERICAN

9

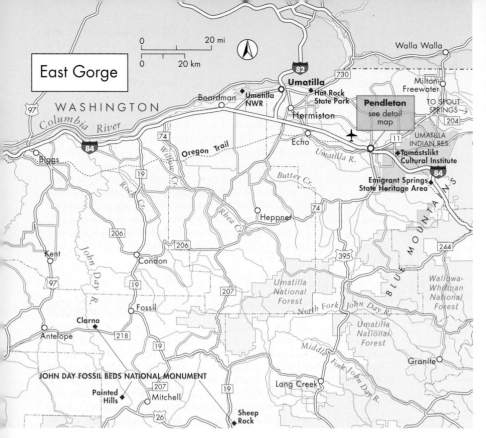

East Gorge

- ℭ 🏨 **Desert River Inn**. The largest and, by far, the best-equipped hotel in Umatilla, the Desert River Inn acts as the centerpiece of the town, with its restaurant, golf course, and banquet rooms making it more than just a place to spend the night. The rooms are large and comfortable, and there is a host of extras available, including Pasco & Hermiston airport pickup on request. **Pros:** some rooms have kitchenettes; horseshoe pits get a lot of action in the summer. **Cons:** not within walking distance into downtown. ⊠ *705 Willamette Ave.* ☎ *541/922–1000 or 877/922–1500* ⊕ *www.desertriverinn.com* ⌂ *66 rooms* ⚒ *In-room: kitchen (some), refrigerator, Wi-Fi, a/c. In-hotel: restaurant, room service, bar, golf course, pool, gym, pets allowed (fee)* ☰ *AE, D, MC, V* ℩⊙∣ *CP.*

SPORTS AND THE OUTDOORS

RECREATIONAL AREAS ℭ **Hat Rock State Park.** On the south shore of Lake Wallula, a 70-foot basalt rock is the first major landmark that Lewis and Clark passed on their expedition down the Columbia. In his notations, William Clark called it "Hat Rock," and the name stuck. Standing tall amid rolling sagebrush hills, it overlooks Lake Wallula, a popular spot for jet skiing, swimming, boating, and fishing for rainbow trout, walleye, and sturgeon. In addition to water sports, the park provides scenic picnic spots and expansive views of the stark, desertlike landscape. But because it abuts an upscale lakeside housing development that's visible from some portions of the park, it might be a challenge to pretend you're back in the days of Lewis and Clark. ✉ *U.S. 730, 9 mi. east of Umatilla, 82375 C St., Hermiston* ☎ *800/551–6949* ⊕ *www.oregonstateparks. org* ✇ *Free* ☼ *Dawn–dusk year-round.*

Umatilla National Wildlife Refuge. The 23,555-acre refuge includes marsh, woodland, and wetland habitats that make it vital to migrating waterfowl and bald eagles, in addition to myriad species of resident wildlife. Although there are numerous routes to access portions of the refuge, the best and easiest way to view wildlife in ponds and wetlands is to drive along the McCormick Auto Tour Route, accessible from Paterson Ferry Road, off Route 730, 9 mi west of Umatilla. ✉ *Stretches from Boardman, 20 mi west of Umatilla, to Irrigon, 9 mi west of Umatilla, north of I–84 along Columbia River* ☎ *509/546–8300* ⊕ *www.fws.gov/ Umatilla* ✇ *Free* ☼ *Daily dawn–dusk on designated roadways only.*

PENDLETON

210 mi east of Portland, 130 mi east of the Dalles on I–84.

At the foot of the Blue Mountains amid waving wheat fields and cattle ranches, Pendleton is a quintessential western town with a rip-snorting history. It was originally acquired in a swap for a couple of horses, and the town's history of wild behavior was evident from the first city ordinance, which outlawed public drunkenness, fights, and shooting off one's guns within the city limits. But Pendleton is also the land of the Umatilla Tribe—the herds of wild horses that once thundered across this rolling landscape were at the center of the area's early Native American culture. Later Pendleton became an important pioneer junction and home to a sizable Chinese community. Today's cityscape still carries the vestiges of yesteryear, with many of its century-old homes still standing, from simple farmhouses to stately Queen Annes.

Given its raucous past teeming with cattle rustlers, saloons, and bordellos, the largest city in eastern Oregon (population 17,500) looks unusually sedate. But all that changes in September when the **Pendleton Round-Up** *(⇨ Sports & the Outdoors)* draws thousands.

GETTING HERE

Pendleton has the region's only airport, the Eastern Oregon Regional Airport, which has incoming and outgoing flights daily on SeaPort Air to Portland and Seattle. Pendleton is located right on I–84 and is serviced by Greyhound.

VISITOR INFORMATION

Pendleton Chamber of Commerce (✉ *501 S. Main St.* ☎ *541/246–7411 or 800/547–9811* ⊕ *www.pendletonchamber.com*).

EXPLORING

Fodor'sChoice
★

Pendleton Underground Tours. This 90-minute tour transports you below ground and back through Pendleton's history of gambling, girls, and gold. Originating in 1989, the Underground Tours depict town life from more than a century ago (when 32 saloons and 18 brothels were operating in full swing) to the 1953 closure of the Cozy Rooms, the best-known bordello in town. The Underground Tour

9

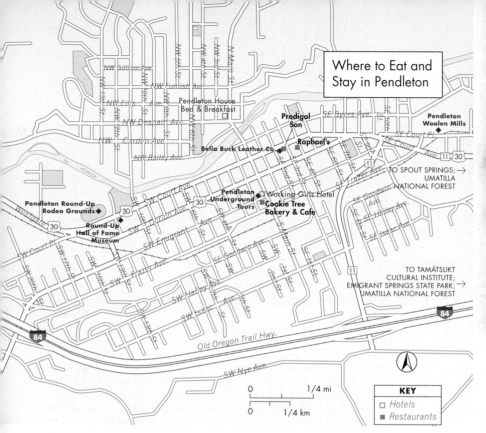

Pendleton House
Bed & Breakfast

Prodigal
Son

Pendleton
Woolen Mills

Raphael's

Bella Buck Leather Co.

Pendleton
Underground
Tours

Working Girls Hotel

Cookie Tree
Bakery & Cafe

Pendleton Round-Up
Rodeo Grounds

Round-Up
Hall of Fame
Museum

TO SPOUT SPRINGS;
UMATILLA
NATIONAL FOREST

TO TAMÁTSLIKT
CULTURAL INSTITUTE;
EMIGRANT SPRINGS STATE PARK; →
UMATILLA NATIONAL FOREST

Old Oregon Trail Hwy.

SW Nye Ave.

| 0 | 1/4 mi |
| 0 | 1/4 km |

KEY	
☐	Hotels
■	Restaurants

eventually resurfaces, climbing the "31 Steps to Heaven" to those
Cozy Rooms, where madam Stella Darby reigned. The secret gambling
lairs, opium dens, and bathhouses that lie directly below the pave-
ment will give you a whole new perspective of the streets of Pendleton.
⌧ 37 SW Emigrant Ave. ☎ 541/276–0730 or 800/226–6398 ⊕ www.
pendletonundergroundtours.com ⌇ $15 ⊙ year-round, reservations
necessary.

Pendleton Woolen Mills. Perhaps Pendleton's main source of name-rec-
ognition in the country today comes from this mill, home of the trade-
mark wool plaid shirts and colorful woolen Indian blankets. If you
want to know more about the weaving process, the company gives
20-minute tours 4 times daily. The mill's retail store stocks blankets
and clothing; there are good bargains on factory seconds. ⌧ 1307 SE
Court Pl. ☎ 541/276–6911 or 800/568–3156 ⊕ www.pendleton-usa.
com ⊙ Mon.–Sat. 8–6, Sun. 9–5; tours weekdays at 9, 11, 1:30, and 3.

☺ **Round-Up Hall of Fame Museum.** The museum's collection spans the
rodeo's history since 1910, with photographs—including glamorous
glossies of prior Rodeo Queens and the Happy Canyon Princesses (all
Native American)—as well as saddles, guns, and costumes. A taxider-
mied championship bronco named War Paint is the museum's cool-
if-slightly-creepy prize artifact. ⌧ 1114 SW Court Ave., across from

Pendleton Underground Tours

Round-Up grounds ☎ *541/278–0815* ⊕ *www.pendletonroundup.com*
✉ *$5* ⊘ *Mon.–Sat. 10–4.*

☉ **Tamástslikt Cultural Institute.** Located at the Wildhorse Resort and Casino, the 45,000-square-foot building depicts history from the perspective of the Cayuse, Umatilla, and Walla Walla tribes. (*Tamástslikt* means "interpret" in the Walla Walla native language.) An art gallery showcases art of local and regional tribal artists. There's also a museum gift shop, theater, and café. ✉ *72789 Hwy. 331, north of I–84 at Exit 216* ☎ *541/966–9748* ⊕ *www.tamastslikt.org* ✉ *$8* ⊘ *Daily 9–5, except closed Sun. Nov–Mar.*

9

NEED A BREAK? A popular laid-back spot across from the Underground Tours, the **Cookie Tree** (✉ *39 SW Emigrant Ave.* ☎ *541/278–0343*) is good for a quick breakfast, sandwich, pastry, or fresh bread.

WHERE TO EAT AND STAY

¢ ✕ **The Prodigal Son.** This is one of the newest brewpub entries in eastern
AMERICAN   Oregon's ambitious bid to catch up with the rest of this ale-obsessed state. A cavernous former car dealership (think Model Ts) houses this oh-so-hip hangout, complete with leather couches, tabletop Pac-Man, and a minilibrary. The strong, malty house porter is a hit with young locals, and the menu sticks to tasty pub-food classics: fish-and-chips, Reubens, and Scotch eggs. ✉ *230 SE Court Ave.* ☎ *541/276–6090* ⊕ *www.prodigalsonbrewery.com* ▭ *MC, V.*

$$$ ✕ **Raphael's.** Is it a restaurant—or a millionaire's seven-gabled home?
NEW AMERICAN   It's both! The 1904 Raley House was sold and converted in 1991 to its current gastronomic glory, where art deco meets Native American

cultural sensibilities. Husband/co-owner/chef Rob Hoffman is crazy for huckleberries—you might find them integrated in the Indian salmon, the pastas, chicken, or wild game (elk, pheasant, buffalo), as well as the crème brûlée. If you'd rather drink your berries, consider Raphael's signature huckleberry martinis and daiquiris. When chef Rob's not using huckleberries, he might mingle apples in his smoked prime rib, or apricots in a pork loin sauce. In sunnier months, consider dining alfresco in the garden out back. ⊠ *233 SE 4th St.* ☎ *541/276–8500 or 888/944–2433* ⊕ *www.raphaelsrestaurant.com* ▭ *AE, D, DC, MC, V* ⊗ *Closed Sun. and Mon. No lunch.*

$ 🏠 **The Pendleton House Bed & Breakfast.** This gorgeous, 6,000 square-foot pink stucco home hasn't changed much since it was built in 1917. The Chinese wallpaper, custom fittings, woodwork—all original in this blend of French neoclassical and Italianate architecture. Located in Pendleton's North Hill neighborhood, the bed-and-breakfast is a grand reminder that the Old West had its share of wealth and worldly sophistication. Furnished with period furniture, the rooms are quiet and comfortable. Four of them share one bathroom, designed by Pittock Mansion architect Edward T. Foulkes; according to the owner, it's so stunning that guests don't seem to mind the inconvenience. Gourmet breakfasts might include eggs Benedict with proscuitto, toasted pecan-and-cranberry-stuffed French toast, or soufflé frittata ramekins. **Pros:** glorious home; small pets allowed; comp wine-and-cheese hour. **Cons:** one shared bathroom for 4 rooms; owners are somewhat brusque. ⊠ *311 N. Main St.* ☎ *541/276–8581 or 800/700–8581* ⊕ *www. parkerhousebnb.com* ⮥ *5 rooms, 1 with 1/2 bath* ⟁ *In-room: no phone, no TV, Wi-Fi (some). In-hotel: parking (free), some pets allowed (fee), no kids under 14* ▭ *AE, MC, V* ⟡ *BP.*

¢ 🏠 **Working Girls Hotel.** From boarding house to bordello to hotel, the
Fodor's Choice
★ refurbished 1890s edifice advertises its "Old West Comfort" with a large vertical sign hanging from the top of the building. A redheaded lass looks down from the top of the sign, as if wanting to call to potential customers passing by. Exposed-brick walls and 18-foot ceilings run throughout, but the individual Victorian antiques that decorate the rooms give them all their own personalities. Owned and operated by the Underground Tours, the inn has a full kitchen and dining room available to guests, and with no lobby or front office, you'll feel more like you're renting a historic downtown apartment than booking a hotel room. **Pros:** centrally located in downtown Pendleton; fun decor; great prices. **Cons:** bathrooms in the hall instead of the room; no on-site reception. ⊠ *17 SW Emigrant Ave.* ☎ *541/276–0730 or 800/226–6398* ⊕ *www.pendletonundergroundtours.com* ⮥ *4 rooms with 2 shared baths, 1 suite* ⟁ *In-room: a/c, no phone, no TV (some), no kids under 14* ▭ *MC, V.*

SPORTS AND THE OUTDOORS

RECREATIONAL   **Emigrant Springs State Heritage Area.** Near the summit of the Blue Moun-
AREAS   tains, this park in an old-growth forest is the site of a popular pioneer stopover along the Oregon Trail. The park has picnic areas, hiking trails, historical information, and gathering spaces for special events.

At the campground, in addition to 18 full hookups and 32 tent sites, there are seven rustic cabins, including two totem cabins. ✉ *Off I–84 at Exit 234, 65068, Old Oregon Trail, Meacham* ☎ *541/983–2277 or 800/551–6949* ⊕ *www.oregonstateparks.org* 🗓 *Day use free* ☯ *Year-round.*

Umatilla National Forest. Three rugged, secluded wilderness areas attract backpackers to this 1.4-million-acre forest: the Wenaha-Tucannon, the North Fork Umatilla, and the North Fork John Day. *Umatilla* is derived from a word in the indigenous Shahaptian language meaning "water rippling over sand," and the forest has its share of fishable rivers and streams as well. Home to the Blue Mountain Scenic Byway and 22 campgrounds, the diverse forestland is found both east and south of Pendleton, and extends south almost as far as John Day, where it borders the Malheur National Forest. To the east it is bordered by the Wallowa-Whitman National Forest. Major thoroughfares through the forest include I–84, U.S. 395, and routes 204 and 244. ✉ *Forest Headquarters: 2517 SW Hailey Ave.* ☎ *541/278–3716* ⊕ *www.fs.fed.us/r6/uma* 🗓 *Northwest Forest Pass required at some trailheads, $5/day or $30 annual.*

RODEO **Pendleton Round-Up.** More than 50,000 people roll into town during the second full week in September for one of the oldest and most prominent rodeos in the United States. With its famous slogan of "Let 'er Buck," the Round-Up features eight days of parades, races, beauty contests, and children's rodeos, culminating in four days of rodeo events. Vendors line the length of Court Avenue and Main Street, selling beadwork and curios, while country bands twang in the background. ✉ *Rodeo grounds: 1205 SW Court Ave., at SW 12th St.* ✉ *Office, open year-round: 1114 SW Court Ave.* ☎ *541/276–2553 or 800/457–6336* ⊕ *www.pendletonroundup.com.*

SKIING **Spout Springs.** This ski resort in the Umatilla National Forest has an elevation of 4,950 feet at the base, 5,550 feet at the top, and a vertical drop of 550 feet. There are 11 runs and 21 km of Nordic trails, as well as a terrain park and large freestyle tubing hill. ✉ *Summit of Hwy. 204 at Tollgate, Milepost 22; 79327 Highway 204, Weston* ☎ *541/566–0320* ⊕ *www.spoutspringsskiresort.com* 🗓 *$30 adult.*

SHOPPING

Bella Buck Leather Co. Though it shares space with a traditional tackle shop, this boutique puts a New West, punk-a-billy spin on frilly leather goods. Think skulls and mud flaps, ladies. ✉ *224 SE Court Ave.* ☎ *541/410–4023.*

Hamley & Co. Western Store & Custom Saddlery. On-site craftspeople at this Western superstore fashion hand-tooled saddles considered among the best in the world. You'll also find authentic cowboy/cowgirl gear and quality leather products, plus gifts and art. Bonus: in 2007 Hamley's opened a huge steak house on-site for lunch, dinner, and drinks. ✉ *30 SE Court Ave.* ☎ *541/278–1100 or 877/342–6539* ⊕ *www.hamley.com*

NORTHEAST OREGON

No part of eastern Oregon repudiates the region's reputation for flat and barren landscapes quite like its lush and mountainous northeast corner. Simply put, the Wallowa Mountains are among the most underrated outdoor-rec hot spots in the Rockies, with 565 square mi of backpacker-friendly wilderness, abundant wildlife, and proximity to Hells Canyon, North America's deepest gorge. The nearby Blue Mountains are no slouches either, home to some of the state's best alpine and Nordic skiing. Towns like Baker City, Joseph, and La Grande have transitioned more thoroughly than much of the region from pastoral and extractive economies to hospitality and recreation, making them eastern Oregon's de facto capitals of art, food, and culture. Each city has a vibrant downtown and a chillbilly vibe, and you'll find locals swapping fish stories and trail tales in one of the area's excellent brewpubs. Baker City in particular has maintained its mining-era integrity—the restored Geiser Grand Hotel is a must-visit, especially for history buffs.

LA GRANDE

56 mi southeast of Pendleton on I–84 at Hwy. 82.

La Grande started life in the late 1800s as a farming community. It grew slowly while most towns along the Blue Mountains were booming or busting in the violent throes of gold-fueled stampedes. When the railroad companies were deciding where to lay their tracks through the valley, a clever local farmer donated 150 acres to ensure that the Iron Horse would run through La Grande. With steam power fueling a new boom, the town quickly outgrew its neighbors, took the title of county seat from fading Union City (Union City claims it "was robbed"), and with its current population of 12 thousand sits at the urban center of the Grand Ronde Valley. Though you can appreciate it for its own charms, La Grande is a convenient stop if you're heading to the nearby Wallowa Mountains.

GETTING HERE

La Grande sits at the intersection of I–84 and Highway 82, the primary route through the Wallowa Valley to Joseph and Enterprise. Cars and busses will get you into town from Portland, 260 mi west, and Boise, Idaho, 170 mi east. The closest airport is Eastern Oregon Regional, 50 mi northeast in Pendleton. The **Wallowa Link Bus** (☎ *541/963–2877* ⊕ *www.neotransit.org*) runs twice a week between La Grande and Joseph, stopping in Enterprise. The **Baker Bow** shuttle bus (☎ *541/963–2877* ⊕ *www.neotransit.org*) runs Monday to Friday to Baker City and Haines. **Greyhound** also makes stops here.

VISITOR INFORMATION

La Grande Visitor Center (✉ *102 Elm St.* ☎ *541/963–8588 or 800/848–9969* ⊕ *www.visitlagrande.com*).

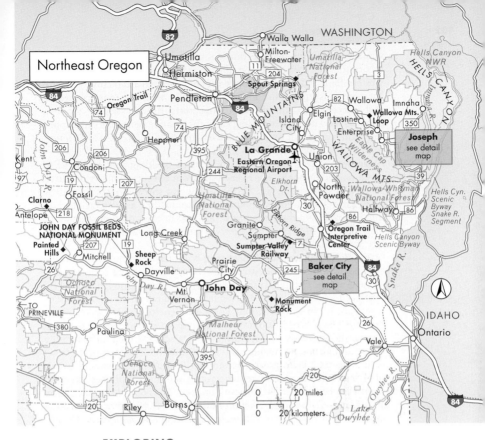

EXPLORING

Union's National Historic District. Fourteen miles southeast of La Grande is a Victorian-era town that's working to restore many of its historic buildings. In addition to the picturesque buildings lining Union's Main Street, the main attractions are the **Union Hotel** (⊠ *326 N. Main St.* ☎ *541/562–6135* ⊕ *www.theunionhotel.com*), a beautifully restored hotel with a restaurant and parlor (⇨ *Where to Eat and Stay*), and the **Union County Museum** (⊠ *331 S. Main St.* ☎ *541/562–6003* 🖾 *$4* ⏱ *mid-May–mid-Oct., Mon.–Sat. 10–4, or by appointment*), which has a fascinating exhibit on the Ku Klux Klan in Oregon, among other things.

NEED A BREAK? If you want to remain an anonymous tourist, don't visit **Joe and Sugar's** (⊠ *1119 Adams Ave.* ☎ *541/975–5282*). You can't avoid being chatted up by the funny, friendly, and helpful owner of this sweet-smelling café and coffee shop.

WHERE TO EAT AND STAY

$$$
NEW AMERICAN ✕**Foley Station.** This local favorite has an antique pressed-tin ceiling, an open kitchen, exposed-brick walls, and high-backed, rich wood-paneled booths. The snazzy bar has multiple happy hours, namely Martinis & Munchies in the Lounge, 3 to 5 and 8 to closing. The seasonal menu

wanders from inexpensive burgers to high-end lobsters and steaks, incorporating Northwest ingredients as well as a pronounced Southwestern flair, and hush puppies with jalapeño jelly keep company with Vietnamese spring rolls. There's a full bar, with wines, microbrews, and a decent selection of after-dinner ports. Brunch starts at 9 AM on Sundays, and it's worth coming early for creative Benedicts (think pork loin and ahi tuna). ⊠ *1114 Adams Ave.* ☎ *541/963–7473* ⊕ *www. foleystation.com* ⊟ *D, MC, V.*

$$$
AMERICAN

✕ **Ten Depot St.** In a stylish historic brick building that has a VFW upstairs, Ten Depot St. has everything from burgers to nicely prepared steak and seafood dishes. With dark wood throughout accented by plum tablecloths and teal plates and napkins, it's an elegant place to dine. Start off your evening with a drink at the adjoining bar. ⊠ *10 Depot St.* ☎ *541/963–8766* ⊕ *www.tendepotstreet.com* ⊟ *AE, MC, V* ⊗ *Closed Sun. No lunch.*

¢ 🏨 **The Historic Union Hotel.** Cast-iron Victorian lampposts frame the entrance to this three-story, redbrick building, its white trim standing out against the red like icing on a cake. The Union Hotel, about 14 mi south of La Grande, offers 16 elegant, individually themed rooms. The forest-green Northwest Room has a kitchenette and a jetted tub for two; the Davis Bros.' Room comes with a wood-paneled shower with double showerheads; and for large parties up to 6, the Huffman Suite has a full kitchen. Per owners Dave and Rob, the best part of the hotel is "the guests." **Pros:** great prices; visual/historic treat; owners go out of their way to accommodate; RV spots. **Cons:** no TV, phones, Internet; front view of a trailer park doesn't impress. ⊠ *326 N. Main St., Union* ☎ *541/562–6135* ⊕ *www.theunionhotel.com* ⟿ *16 rooms; RV accommodations, 8 spaces, for $25/night* ⟁ *In-room: no phone, no TV, a/c. In-hotel: restaurant, parking (free), some pets allowed (fee), kids under 9 discouraged* ⊟ *D, MC, V.*

SHOPPING

Sunflower Books, Etc. This unassuming yellow bungalow has been a cozy indie bookstore and coffeeshop for more than two decades. Find cookbooks in the kitchen and coffee table books in the living room, then grab some shade-grown joe in the dining room before sitting down to use the free Wi-Fi. ⊠ *1114 Washington Ave.* ☎ *541/963–5242* ⊕ *www. sunflowerbookstore.com.*

SPORTS AND THE OUTDOORS

RECREATIONAL
AREAS

Eagle Cap Wilderness. At more than 350,000 acres, this is the largest wilderness in Oregon, encompassing most of the Wallowa range with 534 mi of trails for hard-core backpackers and horseback riders. Most of the popular trail heads are along Eagle Cap's northern edge, accessible from Enterprise or Joseph, but you also can find several trailheads 20 to 30 mi southeast of La Grande along Route 203. (Some areas of the wilderness are accessible year-round, while the high-elevation areas are accessible only for a few months in summer.) To park at many trailheads you must purchase a Northwest Forest Pass for $5 per day, or $30 per year. To hike into the wilderness, you also need to get a free permit that will alert rangers of your plans. ⊠ *East of La Grande, via*

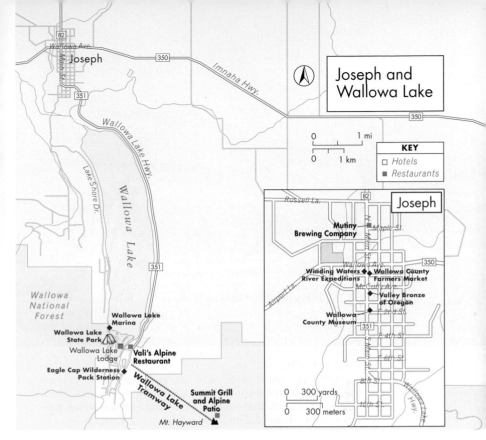

Hwy. 82 and Hwy. 203. *Wallowa Mountains Visitor Center: 115 Tejaka Ln., off Hwy. 82, Enterprise* ☎ *541/426–4978* ⊕ *www.fs.fed.us/r6/w-w.*

Fodor's Choice **Wallowa Mountains.** Forming a rugged U-shape fortress between Hells
★ Canyon on the Idaho border and the Blue Mountains, the Wallowas are
sometimes called the American Alps or Little Switzerland. The granite
peaks in this range are between 5,000 and 9,000 feet in height. Dotted
with crystalline alpine lakes and meadows, rushing rivers, and thickly
forested valleys that fall between the mountain ridges, the Wallowas
have a grandeur that can take your breath away. Bighorn sheep, elk,
deer, and mountain goats populate the area. Nearly all the trails in the
Wallowa Mountains are at least partially contained within the Eagle
Cap Wilderness. The offices and visitor center for the mountains are in
Enterprise, but La Grande makes a good home base for exploring both
sides of the range. ✉ *Wallowa Mountains Visitor Center: 115 Tejaka
Ln., off Hwy. 82, Enterprise* ☎ *541/426–4978* ⊕ *www.fs.fed.us/r6/w-w.*

JOSEPH

80 mi east of La Grande on Hwy. 82.

The area around Wallowa Lake was the traditional home of the Nez
Perce Indians—the town of Joseph is named for Chief Joseph, their

Teepees overlooking Joseph Canyon

famous leader. The peaks of the Wallowa Mountains, snow-covered until July, tower 5,000 feet above the regional tourist hubs of the town. Joseph itself isn't much more than a nice Main Street speckled with shops and cafés. Follow Main Street a mile out of town, though, to reach the gorgeous Wallowa Lake, where you'll find a whole separate hospitality village of rental cabins, outfitters, go-karts, and ice-cream stands. The busy area on the south end of the lake is also the site of two of the most popular access points for the mountains, the Wallowa Lake trail head and the Wallowa Lake Tramway.

GETTING HERE
Hwy. 82 ends at Joseph, which is reachable primarily by car (or private plane at the town's postage-stamp airport). The **Wallowa Link Bus** (☎ *541/963–2877* ⊕ *www.neotransit.org*) runs twice weekly to and from La Grande, with a stop in Enterprise.

Main St. bisects tiny Joseph, then bends around Wallowa Lake to reach the tourism village on the south shore. In the summer a **shuttle bus** runs throughout the day among Joseph, Enterprise, and the south end of the lake (☎ *541/426–3840*).

VISITOR INFORMATION
Joseph Chamber of Commerce (✉ *Kiosk at Main St. & Joseph Ave.* ☎ *541/432–1015* ⊕ *www.josephoregon.com*).

EXPLORING
Valley Bronze of Oregon. This extensive gallery displays sculptures by the many artists who cast their work at the nearby foundry, plus the work of other artists from around the world. Generally, the gallery is open

Memorial Day to October, daily 10 to 5, but as winter settles in it's Saturdays only, and hours vary. The foundry itself is a half mile away, and your tour guide will lead you there after the group has gathered at the showroom. ✉ *18 S. Main St.* ☎ *541/432–7551* ⊕ *www.valleybronze. com* ✍ *$15* ⊙ *Tours daily: Mon.–Thurs. at 10:30, weekends at 1.*

Wallowa County Farmers Market. More than just a cluster of produce tents, Joseph's Saturday markets are the social hub of the community. Grab groceries or treats from rows of veggie vendors, chocolatiers, and sustainable cattle ranchers, then hang around for the live outdoor music and the bronze-sculpture street art. ✉ *Main St. and Joseph Ave.* ⊙ *Memorial Day–mid-Oct., Sat. 10–2.*

Wallowa County Museum. Joseph's volunteer-run museum has a small but poignant collection of artifacts and photographs chronicling the flight of the Nez Perce, a series of battles against the U.S. Army that took place in the late 1870s. Built as a bank in 1888, the building was robbed in 1896, an event commemorated by a number of the museum's artifacts, including a massive old safe and some yellowing newspaper accounts. ✉ *110 S. Main St.* ☎ *541/432–6095* ⊕ *www.co.wallowa.or.us/museum* ✍ *$2.50* ⊙ *Memorial Day–3rd weekend in Sept., daily 10–5.*

Wallowa Lake Tramway. The steepest tram in North America rises 3,700 feet in 15 minutes, rushing you up to the top of 8,150-foot Mt. Howard. Vistas of mountain peaks, forest, and Wallowa Lake far below will dazzle you, both on the way up and at the summit. Early and late in the season, 2½ mi of cross-country skiing trails await at the top, and the interpretive trails are open for hiking during the snowless months of midsummer. Enjoy casual lunch with great views at the Summit Grill and Alpine Patio before making your return trip back down to earth. ✉ *59919 Wallowa Lake Hwy.* ☎ *541/432–5331* ⊕ *www. wallowalaketramway.com* ✍ *$24* ⊙ *May–Sept., daily 10–4; Oct. 11–3. Tram runs sporadically in winter.*

EN ROUTE **Wallowa Mountain Loop.** This is a relatively easy way to take in the natural splendor of the Eagle Cap Wilderness and reach Baker City without backtracking to La Grande. The three-hour trip from Joseph to Baker City, designated the Hells Canyon Scenic Byway, winds through the national forest and part of Hells Canyon Recreation Area, passing over forested mountains, creeks, and rivers. Before you travel the loop, check with the Forest Service about road conditions; the route can be impassable when snowed over. ✉ *From Joseph, take Hwy. 350 east for 8 mi, turn south onto Forest Service Rd. 39, and continue until it meets Hwy. 86, which winds past town of Halfway to Baker City* ⊕ *www.fs.fed.us/ r6/w-w/recreation/byway/byway-hc.shtml.*

WHERE TO EAT

AMERICAN ✗ **Mutiny Brewing Company.** A small brewpub with a bistro feel, Mutiny churns out a couple of respectable microbrews, but puts an equal focus on the food. Locally-sourced ingredients fill out a simple menu of creative sandwiches and knockout burgers, and locals crowd the place during weekend brunch for huevos and beer shandies. There's patio seating with excellent mountain views. ✉ *600 N. Main St.* ☎ *541/432–5274* ⊕ *www.mutinybrewing.blogspot.com* ➟ *MC, V* ⊙ *Closed Mon.*

DID YOU KNOW?

The Eagle Cap Wilderness area is one of Oregon's premier backpacking destinations, with more than 500 miles of trails. It is home to more than 50 alpine lakes, including the highest lake in Oregon, Legore Lake.

¢ ✕**Terminal Gravity Brew Pub.** Beer connoisseurs from across the state, and just about all the locals, rave about the India Pale Ale at this tiny microbrewery in a canary-yellow house 6 mi north of Joseph in Enterprise. Aspens wave on a front yard dotted with picnic tables, and kids and dogs lounge on the wooden front porch. Between the indoor customers strumming guitars and outdoor customers playing volleyball, it can't just be about the hops at this friendly local hangout. The menu is short and simple, with creative sandwiches and burgers. There's a rotating selection of house-brewed beers on tap, complete with seasonals. The suds stack up favorably against the gazillion beers brewed over in Portland, but it's the vibe that really sells this place. ✉ *803 SE School St., Enterprise* ☎ *541/426–3000* ⊕ *www.terminalgravitybrewing.com* 〓 *MC, V* ⊙ *Closed Sun.–Tues. No lunch.*

AMERICAN
Fodor'sChoice
★

$ ✕**Vali's Alpine Restaurant.** This Wallowa Lake institution serves a rotating, single-entrée menu of classic Hungarian dishes like cabbage rolls and goulash. Drop in before 11 AM weekends for the out-of-this-world homemade donuts. ✉ *59811 Wallowa Lake Hwy.* ☎ *541/432–5691* ⊕ *www.valisrestaurant.com* ⚲ *Reservations required* 〓 *No credit cards* ⊙ *Closed Labor Day–March. No lunch.*

EASTERN
EUROPEAN

$$ ✕🍴 **Wallowa Lake Lodge.** At this friendly 1920s lodge, handmade replicas of the structure's original furniture fill a large common area with a massive fireplace. The lodge's rooms are simple yet appealing; the grandest have balconies facing the lake. The cabins, some with fireplaces and lake views, are small, old-fashioned havens of knotty pine. The onsite restaurant serves standard American fare for breakfast, lunch, and dinner. **Pros:** affordable; visual/historical treat; owners go out of their way to accommodate. **Cons:** no TV, phones, Internet. ✉ *60060 Wallowa Lake Hwy., Wallowa Lake* ☎ *541/432–9821* ⊕ *www.wallowalake.com* ⇆ *22 rooms, 8 cabins* ⚿ *In-room: no phone, no TV, Wi-Fi. In-hotel: restaurant, bar* 〓 *D, MC, V* ⊙ *Closed mid-Sept.–Memorial Day.*

SPORTS AND THE OUTDOORS

RECREATIONAL
AREAS

Wallowa Lake. A few miles south of Joseph proper on Highway 351 (or the Wallowa Lake Highway), sparkling, blue-green Wallowa Lake is the highest body of water in eastern Oregon (elevation 5,000 feet). Boating and fishing are popular, and the lake supports a whole vacation village on its southern end, complete with cabins, restaurants, and miniature golf. ✉ *Wallowa Lake Hwy.*

Wallowa Lake State Park. On the south shore of Wallowa Lake is a campground surrounded on three sides by 9,000-foot-tall snowcapped mountains. If you'd rather lose elevation than gain it, Hells Canyon is just 30 mi east. The park campground has 121 full hookups, 89 tent sites, a 2-story cabin (sleeps 8), and 2 yurts. Popular activities include fishing and powerboating on the adjacent Wallowa Lake, plus hiking on wilderness trails, horseback riding, and canoeing. Nearby are bumper boats, miniature golf, and the tramway to the top of Mt. Howard. ✉ *Off Hwy. 82, 6 mi south of Joseph, 72214 Marina La.* ☎ *541/432–4185 or 800/551–6949* ⊕ *www.oregonstateparks.org* 🎫 *$5 per vehicle* ⊙ *Daily.*

HORSEBACK RIDING	**Eagle Cap Wilderness Pack Station.** Book a short guided ride and/or a multiday summer pack trip from the south end of Wallowa Lake into the Eagle Cap Wilderness. ✉ *59761 Wallowa Lake Hwy.* ☏ *541/432–4145 or 800/681–6222* ⊕ *www.eaglecapwildernesspackstation.com.*
RAFTING AND BOATING	**Winding Waters River Expeditions.** Experienced river guides lead whitewater rafting and kayaking trips on the Snake River and the nearby Grande Ronde River. ☏ *877/426–7238* ⊕ *www.windingwatersrafting. com.*
	Wallowa Lake Marina Inc. From May to mid-September, rent paddleboats, motorboats, rowboats, and canoes by the hour or by the day. ✉ *Wallowa Lake, south end* ☏ *541/432–9115* ⊕ *www.wallowalakemarina. com.*

HELLS CANYON

Fodor's Choice ★

30 mi northeast of Joseph on Route 350.

This remote place along the Snake River is the deepest river-carved gorge in North America (7,900 feet), with many rare and endangered animal species. There are three different routes from which to view and experience the canyon, though only one is accessible year-round.

Most travelers take a scenic peek from the overlook on the 45-mi **Wallowa Mountain Loop,** which follows Route 39 (part of the Hells Canyon National Scenic Byway) from just east of Halfway on Route 86 to just east of Joseph on Route 350. At the junction of Route 39 and Forest Road 3965, take the 6-mi round-trip spur to the 5,400-foot-high rim at Hells Canyon Overlook. This is the easiest way to get a glimpse of the canyon, but be aware that Route 39 is open only during summer and early fall. During the late fall, winter, and spring the best way to experience Hells Canyon is to follow a slightly more out-of-the-way route along the **Snake River Segment** of the Wallowa Mountain Loop. Following Snake River Road north from Oxbow, the 60-mi round-trip route winds along the edge of Hells Canyon Reservoir on the Idaho side, crossing the Snake River at Hells Canyon Dam on the Oregon-Idaho border. In some places the canyon is 10 mi wide. There's a visitor center near the dam, and hiking trails continue on into the Hells Canyon Wilderness and National Recreation Area. Be sure you have a full tank before starting out, since there are no gas stations anywhere along the route. If you're starting from Joseph, you also have the option of heading to the **Hat Point Overlook.** From Joseph, take Route 350 northeast to Imnaha, a tiny town along the Imnaha River. From there, Forest Road 4240 leads southeast to Route 315, which in turn heads northeast up a steep gravel road to the overlook. This route is also open only during the summer. Carry plenty of water.

GETTING HERE

Many seasonal Forest Service roads access Hells Canyon from Imnaha east of Joseph and the Wallowa Mountain Loop. Four-wheel drive may be necessary; check with rangers at the Wallowa Mountains Visitor Center. Most float trips originate from the Hells Canyon Creek site below the Hells Canyon Dam.

9

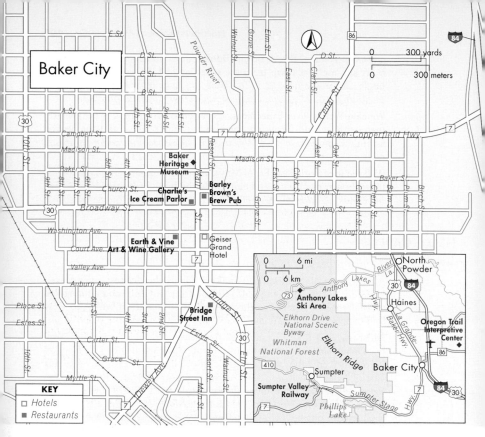

Baker City

KEY
□ *Hotels*
■ *Restaurants*

VISITOR INFORMATION
Wallowa Mountains Visitor Center (✉ *115 Tejaka Ln., off Hwy. 82, Enterprise* ☎ *541/426–4978* ⊕ *www.fs.fed.us/r6/w-w)*

SPORTS AND THE OUTDOORS

RECREATIONAL
AREAS

Hells Canyon National Recreation Area. This is the site of one of the largest elk herds in the United States, plus 422 other species, including bald eagles, bighorn sheep, mule deer, white-tailed deer, black bears, bobcats, cougars, beavers, otters, and rattlesnakes. The peregrine falcon has also been reintroduced here. Part of the area was designated as Hells Canyon Wilderness, in parts of Oregon and Idaho, with the establishment of the Hells Canyon National Recreation Area in 1975. Additional acres were added as part of the Oregon Wilderness Act of 1984, and the recreation area currently extends across more than 650,000 wild and rugged acres. Nine hundred miles of trails wind through the wilderness area, closed to all mechanized travel. If you want to visit the wilderness it must be on foot, mountain bike, or horseback. Three of its rivers, the Snake, Imnaha, and Rapid have all been designated as Wild and Scenic. Environmental groups have proposed the creation of Hells Canyon National Park to better manage the area's critical habitat. A wildlife-viewing guide is available from the Idaho Department of Fish and Game. ⊠ *115 Tejaka Ln., off Hwy. 82, Enterprise* ☎ *541/426–4978 or 541/426–5546* ⊕ *www.fs.fed.us/hellscanyon.*

Wild and Scenic Snake River Corridor. Sixty-seven miles of river are federally designated as part of the National Wild and Scenic Rivers system. Extending ¼ mi back from the high-water mark on each shore, the corridor is available for managed public use. Since the corridor itself is not designated as "wilderness," and wilderness area regulations do not therefore apply, there are developed campsites and man-made structures, and some motorized equipment is allowed. In season, both powerboaters and rafters must make reservations and obtain permits for access to the river corridor. ☎ *509/758–0616 general information; 509/758–1957 noncommercial float reservations; 509/758–0270 powerboat reservations* ⊙ *Daily Memorial Day–early Sept.*

BAKER CITY

44 mi south of La Grande on U.S. 30 off I–84.

During the 1860s gold rush, Baker City was the hub. The Big Apple, or rather, the Big Nugget. Many smaller towns dried up after the gold rush, but Baker City transformed itself into the seat of the regional logging and ranching industries that are still around today. Remnants of its turn-of-the-century opulence, when it was the largest city between Salt Lake and Portland, are still visible in the many restored Victorian houses and downtown storefronts.

Baker City may not have that much gold left in its surrounding hills—but what hills they are. The Wallowas and Eagle Cap, the Elkhorn Ridge of the Blue Mountains, the Umatilla National Forest, the Wallowa-Whitman, Hells Canyon, Monument Rock—the panorama almost completes a full circle. Outdoor enthusiasts flock here for the climbing, fishing, hunting, waterskiing, canoeing, hiking, cycling, and skiing. Baker City's gold rush has been supplanted by the "green rush."

GETTING HERE

Baker City is easily accessed by I–84, 305 mi east of Portland and 127 mi west of Boise, Idaho. The city is the hub for several smaller highways as well, including scenic Hwy. 7 through the Blue Mountains to John Day. The **Baker Bow** (☎ *541/963–2877* ⊕ *www.neotransit.org*) shuttle bus runs Monday to Friday to La Grande and nearby Haines, and the **Baker City Trolley** services the city Monday to Saturday (☎ *541/963–2877* ⊕ *www.neotransit.org*). **Greyhound** also makes stops here. The closest airport is Eastern Oregon Regional, 95 mi northeast in Pendleton.

VISITOR INFORMATION

Baker County Chamber of Commerce and Visitors Bureau (⊠ *490 Campbell St.* ☎ *541/523–5855* ⊕ *www.visitbaker.com*).

EXPLORING

Baker Heritage Museum. Located in a stately brick building that once housed the community's swimming pool, Baker's history center has one of the most impressive rock collections in the West. Assembled over a lifetime by a local amateur geologist, the Cavin-Warfel Collection includes thunder eggs, glowing phosphorescent rocks, and a 950-pound

9

hunk of quartz. Other exhibits highlight pioneering, ranching, mining, and antique furniture. The museum also operates the nearby **Adler House Museum** (⊠ *2305 Main St.* ⊠ *$6* ⊗ *Memorial Day–Labor Day*), an 1889 Italianate house that was once home to an eccentric publishing magnate and philanthropist. ⊠ *2480 Grove St., at Campbell St.* ☎ *541/523–9308* ⊠ *$6* ⊗ *Mid-Mar.–Oct., daily 9–4.*

EN
ROUTE

Elkhorn Drive. This scenic 106-mi loop winds from Baker City through the Elkhorn Range of the Blue Mountains. Only white-bark pine can survive on the range's sharp ridges and peaks, which top 8,000 feet; spruce, larch, Douglas fir, and ponderosa pine thrive on the lower slopes. The route is well marked; start on Highway 7 west of Baker City, turn onto County Road 24 toward Sumpter, pass Granite on Forest Service Road 73, and then return to Baker City along U.S. 30.

National Historic Oregon Trail Interpretive Center. Head 5 mi east of Baker City to this sprawling facility perched on a high hillside for a superb exploration of pioneer life in the mid-1800s. From 1841 to 1861 about 300,000 people made the 2,000-mi journey from western Missouri to the Columbia River and the Oregon coast, looking for agricultural land in the West. A simulated section of the Oregon Trail will give you a feel for camp life and the settlers' impact on Native Americans; an indoor theater presents movies and plays. A 4-mi round-trip trail winds from the center to the actual ruts left by the wagons. ⊠ *22267 Oregon Hwy. 86* ☎ *541/523–1843* ⊕ *www.blm.gov/or/oregontrail* ⊠ *$8* ⊗ *Apr.–Oct., daily 9–6; Nov.–Mar., daily 9–4.*

Sumpter Valley Railway. Though the original track was scrapped in 1947, an all-volunteer work force has rebuilt more than 7 mi of track on the railroad's original right-of-way. Today the train operates along a 5 mi route in Sumpter. Trains leave from the McEwen and Sumpter stations; call for departure information. ⊠ *On Hwy. 7, 22 mi west of Baker City* ☎ *541/894–2268 or 866/894–2268* ⊕ *www.svry.com* ⊠ *$15* ⊗ *Memorial Day–Sept., weekends and holidays; Mid-Oct., 1-day fall foliage excursion.*

NEED A
BREAK?

No historic Main Street would be complete without its soda fountain, and **Charley's Ice Cream Parlor** fits the bill, serving all manner of treats, frozen and otherwise. ⊠ *2101 Main St.* ☎ *541/524–9307* ▭ *AE, D, DC, MC, V* ⊗ *Closed Sun.*

WHERE TO EAT AND STAY

$

AMERICAN

✕ **Barley Brown's.** It's the "Cheers" of Baker City–and everyone knows owner Tyler's name. A perennial winner at American beer festivals, their "Shredder's Wheat" American Wheat Ale recently beat out international contenders for a gold at the World Beer Cup. You can watch the process behind glass windows as they brew some eight different beers (for example, Hot Blonde jalapeño ale, Tank Slapper India pale ale). Barley Brown's also makes tasty grub, from burgers and quesadillas to spicy pastas and the occasional alligator. Tyler is committed to using local produce (the hand-cut fries are Baker County potatoes) and hormone-free beef. ⊠ *2190 Main St.* ☎ *541/523–4266* ▭ *AE, MC, V* ⊗ *Closed Sun. No lunch.*

Historic Baker City mural in downtown Baker City

$ ✕ **Earth & Vine Art & Wine Gallery.** A chic little café on the ground-floor
NEW AMERICAN   corner of one of Baker's numerous historic buildings, Earth & Vine
sticks to sandwiches, flatbread pizza, fondue, and other simple treats.
Regional varieties occupy much of the short wine list, but owner Mary
Ellen Stevenson keeps many more bottles in the cellar than she prints
on the menu, so ask for a recommendation. Local art, live music, and
periodic sushi nights pack in the Baker City creative class. ✉ *2001
Washington Ave.* ☎ *541/523–1687* ▭ *AE, D, V, MC.*

¢   🛏 **Bridge Street Inn.** Right off Main Street, the Bridge Street Inn is one
of the least-expensive motels in town. With rooms that are clean and
reliable, it is an excellent option if you're short on funds. All rooms
have microwaves and refrigerators, new sinks, and double-pane windows. A substantial Continental breakfast is included, and owner Thoy
occasionally serves up free dinners in the lobby as well. **Pros:** inexpensive; well-insulated; comp breakfast. **Cons:** with 41 ground-floor
units, neighbors may be noisy. ✉ *134 Bridge St.* ☎ *541/523–6571 or
800/932–9220* ⊕ *www.bridgestreetinn.net* ⤳ *41 rooms* ⌂ *In-room:
Wi-Fi, kitchen (some). In-hotel: parking (free), laundry facilities, some
pets allowed* ▭ *MC, V* ❚⚬❙ *CP.*

$ 🛏 **Geiser Grand Hotel.** She sits like the dowager duchess of Main Street,
Fodor's Choice   her cupola clock tower still cutting a sharp figure against a wide Baker
★   City sky. It's the Geiser Grand, built in 1889, the Italianate Renaissance
Revival that was once known as the finest hotel between Portland and
Salt Lake City—and arguably still is. Reopened in 1998 after an $8
million restoration, the rooms still have those 14-foot ceilings, old-
fashioned transoms above the door, and 10-foot-tall windows. But of
all the fascinating features, it's the custom-built stained-glass ceiling

9

in hues of green, blue, purple, and red that takes center stage. The fact that it was created from photographs and an old timer's memory makes it even more astounding. No gym on-site, but guests have complimentary access to one across the street, plus nearby tennis courts. **Pros:** great downtown location; fascinating history; if possible, take the Saturday afternoon hotel tour. **Cons:** rooms, while well-appointed, have a distinct femininity; Wi-Fi spotty in some rooms. ⊠ *1996 Main St.* ☎ *541/523–1889 or 888/434–7374* ⊕ *www.geisergrand.com* ⌤ *30 rooms* ♿ *In-room: Wi-Fi, DVD. In-hotel: restaurant, bar, parking (free), some pets allowed* ☰ *AE, D, MC, V.*

SPORTS AND THE OUTDOORS

SKIING   **Anthony Lakes Ski Area.** Find some of the state's best powder at this hill in the Wallowa-Whitman National Forest, along with a vertical drop of 900 feet and a top elevation of 8,000 feet. There are 21 trails, one triple chairlift, and a 30-km cross-country network. Snowboards are permitted. ⊠ *47500 Anthony Lake Hwy., North Powder* ☎ *541/856–3277* ⊕ *www.anthonylakes.com* ⌤ *Lift tickets $39* ☉ *Nov.–Apr., Thurs.– Sun. 9–4.*

JOHN DAY

80 mi west of Baker City on U.S. 26.

More than $26 million in gold was mined in the John Day area. The town was founded shortly after gold was discovered there in 1862. Yet John Day is better known to contemporaries for the plentiful outdoor recreation it offers and for the nearby John Day Fossil Beds. The town is also a central location for trips to the Malheur National Wildlife Refuge and the towns of Burns, Frenchglen, and Diamond to the south.

As you drive west through the dry, shimmering heat of the John Day Valley on U.S. 26, it may be hard to imagine this area as a humid subtropical forest filled with lumbering 50-ton brontosauruses and 50-foot-long crocodiles. But so it was, and the eroded hills and sharp, barren-looking ridges contain the richest concentration of prehistoric plant and animal fossils in the world.

GETTING HERE

You can get to John Day on the thrice-weekly **People Mover** (☎ *541/575– 2370*) bus from Bend, but you really need a car to explore the nearby forests and fossil beds. The town is a scenic, 80-mi drive from Baker City on Highways 7 and 26. To the west, it's 152 mi to Bend and the closest commercial airport, primarily on U.S. 26.

VISITOR INFORMATION

Grant County Chamber of Commerce (⊠ *301 W. Main St., John Day* ☎ *551/575–0547 or 800/769–5664* ⊕ *gcoregonlive.com*).

EXPLORING

Grant County Historical Museum. Two miles south of John Day, Canyon City is a small town that feels as if it hasn't changed much since the Old West days. Memorabilia from the gold rush is on display at the town's small museum, along with Native American artifacts and antique musical instruments. Drop in at the neighboring pioneer jail, which the locals pilfered years ago from a nearby crumbling ghost town. ✉ *101 S. Canyon City Blvd., 2 mi south of John Day, Canyon City* ☏ *541/575– 0362; 541/575–0509 off-season* ⊕ *wwwgchistoricalmuseum.com* ☑ *$4* ⊙ *May–Sept., Mon.–Sat. 9–4:30.*

Kam Wah Chung & Co. Museum. This ramshackle building was a trading post on The Dalles Military Road in 1866 and 1867, then later served as a general store, a Chinese labor exchange for the area's mines, a doctor's shop, and an opium den. Having been listed on the National Register of Historic Places in 1973, the museum is an extraordinary testament to the early Chinese community in Oregon. Tours are on the hour with groups limited to 10 people; if you miss it, you can always catch the 19-minute video lecture given by the curator. ✉ *125 N.W. Canton* ☏ *541/575–2800* ☑ *Free; donations accepted* ⊙ *May–Oct., daily 9–5.*

WHERE TO EAT

$ ✕ **The Grubsteak Mining Co.** With old mining equipment hanging from

AMERICAN   the walls and a large painted mural of miners from the 1860s, this eatery is representative of its name. The neighborhood joint does its job, cooking up good, simple food for breakfast, lunch, and dinner. The house dinner favorites include the Fergus Burger (2/3 pound of sirloin) and a Jack Daniels flatiron steak. Locals can be found playing pool in the bar at the back of the house long after the sun goes down—until 2 AM, to be exact. ✉ *149 E. Main St.* ☏ *541/575–1970* ▭ *AE, D, MC, V.*

JOHN DAY FOSSIL BEDS NATIONAL MONUMENT

40 mi from John Day, west 38 mi on U.S. 26 and north 2 mi on Hwy. 19.

ℭ   The geological formations that compose this peculiar monument cover

Fodor'sChoice   hundreds of square miles and preserve a diverse record of plant and

★   animal life spanning more than 40 million years of the Age of Mammals. The national monument itself is divided into three units: Sheep Rock, Painted Hills, and Clarno—each of which looks vastly different and tells a different part of the story of Oregon's history. Each unit has picnic areas, restrooms, visitor information, and hiking trails. The main visitor center is in the Sheep Rock Unit, 40 mi northwest of John Day; Painted Hills and Clarno are about 70 and 115 mi northwest of John Day, respectively. If you only have time for one unit of the park, make it Painted Hills, where the namesake psychedelic mounds most vividly expose the region's unique geology.

GETTING HERE

Reach the Sheep Rock Unit of the John Day Fossil Beds Monument driving 38 mi west of John Day on U.S. 26, then 2 mi north on Highway 19. The Painted Hills unit is an additional 35 mi west on U.S. 26. To reach the Clarno unit, follow Highway 19 north from the Sheep Rock Unit, 60 mi northwest to Fossil. From Fossil, drive west on Highway 218 for 20 mi to the entrance. Be prepared to stop for frequent roadside interpretive exhibits between the three units. The fossil beds are between Eastern Oregon Regional Airport, 144 mi northeast in Pendleton, and Roberts Field-Redmond Municipal Airport, 104 mi west in Redmond.

9

VISITOR INFORMATION

Thomas Condon Paleontology Center (✉ *Hwy. 19, 2 mi north of U.S. 26, Kimberly* ☎ *541/987–2333* ⊕ *www.nps.gov/joda*).

EXPLORING

Clarno. The 48-million-year-old fossil beds in this small section have yielded the oldest remains in the John Day Fossil Beds National Monument. The drive to the beds traverses forests of ponderosa pines and sparsely populated valleys along the John Day River before traveling through a landscape filled with spires and outcroppings that attest to the region's volcanic past. A short trail that runs between the two parking lots contains fossilized evidence of an ancient subtropical forest. Another trail climbs ½ mi from the second parking lot to the base of the Palisades, a series of abrupt, irregular cliffs created by ancient volcanic mud flows. ✉ *Off Hwy. 218, 20 mi west of Fossil* ☎ *541/763–2203* ⊕ *www.nps.gov/joda* ☉ *Daily, during daylight hrs.*

Painted Hills. The fossils at Painted Hills, a unit of the John Day Fossil Beds National Monument, date back about 33 million years, and reveal a climate that has become noticeably drier than that of Sheep Rock's era. The eroded buff-color hills reveal striking red and green striations created by minerals in the clay. Come at dusk or just after it rains, when the colors are most vivid. If traveling in spring, the desert wildflowers are most intense between late April and early May. Take the steep, ¾-mi **Carroll Rim Trail** for a commanding view of the hills or sneak a peek from the parking lot at the trailhead, about 2 mi beyond the picnic area. A few Forest Service roads lead north toward the Spring Basin Wilderness and the town of Antelope, but these are appropriate only for high-clearance vehicles and only when dry. ✉ *Off U.S. 26, 9 mi west of Mitchell* ☎ *541/462–3961* ⊕ *www.nps.gov/joda* ☉ *Daily, during daylight hrs.*

Sheep Rock. The **Thomas Condon Paleontology Center** at Sheep Rock serves as the primary visitor center, with a museum dedicated to the fossil beds, fossils on display, in-depth informational panels, handouts, and an orientation movie. Two miles north of the visitor center on Highway 19 is the impressive **Blue Basin**, a badlands canyon with sinuous blue-green spires. Winding through this basin is the ½-mi **Island in Time Trail,** where trailside exhibits explain the area's 28-million-year-old fossils. The 3-mi Blue Basin Overlook Trail loops around the rim of the canyon, yielding some splendid views. Blue Basin is a hike with a high effort-to-reward ratio, and in summer rangers lead interpretive jaunts Friday to Sunday at 10 AM. ✉ *32651 Hwy. 19, Kimberly* ☎ *541/987–2333* ⊕ *www.nps.gov/joda* ☉ *Daily, during daylight hrs.*

WHERE TO STAY

¢ ⛺ **Fish House Inn and RV Park.** One of the only places to stay near the Sheep Rock fossil beds is 9 mi east, in the small town of Dayville. The piscatory touches at this lovely inn include fishing gear, nets, and framed prints of fish. The main house, built in 1908, has three bedrooms upstairs that share an outdoor deck and a separate entrance, and behind it is a cottage with a large bedroom and suite. The downstairs is available as a full suite with three bedrooms, one bath, kitchen, dining room,

John Day Fossil Beds

and living room. With a general store, a bar, and a gas station, Dayville can fill most of your traveling needs and has the only services in the area. **Pros:** great prices; fun atmosphere; ground floor of main house is great for a group traveling together. **Cons:** no food service other than the small mercantile. ⊠ *110 Franklin St., Dayville* ☎ *541/987–2124 or 888/286–3474* ⊕ *www.fishhouseinn.com* ⤢ *5 rooms, 2 with shared bath, 1 suite* ⚷ *In-room: no phone, refrigerator. In-hotel: some pets allowed* ⊟ *AE, D, MC, V.*

SOUTHEAST OREGON

Oregon's outback is indeed a high and lonesome setting of sagebrush desert, one-horse towns, and acre after acre of grazing cattle. And while the region may be light-years away from cosmopolitan, southeast Oregon has historically been one of the West's more demographically diverse regions. The area's indigenous Paiute and Shoshone residents came to share the land with white pioneer families, Basque herders, Mexican bracero cowboys, Chinese mine workers, and a number of other groups who've helped to shape Oregon's high desert culturally. The impressively spare scenery, meanwhile, has been a constant. While the sagebrush horizon can be beautiful in its constancy, visitors need only to brave some of the region's gravel backroads to discover a collection of diverse and singular landscapes. Places like the blistering white Alvord Desert, the dramatic Owyhee Canyon, and the sculptural rock formations of Leslie Gulch can go toe-to-toe with any national park for straight-up natural beauty, but they host a comparative sliver of visitors each year.

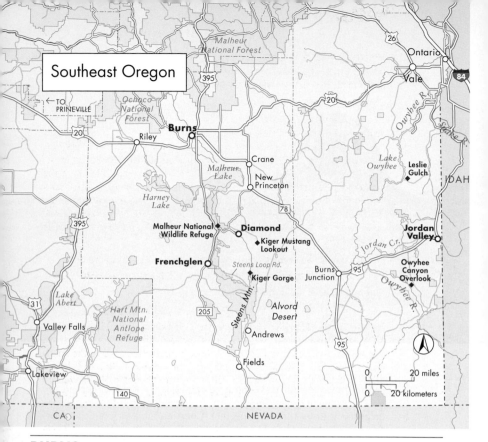

BURNS

76 mi south of the town of John Day on U.S. 395.

Named after poet Robert Burns, this town was the unofficial capital of the 19th-century cattle empires that staked claims to these southeastern Oregon high-plateau grasslands. Today Burns is a working-class town of 3,000 residents, surrounded by the 10,185 square mi of sagebrush, rimrock, and grassy plains that compose Harney County, the ninth-largest county in the United States. As the only place in the county with basic tourist amenities, Burns serves as a convenient stopover for many travelers. However, its usefulness as a source of modern convenience goes hand in hand with the sense that, unlike many of the region's smaller outposts, its Old West flavor has largely been lost. Rather than a final destination, think of Burns as a jumping-off point for exploring the poetry of the Malheur National Wildlife Refuge, Steens Mountain, and the Alvord Desert. Outdoor recreation at this gateway to Steens Mountain includes fishing, backpacking, camping, boating, and hiking.

GETTING HERE

Bend and the nearest commercial airport are 130 mi west of Burns on U.S. 20. From John Day to the north, it's a 70-mi drive through the sage-brush scrub along U.S. 395. **Porter Stage Lines** (☎ *541/269–7183*) runs a daily bus east to Ontario and west to the coast via Bend and Eugene.

VISITOR INFORMATION

Harney County Chamber of Commerce (✉ *484 N. Broadway, Burns* ☎ *541/573-2636* ⊕ *www.harneycounty.com*).

EXPLORING

Harney County Historical Museum. More like a cluttered antique super-store than a traditional museum, the county's treasure trove keeps a photo collection documenting the area's history, along with taxider-mied animals, interesting rocks, old dental equipment, and all sorts of other bric-a-brac. There's a scale replica of the Liberty Bell (with the crack) made entirely of pinecones, a display of handmade quilts, and a whole lot of handmade placards exhibiting folksy Westernisms. ✉ *18 W. D St.* ☎ *541/573-5618 or 541/573-7225* ⊕ *www.burnsmuseum. com* ⬛ *$4* ⊙ *Apr.–Sept., Tues.–Fri. 10–4, Sat. 10–3. Tours available in closed months.*

NEED A BREAK? Sip an espresso and browse through cards, gifts, and books at the **Book Parlor** (✉ *433 N. Broadway* ☎ *541/573-2665* ⊙ *Tues.–Sat. 10–5:30. Closed Sun. and Mon.*) in the center of town.

WHERE TO EAT

¢ ✕ **Bella Java & Bistro.** This simple, but elegant café is in a historic store-

CAFÉ front downtown, with high ceilings and an eclectic decor. Pastries, simple sandwiches, and delicious, house-made soups anchor the small menu. Locals are in and out all day for their espresso fix, and there's local beer and wine behind the counter, too. ✉ *314A N. Broadway* ☎ *541/573-3077* ▭ *MC, V* ⊙ *Mon.–Fri. 7:30–3, Sat. 9–3. No dinner.*

SPORTS AND THE OUTDOORS

RECREATIONAL **Malheur National Forest.** You can cut through this 1.4-million-acre forest

AREAS in the Blue Mountains as you drive from John Day to Burns on U.S. 395. It has alpine lakes, meadows, creeks, and grasslands. Black bears, bighorn sheep, elk, and wolverines inhabit dense stands of pine, fir, and cedar. Near Burns the trees dwindle in number and the landscape changes from mountainous forest to open areas covered with sagebrush and dotted with junipers. ✉ *Between U.S. 26 and U.S. 20, accessible via U.S. 395 Emigrant Creek Ranger District Office:265 Hwy. 20 S., Hines* ☎ *541/573–4300* ⊕ *www.fs.fed.us/r6/malheur* ⬛ *Free* ⊙ *Daily.*

Malheur National Wildlife Refuge. This unusual desert environment covers 187,000 acres. The squat, snow-covered summit of Steens Mountain is the only landmark in this area of alkali playas, buttes, scrubby mead-ows, and, most surprising of all, marshy lakes. It's arid and scorching hot in summer, but in the spring and early summer more than 320 species of migrating birds descend on the refuge's wetlands for their annual nesting and mating rituals. Following an ancient migratory fly-way, they've been coming here for nearly a million years. The 30-mi Central Patrol Road, which runs through the heart of the refuge, is your best bet for viewing birds. But first stop at the **Malheur National Wild-life Refuge Headquarters,** where you can pick up leaflets and a free map. The staff will tell you where you're most likely to see the refuge's winged inhabitants. The refuge is a short way from local petroglyphs (ask at the headquarters); a remarkable pioneer structure called the **Round**

9

Barn (head east from the headquarters on Narrows–Princeton Road for 9 mi; road turns to gravel and then runs into Diamond Highway, a paved road that leads south 12 mi to the barn); and **Diamond Craters,** a series of volcanic domes, craters, and lava tubes (continue south from the barn 6 mi on Diamond Highway). Just outside the refuge is a rare sagebrush lek, the spring mating grounds where clusters of gray-brown sage grouse conduct morning strutting routines with fanned-out feathers. Visit at sunrise between mid-March and mid-June to see this peculiar display (8 mi west on Foster Flat Road; ask at the headquarters for more info). You'll need a car to get around Malheur National Wildlife Refuge, although the adventurous might enjoy exploring by bike or on foot. ⊠ *3691 Sodhouse La., Princeton* ☎ *541/493–2612* ⊕ *www.fws. gov/malheur* ☞ *Free* ☉ *Park daily dawn–dusk; headquarters daily 8–4.*

DIAMOND

54 mi from Burns, south on Hwy. 205 and east on Diamond–Grand Camp Rd.

Though it's tucked into a verdant little valley just east of Malheur National Wildlife Refuge, Diamond has an average year-round population of something like seven people. You could probably do your own census as you take in the undisturbed cluster of a few houses and the hotel in the midst of this wildlife-rich, wide-open country. During its heyday at the turn of the 20th century, Diamond had a population of about 50, including the McCoy family ranchers, who continue to run the town's hotel today.

GETTING HERE

Diamond Lane turns off Hwy. 205 about 42 mi south of Burns, heading east through the Malheur National Wildlife Refuge for 12 mi. The last few miles are unpaved, but manageable for any passenger car. You can also catch up with Diamond Lane heading south from the refuge's Diamond Craters area. Eastern Oregon Regional Airport in Pendleton is the closest airport.

EXPLORING

Kiger Mustang Lookout. Not far from town is this wild-horse viewing area run by the Bureau of Land Management. With their dun-color coats, zebra stripes on knees and hocks, and hooked ear tips, the Kiger mustangs are perhaps one of the purest herds of wild Spanish mustangs in the world today. Once thought to be the descendants of Barb horses brought by the Spanish to North America in the 16th century, the Kiger horses remain the most sought-after for adoption throughout the country. The viewing area is accessible to high-clearance vehicles only, and is passable only in dry weather. ⊠ *11 mi from Happy Valley Rd.* ☎ *541/573–4400* ☞ *Free* ☉ *May–Oct., dawn–dusk.*

WHERE TO EAT AND STAY

¢   ✕ **Frazier's.** Owned by the Hotel Diamond, Frazier's is a small pub-style
AMERICAN   restaurant in a renovated stone icehouse, the oldest building in Diamond and maybe the coolest little bar in southeastern Oregon. Burgers, steaks, salads, and sandwiches are served for lunch. Aside from

the dinners served in the hotel, this is the only place in town to buy a meal. And as the Bureau of Land Management firefighters can tell you, it's also the only place for many miles to play a game of pool. The unmarked restaurant is found around the back of the Hotel Diamond, and often looks like it might not be open, but head on in for friendly service in what feels like a subterranean speakeasy. ⊠ *Hotel Diamond, 49130 Main St.* ☎ *541/493–1898* ▭ *MC, V* ✪ *No dinner.*

¢ 🏨 **Hotel Diamond.** In the early 1900s the Hotel Diamond served the local population of ranchers, Basque sheepherders, and cowhands. Now it caters to the birders, naturalists, and high-desert lovers who flock to the Malheur refuge. The air-conditioned rooms are clean, comfortable, and pleasantly furnished with an eclectic mix of furniture, including wicker chairs, old wooden desks, and four-poster beds. From the comfortable screen porch guests can look out on the hotel's towering, narrow Lombardy poplars, often planted as de facto fences in ranch country. Family-style meals are served both to hotel guests and to the general public at 6:30 PM, by reservation only. A complimentary breakfast is served in the lounge. The hotel, owned and operated by a fifth-generation ranch family, is also the only place in town to buy gas or groceries. **Pros:** affordable; idyllic location; friendly owners. **Cons:** isolated; no Internet. ⊠ *49130 Main St., 10 mi east of Hwy. 205* ☎ *541/493–1898* ⊕ *www.central-oregon.com/hoteldiamond* ⇗ *8 rooms: 5 upstairs with 2 shared baths; 3 suites downstairs, each with private bath* ⚬ *In-room: no phone, no TV, a/c. In-hotel: restaurant, bar* ▭ *MC, V* ❢❢ *CP* ✪ *Closed Nov.–March.*

Fodor's Choice
★

FRENCHGLEN

61 mi south of Burns on Hwy. 205.

Frenchglen, the tiny town near the base of Steens Mountain, has no more than a handful of residents, and in the off-season offers no basic services to travelers. In other words: eat first. The only lodging in town, the historic Frenchglen Hotel, is a true classic of Oregon hostelry. In the spring and summer Frenchglen's main street is crowded with birders on break from exploring the adjacent Malheur refuge. The popular Steens Mountain Loop begins and ends here, and the town makes a nice setting-off point for adventures in the remote Alvord Desert.

9

GETTING HERE

Frenchglen is 60 mi south of Burns on Hwy. 205. It's an isolated, one-street town with minimal services, and the only gas station keeps sporadic hours. Fill up in Burns before heading down. Eastern Oregon Regional Airport in Pendleton is the closest airport.

VISITOR INFORMATION

Harney County Chamber of Commerce (⊠ *484 N. Broadway, Burns* ☎ *541/573-2636* ⊕ *www.harneycounty.com*).

WHERE TO STAY

¢ 🏨 **Frenchglen Hotel.** A historic example of the 1895–1930 architecture called "American Foursquare," the 1920 Frenchglen Hotel is a simple white wooden house with a porch—Americana at its renovated best.

State-owned, managed by John Ross, the hotel serves up a family-style dinner (reservations essential) to guests and the public at the long wooden tables in the combination lobby-dining room. Breakfast and lunch are also served, and meals sometimes incorporate produce grown in the cute garden out back. The small bedrooms, upstairs off a single hallway, share two bathrooms; five modern units with queen beds and private baths are in the back. Though still a part of the Frenchglen Hotel, the newer addition is called Drover's Inn. **Pros:** historic round barn is on-site; close to Steens Mountain and Malheur Refuge; stay overnight in an authentic 1920s, rural American home. **Cons:** shared bathrooms; no phones or TV. ⊠ *39184 Hwy. 205* ☏ *541/493–2825* ⌂*8 rooms* ♿ *In-room: no phone, no TV. In-hotel: restaurant, some pets allowed* ▭ *D, MC, V* ☻ *Closed Nov.–mid-Mar.*

SHOPPING

Frenchglen Mercantile. Frenchglen's only store has a small display of historic ranch items like old branding tools and turn-of-the-20th-century toiletries. Cold drinks, film, sunscreen, good coffee, snacks, and canned goods are also for sale. The store is only open in the summer, and the dates may change each year. It's also the only place in town for gas, and the owner has a sign on the door with a number to call if the store's closed—it's a $40 minimum charge, though, so fill up in Burns if you can. ⊠ *Hwy. 205* ☏ *541/493–2738.*

SPORTS AND THE OUTDOORS

HIKING   **Steens Mountain.** Amid the flat landscape of southeastern Oregon, the mountain is hard to miss, although the sight of its 9,700-foot summit is more remarkable from the east. There, its sheer face rises from the flat basin of the desolate Alvord Desert, which stretches into Idaho and Nevada. On the western side, Steens Mountain slopes gently upward over a distance of about 20 mi and is less astonishing. Steens is not your average mountain—it's a huge fault block created when the ancient lava that covered this area fractured. Except for groves of aspen, juniper, and a few mountain mahogany, Steens is almost entirely devoid of trees and resembles alpine tundra. But starting in June the wildflower displays are nothing short of breathtaking, as are the views: on Steens you'll encounter some of the grandest scenery in the West.

The mountain is a great spot for hiking over untrammeled and unpopulated ground, but you can also see it by car (preferably one with four-wheel drive) on the rough but passable 52-mi **Steens Loop Road,** open mid-July–October. You need to take reasonable precautions; storms can whip up out of the blue, creating hazardous conditions. On the drive up you might spot golden eagles, bighorn sheep, and deer. The view out over **Kiger Gorge,** on the southeastern rim of the mountain, includes a dramatic U-shape path carved out by a glacier. A few miles farther along the loop road, the equally stunning **East Rim viewpoint** is more than 5,000 feet above the valley floor. The view on a clear day takes in the Alvord Desert. ⊠ *Northern entrance to Steens Loop Rd. leaves Hwy. 205 at south end of Frenchglen and returns to Hwy. 205 about 9 mi south of Frenchglen.*

**OFF THE
BEATEN
PATH**

Alvord Desert. With the eastern face of Steens Mountain in the background, the Alvord Desert conjures up Western movie scenes of parched cowboys riding through the desert—though today you're more likely to see wind sailors scooting across these hard-packed alkali flats (the "playa") and glider pilots using the basin as a runway. But once they go home, this desert is deserted. Snowmelt from Steens Mountain can turn it into a shallow lake until as late as mid-July. The mostly gravel Fields-Denio Road runs alongside the playa, accessing a number of rutted tracks maintained by the Bureau of Land Management. At the south end of the road, **Fields Station** (⊠ *22276 Fields Dr.* ☎ *541/495–2275* ⊕ *www.fieldsoregon.com*) pretty much *is* the town of Fields, an all-in-one post office, general store, motel, and café. The old-fashioned milkshakes at this desert outpost are themselves worth the drive, made with old-school fountain syrups and served in enormous, 24-oz plastic cups. If the milkshakes aren't enough to justify a desert trip, then come for the **Alvord Hot Springs** (⊠ *Off Fields–Denio Rd., 23 mi north of Fields* ☙ *Free*). Though the land is privately owned, the public is welcome to use the two concrete pools taking on superheated water from the nearby springs. From this roadside, ramshackle soaking station, the view of Steens Mountain is superb. Be warned, though, Alvord is a nudity-friendly spring. ⊠ *From Frenchglen take Hwy. 205 south for about 33 mi until road ends at T-junction near town of Fields; go left (north) to Alvord Desert and Alvord Hot Springs.*

JORDAN VALLEY

137 mi southeast of Burns on Hwy. 78 and U.S. 95.

The canyon country of the 280-mi Owyhee River extends through parts of Nevada, Idaho, and southeast Oregon, a sparsely populated area of deep gorges that cut through the high Owyhee Plateau. Jordan Valley is named for Jordan Creek, the Owyhee tributary that flows through town. The outpost was settled by cattlemen and miners in the late nineteenth century, and in the early twentieth century became a hub for Basque immigrants, who traveled from the Spanish Pyrenees to herd cattle and sheep in the American West. Several buildings in town once served as boarding houses for Basque herdsmen and their families, and at the center of town stands one of the country's few remaining original pelota courts, built in 1915 to host matches of the traditional Basque game of handball. Today the presence of both cattle ranchers and Basque families remains significant, and Jordan Valley is increasingly becoming the service hub for travelers in the rugged Owyhee canyonlands.

GETTING HERE

Jordan Valley is on the Oregon–Idaho border, and Boise and its airport are 80 mi northeast. High-clearance vehicles will have an easier time exploring the backroads of the nearby Owyhee canyonlands.

VISITOR INFORMATION

Ontario Chamber of Commerce (⊠ *876 SW 4th Ave., Ontario* ☎ *541/889–8012 or 866/989–8012* ⊕ *www.ontariochamber.com*).

9

EXPLORING

I.O.N. Heritage Museum. The name refers to the tri-state area of Idaho, Oregon, and Nevada, but this humble museum actually focuses almost exclusively on Jordan Valley and the surrounding Oregon Owyhee country. The boxy house-turned-museum was originally built by Ambrose Elorriago, a Basque immigrant whose wife, Maria, refused to emigrate until her husband built a house identical to her family home in Spain. Many of the early-20th-century items around the home are from the Elorriaga family collection. Joanne, the friendly and knowledgeable sole curator, can elaborate on the region's ranching history and Basque heritage. ⊠ *502 Swisher Ave.* ☎ *541/586–2100* ⊕ *www. cityofjordanvalley.com* 🖃 *Free* ☉ *Memorial Day–Labor Day, Thurs.– Sat. 1–4 and by appointment.*

SPORTS AND THE OUTDOORS

RECREATIONAL AREAS
Fodor's Choice
★

Leslie Gulch. The gnarly spires of rock at Leslie Gulch are made from volcanic-ash tuff, rhyolitic leftovers from ancient eruptions, sculpted by erosion into towers and pinnacles. Much of Leslie Gulch is designated as Wilderness Study Area, and the canyon cliffs are home to a resident herd of bighorn sheep, along with coyotes, bobcats, mule deer, and the occasional elk. The 15-mi drive along Leslie Gulch Road descends from the Owyhee uplands into the river canyon, showing off dozens of spectacular formations along the way. At the end of the road are a boat launch and a free, 12-site primitive campground. You can only go a couple of miles up the side canyon of Juniper Gulch before it's too narrow to travel, but bring a camera along for a short hike past bizarre, pockmarked citadels. Keep your eyes peeled for rattlesnakes, too. ⊠ *Off U.S. 95, 19 mi north of Jordan Valley* ☎ *541/473–3144* ⊕ *www.blm. gov/or* 🖃 *Free* ☉ *March–mid-Nov.*

Owyhee Canyon Overlook. The peculiar thing about stunning Owyhee Canyon, with its sheer stone walls up to 1,000 feet tall, is that you wouldn't even know it was there without heading into the backcountry. This canyon overlook, north of the Three Forks put-in popular with rafters and kayakers, shows off both the gorge's dizzying depth and its remoteness. High-clearance vehicles will have the best luck on the 18 mi of rutted jeep track that leads to the signed overlook, and passenger cars should avoid the route when wet. Set aside a couple of hours for the trip, and expect a cattle jam or two along the way. ⊠ *Off U.S. 95, 15 mi west of Jordan Valley. Follow signed road 18 mi south to overlook* ☎ *541/473–3144* ⊕ *www.blm.gov/or* 🖃 *Free.*

Travel Smart Oregon

WORD OF MOUTH

"Yes, you will definitely need a jacket. Nothing heavy, but rather layers work better here. Fleece and a rain jacket are staples in our wardrobes. If we have an unusual warm spell, you might get away with shorts for part of the day, but you will most likely still have fleece or a sweatshirt on at the same time. Just bring some layers and you will be fine."

—mms

GETTING HERE AND AROUND

Except for Portland, you'll need a car to enjoy Oregon's cities, towns, coast, mountains, and wine country. Portland has outstanding public transportation options, such as a light rail (that goes to the airport), streetcar, buses, and taxis. This is not the case in most other towns in the state, so even if bus or train service exists between two points, you may need a car to get around once you reach your destination.

TRAVEL TIMES FROM PORTLAND TO	BY AIR	BY CAR
Ashland	N/A	5 hr
Astoria	35 min	1 hr, 50 min
Bend	40 min	3 hr, 25 min
Columbia River Gorge/ Hood River	N/A	1 hr
Coos Bay	55 min	4 hr, 15 min
Crater Lake National Park	N/A	4½–5 hr
Dundee	N/A	45 min
Eugene	40 min	2 hr, 5 min
Medford	55 min	4 hr, 55 min
Newport	40 min	2 hr, 40 min
Mt. Hood	N/A	1½ hr
Pendleton	1 hr	3½ hr
Salem	N/A	1½–2 hr

▌ AIR TRAVEL

Flying times to Oregon vary based on the city you're flying to, but to Portland, typical times are 5 hours from New York, 4 hours from Chicago, 2½ from Los Angeles, and 3¼ hours from Dallas.

AIRPORTS

Portland International Airport (PDX) is one of the best airports in the United States, thanks to a spacious layout, wealth of dining facilities, terminal-wide Wi-Fi, moving sidewalks, and smooth TSA processing. It serves as the primary gateway to the state, with shuttle connections to smaller airports on the Oregon Coast, Willamette Valley, and southern, central, and eastern Oregon.

Airport Info Portland International Airport (PDX) (☎ 503/460–4040 or 877/739–4636 ⊕ www.portofportland.com/PDX_home.aspx).

GROUND TRANSPORTATION

PDX is just 30 minutes by car from downtown Portland, and is served by taxi (about $35), light rail and bus ($2.30), and airport shuttle service ($14).

Contacts Blue Star Airporter (☎ 503/249–1837 ⊕ www.bluestarbus.com). **Broadway Cab** (☎ 503/227–1234 ⊕ www.broadwaycab. com). **Green Cab and Shuttle** (☎ 503/234–1414 or 877/853–3577 ⊕ www.greentrans. com). **New Rose City Cab** (☎ 503/282–7707 ⊕ www.newrosecitycabco.com). **Portland Shuttle Service** (☎ 503/860–5398 ⊕ www. portlandshuttles.com). **Radio Cab** (☎ 503/227–1212 ⊕ www.radiocab.net). **Portland Taxicab** (☎ 503/256–5400 ⊕ www.portlandtaxi.net).

FLIGHTS

Airline Contacts Air Canada (☎ 888/247–2262 ⊕ www.aircanada.com). **Alaska Airlines/Horizon Air** (☎ 800/252–7522 ⊕ www. alaskaair.com). **Allegiant Air** (☎ 702/505–8888 ⊕ www.allegiantair.com). **American Airlines** (☎ 800/433–7300 ⊕ www.aa.com). **Continental Airlines** (☎ 800/523–3273 ⊕ www.continental.com). **Delta Airlines** (☎ 800/221–1212 ⊕ www.delta.com). **Frontier Airlines** (☎ 800/432–1359 ⊕ www. frontierairlines.com). **Hawaiian Airlines** (☎ 800/367–5320 ⊕ www.hawaiianair.com). **jetBlue** (☎ 800/538–2583 ⊕ www.jetblue. com). **SeaPort Airlines** (☎ 888/573–2767

⊕ *www.seaportair.com*). **Southwest Airlines** (☎ *800/435-9792* ⊕ *www.southwest.com*). **United Airlines/United Express** (☎ *800/864-8331* ⊕ *www.united.com*). **USAirways** (☎ *800/428-4322 800/622-1015* ⊕ *www.usairways.com*).

Charter Companies Express Jet (☎ *877/958-2677* ⊕ *expressjet.com*). **Executive Flight, Inc.** (☎ *800/762-8253* ⊕ *www.execflight.com*). **Premier Jets** (☎ *503/640-2927 or 800/635-8583* ⊕ *premierjets.com*).

▪ BOAT TRAVEL

CRUISES

The following cruise lines stop in Astoria, generally as part of a Pacific Northwest or Alaskan cruise. Most stops are for a day, and often include optional side trips to Fort Stevens and into town for shopping, touring, and dining. For more information on the upcoming cruise calendar, contact **Port of Astoria** (☎ *800/860-4093* ⊕ *www.portofastoria.com*).

Cruise Lines Celebrity Cruises (☎ *800/647-2251* ⊕ *www.celebrity.com*). **Holland America Line** (☎ *206/281-3535 or 877/932-4259* ⊕ *www.hollandamerica.com*). **Norwegian Cruise Line** (☎ *305/436-4000 or 800/327-7030* ⊕ *www.ncl.com*). **Oceania Cruises** (☎ *305/514-2300 or 800/531-5658* ⊕ *www.oceaniacruises.com*). **Princess Cruises** (☎ *661/753-0000 or 800/774-6237* ⊕ *www.princess.com*). **Regent Seven Seas Cruises** (☎ *954/776-6123 or 800/477-7500* ⊕ *www.rssc.com*).

▪ BUS TRAVEL

Greyhound buses travel to and within Oregon, providing frequent service on popular runs. Sunset Empire Transportation provides transportation between Portland and Astoria Monday, Wednesday, and Friday, and also serves the north coast cities of Astoria, Warrenton, Hammond, Gearhart, Seaside, and Cannon Beach. Porter Stage Lines connects Florence and Coos Bay with Eugene. People

Mover travels on Highway 26 between Bend and John Day.

Bus Info Greyhound Lines (☎ *800/231-2222* ⊕ *www.greyhound.com*). **People Mover** (☎ *541/575-2370*). **Porter Stage Lines Coos Bay** (☎ *541/269-7183*). **Sunset Empire Transportation Astoria** (☎ *503/861-7433* ⊕ *www.ridethebus.org*).

In Portland, TriMet provides one of the finest mass transit systems in the country. Its downtown bus is free, and connects to MAX light rail stations for faster commutes in and out of town to the suburbs and to the airport. It runs about every 15 minutes most of the day, every day. Service is less frequent in the early morning, at midday, and in the evening.

TICKET/PASS	PRICE
Single Fare	$2.30
Weekly Pass	$22.50
Monthly Unlimited Pass	$86

TriMet Mass Transit (☎ *503/238-7433* ⊕ *trimet.org/max*).

▪ CAR TRAVEL

I–5 is the major north–south conduit for the region, providing a straight shot at high speeds from California to Washington—provided there aren't traffic snarls due to slick conditions or summer road construction. Most of Oregon's largest cities, such as Portland, Salem, Albany, Eugene, Medford, and Ashland, are along I–5. This makes driving between the major hubs an easy option, though it's also possible to travel between them by train or bus.

For those who have the time, traveling U.S. 101 is an attraction in itself, as it hugs the Oregon Coast almost the entire length of the state. Most of the road is incredibly scenic—the loveliest stretches are in northern and central Oregon. Make sure you want to commit to the coastal drive, which may be slow going in some parts, before getting on 101, because jumping back and forth to I–5 can be very time-consuming.

The Cascade Range cuts through the middle of Oregon, which means that east–west journeys often wind through mountain passes, and can be either simply breathtaking (summer) or beautiful, slow, and treacherous (winter).

I–84 is Oregon's major east–west artery, which enters the majestic Columbia River Gorge near Portland and continues east to Hood River, The Dalles, Pendleton, LaGrande, and Baker City. U.S. 26 provides access to Mt. Hood from Portland.

GASOLINE

The first thing visitors notice in Oregon is that it is illegal for customers to pump their own gas. Gas stations are plentiful in major metropolitan areas and along major highways such as I–5. Most major credit and debit cards are accepted, and stations often stay open late; except in rural areas, where you may drive long stretches without a refueling opportunity. ■ TIP→ Keep an eye on the gauge when traveling to national parks and off-the-beaten-path trails, particularly if you'll be heading down Forest Service roads. A good rule of thumb is to fill up before you get off (or too far away from) a major highway like I–5 or I–84.

PARKING

In general, Oregon offers plenty of on-street parking and pay lots. In certain urban areas, specifically Portland and Eugene, there are sections of town where street parking is difficult, particularly during festivals, sports, and other special events. Mass transit in these urban areas is plentiful and efficient, and is the preferred way of travel when big events are going on. Parking enforcement is fairly stringent in Portland, so visitors will want to adhere to posted time limits.

ROAD CONDITIONS

Winter driving can present challenges; in coastal areas the mild, damp climate contributes to frequently wet roadways. Snowfalls generally occur only once or twice a year, but when snow does fall, traffic grinds to a halt and roadways become treacherous and stay that way until the snow melts.

Tire chains, studs, or snow tires are essential equipment for winter travel in mountain areas. If you're planning to drive into high elevations, be sure to check the weather forecast beforehand. Even the main-highway mountain passes can close because of snow conditions. In winter, state and county highway departments operate snow-advisory telephone lines that give pass conditions.

ROADSIDE EMERGENCIES

Emergency Services AAA Oregon (☎ 800/222–4357 ⊕ www.aaa.com).

Oregon State Police (☎ 503/378–3720 or 800/452–7888).

RULES OF THE ROAD

Oregon drivers tend to be fairly polite and slower going, which can be a bit maddening for those in a hurry. Bicyclists are plentiful in Oregon cities and rural highways; drivers need to be especially alert to avert tragedies, including when opening the car door after parking.

Car seats are compulsory for children under four years *and* 40 pounds; older children are required to sit in booster seats until they are eight years old *and* 80 pounds.

Oregon is a hands-free state. It is illegal to talk or text on a cell phone while operating a motor vehicle, and doing so will net you a heavy traffic ticket. Use a wireless headset device if you need to stay connected.

CAR RENTAL

Unless you're only visiting downtown Portland, you will need a car for at least part of your trip. It's possible to get around the big cities by public transportation and taxis, but once outside city limits, your options are limited.

Rates in Portland begin at $64 a day and $276 a week, not including the 12.5% tax. You must be 21 to rent a car. Non-U.S. citizens need a reservation voucher, passport, driver's license, and insurance for each driver.

Major Rental Agencies Alamo (☎ 503/249-4900 or 877/222-9075 ⊕ www.alamo.com). **Avis** (☎ 503/249-4950 or 800/331-1212 ⊕ www.avis.com). **Budget** (☎ 503/249-4556 or 800/527-0700 ⊕ www.budget.com).**Dollar** (☎ 503/249-4793 or 800/800-3665 ⊕ www.dollar.com). **Enterprise** (☎ 503/252-1500 or 800/261-7331 ⊕ www.enterprise.com). **Hertz** (☎ 503/249-8216 or 800/654-3131 ⊕ www.hertz.com). **National Car Rental** (☎ 503/249-4900 or 877/222-9058 ⊕ www.nationalcar.com). **Thrifty** (☎ 503/254-6563 ⊕ www.thrifty.com).

▌TAXI TRAVEL

Taxis in Oregon are easy, convenient, and available in most larger communities. In Portland the flag-drop rate is $2.50 and then $2.30 per mile. Make sure to ask whether the driver takes credit cards, whether there's a minimum fare, and whether there are charges for extra passengers. Other charges may include waiting times and airport minimums.

Portland Taxi Companies Broadway Cab (☎ 503/227-1234 ⊕ www.broadwaycab.com). **Green Cab and Shuttle** (☎ 503/234-1414 or 877/853-3577 ⊕ www.greentrans.com). **New Rose City Cab** (☎ 503/282-7707 ⊕ www.newrosecitycabco.com).

Eugene Taxi Companies Bio Taxi (☎ 541/747-2583 ⊕ www.biotaxi.us). **Eugene Hybrid Taxi** (☎ 541/357-8294 ⊕ eugenehybridtaxis.com).

▌TRAIN TRAVEL

Amtrak, the U.S. passenger rail system, has daily service to the Pacific Northwest from the Midwest and California. The *Coast Starlight* begins in Los Angeles; makes stops throughout California, western Oregon, and Washington; and terminates in Seattle. There are stops in both Portland and Eugene; the 2½-hour trip between Portland and Eugene costs $33.

Amtrak's *Cascades* begins in Vancouver, B.C.; makes stops in Seattle, Tacoma, Portland, and Salem; and terminates in Eugene. The *Empire Builder* begins in Chicago; makes stops in Milwaukee, WI; St. Paul, MN; Spokane, WA; and other cities before arriving in Portland. The journey from Spokane to Portland is 7½ hours ($105), with part of the route running through the Columbia River Gorge.

▌TIP➜ Book Amtrak tickets at least a few days in advance, especially if you're traveling between Seattle and Portland on the weekend.

Train Info Amtrak (☎ 800/872-7245 ⊕ www.amtrak.com).

ESSENTIALS

■ ACCOMMODATIONS

The lodgings we list are the cream of the crop in each price category. We always list the facilities that are available, but we don't specify whether they cost extra; when pricing accommodations, always ask what's included and what costs extra. Properties are assigned price categories based on a standard double room in high season (excluding holidays), and excluding tax and service charges. Portland room tax: 12.5%. Elsewhere in Oregon: ranges from 6 to 10%. ⇨ *For price categories, see individual chapters.*

■ TIP→ Assume that hotels operate on the European Plan (**EP, no meals**), unless we specify that they use the Breakfast Plan (**BP, with full breakfast**), Continental Plan (**CP, continental breakfast**), Full American Plan (**FAP, all meals**), or Modified American Plan (**MAP, breakfast and dinner**), or are **all-inclusive** (**AI, all meals and most activities**).

APARTMENT AND HOUSE RENTALS

An alternative to staying in a hotel is to spread out a bit and relax in a vacation rental. There are plenty of choices, particularly along the Oregon Coast, near Mt. Hood, and in Central Oregon resort areas near Bend. Renting an apartment or a house is an especially attractive idea for long-term visitors or large groups and families.

Contacts ForGetaway (⊕ *www.forgetaway. com*). **Home Away** (⊕ *www.homeaway.com*).

BED-AND-BREAKFASTS

Oregon is renowned for its range of bed-and-breakfast options, which are found everywhere from busy urban areas to casual country farms and windswept coastal retreats. Many bed-and-breakfasts in Oregon provide full gourmet breakfasts, and some have kitchens that guests can use. Other popular amenities to ask about are fireplaces, jetted bathtubs, outdoor hot tubs, and proximity to area activities. The regional bed-and-breakfast organizations listed below can provide information on reputable establishments.

Contacts Bed & Breakfast.com (🖀 512/ 322-2710 or 800/462-2632 ⊕ *www. bedandbreakfast.com*). **Bed & Breakfast Inns Online** (🖀 310/280-4363 or 800/215-7365 ⊕ *www.bbonline.com*). **BnB Finder.com** (🖀 888/469-6663 ⊕ *www.bnbfinder.com*). **Oregon Bed & Breakfast Guild** (🖀 800/944-6196 ⊕ *www.obbg.org*).

CAMPING

Oregon has excellent state-run campgrounds. Half accept advance camping reservations, and the others are first come, first served. Campgrounds range from primitive tent sites to parks with yurts, cabins, and full hookups. Sites are located in and around Oregon's more spectacular natural sites, be it on the coast, the Cascade Range, or near the wine country. Privately operated campgrounds sometimes have extra amenities such as laundry rooms and swimming pools. For more information, contact the state or county tourism department.

Campground Reservations Oregon Camping Guide (⊕ *www.ocnsignal.com/oregon-camping-guide.html*). **Oregon Parks and Recreation Dept.** (🖀 800/452-5687 *reservations* ⊕ *www.oregon.gov/oprd/parks*).

HOSTELS

Contacts Hostels.com (⊕ *www.hostels.com/ oregon-state/usa*). **Hostelling International— USA** (🖀 301/495-1240 ⊕ *www.hiusa.org*). **Oregon Hostels Guide** (⊕ *www.ocnsignal. com/oregon-hostels.html*).

■ COMMUNICATIONS

INTERNET

The Pacific Northwest is well wired, and it's difficult to find a hotel in a major city that doesn't offer either Ethernet connections, Wi-Fi, or both. In most cases the service is a standard room amenity.

Coffeehouses almost always have reliable Wi-Fi, and the service often is free (assuming, of course, that you at least buy a cup of coffee); a few have a communal computer or two if you didn't bring the laptop. Portland International Airport also has free Wi-Fi.

For a list of wired coffee shops in Portland, check out ⊕ *http://portland.wifimug. org*. For more Portland hotspots, check out ⊕ *www.wifipdx.com*; ⊕ *www.wififreespot. com* and ⊕ *www.jwire.com*.

Contacts Cybercafes (⊕ *www.cybercafes. com*).

▌EATING OUT

The farm-to-table concept is in full bloom in Oregon. Its cuisine highlights regional seafood, locally raised meat, and organic produce. Farm stands are plentiful in the rural areas and are definitely worth a stop; almost all cities have at least a weekly farmers' market.

Almost every city in Oregon has a stellar dining spot. Portland takes a back seat to no city in terms of culinary excellence in all price ranges. The city's latest rage are the food carts that are springing up in parking lots and along roadsides.

Oregon's wines are well regarded throughout the world, particularly those produced in the Willamette Valley. Almost every town has its own local brewery. Coffee, of course, is a staple in Portland, and every community has at least one espresso joint. The restaurants listed in the chapters are the cream of the crop in each price category. ➪ *For price categories, see individual chapters. For information on food-related health issues, see Health below.*

MEALS AND MEALTIMES

Unless otherwise noted, the restaurants listed in this guide are open daily for lunch and dinner. Most people eat dinner between 6 and 8 PM.

RESERVATIONS AND DRESS

Regardless of the venue, it's a good idea to inquire whether reservations are needed on a weekend evening. We only mention them specifically when reservations are essential (there's no other way you'll ever get a table) or when they are not accepted. For popular restaurants, book as far ahead as you can (often a week is more than ample), and reconfirm as soon as you arrive. (Large parties should always call ahead to check the reservations policy.) We mention dress only when men are required to wear a jacket or a jacket and tie.

Contacts OpenTable (⊕ *www.opentable.com*).

WINE, BEER, AND SPIRITS

Oregon's wineries mostly lie in the Willamette Valley between the northern Cascades and the coast. The Oregon Wine Board maintains a helpful Web site, with facts, history, and information on local wineries.

Oregon has more than 60 microbreweries, with plenty of festivals and events celebrating its brews. The Oregon Brewers Guild also has links to breweries and information on events.

You must be 21 to buy alcohol in Oregon.

Contacts Oregon Brewers Guild (⊕ *www. oregonbeer.org*).**Oregon Wine Board** (⊕ *www. oregonwine.org*).

FOR INTERNATIONAL TRAVELERS

CURRENCY

The dollar is the basic unit of U.S. currency. It has 100 cents. Coins are the penny (1¢), the nickel (5¢), dime (10¢), quarter (25¢), half dollar (50¢), and the rare golden $1 coin and rarer silver $1. Bills are denominated $1, $5, $10, $20, $50, and $100, all mostly green and identical in size; designs and background tints vary. A $2 bill exists but is extremely rare.

CUSTOMS

Information U.S. Customs and Border Protection (⊕ *www.cbp.gov*).

DRIVING

Driving in the United States is on the right. Speed limits are posted in miles per hour (usually between 55 mph and 70 mph). In small towns and on back roads limits are usually 30 mph to 40 mph. Most states require front-seat passengers to wear seat belts; children should be in the back seat and buckled up. In major cities rush hours are 7 to 10 AM and 4 to 7 PM. Some freeways have high-occupancy vehicle (HOV) lanes, ordinarily marked with a diamond, for cars carrying two people or more.

Highways are well paved. Interstates— limited-access, multilane highways designated with an "I-" before the number—are fastest. Interstates with three-digit numbers circle urban areas, which may also have other expressways, freeways, and parkways. Limited-access highways sometimes have tolls.

Oregon drivers can be fairly polite and slower going, which can be a bit maddening for those in a hurry. Wet roads are frequent, and extra care is required on roadways, particularly side roads.

Bicyclists are plentiful in Oregon cities and rural highways. Drivers need to be especially alert to avert tragedies, including when opening the car door after parking.

Oregon is a hands-free state. It is illegal to talk or text on a cell phone while operating a motor vehicle, and doing so will net you a heavy traffic ticket. Use a wireless headset device if you need to stay connected.

Gas stations are plentiful, except in rural areas. Most stay open late (some 24 hours). Along larger highways, roadside stops with restrooms, fast-food restaurants, and sundries stores are well spaced. State police and tow trucks patrol major highways. If your car breaks down, pull onto the shoulder and wait, or have passengers wait while you walk to a roadside emergency phone (most states). On a cell phone, dial *55.

ELECTRICITY

The U.S. standard is AC, 110 volts/60 cycles. Plugs have two flat pins set parallel to each other.

EMBASSIES

Contacts Australia (☎ *202/797–3000* ⊕ *www.austemb.org*). **Canada** (☎ *202/682–1740* ⊕ *www.canadianembassy.org*). **UK** (☎ *202/588–7800* ⊕ *ukinusa.fco.gov.uk*).

EMERGENCIES

For police, fire, or ambulance, dial 911 (0 in rural areas).

MAIL

You can buy stamps and send letters and parcels in post offices. Stamp-dispensing machines can occasionally be found in airports, bus and train stations, office buildings, drugstores, convenience stores, and in ATMs. U.S. mailboxes are stout, dark-blue steel bins; pickup schedules are posted inside the bin (pull the handle). Mail parcels over a pound at a post office.

A first-class letter weighing 1 ounce or less costs 44¢; each additional ounce costs 17¢. Postcards cost 28¢. Postcards or 1-ounce airmail letters to most countries cost 98¢; postcards or 1-ounce letters to Canada or Mexico cost 75¢.

Contacts **DHL** (☎ *800/225-5345* ⊕ *www. dhl.com*). **FedEx** (☎ *800/463-3339* ⊕ *www. fedex.com*). **Mail Boxes, Etc./The UPS Store** (☎ *800/789-4623* ⊕ *www.mbe.com*). **USPS** (☎ *800/275-8777* ⊕ *www.usps.com*).

PASSPORTS AND VISAS

Visitor visas aren't necessary for citizens of Australia, Canada, the United Kingdom, or most citizens of EU countries coming for tourism and staying for under 90 days. A visa is $100, and waiting time can be substantial. Apply for a visa at the U.S. consulate in your place of residence.

Visa Information Destination USA (⊕ *travel.state.gov/visa/*).

PHONES

Numbers consist of a three-digit area code and a seven-digit local number. In Oregon the area code is 503; surrounding areas use 541 or 971.Within many local calling areas, dial just seven digits. In others, dial "1" first and all 10 digits; this is true for calling toll-free numbers—prefixed by "800," "888," "866," and "877." Dial "1" before "900" numbers, too, but know that they're very expensive.

For international calls, dial "011," the country code, and the number. For help, dial "0" and ask for an overseas operator. Most phone books list country codes and U.S. area codes. The country code for Australia is 61, for New Zealand 64, for the United Kingdom 44. Calling Canada is the same as calling within the United States (country code: 1).

For operator assistance, dial "0." For directory assistance, call 555-1212 or 411 (free at many public phones). To call "collect" (reverse charges), dial "0" instead of "1" before the 10-digit number.

Instructions are generally posted on pay phones. Usually you insert coins in a slot (usually 25¢–50¢ for local calls) and wait for a steady tone before dialing. On long-distance calls the operator tells you how much to insert; prepaid phone cards, widely available, can be used from any phone. Follow the directions to activate the card, then dial your number.

Cell Phones The United States has several GSM (Global System for Mobile Communications) networks, so multiband mobiles from most countries (except Japan) work here. It's almost impossible to buy just a pay-as-you-go mobile SIM card in the United States—needed to avoid roaming charges—but cell phones with pay-as-you-go plans are available for well under $100. AT&T (GoPhone) and Virgin Mobile have the cheapest, with national coverage.

▮ HOURS OF OPERATION

Oregon store hours are fairly standard compared to the rest of the continental United States. Major department stores or shops in the downtown areas including Portland generally follow the 10-to-6 rule, but you should always phone ahead if you have your heart set on visiting a smaller shop. Never assume that a store is open on Sunday, even in the major cities; many smaller shops have truncated Saturday hours as well. Thankfully, coffeehouses tend to keep regular and long hours, so you'll have no problem finding one to kill time in if you have to wait for a store to open.

Note that bars in Oregon close at 2 AM, with last call coming as early as 1:30.

▮ MONEY

Prices throughout this guide are given for adults. Substantially reduced fees are almost always available for children, students, and senior citizens.

In Portland, downtown parking meters take credit cards.

ITEM	AVERAGE COST
Cup of Coffee	$1.50
Glass of Wine	$6–$9
Glass of Beer	$4–$6
Sandwich	$5–$8
One-Mile Taxi Ride in Portland	$2.30
Museum Admission	$10–$15

CREDIT CARDS

Debit cards and major credit cards are accepted almost everywhere—some cafés will even let you charge a single cup of coffee—so don't worry about carrying around wads of cash.

Throughout this guide, the following abbreviations are used: **AE**, American Express; **D**, Discover; **DC**, Diners Club; **MC**, MasterCard; and **V**, Visa.

▮ PACKING

It's all about the layers here, as there's no other way to keep up with the weather, which can morph from cold and overcast to warm and sunny and back again in the course of a few hours, especially in spring and early fall. Summer days are warm and more consistent, but evenings can cool off substantially. August and September are the glorious, warm, clear months that remind Oregonians why they live there. Bring an umbrella or raincoat for unpredictable fall and winter weather. Hikers will want to bring rain gear and a hat with them, even if they're visiting in summer; insect repellent is also a good idea if you'll be hiking along mountain trails or beaches.

▮ SAFETY

The greatest dangers in the Northwest are becoming lost or suffering an accident in the great outdoors. Don't hike alone, and make sure you bring enough water plus basic first-aid items. If you're not an experienced hiker, stick to tourist-friendly spots such as the well-marked trails in the national parks; if you have to drive 30 mi down a Forest Service road to reach a trail, it's possible you might be the only one hiking on it.

▮ TAXES

Oregon has no sales tax, although many cities and counties levy a tax on lodging and services. Room taxes, for example, vary from 6%–9½%. In Portland they are 12.5%.

▮ TIME

Most of Oregon is in the Pacific Time Zone, except for Malheur County in Eastern Oregon, which is in the Mountain Time Zone.

▮ TIPPING

TIPPING GUIDELINES FOR OREGON	
Bartender	$1 to $5 per round of drinks, depending on the number of drinks
Bellhop	$1 to $5 per bag, depending on the level of the hotel
Hotel Concierge	$5 or more, if he or she performs a service for you
Hotel Doorman	$1–$2 if he helps you get a cab
Hotel Maid	1$–$3 a day (either daily or at the end of your stay, in cash)
Hotel Room-Service Waiter	$1 to $2 per delivery, even if a service charge has been added
Porter at Airport or Train Station	$1 per bag
Skycap at Airport	$1 to $3 per bag checked
Taxi Driver	15%–20%, but round up the fare to the next dollar amount
Tour Guide	10% of the cost of the tour
Valet Parking Attendant	$1–$2, but only when you get your car
Waiter	15%–20%, with 20% being the norm at high-end restaurants; nothing additional if a service charge is added to the bill
Coat Check	$1–$2 per item checked unless there is a fee, then nothing

▮ TRIP INSURANCE

Comprehensive trip insurance is valuable if you're booking a very expensive or complicated trip (particularly to an isolated region) or if you're booking far in advance. Comprehensive policies typically cover trip cancellation and interruption, letting you cancel or cut your trip short because of illness, or, in some cases, acts of terrorism in your destination. Such policies might also cover evacuation and medical care. Some also cover you for trip delays because of bad weather or mechanical problems as well as for lost or delayed luggage.

Another type of coverage to consider is financial default—that is, when your trip is disrupted because a tour operator, airline, or cruise line goes out of business. Generally you must buy this when you book your trip or shortly thereafter, and it's available to you only if your operator isn't on a list of excluded companies.

Always read the fine print of your policy to make sure that you're covered for the risks that most concern you. Compare several policies to be sure you're getting the best price and range of coverage available.

Insurance Comparison Info Insure My Trip (☎ 800/487–4722 ⊕ www.insuremytrip.com). **Square Mouth** (☎ 800/240–0369 ⊕ www.squaremouth.com).

Comprehensive Insurers Access America (☎ 800/284–8300 ⊕ www.accessamerica.com). **AIG Travel Guard** (☎ 800/826–4919 ⊕ www.travelguard.com). **CSA Travel Protection** (☎ 800/348–9505 ⊕ www.csatravelprotection.com). **Travelex Insurance** (☎ 888/228–9792 ⊕ www.travelex-insurance.com). **Travel Insured International** (☎ 800/243–3174 ⊕ www.travelinsured.com).

▮ VISITOR INFORMATION

Travel Oregon (☎ 503/284–4620 ⊕ www.traveloregon.com). **Travel Portland** (☎ 503/275–9750 or 800/962–3700 ⊕ www.travelportland.com).

INDEX

PHOTO CREDITS

1, Greg Vaughn. 2, Jeanne Hatch/iStockPhoto. **Chapter 1: Experience Oregon:** 8-9, zack schnepf/ iStockphoto. 10, Capricornis Photographic Inc./Shutterstock. 11 (left), Rachell Coe/Shutterstock. 11 (right), Aimin Tang/iStockphoto. 14, kun0me/flickr. 15 (left), eyeliam/flickr. 15 (right), Jeremy Dunham. 16 (left), Norman Eder/iStockphoto. 16 (top center), Zachary Collie/Flickr. 16 (bottom right), Vivian Fung/Shutterstock. 16 (top right), James Horning/Shutterstock. 17 (top left), Lawrence Freytag/iStockphoto. 17 (bottom left), Ewan-M/Ewan Munro/Flickr. 17 (top center), Brian A. Ridder/Flickr. 17 (bottom center), SEAN POWELL @ TREE FARM FOTOGRAPHY/iStockphoto. 17 (left), EyeMindSoul/ Flickr. 18, eyeliam/flickr. 19 (left), Richard Hallman / Freelanceimaging.com. 19 (right), Xuanlu Wang/ Shutterstock. 20, Eric Cable. 21 (left), Julie DeGuia/Shutterstock. 21 (right), vis-a-v./Flickr. 22, Matt McGee/flickr. 23, Argyle Winery. 24, TFoxFoto/Shutterstock. 25 (left), CrackerClips/Shutterstock. 25 (right), Timberline Lodge. 26, William Blacke/iStockphoto. **Chapter 2: Portland:** 27, Brian A. Ridder/ Flickr. 28, --b--/Flickr. 29 (left), David Owen/Flickr. 29 (right), Michael Hashizume/Flickr. 30, Daivd L Reamer. 31 (bottom), Michael S. Barr Photography. 31 (top), eyeliam/flickr. 32, Jason Brisch/Flickr. 33 (bottom), Upright Brewing. 33 (top), Jason McArthur/Flickr. 34, Christian Reed/Flickr. 35 (bottom), eyeliam/Flickr. 35 (top), Rebecca Wilson/Flickr. 36, m_e_mccarron/Flickr., 37 (bottom), Gabriel Amadeus/Flickr. 37 (top), periwinklekog/Flickr. 38, Mike Rohrig/Flickr. 39 (bottom), Michael Silberstein/ Flickr. 39 (top), Ian Sane™/Flickr. 40, Greg Vaughn. 41, Sam Churchill/Flickr. 45, Karen Massier/ iStockphoto. 50 and 55, Greg Vaughn. 62, Rigucci/Shutterstock. 69, Jeff Hobson. 74, Basil Childers. 83, Charles A. Blakeslee / age footstock. 90, Rigucci/Shutterstock. 100 (top), McMenamins Kennedy School. 100 (bottom left), Hotel deLuxe. 100 (bottom right), Heathman Hotel. 109, Greg Vaughn. 114, EvanLovely/Flickr., 122, LWY/Flickr. 129, Jason Vandehey/Shutterstock. **Chapter 3: The Willamette Valley and Wine Country:** 133, Greg Vaughn. 134 (bottom), Gathering Together Farms. 134 (top), Don Hankins/Flickr. 135, Doreen L. Wynja. 138, Craig Sherod. 145, Greg Vaughn. 148, Randy Kashka/Flickr. 158, Jason Tomczak. 159, Greg Vaughn. 160, Rex Hill. 162 (left), Jason Tomczak. 162 (right), Rex Hill, 163, Doreen L. Wynja. 164 (top), Polara Studio. 164 (bottom), Rich Stanton. 165 (left), Kent Derek. 165 (center), Rex Hill. 165 (right), Norman Eder/iStockphoto. 167 (left), Andrea Johnson Photography. 167 (center), Polara Studio. 167 (right), Dundee Bistro. 171-90, Greg Vaughn. **Chapter 4: The Oregon Coast:** 195, Greg Vaughn. 196 (bottom), Jeramey Jannene/Flickr. 196 (top left), Aimin Tang/iStockphoto. 196 (top right), scaredy_kat/Flickr. 197 (top), Oksana Perkins/iStockphoto. 197 (bottom), OCVA/Flickr. 200, Tom Wald/iStockphoto. 201 (bottom), John Norris/Flickr. 201 (top), Scott Catron/wikipedia.org. 202, Pacific Northwest USCG/Flickr. 209-19, Greg Vaughn. 223, OCVA/Flickr. 229, Greg Vaughn. 233, Stuart Westmorland / age footstock. 235, Thomas Kitchin & Vict / age footstock. 236, San Juan Safaris. 241, Oregon Coast Aquarium. 246-58, Greg Vaughn. **Chapter 5: The Columbia River Gorge and Mt. Hood:** 261, Laura Cebulski/iStockphoto. 262, Timberline Lodge. 263 (top), Robert Crum/iStockphoto. 263 (bottom), Christian Sawicki/iStockphoto. 266, Rigucci/Shutterstock. 273, zschnepf/Shutterstock. 274-83, Greg Vaughn. 289, William Blacke/iStockphoto. 291, Gabriel Amadeus/Flickr. 292 (top and bottom), Danny Warren/iStockphoto. 293 (left), SarahMcD /Flickr. 293 (right), Zachary Collier/Flickr. 296, Zachary Collier/Flickr. 297 and 298, Greg Vaughn. 299, Brendan McMurrer/Flickr. 300 (top), Melissa & Bryan Ripka/Flickr. 300 (bottom), Brian W. Robb. **Chapter 6: Central Oregon:** 305, Mike Houska. 306 (bottom), Black Butte Ranch. 306 (top), Robert O. Brown Photography/iStockphoto. 307, JonDissed/flickr. 310, Sunriver Resort. 315, USGS photo by Lyn Topinka/wikimedia. 319, Sunriver Resort. 320, Greg Vaughn. 325, mccun934/flickr. 331, mariachily/flickr. **Chapter 7: Southern Oregon:** 335, Greg Vaughn. 336, Michael Dunn~!/flickr. 337 (top), Michael (a.k.a. moik) McCullough/wikimedia. 337 (bottom), Ellen C Campbell/Chanticleer Inn. 340, Paula C. Caudill. 343, Larry Turner. 346, nwrafting/flickr. 351, Rogue Creamery. 356-63, Greg Vaughn. 365, T Charles Erickson. 369, Running Y Ranch. **Chapter 8: Crater Lake National Park:** 373, William A. McConnell. 374 (bottom), Aimin Tang/iStockphoto. 374 (top left), Steve Terrill. 374 (top right), Ashok Rodrigues/iStockphoto. 375, Michael Rubin/iStockphoto. 377, Vivian Fung/Shutterstock. 382-83, Zack Schnepf/iStockphoto. **Chapter 9: Eastern Oregon:** 387 and 388 (top), Fokket/flickr. 388 (bottom), Jan Tik/flickr. 389, salvez/flickr. 392, Jeffrey T. Kreulen/iStockphoto. 397, Pendleton Underground Tours. 404, IDAK/Shutterstock. 406-07, Danny Warren/iStockphoto. 413, Cacophony/ wikimedia. 417, AmySelleck/flickr

ABOUT OUR WRITERS

Andrew Collins, a Portland resident since 2007, has authored more than a dozen guidebooks and is the gay travel expert for *The New York Times* Web site, About. com. The former Fodor's editor updated our Southern Oregon and Experience chapters, and wrote the whale watching feature in chapter 4.

Sarah Cypher is a freelance writer, book reviewer, and manuscript editor. While living in Oregon she learned how to fix a derailleur, make good coffee, and travel from downtown Portland to Mt. Hood by back roads on skinny tires. Sarah wrote our Portland bike feature.

England-born and Midwest-raised, **Mike Francis** has worked as a reporter, editor, and producer in Oregon for 27 years. He lives with his family in Portland, where he is an associate editor for *The Oregonian*. Mike updated our Central Oregon chapter.

A writer by vocation, troubadour by avocation, **Matt Graham** has performed and watched shows all over the City of Roses, making him a well-versed person to write our Portland music feature.

Brian Kevin explored Mt. Hood, the Columbia River Gorge, and the high desert country of eastern Oregon from a home base in the Wallowa Mountains. He writes about travel and adventure for publications such as *Outside*, *Sierra*, and *Afar*, and he tweets about the same at twitter.com/brianMT.

Janna Mock-Lopez is enamored of the spirit, beauty, and vitality of Portland, and loved writing the city chapter. Janna is a publisher of two magazines: *Portland Family* and *Goodness*, of which more than 60,000 copies are distributed monthly in the greater metropolitan area.

Kerry Newberry is a Portland-based writer covering food and drink, travel, and lifestyle for a variety of regional and national publications. As an East Coast transplant lured to the West Coast by ample farmers' markets, she now finds the microbrewing, indie-coffee roasting culture hard to ever leave behind, and enjoyed writing our Portland beer feature.

A sixth-generation Oregonian, **Deston S. Nokes** spent his childhood traveling Latin America and the East Coast. Today he makes Portland his home, where he works as a travel journalist and business communications consultant. He explored the Oregon coast and the Willamette Valley for our book.

Dave Sandage is a software engineer living in the heart of Willamette Valley wine country. In his spare time he enjoys cooking, wine tasting, and making his own beer and wine. Dave wrote our Willamette Valley wine feature.

Jenie Skoy is a freelance writer based in Oregon's Willamette Valley. She recently learned to windsurf in the brisk wind off the Columbia River, and climbed a 400-year old tree in one of Oregon's old growth forests. Her adventurous spirit came in handy when writing our Mt. Hood and Columbia River Gorge sports feature.

Allecia Vermillion is a Portland native who loves dining out and drinking local. She is a freelance writer pleased to once again reside in the Pacific Northwest after stints in San Francisco and Chicago. Allecia wrote our food features in the Experience and Portland chapters.

Christine Vovakes's travel articles and photographs have appeared in publications including *The Washington Post*, *The Christian Science Monitor*, *The Sacramento Bee* and the *San Francisco Chronicle*. For this book, Christine wrote our Crater Lake chapter.

After more than ten years living in Oregon, **Crystal Wood** still loves playing tour guide to friends and family. Crystal's vast knowledge of Portland made her the perfect person to update that chapter and write the Portland parks feature.